Christmas 2011

CW01019999

To Chris

Wishing you a very

happy 'down-under' Christmas!

With love from

Simon and Norma

xxxx

# 125 YEARS OF THE BLUES

## THE HISTORY OF THE BEDFORD BLUES 1886-2011

INCORPORATING
THE BEDFORDSHIRE TIMES CENTENARY
HISTORY OF BEDFORD RUFC

Neil Roy
with Phil Beard

Doug Bowker, Marie Davies, Peter John Gates, Richard Glasspool, Mike Green,
Victor Head, Simon Hutchinson, Jackie Markham, Phil Novis, Jane Roberts,
Sam Roberts, Nigel Rudgard, Terry Stark, Chris Ward, Matt Webb, Richard Wildman

First published in 2011 by Bedford Blues Ltd



Pictures are used with grateful thanks to the relevant photographers, newspapers and archives who have provided them

ISBN 978-0-9570345-0-1

Layout and design by Bluegreen Design Consultants,
The Old Mill, 34a Gladstone Street, Bedford MK41 7RR
www.bluegreendesign.co.uk

Jacket design by Dave Brown

Printed and bound in England by Information Press, Eynsham, Oxford

# CONTENTS



## 125 YEARS OF THE BLUES

## WHO'S WHO AT THE BLUES



## FOR THE RECORD



## SEASON BY SEASON



## POSTSCRIPT

# BEDFORD BLUES

1886

# THE PRESIDENT

Twenty five years on and the values and traditions established in the first hundred years continue to be upheld. We remain a family club with secure support from the people of Bedford and our team continues to play the club's trademark open, attractive, running rugby.

Young players still have the opportunity to develop in our excellent Colts Academy and in the thriving Junior Blues first established in 1973. Although, since the professional era, our former player base has extended worldwide a special bond with the club remains.

Personally, I feel privileged and honoured to be Club President for its 125th anniversary and look forward to the celebrations, both on and off the field. With our present financial stability, enviable fan base and a team secure at the top of the second tier of English rugby we can look forward to the Blues remaining 'first class'.

G. W. Davies

**Gareth Davies**

President Bedford Blues

2011

# THE CHAIRMAN

When Harry Elliott wrote about the difficulties the club was encountering at the time of the Centenary in 1986, he could never have predicted what was to come. Professional rugby was officially launched in 1995-96 and the game which had served us so well was never to be the same.

There were some who could not deal with this concept and would forever mourn the passing of amateur rugby.

Despite the ups and downs of recent years I would like to think that the Bedford Blues have found its place in the overall scheme that has evolved.

We are a very successful Championship club who still embrace the principles of the proper rugby club and for that, as we celebrate 125 years, we should be eternally grateful.

I do hope you enjoy this book on which Neil Roy and his team have worked so hard.

Best wishes.

**Geoff Irvine**

Chairman Bedford Blues

2011

# MESSAGES

The Bedford Former Players Association had the idea to update the records to celebrate the club's 125th year. Phil Beard and Tony Mills were the prime movers back in 2006. And this book is the end product.

It has been a labour of love for many people, not least Neil Roy who was responsible for the book marking the club's Centenary. We set the broad guidelines for this one based on that and helped where we could. He set about forming a team from within the club to help him produce it. And the result is something we can all be proud of.

**Leigh Mansell**

Chairman, Bedford Former Players Association

The Followers are delighted to be involved with this book. Many of our members are among those who helped in some way to put it together.

Our secretary Jane Roberts, for instance, retyped the entire Centenary publication so that it could be updated. When you look at all the information it contains, it makes you realize the enormous effort that has gone into producing it.

Congratulations to everyone. It is a wonderful reflection of a wonderful rugby club.

**Peter Smith**

Chairman, Bedford Rugby Followers Association

I'm delighted to endorse Neil Roy's update to his original *Bedfordshire Times Centenary History*, written when he was our sports editor. His enthusiasm, knowledge and sharp journalistic skills ensure we are treated to a fascinating read.

Both the Bedford Blues and the *Bedfordshire Times*, now the *Times & Citizen*, have been part of the fabric of the town community since Victorian times.

We've been there to report this amazing sporting story in words and pictures - in print, and now online too - and it's satisfying to see so much of this coverage contained in this updated publication.

We were backing the Blues when the first ball was kicked in 1886. We're proud and privileged to still do so today.

**Jim Stewart**

Editor, *Bedfordshire Times & Citizen*

# PREFACE AND ACKNOWLEDGEMENTS

The turmoil at Bedford Rugby Club in 1998 and 1999 would have been worthy of a book on its own. It certainly earned a chapter, *Bedford Main Line*, in an essential work on the start of the professional era - *Midnight Rugby* by Stephen Jones of *The Sunday Times*. He was a well informed journalist of all things at Goldington Road and in 1982, in the magazine *Rugby World*, he nominated the club's supporters as the best in the country. He would not have been surprised by what they achieved in saving the Blues in 1999, nor in seeing an entire book devoted to that era.

But the brief for this book outlined by the Bedford Former Players Association was to produce an account of 125 years, incorporating the Centenary history which was published in 1986. That book was made possible by journalists and printers at the *Bedfordshire Times* and by the newspaper's archives being available to the club's then Keeper of the Records, Jack Pope. He and I went back to the beginning and checked facts and figures against newspaper reports and official records compiled mainly by Don Riddy. He worked full time at it; I worked in my spare time from the sports desk of the newspaper and together we travelled all over the area to interview players and officials of the past. We were lucky to get help from many people including the legendary rugby reporter Doug Bowker, the *Daily Telegraph* writer Victor Head and the local historian Richard Wildman – all of whom had worked on the *Bedfordshire Times*. The printers worked for nothing to help complete what was received as an excellent work recognized as a credit to the newspaper and the club. Geoffrey Nicholson of *The Independent* described it as one of the best of its sort.

This book has been produced using more sources, more newspapers and, of course, the internet. Phil Beard, Keeper of the Records, got the project going, took charge of the records and read every word in the book more than once. Marie Davies, who in 2011 profiled former players in the match programme, provided valuable research, insights and pictures. Former local journalists Matt Webb and Mike Green and broadcaster Sam Roberts, the match day announcer in 2011, wrote articles based on their time in the grandstand. Local accountant Chris Ward used to write match reports on the club's website. He has provided an expert's feature on finances.

Perhaps the greatest contribution was made by Jane Roberts, secretary of the Followers. She retyped the entire original book, including all the statistics, and put some of the new sections into the same style as well. Whenever there was a computer issue that my wife couldn't resolve, she did. Jackie Markham, President of the Followers, proof read all of Jane's work and made suggestions after reading other sections.

Many other people have helped. Most were from the terraces of the club. Terry Stark was a ruthless proof reader who we were often unable to satisfy when he noticed a discrepancy. Phil Novis located photographs for the project and Peter John Gates copied them, using a special technique he had developed, from pictures on walls in various bars around the ground. Nigel Rudgard, the club photographer for the previous decade or so provided many of the pictures, including the one on the front and the entire colour section.

Jeff Cox, Mick Meadows and Rob Crowle had memories to rely on, Geoff Appleton and John Saunders had records, Steve Ashton, Jez Keates, Isabel Britton, Denis Ormesher, Bernie McGee and others remembered much that was off the radar of those who follow only the first team.

At the design stage we were lucky to have Dave Brown of Bluegreen Design on the job. A regular supporter, he was the person who put together the match day programme and someone who knew how to spot a problem in a table of tries, conversions and penalties.

It was fun chasing leads from people who had an idea that, for instance, a former player was an international; but we always looked for other sources to support the claim and sometimes couldn't find any. Some unions, like the Russian or the Dutch, were quick to reply to queries. Others didn't reply at all – possibly through no fault of their own. Michael Rowe at the RFU press office was extremely helpful. So was Chris Wearmouth at Northampton and Dave Fuge at Plymouth Albion.

Not all games that have taken place on the pitch at Goldington Road have been recorded. Some testimonial, tribute and friendly matches which were often used as fundraisers or trials have been left out. Sometimes the committee decided that a match should not count in the records but then two or three years later it decided the same fixture should. Some matches weren't covered by the press; there were no programmes, no team announcements and difficulties in finding out who some players were. From 2008, the Mobbs Memorial Match against the Barbarians became a Bedford fixture and because of the status of the match its details are included in the records for the season – even though it was often used as a trial game rather than a genuine first team one. From 2012 the format is due to change again.

Even in the professional era there are instances where the initials of some players aren't known and where scores and scorers haven't been recorded properly. Also there have been changes in the way newspapers and programmes refer to players. Once, someone was recorded by his full initials and surname. By 2011, newspapers tended to use just surnames or one initial and surname. Programmes tended to use one first name and surname. Where we have profiled someone we have attempted to find out that person's full set of initials but the same person will often appear in the various lists of players or scorers using the initial of the first name he was known by. In some eras there are no team photographs for certain seasons. From the Centenary, statistics are recorded in a slightly different way, reflecting the emphasis on try scoring.

I should like to thank everyone who helped with both books. They know who they are and what they did; but apologies to anyone who didn't get his or her due. It was difficult at times but always enjoyable. In one case we spent nearly a week looking for five points in James Pritchard's career total of more than 2,000. The issue was only resolved when he dug out an old film of a particular match.

If the experience of the first book is anything to go by there will be corrections needed for the next one – whatever form it takes. But one thing is certain, I will not be available to help with the 150th anniversary edition of the history of the Bedford Blues. My advice to those who are likely to be charged with compiling it is that they should start now and anyone who thinks something has been missed out of this edition should make sure it gets in the next one. I should also like to see the setting up of a heritage group involving interested people in all sections of the club to address and make policy on the sort of issues that we have encountered. Those who have played a role in producing this book would be a credit to it.

**Neil Roy**

May 2011

# 125 YEARS OF THE BLUES

James Pritchard, captain of the Blues in 2010-11, with Gregor Gillanders in support, left, and Darryl Veenendaal, right. Pritchard became the first Bedford player to score 400 points in a season

# 2010-11: A SEASON TO REMEMBER

Bedford's 125th season was one of the best. And when Geoff Irvine, the club Chairman, told shareholders at the annual meeting of Bedford Blues Ltd in March 2011 that they were seeing the best rugby since the days of Frank Warren he was absolutely right.

The 2010-11 rugby union campaign was one to remember for a number of reasons. For many it was the moment when the Blues captain James Pritchard became the first player ever to score 400 points in a season when he set a new club record of 403 with three penalties in the British and Irish Cup Final defeat at Bristol. For others it came early in the amazing 23-22 defeat in the Championship play-off semi final at Worcester when player of the season Paul Tupai crashed into an opponent and ran straight through him to set down a marker that told everyone it was going to be some encounter; or right at the end of the same game in that dramatic instant when the TV match official was asked to establish whether Duncan Taylor had scored the opportunist try that stunned the stadium and would have pinched the tie.

For others it came in the cup semi final when Handre Schmidt, needing one try to equal Ben Whetstone's modern-era record, passed the ball with the line at his mercy for his nearest challenger in the race to be top try scorer to touch down. The modest winger, who scored 25 times in his first season, said in interview afterwards: "It's a team game. He'd have done the same".

Player of the season 2010-11 Paul Tupai

Top try scorer in 2010-11 Handre Schmidt

Everyone will have his or her own favourite memories. But the biggest crowd of the season, 4,150, experienced something on Boxing Day 2010 that few thought possible – an actual match after hundreds of supporters cleared the pitch of snow. And for many that was the moment that summed it all up. All hands on deck and a 39-22 win. Certainly at the end-of-season black tie dinner organized by the Former Players Association in May 2011, it was deemed worthy of a short film. Mike Rayer, former player and Director of Rugby since 2005, told guests he thought that day was what the club was all about.

The Chairman's claim was made in March when defeats were still in single figures. But it was still true at the end – perhaps even more so. The Blues were recognized as one of the most attractive sides in the Championship, then in its second year. No less a figure than Rob Andrew, the former England fly half and the new Director of Operations at the Rugby Football Union told *The Independent* on May 11 that Bedford's one point defeat at Worcester in the Championship play-off semi final which was shown live on Sky TV "was the best piece of rugby theatre we've seen all season." *Rugby Times* of May 27 said the Blues "were the real winners on the day as was the Championship because this was a marvellous advertisement for the competition". Editor Jon Newcombe went on: "It has to be one of the games of the season, if not the last decade, such was the drama, tension and skill on show".

The facts supported the Chairman too. In statistical terms, the club's 125th season was one of the most successful ever. The 2010-11 campaign saw 27 wins in 38 games. Only six other seasons in the club's history saw more, the record being 29 in 1971-72 and 1997-98. Including the match against the Barbarians, the side scored 144 tries (and four penalty tries). Only the All Stars of 1996-97 and 1997-98 at the start of the professional era and the 1975-76 side scored more. Only in the Warren era, 1996-98, were more than 1200 points scored in a season. The 2010-11 vintage got 1216 – of which 910 were in the Championship, 271 in the British and Irish Cup and 35 in the Mobbs Memorial Match against the Barbarians.

Of course 100 or more tries a season was the norm in a golden age between 1967 and 1980 and there were more wins than defeats in successive seasons from 1957 until 1977. But after the trauma of 1999, the Blues recorded more wins than losses in every season from 2004-05 and more than 100 tries from 2005-06 onwards – save in 2007-08.

The record of the 2005-06 side was impressive – in some ways better than the 2010-11 totals with the same amount of league and cup tries, 139, in six fewer games. It too, like the 2010-11 squad, finished second in the league and was the losing finalist in the cup – both times Harlequins were the winners. In 2011, in the new play-off format, Worcester, were promoted and Bristol won the British and Irish Cup, also in its second year, by 17-14 on a rainy evening in one of the driest Springs on record. Supporters, knowing they couldn't be promoted even if they'd beaten Worcester because their Goldington Road ground wasn't up to standard, were keen for a cup win in the club's 125th year to sit alongside others in 1975 and 2005. But it wasn't to be.

That defeat was something of a reality check to a season which started with a 50 point win over Plymouth Albion and later saw 80 points notched up against Rotherham – Bedford's second highest total ever in one game. Ollie Dodge's three tries on the opening day was the first of eight hat-tricks in the season. Dodge was part of the new breed of professional rugby player – nurtured in an academy (in his case Leicester) and blooded through England age group teams. He completed his 100th match for Bedford in that defeat at Bristol.

The Blues had previous relationships with both Leicester and Northampton which gave players on the books of the Premiership clubs the chance to develop in the second tier of rugby. But in 2010-11, seven young players from Saracens were made available under the new 'dual registered' regulations. One of them, Jake Sharp, made more than 20 appearances, another, James Short, scored four tries in the home win against Moseley and a third Owen Farrell kicked Saracens into the Premiership final to face Leicester and then, with Short scoring a try, landed 17 points to steer them to victory.

The Saracens link, according to the Chairman at the annual meeting, was triggered by former Bedford player Mouritz Botha who signed for the London club in 2009 after joining the Blues in 2006 from Bedford Athletic. 'Big Mo', who played cricket for the 'Ath' as well, and Soane Tonga'uiha, who was at Bedford from 2004 until 2006 before moving on to Northampton, were old boys who made a big impression in the 2010-11 season and both were included in Will Greenwood's *Daily Telegraph* Premiership Team of the Season.

Players moved onwards and upwards with the club's blessing, said Mr Irvine, adding that others were queuing up to take their places. Scrum half Karl Dickson had gone to the Harlequins in 2009 and that provided the chance for Will Chudley who himself was off to Newcastle for the 2011-12 season. Myles Dorrian, who charmed guests at the Followers' May Ball with his talent at singing - just as he did the players on the team bus - had secured a Premiership contract at Exeter where the former Bedford, and Northampton, fly half Ali Hepher was the backs coach. Duncan Taylor, who 'touched down' at Worcester after Dorrian's dropped goal attempt hit the post, got a deal from Saracens.

It was also true that young players from the Bedford Academy were breaking into the first team. Three, Josh Bassett, Elliot Bale and Steve Smith, made debuts in the 2010-11 season. Five members of the first team squad had come out of the Academy; one, flanker Sacha Harding, had reached 150 appearances in his career while Chudley, who was nominated in the *The Rugby Paper's* Championship Team of the Season, passed 70. The Bedford Academy was outside the funded elite but in 2011 the Colts completed a fourth victory in the National Cup competition in five years to show that they were still nurturing players of promise for the future.

Twenty five years after the Centenary, the club was operating with confidence on and off the field. Even the finances were improving in line with the Chairman's determination to balance the books. Accounts to the end of June 2010, showed a loss of £189,000. But ever the optimist Mr Irvine told the annual meeting: "I am pleased to say that figures up to Christmas show us in a slight profit."

Average gates, still hadn't reached 3,000 but that match on Boxing Day, the only one in the division to go ahead, certainly helped. Simon Hutchinson, a former reporter on *Bedford on Sunday* was at the ground early in his role as press officer at the Blues. He made the film and he wrote:

"In all honesty, a game of rugby should not have taken place at Goldington Road on Boxing Day 2010. Sledging or a snowball fight – yes. Rugby – no."

The days running up to Christmas had seen snow falling all over the UK and the Bedford Blues had already endured one cancellation with their British & Irish Cup match away to Neath the previous weekend falling foul of the weather.

Despite the Goldington Road pitch bearing more resemblance to the Cresta Run, the Bedford Blues management was determined that the post-Christmas match should go ahead. The only problem was the four inches of snow that had covered the playing surface for over a week. Not to be perturbed, the ground staff at the club knew that the snow would be acting as insulation and that the ground was soft and more than playable – if they could get to it.

It was at this point that the call to arms was made.

Earlier in the season, Bedford Blues had started to take full advantage of social media in all its glory. A successful website had been run for a number of years, but now fans could 'like' Bedford Blues Rugby Club on Facebook or follow BedfordBluesRFC on Twitter to get the latest news and match day scores.

The first message sent out to the fans was simple - "We need help". From there, the request for people to give up a couple of hours of their time to help shift snow of the pitch was made.

Those interested were asked to bring a shovel if they had a spare and drop the club an email to let them know who was coming so that complimentary tickets could be issued to the volunteers.

What then happened on Boxing Day morning exemplified exactly what supporting your club is all about. Around 300 people of all ages and walks of life descended on Goldington Road armed with spades, brushes, wheelbarrows and much more. Their one aim was to ensure that the game went ahead

A local company had donated diggers so that the removed snow could be shifted away from the pitch, large heaters were brought in so that any frozen spots could be blasted and the Highways Agency would have been proud of how the walkways and stand were gritted to reduce the risk of slipping.

"It was truly a wonderful sight to see and one that will stick with me for a very long time," said ground manager Pete Beard.

"We had no idea how many people were likely to turn up. We thought a few dozen would shake off the after effects of Christmas and head down, but we received about 150 emails pledging to help out. On the day more and more just flooded through the gates with everyone rolling up their sleeves to get the job done and everything else, including the result, went as planned."

Beyond all belief, this band of loyal supporters eclipsed events on the field to create what was quite possibly the highlight of the season (which can be viewed on Youtube at www.youtube.com/watch?v=1BUa_h_ce7Q).

# IN THE BEGINNING

This stone commemorates the exploit of William Webb Ellis who, with a fine disregard for the rules of football as played in his time, first took the ball in his hands and ran with it, thus originating the distinctive feature of the rugby game. AD 1823. He should, of course, having caught the ball, kicked it. But was it really Webb Ellis? Was it even in 1823?

O L Owen in his *History of the Rugby Football Union* written in 1955, claims that "someone or some persons about that period ran rather than kicked." And that "by common consent" a centenary match representative of the four Home Unions was played on the Rugby School ground in 1923, and a tablet bearing the Webb Ellis declaration is set in the wall of Rugby Close.

In 1970 U A Titley and A R McWhirter marked the undoubted Centenary of the Rugby Football Union with their *History*, and in rather more reckless fashion declared that if they couldn't prove Webb Ellis invented Rugby Football, they didn't really care.

"Who but a curmudgeon would question the factual origin of Camelot or the Arthurian legend?" they asked. Fair enough, but those Round Table doings, fact or legend, were rather farther back in time than Webb Ellis or his like on a rectangular field at Rugby School. It seems curious today that such a momentous charge was not more fully chronicled at the time.

The trouble is that not until 1895 was a sub committee of Old Rugbeians assembled to "enquire into the origins of Rugby football". By then, the chief protagonist, Webb Ellis, had died after a career in the Church, and so had the antiquarian, Matthew Bloxham, on whose written testimony the Webb Ellis story chiefly rests.

Even Bloxham's evidence contained in the school's *Meteor* was circumstantial, he having left Rugby three years before Webb Ellis ran rather than kicked.

At least Bloxham's view of what Webb Ellis should have done is valid and worth setting down: "according to the then rules he ought to have retired back as far as he pleased... for the combatants on the other side could only advance to the spot where he had caught the ball, and were unable to rush forward until he had either punted it or placed it for someone else to kick".

All this still leaves unanswered the really intriguing question: What happened when Webb Ellis disregarded the rules and ran? Interestingly, one witness before the 1895 committee, T Harris, remembered Webb Ellis best as a cricketer, adding that at football "he was inclined to take unfair advantage," and that the cry of "hack him over" was always raised against any player who was seen running with the ball in his hands.

Another celebrated old Rugbeian, author of *Tom Brown's School Days*, Thomas Hughes, wrote that in his first year (1834) "running with the ball to get a try by touching down within goal was not absolutely forbidden, but a jury of Rugby boys of that day would almost certainly have found a verdict of 'justifiable homicide' if a boy had been killed in running in."

Not until 1841-42 was 'running in' made legal and even then with limitations – the ball must be caught on the bound, the catcher must not be off his side, there should be no handing on but the catcher must carry the ball in and touch down himself. Picking up on the ground was absolutely illegal.

Hughes, who died in 1896, thought by that time the game had developed into "too much of handball"; he felt the football of 1850s and 1860s was the finest form ever attained.

The most likeable explanation for Webb Ellis taking flight is that contained in the RFU centenary volume. "He thought it safest to run away with the ball being a member of the Town House which, at that period, was extremely unpopular."

Such a suggestion leads us neatly into what must surely be more legend than fact, the history of football itself.

Whether it was the Chinese who seem to be credited with inventing everything, some primitive tribe, or the more disciplined Romans who played 'harpastum' as a means of keeping their legions fit, football in its many variants always seems to have been pretty rough. In England, Kings (Edward II and III, and Henry VIII)) and Queens (Elizabeth I) enacted laws against football.

In 1853, Stubbes, in his *Anatomie of Abuses*, referred to football as "a devilish pastime ... and hereof growth envy, rancour and malice, and sometimes brawling, murther, homicide and great effusion of blood."

But football struggled on, and that merrier monarch, Charles II, lent an air of respectability by attending a match between the royal servants and those of the Duke of Albermarle; alas, Samuel Pepys was not present otherwise we might have knowledge of the teams, their attire and style of play.

There seemed no limit to numbers - whole villages and parishes were pitched against neighbouring ones – and nor was distance covered or time spent of much consequence.

Richard Carew in his *Survey of Cornwall*, talks of the hurlers taking their way "over hilles, dales, hedges, ditches, yea, and thorow bushes, briars, mires, plashes and rivers whatsoever."

A Frenchman remarked that if Englishmen called this playing, it would be impossible to say what they would call fighting.

These barbaric encounters continued well into the 19th century until a Victorian age brought a semblance of law and order which drove the game from the street to the playing field. Football became respectable for public schools and universities, leading to 1871 and the formation of the RFU to provide a common code of rules – Laws of the Game.

One hundred years and more later those Laws continue to be shaped and changed to meet ever-changing conditions, and to counter players like Webb Ellis who still choose to disregard them.

But as our authors of the *Centenary History* declare: "If it was cheating (by Webb Ellis) few could now fail to regard it as quite inspired cheating."

# THE RIOT OF 1859

It was from Rugby that the game spread says B Fletcher Robinson in his book *Rugby Football* (A D Innes and Co 1896). It was carried by Old Rugbeians to other schools where they went as masters, to the universities or to clubs which they had founded to keep alive the game they had learned to love at school.

In 1865 old boys from Rugby and Marlborough formed the entire Richmond team. After the foundation of the Rugby Union in 1871, the first five presidents were all former Rugby boys. At Oxford one of the original rules was that the captain, the secretary and at least one of three committee men had to be a Rugbeian.

The early nurseries of the game were at Rugby, where they didn't accept the Rugby Union's rules en bloc until 1890, Marlborough, Wellington, Cheltenham, Clifton, Haileybury, Tonbridge and Leys. They were what Fletcher Robinson called the Fons et Origo of the game. He adds "at Bedford there are two great football schools, Bedford Grammar and Bedford Modern which turn out many fine players."

The schools were great rivals and early accounts of organised games reflect this. The authority on the history of Bedford in 2011 was *Richard Wildman*, formerly honorary secretary (later chairman) of the Bedford Society and the author of *Bygone Bedford* (1974), *Bedford Past and Present* (1975), *Victorian and Edwardian Bedfordshire from Old Photographs* (1978), *Bedford: A Pictorial History* (1991), *Britain in Old Photographs: Bedford* (1994, re-issued 2009) and *Bedford's Motoring Heritage* (with Alan Crawley, 2003). A second-hand bookseller with a shop in Mill Street between 1978 and 1996, he was an occasional contributor to the *Bedfordshire Times* from 1967. From 1999 he was archivist of Bedford Modern School and secretary of the OBM Club. This article on Bedford's schools, the Goldington Road Field and the Bedford Riot of 1859 was published in 1986.

"Dr Robert Burton Poole (1841-1908), Headmaster of Bedford Modern School from 1877 to 1900, was educated at Rugby, and in his early years at BMS he sometimes played in the 1st XV (the practice of including masters in the teams ceased at the school in 1888). In *Bedford Modern School of the Black and Red* (1981, re-issued 2010), Andrew Underwood refers to one of Poole's former pupils recalling that 'the Doctor' once drop-kicked a ball over an elm tree at the Goldington Road field. Poole was probably the only headmaster of either of the Bedford schools to do this. The occasion may have been a match against one of the clubs, which later merged into Bedford RUFC. (See E J Cooper on BMS Rugby in *The Eagle*, Christmas 1955).

Organised games at the two schools for boys in Bedford had to wait for the provision of a suitable playing field, which did not occur until the 1840s. Bedford Grammar School (renamed Bedford School in 1917) was founded in 1552 to replace the school run by Newnham Priory, which had been dissolved by Henry VIII. In 1566, Sir William Harpur, a former Lord Mayor of London and past Master of the Merchant Taylors' Company, who had been born in Bedford, endowed the school with 13 acres of meadowland in Holborn, thereby creating the Bedford Charity. This was controlled by Bedford Corporation until 1764, when a separate board of trustees (the Harpur Trust) was set up to administer the Grammar School and a Writing or English School teaching (as the name suggests) subjects other than Latin and Greek. Both schools shared the same building in St Paul's Square (the Old Town Hall and Tourist Information Office) until early in the 19th century. The Writing School became the

Commercial School and as such moved into part of the new range of Harpur Trust buildings in Harpur Street, designed by Edward Blore, which survives as the Blore Façade of the Harpur Centre. The Commercial School was finally renamed Bedford Modern School in 1873, and left Harpur Street for a new site in Manton Lane in 1974. The Grammar School, meanwhile, stayed in St Paul's Square until 1892, when it moved to the present Bedford School buildings to the north of St Peter's Street.

By 1841 there were 300 boys at the two schools, records Joyce Godber in *The Harpur Trust 1552-1973* and to avoid dangerous out of school activities including bullying of younger pupils, the Trust rented a six acre field along Goldington Road from the House of Industry (the Workhouse, later the North Wing Hospital). Normally used for cattle fairs, the field was mainly used for playing cricket, but levelling-off did not take place until 1847. None of the printed sources consulted for this article equates this field with the present Bedford ground, but Mercer's Map of Bedford (1878), which is precisely scaled, shows the field which is now the club ground as having an area of almost exactly six acres, and this is confirmed by the Ordnance Survey Map (1882).

It was intended that the Grammar and Commercial Schools should use the Goldington Road field on different afternoons, but on Thursday June 2, 1859, a crowd of Commercial schoolboys arrived to find the Grammar School – who had been given an extra half-holiday – in possession of the cricket pitch. The story of what happened next has been told in amusing detail by L R Conisbee in two articles in the *Bedfordshire Magazine* (Summer and Autumn issues, 1964). The 'Bedford Riot' of 1859 is still the most serious incident of its kind to have occurred in the town, and although it was occasioned by a cricket-match, its origin was at the club ground, which was then the House of Industry field. (The House of Industry estate was taken over by the Borough Council in 1964).

After abandoning their game because of the increasingly hostile behaviour of the spectators, the Grammar schoolboys, outnumbered by at least two to one, were pursued back towards the town centre. At St Peter's Green, one of their number, Augustine Lemprière Foulkes, aged 19, knocked out a 14-year-old Commercial schoolboy named Adderley Clarke, with a stick, causing a three-inch scalp wound. Foulkes might have been beaten up or worse by his antagonists and passers-by, had not the heavily-built, fox-hunting Rector of St Peter's, the Revd Gustavus Burnaby, appeared and scattered the boys. On the evening of the following day, Friday June 3, the 'Bedford Riot' really ensued when a mob of possibly 2,000 people besieged Foulkes (who was being summoned for assault), the Head Master of the Grammar School, and his solicitor in the solicitor's office in St Peter's Street. All the front windows were broken and Head Master and pupil had to make a rapid departure over the back garden wall into Lurke Street. Fortunately a shower of rain dispersed the mob. Clarke recovered from his blow on the head and Foulkes, who later became Vicar of Steventon in Berkshire, was eventually fined £5 with costs by the magistrates.

The Foulkes incident sparked off a riot because there was at that time very bad feeling in Bedford between supporters of the Commercial School, whose pupils were mostly Bedford-born, and parents and boys of the Grammar School, who were largely from the professional classes and often 'Squatters', that is, not local people but resident in Bedford for the sake of the education offered by the Harpur Trust. Education was indeed Bedford's principal 'industry' for most of the 19th century. The town's first premises for large-scale manufacture were the Britannia Ironworks (later George Fischer Castings), opened by the brothers James and Frederick Howard, makers of steel ploughs, in the year of the Foulkes riot, 1859, but Bedford's growth as a residential centre was almost entirely the result of the educational attractions of the Harpur Trust.

Understandably, the Goldington Road field seems to have fallen out of favour with both schools, which found alternative (and separate) playing fields west of the railway line from Bedford to Hitchin. When the Midland Railway built its direct link to London (St Pancras) in 1868, the Grammar School field was affected and a substitute was found in the glebe land belonging to St Peter's Church. Rent of a cricket field from the Rector eventually led to the purchase by the Harpur Trust of the future site of Bedford School and its present playing field. John Sargeaunt states in *A History of Bedford School* (1926) that the football game played by the Grammar School was called Rugby, but that originally the school had its own rules.

Bedford Modern School (formerly the Commercial School) used a field in Ford End Road, near the Gas Works, until the Clarendon Street playing field opened in 1884. In his history of BMS already referred to, Andrew Underwood records that the pavilion, although new in 1884, offered rather primitive facilities for rugby players. Two zinc baths were filled with hot water and set out with soap and towels by the groundsman ("those who got there first had the benefit of the water at its warmest and cleanest").

It may be of interest to note that the section on Football in the *Victorian History of the County of Bedford* (1908), Vol 2, was written by Arthur Ransom (1831-1912), who was Editor of the *Bedfordshire Times* from 1879 to 1895, and co-proprietor (with Joshua Hawkins) from 1879 to 1893. Despite his contemporary reputation as a local historian, Ransom's writings have not stood the test of time as well as those of his subordinate, John Hamson, who was Assistant Editor of the paper for many years. Ransom's account of the development of rugby at the schools in Bedford (and where they played it) is garbled and more than slightly inaccurate. It seems unlikely that "when Rugby football first became an institution at the Bedford Modern School, it was played at Goldington village." Ransom was elderly when he wrote that, but as he had first come to Bedford in 1879, just after Dr Poole introduced rugby at BMS, he presumably had some reason for his statement. As Bedford Modern School's field was at Ford End Road in the late 1870s and at Clarendon Street from 1884, it might possibly refer to some forgotten match on Goldington Green."

# THE OLD SCHOOL TIE

Rugby football was born and nurtured in public schools and with two of them in a small market town, school teams existed before Bedford had one it could call its own. Both Bedford School and Bedford Modern had fixtures with other schools, of course, and also with the club sides that existed in the area before the birth of the Blues. *The Leicester Centenary* (David Hands, 1981) records fixtures against Bedford School from its third season in 1882-83 right up to 1900. The school won its fair share of games as well, twice in fact, in the season 1892-93 when a side recorded as 'Bedford Town' actually lost. Leicester played the Bedford Rovers in their first season, 1880-81, and by their fifth they had added the Bedford Swifts to their list.

The contribution of two public schools for boys in the town was the strongest theme in the history of the club – certainly until the advent of professionalism. There are others, like the works sides that developed, the junior clubs in the county, other schools, and the universities, particularly Cambridge, but the Harpur Trust schools, in producing players, coaches, administrators and arenas of employment made the club into the respected force it was to become. Right up until its Centenary, more than half of its captains, coaches, presidents and principal office holders were either former pupils of, or masters at, one or other of the schools. Education being one of its main industries, the town attracted not just 'squatters' to board at, mainly, Bedford School, but whole families who often moved to the large houses by the railway station so that they could commute and their sons could be educated, relatively cheaply, at Harpur Trust schools. Great players like Maurice Pugh and Doug Cotton moved to the town with their families for no other reason, they said, than the education.

Fletcher Robinson referred to the 'great rugby schools'. So not unnaturally, someone decided to produce a table designed to determine which ones they were. Wallace Reyburn in the *Men in White – the Story of English Rugby*, 1975, listed schools and the English internationals they had produced and then listed the 'great' players and where they had been educated. He understates the case as far as Bedford School and Bedford Modern are concerned but he concludes "that the game is now dominated by others than of public school background". Reyburn's table is an illuminating one.

With a head start Rugby School, not surprisingly, led it with 41 internationals, Bedford School being placed ninth with 12 and the Modern School not appearing at all. The facts are different though and Bedford School can claim 15 English internationals, two Irish, one Scottish and one Welsh, and Bedford Modern can claim eight English internationals, which would have put them into 13th place in Reyburn's table.

Bedford School records show that organised fixtures were taking place in 1870. The earliest rugby honours board in the school pavilion is of the 1870 team captained by H B Barnes. Hockey had been played by the river in the playground during headmaster Brereton's days and a form of football became possible when the school rented a field. There would have been, said Murray Fletcher, player, coach and historian at Bedford School and the Blues' scrum half for many years, no regular rules. Tripping and hacking would have been allowed and everyone joined in. By the 1870s, inter-school matches were being played against Bedford County School, Perse, King's Ely, St Paul's College, Stony Stratford and Magdalene College School, Oxford. Bell's *Life in London*, in 1870, reported on a match between Bedford Grammar and Christ's College, Cambridge, and of local fixtures there are reports of a match played against a town club which the school lost by three 'rouges' to one.

The first record of a rugby XV at Bedford Modern was in 1878, said PJ King, legendary coach and master there as well as a hooker at the Bedford club. It was a match played against an Old Boys' side. The first inter-school game was in 1880 – against the County School, which then occupied the site of the 'Granada' building in Ampthill Road. In the 1883-84 season, home and away fixtures were initiated against Leys School, Cambridge and King Henry's School, Coventry. Mill Hill joined the list in 1885. Until the season 1885-86 masters were included in the team – with, of course, the agreement of opponents.

Both schools have produced great players, not all of whom made their names with the Bedford club. In the early days, many boys from the Grammar School went to Blackheath. Others who had boarded went to clubs nearer their homes and others to clubs in areas where they were to pursue their careers. The roll of honour from Bedford School is 19 internationals, five British Isles tourists, as well as many Barbarians, Blues and county players. The internationals and the date of their first cap are: P Christopherson (1891), P G Jacob (1898), J G Milton (1904), C E L Hammond (1905), B Maclear (Ireland, 1905), F H Palmer (1905), C H Milton (1906), F G Brooks (1906), H H Vassall (1908), E L Chambers (1908), B A T McFarland (Ireland, 1920), S W Harris (1920), R Jones (Wales, 1926), J G Cook (1937), L F L Oakley (1951), D P Rogers (1961), M C Bayfield (1991), A C T Gomarsall (1996), D A Callam (Scotland, 2006). W J Carey, never capped for England, Vassall, Harris, Rogers and Bayfield all toured abroad with British Isles teams, nicknamed, in 1924, 'The Lions'. A F Blakiston, first capped by England in 1920 and by the Lions in 1924, attended Bedford School for a short period, as did K C Fyfe, capped by Scotland in 1933. Mr Fletcher, though, would not claim them from either Trent or Oundle.

Bedford Modern School produced eight full internationals: W B Thomson (1892), H W Finlinson (1895), E R Mobbs (1909), R C Stafford (1912), A G Bull (1914), H L V Day (1920), R E G Jeeps (1956) and L E Weston (1972). Weston, who played occasionally for Bedford in the mid 1960s, was at scrum half for Rosslyn Park when Bedford beat them at Twickenham in 1975. R Willsher and G T Dancer played in wartime internationals. A O Jones, the Test cricketer, G U A Read, A J Turner, G A de Smidt and J G Rogers all played in trials. Mr King is convinced that Jack Rogers would have been capped had he not lost a leg in a wartime air crash. R E G 'Dickie' Jeeps, an England captain who played for Northampton, made three tours with the British Isles teams of 1955, 1959 and 1962 and G T 'Beef' Dancer, though never capped by England, toured with the Lions in 1938 playing in all three matches against South Africa.

Coaches from the schools have always had a close relationship with the club. The man who put the Grammar School on the map was the remarkable E H Dasent who, in the early days, sent boys to Blackheath but later became the Bedford President. He coached the school from 1884 until 1909. For eight consecutive seasons before 1900 the XV went unbeaten by school opposition and for five football terms, no boy crossed the school line. In those days, not just Leicester but other club sides – Richmond, Blackheath and Harlequins – were often beaten. Dasent set the standard, others followed and maintained the reputation: among them E L Chambers, T T Shaw, H A Henderson, O V Bevan, N E Browning, F M Fletcher, A C Fitt, A M Thorp, P D Briggs and GMK Fletcher. The 1941 side was the first to win all its matches. It produced the celebrated Haynes, Oakley and Fletcher. The 1955 side produced D P Rogers, an all time great and captain of the Bedford side that in 1975 won the 'cup' with P D Briggs as its coach. (The 'cup' was officially known until the next year as the 'RFU Club Competition' but here it will be referred to as the 'cup' and later by the name of its sponsor).

The 1900-01 Bedford School team with E Hastings Dasent and three future internationals in FG Brooks, captain, EL Chambers and CH Milton. Picture: The Bedford Archive, Bedford School

Mr King selects as the great team from the Modern School, the one of 1900, coached by Alf Parrott, the first captain of the Blues. That team included G U A Read, a local boy from Pavenham affectionately known as 'Daddy' and G A de Smidt. It won all ten matches. The association between the school and the Blues has stood the test of time. The Rev S V Hartley became chairman after coaching at the school from 1919 until 1927, P J King played and became a committee man, Harry Bitton became President, George Cullen served on committees and Richard Chadwick played in the side that won the 'cup' and later coached the team. Old Modernians Roger Slaughter and Mike Fitzgerald also coached the club in the 1980s. The story with administrators and committee men is the same. In the professional era Bruce Willey, Ian Bullerwell and Geoff Irvine were Chairmen, Bruce Willey and John Saunders were Presidents and Tony Mills was the Rugby Administrator. The only two players to make more than 400 appearances for the club were D P Rogers of Bedford School and M A Howe of Bedford Modern.

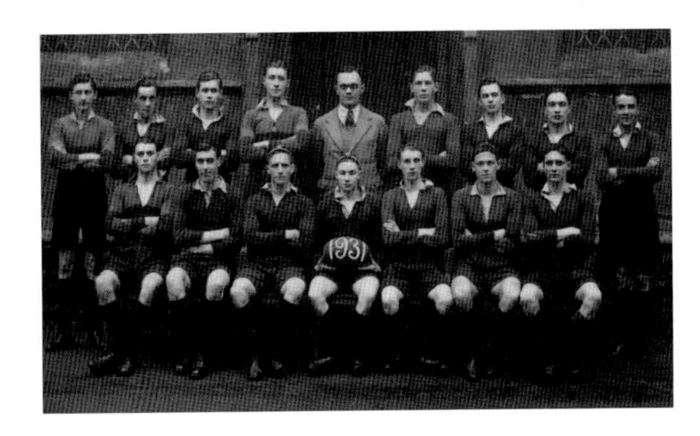


The 1931 Bedford Modern School team showing PJ King. Picture: BMS Archives (gift of Mrs Fay Bradley)

Just as the game spread from Rugby and the universities to schools like Bedford and Bedford Modern, so those great rugby playing institutions influenced the style of recreation in other schools in the area and they in turn produced players, coaches and administrators to serve the town club. One of the 'founders' of the club, 'Pinkie' Booth, attended the County School, a fee-paying school started in 1868 when it was known as the Bedford School for Middle Class People, later to change its name to Elstow School. It produced a Scottish international D M Grant, who was capped while still at the school. One of its headmasters, C F Farrar, wrote the book, *The Ouse's Silent Tide*. The school closed during the First World War.

The exclusivity of rugby football to fee-paying schools in the Bedford area remained for nearly 50 years. It changed first within the Harpur Trust itself when the non-fee-paying Harpur Central School, known as Bates's School, took onto its staff Iorwerth Evans, a Welshman who was capped twice as a member of London Welsh in 1934. His headmaster, Captain A B Wignall, suggested to him that he retire at the top and change the Central from a soccer playing feeder to the town's association teams, principally the 'Eagles,' based in Queen's Park, and teach rugby, which he believed better for the character. "I was nearly lynched" said Iori, who died in Bedford in 1985. But he survived the "angry mob" and so did rugby at a school which produced such players as Brian McCarthy, who played for the Blues more than 300 times, Bob Ingledew, who became President of the East Midlands, and many other players and administrators.

The headmaster of Silver Jubilee, Jack Voyce, was a rugby referee and lover of the game and his son Peter later propped for the Blues. Jim Philbrook, a points record holder at the club, taught the game at Pilgrim, the town's grammar school, and when Iori Evans moved, as he put it, "with his Welsh Mafia" to Westfield, rugby in the new state schools of the mid 1960s took off with men like Don Cottingham and Gareth Davies, once of Llanelli and London Welsh, and later club President, preaching the gospel. So too Keith Roberts, who also became President of the East Midlands. "We were missionaries," he once said, only half joking.

In 1986 it was established at the *Bedfordshire Times* that all of the upper schools and most of the middle schools in the Bedford area taught rugby at a time when experts thought it a game in decline because of the death of the grammar school. It flourished at schools such as Sharnbrook Upper where head teachers included ex Bedford first teamers David Jackson and John Clemence. The one-time British and Commonwealth Heavyweight Boxing Champion Matt Skelton said he was inspired to play rugby at Silver Jubilee School by teacher Neil Thomas who, after his retirement, ran a food bar at the club and cooked for the players. Once international school teams had been the province of the public schools but the England U18 side of 1981 included, besides Simon Smith of Bedford School, Paul Alston of Wootton Upper, a future four term club captain.

Professionalism, though, changed things again. One of the star players of the unbeaten Bedford School team of 2009 was Jamie Elliott, grandson of the Centenary President, Harry Elliott. He started at a very early age by kicking a ball around on the pitch at Goldington Road after first team games. He joined the Bedford mini section, played for the juniors, represented the England Under 16s and 18s and was actually contracted to Northampton while still at school. Others from the unbeaten Bedford School team of 2000 made their mark elsewhere. Will Skinner captained the Harlequins. David Callam was a Scottish international on the books at Edinburgh. Of those who regularly played in the league squad at Bedford in 2010-11, not one had been educated at a school in the town. However in the bigger squad used for the cup matches and the Barbarians fixture there were several locally educated players including

Josh Bassett (Harlington Upper), Steve Smith (Hastingsbury), Harry Peck (Bedford School) and Henry Staff (Bedford Modern School). The first two were in the Bedford Academy. The other two were registered at the time at Tynedale and Saracens respectively though Staff signed for Bedford in May 2011.

Several regulars, including Sacha Harding, Will Chudley, Darryl Veenendaal, Duncan Taylor and Chris Locke had come through the Bedford Academy and the Bedford Colts. The Colts, winners of the National Cup (for academies not funded by the RFU) in 2007, 2008, 2010 and 2011 set out to attract ambitious young players not just from the town and the county but from all over the region. Courtney Lawes, coached at school by the former Bedford hooker Norman Barker and capped by England at the age 20 in 2009, was a member at the Old Scouts in Northampton when he represented the Colts for the 2006-07 season and played in the semi final and final of the cup. At about the same time a number of England age group players were recruited from Leicester where they had progressed through their academy under the former Blues captain Andy Key, a part time backs coach at Goldington Road. They joined Bedford and quickly made a mark. Some of them, like Billy Twelvetrees, Dan Cole and Tom Youngs moved on again. Others, like Ollie Dodge and Gregor Gillanders, signed contracts to stay and looked set to join the elite group who made more than 100 appearances for the club. In 2011 it was quite clear that the old school tie had been well and truly loosened - but not discarded.

# THE BIRTH OF THE BLUES

Schools were the original nurseries of the game. But when boys left, they formed the clubs that were to keep alive their passion for rugby. The clubs themselves took over the responsibility for the sport's well being. Many had obvious allegiances to schools, universities and hospitals. When the Rugby Football Union was formed in 1871, Wellington College, King's College, St Paul's School and Guy's Hospital were among the 21 founder members. Together with four others, Blackheath, Richmond, Harlequins and the Civil Service, they were still in existence in 2011.

The first club in Bedford, outside of the schools, was the Bedford Britannia club. It was attached to the Britannia Ironworks and played organised fixtures in the Midland Road area. The first mention of it in the *Bedfordshire Times and Independent* was on November 22, 1873, when they played Hitchin on the Gas Works field. We are told that "the Britannia pack deserted their posts in the excitement and this led to defeat." In the same month they defeated Cleveland College Northampton, by "one poster, one try and one touch in goal to nil." The laws of the game and the methods of scoring were still evolving and were by no means universally accepted until the Rugby Union had established itself. Association football was introduced to the Britannia club at the same time and its members took on all comers at whichever game they chose. Eventually the club adopted the association code and those members who wanted to continue to play rugby joined a club known as the Swifts which was set up in 1882. The Britannia company was described in 1874 as 'vast'. It was the largest employer, it covered 15 acres and its product 'the champion plough of England', was sold world wide. In 1863, the company had been visited by the Italian President, General Garibaldi. James Howard was Mayor at the time and a commemoration tree was planted. Real industry played its part along with schools.

The Swifts were often described as a 'working man's team'. They had strong links with the Modern School through both pupils and masters, being set up by Alf Parrott and his colleagues on the staff there, the Reverend H E 'Tubby' Evans and A W 'Kipper' Allen. Parrott had been a boy at the school and later became its rugby coach. A E 'Josh' Hawkins was another on the staff of the Modern School with an interest in rugby and he later played for the Bedford club.

Just as the schools were rivals in the town's industry of education, so the Swifts had rivals in the rugby field. They were known as the Rovers, referred to as a 'gentlemen's team', with strong links to both the Grammar School and the County School. One of its founder members was H 'Pinkie' Booth who later came upon hard times and wrote an article for the *Bedfordshire Standard* which gives a useful first hand account of rugby in the town and the formation of the Rovers. E Hastings Dasent, the Grammar School legend, appointed in 1883, became a playing member.

The Rovers were formed in 1876 after a meeting in the Working Men's Institute in Harpur Street on October 12. The day before they had already played one match using the style of the Bedford Wanderers and they beat the Grammar School. In its first year the club was known as the Bedford Athletic and Football club and besides Booth's account there are many romantic reminiscences of their early days. "Booth, the Pursers, the Tudballs were names to conjure with", wrote the columnist in the Bedfordian's Diary in the *Bedfordshire Times* of 1943. "Purser was the captain and Charles Stimson, later to be Town Clerk, fulfilled the triple role of vice-captain, hon secretary and half-back".

The Rovers' first match after its inaugural meeting was against the Leys School and it ended in a win by three goals and three tries to nil. The formation adopted that day was two backs, three halves and ten forwards. In its second game it beat the County School with two backs, two halves, two quarterbacks and nine forwards. A week later the club suffered its first defeat when it lost to Britannia "by one try to three touches down; no goal was obtained by either party". Britannia lined up with one back, three three-quarters, four halves and only seven forwards, but the Rovers didn't ascribe its first defeat to "faulty distribution of its playing resources". In its next game, a defeat at St Paul's College, Stony Stratford, it used 16 players. There should have been nothing strange about that. The first England-Scotland international in 1871 saw Scotland and England both field 20 men, 13 of them forwards. There was no law about the numbers in a team until 1882, and even then it seemed advisory.

The Rovers

The Rovers' home ground was the House of Industry field in Goldington Road, to all intents and purposes the Bedford club's present headquarters, though slightly farther west and closer to the centre of the town. The Bedford Cricket Club, formed in 1875, used a square on what was known as the top pitch while the schools, with pitches near the railway station, often used what became the first team pitch. The Rovers moved nearer the station themselves, probably to a pitch near one already vacated by the Grammar School, before it was fully developed by the railway company. The railway had developed rapidly with lines to Bletchley in 1846, Cambridge in 1862, St Pancras in 1868 and Northampton in 1872. The Goldington Road ground, which the Swifts took over, was considered too far out of the way. Clubs wanted to play by the railway, which itself wanted ground for its own further expansion. The legend exists that W H Allen saw games on a field while travelling through Bedford by train and bought it, later to establish a firm which employed many rugby lovers and set up its own team, Queens Works, in 1918. Other clubs in the area were developing at Olney, Rushden, Bozeat, Wolverton, Stony Stratford, Northampton, Ampthill and Kempston.

The House of Industry ground was on a pronounced slope and it was unfenced, so no admission charges could be made. The Rovers had little business acumen within their ranks and after ten years of life, they ran into serious financial trouble. The Swifts, on the other hand, formed because of the overflow of available talent, were better organised.

They held their meetings at the Clarence Hotel where people other than players and schoolmasters took an interest in their wellbeing. By the autumn of 1886, the Swifts were going from strength to strength while the Rovers were in decline and, in effect, the Swifts took the Rovers over, though records show that the two clubs decided to amalgamate. The Swifts captain, Alf Parrott, was the first captain of the new team, the Swifts secretary, the businessman and player A F Dudley, became the new club's first secretary and treasurer and the Swifts ground in Goldington Road became its home. The new club was called the Swifts for its first year and then at its annual meeting on September 14, 1887, again at The Clarence Hotel in St John's, it was, said the *Bedfordshire Standard*, resolved "that the club in future be known as Bedford Rugby Football Club". Mr Parrott was again elected as captain. About 30 members were present. "Matches" continued the report, "have already been arranged with Leicester, Northampton, Olney, Charing Cross Hospital, St Mary's Hospital, Grammar and Modern Schools and Kempston. All communications should be addressed to the Hon Secretary A F Dudley, 81 Tavistock Street, Bedford." The Blues were born.

The Swifts

# HOW IT ALL BEGAN

The *Bedfordshire Standard* of September 19, 1930, carried something of a scoop by way of an account from a man who, in his last paragraph. claimed to have started the club. "How the Bedford Rugby Club began" was the heading. "What the game was like 60 years ago" was the subhead.

"Below Mr Herbert Booth, for long known as 'Pinkie', one of the stalwarts of Bedford 'Rugger' in the seventies and eighties, and a notable three-quarter, strong and fast, in his prime, writes of the clubs which existed in those days, and which, from necessarily primitive beginnings, laid the foundations of the present flourishing Town Club. Mr Booth, who is now living in Kilburn, can justly claim to be one of the pioneers of the Bedford club of today, and though he is now 72 years old, and for the last two years has been suffering from bad health, he still takes a lively interest in the game in general and in the fortunes of the 'Blues' in particular. As our readers doubtless know, the Bedford Rugby Club was formed about 1886-87 by the fusion of two rival clubs – the Rovers and the Swifts. 'Pinkie' Booth was one of the leading lights of the Rovers, and afterwards played for Olney, Southport, and Leigh (before the latter club joined the Northern Union). When Mr Booth was 60 years old he weighed 14st 8lb and measured 44 inches round the chest and 12 inches round the forearm, and, to use his own words, was 'as hard as iron'. A photograph of his torso, taken at that time, certainly shows a remarkable muscular development for a man of that age. Up to two years ago Mr Booth regularly used his clubs and dumb-bells before breakfast, but since then heart trouble and gout have compelled him, much to his regret, to abstain from the strenuous physical exercise in which he delighted. His article will interest Bedfordians of senior generations as well as players and supporters of the club which has just entered on what there is every reason for believing will be one of its most successful seasons.

**Mr Booth's Story**

Very little Rugby Football was played in Bedford before 1869, when I was a boy of eleven. I had not long come from the Cape, where I was born, and the nickname 'Pinkie' was given to me by my Kaffir nurse and has stuck with me ever since. The Bedford Grammar School, as far back as I can remember (when the Rev T Fanshawe was Headmaster) could always place a good Rugby fifteen in the field, all turning out in red jerseys, with the spread-eagle across the chest, looking neat, tidy and businesslike. The old Commercial School, now called the Modern School, under Mr Finlinson, did not possess a regular football team; neither did they play many matches. I think that was through want of encouragement.

**When Hacking was Allowed**

Many of the rugby rules have been altered since those days. Hacking and tripping were allowed. You could hack a man off his legs if he held the ball, or you could trip him up instead of tackling him. One of the best trips was the back heel, but you required to be faster than your opponent to execute it. Many old scores were paid off in scrimmages when hacking was allowed, especially when a Masters v Boys match was played. One would often see a master hopping out of the scrum on one leg and carefully nursing the other! Football in those days was very vicious and rough. At this time (about 1870) a large school was built on Ampthill Road, called the Bedford County School. (The first Headmaster was Mr Morris, MA). On completion, it was soon filled, mostly with farmers' sons from the surrounding shires. Taking them as a whole, they were a sturdy lot of boys, and very soon placed a smart Rugby team on the go, their colours being dark blue and yellow hoops. They, like the Grammar School, had matches nearly every Wednesday and Saturday with other schools, Cambridge and Oxford colleges, and a few towns – Northampton, Leicester and Luton. I was at the County School and played three-quarter back for the first team.

### The First Town Rugby Club

I left school in 1876. At that time Bedford had no football club, only scratch teams we managed to get together to play the schools. An old schoolboy friend of mine, Walter Stimson, who was killed in the Zulu War (brother to Charles Stimson, late Town Clerk of Bedford, who was our first football captain), and I, made up our minds to form a Town Football Club and we soon made a start. The first subscription we obtained was from Mr Frederic Hockliffe, father of the late Ald F R Hockliffe of High Street, Bedford, who set the ball rolling with 10/-. This gave us great encouragement, and we next called on Mr George Hurst, known as 'Old Georgie', who was Mayor at the time. Here we received a quick damper as 'Old Georgie' told us he didn't encourage laziness! But a few weeks after that he gave us a guinea. After much tramping about we managed to collect a little over £10. With this we bought two footballs and the goal-posts, and some kind ladies made the touch-flags. Our ground was the House of Industry field on the Goldington Road. There was no charge for admission, on account of the ground being so open. Our first football meeting was held at the Working Men's Institute. Our president was Captain Polhill-Turner of Howbury Hall, who kindly subscribed two guineas; our vice-president was Mr Hugh Jackson, and Charles Stimson was elected captain. The club was called the Bedford Football and Athletic Club. The colours were black, and the subscription was 5/- per annum. We got about thirty members, but out of these we could only place about ten good men in the field. It was a hard job to get fifteen playing members together and every weekend Walter Stimson and myself had to call at the members' houses to see if they could play. If it was a home match we did not have so much trouble to get the men together, but if the match was away from home there were many excuses for not playing. The consequence was, we often had to go away with a weak team, and then there was trouble on account of not playing some of the members in home matches who had willingly played away.

### The Bedford Rovers

As time went on we thought it best to alter the name of the club, so we called a meeting together and had the name changed to The Bedford Rovers, and the colours were changed from black to light and dark crimson four-inch hoops. At the same time we passed a rule that boys from the Grammar and Modern Schools could join by paying half the membership fee. This was a good idea, as it gave us more members and strengthened the team. We had from the Grammar School, Eicke, Pym, Sargeaunt and others; from the Modern School, Vivian, Allen, Walling and Boucher. I proposed that we should allow any townsman to join as long as he was a decent fellow. I proposed Tom Fowler, who eventually became one of our best forwards. He was a good rowing man, which kept him in good condition. He was always quiet and inoffensive, and played for the Rovers the same time that I did. I believe he afterwards became a faithful servant to the Club for many years.

In those days the following players made a strong team – Jack Purser, as full-back, was a good kick and tackled well. He was rather fond of holding the ball too long, for being a strong man, he seemed to enjoy handing off his opponents before he got his kick in; but he was safe. Our three-quarters were composed of Tommy Boucher, the Rev Hugh Evans and myself. The half-backs were Charles Stimson and Stanley Orr. Charles Stimson having twisted his knee, had to give up football and A W Allen took his place. Among our forwards were Eicke, Tom Fowler, Dr Hacon, Vere, Frank Mitchell, Edgar Kempson (who afterwards became captain), Owen Carpenter, and Maldon. Lieutenant Couper Coles, then of the 16th Regiment of Foot, used to be one of the full-backs. He was very reliable, and a good kick. Herbert Castens, a study young fellow, was a very good forward. I am sorry to say he died last year after a long illness.

Believed to be the first Bedford team combining the Rovers and the Swifts

**No Charge at the Gates**

With this team we could hold our own against most of our opponents, and as the Club made progress we began to get a fairly good 'gate', but we made no charge, on account of the ground being so open; and the same thing happened when we had to give up the House of Industry field, our new ground being a large field just over the Midland Railway Bridge. Here again we could make no charge. This always kept the Club poor and it was only through the energy of a few of us that it was kept going. About this time another football club started in Bedford, called the Bedford Swifts. Alfred Parrott was the captain. I did not know much about them. I know they did fairly well and had a few fast men among them – Tom Foster, Reeves and others.

**When 'Seppy' played**

On another occasion when the Bedford Rovers were playing the Grammar School on their ground, the school included among their forwards one of the masters, the Rev Septimus Phillpott (brother to the Headmaster), who played for the school on many occasions. He was very eccentric, but a kind and good man and a good sportsman. As the game advanced, there were some hot scrimmages and hard kicking, resulting in Frank Mitchell, a Rovers forward, hopping out of the scrum nursing a wound and using some swear-words. On hearing this, the Rev Septimus Phillpott stopped the game, divided the two teams, offered up a prayer and gave the signal to start again, which we did with renewed energy.

### A Remarkable Match

In the early days of the Bedford Football and Athletic Club we had fixed up a match with a club called the Irthlingborough Hawks, on our ground. It appeared they had arranged an Association match with the Britannia Football Club the same afternoon, before they played us. In due course the Hawks arrived, with twelve men, and they would not play the match unless we played the same number. This being settled, it came to the matter of boots. As we found they were going to play in the same boots they were wearing, the soles of which were studded with hobnails and tips, we objected to them, unless they did not kick in the scrums. Some of the Hawks played in their trousers and shirts, and a few in knickers, and so the game started. We scored tries as we wanted them, but towards the finish of the game, while an argument was taking place, a big Hawk pounced on the ball, ran down the ground and threw the ball over the cross-bar, and a goal was claimed by them. The referee immediately squashed this. Soon after the whistle blew and thus ended the eventful (!) match.

### Start of the Olney Club

I left Bedford when I was 21 and went to reside at Olney. Here, with the help of Mr Charles Hipwell, we called a football meeting at The Bull Inn. Mr Charles Hipwell was elected captain. He was a splendid three-quarter back, running, dodging and tackling well, and played for the Bedford Rovers on several occasions. The colours of Olney Rugby Club were cerise and French grey. Mr Hipwell kindly lent us the field, many of our Bedford men joined the club, and it became a success.

My career as a footballer ended in Lancashire. I became captain of the Southport rugby team and on leaving Southport I went to reside at Leigh and played three-quarter back for their rugby team, which now belongs to the Northern Union. I believe the old Bedford Rovers club is now called the Bedford Town Football Club – a more appropriate name. Mr W N Blake has been a supporter of the club for many years, and has taken a great interest in its progress. As I started the club fifty-five years ago, nothing gives me greater pleasure than to see a man like Mr Blake and other fine sportsmen carrying on the good work. I wish the club every success."

Olney in 1877. Pinkie Booth is standing on the extreme right

# THE INVINCIBLES

In its first season, the new club was still referred to as the Swifts, and the early teams consisted mainly of those who had been in their ranks the year before. Some of the Rovers continued to play, but others, most noticeably E H Dasent never played for the new club, though he was to become its second President in 1921. The Swifts captain, secretary, players, colours and ground formed the basis for the new club but within their ranks they contained several who had served both clubs in spite of their supposed divisions. One of the most remarkable of them was Tommy Fowler, an iron moulder by trade at J and F Howard, whose grandson Doug was the club President in its 100th year.

Tommy was an artisan with friends in all places and the tastes of a Corinthian. He played both soccer and rugby for the Britannia club where he was a founder member and pursued an athletics career at the Achilles. He rowed and later organised the enclosure at the Regatta. He played for both the Swifts and the Rovers, turned out in most of the matches in the first season and served rugby in the town for more than 50 years, retiring in 1928 as groundsman at Goldington Road.

The new club's first ever match was against Olney, formed in 1877, and played at Goldington Road, on October 9, 1886. Bedford won by 10-3 after Olney had opened with a goal, worth three points. Ransom, Bastock, Garner and Joseph Foster scored tries, worth one point; Jones kicked two goals, worth three points each. The press report of the match said that Parrott and Harris, as well as the scorers, played well for the Swifts; Farrar and Church showed up best for Olney. The club beat the Grammar, 8-0, Modern, 1-0, and County School 12-0 and made an auspicious start winning 17 of its 20 games with its only defeat coming at Leicester on December 27 by 10-0. In its second season, the team did even better losing just one game in 25 and that to a composite London XV, by 16-0, its first defeat at home.

For that second season, the club seems to have preferred to play on the ground at Midland Road in its attempt to expand its fixtures with clubs with London bases. The railway provided easy access to and from the capital to a rapidly growing town whose population rose from 16,850 in1871, 19,533 in 1881, 28,033 in 1891 to 35,144 by 1901.

The schools by now had completely vacated their sites at Midland Road. The line to St Pancras went through the old Grammar School pitch, while that once used by the Modern School was required for engine sheds. There was, though, a pitch still in use between the railway and the gas works in Ford End Road which used to stage matches for both the 'town' club and the county – the South Midlands, forerunners of the East Midlands. The ground on the other side of Ford End Road was also used and a *Bedfordshire Times* report in November 1890, says that the gate at a match against Leicester was poor because spectators were standing on the new railway bridge, the Bromham Road Bridge, and they could see just as well as if they had been on the touchline.

With the expansion of the railways, industry and houses for commuters and workers, the club was squeezed out of the Midland Road area and by 1893, they were forced to move to a ground in Goldington Avenue using the cricket club's new pavilion on the House of Industry ground. "It is a sombre looking iron structure well adapted for its purpose and a great improvement on the old cow hovel which formerly adorned the spot" said the *Bedfordshire Times*. Spectators were asked not to walk across the cricket square on their way to the rugby pitch.

The ground created problems for a number of years and made gate collecting difficult. Support for the new team, however, was substantial and there are reports of crowds of

2-3,000 spectators paying 3d or 6d to watch fixtures which in 1893-94 included London Welsh, Leicester, Northampton, Coventry, the Grammar and Modern Schools, and, on February 5, Stade Francais of Paris, and, on February 21, the Barbarians, for the first time.

When the club moved back to Goldington Road, they little thought that they were on the threshold of one of the most remarkable seasons in their history. How could they have dreamed they were to become known as the 'Invincibles'. Their annual meeting disclosed that the 1892-93 season had been a disappointing one. Their best performance was a win over Clapham Rovers; the gate money, which usually averaged about £20 a match had only totalled £8 6s 11d. Games had been cancelled because of frost and, with a deficiency of £7 in the books, the players and committee had agreed to "defray out of their own pockets."

The Invincibles of 1893-94

"Well", said the *Bedfordshire Times*, "the miracle happened. The new captain Billy Rees inspired confidence in his men from the start, and built up that wonderful team, that happy band of brothers, that perfect blend of the two schools, trained and tempered into a first class attacking machine. When Leicester were beaten, you could feel it in the air. Bedford has seldom been so excited in the whole course of its rather phlegmatic existence."

The 1893-94 team was the most successful in the club's 125 year history. It played 29 games, drew one, 0-0 with Northampton, and lost one, a challenge match at Coventry on Easter Monday by 12-0. Several members of the Bedford team had prior engagements at the Oakley Hunt Steeplechase meeting that day but the defeat stands even though it isn't recorded in the earlier edition of the *Guinness Book of Rugby Facts and Figures*.

Bedford beat Stade Francais at Goldington Avenue by 22-0. They then beat the Barbarians by 7-3, in front of their largest crowd, estimated at 6,000 people. At least 12 of the Bedford team had allegiances with either the Grammar or the Modern School, while the Barbarians contained F A Cory, a pupil at the Grammar, and H W Finlinson, formerly of the Modern School. They were captained by their founder, W P Carpmael of Blackheath.

The Bedford team was: A G Goodison, H H Morris, P G Jacob, W F Surtees, F W Potter, W K Roberts, B G N Knight, W Rees, capt, R Thompson, H Cross, J Niven, A H Griffith, G L Hamilton, W J Carey, G Crampton.

The Barbarian team was: E Field, W G Druce, W Neilson, C Wells, L Mortimer, W P Donaldson, F H Maturin, W P Carpmael, capt, E Bonham Carter, J C A Rigby, S W Whiteway, A F Todd, C Dixon, H W Finlinson, F A Cory.

The referee was Mr A Parrott and the touch judges were Messrs W Browne and H Sharman. Druce scored a try for the visitors, Hamilton for Bedford and Jacob, still a pupil at the Grammar School, dropped a goal to win the match. It was their 26th in succession.

Years later, former players, 'Daddy' Read, the Pavenham farmer, and A Udal, a member of a well known sporting family, remembered the song of the day, perpetuated by a local scribe and sung to the tune of 'After the ball was over.' Four long verses made references to every member of the team. The chorus went:

*After the football is over, after the match is done*
*You will hear people shout, Bedford have again won*
*Twenty-six matches they have played, nay friends 26 they have won*
*So give them a cheer, they never see fear*
*And they'll beat the next team that come.*

In just a few years, Bedford had emerged from obscurity to beat the best rugby union clubs in the land.

# CLOSED DOWN - BY ORDER

The 1893-94 season put the Bedford rugby club on the map. Many of the records achieved that season stood for many years. H H Morris's feat of 38 tries in a season still stood in 2011, as did the playing record with just one defeat in 29 games. The town was growing in the late Victorian era with W H Allen opening their Queen's Works in 1894. The last public execution in Bedford was in 1868, the Corn Exchange was built in 1873, John Bunyan's statue was unveiled in 1874 and Kempston Barracks opened in 1877. Bedford Rowing Club was formed in 1886, and sports were booming with the opening of Bedford Park and the suspension bridge on the same day in 1888.

Large crowds were recorded at rugby matches and fixtures improved. In January 1895, Bedford made their first visit to Wales, playing Swansea and Aberavon; but they still didn't have a ground they could call their own. In 1895, Goldington Avenue was extended and the club lost its pitch but came to an agreement with the cricket club to lease a pitch roughly where they were to find a permanent place. It still took time to work out a deal with the cricket club and in order that the square could be prepared, they were forced to vacate the site and take on Leicester, in front of 3,000 people, in a field in Ampthill Road with an entrance on Victoria Road. In 1896 they entertained Abercarn and Llwynpia from Wales on Easter Saturday and Monday in the same place.

The town of Bedford soon produced another side. The Wanderers, who were formed in 1894-95, beat Northampton, away, and played on the Ampthill Road pitch. They operated until 1899 but then ran into financial difficulties owing £17 11s 10d. They had a close relationship with Bedford and frequently exchanged players, and it was no surprise when they were invited to join forces. Bedford paid off the debt, having themselves made a profit of £42 9s 6d on the season 1898-99. J R D Glascott had been captain of the Wanderers and he became a captain of Bedford.

The Kempston Rovers club had played the new Bedford in the first match of 1887-88 and they continued until 1911, playing mostly the Bedford second team, the 'A team', and supplying players like the Cocking brothers, Alf Osbourn and the Hall brothers to the senior club. Alf Hall, later a captain, was remembered for wearing his cap in the streets of Kempston if Bedford had won its match. Caps were introduced in the 1890s. They were black, after the Swifts colours, and cerise, after the Rovers who played in dark red and pink. In 1923 caps were changed to the new colours, dark blue and light blue, the colours adopted by Bedford as soon as they changed their name from the Swifts. The club experimented with a white strip for one season and white was the recognised change until 1985 when a variation of the two blues was introduced. Light and dark blue, black and cerise are the colours incorporated into the club's insignia.

With new responsibilities on a permanent pitch, the club hired Tommy Fowler as part-time groundsman at ten shillings a week and they made the first attempt to level the pitch in 1898. Cherry and Rogers carried out the work at a cost of £170, borrowed from the London and Midland bank at 4½ per cent. The club's finances were in good order having recovered from the 1892-93 season of lost gate money and 'certain irregularities' the year after.

By 1900, the club had a thriving fixture list. In 1898-99 leading Irish teams Monkstown and Bective Rangers were visitors to Goldington Road. Membership had increased to more than 100, members paying a minimum of five shillings, entrance to a match was 3d or 6d and advertisers were charged for space in the match card. On the outgoings, players were entitled to expenses for travelling, lemons for half-time worked out at 6d a match, the Bedford Town Band cost ten shillings per game and visiting sides were guaranteed money to appear. In the case of Burton on Trent, one of the top Midland clubs, it was £10 for a Boxing Day visit.

Police officers cost five shillings per match and on one day in 1901 they had the opportunity to earn their money. The occasion was the Bedford-Northampton game on February 23, which the home side lost by 3-14. Spectators showed their disapproval after the match by jostling the referee and visiting players and the East Midlands closed the ground down from March 9 until March 29. Already that year games on January 26 and February 2 had been scratched in accordance with Rugby Union instructions for the death and funeral of Queen Victoria.

The *Bedfordshire Standard's* report the following week read: "Bedford: F Redman, F G Brooks, M E Finlinson, DeSchmitt, E Kelberer, C Randall, A Mender, F S P Saunders, J R D Glascott, R Maclear, F W Tucker, W F Bryant, J Foster, C Parsons, A Chambers. Results – 3-14, F G Brooks scoring a try ... Shortly before the interval Mender broke his leg ... Foster had the misfortune to break his nose but he is going to play tomorrow ... In the second half after the referee had ruled that Kingston beat Brooks (Bedford) to the touch down after the latter had kicked ahead ... The crowd again let out their disapproval. Of course it was a real disappointment and Bedford were allowed no points but the spectators must really learn to curb their feelings or they will be getting their club into trouble and possibly earn the suspension of their ground, which I am sure they have no wish to do ... As soon as the game was over the spectators on the 'threepenny' side swarmed round the players and booed both the Northampton team and the referee. It could hardly be called a mobbing, but I understand that the latter official said nothing and was escorted out of the ground and into a cab by the Bedford players. It was a regrettable incident and I hope will not be repeated or the Bedford club will certainly be brought into trouble through no fault of their own."

On March 8, the paper reported that following the report of the referee Mr McGawley, the ground was to be closed: "I believe this is the first time the Bedford ground has been suspended in this way and I remember only one other occasion when the club deemed it advisable to distribute hand bills on the ground giving warning that it might be closed if hostile demonstrations were made regarding the referee. In the present instance I am happy to report the referee-baiting was not indulged in by the regular attendants but only by a certain number of irresponsible rowdies who attend only on such extra special occasions as the match with Northampton and as they go for the express purpose of seeing their own side win, when losing if the opposing side proves the better it is through the favours of the referee, upon whom, therefore, they vent their displeasure. Such 'patriotism' should not be underestimated, their presence being an infliction on the club. But they must be educated as good sportsmen and I would appeal to the orderly loving regulars of the ground to use their best endeavours by courteous and other legitimate means to check any future display of undesirable feeling. One of the findings of the East Midlands Union is "that the team and officials tried their utmost to prevent the demonstrations and are completely exonerated from any blame in the matter. That is only fair and just but what about the next occasion."

In another part of the same paper under the heading "An Appeal from the Club Office" was a letter from Mr R Thompson, Hon Sec of the club, referring to the Bedford v Northampton game. "In consequence of the disgraceful behaviour of a section of the spectators at the above match (Bedford v Northampton) the office of the Football Club has decided to make this appeal to their regular supporters asking them to use every endeavour to assist in keeping order.

Spectators like players, must bear in mind that the referee is the sole judge of the game and his decisions are final and must be accepted by all in a true sportsmanlike manner (as the press reporter wrote). The referee at the above match, after the abominable treatment he received had no other alternative than to report the matter to the RU authorities, with the result that the ground has been suspended until March 29. The punishment, (the results of the conduct of a few ignorant and unsportsmanlike persons), falls heavily on the innocent, both players and orderly spectators. The latter, let it be definitely understood that they, on their part, will need to prevent a repetition of this inexcusable behaviour and that if, in the future, a referee's decisions are received with any booing and open manifestations of dissent, as occurred in the above match they have requested the Captain to withdraw his team from the field as a protest against such conduct."

The New Zealand tourists of 1905

# BEDFORD V NEW ZEALAND

In 1987 rugby's first World Cup was scheduled to be staged 100 years after the birth of the Blues and the formation of the International Board. In 2011, the seventh tournament was scheduled. On both occasions, New Zealand were the pre-tournament favourites, a reflection of their pre-eminence in the game established, it could be argued, as long ago as 1905 when the first All Blacks came to Britain.

Eighty years on, the *Bedfordshire Times* met a supporter who was introduced to rugby the day Bedford played New Zealand. Yes, New Zealand. It was November 15, 1905, and it was surely one of the greatest days in the club's history. The supporter was Arthur Clarke who lived in Bromham and, at the age of 90, still had a razor sharp brain. The edition of November 14, 1985 took up three-quarters of a broadsheet page to celebrate the anniversary of the match against the All Blacks through the eyes of a man who sneaked in under the hedge.

A forward thinking committee had secured a fixture with the tourists by guaranteeing £35 and 70 per cent of the gate. More than 6,000 people turned up to watch the match. The town closed down for a half day to give its citizens the chance to go along to Goldington Road to see what became known as one of the greatest touring sides ever.

Arthur Clarke was a ten year-old at Clapham Road School when a rugby keen headmaster, Mr Guppy, announced a half day off. He went along to the ground with a number of his chums but when he saw the prices – 3/6, 2/6, 1/- and 6d – he decided against going in. So, along with countless others, he 'bought' what he called a 'hedge ticket', sneaked in under the fence, liked what he saw and used it on and off for a number of years thereafter. Say no more.

The 1905 touring team is remembered in New Zealand as one of the greatest. They followed the 1888-89 Maoris and changed the game by the use of specialist positions and skills while the Home Unions still hadn't settled on the positioning of 15 players.

The New Zealanders actually planned moves; they developed the ruck, the wing forward, the five eighths, the attacking full-back and the miss pass. They used the hooker to throw in at the line-outs at a time when in England the hooker was the first man to arrive at the lineout or scrum. The next to get there became the prop and so on.

Not surprisingly our 'colonial cousins' swept all before them and set many records. They beat Scotland, Ireland, England and France, with ten tries, and lost just once in 33 matches. On December 16, in front of 25,000 at Cardiff, they went down 3-0. It still hurts, they say, that a famous try wasn't allowed. The Welsh had plenty of time to prepare for the game and work out their plans to counter the 'pioneers'. But teams who met the tourists early on were caught cold. They opened with a 55-0 win against the county champions, Devon, and Fleet Street changed the result because they didn't believe it possible.

For ten year-old Arthur Clarke, the day off from school and the taste of adventure was more important than the detail of the day. But the late Brigadier M C T Gompertz, an Old Bedfordian, has provided an account for the Bedford records in a letter to Don Riddy, the club's first Keeper of the Records. "Bedford", he wrote, "were appalled at what they had taken on. So they went out into the highways and byeways and collected a pretty hot side. They got Hudson, an international, and Romans, from Gloucester; Anderson and Basil Maclear, the Old Bedfordian and Irish international, the Northampton halves and Edgar Mobbs, an Old Modernian born in Olney in 1892, capped seven times for England and killed in the First World War."

The Brigadier implies that this made the tourists put out a stronger side than they wanted to with their first international – against Scotland – to follow on the Saturday.

The All Blacks certainly gave an amazing display and they won with four tries in the first half and one conversion, making it 14-0, five tries in the second half, of which four were converted, and a dropped goal from a mark. Their scrum half, Hunter, scored five tries. The tourists then moved on up to Inverleith, where they beat Scotland 12-7 on November 18. Arthur Clarke and his mates and many more were hooked for life.

The line-up at Goldington Road that Wednesday afternoon was Bedford: J Romans, E R Mobbs, M E Finlinson, B Maclear, H J Anderson, A Hudson, H C Palmer, T N Preston, J Mason, N G Follitt, W Johns, A L Rogers, R B Campbell, A V Manton, R Maclear (captain).

New Zealand: G Gillet, D McGregor, R G Deans, E Harper, H J Mynott, J Hunter, F Roberts S Casey, G Tyler, J Corbett, F Newton, G Nicholson, A McDonald, C Seeling, D Gallaher (captain). Referee: Mr F W Nicholls (Leicester).

Of the New Zealand team, their captain, Dave Gallaher, is the man credited with introducing the specialist wing forward position in a party that changed the way the game was played for ever after. Bob Deans is the player who 'scored' the disputed try that lost the tourists their 100 per cent record in the 3-0 defeat by Wales, the defeat all subsequent touring teams have set out to avenge.

With such an introduction to the game, Arthur Clarke became a devoted Bedford fan and he followed them for 80 years, seeing all their ups and downs and all their great players. He rated Arthur Heard, Dick Stafford, 'Daddy' Read and 'Budge' Rogers as the best the club had.

How did the *Bedfordshire Times* see the big match? The November 10 issue of 1905 reads thus: "New Zealanders have shown the mother country that she does not know how to play football. That is so far. But next Wednesday they have to face Bedford, and Bedford, we understand on good authority, will show no mercy whatever. It may be that the New Zealanders will regret that they did not yield to the persuasion of Lancashire and give up the Bedford match in favour of a new fixture in Manchester." It goes on in a style of the time: "The colonials have already beaten Devon, Cornwall, Bristol, etc ... Rather than jeopardise those beautifully poetic love bonds which, according to politicians, bind the colonies to Britain, we would beg of the Bedfordians to let their visitors down lightly."

The *Bedfordshire Times and Independent* produced the official programme for the match, price 2d, and Huntley and Palmer handed out big match memorabilia. Special trains were laid on to bring spectators from Northampton, London and Luton. The November 14 issue of the *Bedford Record* took note of the warning of one London newspaper that the contest "would be a picnic for the New Zealanders." And so it proved. The tourists arrived in Bedford on Monday and straightaway went from their headquarters at the Swan Hotel to the park for kicking and passing practice. In the evening they occupied the dress circle at the Royal County Theatre. Their management complained about the inclusion of Basil Maclear in the team, but it was pointed out that he was an Old Bedford Grammar School boy and that was good enough. There were 11 in the team.

The ball by ball match report on Friday, November 17, took up an entire column. It was much more restrained and humble than the preview, of course: "A mere provincial writer is not fit to tell of their merits." Quite so.

# PRIDE AND JOY

In less than 20 years, Bedford had secured fixtures against the club side which was to become the most respected in the world and the touring team from one of the greatest rugby countries. By the time the war broke out in 1914, it had established itself as one of the leading clubs in the land with a permanent home, a strong fixture list, a regular supply of players from its schools and a number of internationals to its credit.

The season before they played New Zealand, the club opened its first grandstand, built by the contractors Chas Negus at the cost of £201 and opened by the wife of the President on February 11, 1905, before a match against London Welsh. At the meeting of the committee in the Lion Hotel on January 30, it was resolved that Mrs Guy Pym should receive a bouquet of flowers in the club colours of light and dark blue. Her husband Guy Pym was the club's first President and as the town's MP until 1906 he held similar offices in many other sporting arenas. Conditions of membership were altered to encourage some to pay more. For the match against New Zealand £42 was realised from the grandstand and £310 3s 7d from the gate. By then, the club had in excess of 200 members.

Big matches generated enormous interest in the town and gates boomed in a flourishing era. The new stand was a welcome improvement but the players' and referees' changing facilities were not of a very high standard. In 1909, the Bedford committee explored the possibility of building a new pavilion which could also be used for scrummage practice on winter evenings. At the time, the Bedford Cricket Club held the lease on the ground from the House of Industry and they sub-let it to the rugby club. But in 1910, the rugby club took it over and sub-let to the cricket club, acquiring, at the same time, an additional strip of land on which to build the new pavilion.

The stand opened in 1905

The Scrum Hall opened in 1910 was a bar 100 years later

Detailed plans were prepared by E H C Inskip, a well known local architect and a vice-president and committee man. A tender of £574 from Melcombe and Sons was accepted on condition that the project was completed by August 1, 1910. The London City and Midland Bank agreed a loan of £300 at 4½ per cent per annum. Mr Inskip, as well as former captain, Charles Franklin, whose family were coal merchants, S R Wells, a member of the brewing family and later President, and J W Carter, a wholesale confectioner, later the club's first official Chairman, agreed to act as guarantors.

The Scrum Hall, as it came to be known, was completed in time and used first for the opening match of the 1910-11 season for a game against Bedfordshire RU. "It comes into use tomorrow" said the *Bedfordshire Times* of September 2, 1910, "when the teams and referee will dress there and can have their bath and rub down after the match. A gate opposite the Hall runs into the arena. The Hall is furnished with a few seats and the lock up shelves will be useful for Mr T Fowler to store footballs and other equipment in." Mr Fowler, the groundsman, ruled from the Scrum Hall. Towards the end of that season, his son Ralph played five times as a young full back, and 75 years later, his grandson Doug, the Bedford President, proposed the toast to the building that became the club's pride and joy.

The Bedfordshire team for that first match of 1910-11 was: W Hills, O Whaley (Bedford Athletic), F Harrison (Kempston), C C Stafford, L Bennett (Bedford A), E Childs, B Catlin, C Piercey (Bedford Athletic), C Hall (Bedford Nomads), Lansberry (Old Modernians), L Kingston (Kempston), F Osbourn, A Leach (Bedford Athletic), E Jarvis (Old Bedford Grammar), E Fowler (Bedford Nomads).

Visiting teams spoke highly of the new facility. The *Bedfordshire Times* of October 21, reported that the Harlequins, the leading team in the country "considered them the best dressing rooms in England." They had just run in 11 tries in a 47-7 win with Adrian Stoop, John Birkett and Ronnie Poulton in their side.

The Scrum Hall was turned into a quartermaster's store in the First World War and used as a classroom for children evacuated from London in the second. When a new pavilion was opened in 1960, the Scrum Hall took on a new lease of life and became the club bar. In 1968, the dining hall and kitchen extension was added and in 1969, the honours board was unveiled there by L H Nicholson, the oldest surviving captain.

# DICK STAFFORD

The pride and joy of Bedford in 1905 was its rugby captain, Ronnie Maclear, a former pupil of the Grammar School and the son of a doctor who practised in The Crescent. "Ronnie Maclear has been elected captain" said the *Bedfordshire Times* of September 8, 1905. "What would ye more? He is the synonym of a good footballer as Bedfordians very well know. He has rendered yeoman service to the Bedford club while others have fallen to the blandishments of other, perhaps more brilliant clubs. Ronnie has been faithful."

He led the side against the New Zealanders and later became a trainer at Bedford Athletic. The 'Ath' were formed in 1908 when the Royal Army Medical Corps moved its depot to Luton and the team who played for them, The Rams, after RAMC, decided at a meeting at the Kings Arms to carry on playing in Bedford at a field opposite the Park Hotel. Arthur 'Shaver' Leach was their first secretary and Ronnie is remembered by the Athletic as the man who taught the game to players from the elementary rather than Harpur Trust schools at a time when the town club expected to take its pick of the best from the Grammar and Modern. Joe Foster, a former Bedford player, was a founder member of the 'Ath'. W C Chalker, educated at Elstow School, was its first captain.

Ronnie Maclear

Basil Maclear

Ronnie's brother Basil, the youngest of five sons of a local doctor, was probably one of those the newspapers considered had left the town for more 'brilliant clubs', in his case Blackheath, where many of Hastings Dasent's protégés from the Grammar School were directed. One of the reasons was Blackheath's proximity to Woolwich and the great tradition between the Grammar School and the Army. Basil was gazetted from Sandhurst into the Royal Dublin Fusiliers and saw action in the Boer War, fighting at Spion Kop, and like the great Bedford Modern School hero E R Mobbs, he was killed in action in the First World War. Two of his brothers also lost their lives while serving in the Army.

Basil Maclear is best known in rugby for playing against the 1905 New Zealanders four times in a month, turning out in the threequarters for Blackheath on November 4, Bedford on the 15th, Ireland on the 25th and Munster on the 28th – losing each time. In all, he won 11 caps for Ireland, making his debut against England as a member of Cork County in February 1905. He also played for Monkstown, Sandhurst, the Army and the Barbarians as well as Blackheath and, of course, Bedford for whom he turned out at least 17 times between 1896 and 1906. Along with Mobbs, who played twice for Bedford, he was considered a legitimate 'guest' in the famous match against the All Blacks. His brother, of course, was captain.

The Grammar School produced its first international long before the town club did. Percy Christopherson of Blackheath in 1891, holds that distinction while P G Jacob, who dropped the goal for Bedford to beat the Barbarians while he was still at school in 1894, was its second, also as a member of Blackheath, in 1898. The School's third international was the club's first, J G Milton, capped for England while still a schoolboy. 'Jumbo' Milton was captain of the XV in 1903-04 and in that same season he played for Bedford in October and December of 1903 and February and March of 1904. In between, he was capped for England as a forward, against Wales on January 9, 1904, in a match played at Leicester that finished in a 14-14 draw. He was capped twice more that season while a member of Bedford and then twice more while a member of the Camborne School of Mines. His brother C H Milton was also educated at the Grammar School and he too was capped for England in 1906 while at the Camborne School of Mines. The Milton family is unique in the history of English rugby. Sir William Henry Milton, father of the two boys, was also capped by England, in 1874 and 1875. Later he captained South Africa at cricket.

Bedford's first three internationals, J G Milton, F G Brooks and E L Chambers were all products of the Grammar School. Milton played for the club just four times, Brooks 17, and Chambers, who later returned as a master, four. The club's fourth international was D M Grant who was capped twice for Scotland in 1911 while still a pupil at the Elstow School at which also 'Pinkie' Booth and many of the Rovers had been educated. He played for Bedford 25 times before joining London Scottish.

Bedford Modern School's first two internationals were both Blackheath players. W B Thomson was capped four times between 1892 and 1895 and its second H W Finlinson, later the fifth President of the Blues, three times in 1895. The school's third, Edgar Mobbs, made little impact while a pupil but he was capped seven times between 1909 and 1910 as a member of the Northampton club. Legend has it that he led his men in the First World War by kicking a rugby ball 'over the top' and following it up. The annual match between the Barbarians and the East Midlands, instituted in 1921, was played in his memory. In March 2008 Bedford took over the fixture.

If the Maclears were the early epitome of the Grammar School rugby player, then R C 'Dick' Stafford was the same to the Bedford Modern School. To the club, he was the first "born and bred in our midst, to play for no other, to become its captain and to be called on by his country." Dick Stafford attended the school from 1900-1910 and had a trial for the club in September 1908 at the age of 15. He made his debut for Bedford in March 1909, against Old Charltonians and played for the East Midlands while still at school. He was named vice-captain of the club in 1910-11 and 'assisted' Northampton on their Easter tour of 1911, having played for the South v England in the international trial at Twickenham in December 1910. He was elected captain of Bedford in 1911-12 at the age of 18 and in 1912 played four times for England. He was elected captain for a second term but was taken ill on October 27, 1912, aged 19 years and four months. Newspaper reports showed just what the young rugby captain meant to the town.

The *Bedfordshire Times* of November 15, 1912, reported on the game between Bedford and St Bartholomew's Hospital the previous Saturday: "We understand a proposal was made on Saturday to postpone this game in sympathy and honour of the brave spirit that lay, not far away, in extremis. The game was played, but the team had no heart for it. A gloom was over the play, for all spectators and players seemed to be living under the shadow of a great tragedy. The news that morning that the popular young skipper, the very embodiment it had seemed of all the athletic virtues, a giant among his fellows in stature and of perfect physique lay near unto death and that his life was despaired of, was present in every mind."

The *Bedfordshire Times* of December 6, 1912, devoted almost a whole page to the death and funeral of R C Stafford who had died on Sunday morning shortly before daybreak. "His last game had been on October 24, when he helped East Midlands to win their first county match of the season handsomely. Three days later he took to his bed but it was not until Friday, November 8, that it was realised that his condition was dangerous. Then came with awful suddenness the announcement that a London specialist had been called in, had pronounced his case hopeless and refused to operate and that, at the outside, Dick Stafford had but one month to live. He was the fourth in line of Old Modernian internationals and was the first Bedford born and bred who had grown up in our midst. Though born to greatness on the football field he had no 'side', was a staunch friend and an extremely popular leader

"The funeral service took place in St Mary's Church. The streets were thronged with people, blinds were drawn and windows shuttered on the route. A reserved space in the nave was filled by members of firm and staff of Messrs Stafford and Rogers and their friends. Buried in Bedford Cemetery. There was a greater multitude than at any funeral within our recollection for 20 years. He made his debut in the Bedford pack during the 1908-09 season at one of the holiday matches. He had first played as a 'pick up' for an opposing team. He was said to have played a great game for East Midlands against the Midlands in 1909-10 when he was barely 17, stood about 6ft and weighed over 13 stone and was spoken of thus early as a possible candidate for international honours.

"During 1910-11 he appeared in the International Trials. When prior to the 1911-12 season H Willett laid down the captaincy, his mantle naturally fell upon R C Stafford though not yet 19. He set to work to mould a team which would win back Bedford's prestige. He succeeded in a most surprising manner. The Bedford pack led by the indomitable Stafford himself, became known and respected in the best class of football and before Christmas had an unprecedented run of successes especially against Metropolitan clubs. He had a devastating tackle and anyone who has ever seen one of Stafford's tremendous dashes for the line, leaving a trail of fallen foes in his wake, will not easily forget it. He never stood out more splendidly than in a forlorn hope.

"He was still at school when he first played for East Midlands and from then never missed a county game. In his last game he had led the E M forwards brilliantly at Franklin's Gardens scoring against Surrey a couple of the best tries, both great individual feats. The closest bond of good fellowship existed between him and that other great Old Modernian, E R Mobbs, the East's skipper.

"As an oarsman and a runner, young Stafford also ranked among the first class. At the Inter Schools Sports between BMS and Elstow, he won the Mile Flat Open, the Long Jump in which he cleared 20ft and set up a new BMS record, the Hundred Yards in 11 seconds and finished by defeating D M Grant in the Hundred and Fifty Yards inter schools race by 2in in a shade under 16 secs. That spring in the Public Schools Championship he ran second by about a foot although not in training, being practising for rowing.

" As a mark of respect Bedford scratched their game with Upper Clapton."

The East Midlands of 1910.
ER Mobbs is captain, DM Grant is extreme left in the back row and RC Stafford is seated second from right.

# A TERRIBLE DEFEAT

The death of Dick Stafford and the First World War ended an era at the Blues. The club had expected to build a great team around its young hero. Even without him it had an impressive record in 1913-14 of 23 wins from 35 matches under the captaincy of the experienced Alf Manton. Among the victories was one over a scratch side known as the London Clergy. It had been raised by W K Roberts, a former Bedford captain, to support a church charity. The team consisted of 15 clerics and the Bedford vice-captain, the Reverend W W Vassel, turned out against his own club.

The war started a month before the new season was due and Bedford players, like others throughout the land, answered their country's call – some making the supreme sacrifice. It is a matter of regret that the club kept no record of those of its members who gave their lives in the 1914-1918 war. One of the first to fall was Lieutenant C C Stafford, elder brother of R C Stafford. He was a member of the Rowing Club, Bedford Athletic and a former Blues player who made 20 appearances for the first team between 1908 and 1912. Others who died were Basil Maclear and Tommy's son, Claude Fowler, and these three, representing the three main roots of the club are remembered as standard bearers for all the others.

Soon after the outbreak of hostilities, the ground was taken over and used by the Scottish Division stationed in the town. The Scrum Hall became the Quarter-master's Stores and in the middle of the playing field a cook house and 'cinema' was erected. Club rugby ceased but games continued in the schools.

The armistice was signed in 1918 and some clubs were able to get going again straight away. In Bedford, it was different because the Army refused to release the ground and no official Bedford club match was played in 1918-19. One game that did take place became the subject of much debate and not until a heavy defeat at home to Leicester in 1983 was it finally laid to rest. The occasion was a game at Welford Road on February 15, 1919, when the 'Tigers' beat a team billed as 'Bedford' by 71-0. In 1983 after a 68-3 defeat by Leicester, the 1919 scoreline was claimed by some as the record. It wasn't, of course, because Bedford had no matches at all in that season. Press reports put the record straight and showed the mood of the day.

The *Bedford Record* of February 18 reads: "According to the London press, 'Bedford' visited Leicester and sustained a terrible defeat at the hands of the ferocious Tigers. Lieut H L V Day, an OBM, was playing for Leicester and scored four tries besides placing three goals. The team, we understand, was raised by Mr A W Leach in Bedford and District. But why it should play under the name of Bedford and thus give the world to understand that it was a team from the Bedford RUFC requires some explanation. A defeat such as this is calculated to do the reputation of the Bedford club, which was at its highest when war stopped play, great harm, and may seriously prejudice it when it gets into working order again. Lieut Day has been selected to play right wing threequarter in the Army trial at Richmond."

What in fact had happened was that Arthur Leach, who was known as 'Shaver' in rugby circles had raised a team principally from the two schools. The boys themselves thought that they were going to play a similar side in the Leicester area. The young Maurice Pugh was in the team. "There was a huge crowd," he recalled, "and a number of internationals up against us. We had no chance."

A letter to the *Record* put the blame on the custodians of the Bedford club: "It should have been up to our officials to have made it known and so keep the good name of Bedford untarnished in the rugby world. I am of the hope that this will catch the eye of our officials," it went on, "and if they leave us too long without a little light on the subject, I am afraid that they will find some of their old supporters turned over to the soccer game with the idea that rugby was dead in Bedford."

After more public pressure an open meeting was called at the King's Arms in St Mary's to discuss the affairs of the club. The *Bedfordshire Times* of August 29, 1919, reported it in full. Voted to the chair was J W Carter, later to become the club's first Chairman. Players were asked to sign on and to ask others to join. 'Alf' Hall and R S Mackinder were the first to do so, reported the newspaper; Alf Manton though not at the meeting, had agreed to lead the team. Mr Cannon agreed to serve as secretary and Mr Plowman as treasurer. 'Shaver' Leach, the man who raised the County side to play the Blues when the Scrum Hall was opened in 1910-11 and the 'Bedford' team that played 'Leicester' that year, was invited to become team secretary. Later when young reporters were sent to watch matches at Bedford School, even though they knew nothing about the game, they were told to search out 'Shaver' and just write down what he told them.

At that meeting in the King's Arms on August 21, the headmasters of both schools had promised to lend their pitches. Bedford Park was to be used for training. Seven of the 14 matches in 1919-20 were at home, four at Bedford School and three at the Modern. Both matches against Northampton were played away and both resulted in heavy defeats, by 40-5 and by 53-3. Manton played in just one match and Hall took over the captaincy.

For 1920-21, A F Wesley took over after the annual meeting, the first since 1914. Though the Army had started to move off the ground, the club was still unable to use the regular pitch, the grandstand and the Scrum Hall. Early season matches were still played on the school grounds but on November 9, 1920, Bedford came 'home' even though it was to the second team pitch. The third match of that season saw a defeat even greater than the one at Leicester. On September 25, Bedford lost 76-0 at the Harlequins, conceding 17 tries, each one then being worth three points. The scoreline represented the club's heaviest defeat until it was matched at Bath in January, 1990 when, since 1971-72, a try was worth four points. It was increased in value to five points in 1992-93 and an even heavier defeat was to come when the Blues fielded a weakened team at home to Richmond on May 16, 1999 in order to concentrate on the relegation play-offs against Rotherham on May 20 and 23. They lost 106-12 to Richmond, conceding 16 tries and 13 conversions, but survived in the play-offs – just. Hardly a voice was raised against the decision.

# GREAT LEAP FORWARD

Goldington Road was finally handed back to the club in 1922 and the occasion was marked with a match against Coventry on January 14 of that year. The opening ceremony was performed by the President, E Hastings Dasent. Coventry won the match 8-5, but for Bedford supporters there was immense relief at having once again their own pitch, grandstand and Scrum Hall. The next 17 years saw tremendous strides forward in administration, facilities, and status and in the late 1930s, Bedford once again produced another great team before war was to call 'no side' for the second time in 25 years.

Businessmen took on important positions at the club and provided the impetus to erect a covered section behind the west goal in 1927, a scoreboard and clock in 1930 and a new entrance in 1931. Then in 1933, the club opened a new grandstand, the equal of most in the country and the one still in use in 2011. It was made possible through the generosity of the Blake family, pioneers of the cinema business in the area. It was completed at a cost of £1,760 and opened on September 7, 1933, with a game against Northampton which Bedford won by 10-5.

The 'A' team had been revived in 1920-21 but with the first XV staging most of their games at home and paying guarantees to visitors they often had difficulty in finding a pitch. Ground was rented behind the Fox and Hounds public house in Goldington Road. It was owned by Mr Cave and often used by the Athletic and by the Bedford Thursday Club, a town team made up of Blues players, for the most part, who had Thursday afternoons off work. There were discussions in committee about trying to buy the ground for the reserve side but the matter wasn't pursued.

In 1931, the 'A' team changed its name to the Wanderers and the next year the club rented a sports field in High Street, Kempston, for £35 per annum plus rates, to give its reserve side a base. Previously, the ground had been used by J and F Howard but when the town's first great company failed in the depression, the club rented its sports field from Mr W Harter, of The Bury, Kempston. It was given up in 1935 when the Igranic Company took over. In 1986, the Cutler-Hammer club used it. By then, of course, the Wanderers and the other teams at the club were able to use the top pitch at the Goldington Road ground throughout the season. The cricket area used by Bedfordshire Club and Ground, the county second XI, was handed over to the rugby club in 1938. Previously it had to be vacated in time for the cricketers to start work on the square.

During the First World War, the top pitch had been used for stabling mules and before the ground could be used again it had to be relaid. The man given the job was Dick Rogers, the groundsman at Bedford Modern School and their former cricket professional who joined them from Felstead in 1883. He had produced some fine players and had converted the waste land in Clarendon Street into playing fields. The top pitch was separated from the main one by a sharp drop which was 'levelled' by Bob Reynolds who had taken over as groundsman in 1930 on the recommendation of Arthur Marshall, captain in 1932-33, club President from 1962 until 1965 and the 50th President of the Rugby Football Union.

Bob had worked in Laxton's nursery in Goldington, been gardener to the headmaster at Bedford School, worked in the brickworks at Wootton Pillinge and, during spells of unemployment, had laboured in the telephone gangs that were laying wires around the town. He had been to school with Arthur Marshall at Goldington and the pair picked up rugby from the Bandey brothers, one of whom became club secretary. Bob played for the

Queens during the war and then joined Arthur at Bedford Athletic.

In the 1920s with the club still trying to find its feet, there was a great deal of player movement, particularly with the Athletic and Olney. Sam Kitchener, the Olney lay preacher and sometime booth boxer who also played for Northampton, was captain at Bedford in 1923-24 at the age of 37. His influence in the community was seen as very useful in attracting players, though Northampton with its shoe industry was a formidable rival. One of Bedford's great captures was that of the Llanelli and Wales scrum-half D E John who played 18 times for the Blues in 1926-27 having been found employment by the team's secretary Sid Crawley. He later returned to Wales and was capped again.

Frank Phypers, P J King and Bob Reynolds all played for the 'A' team, the Athletic and the Thursday Club while competing for the hooker's position at the town. In 1927-28 that role was taken over by the Olney undertaker Roger Perkins who held it for ten years, making a total of 283 appearances and starting a sequence of long-serving hookers that continued with Brian McCarthy, Norman Baker and Mark Howe.

In 1925, Aubrey Fensome was elected captain. He had attended the meeting at the King's Arms in 1919 and had developed into a fine winger. On the left wing at the same time was Rex Alston, a master at Bedford School who later became a journalist and broadcaster with *The Daily Telegraph* and the BBC. His obituary appeared in *The Times* in 1985, but he was alive and well in 1986 talking to the *Bedfordshire Times* about his days at the Blues.

"When I joined in 1924," he said, "the leading lights were F G Hore, C J Churchill and, of course, L A R Fensome, an elusive runner and a fine defensive player. L H Nicholson was our line-out expert and C H Tomkins, a goalkicking loose forward, our expert at getting hurt in his own 25 to give colleagues a breather.

"The outstanding personality was Charlie Brumwell, a fine all-round sportsman, a thrusting centre, clever seller of dummies and forthright tackler who, with a little more pace, would have been England class. His partner in the centre was often the big, long-striding R D Cotton. I owed many of my tries to their openings.

"At full back we had Ronnie Eidsforth, a long-kicking and courageous player, and others in our back division were B A Begg, Len Ashwell, TEK Williams and N F Reed. We had great support from RAF Henlow with Messrs Cockell and Munckley forming a solid front row and Lieutenant Carter, a fine scrum-half. In the second row were N B Larby and D C Riddy, and at number eight the tall goalkicking C H Williams.

"We owed much in my six years with the club to G U A 'Daddy' Read, a knowledgeable tactician and shrewd adviser, and to Peter Perkins, a wholehearted supporter. I was no great footballer, but being a fast runner I could usually outpace most of my opponents and providing my colleagues gave me the ball with space, I could usually run in the tries.

"I don't think that wing threequarter was a good place to captain the side from, but I was honoured to take over from Fred Hore and from Aubrey. My greatest thrill was to score the first try against Northampton on October 29, 1927, when we beat them 6-5 at Franklins Gardens, the first time we had done so since the war. I remember scoring three tries for the East Midlands against Warwickshire to win the group championship and playing four times in the Mobbs match against all the class players of the day. I also recall that in 1930, I had to mark C C Tanner who had come to prominence playing for Cambridge University. He scored three tries in the match, handing me off each time right in front of the England selectors. A fortnight later he won his first cap. I reckon he owes me a large drink!"

The stand that was still in use in 2011 was opened in 1933

# THE LION OF BEDFORD

Rex Alston was succeeded as captain of the Blues by Charlie Brumwell, an Old Bedfordian who was elected four times in succession. He handed over to Arthur Marshall for the 1932-33 season before Arnold Sime took over in 1933 to be elected a record five times and to build what many people thought the best team that Bedford ever had. Rex Alston, who was a correspondent when Bedford, under Pat Briggs, won the English-Welsh Pennant in 1969-70 and under 'Budge' Rogers, with Briggs as coach, won the RFU Club Competition in 1975, thought that the teams of the late 1930s the best ever. They never, of course, saw the Invincibles of 1893-94, nor the All Star teams of 1997-98 but Bob Reynolds, Aubrey Fensome, P J King and the Centenary Year President Harry Elliott, all rated the 1938-39 side the best they ever saw. J G Cook was its captain, Sime having retired at the end of the previous season to pursue his career at the Bar and in other sports.

Sime was a talented all round sportsman who, like Alston before and Ian Peck later, also captained Bedfordshire at cricket. He was a born leader who, it was said, instructed referees in the fine arts of play to Bedford's advantage while from his position at scrum-half he commanded some of the finest forwards the club ever knew, like a huntsman whipping in to hounds.

The teams of the late 1930s couldn't match the record of the 1893-94 side who drew once, with Northampton, and lost once, to Coventry, in 29 matches. Nor could it win competitions like the unofficial one in 1969-70 or the RFU's own in 1975 because they didn't then exist. They didn't contain either the international captains (D P Rogers and D G Perry of the late 60s) nor the capped players who graced Goldington Road in another golden age after the advent of professionalism, but they did have trialists in virtually every position, top quality men in reserve and the 1938-39 team had a record of just four defeats in 32 matches which is as good as any save the Invincibles and the 1997-98 team which lost four times, all away from home, and set a new points for record in 33 games in the second tier. Northampton and Coventry were both beaten twice in the 1938-39 season. Moseley, Sale, Old Merchant Taylors and the RAF inflicted the only defeats. Like another before, it never realised its full promise because of war, but it attained legendary status and old players and supporters spoke about it in awe.

Bedford didn't produce an international after Dick Stafford in 1912 until their RAF flanker C R Davies was capped once by Wales in 1934 and then D L K Milman played for England in 1937 and 1938 and twice in 1939. Gilbert Cook won a cap in 1937 and Vic Lyttle three, for Ireland, once in 1938 and twice in 1939. In the final Irish trial of 1939 the winger, Lyttle, was joined by a forward George O'Brien Power and a three-quarter Ellis Walshe, two Old Bedfordians. George's brother Jimmy, 1936, J G Rogers and O V Bevan in 1937 and T D Thevenard, 1936, were all trialists who played in the 1938-39 back division. Brumwell had a trial in 1931, Sime in 1932 and among the forwards Rex Willsher and Gerry Dancer had many from 1934-35 onwards. They were also often named as reserves.

There was a feeling on Bedford terraces, once again grown used to success, that Blues players of the age suffered injustices at the hands of the England selectors. In no case did supporters find that to be as true as in the case of Gerald Thomas Dancer, known to all as 'Beef'. He became the club's first British Lion, but he never won a full cap for England.

Born in Ford End Road, Queen's Park, on January 15, 1911, 'Beef' started his working life as a dairyman with his father. Briefly they ran a tobacconists' shop, then they went into the building trade. Later 'Beef' became an animal foods rep, took a pub at Kempston and finished work in 1975 as mine host of the Seven Wives pub in St Ives where he fell in with Andy Smith and his stable of boxers that at one time included champions Joe Bugner, who grew up within a clearance kick of the ground at Goldington Road, Des Morrison, who lived next to the Eagles ground in Nelson Street, and Dave 'Boy' Green. "Building work really hardened me for rugby," he said, "I became a bricklayer and my mates at the time were local boxers like Johnny Seamarks and Reg Perkins. We used to train together. The 1930s were a marvellous years for sportsmen. I knew all the soccer players at the Eagles and followed them right up to the end. I think it's a tragedy when I read that there is no team any more," he said in an interview with the *Bedfordshire Times* in 1983. Of course the Eagles re-formed later with former captain Ian Peck's sister in law, Penny Young, among the driving forces.

At school 'Beef' was always "barging about and getting into trouble". He couldn't leave early enough. He started life at Queen's Park School but when his friends won scholarships to Bedford Modern, his father paid for him to go there as well. "I left at 16. I wasn't a good pupil. I never made the First XV but I did captain the Under 14s. We were taken for rugby, I remember, by the Rev Mr Hartley, vicar of Elstow. I thought the school would be glad to see the back of me when I persuaded my father to let me leave, but strangely enough the headmaster came around to persuade him to keep me on. It might have been because they wanted me for rugby, I really don't know. Anyway my rugby career started at Bedford Modern."

Finally into the world that he couldn't wait to be let loose on, he joined Bedford Athletic Rugby Club and played for them at their ground just off Newnham Avenue, thoroughly enjoying himself. On April 9, 1928, he made a debut for Bedford having been invited to play against the Old Bedford Modernians. He made his second appearance for the Blues in the final game of the season, a 9-0 defeat by Coventry. Rex Alston was skipper at the time. 'Beef' was 17. He thinks he played in the second row. "In those days it was often a case of the first men to the scrum packing down first."

'Beef' Dancer on the rampage with the Lions in South Africa

He didn't appear in a Bedford shirt again until the season 1931-32. He went back to the Athletic and made the most of life. Then he had a year out altogether and got married at the age of 20. One night he was coming out of the old Empire cinema in Midland Road when the Bedford captain, Charlie Brumwell, 'ambushed' him and asked him to go back to the Blues. "My wife wanted me to play, so I agreed there and then. Charlie was a real tough centre and would have made it as a boxer. I always thought he should have played for England." From the beginning he went straight in as prop and earned the reputation of a tough customer. He played 29 times in his first season, 33 in his second and finished up with 310 appearances.

"I never wanted to be captain and I never had much time for committees but you know we had some marvellous people around the club in those days; good captains. Sime could talk the hind legs off all the referees; and good people like Bob Reynolds the groundsman who was always on at me. Ernie Blake, Peter Perkins, Jack Nightingale. If someone needed a job, they made sure he got one. Because if they didn't find him one, Northampton would."

Both Leeds and Hunslet made him offers to turn to Rugby League and he thought seriously about going north. During the war he played in a special match where the League met the Union and drew 10-10. "The League boys love the game even more than we do," he said. "I think some clubs, Bedford included, take this amateur business too far."

By 1936 he had represented East Midlands and Barbarians and played in England trials. On one of his three Baa Baas tours he shared a room in Penarth with Prince Obolensky, the Rosslyn Park and England winger. He played against the New Zealanders of 1935-36 and saw all the great players of the day.

"It never bothered me that I might have been with famous players or whatever, and it's only now when I think back that I realise how good some of them must have been. I enjoyed playing so much and that's all I wanted to do. It didn't matter who it was for or with.

"I was never interested in statistics but I do know this. The best hooker I ever played with was Roger Perkins of Bedford. Roger was a real mate of mine. He was a country boy from Olney, which used to be a sort of nursery at the time for both us and Northampton. We had some great times together. I remember one year, I got him drunk before the Old Paulines match and we tried to bring him round with cold water. During the game, the referee asked our captain to send him off. "Some mate you are" he said to me afterwards.

"I asked him once what a 'dominoe' move was. "Wait until the next scrum," he said, and then wham. This bloke who'd been hitting him went out like a light. That's a dominoe, says old Roger. Double six. I can see him now. I went to visit him a couple of years ago just before he died.

"I think the game was harder in those days than it is now," he said. "But the one thing we never had was some of this raking and use of the boot. Fists would often fly but we never used the boot. Games with the Midland clubs were often real wars. I remember the Wheatleys from Coventry. There were three brothers in a coal business. One of them, Neb, used to frighten me to death, just looking at him. He was huge and real ugly, but you know we all got on well after the game and on England trials and the like we used to stick together. We liked London clubs even less."

'Beef' was a popular tourist and got on well with the Barbarians, and when the team for the Lions tour to South Africa in 1938 was due to be announced, he had a feeling he'd be in it even though he'd been overlooked by England. The men who chose the Lions were often the men who chose the Baa Baas. They knew he'd be a good tourist and a hard enough player to stand up to the Springboks.

The journey to South Africa took two weeks and the party was away for five months. The previous Lions' tour had been a rough one and the order of the day from the captain, Sam Walker, was that they should play like gentlemen. 'Beef' missed the first game but played in 20 out of the remaining 22. At his very first scrum he remembers it was bang, bang, bang. "There was a profile of me in the 'Outspan' magazine that painted me as a right villain. On my passport on the way out, I wrote 'cauliflower ear' in the section where it wanted 'distinguishing marks'. On the way back the boys said I wouldn't be let in because I'd grown another one. It was really rough, but I enjoyed the games."

"It was a marvellous tour and the hospitality was terrific. I didn't spend a halfpenny until I started buying presents to bring home. I even made friends with a man from Coventry, Jimmy Giles, the scrum half. The front row was Eddie Morgan, Swansea, Bill Travers, Newport, and Gerry Dancer, Bedford. We played together in most of the games. They were great days. I remember them well." The Lions lost the first two Tests 26-12 in Johannesburg and 19-3 in Port Elizabeth and on the way to Cape Town for the final game they had a big party. "All the papers wrote us off," he recalls, "but we actually won. I reprieved myself when I scored a try because earlier my name was mud when I put out a pass that was intercepted and the South Africans scored."

When he got back home near the end of September, 'Beef' decided to take a rest after playing non-stop rugby for 12 months; but the East Midlands selectors were soon knocking on the door and before long it was time for another round of England trials. He was selected for the first but left out of the second. "I asked Arthur Marshall what the excuse was that time. He told me that the selectors reckoned I wasn't fit enough. What a laugh. Not fit enough after a year's rugby and a Lions' tour. If I had been everything they wanted me to be I would have been a complete team."

# FLETCHER, HAYNES AND OAKLEY

The Second World War, 1939-1945, meant that the great team of 1938-39 was denied the chance to prove itself again. It also meant that players who would surely have become internationals were to remain uncapped. All the same, a number of them played in Red Cross and Service Internationals and, this time, rugby carried on. The club was not to make the mistakes that cost it dear during the First World War.

The day before war was declared, Bedford were due to open their season at Leicester. But because so many of its players were in the Regular Forces, the Territorials or the RAF Reserve, the club had most of its team unavailable for the match and it had to call the game off. Attempts to inform people proved difficult, but only one of the XV actually arrived at Leicester and that was Vic Lyttle who lived very near to the Moseley ground in Birmingham. He turned up that afternoon of September 2 and, when it became clear that no-one else was arriving, helped raise a scratch side from people in the ground so that a game could be played.

Most rugby stopped after the declaration of war. The national emergency saw many children from London evacuated to Bedford and the local authority "required use of the Goldington Road ground for organised games and outside classes." They wanted the Scrum Hall for "cleansing purposes". In 1940, field kitchens and Nissen huts were erected on the top pitch to provide facilities for feeding troops. But remembering what had happened 25 years earlier, the club made certain that its main pitch was kept available for rugby, if only to ensure that it didn't lose out again when hostilities ended.

The question of keeping the game alive and the demand evident in the town for rugby matches was considered by the committee at their meeting on October 20, 1939, held at the Swan Hotel. Present were H W Finlinson (in the chair), L P New, N J Timmins, F Holmes, B Edgington, D J V Bilham, A H Perkins, O V Bevan, E E Blake and L A R Fensome. It was reported that the Borough Education Committee had raised no objection to the ground being used for occasional matches on Saturday afternoons but that "Captain Wignall wanted good notice of any fixtures that were made." The club had to pay the Education Authority £1 per match.

The 1941 Bedford School team containing in the middle row Murray Fletcher, third left, 'Tich' Haynes, right, and Leo Oakley, left. Picture: The Bedford Archive, Bedford School

The man who took it upon himself to ensure that rugby continued was A H 'Peter' Perkins, the team secretary and chairman of selectors, who became club Chairman in 1945. With copper plate-style handwriting he stayed in touch with players in whichever theatre of war they were serving and he produced a newsletter which many valued among their fondest wartime memories. Matches were arranged mainly with London clubs, hospitals and universities. Servicemen on leave or stationed locally, as well as students, schoolboys and those in essential services at home, made certain that sides were raised and fixtures honoured. "We used to meet in the waiting room of St Pancras station," recalls Bob Reynolds, the groundsman who took on the job of looking after shirts, shorts and boots. "Most times we weren't sure who would turn up. I remember once Gilbert Cook arriving, having been in action in Germany the night before."

A special relationship was established with Rosslyn Park, with players turning out for either club, depending on which one had a game. In Arthur Trollope, Bedford had a friend who could always be relied upon to provide a referee. A player at the club between 1894 and 1902 and a former pupil at the Elstow School, he was secretary of the London Society of Referees. P J King remembered how Peter Perkins would adjust kick-off times at home games and order a taxi to wait for the final whistle at a school match then to drive the referee, often P J himself, to take charge of a Blues match at Goldington Road.

Between November 1939 and March 1945, the club played 56 matches and used at least 215 players, many of whom made only one appearance. In 1943-44, for instance, 11 games were arranged and around 70 players used, 35 of them turning out just once. Against Guy's Hospital on January 8, 1944, the then current captains of both Cambridge, J H Langham, and Oxford, D A B Garton-Sprenger, played for Bedford. It was a great morale-booster to both the club and the town when Ronnie Eidsforth, their pre-war full-back, made his first wartime appearance in the colours. He had made his debut back in 1924 and had overtaken Alf Hall's appearance record of 272. He'd been captured in Germany early in the war but was one of the first prisoners to be repatriated.

The thrust of policy at home during the Second World War was that life should go on as normal. Education was encouraged for all those who could take advantage of it and schools rugby continued virtually uninterrupted, as indeed it had in the Great War. At Bedford School, it was something of a golden age for the game. Owen Bevan, the coach there at the time, produced perhaps the best team the school has ever known, and the fact that the town club was able to stay open for business during the war established the allegiances of several boys who were to become post-war greats. Under different circumstances they could have been lost to other clubs.

Bevan's XV of 1939, 1940 and 1941 won all of their school matches. They won the Public Schools Sevens in 1940-41 and 1941-42 and were losing finalists in 1942-43. The 1941 XV was the first at Bedford School to win all its matches; the 1942 XV drew once and won all the others. Captain of the 1941 team was Murray Fletcher, the scrum-half. Captain of the 1942 side was Leo Oakley, a centre, and in between them at stand-off was Reg Haynes, a mercurial player known as 'Tich'. The three had played together in the Bedford Lower School XV of 1937. Fletcher and Oakley made the first team in 1940 and Haynes joined them in 1941. While still at school, all three were chosen to play in an RAF benevolent match against the Midlands staged at Goldington Road in 1942. The dashing Peter Ralphs, who made 86 consecutive appearances, was another of the vintage – as was Peter, later Sir Peter, Parker.

Haynes went to Queen's Park School before going to Bedford, and Fletcher was at Goldington.

They made their Bedford debuts on March 20, 1943, while on leave from Army university courses, Haynes scoring two tries in a 29-9 win over Rosslyn Park. The next week the club selected the entire 1941 Bedford School back division against St Mary's Hospital. One of them was unable to play but Oakley did and so did Peter Parker and the legend of the 'musketeers' was born. There were nine OBs and two OBMs, Willsher and Dancer, in that team.

Oakley had scored 37 tries, eight in one match, for the 1941 team. A modest, unflappable character with a cavalier approach to the game, he was immensely strong and fast. He had a great change of speed, lethal tackle and a devastating hand-off. Haynes was the rapier, a natural ball-player with superb hands, a quick brain and perfect timing. "Fletcher," wrote Doddy Hay in an edition of the magazine *Rugby World* in 1966, "was tough, dark and muscular. For 20 minutes he would sling out conveyor belt passes ... then, woosh, he would be through like a rocket to show you, too late, that both members of the half-back partnership could run." He had a remarkable one-handed pass and a superb over-the-shoulder kick, being remembered once for an astonishing dropped goal with his back to the posts. He was the first to return home after military service and played 148 times for the club. Oakley made one appearance for England. Haynes had a trial but Fletcher was unlucky though he was a popular Barbarian.

Fletcher was so highly rated that Bedford later felt themselves sufficiently well served at scrum-half to make no effort to get R E G Jeeps to Goldington Road even as his deputy! Jeeps left the Modern School in 1949 and played for Cambridge City for a year before joining Northampton. He went on to play 24 times for England and 13 Tests for the British Lions. Fletcher played in three championship finals for the East Midlands, against Cheshire in 1950, Middlesex in 1951 and Yorkshire in 1953. He became a master and coach at Bedford School and his son, Guy, later played 77 times for the Blues in the same position as his father during an era when the club was blessed with outstanding scrum-halves. He, too, was a master and coach at the school, responsible for the likes of M C Bayfield and A C T Gomarsall and for other unbeaten XVs in 1991 and 2000.

# WE WILL REMEMBER THEM

Bedford's reputation in the rugby world had never been higher than it was in 1939. As a result of its efforts during the war, the club was in a far stronger position for the resumption than it had been in 1918. The legendary *Bedfordshire Times* correspondent, Harry Dutton, wrote in May 1946: "Above all consideration is the fact that we have had a full programme in which there were a few poor games, many good ones and several that provided rugby of the highest order. The regular supporter can look back with pleasure on the season and thank Mr Peter Perkins, his fellow officials and all the players who have done so much to restore the club's fortunes and open the way to a bright future."

The official team picture for 1941-42

This time the club made sure that it honoured those of its members who had given their lives and others who had been recognised for distinguished service. It produced a "Review of the War Time Period" in which it listed those who had been decorated. There must have been others whose bravery was never reported but the following were honoured publicly.

W/Commander W M Brereton, MBE, AFC; S/Ldr N E Browning, MBE; S/Ldr A E Cook, DFC; S/Ldr C R Davies, mentioned in despatches (MID); Capt A R P Ellis, DSO; Major H Elliott, MC; Capt N H Golding (MID); Major A E P Joy, MBE (MID); L/Col C Lincoln (MID); F/Lt B McMaster, DFC; Major D Milman, MC; S/Ldr A Panton, DFC; Lt P Perks, MC; Sub Lieut L Pollard (MID); Supt M D Pugh, Indian Police Medal.

***Pro Patria***

*D G Allen* — *RNVR*
*R M Andrews* — *RN*
*R Angus* — *RAF*
*J C Atkins* — *RAF*

*J E Bartrum* — *RAF*
*A J Bell* — *RAC*
*Stanley Blincow* — *Bedfs & Herts Regt*
*Sydney Blincow* — *RA*
*R G Brimley* — *RN*
*Neil Buchanan* — *RNVR*

*K C Campin* — *RAF*
*A E Cook* — *RAF*
*J C W Cousins* — *RASC*

*C R Davies* — *RAF*
*C B Donovan* — *Gurkha Rifles*

*L A Emmerton* — *RAF*

*H D N Ffinch* — *Gurkha Rifles*
*I J Fitch* — *RAF*
*R A D Foster* — *RAF*

*T B Garland* — *RAF*

*P H Lawless* — *War Correspondent*
*C H Lichford* — *Anti-Tank Regt*
*R K Luddington* — *RAF*

*A C Marston* — *Rajputana Rifles*
*B J McMaster* — *RAF*
*A R J Medcalf* — *RAF*
*G I R Milliken* — *RA*
*J S Moll* — *Queen's R Regt*
*D W Moore* — *RNVR*

*D J Neal* — *RAF*

*D A O'Hare* — *RN*

*Alan Parker* — *RAF*
*H A Pickering* — *RAF*
*J O'B Power* — *RAF*
*D A Prothero* — *RN*
*C A Pryor* — *RAF*

*S H Raw* — *Frontier Force Rifles*
*A K Rogers* — *RAF*

*L Dalrymple Sandes* — *RAF*
*N B Sanford* — *Gloucester Regt*
*P R D Shaw* — *IOC Regt*
*P R Sinclair* — *RE*
*M E Staples* — *RAF*

*T D Thevenard* — *FAA*
*R C W Timmins* — *RA*
*L R Trueman* — *RAF*

*A T A Wallace* — *Bedfs & Herts Regt*
*Hugh Ward* — *RA*
*Ronald Warren* — *RAF*
*F K Webster* — *RAF*
*R A West* — *RAF*
*J P Whitaker* — *RNVR*
*K T White* — *RAF*
*G M Wilkins* — *N Staffs Regt*
*C A Wood* — *RAF*

# AFTER THE WAR

In his review of the wartime period, published in July 1944, the club President Ernie Blake wrote: "We have no players whatever on National Work in the district, so we have no resident nucleus of a team upon which to rely. The raising of 15 men to form a side, even to play occasional games, had become very difficult by March 1944. By the time October 1944 comes around it may be impossible."

But the Blues had responded to their President's appeal to keep going during the war and they soldiered on with a programme of ten matches, of which seven were won, in 1944-45. The club also provided its full share of players for the wartime showcase matches that were staged. Rex Willsher and C G Gilthorpe played in the Red Cross games of 1939-40. In the service internationals that were held, with no caps being awarded, G T Dancer, L F L Oakley, H R Peel, B J McMaster and Rex Willsher all represented the Blues. R Furbank, D L K Milman, L F L Oakley played for the Army, G T Dancer, J E L Grey and B J McMaster for the RAF, Willsher for the Civil Defence, and Dancer, McMaster and Willsher for the Barbarians. Among those who missed these and possibly higher honours was J G Rogers, who lost a leg in the war and whose brother, A K Rogers was killed. "Jack would certainly have been an international," said P J King.

The four home countries plus France and the Kiwis – mainly New Zealand forces stationed in the country – played a number of Victory Internationals for which, again, no caps were awarded. G A Kelly played in six of these games and C G Gilthorpe, an RAF officer stationed locally, in three of them. Kelly, however, became Bedford's first capped player after the war when, along with 14 others making their full international debuts, he turned out against Wales at Cardiff in January 1947 for England's first recognised international since 1939.

The Bedford committee wasted no time in restoring business as usual at Goldington Road and they arranged a full programme of fixtures for the 1945-46 season. Rex Willsher was the captain of a side who used more than 60 players in 31 matches of which 17 were won. Willsher was the heir of Dick Stafford and the forerunner of Roger 'Tod' Slaughter as Modern School boys who were captains of the Blues, flankers at rugby and outstanding all-rounders, especially in the athletics field, at school.

The Education Authority had vacated their responsibility at the ground by September 1945, though the Army were slower to move out. They didn't clear the top pitch until the summer of 1947, following a severe winter in which eight matches between January 25 and March 15 were lost. In 1945, the groundsman, Bob Reynolds, was re-engaged by an eager committee at a wage of £5 a week. He planted the lime trees on the east side in honour of the war dead.

Cost of admission to the grandstand in 1945 was two shillings, ground admission was 7d and the programme 3d. The rules of the club had been brought up to date, and widows and children of those members who had made the 'great sacrifice' were offered honorary membership of the club. It was decided that £5 "be paid to Mr C A E C Howard for the benefit of A Leach in view of his past services to Rugby Football in Bedford."

'Shaver' Leach, the man who raised the team that played the Blues when the Scrum Hall was opened in1910 and then the side of schoolboys that took on Leicester in 1919, had fallen on "evil days". He was to benefit by the equivalent of a week's wages.

By 1947-48 more players had been demobilised from the services and the side had a settled look about it, though conscription still continued to make its claims.

Fletcher, Haynes and Oakley were back at the Blues and other former pupils of the schools were making their mark. "Has there ever before or since been a period in which so many great players were coming out of our local schools?" asked the *Bedfordshire Times* journalist Dick Dellow, referring to H W Rose, B J Hazell, P G Miller and R E G Jeeps, all coming from the Modern School. The Bedford Colts were set up by Messrs McCulloch and Wells with a loose relationship to the club. 'Jock' McCulloch was invited onto the committee in 1948. The Colts had been formed in the main by boys from the Harpur Central School. When they became over age, they formed a new club which they appropriately named the Swifts. A third team at the Blues was set up in 1961-62 – and called the Rovers.

# FROM THE PRESS BOX

Rex Willsher was succeeded as captain by the Huntingdon farmer Dick Furbank and by 1950-51 the club had built another team to rank with the best in the country. The side, captained by George Jenkins, lost just five times in 33 matches, conceding 18 tries and scoring 90. John Bance's 1951-52 team lost only six times in 36 outings, conceding 30 tries and scoring 95. In 1950-51, Oakley and A C Towell played one game each in the England centre and 'Bill' Rose was a travelling reserve.

A successful team played to full houses as sport in general boomed after the war and media interest was high. The committee gave its permission for former Bedford captain Rex Alston to commentate for BBC radio on the second half of the Rosslyn Park match in December 1949.

The *Bedfordshire Times* always had its own man at matches and results were relayed at speed to their offices in Mill Street and displayed, along with those from the Eagles, the town's soccer club, Kempston Rovers and other local teams. On the staff from 1948 until 1958 was *Victor Head* who later joined *The Daily Telegraph* as a rugby and sports writer between 1964 and 1986. He had an eventful apprenticeship as he recalled:

"Returning to Goldington Road as Rugby correspondent for *The Daily Telegraph* was a curious experience for someone whose baptism in sports reporting had been on that very turf a decade or so earlier around 1949. Bedford then seemed to be a giant among clubs attracting to its banner a round table of heroes among players at a time when 'training' still carried the odour of sanctity.

Saturday afternoons at Goldington Road's Camelot in those long ago days, seen now through the lenses of memory, seem bathed in the harsh, bright light of winter sunshine, glinting on the windows of the North Wing hospital beyond the Wanderers' pitch. Surely players and crowds were larger then, shadows darker in contrast and the Press bench bulging with men of magisterial dignity, sporting some of the most expensive complexions in post-war Britain. Even such eminent local rugby scribes as Chris Carter, Harry Dutton and Derek Parrott seemed overshadowed.

Towering among them was the correspondent of a London evening newspaper, Mr Hylton Cleaver. Being assigned to him as copy runner and telephonist proved an eventful introduction to sports journalism, partly because he was central to the events taking place and not merely a peripheral onlooker.

Thus the fact that Oakley was going over in the corner right in the eye of the setting sun was not sufficient cause for Cleaver to interrupt his learned debate with a colleague on the latest tinkering with the Laws. Mere details such as tries could be confirmed by his copy-runner whose duties were more varied than simply dashing off importantly at 20-minute intervals to phone the great Hylton's immortal prose to the waiting presses.

Since Hylton, long a boyhood favourite as the author of school yarns featuring Biggles-type heroes of the 1st XV at St Oswald's, had not perfected the knack of consistently legible longhand, it was sometimes necessary to fill in the gaps for him. It was a form of apprenticeship much to be recommended providing one had a mentor as genial and indulgent as Hylton Cleaver.

Quite aside from such mundane chores, the copy-runner, in the middle of an exciting period of play, might be dispatched to the pitch to "check that red-haired fellow's Christian name and ask him if he missed the tackle that gave away the last try." I have often mused, since then, that SAS training might, with advantage, include such tests of character and nerve.

For an ex-student of English the experience was useful in other ways. It certainly widened one's knowledge of the language and its piquancy. One also had the opportunity of observing the truth of Paddy Campbell's description of a rugger scrum as being 'redolent of pink gin and cigars'.

In later years it became easier to believe, for example, the story of the anguished referee who, having sent off a Coventry forward for smoking in the scrum, explained afterwards in the bar: "It wasn't so much the smoking I objected to. It was when he asked me for a light..."

The Press box at Goldington Road, and other grounds, was the realm of such other daunting character as *The Times* correspondent, august as a bishop, with a terrible wrath for unseemly behaviour among his colleagues. This disapproval could be incurred by chewing, chattering and exhibiting partisanship as might well happen when the local newspaper correspondent failed to stifle a cheer if the home team scored. The glittering eye then cast upon the hapless victim had more than a hint of the Ancient Mariner about it.

Another well-remembered glittering eye was the monocle worn by that irascible lawyer 'Baron' Mike Rothschild who was a regular and unofficial adviser to the Press, always occupying a seat adjacent to it, from where he was generous with pungent comment on the players, the committee, the crowd and the correspondents. Mike became a firm friend and wise counsellor. Not until after he died, was I, having promised, allowed to refer in print to his war-time exploits – as a member of the SAS forerunner, and as a special agent dropped into Occupied Europe from whence, having completed a mission, he was said to have once escaped to Vichy France disguised as a peasant and pushing a wheelbarrow. Ski-ing for Oxford, playing bridge for England and taking part (on the pacifist side, ironically), in the famous pre-war 'King and Country' Oxford Union debate were among other incidents in an eventful life, much of which is unrecorded.

Mike's monocle occasionally hid his glass eye, a war-time memento that often, in the bar after a game, reminded some of a pre-war Bedford hooker, noted for his toughness. He always signalled the outbreak of hostilities in fierce encounters with, say, Coventry or Northampton, by pausing to remove his glass eye and putting it carefully in his pocket. This sounds authentic. A more apocryphal version would have had him handing it to the referee for safe keeping.

Another popular incumbent of the Press box was Pat Marshall of the *Daily Express* whose 'brief' was to write about personalities, hang the match. It is alleged that he became the butt of many a hoax among the players who plied him with all sorts of tall yarns such as Bedford acquiring the services of a Siamese prince on the wing – and the story about a Bedford player becoming a sensation in American grid-iron football because he refused to wear the heavy body armour and, unencumbered, was able to skip past the opposition at will.

Such tales are probably folklore because Pat was not only a well-informed rugby observer but a bit too wise to be taken in. If he ever used such stories, I suspect he did so on the basis that they were 'good copy' even if the source was dubious.

Pat would have appreciated the story told of a Bedford back of those days, P J 'Smokey Joe' Wootton (subsequently my brother-in-law) who hotly denies once scoring a try with a fag in his mouth rather in the style of that Victorian Oxford Blue reputed to have broken the world's high jump record without removing his top hat or pausing to stub out his cheroot.

Peter Wootton was a product of that fine generation of wassailers at Bedford Modern School under P J King which yielded such formidable contemporaries as Les Dilley, Bill Rose and John Arnold, all at Loughborough College, together with Murray Fletcher, Paddy Adkins and Peter Collingridge.

Peter, later a headmaster in Worcester, played centre, wing and outside-half for Bedford, East Midlands and latterly for the Wanderers whose captain he was from 1952 until 1956. He remembers with a chuckle some of the characters with whom he played in the halcyon days of 1949-1954. Looming large among them was Leo Oakley, that explosive threequarter of immense strength with biceps "like some people's thighs". Peter and Leo weighed about the same in those days, 11st 10lb, and on one occasion for a bet, Peter laid stiffly on the floor, hand across chest, and Leo stooped, picked him up and held him aloft above his head.

There were durable skippers like George Jenkins who was open side wing-forward around 1949, having played for Esher well before the World War (which was open to dispute). Despite repeated probing about his age from the 'young 'uns', who regarded George as Methusela, he was never drawn.

Farmers have provided Bedford with many a stout prop and none tougher than Dickie Furbank, 'strong as an ox', who had his finest hour when well and truly psyched up against Percy Park on an Easter tour. Peter recalls Furbank playing like a human tank on that day – "he took on their pack almost single-handed".

That tour to the north-east was, Peter recalls, "the booziest Easter ever," their self-appointed host being an inebriated Old Bedfordian who apparently owned a brewery and generously entertained the team in his sampling room. This probably explains one of the subsequent escapades that led to Gus Hale appearing at breakfast minus half his luxurious moustache.

Gus was a large second-row forward and the impromptu barber-shop session required the combined efforts of, among others, Leo Oakley, 'Tich' Haynes – both noted pranksters – John Taylor and others to hold him down. Gus entered into the spirit by appearing for breakfast wearing a schoolboy's cap and turning his head when ordering, thus showing the waiter only a clean upper lip.

When the waiter returned Gus had altered his position to display the be-whiskered half of his face and the waiter's expression amply rewarded his sacrifice. Hale, apart from an impressive thirst – "I've seen him consume at least 18 pints on one occasion after a game but he always reckoned he lost at least 5lb a match," says Peter – may have cherished his moustache as some compensation for being somewhat thin on top. A radio commentator, influenced by that glistening pate, once described him as "that veteran Hale" when Gus was all of 24 years old.

Bald men seemed more abundant in those days and a shining example was Mike Henderson who at Coventry one day was involved in an off-the-ball incident with one of the Wheatley brothers. This riled the Coundon Road aficionados and as the players left the field and trooped down the tunnel in the centre of the main stand, an irate lady leaned over the side and whacked a bald Bedfordian with her umbrella, exclaiming, "Take that, you dirty bugger!"

Joe Brown, the hooker, was most upset at being mistaken for Henderson. Says Peter, "Unfortunately, Joe too, was rather bald on top."

Another farmer captain was John Bance who had the most enormous hands. "In them a pint pot looked like a half-pint," remembers Peter. Bance was a gentle giant and nothing ever disturbed that easy-going nature. Against Coventry – how often they crop up in ex-players' memories – on one occasion Bedford were well on top but had suffered more than a fair share of knocks.

"Our hooker scored a try and went off, mysteriously injured, and then Jock Hazell's chat provoked some of the Coventry players – he could never keep quiet – and they nobbled him, too. We led 9-3 but to our consternation John Bance was felled. As we crowded round his apparently senseless figure the thought of holding on with only 12 men was not encouraging.

"Then John opened one eye, saw no opponents, and gave us a reassuring wink. He was, of course, taking a well earned rest and we held on for a 9-9 draw."

Like those of so many ex-players of that era, Peter's recollections largely concern the off-the-pitch fun that was the essence of rugby and, one hopes, still is despite neo-professionalism, league tables and obsessive coaching dogma. But, when forced, he does recall some of the outstanding performers, such as Alan Towell – "probably the best centre I ever played outside. He was certainly the best timer of a pass."

Murray Fletcher could read a game better than most and he had a tremendous pass that made the lives of fly-halves so much easier. 'Tich' Haynes, his regular partner, was brilliant in his own right, but playing with Fletcher was very under-rated by the England selectors and should have done better than gain just a trial.

Haynes, the supreme individualist, often took his own side by surprise. Although only 9st 10lb he was strong, agile, could turn 'on a sixpence' and, being so light, was able to stop suddenly – a tremendous asset. "Against Met Police he made four quite large gentlemen in blue look very silly. He offered the ball to one, sidestepped the next, dummied the third, and then chipped over the last before rounding him and going for the line."

'Tich' was also a considerable kicker. At Twickenham against the Harlequins, Bedford were awarded a penalty kick on the centre spot and there was considerable amusement among the opposition when this tiny figure stepped up to take it. Only a last-minute gust of wind at the South end diverted the ball against an upright, well above the cross-bar, and Quins gave 'Tich' much more respect after that.

The tilted stage at Goldington Road – always worth a point or two to Bedford, "particularly if we used the slope in the second half" – has seen hundreds of memorable scenes and actors whose names echo down the years, Hazell, Bance, Lovell, Rose, Fletcher, Rogers, Haynes, Ralphs ('a good, hard, straight runner'), Peter Parker ('more than useful but he always seemed to have other things on his mind') ... and so on and on.

But, if such things as apparitions do occur and some events do leave behind something indelible, then that spot will surely be haunted for centuries by a fleeting moment in 1953. On that January afternoon Leo Oakley, the pride of Bedford, was halted in full flight by a crash tackle that broke his leg and ended his career. That instant of frozen horror, following the audible impact which told everyone the worst, still remains in the minds of those who were there."

# THE BEDFORD CHARACTER

What was the Bedford character? How was the club seen in rugby's wider world? An article held in esteem in club archives as much as the 'Pinkie' Booth story appeared in the March 1966 edition of the magazine *Rugby World*'. Written by Doddy Hay, it was often produced at times of low ebb to remind players of their glorious tradition.

Under the headline "Famous clubs – number 18 – Bedford". Mr Hay wrote: "A match against them always serves to separate the men from the boys."

The article continued: "Bedford, the rugby team, is a magnificent Trial Horse. Now, before the stands at Goldington Road rise in their wrath, let me make it clear that this is intended as a compliment. That Bedford are also one of the great provincial clubs no one would deny – but the essential quality of their greatness, and the attribute that abides in the memory, is the fact that when you've played against them, win or lose, you always know you've been in a game. That sloping pitch – absolute murder in the second half when you're grinding your way uphill against a three point lead – the roaring, appreciative, partisan crowd; the light and dark blue jerseys, bulging with muscle and purpose, that come at you in waves – all this adds up to one of the hardest sides in the country to beat, or even to play as well against as you know you can when faced with less dedicated, determined opposition.

"The Bedford match is one of those invaluable few that always serves to separate the men from the boys. The Universities know this, and so do the Services, and both groups regard Goldington Road as a significant milestone on the road to Twickenham. To understand the peculiar power of Bedford Rugby one need only compare the club's match record and score-sheet over the years with its list of international players. The first is impressive, the second sparse – less than thirty, all told, between the four home countries.

"Bedford have, to be sure, had their stars, but those who have received the accolade of international recognition are precious few. The real strength of the club has always rested on its teams – and this, surely, is the most admirable attribute of them all."

The retirement of Fletcher, Haynes, Oakley and the Old Bedford Modernian Bill Rose, one of the first genuinely attacking full backs, saw the end of another outstanding team at Goldington Road. Results in the six seasons from 1947 until 1953 were, in terms of matches lost as a percentage of the total, inferior only to those in the six seasons immediately before the Second World War. Not until the period 1968-1972 were records as good by the same criterion.

In 1956-57, Bedford actually lost more matches in a season than it won, something it hadn't done since 1919-20 and 1920-21, and before that just fives times after its formation.

It didn't do so again until 1977-78 but in the last 10 seasons of its first 100 years, it did so eight times – something it had done just eight times in its previous 90 seasons.

There were good records of course in the cycle and in the 1959-60 season an outstanding one in a team captained by Peter Avery, a schoolmaster at St Albans School, later to introduce Bob Wilkinson and Alan Towersey to the club. Avery's team lost seven times in 37 matches, beating Leicester twice, winning and losing to Northampton, and drawing away at Coventry.

The 'Rugby World' article suggests that Bedford at the time were recognised as a hard physical team. Styles, of course, changed, often because of the laws, often because of the players available. The post war sides were based on mobile forwards and speedy backs, the same ingredients that made up the teams that won the English-Welsh Pennant in 1969-70 and the cup in 1975. In between there was an era of hard forward play in which backs were thought to be surplus and the game in essence a battle between opposing packs with back row forwards expected to do most of the scoring.

At the time of the Doddy Hay article, Bedford's list of internationals numbered in fact less that 20. Five club members had been capped before the First World War and four between the wars. A number were recognised in war-time matches for which no caps were awarded, but in England's first full international after the war, the Bedford prop Geoff Kelly was capped against Wales in 1947, and then twice more that year and once in 1948.

In 1951 both Bedford centres, Alan Towell and Leo Oakley, were capped once. In 1954 John Bance was capped against Scotland and in 1959, Larry Webb played four times for England. He was selected for the opening game the following season but had to withdraw through injury. Ron Jacobs, of Northampton, took his place and stayed in the team. Larry was one of the club giants and like his front row colleagues, Alan Lovell and Brian McCarthy, was to make more than 300 appearances for the Blues. Like Lovell, he died before his time, a helicopter accident in 1978 claiming his wife and daughter as well.

Seven of the club's internationals were capped in the 1970s, in a prolific period between 1971 and 1976, but Bedford's reputation as the home of great players and its status as a first class club was perhaps never clearer than it was in March 1966 when Doddy Hay's article appeared in 'Rugby World'.

In the winter of 1962-63, 12 games were lost because of snow and ice, just one match being played, on the top pitch, against the Argentine tourists San Isidro. December 1963, though, brought a unique occasion, the staging of a Probables v Possibles England trial at Goldington Road with more than 5,000 spectators in the ground. Two of the trialists in the match were back row forwards D P 'Budge' Rogers and David Perry. Both had been capped previously and both were England regulars between 1963 and 1966. In 1964-65, Rogers captained Bedford and Perry captained England while in 1965-66 Rogers captained England while Perry captained Bedford. They were the only players to have captained England while at Bedford in the club's first 100 years: a formidable destroying flanker and an elegant ball playing number eight: a unique partnership. Later, John Orwin was to join them as a Bedford forward who became captain of England.

Another Bedford player, Geoff Frankcom, played in all four games under Perry's captaincy, to give Bedford three internationals in the same team for the first time. In February 1966, the Rugby Followers went to Paris to see Danny Hearn, another centre join Rogers and Perry in the England side that played France. A celebratory dinner followed at the Bridge Hotel when the England men in the Bedford ranks were joined by several of its earlier international heroes. No wonder the rugby world was impressed.

An international line up at the Bridge Hotel in 1966.
Left to right, standing: Geoff Frankcom, Budge Rogers, David Perry, Larry Webb, John Bance, Leo Oakley.
Sitting: Ron Peel, Gilbert Cook, Rex Willsher, Dermot Milman, Vic Lyttle and Geoff Kelly.

# D P ROGERS – THE GREATEST

The club's first British Lion Gerry Dancer kept the Griffin pub in Kempston until he moved to the Seven Wives in St Ives in the early 1960s. Rugby men used to visit him to listen to his tales of the battles in South Africa on the 1938 tour. Just along the road from the pub in Kempston, one of his successors in the Bedford front row, Alan Lovell, was the son of a former police officer who kept the Half Moon. Still in Kempston, the club's second Lion lived with his parents at the King William pub. D P 'Budge' Rogers, who toured South Africa in 1962, was a teetotaller and a dedicated trainer with such a zeal for the game and the art of flanking that more than anyone else he put Bedford on the sporting map. For many years when people spoke about sport in Bedford they spoke about Derek Prior 'Budge' Rogers OBE, captain of England, at one time his country's most capped player, chairman of selectors when England won a Five Nations Grand Slam in 1980 and President of the Rugby Football Union in 2000-2001.

*Doug Bowker* was rugby correspondent of the *Bedfordshire Times* throughout the entire career of the man whose record stands alone in the club's history. Statistical references in his original article have been updated. He wrote:

"For long years Bedford used a Boxing Day fixture against Old Paulines as an occasion to 'blood' promising schoolboys. Blues were supposed to win, but on Boxing Day 1956, the Old Boys achieved a rare victory, six points (two penalty goals) to nil.

The game marked the debut of 'Budge' Rogers, then a 16 year-old at Bedford School, and I gave him two lines in my report: "kept well with the ball and tackled keenly."

For the next 20 years, at club, county and international level, these remained the chief Rogers characteristics, confirmed not just in words by sports writers but in photographs: picture the action and almost inevitably 'Budge' Rogers was in that picture.

It could be argued that he wasn't a natural ball player; he could drop a pass and give a bad 'un with the best at times.

That he was a defensive 'Death to the fly half' player, rather than an attacking one, is not borne out by the fact that he scored 126 tries for Bedford, a figure exceeded only by winger Derek Wyatt (145).

Nonetheless, hard work and durability based on supreme fitness (he didn't smoke or drink though home was a pub), were the hallmark of his success. And he was an instinctive player.

I remember his colleague in the back row, David Jackson, once explaining a difference between Budge and himself. In so many words David said that at a 50-50 ball situation on the 'deck' while he considered for a second "if it was worth it", he found 'Budge' had dived on the ball.

It undoubtedly cost 'Budge' a few more bumps and bruises; at the end of a long season it was reckoned you couldn't put a finger on his body without striking some scar of battle.

Some of these marks were carelessly, maybe deliberately handed out, yet 'Budge' was never seen to retaliate or 'dish out the dirt' himself.

Perhaps the best tribute to him was paid by the man whose title of the most capped Englishman 'Budge' took over. Said Lord Wakefield: "There could not be a better guardian of our traditions on the field of play, nor a better exponent of the spirit and manner in which our game should be played."

'Budge' achieved that signal honour, his 32nd cap, in February 1969. On the evening before the match at Twickenham, skipper Dick Greenwood had to drop out, so 'Budge' led England, and to an emphatic victory, 22-8, over France.

Back home his achievement was recognised by a mayoral reception, and later he was honoured with the OBE for services to rugby football.

Not bad for a six stone, under five foot, 11 year-old described as "disgusted" when torn away from his beloved soccer to play rugby football. Murray Fletcher is always credited with converting 'Budge' from a rather ordinary scrum half into arguably the greatest wing forward of his time. Yet his first match in an Under 12 Bedford School side (against Dunstable GS) was at wing forward, conversion to scrum half following "because he was so small."

It was three years later, when he arrived as possible 1st XV material, that Mr Fletcher (who knew a good scrum half when he saw one) felt there were two better for the role than 'Budge'. But all that tireless covering, that ferocious tackling... maybe a wing forward?

The rest is not quite history. At that time, 'Budge' almost had to give up the game altogether. After every game a knee "blew up", a mysterious happening which happily cleared up.

For those who like statistics, 'Budge' made 485 appearances for Bedford – a club record – scored 126 tries as we've said, oh, and at Bath in 1964, one dropped goal to make a round total of 400 points.

At one time this was the 12th highest total by a player for the club (under modern scoring values the tally would be nearer 500).

He played 34 times for England between 1961 and 1969, captained the side seven times, and toured with the British Lions to South Africa in 1962, playing two Tests.

He scored three tries in internationals, one in his first against Ireland in February 1961.

He played for and captained East Midlands and The Barbarians an unrecorded number of times, and overall must have played in excess of 600 first-class matches. It is unlikely any other player was on the first class scene for so long.

Playing days over, he sat on the Mallaby committee, became an England selector in 1976 and was chairman of selectors in the Grand Slam season of 1979-80.

Everyone will have memories of 'Budge', but, common to us all, acknowledgement of a most modest sportsman despite those supreme honours, a one-club man, who, whenever he was away on international or representative duty, always first asked, "How did Bedford get on?"

In May 1975, Bedford gave him the proudest day in his career when they won the 'cup' by beating Rosslyn Park in a game which will for ever rank as an example of rugby football at its best.

We will remember it for exciting running and passing culminating in glorious tries. But also for 'Budge' Rogers, at the end of a career, still with the ball and tackling to oblivion.

Bedford's greatest? Certainly the greatest for any young player just setting out to try and emulate."

'Budge' Rogers is first to the ball. Fellow back rowers and captains
David Jackson and 'Tod' Slaughter, right, are in support

# NEVER HAD IT SO GOOD

Budge Rogers was held in such esteem, that when asked, by his old school to raise sides to play, what they hoped, would form the XV for the next year, he could invariably produce one that contained internationals, trialists and well established players. The status this gave to the school was enormous. The benefits to the club, at a time when top class players were regular visitors at arenas like Bedford School and Goldington Road were obvious.

Whereas, by the year 2000, future stars were spotted and courted in the pyramid of mini, junior, schoolboy, colts, academy and club rugby, in the 1960s their stages were often confined to Oxbridge, other clubs or the Services. They were secured by clubs with offers of employment, not in building societies, leisure centres or big businesses, as often became the case, but at public schools and grammar schools.

In Bedford's case that meant at either Bedford School or Bedford Modern School and it also meant that masters at the schools like Murray Fletcher and George Cullen who were in charge of rugby did an important scouting job for the club. With sympathetic headmasters, they were often able to place players the club was keen to attract.

The 1950s and 60s saw a golden age of university rugby and though it has always been accepted that the Bedford colours of light and dark blue were chosen because of the town's proximity to both Oxford and Cambridge, it was usually in Cambridge that links were stronger. For one thing Cambridge was about 20 miles nearer and so more local boys went there to make their mark not just as scholars but as sportsmen and administrators. In days when travel wasn't as easy as it was to become with universal car ownership and networks of motorways across the country, convenient road and rail connections existed with Bedford, a pleasant market town with two top drawer public schools and a number of others, plenty of employment prospects, and a first class rugby club. With some hard men in the front five and two men in the back row who were to captain England, the Blues were a great attraction to top class backs in particular.

In July 1957 the new Prime Minister Harold Macmillan made a famous speech at a Conservative Party rally at 'The Eyrie', home of the Eagles, the town's Southern League soccer team in Nelson Street. "Most of our people have never had it so good," he said. Abridged, it was to become the catchphrase of the 1960s. It was certainly true at the Blues by 1966 when the Doddy Hay article was published.

The Bedford connection at Cambridge in the early 1960s centred on Christ's College. The secretary of its team was Roger Dalzell an Old Bedfordian who made 19 appearances at scrum half for the Blues. Christ's at the time was brimming with rugby talent that had been assembled there by Dr C G Pratt. They included Tony Lewis, Ian Balding, Bev Dovey, Dave Wrench, John Brash, Vic Harding, Trevor Wintle and Brian Thomas all of whom were to make their mark in international sport. One of their number was Pat Briggs who won a Blue at fly half in 1962 in between Gordon Waddell of Scotland and Mike Gibson of Ireland. At a scratch match against a School XV he was introduced to William Brown, headmaster of Bedford School, and later accepted a position there. His brother Paul, in fact, played once for Bedford in 1962-63 but Pat made the first of his 238 appearances on February 1, 1964, going on to captain the side that won the equivalent of the league in 1969-70 and to coach the side that won the 'cup' in 1975.

Mike Lord, later Deputy Speaker of the House of Commons, a Knight and then a Lord, and Freddie Booth were other Christ's players who followed him to Bedford. Geoff Frankcom, capped while still at Cambridge, joined him at both the club and the school the season after and so did Danny Hearn, an Oxford graduate who did his teaching practice at Bedford School before accepting a post at Haileybury. He became the Blues' fourth international of the 1960s but his career was cut tragically short after an accident in a match against the All Blacks at Leicester in 1967. He made a strong tackle in the game and was left paralysed. Rebuilding his life with courage he continued to teach and coach the game at Haileybury School.

With a honeypot effect, the Blues were able to attract players not just from Cambridge, the town and the University, but from all over the region as well. Larry Webb was a great magnet for the men of Hertfordshire and with Geoff Kelly an administrator in that area, players like Tony Else, John Bardner, John Bridges, Wyn Mathews and Jack Smith, an Old Bedfordian who played more than 300 times and captained the county at cricket, all found their way to Goldington Road. The Eastern Counties connection was strong as well with men like Dennis Hart, Brian Arthur and Peter Green, two who were to die in an aircrash bringing supporters back from an international in France in 1974, all seeing Bedford as the place to get on. Internationals of the 1970s like Jeremy Janion, Tony Jorden and Derek Wyatt, another who became an MP, all came through the Eastern Counties but their successors in England teams of the 1980s like Nick Youngs and Mark Bailey found they had to leave Bedford to further their international careers.

By then much had changed. The hard men had left the pack and giants like Rogers and Perry had proved irreplaceable. The Universities and the Services, traditional recruiting areas, were no longer the power they once were. Players were spotted and scouted in different arenas at an earlier age; their expectations were more short term; new roads and motorways meant they could travel farther. In the steps towards merit tables, leagues and professionalism many thought that national selection would demand that potential internationals should play for a small number of clubs.

The schools in Bedford still produced players and had sportsmen on their staff. The club, along with others in the rest of the country, developed youth policies to grow their own, it improved facilities and it nurtured its reputation as a rugby town. It had a sympathetic press locally and nationally and a near monopoly in spectator sport in the town, but it needed more to compete at the top level of rugby where it was to have two opportunities it could not sustain - in 1989-90 and 1998-2000. Perhaps it was another 'Budge' Rogers? Or another Alan Lovell? Or a Mark Howe, one of the last great amateurs and another one club man. But in the 'professional' era, would players of their stature have stayed at Bedford?

What determined a club's status after 1995 was first and foremost money. And lots of it.

'Budge' Rogers, right, is introduced to Prime Minister Harold Macmillan at Twickenham.

Pat Briggs, captain and the Blues' first official coach

'Tod' Slaughter

# THE PENNANT FLIES HIGH

In spite of international and representative calls made on his time, 'Budge' Rogers played more games for the Blues than anyone else. He, like another Old Bedfordian, Arnold Sime, also captained the side for five seasons, though in his case, his captaincy was in three terms. He took over from David Perry in 1963-64 and handed back to Perry at the end of 1965-1966. He took over from Perry again for 1966-67 and then returned to the role in the twilight of his career for two seasons starting in 1973-74. In 1968-69 he became the most capped English player and then in 1969-70 he was awarded the OBE for services to rugby.

He was succeeded as captain in 1967-68 by Roger 'Tod' Slaughter, an OBM, who started his career as a three-quarter, but who was given a chance in the back row, when he stepped in as travelling reserve on one occasion when Rogers missed the train. In spite of terrific competition for a back-row position, he still managed to make over 300 first team appearances, playing 38 times in 1966-67, the same number as the prolific winger, Jim Philbrook and hooker Norman Barker.

Slaughter concentrated the minds of his teams on fitness and the record of his first side indicates just that. It lost nine games out of 15 by the end of November, but then, in the next five months, it lost just three more. In the process, Philbrook became the first Bedford player to score 200 points in a season. His second season saw the team make a better start and finish with just nine defeats in 34 games. Significantly, just 36 players were used for a full campaign, at the time the lowest figure per season in reliable records.

The fitness fanatic, Slaughter, was succeeded as captain by one of the great thinkers of the game, Pat Briggs, and with the club firing on all cylinders and class players from all over striving for a place, Bedford enjoyed three years under Briggs, of single figure defeats. His side of 1969-70 was one of the most successful ever, losing just six times in 35 matches, each of them away from home. A draw against Cambridge University at Goldington Road prevented it from matching the Invincibles of 1893-94, the All Stars of 1997-98 and the sides of the very early years as a team that won all its home matches. In 1969-70, Brian Page, who left Northampton to join the Blues, kicked a new points record of 229. In 1971-72 he extended it to 296.

The 1969-70 side won *The Sunday Telegraph* English-Welsh Pennant, a sort of unofficial league table, organised by that newspaper and based on matches between leading clubs.

The Blues just missed another title as well in that successful season. Just as Coventry denied the Invincibles an unbeaten record, so Northampton, who had already been beaten twice that season, denied Briggs' team *The Sunday Telegraph's* English table. The East Midlands arranged a charity match, against Bedford, for the benefit of George Thorpe, who was paralysed as the result of an accident sustained when he was playing for Stockwood Park. Saints won 12-8, but a successful season was immeasurably saddened by the death of the Blues' President and Honorary Secretary, Eric King, who suffered a heart attack in the stand at Franklin's Gardens. Coventry won the Pennant and Bedford finished second as a result of the defeat at Northampton, a match which no one regretted playing for a good cause. "The Pennant will fly high", screamed the *Bedfordshire Times*, and it was presented in September 1970 by Jack Bailey, a former master at Bedford School, then assistant secretary of the MCC.

# WE MUST REMAIN FIRST CLASS

Our first duty, said the Bedford secretary Eric King in an interview in 1967, "is to ensure that Bedford remains first class. When you're down, tradition doesn't count at all. The only way back is the hard way." Mr King had been a captain of the Modern School XV and he joined the club in the late 1920s taking over responsibility for fixtures from his father, later handing it on to his brother. He saw the black days after the First World War when many of the best fixtures were lost and he played a major part in re-establishing the club as a first class force. While large crowds turned up to the 1963 England trial and to the occasional East Midlands v Barbarians match played on the Bedford ground, the club, in the mid 1960s, with a host of stars in its ranks, was drawing around 2,000 people for an attractive match. "Not nearly enough" said Mr King. "You can't rely on your gates now if you want to survive. A strong social side is an absolute essential. Especially with the Rovers and Rams fielded from 1961-62 and 1966-67."

The fact that an England trial was held at the ground in 1963 indicates that the club had facilities rated as first class as well as a team. An apron had been added to the front of the main stand in 1949-50 and new dressing rooms were opened in 1961 by Major Simon Whitbread with two former Presidents of the RFU in attendance. The dressing rooms had been donated, at a cost of more than £3,000, by the club President, Ernie Blake, the same benefactor who had provided much of the finance for the main stand opened in 1933-34. Mr Blake sadly died before the official opening on September 2, a day marked with Leicester agreeing to play at Goldington Road instead of at home, and Bedford winning the match 21-13 with the second half televised live on BBC TV. Rex Alston, the former Bedford captain, was the commentator, and the club received a fee of £125.

With new changing rooms, the Scrum Hall took on a new lease of life as the club's bar and in 1968 it was extended to provide a tea room at a cost of £12,000, £3,000 of that coming in the form of a grant from the Ministry of Education. Again Major Whitbread, Lord Lieutenant of the county, did the honours, this time before a match with London Scottish on October 26. Danny Hearn was among those present at the ceremony. On April 26, 1969, the club's honours board was unveiled by its oldest surviving captain, L H Nicholson, and on November 11, 1975, Don King, the President, switched on the floodlights in memory of his brother, Eric. Laurie Bridgeman, the Bedford secretary, secured a grant from his employers, the Sports Council, the total cost of the project being around £10,000.

The most ambitious of all the post war projects was the new clubhouse. In issue number 5, September 1976, of *Blue Print*, a club news sheet edited by Doug Fowler and Derek Wyatt, an appeal read: "Bedford Rugby Football Club is rated as a top class club, it has a first class ground by Rugby Union standards with excellent floodlights. Unfortunately the changing rooms and clubhouse facilities are not comparable with many other first class clubs who have brought their facilities up to modern requirements and expectations.

"Such improvements are essential to Bedford RUFC to maintain its well earned position among the top few rugby clubs. It is to this end that a project committee has sat for eighteen months considering how to replace the existing outmoded amenities, and a 'fund raising' committee is now running the appeal.

"Go ahead has been given conditionally for the money needed to fund the project to be raised by the club's own resources and initiative, all depending on planning permission etc.

Not only the money to build is needed, but all the building interior has to be furnished in keeping with modern standards. With the addition of first class changing accommodation and clubhouse it may be possible to stage grander rugby occasions and increase the prestige of Bedford Town itself.

"The Club cannot expect any assistance from public funds, therefore, this appeal with other means of raising money is necessary and must be successful. Already offers of help have been received. It is hoped that sports lovers, particularly rugby supporters, townspeople, companies, local industry, will subscribe to this venture and enable their Town's Rugby Club to compete on equal terms and entice the best clubs to visit Bedford."

Old players, among them Larry Webb, are known to have made substantial donations and fund raising schemes like 'Buy a Brick' and the '200 Club' were launched. At a cost of £78,000 the new clubhouse and dressing rooms were built and opened on April 4, 1978, by John Wells of the Charles Wells Brewery, still the club's main sponsor in 2011. 'Mr John' was a grandson of S R Wells, one of the guarantors of the original Scrum Hall back in 1910. The brewery provided an interest-free loan guaranteed by the North Bedfordshire Borough Council. The occasion was marked by a match between the Blues and a 'Budge' Rogers International XV.

'Budge' himself opened the new ground entrance on December 11, 1982, 'favourable conditions' this time coming from John Willmott (Bedford) Ltd. In 1986, plans were unveiled for improved car parking, lighting of the training pitch and general refurbishment of the club's facilities. What Eric King's view on rugby turning professional might have been, we can only guess. But he would surely have approved of the new stands – albeit temporary ones – erected during the premiership era and of the general sprucing up of the ground and the erection of a large marquee during the stewardship of Geoff Irvine, another OBM, in the first decade of the new millennium. And, as a Bank of England man, he may well have been excited at the club being run by a board of directors and of fund raising not just through raffles and the like but through rights issues to shareholders - which became the order of the day in the years after the buy-back of 1999. By 2010, Bedford was held up as a model run club by no less an authority than the relatively new weekly *Rugby Times*.

Richard Sharp, in white, and Mike Weston in opposition in the England trial at Goldington Road in 1963.

Neil Bennett, England international fly half and the first Bedford player to score 300 points in a season

# MAGNIFICENT SEVENTIES

The early 1970s were years of fabulous success at Goldington Road. The Pat Briggs teams of 1969-1972, carried on from Slaughter's with single figure totals of defeats in a season. Briggs represented the exciting traditions of Cambridge back play, Slaughter stood for fitness and hard forwards and with Rogers the supreme professional, in his attitude to the game, the Blues had a blend that attracted class men from all over the region. They used few players per season, but had top quality reserves, many of whom were denied a place in the club's imaginary Hall of Fame because they couldn't get into a first team bursting with talent. The Blues second team was the equal of many a self respecting club's first XV. Briggs, Slaughter and Rogers were among the few who actually lived in Bedford, but ambitious players were prepared to travel just to be part of a success story that had won the equivalent of the league championship and was to go on to win the 'cup'.

The 1970s saw more Bedford men capped for their country than in any previous decade at the Blues. Seven of them were honoured before 1976. The Rugby Union's Centenary in 1970-71 brought a record 15 caps in a season. Jeremy Janion earned six, Billy Steele five, for Scotland, and Jacko Page four. All three played in the Calcutta Cup match of 1971. Tony Jorden, Neil Bennett, Bob Wilkinson and Derek Wyatt were all capped by 1976, and in the Calcutta Cup match of that year, England started with one Bedford man on the field and finished with three while a former Blues player was on the wing for Scotland. The club was a real force in the international arena. When Rogers retired he became an England selector, chairing them when the national side won the Grand Slam in 1980.

Briggs handed over the captaincy to his scrum half Vic Lewis, and then retired through injury in 1972. In those days, the captain was responsible for coaching, but a succession of them invited P D Briggs to look after their teams and he did so until 1981. As a player and captain, he always believed that he was at his best as a coach and with class players at his disposal, he was able to produce teams that people wanted to watch and play for. The hallmark of them was their support play, with mobile forwards, decisive tackling and keen team awareness. He would prepare dossiers on the opposition's strengths and weaknesses and spend hours with individuals making sure they knew what their job was. He went on to coach the England Under 23s and could have gone higher had he not put first his responsibilities at Bedford School.

The 1970s saw tangible success at Goldington Road and a host of new records established as well. Brian Page and Neil Bennett set new points totals with Bennett becoming the first to score 300 in a season. His 35 points in a match was a record and the 71-7 win over the Wasps in 1974 another. Derek Wyatt and Alan Towersey joined the select few to score more than 100 tries in a career at Bedford, with Wyatt setting the highest ever total, and many other records, including three tries in a game 17 times. The 1975-76 points total of 1,043 and the try total of 151, were records at the time and with points against, 731, also a record they were exciting times – for spectators and players. In April, 1974, Bedford staged a game for the dependents of the Paris air crash. Blues players Brian Arthur and Peter Green were among those killed in the tragedy. A match between the Bosuns and Midland Counties raised £2,750 and established a ground record with a scoreline of 72-56. For the rugby follower, those were the days. And the greatest of them all was April 26, 1975.

# THEIR FINEST HOUR

Games against the Barbarians and New Zealand were momentous occasions in Bedford's history. So were the matches against other touring sides and the great Welsh clubs, with their star players. The 'All Star' period of the early professional era broke many of the records set in the 1970s and produced many memorable matches. The Blues went on to win the level two 'cup' at Twickenham in 2005 and were runners up in 2006 and 2011. But who could deny that, having won the equivalent of the 'league', the club's finest hour was when it went on to win the equivalent of the 'cup' against Rosslyn Park by 28-12 on April 26, 1975. The game, in front of a then record crowd for the competition at Twickenham was spoken and written about as one of the greatest ever. The RFU, at first, provided no cup to the winners and sought no sponsor. But from 1975-76 it did and its name and format changed regularly ever after. In 2011, the 'cup' was an Anglo-Welsh competition. The Blues played in the level two British and Irish Cup.

In 1974-75, the 'cup' was known as The RFU Club Competition. The first four winners were Gloucester, Coventry, twice, and Bedford. To mark its achievement the club produced a booklet written by Don Riddy and Doug Bowker and printed by Doug Fowler's Office Aid Press. Proceeds from the sale went to the Floodlight Fund.

One of the chapters was entitled 'The RFU Club Competition and Bedford's part in it before 1974-75.'

"The RFU Club Competition is organised on 'knock-out' principles. It started in 1971-72, in response to a fairly general desire for some kind of officially-recognised national competition between clubs (as distinct from counties). Thirty-two clubs take part in the first round. Most of them are senior clubs nominated because of their good playing records the previous season, but a few qualify as winners of county or divisional competitions. The draw for the first round is made on a regional basis, and so originally was the draw for the second round. But for 1973-74 the second-round draw was made nationally, without regard to geographical area, and the draw for the third and later rounds has always been so made.

In the first two seasons of the Competition, certain matches – notably the finals at Twickenham – had been largely ruined for all concerned through injuries to players, which had left teams at a numerical disadvantage to their opponents. Thereafter the RFU extended to the Competition the rule about replacements which was already in force for international matches. Clubs may now nominate six reserves and call upon any one, or if need be two, to replace players who suffer an injury during the course of a game which, in the opinion of a medical practitioner, makes it unwise for them to continue to play. It was by virtue of this rule that David Jackson replaced Foster Edwards at half-time in our third-round Competition match of 1974-75. He thus became the first Bedford player to replace a colleague in the course of a game, though not the first Bedford player to act as replacement in a match in which we were engaged, since in 1894 a Bedford man was allowed – legally or otherwise – to take the place of an injured opponent towards the end of the first half of a game in which the score stood at 0-0 (but which we eventually won by 14-0).

In 1971-72 we drew Rugby away for our first-round match. The game, the first we had ever played on a Sunday, attracted over 2,000 spectators even though the weather was most unfavourable. We started badly despite the fact that we had the wind and the rain at our backs in the first half, and we were 3-12 down just before the interval. We reduced our leeway with a try and in the second half went ahead thanks to two tries scored by Peter Green (who was so tragically to lose his life in the Paris air disaster 18 months later) and a conversion kicked by Brian Page. But it had been a close call for us. In the second round we were again drawn away, this time against Moseley. The game took place under floodlights on a late-January evening in conditions that were so bad, with heavy rain falling on an already waterlogged pitch, that it would never have been started as a normal club fixture. We lost by 9-16, and Moseley went on to reach the final, where – seriously depleted well before the end of the game – they lost by 6-17 to Gloucester.

The following season we had our first home tie, against Leicester. Playing just before Christmas, we were unlucky in that 'Budge' Rogers was unable to turn out because of injury. But it was indifferent tackling that led to our defeat by 17-21. Only a month later we trounced the Tigers in our normal home game with them by 37-9! The final that season was contested by Coventry and Bristol. Coventry won by 27-15, Bristol having fought bravely but unavailingly to make up for the loss of their hooker, John Pullin, at the very start of the game.

In 1973-74 we did not enter for the Competition, having failed to qualify by nomination for the first round. The ultimate winners were again Coventry – in fact, until they were beaten at Goldington Road in 1974-75, Coventry had never lost a Competition match, although they had been eliminated in the semi-final round of the first season by reason of being the home team in a 6-6 draw (with Gloucester).

## The RFU Club Competition 1974-75

### First Round

The North-cum-Midlands region in which we were placed for the first-round draw of the 1974-75 Competition looked strange on the map, since it was extended to include Bournemouth; and it was to Bournemouth that we had to travel. The game was played on Sunday, November 3. The team had made the journey the previous day and were able to practise that afternoon on the well-appointed ground of the local club. The match was favoured by summer-like conditions.

In spite of the big score that was steadily piled up against them, the home side displayed great spirit and kept going hard to the bitter end – indeed, it was their try and conversion which, to well-merited applause, rounded off the afternoon's scoring. Before that, however, we had crossed their line eleven times, and there were two penalty goals to add to eight try-conversions, making the final score 66-6. Our points total is the biggest record in the Competition since its inception, and it ranks as the (then) second highest score that we have ever registered away from home, coming after the 71 points (against 7) which we ran up in our game with the Wasps at Sudbury on April 6, 1974. Derek Wyatt's six tries established a new Bedford record for a player in any one match – five tries had been scored on a number of occasions, most recently by R Fletcher in 1964-65, against the RAF. (Actually six tries equalled the record of H Willett in 1907 and A D Heard in 1908).

**Team:** A M Jorden, A K Towersey, J M Howard, S Wells, D M Wyatt, W N Bennett, P Evans, C J Bailward, M Hempstead, A Johnson, C Hooker, R M Wilkinson, D P Rogers (capt), D Jackson (No 8), E F Edwards.

**Scorers:** W N Bennett (8C, 2P), E F Edwards (1T), D Jackson (1T), A K Towersey (2T), S Wells (1T), D M Wyatt (6T).

**Reserves:** B Page, R Smith, C Davies, A J Hollins.

### Second Round

The draw for the second round gave us home advantage against Sale, and the game was arranged to take place on February 8, just a month after we had entertained the Cheshire side in our normal Club fixture. The 'dress rehearsal' of the Competition match had resulted in a very good game, which we had won by 19-4, a gratifying score since our Hertfordshire players had not been available for selection because of the county's quarter-final match of the County Championship with Gloucestershire. John Howard could not be chosen for the Competition game owing to injury, and Richard Chadwick took his pace, making only his second nominated appearance as a three-quarter for the First XV (he had earlier played at centre in the game with Percy Park on the Club's Easter tour of 1973).

The winter had been very wet, as most of the spring was to be; but conditions were excellent for the Competition match, which was witnessed by a good-sized all-paying crowd. The game was hard fought and closer than the final score of 23-3 might suggest, our visitors having a potential which they were never quite able to deploy to the full, perhaps because of the activities of Steve Smith, their England scrum-half, were much cramped by those of his opposite number, Alun Lewis, who had come into the Bedford team since the Bournemouth game and had quickly struck up a fruitful partnership with Neil Bennett. The score at half-time was 16-3, but nine of our points had come only in the last five minutes of the half. Neil Bennett had scored all our first-half points, and in the second half he added three more, before Richard Chadwick completed our scoring with an excellent try to finish off a good passing movement.

**Team:** A M Jorden, A K Towersey, S Wells, R Chadwick, D M Wyatt, W N Bennett, A D Lewis, C J Bailward, N Barker, B Keen, C Hooker, R M Wilkinson, D P Rogers (capt), E F Edwards (No 8), A J Hollins.

**Scorers:** W N Bennett (1C, 1D, 2P, 2T), R Chadwick (1T)

**Reserves:** B Page, G Fletcher, C Davies, A Johnson, D Jackson.

### Third Round

For the third round of the Competition we were again drawn at home, this time against Gosforth. It was a match we could look forward to with no great confidence since, although we had beaten Gosforth seven times in eight encounters, four times on their ground, they had fairly routed us at the eighth time of asking, in 1973-74, inflicting on us our heaviest defeat but one (0-32) at home since The First World War. Gosforth had all-round ability, and their pack was especially powerful, containing three current internationals, including the Scottish hooker.

Since our Competition match with Sale, our away game with Neath had been washed out by rain; but we had shown good form in beating Blackheath (28-13) and RAF (51-0) at home. Unfortunately, on the day of the Competition game, playing conditions were all too reminiscent of those which prevailed when we met Gosforth the previous season, with heavy rain falling on an already sodden playing surface. The game itself was a hard, bruising business, in which our opponents seemed determined to take the utmost advantage of their physical strength. Alas for them, one of their three-quarters sinned and was ordered off the field.

Sustained handling movements were understandably few, and only one try was scored – but it was a remarkable one in the circumstances. Gosforth made a high clearing kick from their 25-yard area, and their fast follow-up was full of menace; but Derek Wyatt, running at top pace counter to their advance took the ball cleanly, and his speed carried him right through the defending ranks for a try near the corner flag, which Neil Bennett improved upon with a great kick at the second attempt, the first having been prematurely charged by certain of the Gosforth players. Our half-time lead of 6-3 (two penalties to one) was thus extended to 12-3, and although play continued exciting to the very end and Gosforth reduced the lead with another penalty goal, we were left winners by 12-6.

The match was noteworthy on several counts. To begin with, Neil Bennett had been chosen to play the following week in his first international game, but he elected to depart from the long tradition of resting from rugby on the previous Saturday. Second, as already mentioned, we introduced a replacement in the course of the game for the first time in our history. Third, the gate was very good, in spite of the weather, the total takings exceeding £1,000, at that time a Club record.

**Team:** A M Jorden, R Demming, R Chadwick, J M Howard, D M Wyatt, W N Bennett, A D Lewis, C J Bailward, N Barker, B Keen, C Hooker, R M Wilkinson, D P Rogers (Capt), E F Edwards (No 8) (replacement: D Jackson), A J Hollins.

**Scorers:** W N Bennett (1C, 2P), D M Wyatt (1T).

**Reserves:** J Cooley, G Fletcher, C Davies, A Johnson (as well as D Jackson).

### Semi-Final Round

For the third time in succession the luck of the draw was with us for the semi-final round of the Competition, giving us home advantage against our old friends and rivals Coventry. In the season's normal home fixture with them, towards the end of the previous November, they had come out on top, but only by the narrow margin of 16-19 and only after we had virtually presented them with six points in the first minute of the game. At half-time we had been 6-16 behind, but in the end they had won by a very shaky dropped goal scored just before no-side.

Once more the ground was very heavy for the Competition game, following a snow storm during the Thursday night and other frequent snow showers, including one just before the game started. Happily, the threat of further climatic interference with proceedings did not materialise, thought it was present for much of the match. The stand was filled to capacity long before the game got under way, the total number of spectators was over 3,000. The 'takings' topped £2,000, establishing a new record for the Club.

It was an extremely exciting game, played against a positive hubbub of background noise, which rose to a crescendo of almost deafening proportions when Bedford scored; but it is very pleasant to record that the crowd fell silent when either side was attempting a kick at goal, thereby setting an example which other crowds might well follow, particularly those watching international matches. A stiffish east wind neutralised whatever advantage there might have been in playing down the slight slope, the effect of which had been much magnified in pre-match press reporting.

This time, with the slope in our favour but against the wind, we did not allow Coventry the psychological advantage of an early score. Instead, we went in front after eight minutes, when John Howard kicked ahead and touched down for a try, which Neil Bennett converted. An interchange of penalty goals left us six points up at half-time, but the margin was reduced soon after the restart, when Coventry kicked a second penalty goal (9-6). The score remained unchanged for the next half-hour, during which we were forced on to grim defence in our own half and often in our own 25. It seemed that we must crack eventually. But just when our cause looked desperate, especially in view of Coventry's renowned ability to raise their game in the last ten minutes, we drove forward to the other end and stayed there.

Under intense pressure, the Midlanders' scrum half, who had played an excellent game, threw out a pass which eluded his colleagues but not Andy Hollins, who pounced upon the ball and scored a try amidst a tumult of cheering. So Coventry, at last, but worthily, yielded their proud record of never losing a game in the Club Competition, and we were able to look forward to our visit to Twickenham in three weeks' time. It had been a magnificent match, which we just deserved to win because of our masterly defence and our ability to turn half chances to account.

**Team:** A M Jorden, R Demming, R Chadwick, J M Howard, D M Wyatt, W N Bennett, A D Lewis, C J Bailward, N Barker, B Keen, C Hooker, R M Wilkinson, D P Rogers, E F Edwards (No 8), A J Hollins.

**Scorers:** W N Bennett (1C, 1P), A J Hollins (1T), J M Howard (1T).

**Reserves:** S Wells, P Evans, C Davies, A Johnson, D Jackson.

### Final Round, at Twickenham, April 26, 1975

The supporters of the two finalists, if not the players most nearly concerned, must have spent many hours weighing up the arguments for and against success for their side on the great day. From a Bedford view-point the chances seemed to be very evenly balanced indeed. The record book showed that, up to and including 1973-74, each club had won 30 of the 66 games played in the series of fixtures, which dated back from 1897-98. Bedford had been slightly ahead on points scored (649-602). Against this, Rosslyn Park had won the latest game between the two teams, played at Bedford on December 28, 1974 – but only by 16-20, the decisive try coming in the third minute of 'injury' time, after our vice-captain John Howard had been badly injured early on in the game – he had pluckily remained on the field but had been compelled to move from centre to blind side wing threequarter, where he had done whatever he could. However, the Park were having their best-ever playing season, and when the curtain was finally rung down they headed *The Sunday Telegraph's* merit table for clubs in England, in which our own position was ninth. Then again, no one who, on the evening of semi-final day, had seen the BBC2 tele-recording of Rosslyn Park's match at Morpeth could have any illusions about their strength and especially about the devastating power of their big forwards.

The Bedford squad pictured with the match officials before kick-off at Twickenham

There was another point to bear in mind. London had rarely been our happiest hunting ground. Too often we had to finish a game a man short through injury, or else our opponents had pulled off some monstrous 'long shot' – or else, quite simply, we had failed to reproduce our home form. Only five weeks before the final, we had lost 7-24 at Blackheath, whom we had beaten at Goldington Road a month earlier by 28-13. On the other hand, we had achieved some outstanding performances this season away from home: we had, for instance, registered our biggest-ever win against Northampton at Franklin's Gardens (29-9) and had beaten Waterloo at Blundellsands by 37-7. Even in London, we had had an early-season win against London Irish (24-0) – and, perhaps best of all, we had beaten London Welsh at Old Deer Park in February by 17-6, even though we had lost a player very early on and had accordingly been forced to move 'Budge' Rogers from the pack to centre threequarter. And lastly, only a fortnight before, we had beaten Northampton by 40-16 at Goldington Road, thus running up our biggest-ever score against our East Midlands neighbours, in a series that is as old as the Club itself – indeed older, if one takes into account, the fixtures of the old Rovers and Swifts!

For the Competition final, the weather was as different as could be from that for the three preceding rounds, being gloriously sunny and windless, perfect for back play if too warm for toiling forwards. There was certainly no complaint about the weather from spectators, many of whom came from Bedford and the surrounding area, and by their well co-ordinated and vociferous support, were to do much to inspire the team to raise their game.

Play in the early stages was probably what most spectators either hoped for or feared, depending upon the team they favoured. Rosslyn Park were clearly bent on making the most of their forward power, and the Bedford front row had a torrid time in the first few set scrums. It came as no great surprise when, after twenty minutes, the Park went ahead with a try by their left wing threequarter (0-4). But our forwards, playing superbly, weathered the storm and, though outweighed by some 6lb a man, began to get the upper hand in line-out, maul and loose. The longer the first half went on, the better our men played, and our backs looked definitely superior to their opposite numbers in their defence, in their combination, in their quick thinking, and in their readiness to attack from almost any position. Just before half-time the Bedford backs handled safely and at speed, and Derek Wyatt raced over for a try far out, which Neil Bennett converted with a beautiful kick to put us in the lead (6-4).

The second half opened with what Monday's *Daily Telegraph* headlined as a 'wonder' try. The Park kicked off deep into our half. Bob Wilkinson, under pressure, made a clean catch and sent our back-row forwards away with a splendidly-timed pass. From then on, the ball was moved swiftly and purposefully from man to man and back again, until finally Chris Bailward was given it with the Park's posts ahead. A few paces, and he plunged over for a try with what must have been Twickenham's most exultant leap and dive. With Neil Bennett again converting, Bedford were 12-4 ahead, and for the next twenty minutes or so the Park were almost run off their feet; two tries were scored by Bob Demming, the second being converted, and another try was added by Brian Keen, which was also 'majorised'. So in less than half an hour we had taken the score to 28-4, with three tries by wing threequarters and two by front-row forwards. Two more tries were missed by the narrowest of margins. Then, with the sun still blazing down and the outcome of the match no longer in doubt, we may have eased up a little – in any case, Rosslyn Park took another hand in the scoring, with two tries.

However, the day had unquestionably been ours and must have been one of the finest in the long history of the club, whose steadfast belief in the virtues of clean, open, 15-man rugger had been thus joyously vindicated. It had been a well-nigh perfect application of the principles expounded and illustrated by Pat Briggs, coach and former captain of the XV, and a full justification of the faith and judgement of 'Tich' Haynes and his fellow selectors. And how appropriately it rounded off the third period of captaincy of 'Budge' Rogers, who had first played for the XV over 18 years earlier and had demonstrated most aptly at the headquarters of the RFU that his stamina and his skill in all aspects of play were no less remarkable than when he captained England!

Brian Keen on the ball with Chris Bailward, Andy Hollins and 'Budge' Rogers in support in the final

It is fitting that this account of the final round of the RFU Club Competition of 1974-75 should end with a tribute to both teams. Rosslyn Park and Bedford have always maintained close and friendly relations, for all their determination to beat each other on the field of play. John Reason, rugby correspondent of *The Daily Telegraph*, had written on the morning of the final match: "At least though the way is now clear for what should be the best tempered final in the brief history of the competition ... it looks as if all the referee will have to do is to blow his whistle at the start and blow it again at the finish." Writing after the game, Peter West opened his account in *The Times* thus: "Bedford and Rosslyn Park produced a final at Twickenham on Saturday that did the game and the knock-out competition proud"; and in *The Guardian* of April 28, under the heading "Twickenham enjoys return to chivalry", David Frost put it: "Bedford and Rosslyn Park brought Twickenham and the National Knock-out Cup Competition to life on Saturday with a captivating display of non-stop, aggressive, creative rugby much to the liking of a happy, shirt-sleeved crowd." It remains only to add that, although the referee had to blow his whistle more than twice, he and the touch judges did their job to perfection, keeping the game flowing all the time.

Of course Bedford had already beaten the Barbarians, played New Zealand and won The *Sunday Telegraph* English–Welsh Pennant. Later, following the introduction of leagues, they twice won promotion to level one and 30 years after the Twickenham triumph they returned to win the level two knock out competition. But few would deny that that day in 1975 was their finest hour.

**Bedford:**

A M Jorden, R Demming, J M Howard, R Chadwick, D M Wyatt, W N Bennett, A D Lewis, B Keen, N Barker, C J Bailward, C Hooker, R M Wilkinson, D P Rogers (Capt), E F Edwards (No 8), A J Hollins. **Reserves:** B Page, S Wells, G Fletcher, C Davies, A Johnson, D Jackson.

**Rosslyn Park:**

R A Codd, R G Fisher, C D Saville, M B Bazalgette, D J McKay, P A Treseder, L E Weston, R L Barlow, P d'A Keith-Roach (Capt), N P Hinton, A K Rogers, N D Mantell, P G Anderson, A G Ripley (No 8), G Ling. **Reserves:** C P Kent, C Dunsford, G Lloyd-Roberts, I Smith, D J Sterling, S Johnson.

**Scorers:**

**For Bedford:** C J Bailward (1T), W N Bennett (4C), R Demming (2T), B Keen (1T), D M Wyatt (1T);
**For Rosslyn Park:** R G Fisher (1T), D J McKay (2T).

**Referee:**

Mr R F Johnson (Kent and London Societies of RFU Referees).

**Touch judges:**

Mr D E Coombes (London Society of RFU Referees) and Capt P L Lillington (The Army/London Society of RFU Referees).

Budge Rogers with the 'cup'

# RECORD OF RFU CLUB COMPETITION 1974/75

| 1st Round | | 2nd Round | | 3rd Round | | Semi-Final | | Final | | |
|---|---|---|---|---|---|---|---|---|---|---|
| Bournemouth | 6 | Bedford | 23 | Bedford | 13 | Bedford | 12 | Bedford | 28 | **Bedford** |
| Bedford | 66 | | | | | | | | | |
| Nottingham | 6 | Sale | 3 | | | | | | | |
| Sale | 16 | | | | | | | | | |
| Bristol | 7 | Bristol | 3 | Gosforth | 6 | | | | | |
| Plymouth Albion | 6 | | | | | | | | | |
| Northampton | 4 | Gosforth | 13 | | | | | | | |
| Gosforth | 7 | | | | | | | | | |
| Streatham-Croydon | 3 | Richmond | 14 | Richmond | 0 | Coventry | 6 | | | |
| Richmond | 10 | | | | | | | | | |
| Morley | 16 | Morley | 6 | | | | | | | |
| Waterloo | 7 | | | | | | | | | |
| Blackheath | 9 | Blackheath | 6 | Coventry | 3 | | | | | |
| Wasps | 3 | | | | | | | | | |
| Coventry | 40 | Coventry | 32 | | | | | | | |
| Bradford | 10 | | | | | | | | | |
| Solihull | 6 | Liverpool | 6 | Bath | 9 | Morpeth | 6 | Rosslyn Park | 12 | |
| Liverpool | 7 | | | | | | | | | |
| Falmouth | 9 | Bath | 12 | | | | | | | |
| Bath | 9 | | | | | | | | | |
| Morpeth | 12 | Morpeth | 19 | Morpeth | 13 | | | | | |
| Stockwood Park | 0 | | | | | | | | | |
| Maidstone | 16 | London Irish | 3 | | | | | | | |
| London Irish | 19 | | | | | | | | | |
| Aylesbury | 12 | London Scottish | 6 | Rosslyn Park | 21 | Rosslyn Park | 28 | | | |
| London Scottish | 39 | | | | | | | | | |
| Rosslyn Park | 22 | Rosslyn Park | 11 | | | | | | | |
| London Welsh | 9 | | | | | | | | | |
| Moseley | 15 | Moseley | 10 | Moseley | 7 | | | | | |
| Wilmslow | 7 | | | | | | | | | |
| Gloucester | 21 | Gloucester | 7 | | | | | | | |
| St Luke's College | 3 | | | | | | | | | |

NB: The home side is given first in all ties except the final

# ONLY ONE WAY TO GO

The triumph of 1975 was followed by a record-breaking season of celebration under the captaincy of John Howard, with Neil Bennett setting a total of 351 as the Blues passed 1,000 points and 150 tries in a season for the first time. The 1976-77 season opened with the name of D P Rogers missing for the first time in 20 years and after his retirement the great team broke up and could not be replaced. Bennett set new records and then moved to London Welsh to team up again with Alun Lewis, the man Pat Briggs had described as the 'missing link' in 1974-75. Derek Wyatt set more try-scoring records and then moved on to Bath and to Oxford University; Jorden played junior rugby and then became an England selector, and others just retired. Wilkinson joined the 300 club, and having played in the famous match against the All Blacks for the Barbarians in 1973, he put in a marvellous performance for the Midlands in another famous win against the New Zealanders, ten years later. In 1984, he retired and so did his second row partner from 1975, Clive Hooker. The club was asked, by the players involved, to make an agonising choice between its two England ranked scrum halves, Nick Youngs and Ian Peck, and when Youngs, the one they chose, moved to Leicester in 1981, he set a trend whereby it seemed that players had to leave Bedford to make progress.

There was greater movement among players than ever before. Everyone had cars, a new motorway network meant that players from the east needn't gravitate to Bedford because it was just as easy to get to London. Teaching posts that once attracted people to Bedford suddenly weren't the glamorous incentives that they once were in an era when big money was to be made in jobs in the City or in London real estate. Some clubs had people on their committees who could open doors to a much richer lifestyle for the ambitious player. Just as Bedford became a force in the game by attracting quality backs from Cambridge and the east who wanted to play behind hard edged forwards so other clubs were able to become powers in the game in their own way. Bath, for instance, won the cup five times in the 1980s and five times in the 1990s as well. They were one of the most successful clubs of the time. Leicester were another. Wasps another. The likes of Bedford found it hard to compete in the player 'market' but with a fixture list established in their glory days those who did turn out for the Blues performed heroically to make sure that the club retained its first class status.

Wilkinson, Dave Jackson and Nick Martin skippered teams in the late 1970s and a succession of captains and coaches in the first half of the 1980s tried to hold the ship steady. Graham Phillips, John Mawle, Peck and Andy Key all had their moments with teams that beat the likes of Llanelli, Pontypool, with three debutants in the front row, and Swansea. They were supported by coaches in Briggs, Slaughter and Mike Fitzgerald who worked as hard as anyone could have without always the same sort of raw material and resources at their disposal.

In spite of success on the junior front, and especially at Colts level where it produced a number of England players, the club went into its Centenary celebrations in 1986-87 with one of its worst ever playing records. None of the teams of the 1980s up to then won more games than they lost. For 13 successive years Blues sides scored more than 100 tries per season but that suddenly stopped in 1980-81 and in its 100th season the try total was the lowest since the war, while the against totals were the highest ever. Fifty-point defeats became the order of the day against clubs who once were Bedford's equal. In merit tables, where ten years earlier they were on the top, Bedford were at the bottom, except in the Midlands edition where the simultaneous decline of their neighbours Northampton, gave them a lifeline that they grabbed gratefully to qualify for the John Player Cup third round in their Centenary.

At the *Bedfordshire Times*, Doug Bowker gently eased himself off the rugby desk and to make up for lost Saturday afternoons he cut all ties with Goldington Road. Then, in October 1985, the BBC TV programme *Rugby Special*, to much criticism, focused in on the Blues for its 'match of the day' against Broughton Park in the John Player Cup second round. Defeat was one of the low points; to be followed by another the next week against Rugby, before a marvellous recovery operation started with a stirring win against Northampton and a hat-trick of tries for Kevin Canning, the first against the Saints since 'Tich' Haynes in 1949. Bowker couldn't resist watching the Broughton Park match on TV and in his weekly column, *In My View*, he summed it all up, as usual, quite perfectly. 'Fallen champs with nowhere to go but up'.

"I half broke a promise on Sunday when I watched Bedford being knocked out of the John Player Cup by Broughton Park in TV's *Rugby Special*. The last time I saw Bedford in a cup game was when they lifted the trophy in the final at Twickenham in April 1975. The country mouse was not given a chance against the town cat, Rosslyn Park, but Bedford smashed them 28-12 in what was a classic performance of running rugby, with forwards sharing the tries with the backs.

Neil Bennett and Alun Lewis at half back, Bob Demming and Derek Wyatt on the wings, 'Budge' Rogers leading a power pack at flanker ... what a side and occasion to savour. More than 10,000 people, mostly from Bedford, were at Twickenham, and I disgraced myself by having too much beer before the game and during it passing to national Pressman, who hadn't given us a chance, notes reading 'What price Bedford now?' Afterwards was near oblivion (of delight, of course).

Our headline was 'Champions of All England', but how soon the decay. A few older heads retired, younger ones moved from the area, the side broke up.

I moved with them (from covering sport) and lost the Goldington Road habit, saying I'd return when they found a team to win the 'cup' again. Alas, appearances in the competition since have been brief, and with 50-point hidings in other games, this season will surely rank the worst in the club's history.

You can't win 'em all, of course, but Bedford have got into a slough of losing 'em all. The slide down the new-fangled league tables could continue. Top clubs, especially Welsh ones, painstakingly built into the fixture list, drop out. Bedford could return to playing old boys' and hospital sides. Every workday I pass the ground, resplendently green, set about with adverts, towering lights, a good clubhouse, all the outward trappings of a successful club. Then I glance at the board showing next Saturday's opponents, shudder, and feel glad I won't be there to watch and report.

Cowardly? To an extent, and part reason for my watching on Sunday was to spot braver supporters who have kept faith. Mind you, in my 20 years covering Blues it wasn't all cup triumphs. They were an up-and-down side, losing games they should have won, then springing a surprise against the best. There was always hope.

I trust players and officials haven't lost that. A Centenary Year must not be used solely to wallow in nostalgia but to make a new beginning to better days. Ten years ago Bedford were at the top and there was only one way to go – down. If they are now truly at the bottom there's only one way to go – up!"

Of course they weren't at the bottom. But they weren't where they wanted to be or where they thought they should be either. The coming of leagues and professionalism, though, meant they were soon where they deserved to be. And it wasn't long before they were on the 'up' again.

# 100 YEARS OF THE BLUES

By the end of the season 1985-86, Bedford's playing record had slumped from the peak of the mid 1970s. Standards on the field could not match the strength of the fixture list established during a golden era. "Those were the days, my friends," said the *Bedford Express* in April 1986, mimicking a popular song. "We thought they would never end." But end they did and a club that had lived well on the success of the 1970s realised that it was losing touch in the 1980s. To its credit it did confront the new reality and it commissioned its officers to use wisely its Centenary celebrations in 1986-87 as a year of grace after which it would be judged like everyone else on its results alone.

The 1985-86 season was one of the worst on record. Yet the club was a happy one and regarded by visitors as one of the most pleasant on the first class circuit. Its Goldington Road ground, originally on a lease from the House of Industry, was, in 1986, managed by a trust through the North Bedfordshire Borough Council. It had two pitches, modern changing rooms, a luxury lounge bar and committee room, the Scrum Hall bar and tea room, a shop and a solid stand that had stood for more than 50 years. Floodlights enabled matches to be played in the evenings and the Blues, Wanderers, Rovers, Rams, Colts and a thriving junior and mini section all made use of the facilities most days of the week. The club paid a peppercorn rent for the ground.

Players built a mini gym under the main stand and lights enabled training to take place on the top pitch. Schools were still enthusiastic supporters and their facilities were readily available. Matches were sponsored by local firms and some games were played in competitions like the John Player Cup, John Smith Merit Table and Midland Merit Table as well as regular friendlies. In 1986 the Blues wore the logo of their sponsors, London Brick Landfill. It cost £2.50 to sit in the stand. £1.50 to get into the ground and 25p for a programme. (The 1945-46 prices were two shillings for the stand, nine pence for the ground and three pence for a programme). The club had nearly 300 Vice-Presidents who paid £27.50 for membership and a grandstand seat for home matches.

In 2010-11, the main sponsors were brewers Wells and Young's, Autoglass, LifesureGroup and KooGa. It cost £320 for a season ticket in the stand and £256 for one in the ground. That got you in to 11 home league matches, three play-off games and three British and Irish Cup matches - though there were deals on offer that took the price down to £256 for the stand and £192 for the ground, including a free lunch, if you bought it by June 30. The prices on match days were £20 for the stand, and £16 for the ground with concessions for students and under 16s. The programme cost £2.50. The average home attendance for league (11 Championship and three play-off) games in 2010-11 was 2,765. For the cup, including the quarter final and semi final, it was 1,958. The gate for a pre-season friendly against Northampton in August 2010 was 3,552.

In the 1985-86 season the club was managed by a General committee, Executive committee and a number of sub committees which included Finance, Centenary, Playing, Selection, Administration, Social and Junior section. Its principal officers were:

President: D Fowler. President Elect: H Elliott; Chairman: K Phillips; Vice-Chairman: P Evans; Secretary: A Mills; Assistant Secretary: R Evans; Treasurer: P Hulance; Assistant Treasurer: J Walker; Fixture Secretary: J Saunders; Team Secretary: J Saunders; Blues Captain: A Key; Wanderers Captain: A Walford; Rovers Captain: S O'Neill; Rams Captain: P Boon; Wanderers Secretary: D Matthews; Rovers Secretary: M Lilley; Sponsorship, Advertising: R Forsyth; Membership Secretary: B Hire; Coaching: M Fitzgerald, B French,

P Evans; General Committee: J Blakemore, I Bullerwell, R Evans, N Everett, E Keep, N J Stillman, K Roberts, B Pinsent, H Johnstone, R Partridge, I Boon, R Forsyth, R Slaughter, J Pope, M Hire; Co-opted, J Lee, G Cullen, M Fitzgerald, D Braybrook; Past Presidents, N J Timmins, H W Nightingale, H W Bitton, R H Haynes, Maj H F Rawkins.

These, in the main, were the members who took the club forward into the Centenary and beyond and, though plenty was going on behind the scenes, the Blues celebrated their 100 years with a series of events. There were fetes, balls, discos, dances and mini festivals. The club staged special matches such as those against Crawshay's XV and Cambridge University Past and Present and it put on the Under 18 Schools international between England and France at Goldington Road. One of the undoubted highlights was the Centenary dinner in the sports hall at Bedford School at which the guest speaker was a former player, Dudley Wood, the highly regarded new Secretary of the RFU. The celebrations ended with a tour to Kenya. The whole year, driven by club Chairman Ken Phillips, was an unqualified success and it concentrated minds wonderfully. This surely was a heritage worth preserving and handing on.

During his stewardship, Mr Phillips was, at one time, also the chairman of the Senior Clubs Association. He, and his deputy at Bedford, Phil Evans, were in favour of merit tables and leagues and they saw the move to professionalism as inevitable given what was already happening in the southern hemisphere. They saw the changes as a way in which the Blues could thrive again and retain its status as a first class club. The Centenary helped showcase the club but at the time it was difficult to attract players, to manage them and to keep them. Players still claimed the game as theirs. They could effectively do what they wanted and the best could play where they fancied because they could travel anywhere. Some would come if the right jobs were offered. Some wanted lavish expenses. It was a hard time for small clubs like Bedford who had always relied on a core of local players who wanted to play for their home town. Professionalism, through having players under contract, got rid of many of those problems. In return for being properly rewarded, players would have greater obligations to clubs who could buy in the talent they wanted according to what they could afford.

As Bedford celebrated, its leading lights looked to the future. This, though, was still the age of the amateur and the 'shamateur.' But times were changing.

Centenary Dinner in the Sports Hall at Bedford School

# LAST OF THE AMATEURS

The Centenary season at Bedford RUFC coincided with the introduction of league rugby in England. Out went the old regional merit tables and in came a national structure. However, wrote Matt Webb, who reported on the Blues between 1989 and 2002 in his role as sports editor of the *Bedford Herald*, the *Citizen*, the *Bedfordshire Times* and the *Times & Citizen*, in a typical RFU compromise, it was seven seasons before teams met each other more than once in a campaign. He wrote:

"Bedford were placed in the second tier and so the brave new world kicked off on September 13, 1986 with a dour 12-6 win over London Irish, courtesy of four penalties by Centenary skipper Andy Key. Only three more league wins followed as Bedford finished ninth in the fledgling John Smiths Merit Table B. In some ways that first season was a snapshot of the following decade at Goldington Road as occasional highs and rather more frequent lows punctuated the mediocrity.

Fifth the following season was followed by the first of the highs as Bedford were promoted to the top division – almost by default in 1988-89. An astonishing final day started with as many as six teams knowing they could be promoted alongside runaway champions Saracens and with the Blues realising victory at Sale would guarantee their place at the top table. A try by future coach Richard Greed, a drop goal from Stuart Vaudin and two Andy Finnie penalties – one a 50-yard monster – were only enough for a 15-15 draw and the atmosphere in the Heywood Road clubhouse was like a wake. But, 25 agonising minutes later, news filtered through that Coventry had been beaten 9-24 at London Scottish while London Irish had let a 21-0 half time lead slip to lose 21-22 to a late Blackheath drop goal. Suddenly the tears of grief turned to tears of joy and Bedford were contemplating life among the elite.

Unfortunately, it was a journey they would have to make without coach Richard Chadwick, talismanic captain John Orwin and nuggety winger Kevin Canning, who all announced their retirements, as well as influential scrum half Brian Gabriel who departed for Nottingham. The captain's armband passed to stalwart hooker Mark Howe, while Orwin's place in the boiler-room was taken by 22-year-old future British Lion Martin Bayfield. The coaching duties were filled by former Taranaki boss Ian Snook, who had the unenviable task of assembling a squad to compete with the best in England.

What followed was nothing short of disastrous as Bedford lost every game and never really threatened to break their duck. In the process they suffered an 8-71 home defeat by Harlequins and a then-record 0-76 battering at Bath. Incredibly coach Snook wrote in the *Bedford Herald*: "It may be difficult to comprehend if you weren't at Bath last Saturday, but I believe that Bedford turned in their best performance this season." It was even more difficult to comprehend for those who had witnessed the debacle at The Rec.

The following two seasons saw the Blues flirt with relegation to the third tier, with only a couple of late-season wins keeping them away from the trap door. They were not so lucky in 1992-93 when, despite finishing seventh, a restructure of the leagues meant they were relegated to the third level of English rugby. Single-point defeats at Morley and Exeter in the final weeks of the 1993-94 season meant they finished second and missed out on an instant return to Courage League Two. But that was remedied the following season as Bedford lifted the league title after a nail-biting end to the season that went down to the final whistle.

Coached by former Bristol and England flanker Mike Rafter and captained by Paul Alston, they made the early running by winning seven of their first eight games, thanks largely to the ever-reliable boot of Finnie, who would be the first player to lift the *Times & Citizen* Cup as player of the year. However, when they travelled to Blackheath in March of that season, it was the home side who were favourites to go up as champions. But Blackheath had no idea what was about to hit them – both on and off the pitch. So many made the journey from Bedford to South-East London, Blackheath ran out of glasses and had to shut the bar until a public address request for their return had been answered. On the field, tries by Alston and Ben Whetstone helped Bedford to a 12-12 draw which turned the title race in their favour.

However, it all came down to the last game of the season against Richmond when Rafter had to gamble on youth to bolster his injury-hit squad. For probably the last time in the club's history they took the field with schoolboys on each wing in the shape of Matt Oliver (Bedford School) and Giles Witheat (Bedford Modern). What followed was the longest afternoon many Blues fans can remember as Finnie converted tries by Whetstone, crowd favourite Steve Harris and Marcus Cook to edge the side into a 21-20 lead with 27 minutes still to play. With many of the 1975 cup-winning side looking on, Richmond bombarded the line but some desperate defending and a couple of missed kicks meant the title came to Bedford rather than Blackheath. The trophy itself went on a joyful, if unofficial, tour of the town and was later seen in the hands of prop Singh Basra as he danced on the tables of the Irish Club.

The following season back in Courage League Two was tough and, despite two wins and a draw in the opening four matches, the club finished bottom of the table as pressure of business prompted Rafter to resign and just one victory was secured after Christmas. Relegation was avoided due to another restructuring of the leagues.

While the leagues had highs and lows, the cup competition offered little cheer and served up a couple of results that will go down in infamy. A 15-23 defeat at Bradford & Bingley in 1993-94 saw prop Leigh Mansell sent off and flanker Matt Deans earn glowing reviews from the locals for a masterclass in front row play after reluctantly stepping in for his errant team-mate! But the game that came to be known as "The Great Building Society Disaster" was nothing compared to the fate that befell the champion team the following year when they went to Cumbria to take on Division Four side Aspatria. Coach Rafter later bemoaned the fact he had watched other games from that day on Rugby Special being played in bright sunshine while Bedford were greeted by horizontal sleet and a home side determined to take no prisoners. A 6-32 defeat duly followed and poor Ben Whetstone had to be treated for suspected hypothermia before the long journey home.

Another player to suffer real pain in the cup cause was centre Jim Chandler when Bedford pulled out the plum tie of the round in 1991-92. Just weeks after England had reached the World Cup final, and Will Carling's men had catapulted rugby into the national consciousness, Bedford were drawn to host Harlequins, who included World Cup finalists Carling, Jason Leonard, Simon Halliday and Peter Winterbottom in their ranks. Rather than Quins' comfortable 33-3 win, it was flanker Winterbottom who made the headlines in the local press for a punch that removed three of Chandler's teeth. The *Bedfordshire Times* told the whole gruesome story – under the headline *Operation Dracula* – of how Chandler retrieved the teeth, put them in a glass of milk and had them replaced by consultant oral surgeon Michael Simpson, who happened to be sitting in the stand, before being packed off to hospital.

Despite the arrival of leagues, some vestiges of the old days remained and Bedford were able to keep some of their traditional friendlies, including Northampton, Gloucester, Leicester and the odd Welsh visitor. Two new and high profile names appeared on the fixture list as first Auckland and then Canterbury played midweek matches. The idea that such players as Pat Lam and Andrew Mehrtens would ply their trade at Goldington Road for anything more than one evening was fanciful. But professionalism was on its way to the game and, with it, the prospect of the English leagues being awash with some of the top stars. As the money started rolling in towards the end of the 1995-96 season, the game began to change irrevocably – and Bedford were in the forefront of the revolution."

Mark Howe, hooking between Richard Pascall, left, and Phil Boulding, was one of only two players in 125 years to make more than 400 first team appearances

John Orwin was the third forward to captain both Bedford and England

# DREAMS AND NIGHTMARES

What made tough minded, self made entrepreneurs want to invest in rugby clubs after the sport went professional following the World Cup of 1995? It was elitist, riddled with cliques and run by people, in the main, committed to the ethos of the amateur in spite of the growth of semi professionalism in the southern hemisphere and 'shamateurism' in the northern. Perhaps it was the boost given to the game by Nelson Mandela when he wore the number six Springbok shirt as Francois Pienaar collected the Webb Ellis Cup after South Africa beat New Zealand in the final. Perhaps it was the euphoria, the impact made by Jonah Lomu and 'The World in Union' at the 1995 event and the promise of massive amounts of money from media empires that convinced people that TV and rugby were made for each other – like Premiership soccer. Whatever it was, come forward they did and, to their credit, some were still there in 2011. *Rugby Times* estimated, in October 2010, that Nigel Wray had invested £20million in the Saracens.

Bedford, quaint old Bedford, attracted no less a personality than Frank Warren, the boxing promoter, one of the most charismatic showmen of the age and someone, arguably, with a higher profile than any of the other big investors. He never really said what made him want to invest millions in the club, other than to make it clear that it wasn't to stage boxing tournaments, but as Stephen Jones noted in *Midnight Rugby*, he sat in the stand and roared abuse at the referee with the best of them. And that was good enough for most people. What is significant, though, is that the initial phone call asking if Bedford might be interested came from a rugby contact at ITV, which had the rights to the 1995 World Cup, and Bob Burrows, the respected former head of ITV Sport, later became chief executive at Goldington Road. He told the *Bedford Herald* in June 1996: "We began looking seriously at the club in February and were more than aware of the rich traditions and history that rugby has in the town....quite simply it is the club for us." At a meeting held at what was then known as the County Hotel on June 5, 1996, members grabbed the chance to hand over 90 per cent of the club in exchange for a share certificate and a dream. There were few dissenting voices – perhaps just one vote against.

Frank Warren

Ian Bullerwell, Geoff Cooke and Paul Turner at a 1996 press conference at Goldington Road

For ten years since its birth in 1977, *Bedfordshire on Sunday* didn't cover sport; but the owner, Frank Branston, who was interested, mainly, in local politics and was later to become the first elected Mayor of Bedford, was persuaded by some of his staff that carrying the Saturday results and reports on Sunday was a service readers and advertisers would appreciate and one that would cause problems for rival publications. In 1996, *Mike Green*, who had been editor, was the newspaper's Blues reporter. Among other things, he was chairman of Bedfordshire County Cricket Club when future England Test players Graeme Swann, Monty Panesar and Alastair Cook came into the team as 16 year olds. He wrote:

"For me it all began on a Saturday morning in the office of the then chairman, Ian Bullerwell. Negotiations with Frank Warren's Sports Network Europe had taken place and Mr Bullerwell, who had cancelled a trip to Los Angeles at the last moment, and other committee members, were waiting anxiously for confirmation that the deal had been completed.

The news came through mid-morning and the following day, June 2, 1996, *Bedfordshire on Sunday's* front page screamed – 'Blues set to join giants of rugby.' With Frank Warren's backing - £2.25 million to be spent on players over five years - former England manager Geoff Cooke installed as Director of Rugby with the peerless and apparently ageless Paul Turner as player-coach and any number of internationals ready to sign, there was every justification.

However, just three years and three months later, the only ever midweek edition of *BoS* told fans: "Future hangs on rugby authorities" and owner Frank Branston had pledged £10,000 as the newspaper launched an appeal to save the club.

That things went so terribly wrong was not the fault of Mr Warren. Yes his spat with fellow boxing promoter Don King, which led to his assets being frozen, was at the heart of the problem, but he only ever wanted what was best for Bedford and having said that he would sell the club for a pound to a company ready to invest in the Blues, it was on the advice of certain club officials that he handed over to Jefferson Lloyd International - whoever they were.

Nobody could possibly deny that during the time Sports Network owned the club, we saw some of the best rugby ever played at Goldington Road. In the first season alone, players of the calibre of Scott Murray, Martin Offiah, Junior Paramore, Jeff Probyn, Mike Rayer, Rudi Straeuli, Paul Turner and Roy Winters all pulled on a Bedford shirt. The following season saw the arrival of Alistair Murdoch, Rory Underwood and Jason Forster.

Promotion was not achieved that first season, but there were so many memorable games. The 64-9 demolition of Moseley, the nail-biting 27-26 win away to London Scottish, the agonising 33-34 loss at Richmond and, best of all, the never to be forgotten 34-28 downing of Newcastle at Goldington Road.

That famous win was followed by three straight defeats, but Bedford were still in the play-offs against Bristol. It was not to be though - an 11-20 defeat at home in which Straeuli picked up a serious injury being followed by a 12-19 loss at Bristol. But Bedford kept playing attacking rugby to the end and I can still picture Rayer making a 40-yard break from behind his own line in the dying minutes.

The Welshman, for me, was the star of that season, setting a club record points tally of 361 as his boot unerringly sent the ball over the bar, if usually only with a couple of inches to spare.

It all came right on the field the following season. Rayer beat his own record with 370 points, Ben Whetstone, a survivor from the amateur days, was the leading try-scorer for the second season in a row and the Blues romped to the Allied Dunbar Division Two title. This must have been one of the finest seasons in the history of the club. Bedford did not lose a game in the league until April 11 (Rotherham, who were to feature in Bedford's history in the following two seasons were the victors) and by then promotion had long since been clinched.

Off the field though, the financial problems were beginning to show. Cutbacks saw eight quality players released as early as mid-October. And it was a lack of money that was to end Bedford's hopes of making any real impression on the top league. In the end they stayed up by the flimsiest of margins following a 38-38 tie over two legs with Rotherham in the play-off.

Paul Turner went in September, Geoff Cooke soon after and it was Rudi Straeuli who took over team affairs. There were fantastic wins over Harlequins and Wasps, a double over London Scottish and a late triumph over West Hartlepool but the club conceded a record points against total that season.

And all the time Sports Network and Mr Warren were being backed into a position where they had little option but to look for a way out as the fight with Don King was followed by a bout with HM Customs and Excise.

Geoff Irvine - 'a diamond geezer' in Mr Warren's words - David Gunner and David Ledsom tried to get together a consortium of local businessmen to take over the club as early as Christmas, but could not get the support, and then on to the scene at the end of April came Jefferson Lloyd in the form of Doug Braddock. So began six months of farce which so nearly brought about the death of the Blues.

The sale, supposedly for £1 although Sports Network never actually saw the coin, took place with the summer rapidly approaching. Mr Irvine was bewildered as to why anyone would want to buy a club at that time of the year with wages to pay and no income. The answer proved to be simple.

The alarm bells started ringing for me when I asked Mr Braddock what the company actually did. "My background is stockbroking," he replied. Yet at a press conference a few days later, when asked by a national newspaper journalist if he was a stockbroker, Mr Braddock replied: "I don't know where you got that idea."

Yet supporters were so relieved that the club had apparently been saved that when Mr Braddock started promising the moon, the only person who tried to ask a couple of searching questions at the annual meeting was Paul Bowker, a former committee member of the amateur club who was shouted down with members yelling at him not to be 'negative.' One statement made at that meeting by Mr Braddock was that coach Straeuli would only leave the club 'over my dead body.' Within a matter of days the popular South African had effectively been sacked without any noticeable deterioration in Mr Braddock's health. Paul Turner returned.

*Bedfordshire on Sunday* next revealed that the real man in charge was John Gurney, who, at the time, was under investigation 'in the matter of the Drug Trafficking Act, 1994' and the subject of a restraint order issued in the Queen's Bench Division of the High Court on May 19, 1999. It must be made clear that no charges were brought against him. But it does help explain why he wasn't at Goldington Road for some time. For weeks Mr Braddock denied he had anything to do with Mr Gurney apart from once having shared an office block. But when *BoS* found that the High Court had frozen Mr Gurney's assets, Mr Braddock suddenly changed his mind and admitted that Gurney did have a major shareholding in the club.

The following day, 'heavies' arrived to escort Mr Braddock out of the club offices, take away his car and leave him a forlorn figure clutching a briefcase. Later Mr Gurney arrived in Bedford claiming that Mr Braddock had somehow managed to gain control of Bedford Rugby by using Jefferson Lloyd International's name without Mr Gurney's knowledge.

Caught up in all this nonsense was club administrator Pip August, former chief executive at Gloucestershire County Cricket Club and the wicketkeeper who spectacularly caught Ian Botham when Bedfordshire played Somerset at the Goldington Bury in the 1982 Nat West Trophy. He found himself having to persuade the RFU and the league that the club was in a position to continue while Mr Gurney's behaviour became more and more strange as he took to posting increasingly bizarre comments on the internet, sometimes in the middle of the night. The harassed staff at the club office would arrive for work to receive telephone calls from worried supporters asking for clarification about something in a message that had been posted overnight that they knew absolutely nothing about. On one occasion, Mr August was called from his home late one evening to stop someone trying to get into the bar safe, claiming it was on Mr Gurney's orders.

The players were not paid. Mr Irvine tried to buy the club but was rejected. Then came the bombshell. The club was to be sold and moved lock, stock and barrel to Coventry subject to the approval of the rugby authorities.

The town was in uproar. *BoS* brought out its special edition. Money poured in and the club was given permission to postpone games. Thanks to the efforts of many, rugby in the town survived and after a warm-up game with Cambridge University the new club played its first league game at Leicester on October 30. A 61-12 hammering resulted but the feeling was of relief rather than disappointment.

Alistair Murdoch replaced Turner as Director of Rugby with Andy Gomarsall as captain. It was always going to be an uphill task and it was not until April that the Blues achieved their first league win. Trips to Italy and France in the European Shield helped to create a family spirit, though, and going into the play-offs, inevitably against Rotherham, hopes were high that Bedford could maintain their position in the top flight.

It was not to be. Beaten 40-20 at Rotherham, the return at Goldington Road was played in near water-logged conditions. The Blues pounded away at Rotherham, were awarded two penalty tries and probably should have had a third, but 14-0 it remained and Bedford were down, but certainly not out as had appeared likely back in September."

Martin Offiah, who scored in the Eastern Counties win over Bedford in April 1985, played for the club in 1996-97.

He is pictured celebrating in the win against Newcastle in April 1997.

Mike Rayer, broke the points scoring record in each of his two seasons as a Bedford player

# WHEN THE PEOPLE HAD THEIR SAY

The consortium that eventually took over at the Blues could have bought the club from Frank Warren before it was offered to the John Gurney group for a pound. In the *Bedfordshire on Sunday* midweek supplement of October 6, 1999 a few days after the announcement that the Blues were being sold to Coventry, Geoff Irvine was quoted as saying that he couldn't muster enough support; but that he wished he'd gone ahead.

He said: *"It's an absolute nightmare – a disaster for the town. I can't think of any way to change things round. It's all very well for people to start jumping up and down now but where were they at Christmas when David Gunner, David Ledsom and myself were trying to get a consortium together. Had business people come up with some money then, John Gurney, Doug Braddock and Jefferson Lloyd International would never have been heard of... With hindsight I wished we had bought it but with no income coming in during the summer, I considered anybody who bought a rugby club at that stage of the year would have to be out of their mind."*

People had always spoken about Bedford as a 'rugby town'. But what did that mean? Certainly huge crowds never turned up to matches unless it was something extra special. After the Centenary season most gates were counted in hundreds rather than thousands. Even during the All Star era of 1996-99 when some world famous players on unheard of salaries were in the team few crowds were more than 4,000. The last league match of 1997-98, one of the best seasons on record, saw a crowd at Goldington Road of 2,224. The one on September 26, 1998 in the top tier against Leicester attracted what was described as a 'disappointing' 4,165.

So did being a 'rugby town' merely mean that establishment people were involved with the club and local businesses supported it to some extent? Or that there were a number of other clubs in the town; or that most schools in the area played the game. No one called Bedford a soccer town although there was a time when the Eagles attracted much bigger gates than the Blues and certainly on the sports pages of the *Bedfordshire Times*, in the 1960s and 1970s, there was never any question that football stories sold more papers than rugby ones. Both Frank Warren and John Gurney were always asking where the crowds were in this so-called hotbed of rugby. Both considered moving to where they might be. But they were outsiders who were attracted to the Blues for different reasons. Geoff Irvine's team, part of the town's new movers and shakers, knew exactly where they were. They were following the fortunes of the club from a distance. They were proud of it and thought it important. But only a few did anything to really support it. And it was their commitment and flair for positive publicity that earned the town its reputation.

Nevertheless, in the month of October 1999, all that changed. And when news started to come out at the match at Saracens on October 1 that the players were on their way to Coventry and that the Coventry chairman had just paid their wages that latent support exploded. And it was ordinary supporters and volunteers who mobilised it. People like press officer Howard Travis prepared to give up his job in the police force to get the message across. He wanted a supporters' buy-out and briefed the media to that effect. Members of the Followers stationed themselves at the club – ready for news; prepared for action. Local newspapers and radio were always supportive but suddenly regional TV was carrying interviews that showed the fury and passion of die-hard supporters. One with Norman Flinn of the Followers was worthy of an Oscar - only he wasn't acting. He was livid. "What right has this man got to sell our club.

Who does he think he is," he screamed on *BBC Look East*.

Players and coaches were in a difficult position. They all had contracts. They weren't being paid. Nearly all of them came from out of town and had been brought in or stayed on after assurances of financial stability. But there were still a few locals among them and flank forward Phil Elphick had no hesitation in telling local radio: "I play for Bedford. I will not be playing for Coventry."

On Tuesday October 5, Peter Smith of the Followers had a meeting with John Gurney. He'd organized a briefing of supporters in the bar afterwards. But so many people turned up that it had to be moved from the top bar, to the Scrum Hall and then to the main stand and it became a rally rather than a briefing. It was the moment when the anger, frustration and determination of fans became clear to everyone – when the buy-out plan gathered momentum and took off. Howard Travis accepted three promises on the spot for a total of more than £50,000 – all of which materialized.

In 1999, few people at the club really knew what to make of the new internet forum *Have Your Say*. But Robert Leggat did. He wasn't your average 'rugger bugger' – he was quiet, unassuming, academic, church going, caring and a genuine fan. But when it came to the internet and what it could do, he was years ahead of his time. He set the site up and became its moderator and he showed what a tool for outrage such chat rooms could become with comments and support coming in from all over the world. John Gurney was fascinated by it; and two of the few people he trusted at the Blues were Robert Leggat and the owner of the company that provided the internet service – Mike Kavanagh – who he was later to describe as a 'real hero of Bedford'. Mr Gurney would ring up Mr Leggat day and night for comfort and advice. Later he made it clear he would negotiate with Mr Kavanagh, who he, perhaps, saw as someone cut from a similar diamond as himself, but not with Mr Irvine who he saw as 'too establishment' – educated at Bedford Modern School and someone whose self made wealth enabled him to rub shoulders with gin and tonic celebrities at fancy golf tournaments. Mr Gurney was non league soccer, no disrespect, rather than Ryder Cup.

The furore was reflected in the council where the Mayor, Carole Ellis, whose big civic moment was to come six months later with the visit of Nelson Mandela, described the sale to Coventry as a 'kick in the teeth'. The leader, Shan Hunt, knew all about rugby, its place in the community and its importance to fans. She was Welsh and her husband, also a councillor, was a former player. She got her officers to start wheeling and dealing. One of them was Peter Smith of the Followers, a senior man in the Town Hall finance department, who was able to point everyone in the right direction. MP Patrick Hall knew the game from his days at Bedford Modern School. He promised to get the Sports Minister involved. At least two other MPs, Derek Wyatt and Mike Lord, a Deputy Speaker, who was knighted in 2001 and made a Lord in 2010, were former players. The message, the fury, was everywhere. John Gurney had succeeded in uniting the town behind the club in a matter of days as never before.

The body that ran the Allied Dunbar Premierships One and Two was the English Rugby Partnership Ltd (ERP). It was jointly owned by the Rugby Football Union (RFU), English First Division Rugby (EFDR) and English Second Division Rugby (ESDR). It invited interested parties Keith Fairbrother of Coventry and John Gurney to speak for 15 minutes each at an office in London on October 7. It was also persuaded to hear submissions from Bedford Borough Council and someone else from Bedford Rugby. The person thrust into the limelight was local accountant Dave Rawlinson, who, with Doug Mellon, was one of only two directors left on the board. He was better known as a local tennis champion and administrator but, briefed by businessmen Bernard Henry and David Gunner and a number of lawyers, he had his 15 minutes worth and won the day. Game, set and match.

ERP issued the following press release: *"As a result of a board meeting today, where the proposed purchase of Bedford Rugby by Coventry Blues Ltd was tabled….it is the unanimous decision… that this transaction is not in the best interests of Allied Dunbar Premiership Rugby.*

*In addition and specifically, under the Articles of Association of EFDR it is not possible to register the transfer of a share in EFDR other than through promotion. Neither is it possible under RFU Rules to purchase RFU membership. It is therefore not in the gift of the ERP to approve this transaction.*

*The Board would like to record its hopes that Bedford Rugby can find resources to enable it to continue for the good of Allied Dunbar Premiership Rugby. The Board was encouraged to hear from Gordon Johnston, a representative of Bedford Borough Council, that such support has been promised through local business interests."*

With John Gurney now having no option but to cut and run, Dave Rawlinson called a meeting of around 30 big 'hitters' and they decided to launch an appeal in the *Bedfordshire on Sunday* October 10 edition with Dave Ledsom at its head. The money came rolling in to the offices of Rawlinson Pryde at 5, Goldington Road in front of the cameras of *BBC Look East* which had earlier secured an astonishing interview with Mr Gurney about his plans to turn Goldington Road into a centre for Asian Rugby. Geoff Irvine and his team were ready with their money. Other businesses came forward and all in all some 2,500 people raised more than £500,000 in three weeks.

Mr Ledsom and Mike Kavanagh led the negotiations to buy the club at a hotel in the Watford area. Eventually the deal was signed on October 21 through an off the shelf company called Highernova Ltd which became Bedford Blues Ltd in January 2000. The price? No one really said but the suggestion was that it was around £35,000 and most of the debt. That proved to be substantial and several years later Geoff Irvine asked if the ghost of John Gurney would ever go away after a series of industrial tribunal claims by former players and staff who'd lost their jobs.

But the Blues had been saved and following another rally at the ground on October 28 when Rudi Straeuli made a dramatic entrance, Dave Ledsom was confirmed as chairman and a new board set up. In May 2003, John Gurney turned up in even more bizarre circumstances at Luton Town FC, sacking the manager, appointing another one by a vote and promising an F1 race track. By then, though, there was a clear blueprint about what fans should do to get their club back. Get the council onside, get the backing of local business, call on the club's legacy in the community and, above all, get the supporters to kick up a stink - on the internet and everywhere else.

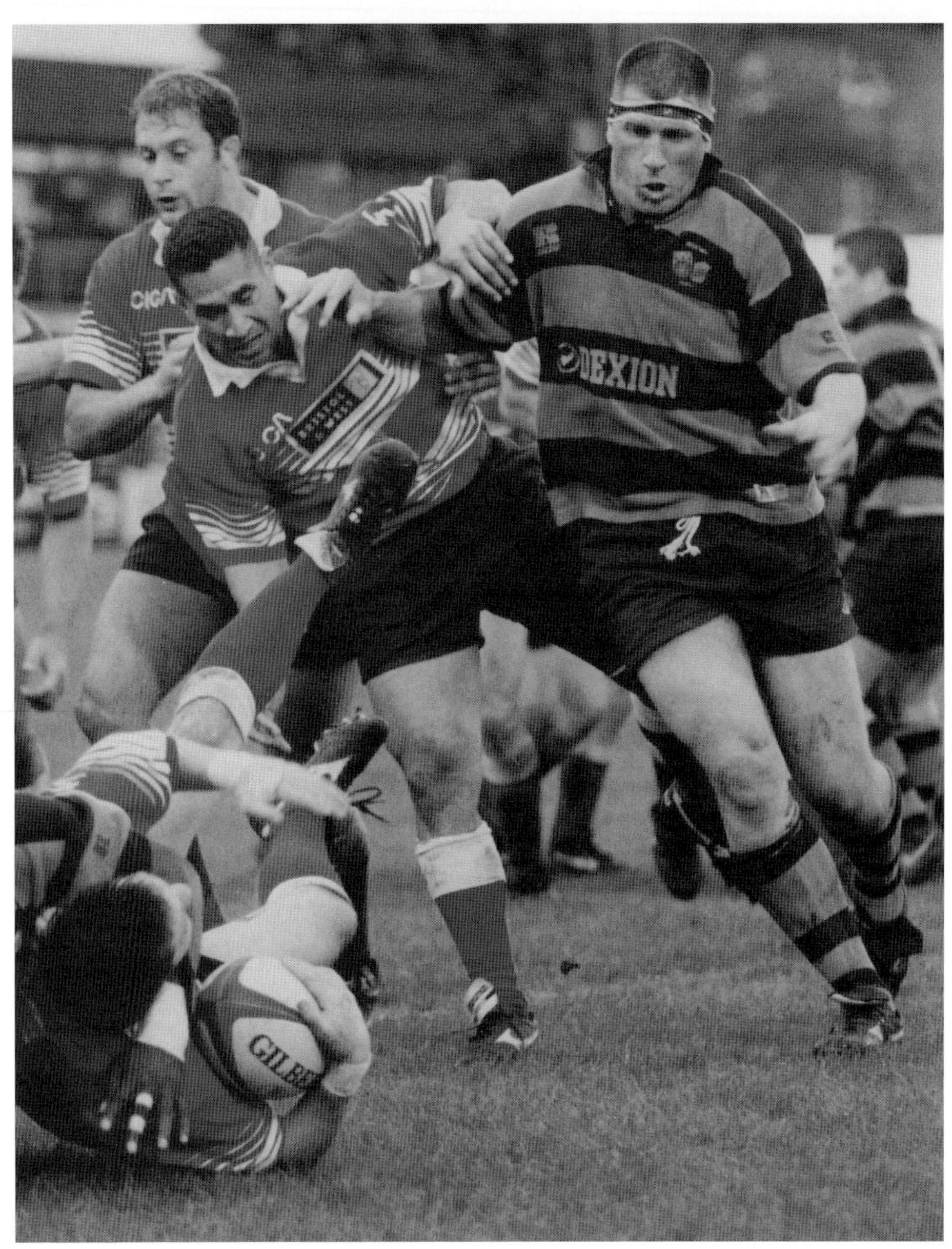


Rudi Straeuli – player, coach and inspiration

# FROM ZERO TO HEROES

The new Millennium dawned at Goldington Road at a time of uncertainty with regards to the club's playing status yet a feeling of great relief that it had been saved and that things could only get better. The new regime, with Dave Ledsom as Chairman and Geoff Irvine as the biggest investor and main man on the board, sought stability above all else after the turmoil of Jefferson Lloyd. They had to clear up the mess left behind; but crucially players and staff were paid on time and debts were honoured – even though some had to be resolved in the courts.

Relegation from the Premiership came inevitably but with dignity and another dose of reality as every single player became out of contract. It was a time to draw a line under the recent past and to start again and Geoff Irvine made an inspired appointment when he recruited Colin Jackson from the successful Dunstablians. The New Zealander was an agent as well as a manager and coach and his job as Director of Rugby was to build a squad to survive in the league and avoid the freefall fate which had obliterated others. That mission was achieved with a draw securing 11th place on the last day of the 2000-2001 season and for the rest of the decade the Blues finished no lower than seventh in the second tier.

Colin Jackson recruited and discovered a number of players who went on to greater things. Among them was James Pritchard, captain during the 125th year of the Blues and one of the all time greats at Goldington Road. When 'Jacko' left to return home to make another step up the rugby ladder after four seasons, Mr Irvine, by then Chairman, played another masterstroke by convincing Rudi Straeuli to take over.

The South African had a mighty reputation as part of the squad that won the World Cup in 1995. But he'd been recruited by Paul Turner for the All Star team as much on the basis of his (Straeuli's) reputation at Penarth in Wales where he'd also played and become a legend. His role at the Blues ended during the Jefferson Lloyd shambles. But he returned home to coach at first club then Super 12 level and then, early in 2002, he became coach of South Africa and all that entailed. He resigned after boot camp controversy, media pressure and a poor World Cup in 2003 but the Bedford Chairman invited him back among friends as much as anything to give him a chance to take stock after the sort of trauma that only rugby mad South Africa could dish out.

Junior Paramore returned, Soane Tonga'uiha was signed and with the record breaking Leigh Hinton taking the kicks, the side won the second tier cup final, the Powergen Challenge Shield, at Twickenham, 30 years after winning there before. It was the perfect way for Bedford to thank the iconic motivator that was Straeuli whose last appearance at 'Headquarters' had been in November 2002 when he was in charge of a Springbok team that lost by 50 points to England. The 14-13 win over Plymouth also convinced supporters that life outside the Premiership could not only be sustainable but enjoyable – perhaps even preferable. Neale Harvey wrote in *Rugby Times*: "...at Bedford, Straeuli is God and to hear 5,000 supporters blasting out 'Rudi, Rudi, Rudi' at the end of the match was as poignant a moment as any he has experienced during a distinguished rugby career."

That win, with Mark Harris scoring a try and Hinton kicking three penalties, raised expectations. It acted as a springboard and the next year the Blues reached the final again, losing this time to the Harlequins. Perhaps more significantly, they finished second to them in the league as well – the best position in the first decade of the new century.

By then another former player, Mike Rayer, was at the helm. The record breaking points scorer of 1996-1998 had a reputation in Wales of playing and preaching an open running game. Sam Roberts, who was the match day announcer for the whole of the decade and who, at one time, profiled players for the programme and later recorded interviews for the internet, wrote: "He identified a style, recruited beautifully and facilitated a belief that enabled some truly enviable rugby to be played." He turned the Blues into a regular top four team and, in five seasons, never lost a match to Coventry. But modestly in an interview in *Bedfordshire on Sunday* in October 2010 he put the success down to the Chairman – the man who controlled the purse strings; the man who made it possible to recruit quality players, once urging shareholders to back a rights issue for that very purpose.

There were some tremendous games during the decade; those battles against Rotherham, Exeter, the Cornish Pirates, London Welsh and Bristol, a 46-45 defeat at Moseley in 2001, the cup runs of 2005 and 2006, a 9-7 home win over Doncaster in 2007, a 27-24 win over Leeds in 2009. Then there was that match at Exeter on March 4, 2006 when fly half Ali Hepher, a Heineken Cup winner with Northampton in 2000, dropped a goal to win the match 37-35 en route to Twickenham.

There were wonderful players too: some who became internationals or Barbarians; others who moved on to a higher level; some like Andre Fox, Hepher and Jon Phillips who weren't captains but had a massive influence on their teams; others who were happy just to make the line up and play. *Sam Roberts* was asked for his favourite XV of the decade and in November 2010 he wrote:

"There were some much loved rugby heroes at Goldington Road between 2000 and 2010: Paramore, Tonga'uiha, Whetstone, Pritchard for a start. But I thought I'd use the opportunity to document those whose work wasn't perhaps as eyecatching or obvious. The following is a team I would love to have seen play together, not because they were necessarily the greatest players to wear the shirt but because wearing the shirt always seemed to mean so much to them.

1. **Matt Volland** – The fans will remember Tonga'uiha's impact and Dan Cole's dynamism, but for me, both on and off the pitch Volland, or 'Q' as he is so fondly known, has been an incredible Blues servant. It's only right he starts things off.

2. **Kramer Ronaki** – Bedford have always fielded a quality hooker. Dan Richmond and Chris Johnson are testament to that but there was something extra special about the Maori Ronaki. Very few would dispute his inclusion here.

3. **John Brooks** – Good tight heads are like hens teeth so Brooks must represent the cockerel's dentures. He was the classic cornerstone, unflinching and constant. Bespectacled, studious and humble off the pitch, he was everything you wanted for your club.

4. **Arthur Brenton** – As far as Bedford records go, no one can live with Brenton during this period. Stooping, grumpy, uncompromising – he was the enforcer par excellence. "No comment" he would offer, with a rare smile, whenever I ventured towards him with my mic – there was rarely anything else needed.

5. **Mouritz Botha** – Edges out Jon Phillips to this shirt. Mo played every game like it was his last and after two full seasons, having playing 62 out of possible 65 games, he got picked up by the Premiership. Incredible work rate, incredibly nice guy, for me, a must have in this side.

6. **Nic Strauss** – Gregor Gillanders has done incredibly well but with over 100 Blues caps, the hirsute South African was twice voted Bedford's best player by the rugby press - he was the archetypal blindside, horrendous to play against, heroic to play alongside.

**7. Sacha Harding** – Laurence White and Ben Lewitt can claim a stake on this berth but Sacha epitomises what it means to play in Blue. Off the pitch he has grown into a fine ambassador - a testimonial in 2010 was richly deserved.

**8. Paul Tupai** – Personally I loved what Shaun Brady brought to GR and Andre Fox was a superb representative for Bedford Blues; but Toops wove a special sort of magic. He never shied away from anything and just got better the more he played for the Blues.

**9. Karl Dickson** – Dicko was by far the best nine we'd had at the club in a long while. He spent a good apprenticeship behind the likes of Malone, Vass and Page but when his time came, he was an irresistible force.

**10. Ali Hepher** – Gets in on one, awkward looking drop goal. Myles Dorrian has, for two seasons, been outstanding for the Blues, perhaps the classiest 10 we've had in the era. But he's never beaten Exeter away. Often bound up and hobbling, Hepher had nous, steering us to a Twickenham trophy. Of course he gets in.

**11. Ollie Dodge** – Fantastic over the hard yards and deceptively quick. His 'body-on-the-line' attitude sometimes led to injury but another man who just loved every moment in a Blues shirt. One of the original dual registered players, and his inclusion is a nice nod to all those who've had split loyalties, but always seemed to adore playing at Goldington Road.

**12. Liam Roberts** – Someone once said that Liam was possibly the best player they'd coached. That someone was Mike Rayer. A wonderful step and great rugby brain, Roberts never quite achieved his potential in rugby but for the Blues, he was always good. A special mention for Ian Vass at 12; reinvention par excellence, nobody was as good defensively as Vassy.

**13. Billy Twelvetrees** – Brendan Burke should have got this spot, of course he should. But Lil' Bill scored great tries, spun enormous passes, kicked outrageous goals and reminded everyone of women's underwear! (He was sponsored by a lingerie shop). He was also better at 13 than 10 in my opinion. I'm sorry Brendan, I really am.

**14. Alex Page** – Page is a famous name to live up to in East Midlands rugby. Alex played on the wing like a man possessed. Ousted from scrum half by Dickson, many would have settled for the bench, not Page. More terrier than greyhound, he scored some great tries and is somewhat of wildcard with the likes of Fielden and Taylor certainly putting their hands up. But nevertheless, he's in.

**15. James Hinkins** – Leigh Hinton could well be included here but Hinko punched above his lightweight frame time and again. The fans loved him, players loved him, Nos loved him – there's no higher endorsement.

Someone I missed out? No doubt. It's all part of the fun. You will all have particular favourites, and there are so many who could make a fine case for inclusion. It's the ultimate Scrum Bar conversation.

But one thing is not up for debate. The coach of this team has to be Mike Rayer. Along with his team of Martin Hynes, Nick Walshe, Matt Volland and Rob Crowle, he has overseen an incredibly exciting and successful period."

Followers Chairman Peter Smith makes a leaving presentation to Colin Jackson, left

Matt Volland and mascot lead the team out

# TWICKENHAM AGAIN

Thirty years after the cup triumph of 1975, Bedford did it again when they beat Plymouth Albion 14-13 in the final of the Powergen Challenge Shield. And they made it to Twickenham for a third time in a knock out competition in 2006 when they lost to Harlequins in the final of the Powergen National Trophy after a memorable win at Exeter in the semi final.

League structures and cup competitions started to change as professionalism took hold - partly to provide increased competition for the elite and partly to satisfy clubs who needed a certain number of meaningful fixtures at regular intervals to help them market their businesses. In 1998 and 1999, Bedford reached the final of the Cheltenham and Gloucester Cup which was considered a 'league' cup, losing on both occasions at Northampton to Gloucester.

To reach the final of the Powergen Challenge Shield, a second tier competition, Bedford were knocked out of the Powergen Cup by Northampton 41-8 in December 2004, having beaten Tabard, Halifax and Exeter en route to Franklin's Gardens. After that defeat in the cup, they were then drawn away at Birmingham and Solihull in the semi final of the shield, winning the match 15-7 with five penalties from Leigh Hinton in March 2005.

And so to Twickenham with more Bedford supporters there on a day of Powergen finals than there had been in 1975. *Mike Green* was among them. Under the headline 'Cool Hinton the Blues Cup hero' he wrote in *Bedfordshire on Sunday*:

"It was heart-stoppingly exciting, nailbitingly tense, but the Blues came through to win the Powergen Challenge Shield at Twickenham.

Behind from the second minute, Bedford spent the rest of the game playing catch up until they were awarded a penalty 25 yards out and to the right of the posts.

Normally it was the sort of kick you would back Leigh Hinton to get, but it had not been his day so far. Two relatively easy penalties and a conversion had been missed and so the pressure was really on.

Some of the players and many in the crowd could not bear to watch but Hinton looked the coolest man on the field although I doubt he felt it. A swig from a water bottle, a glance at the posts and then back came the right boot and over went the ball. Hinton who could so easily have been the scapegoat for a defeat was a victorious hero.

What a game. Bedford left it late, but they deserved to win because it was they who played the attacking rugby. For the most part, Plymouth were content to sit back and counter attack when the Blues made an error.

Leigh Hinton

Their pack was formidable, but Bedford refused to be intimidated with Jon Phillips and Arthur Brenton battling away in the boiler room, the front row showing their mettle and Ben Lewitt and Nic Strauss turning up everywhere. Outside the scrum, there was no contest. The Bedford backs had flair. Plymouth relied on strength. Ian Vass and Ali Hepher were a partnership and a half. Hinton and Matt Allen were always looking for openings and Craig Moir, Mike Staten and Mark Harris ready to punish any errors.

Bedford had their moments of luck, notably when Plymouth had what looked like a perfectly good try ruled out just before the interval, but fortune is expected to follow the brave. But it couldn't have been a worse start as far as Bedford were concerned. Having got a scrum on the Plymouth 22 after a knock on, Paramore picked up at the back of the scrum only for Plymouth to intercept and charge clear. The break was ended five metres from the line by Hinton's tackle but the Plymouth forwards piled in and To'oala went over so close to the line that it must have been touch and go whether he was in touch. The referee was happy and Pritchard's conversion from the touchline made it 7-0 to Plymouth after just two minutes.

Little went right for Bedford as they tried to get back into the game. A couple of knock-ons ended promising moves, they were penalized at a scrum in the Plymouth 22 and then, the unluckiest cut of all, the touch judge deciding that Harris had strayed a fraction of a millimetre outside his own 22 before clearing.

Plymouth attacked from the lineout, Bedford could not get the ball clear and when they were eventually penalized Carrington kicked the penalty.

Nevertheless, despite being ten points down, Bedford were playing the more adventurous rugby and there were breaks by Hinton, Staten and the impressive Lewitt. It took a penalty by Hinton though to get Bedford's first points on the board. And before they had a chance to claw their way any further back, another mistake handed Plymouth three more points. Johnson's throw to the back of the line out had Phillips stretching; he couldn't control the ball and Plymouth pinched it. Their forwards had five charges at the line before the ball finally came back to Carrington who settled for a drop goal.

Back came Bedford with Moir and Harris in full flight and the referee playing a long advantage before deciding to give Hinton a chance to kick a penalty. Another good period of Bedford pressure followed with Vass, Allen and Harris working the ball one way and Vass, Volland and Paramore switching it the other. Unfortunately when the penalty came Hinton missed it.

Bedford were making too many unforced errors both in attack and defence and they had two let-offs in the dying seconds of the half. First the referee called play back for a knock-on after Staten had made a hash of dealing with a kick into the Bedford 22. Then Carrington made a hash of a fairly straightforward penalty. Given those circumstances then, the Blues must have been happy to go in only13-6 down at half time.

Tonga'uiha was on at the start of the second half in place of Volland but soon fell foul of a touch judge which had Bedford surrendering a good position. But they were soon back on the attack with Strauss fly-hacking and charging and Johnson suddenly finding himself in the clear but not trusting his pace and throwing a wild pass.

Time and again though, to their evident frustration, the Blues were pulled up by the referee as the forwards sought to exert pressure. And you really thought it wasn't going to be their trophy when Hinton missed a penalty from right in front of the posts. A minute later they had a line out five metres from the line, but the ball shot forward as the pack started their drive.

From the next lineout much further out, Bedford did get a drive going and when the ball was let out, Hepher's long pass led to Moir making a break. Harris was on hand and although he was tackled just short, he retained possession and dived over. Hinton's conversion would have put the scores level, but he sent it wide.

Sixteen minutes to go, two points in it and already Plymouth started to run the clock down, keeping possession with the forwards and only letting it out as a last possible option.

Bedford can wrestle with the best though and their perseverance was rewarded with five minutes to go when Plymouth conceded a penalty. So it was all eyes on Hinton – and he didn't let his side down. The kick soared between the posts and the Blues were ahead for the first time in the match.

And so followed the most nervous few minutes, Bedford supporters surely ever had to endure. Drop goal attempts were spurned, and although it looked as though Bedford had clinched it when Johnson dived over, the referee decreed the pass to him had been forward.

Plymouth had the ball too often for everyone's nerves in injury time but the Bedford tackling was too good for them. The Powergen Shield was on its way to Goldington Road where the celebrations went on deep into the night.

**Bedford:**

Harris, Moir, Hinton, Allen, Staten (Brown), Hepher, Vass, Volland (Tonga'uiha), Johnson, Brooks, Phillips, Brenton, Strauss, Lewitt, Paramore (Brady).

The winners celebrate

# A MODEL CLUB

No one doubted that professional rugby was going to be mighty difficult to sustain. But that didn't stop experienced entrepreneurs throwing money at it and club committees mortgaging their grounds to claim a slice of whatever they hoped was going to be on offer.

Respected clubs like London Scottish, Richmond, West Hartlepool, Orrell all suffered serious indignities. Others, like Northampton, Worcester and Exeter, saw an opportunity and took it. In September 2010, *Rugby Times* detailed how elite clubs were funded. It claimed that the 11 clubs who had been members of the top tier for the longest time would each receive £2.44m from Premiership Rugby, plus up to £200,000 for fielding a quota of England Qualified Players in their match day squads and more for supplying players to England's elite squads.

Worcester, who were relegated to the Championship, where Bedford played in 2010-11, received £1.44m for being a 'member' of the Premiership 'club' plus a £1m parachute payment to help adjust to relegation, plus £300,000 from the RFU – which is what Bedford got. The Championship itself had been set up for the season 2009-10 during the previous one and the league was brutally reduced from 16 to 12 clubs - by relegating the bottom five and promoting one.

It was complicated all right and in 2010 just Leicester and Northampton, of the 12 Premiership clubs, declared profits. Bath, according to *Rugby Times*, lost £1,259,000. Bedford's Chairman Geoff Irvine told the newspaper that year that the Blues would not meet promotion criteria even if they won the inaugural playoffs. Everyone knew they could not sustain life at the top anyway. Many supporters liked things in the second tier but others longed for another go at the big time.

The season before when three Championship clubs went into administration *Rugby Times* referred to Bedford as a model club. What it meant was that the Blues had worked hard on its core support and had increased gates, it had established other streams of income, including rights issues and cash injections from directors and sponsors, and it had achieved a balance that the annual meeting found acceptable between what it spent on players and other expenditure - like the infrastructure and the ground. The club was successful on the field. But it still made a loss. So how did it work? What made it tick?

In 2007, the *Followers Newsletter*, a regular hand out edited by committee member Adrian Randall ran an article by Richard Glasspool, a member of the club board. He wrote in support of a rights issue:

"In striving to compete at the top of National Division One, the club made operating losses of £119,000 in the year 2005, £101,000 in 2006 and a similar loss is anticipated for the year ending June 30, 2007. (It was £91,000). These losses have to be financed, resulting in the club utilising its maximum over-draft facilities and having to draw upon other sources of funding. Therefore one of the main reasons for the rights issue is to relieve the pressure on the balance sheet and to provide a much-needed injection of working capital. Also, a major benefit from the rights issue is a significant reduction in bank interest charges, money that can be freed up for other uses.

For the current season, the club has budgeted for £1.6 million of income from all sources. The approximate break-down of this amount is 24% from match day and season tickets, 24%

from sponsorship and advertising activities, 10% from the marquee, 7% from other sources (including from The Followers, donations, and the Blues bonus try fund) and 25% from gross sales from the bars and the club shop. The RFU and Premiership Rugby contribute the balance of 10%.

The objective is to achieve a break-even position for the current financial year. The expenditure budget is therefore also set at £1.6 million. Employment related costs account for 50% of total costs, and with player related and ground related costs at 12% and 7% respectively. Costs relating to the marquee are at 5%, general overheads at 10% with financial costs at 3%. The balance of expenditure of 13% comprises cost of sales for the bars and club shop.

The one variable is the Cup competition. The budget does not provide for any income from possible matches drawn at home. Therefore a good cup run involving home matches would provide for much needed incremental revenue.

The budgeted attendance figure for the 15 home league matches is 37,000 at an average of 2,466 and with a net figure of £10.26 per spectator. Prior year figures were 32,755, 2,184 and £9.53 respectively. Thus the Club is looking to achieve a 13% increase in volume terms, which is helped by the presence of Northampton in ND1. After eight home games, the club's cumulative attendance figure is 19,723, close to budget of 19,900. This is good news that we are on track with forecast.... In terms of how Bedford compares with other clubs for this season, after 14 matches, the average home gate for Bedford is 2,465 placing the club in fifth position behind Northampton (10,728), Plymouth (3,603), Exeter (3,564) and Cornish Pirates (3,465).

The marquee, set up in 2005, is proving to be a great success both in terms of generating a profitable revenue stream and in providing for a much needed match day facility. Total bookings for the marquee for the current season will be close to 60, divided evenly between rugby and non-rugby related events. The marquee facility also provides great visibility for the club in the town for being able to host high quality events of a non-rugby nature. In terms of financial performance, after taking into account direct costs, last season the marquee made a net contribution of just over £100,000 and we anticipate a minimum 25% increase for the current season."

That was how Bedford operated at the time and it was public knowledge. But what other clubs envied most was something else – something much more difficult to quantify.

The marquee was erected in 2005 opposite the main clubhouse, built in 1978, on part of what used to be the Wanderers pitch.

Supporters in the marquee

# THE ENVY OF OTHERS?

When Geoff Irvine said that he didn't have the support when he had the chance to buy Bedford from Frank Warren before it was sold to Jefferson Lloyd International he was right because the club was in chaos and about to get worse. Brought up in Bedford and educated at one of its famous schools, he made his money in building – one of the toughest sectors of the economy albeit one that enjoyed boom years between 1997 and 2007. But as a son of Ulster rather than of De Parys Avenue, he was able to detach himself sufficiently from the various mainstream groups which ran his adopted town and to establish for himself what made it work.

That he had ambition to become a success in sport and in business was never in doubt. In his 20s he'd been a director of Bedford Town Football Club, the Eagles. As a youngster, he'd seen astonishing crowds at the Eyrie in Nelson Street. According to David Williams' website *bedfordoldeagles.com*, the 1955-56 average gate was more than 6,000. More than 18,000 packed in to see the fourth round FA Cup tie against eventual winners Everton in February 1966. But later that same year a huge row with the supporters' club erupted over fund raising and finance and by 1982, the club had gone out of business. Mr Williams doesn't argue that one caused the other; but the lesson was clear. Geoff Irvine saw it at first hand and he knew how important support – proper support - was.

Old style soccer chairmen tended to be benevolent despots, putting their own money into the club, getting their own way on the board, employing close contacts and having a manager who sang from the same hymn sheet. They knew what their club meant to the community. They cajoled a supportive press and expected a certain status. Fans then were expected to know their place. As lower league soccer declined much of that model went out of the window. When rugby went professional some saw it as the way forward but those who rode roughshod over their supporters were often in for a shock. Geoff Irvine knew that. And he knew the advantages and disadvantages of the model particularly with regards to supporters in a new age of leisure when people could do many more things on a Saturday afternoon than used to be the case. First and foremost, though, he was a local sportsman and a hard grafter who knew what made sportsmen and supporters tick. He was at ease with fans on the terraces – he felt he was one of them. In the early 1980s a feature in the *Bedford Record* on his sporting prowess described him as a 'Legend in his own lunchtime'.

The Gurney legacy was to unite the Blues from top to bottom. The battle against him was supporter led. It was supporters who suggested a buy out among equals rather than encouraging another sole owner. Supporters became shareholders, they provided management advice through their new internet forums – not that it was always taken up but it kept them involved. It meant that ordinary fans, many of whom had great expertise in a number of relevant fields became genuine stakeholders in the enterprise and determined to make it succeed. The myth of a 'rugby town' suddenly meant something and one of the big challenges taken on by the management and by ordinary fans was to get its citizens down to the ground.

The council was supportive through the generous terms of the new lease on the ground and in other areas. The press was compliant as never before. Hardly a word was raised in criticism in the 12 years after the 1999 buy-out. All of that was just part of what made Bedford the envy of other clubs. It had come through a crisis that threatened its very existence. And it came out as one big team fighting for the same things so that when the club needed more money, supporters were ready to dip into their pockets again and again. An appeal for £75,000 for new floodlights in 2011 was the latest.

The internet meant that anybody could comment on anything. *Chris Ward* was a prominent local accountant who did just that and wrote match reports on *Have Your Say*. He also kept an eye on the small print and in January 2011 he wrote:

"At the meeting of October 28, 1999 it was agreed that larger donors were to be responsible for the day to day running of the club. This was considered reasonable as Geoff Irvine, David Gunner and their team had already contributed £100,000 to pay players in the previous season and had paid players a further £80,000 most recently prior to the Leicester game on October 30. A further £200,000 was guaranteed by the larger donors during that season and thereafter to ensure the club's survival.

No single person or business from the group of larger donors was to have a shareholding of 50% or more. Larger donors were those who had contributed £5,000 or more and were to be called 'consortium' members and allotted 'B' shares and have up to four elected directors on the board of directors. Supporters contributing less than £5,000 were to be allocated 'A' shares of £25 each and entitled to elect two members to the board of directors. Subsequently this was changed to allow the consortium to elect up to eight directors and the Supporters four directors.

Most importantly the supporters with the A shares have veto rights. The holders of 50.1% of the supporters' shares have the right to veto any change in the name of the club, the colours of the strips of the teams, the badge on the jerseys of the players. Also the veto can be used to block any move of the location of the club ground away from Bedford or any disposal of the RFU membership of the club. As early as May 2000 the approval of the shareholders was sought as it was necessary to adopt new colours and a new badge.

The new company's first accounts covered the period from the appeal in October 1999 to June 2000. They reflected the issue of 12,119 supporters shares and 8,500 consortium shares with a combined value of £515,475 – basically the money raised in the appeal. But this was insufficient to cover the huge loss that was to be incurred in the club's first period of trading amounting to £743,192. The club's total income from all sources, but not including the appeal money, was £1,054,881 of which £314,411 came from ticket sales and £372,151 was the contribution from 'English Rugby' (the senior clubs and RFU). The total costs in the first year were £1,798,073, of which nearly £1 million was paid in players and coaches salaries and related costs. The amount by which the loss exceeded the appeal money was covered, basically, by the bank overdraft and private loans.

Drastic action was again needed to ensure the following season's financial survival following relegation from the Premiership to National One. The directors' report for the year to June 2001 was specific. *"During the last financial year it had become very apparent just how disastrous a financial position we had inherited from the previous owners. A whole series of bad business arrangements, poorly written contracts and general incompetence has cost us dearly. Legal fees and associated costs alone in this respect have been in excess of £200,000 since we took over."*

To bolster the funds available the first of several 'rights issues' was undertaken. This involved inviting existing shareholders to buy more shares at £25 each and a further £236,800 was raised this way. But although losses were not incurred at the same level as the previous season they were still huge. Total income fell to £980,713 reflecting lower ticket sales (£208,590) and lower income from English Rugby (£249,729). Costs fell too to £1,295,066, but the loss of £314,353 was still £77,553 less than the monies raised by the rights issue. Further loans made up the balance.

A further rights issue in the year to June 2002 raised £140,150 but losses remained stubbornly high at £258,778, bringing the losses in the first three years of the new entity to £1,316,323. The funds raised and the losses incurred in the 11 years from October 1999 to June 2010 were:

| Years ended June | | Funds Raised | Losses incurred |
|---|---|---|---|
| 2000 | Appeal | 515,475 | 743,192 |
| 2001 | Rights | 236,800 | 314,353 |
| 2002 | Rights | 140,150 | 258,778 |
| 2003 | Other | 30,000 | 155,483 |
| 2004 | Rights | 168,000 | 19,637 |
| 2005 | Other | 20,000 | 119,038 |
| 2006 | | 0 | 101,038 |
| 2007 | | 0 | 91,141 |
| 2008 | Rights | 536,800 | 142,945 |
| 2009 | | 0 | 137,720 |
| 2010 | | 0 | 189,371 |
| **Total** | | 1,647,225 | 2,272,696 |

The rights issue in 2008 included the benefit of a pledge from the Chairman, Geoff Irvine, to match the funds raised in the issue to a total of £250,000. This increased his holding to 18,000 Consortium shares with a nominal value of £450,000 being 27.3% of the total shares issued, and 44.5% of the Consortium shares. The directors of the company hold 64.6% of the consortium shares between them.

The improvement in the club's results on the field have been reflected in rising attendances and hence income from 'spend' on match days. Additionally the construction of the marquee in 2005 opened up the possibility for increased match day hospitality as well as the hiring of the marquee for non-rugby related activities. Initially the building was expected to have a five year life but it turned out to be more robust and was expected to remain serviceable for another five years.

After the near demise of the club in 1999 and subsequent relegation from the top flight, the target for attendances at home games was set at 1500. Nearly 1600 average gates were achieved in 2001 but that fell away to below 1400 in 2002. But gates recovered in 2003 and have risen steadily since and in season 2009-10 topped 2800. Although there was a minor setback to these numbers in 2006-07 there was a rise in gate receipts that season through increased prices. Gate receipts in 2002-03 reached their low point with just £176,000 taken from ticket sales on average gate of 1600, but in the season 2009-10 the total had risen to in excess of £507,000 on average gates of 2827, a significant and very creditable performance, reflecting the improved results and style of play on the field.

English Rugby – a combination of the RFU and the Premiership Clubs - also contributes financial support to the Championship clubs. Excluding the season 1999-2000 the season's average has been just short of £207,000. But the worrying matter is that in the last ten seasons, with one exception in 2007-08, the combined total of gate receipts and English Rugby financial support together has been less than the salary costs of the players. That figure has risen from £488,000 in 2000-01 to £761,000 in 2009-10 at an average of £567,000 per season.

So despite the best endeavours of the board, the generosity of the large donors and small donors alike, the club continues to be dependent on the goodwill of a few to keep it financially alive. Over 11 seasons the business has lost over two and a quarter million pounds - £206,000 per season. At the end of June 2010 the company's liabilities exceeded its assets by £600,000. But with the support of its creditors, mostly willing friendly faces, it can continue. But not like this indefinitely."

In the middle of the severe winter of 2010-11, a lively debate started on the Have Your Say forum about whether or not the Blues had ambition to push on – in effect to go all out for a return to the Premiership. Some thought the club should; others didn't want to get hurt again. It was easy to look at the fantastic facilities and success of Northampton and reflect that around 20 years earlier there was virtually nothing between the two old rivals. But Northampton were ready to take their chance when professionalism came and they took it at the first attempt with the right man at the helm in Keith Barwell, former owner of a newspaper group that had a title in Bedford. And full marks to them. Bedford had a chance and tasted success before it all went wrong.

The Chairman responded at the annual meeting by arguing that had the Blues stayed one more season in the top tier after the buy-out of 1999 the club would have gone bust. "Getting relegated," he said, "saved this club. Premier rugby is just not achievable at the moment. We don't have the money and the ground doesn't conform to requirements. But our league position tells us that we are the 14th best club in the country and compared to where we were ten years ago that is a magnificent achievement. However when the time is right," he said, "we must be ready." Narrow defeats in the Championship semi final and the British and Irish Cup final spoke for themselves. The side gave everything. But they weren't ready on the field and certainly not off it.

So the Bedford model by 2010-11 was to have a strong chairman and a board that had the confidence of the banks and the community. It had directors prepared, old style, to put in their own cash – no one really knew how much. Their view was that the way forward at the time was to invest in a part time team good enough to play attractive rugby and to challenge at the top end of the table rather than to put big money into major infrastructure projects. It had supporters who were genuine stakeholders who could always be relied on for extra money. It had a thriving academy, junior and mini section.

Above all, though, after the experience of 1999 when the club could have gone to the wall, it was united and determined not to put at risk again a heritage created and cherished over 125 years.

Pete Beard, right with Dave the Doorman, organized the Boxing Day 2010 snow clearing operation.

Handre Schmidt with supporters at the 2011 club dinner

James Pritchard celebrates his 403 points for the season with son Lucas and Geoff Appleton, treasurer, and Jackie Markham, President, of the Followers

# 2. WHO'S WHO AT THE BLUES

Captains of Bedford and England:
'Budge' Rogers, left, and David Perry at a reunion and John Orwin in action for England

# THE CAPTAINS

*A Parrott*
*H S Morris*
*H E Vipan*
*W Rees*
*W K Roberts*
*F W Potter*
*R D G Glascott*
*F S P Saunders*
*H B Beddall*
*C R Hoskyn*
*A L Rogers*
*R Maclear*
*C Franklin*
*A W B Gompertz*
*H Willett*
*R C Stafford*
*A V Manton*
*A Hall*
*A F Wesley*
*L H Nicholson*
*E L W Cumming*
*S D Kitchener*

*F G Hore*
*L A R Fensome*
*A R Alston*
*R C Brumwell*
*A Marshall*
*W A Sime*
*J G Cook*
*R Willsher*
*R G Furbank*
*G Jenkins*
*J F Bance*
*A C Towell*
*T R Marshall*
*St L H Webb*
*P Voyce*
*P H Avery*
*B K Williams*
*D G Perry*
*D P Rogers OBE*
*R J Slaughter*
*P D Briggs*
*V J Lewis*

*J M Howard*
*R M Wilkinson*
*D Jackson*
*N O Martin*
*G N Phillips*
*J T Mawle*
*I G Peck*
*A M Key*
*J Orwin*
*M A Howe*
*G Wood*
*R E Pascall*
*P Alston*
*P Turner*
*A R Murdoch*
*A C T Gomarsall MBE*
*B M L Whetstone*
*M J Volland*
*M C Allen*
*D J Richmond*
*J G Pritchard*

Bedford's first captain Alf Parrott

Hugh Willett

Sam Kitchener

Arnold Sime

Dick Furbank

Tony Marshall

There were 65 elected or appointed captains of the Blues in the first 125 years of the club. Of the 52 in the first 100, more than half of them were former pupils or masters of either Bedford School or Bedford Modern School. An Old Bedfordian, W A Sime was elected a record five seasons in succession, another, D P Rogers was captain, with intervals, for five seasons. Two others, R C Brumwell and I G Peck served for four seasons in succession. In the next 25 years, only M A Howe, an OBM, and A C T Gomarsall, an OB, were one season captains who represented the old public school connection. P Alston, a former pupil of Wootton Upper School, and M C Allen were captains for four years in succession. Between 1990 and 2009, five of the club's ten captains had enjoyed substantial careers at Northampton. Three Bedford captains also captained England.

**A Parrott 1886-89**

Alf Parrott was the club's first captain and he held office for three years, later to become secretary. An OBM, he was a master at the school between 1878 and 1923 and coach in 1900. Prior to the formation of the new club he had been captain of the Swifts. He played half-back for Bedford at least 60 times in an era when seasons were fairly short.

**H S Morris 1889-91**

H S Morris was a master at Bedford Grammar School when Mr Phillpotts was the headmaster. He was a forward who first played in 1887, was captain for two seasons, and was still playing in 1893. When he retired, he continued as a vice-president for many years.

**H E Vipan 1891-93**

H E Vipan was the club's third captain. He was an OBM and subsequently became their first secretary. He was a member of the Swifts before the formation of Bedford. He taught at the Modern School and was a keen committee man and administrator, and one of Bedford's delegates at the formation of the East Midlands parent body.

**W Rees 1893-96**

The man who had the distinction of captaining Bedford in its all-conquering season of 1893-94 was Billy Rees, an Old Bedfordian of Welsh extraction who practised as a solicitor in the town before returning to Wales. He was a small, fiery forward who made 134 appearances, seven of them between 1899 and 1902 whilst living in Wales. He stood down in his second term before returning for a third.

**W K Roberts 1894-95**

Bedford's fifth captain was W K Roberts, who took over when his predecessor resigned. One of the half-backs in the great team that beat the Barbarians, he was an OBM who made his debut in 1891 while still at school. The son of Sir Thomas Lee Roberts, he became a clergyman and was vicar of St Mark's, Mitcham. He played at least 64 times for Bedford and in 1914 he brought a first class side to the town to play in a charity match. They were all clergymen and contained internationals, calling themselves the London Clergy. W K Roberts also refereed a Bedford match in 1927.

### F W Potter 1896-98

F W Potter was the club's sixth captain. An OBM, he made his debut whilst still at school and completed 128 appearances at full-back or centre, scoring 252 points. An excellent place kicker, he was the reserve England full-back in 1896 to J F Byrne of Moseley. He was a regular until 1898 when he went to Shanghai and became chief of the Shanghai Gas Works. He returned to the town after 32 years and took a keen interest in the affairs of the club. The cap he was awarded in 1895 is still in the club's possession.

### R D G Glascott 1898-1900

When the Bedford Wanderers got into financial difficulty and joined the Bedford club, their captain, Dick Glascott, was immediately named Blues captain. He was a forward who took place kicks and was in the Wanderers' team that beat Northampton, then known as St James, at Franklin's Gardens on the same day that Bedford beat Leicester at Goldington Road. An OBM, he made 94 appearances and became general manager of the Burma Railway.

### F S P Saunders 1900-02

The treasurer responsible for paying off the Wanderers' debts became the club's eighth captain. F S P Saunders was a forward who captained the club for two seasons, standing down after getting married. He made 78 appearances in four seasons. His well prepared balance sheets for the period are still in the club's possession.

### H B Beddall 1902-03

While H B Beddall was captain, there is the first mention in the minutes of a selection committee. An OB, he was in the school team captained by Basil Maclear. He was a forward who made 39 appearances.

### C R Hoskyn 1903-04

The club's tenth captain was C R Hoskyn, a forward who made 49 appearances. He took a keen interest in the 'A' team and is minuted as calling for all players to wear the correct team shirts. An OB, he became a surgeon and was decorated during The First World War for amputating a soldier's leg with 'improvised equipment' – a pen knife.

### A L Rogers 1904-05

A L Rogers was the force behind the drive to secure a fixture with the New Zealand touring team of 1905. A forward, he played in that great match the following season. He was a keen administrator who always took the chair at meetings. He was eager to improve fixtures with first class clubs and was closely involved with the opening of the first stand in 1905.

### R Maclear 1905-06

Captain of the team that played the All Blacks at Goldington Road was Ronnie Maclear, an OB, who first played for the club while captain of the school in 1896. He was a forward and one of four brothers who all played for the club, the most famous being Basil, the Irish International. Ronnie was a soldier who became coach to Bedford Athletic club after their formation in 1908.

### C Franklin 1906-08

Charles Franklin was an OB who made 161 appearances between 1901 and 1910. A forward, he had an England trial in 1909. He was the son of Chas. Franklin, a well-known coal merchant, and he became a magistrate. He was one of the four who guaranteed the loan to build the scrum hall in 1910 and he remained a vice-president until his death in 1949.

### A W B Gompertz 1908-09

A W B Gompertz was an OB who first played for the club whilst still at school. He became a regular when he left, and was a stand-off and an excellent place kicker who made 65 appearances. He resigned the captaincy to concentrate on army entrance exams and returned to the club as an officer in 1911-12.

### H Willett 1909-11

Hugh Willett, OBM, was an all round athlete who also played cricket for the county. He lived in Bushmead Avenue and his 237 appearances was a club record, turning out on the wing, in the centre or at stand-off. He was club secretary for three years and his brother, also a player, later held this office as well. Although retired, he made a comeback during the 1914-18 war and was made a Barbarian in 1915 while serving under Edgar Mobbs in the 7th Northants Regiment.

### R C Stafford 1911-13

Dick Stafford was a pupil at Bedford Modern School when, aged 15 years and one month, he had a trial for Bedford. He made his debut later that season. He played for the East Midlands while still at school and became captain of the club at the age of 18. He played 67 times at wing-forward and was capped four times for England in 1912. He died of spinal cancer aged 19 and the town went into mourning for the first player born and bred in Bedford to achieve international status.

### A V Manton 1913-19

A V Manton took over as captain on the death of Dick Stafford and held the office as the club started to get on its feet after the First World War. He learned the game in junior clubs, had a spell with Northampton and was considered unlucky not to get an international cap. Rated a brilliant forward, he played 203 times, scoring 73 tries.

### A Hall 1919-20

Alf Hall took over the captaincy as the club struggled after the war. He started playing for Kempston but was a regular choice for Bedford from 1908 until 1923. His 272 appearances was a club record that would surely have been even greater had he not lost five years through war. A fine forward who later took over as captain of the 'A' side, he used to cycle home to Kempston wearing his cap if Bedford won but bareheaded if they had lost. With A J Osbourn and F Millward, he became the first Life Member of the club.

**A F Wesley 1920-21**

A F Wesley first played at Goldington Road when he made up the numbers for Rugby on December 27, 1913. But he played so well that he was selected for Bedford for the rest of the season. An OBM, he was a fly-half whose career was limited by the war. He made only 39 appearances, scoring nine tries, just five after being elected captain before a knee injury ended his career. His family owned the Bridge Hotel.

**L H Nicholson 1921-22**

The club's 20th captain was L H Nicholson, who learned his rugby in his native Bradford and later in the Welsh Guards. He came to Bedford with Messrs Peake Freane & Co, having played for Bristol and Redcliffe. He played as a forward for the East Midlands and made 122 appearances for Bedford, scoring 121 points. He was a loyal committee man with a keen interest in local politics and in 1968 as the oldest surviving captain he unveiled the honours board in the Scrum Hall.

**E L W Cumming 1922-23**

E L W "Jumbo" Cumming was captain in 1922-23. An OB who joined the club on leaving school, he was a forward who made 27 appearances. A talented oarsman, his rugby career was cut short by injury and by his work taking him to Brazil.

**S D Kitchener 1923-24**

Sam Kitchener was appointed captain at the age of 37. He was the first Bedford captain to have come from the Olney club, formed in 1877, and was said to be the club's first 'artisan' captain, being a 'boot' worker. He made his debut in 1905, returned to Olney, then to Bedford, before having a successful career at Northampton and then coming back to Bedford. He made 133 appearances as a forward and scored 23 tries. He was a keen Baptist preacher and a well-known boxer in local booths.

**F G Hore 1924-25**

Fred Hore joined Bedford from Bristol in 1923-24 and was made captain the next season. He was unable to complete his term of office and made a total of only 40 appearances. He later became secretary for two seasons before work took him away from the town. He was made a Life Member.

**L A R Fensome 1925-27**

Aubrey Fensome was a local boy who went to Bates' School and first played for the club in 1921-22. He was a prolific try scoring winger who ran in 97 tries in 196 appearances. He broke his leg against Blackheath on December 18, 1926, and returned to play wing-forward before retiring in 1933. He was President of the club and of the East Midlands and was made a Life Member in 1968. His father was also a great club worker and he was made a Life Member in 1939. They are the only father and son to have achieved this distinction. In the club's 100th year, Aubrey Fensome was its oldest surviving captain.

**A R Alston 1927-28**

The club's 25th captain was Rex Alston, more famous as a broadcaster with the BBC and a writer with the Daily Telegraph, but a very fast winger who scored 96 tries in 120 appearances. He was a master at Bedford School who played until 1929-30 when he moved into journalism and joined Rosslyn Park. He modestly puts down his success to the players inside him who, he says, created the room for him to run in tries unopposed. He also captained the county at cricket.

**R C Brumwell 1928-32**

Charlie Brumwell, known as "Brummy", was an OB whose father owned a fruit business in St Cuthbert's. He first played for the club while at school in 1924-25. An outstanding boxer, oarsman and cricketer as well, he was a versatile centre who could play in any position. He was elected captain for four successive seasons and scored 340 points including 106 tries in 232 appearances. He was reserve scrum-half for an England trial and later centre in an England trial. He also played in the Midland Counties side that beat the Springboks, on their 1931-32 tour of the British Isles - the only team to beat them.

**A Marshall 1932-33**

Arthur Marshall made 251 appearances in nine seasons at Bedford. He was an excellent leader from the front row. A pupil at Goldington School where another great club servant, Bob Reynolds, was his contemporary. Arthur was an administrator in local government. He became club secretary, President of the East Midlands, President of the Rugby Union and President of Bedford. His son, Tony, was later captain of the club as well.

**W A Sime 1933-38**

William Arnold Sime was an OB who studied law at Cambridge and who became a circuit judge. A scrum-half, he scored a record 172 points in his first year as captain and his 546 points in 210 appearances was also a record. He was elected captain in 1933 and then for five consecutive seasons thereafter – another record. An England trialist in 1932, he was a talented golfer and cricketer, captaining Bedfordshire and then Nottinghamshire.

**J G Cook 1938-39**

Gilbert Cook was selected in the centre for Bedford as soon as he left Bedford School. Work took him to Ireland where the England selectors noticed him as a wing-forward. He returned to Bedford and was awarded an international cap at wing-forward against Scotland in 1937. During the war, he was an officer in the RAF playing for the club whenever he could and helping to keep it on its feet. He scored 450 points in 184 appearances and was made a Life Member in 1969.

**R Willsher 1945-47**

Rex Willsher was an outstanding athlete, oarsman and rugby player at Bedford Modern School. He made his debut in 1928-29 and scored 184 points in 354 appearances at wing-forward, the third highest number of appearances in 100 years. During the war he was in food production, a reserved occupation, and did great work trying to keep the club together. He appeared in many trials for England, became a Barbarian in 1934-35 and in 1939-40 played twice for England in Red Cross internationals. He was made a Life Member in 1962.

### R G Furbank 1947-50

Dick Furbank made his debut in 1938-39 and played until 1953, making 249 appearances. He started in the back-row but moved to front-row, sometimes hooking. He made a record 106 consecutive appearances from November 21, 1946 to February 4, 1950 when he was required for an East Midlands county championship semi final against Devon. Murray Fletcher, his vice captain for two years, never led the team because the only time the captain was absent, his deputy was on East Midlands duty as well. A Huntingdon farmer and trustee of the club, he was made a Life Member in 1964.

### G Jenkins 1950-51

George Jenkins joined the club from Esher and played stand-off in the Wanderers until he accepted a challenge to move to wing-forward. He was such a success that he became a regular in 1948-49 and the Welsh selectors came to Bedford to look at him "shutting up the blind side". A civil servant, born in Wales, he retired in 1952 and served as team secretary for three seasons, having made 127 appearances.

### J F Bance 1951-54

John Forsyth Bance made 279 appearances, mainly in the second row. A line out expert he made his debut while at Cambridge University. He became a Barbarian in 1950-51 and played for England against Scotland in 1954. A farmer in Wiston, he played three times for the East Midlands in county championship finals, being on the winning side, with other Bedford players in 1951, when the East beat Middlesex 10-0 at Northampton to win the championship for only the second time. The first win was in 1934.

### A C Towell 1954-55

Alan Towell first played for Bedford in 1946-47 while he was in the RAF. He joined Leicester for three seasons and played at both centre and wing-forward. He won an international cap for England against France in 1948 while at Leicester and another against Scotland, as a centre, while with Bedford in 1951. He was a PE master at Dunstable Grammar and Stratton School, Biggleswade. He scored 25 tries in126 appearances.

### T R Marshall 1955-56

Tony Marshall first played for Bedford as a 15-year-old boy at Bedford School. He started as a back-row forward but switched to the front row. He was awarded a Blue at Cambridge in 1950 and was a Bedford regular when he left. He scored 119 points including 31 tries in 241 appearances, ten fewer than his father Arthur who was captain in 1932-33. They are the only father and son to have captained the club in its 125 years.

### St L H Webb 1956-58, 1961-62

Larry Webb was captain of the club for three seasons scoring 222 points in 336 appearances. Born in Australia, educated in Harpenden, he joined Bedford after service as an officer in the Royal Engineers. He started in the back-row but moved to prop. He became a Barbarian in 1958-59 and played for England against Wales, Ireland, France and Scotland in 1959. An earth moving contractor, he was a generous benefactor to the club especially at the time of the financing the new clubhouse. He was tragically killed, with other members of his family, while piloting his helicopter in 1978. The committee room in the new clubhouse is named after him.

### P Voyce 1958-59

Peter Voyce was an OB whose father, Jack, was headmaster of the Silver Jubilee School. He first played in 1955-56 and became a regular prop the next season. He was elected captain for 1958-59 and had the misfortune to break his leg playing in a social game for Jack Nightingale's XV against a Police team in November 1958. He recovered and regained his place the following season only to break his other leg after 13 matches – this time in a social match for Jack Smith's XV in Luton. He made 76 appearances.

### P H Avery 1959-60

Peter Avery made his reputation as a fit and capable wing-forward who joined the Bedford club from Oxford Rugby Club as a back in 1955-56. A schoolmaster in St Albans, he played mainly full-back but also in the centre and at stand-off. He moved to the pack in the second half of 1957-58 and stayed there. He made 116 appearances, scoring 52 points.

### B K Williams 1960-61

Barrie Williams was born to play for Bedford. His father T E K Williams and his uncle C H Williams were both Bedford players. He started in the centre but played mostly on the wing in a career that lasted from 1958 until 1966. He made 249 appearances scoring 126 tries which, in 2011, was the joint second highest total in the club's history. His best haul in a season was 24 in 1964-65. He was a keen supporter and was still to be found on the touchline 50 years after he was captain.

Barrie Williams was captain in 1960-61 - 50 years before the club's 125th season.

### D G Perry 1962-63, 1965-66

David Gordon Perry won a Blue at Cambridge in 1958 and joined Bedford from the Harlequins in 1961-62, captaining the club in two of his five seasons. A number eight forward he was capped for England fifteen times between 1963 and 1966, captaining his country in all four internationals in 1965. He played 101 times for Bedford scoring 37 tries and his total of 15 international appearances was at one time second in Bedford's history only to D P Rogers who succeeded him as captain both of Bedford and England in 1966.

### D P Rogers OBE 1963-65, 1966-67, 1973-75

Derek Prior 'Budge' Rogers was recognised as Bedford's greatest - someone whose record of achievement is unlikely to be beaten. He made his debut in December 1956 while still at Bedford School and was an automatic choice for the next 19 seasons. He enjoyed five seasons as captain, in three sessions, won 34 caps for England which at the time was a record, led his country seven times, captained the Barbarians and the East Midlands. He was a British Lion, playing in two Tests in South Africa in 1962. He captained the side that won the cup in 1975, became a Life Member of Bedford that same year and was awarded the OBE for services to rugby. A dynamic wing-forward, he made a record 485 appearances scoring 400 points made up of 126 tries and one dropped goal. He was Chairman of Selectors when England completed the Grand Slam in 1980 and President of the RFU in 2000-2001.

### R J Slaughter 1967-69

Roger Slaughter probably wore a Bedford jersey as often as any other player. When not in the first team, he would always turn out gladly for the lower teams. At Bedford Modern School, he was a fine athlete who held a triple jump record that lasted for 25 years and a long jump mark of 6.82ms set in 1958 that still stood in May 2011. He first played for the club in 1960-61 and his last first team appearance was in 1977-78 though he still continued playing in the lower teams. From blind-side wing forward, he turned a struggling team into a successful one in his first season of captaincy and made 334 appearances, scoring 64 tries, and one penalty, in 211 points. Club coach from 1981-84, he was an enthusiastic champion of youth rugby.

### P D Briggs 1969-72

Pat Briggs made his Bedford debut in 1963-64. A Cambridge Blue, he scored 387 points in 238 matches and his total of 33 dropped goals was a club record. His 1969-70 team won the unofficial *Sunday Telegraph* English-Welsh pennant. He was a Barbarian and four times an English trialist who was rated extremely unlucky not to be capped at fly half. On his retirement through injury in 1972-73 he took over the coaching of the team until 1981. A master at Bedford School, he was coach of the side that won the cup in 1975.

### V J Lewis 1972-73

Vic Lewis joined Bedford in 1970-71 from Rosslyn Park at a time when they already had an international in the scrum half position in J J Page. He was an outstanding substitute with what his partner P D Briggs rated "the best quick pass" he had ever seen. When Page moved to Northampton, he made the position his own and the following season he was elected captain. He worked as a representative for a brewery and made 112 appearances.

### J M Howard 1975-76

John Howard was the captain of the team that celebrated its winning of the cup the previous season by setting new points and try scoring records as well as conceding more points than ever before. He joined the club from Cambridge University as a centre and often turned out at fly-half. He was at centre in the 1975 cup winning team and made 110 appearances scoring 138 points before work took him north and to the Headingley club. He died on a walking holiday in the Himalayas in 1990. A Bedford v Cambridge University All Stars match was played in September 1991 in aid of the J M Howard Scholarship Fund.

**R M Wilkinson 1976-9**

Bob Wilkinson first played for Bedford while still a pupil at St Albans School. A Cambridge Blue, he was an uncapped player when he represented the Barbarians in their famous victory over the All Blacks in January 1973 and he went onto become one of their most popular choices and an enthusiastic player with other invitation teams as well as the Midlands and East Midlands. Lock-forward in the Bedford team that won the cup in 1975, he won six England caps, the first in Australia in May 1975, the others in 1976. In spite of years spent studying and responsibilities with his family fruit importing business, he made 311 appearances and scored 37 times. He is one of the few who players who captained Bedford for three years in succession.

**D Jackson 1977-78**

David Jackson took over as captain when Bob Wilkinson had to stand down during 1977-78. At the time he was vice captain, having first played as a number eight in 1971-72. He was a schoolteacher at John Bunyan School and later head at Sharnbrook Upper School which was rated as one of the best in the county. By the time he retired as a player in 1978-79 he had made 212 appearances, scoring 53 tries. He played county rugby for Oxfordshire where he was also rated as a highly skilled ball player.

**N O Martin 1979-80**

Nick Martin moved to Bedford in 1972-73 having been capped by England in the colours of the Harlequins. A Cambridge Blue, he played in the second-row for two seasons before returning to the Quins. He became their captain then came back to Bedford, making seven appearances in 1978-79. He was elected captain the next season and retired from the first class game at the end of a popular term. He scored ten tries in 81 appearances.

**G N Phillips 1980-81**

Graham Phillips joined Bedford from Northampton in 1978-79 having played for the England under 23s, the Midlands and the East Midlands, of whom he was a captain. He played both in the centre and at wing-forward for the Saints, but came to Bedford, on being appointed a master at Bedford School, as a wing-forward. He scored 24 tries in 146 appearances for the Blues, one of them in a famous win over Llanelli. His 41 appearances out of 45 games in 1980-81 was the most ever made by a captain in one season. Graham Phillips was much in demand as an after dinner speaker after retiring.

**J T Mawle 1981-82**

Bedford's 50th captain was John Mawle, a farm manager who first played for the club in 1970-71. He captained the side 11 years later and retired at the end of his term, having made 220 appearances scoring five tries from his position in the second-row. He captained the Wanderers in 1976-77, but first team calls meant that he needed a permanent deputy. He also played for and captained Oxfordshire and represented Southern Counties against both Argentina and Canada. Before emigrating with his family to New Zealand, he was the second chairman of the Former Players Association.

### I G Peck 1982-86

Ian Peck

Ian Peck was elected captain of the Blues for four years in succession, standing down from the post in the fourth following the premature birth of his son Tristan. He captained Bedford School and Cambridge University at both rugby and cricket and led the Blues and East Midlands at rugby and Bedfordshire at cricket in the same year. An outstanding ball player and scrum half, he represented the England Schools, Under 23s, England B and England, on their tour of Fiji. He was 'on the bench' when England won the Five Nations Grand Slam in 1980. He had a keen eye for players and 30 years later was still helping Cambridge University. As captain in Bedford's 100th season, he was proud to see his youngest son, Harry, represent the Blues against the Barbarians in its 125th.

### A M Key 1985-86

Andy Key

Andy Key was a popular choice to take over the captaincy when Ian Peck stood down and at the end of the season he had the honour of being elected for the club's Centenary celebration season. An attacking full back, he joined the Blues from Leicester, making his debut on January 1, 1982, and recording the fastest 100 appearances. As captain of a Bedford team that beat Northampton twice in a season, he joined an elite group that included Alf Parrott, Alf Manton, Charlie Brumwell, Arnold Sime, Gilbert Cook, Dick Furbank, David Perry, Pat Briggs, 'Budge' Rogers and Graham Phillips – as captains to skipper sides who did the double in 125 years. After the Centenary season he returned to Leicester and later became a prominent figure in their academy. He came back to Bedford in 2004-05 as a part time backs coach for three seasons and between 2008 and 2011 was the Director of Rugby at Leeds Carnegie.

### J Orwin 1987-89

John Orwin with Bedford Athletic stalwarts 'Lofty' Norman and Ron Cox

John Orwin was recruited to Bedford in the Centenary season to be the lock forward catalyst around whom the club could revive its flagging fortunes. An England international and a skilful, much respected member of the mighty Gloucester pack whose career had stalled, he took over as captain in 1987-88 and immediately led the Blues to their best record of the decade. In his second season at the helm, he led them to promotion to Courage League One. By then he'd resurrected his international career and become captain of England; but, having been a publican and an estate agent, he left Bedford to seek new challenges on and off the field.

The first was in his native Yorkshire, where the Orwin effect, again, had instant results at Morley, then at Wibsey and later at several other clubs up and down the country – including Altrincham, Datchworth and Biggleswade where he played in the first XV at the age of 50. He is also profiled as an international.

**M A Howe 1989-90**

Mark Howe makes it into the list of the all time top players at Bedford as a captain and one of only two players to turn out for the club more than 400 times. He made his debut as a teenager at Bedford Modern School in 1976 and made the number two – hooker's - jersey his own for the next 20 years, making 478 appearances. He was a one club man –'Bedford to his Boots'– said the magazine *Rugby World*. He represented England Schools, Students, U23s, East Midlands, Midlands, the Barbarians and was a final trialist in 1981. But his commitment to his home town club and his responsibilities to the family farm at Marston Moretaine probably cost him a full cap. "He told me that he would never be able to look his friends in the eye if he left Bedford," said Howard Travis, a former club press officer. Mark Howe captained the Blues for one difficult season in the top tier from where they were quickly relegated. As the club reached its 125th year, he was a member of its board of directors.

**G Wood 1990-91**

Glyn Wood joined the Blues in the Centenary year after three seasons at Northampton and he teamed up again with former colleagues from the Combined Services, John Orwin and Martin Whitcombe. They had served with the RAF but he'd been in the Navy, having joined the Fleet Air Arm at 16. He played services rugby for 11 years, first in the centre but then in the back row and also made his mark as a member of the Fleet Air Arm Field Gun team at the Royal Tournament on three occasions. He turned out for Kettering, United Services Portsmouth and represented the Combined Services against Canada and Australia. When he went to Northampton in 1984 he was reunited with his Kettering coach Dick Tilley who later coached him at the Blues. Glyn Wood, who became an estate agent in Bedford on leaving the Navy, became a coach himself at Kettering when he retired.

**R E Pascall 1991-92**

Richard Pascall played 163 times for the Blues, 112 times between 1978 and 1982 before he left to join Gloucester and 51 times between 1990 and 1993 after he returned with 270 games for them under his belt. He was a man of Kent who went to teacher training college in Cheltenham and represented England Students. He made contact with Bedford when he took up his first teaching job in Wellingborough. Starting in the Rovers and Wanderers he soon found a regular place at loose head prop and to further his education in that position he left to join what was considered the toughest finishing school there was. His return in 1990 along with Gloucester colleagues Nick Marment and John Brain, who later made his mark as a Premiership coach, was something of a coup for the Blues as they strove to consolidate themselves in level two of the leagues at a time when professionalism seemed a long way off.

Paul Alston celebrates with his 1994-95 team after winning promotion

### P Alston 1992-96

Paul Alston was one of just a handful of players in 125 years to captain the Blues for four consecutive seasons. He would most certainly have been among the group who made more than 300 appearances and probably among the elite who made 400 had he not left for Northampton at the age of 19 before returning in 1992 after 195 appearances and 57 tries. He was identified as someone likely to enjoy an outstanding career when, as a pupil at Wootton Upper, he represented the England Schools and later the Colts, in a squad that contained three other members of the successful side at Bedford. Paul Alston was captain when the Blues were relegated from Courage League Two but led them back two seasons later amid great scenes at Goldington Road after a one point win over Richmond in 1995. He joined Luton as player-coach in 1996, but came back to Bedford as forwards coach and made the last of his 153 appearances in 2003 when he came off the bench - 21 years after his Blues debut.

### P Turner 1996-98

Paul Turner was hailed by his many admirers as a rugby magician – especially during his time as player and coach at Sale when he steered that club into the top tier of English rugby and turned it into one of the most attractive sides of the early 1990s. The group that eventually took control of Bedford had tried to do a deal with Sale but when it fell through, Blues members embraced enthusiastically the Holy Trinity of Frank Warren, Geoff Cooke and Paul Turner - who some remembered taking penalties with either foot in the colours of London Welsh in an early league game at Goldington Road. Three Welsh caps between 1988 and 1989 seemed a scant return for someone possessing all the flair, skills and charisma of a fly half who stood flat and who quite literally 'bossed' games. And the Bedford fans saw some scintillating back play during his time as the club's first professional captain – and one nearer 40 years of age than 30 at that. He is also featured in the section on coaches.

### A R Murdoch 1998-99

Alistair Murdoch stepped up to the captaincy as the dream of All Star rugby started to turn sour when Frank Warren's assets were frozen by the courts in litigation that had nothing to do with Bedford. Players and officials weren't paid on time and with their contracts broken many felt they had no option but to leave. Others vowed to stay together for as long as they could after the club's promotion to Allied Dunbar Premiership One at the second attempt. Alistair Murdoch was one of them. He joined the Blues in 1997 as an Australian international threequarter who was rated by his coach, Bob Dwyer, as the strongest player he'd ever trained. He scored 12 tries in 21 matches as the Blues steamrollered through the second division but it was a different story once they'd got to the first with survival on and off the field the only objective. Against the odds they did survive with the skipper, his Director of Rugby, Rudi Straeuli, and many others putting in a heroic effort.

**A C T Gomarsall MBE 1999-2000**

Andy Gomarsall captained the Blues for all of his 26 appearances – bar one. And that was his debut match in 1991 while he was still at school. He joined as an international scrum half from the Wasps – the club he went to on leaving Bedford School – attracted by Paul Turner who had returned to Goldington Road as coaching supremo under the regime of Jefferson Lloyd International. His friend, Paul Sackey, later an England winger, and prop forward Adam Black also came from the Wasps and they were among a whole group of new players recruited to try to keep Bedford's place in Premiership One. But the Jefferson Lloyd project was a disaster and soon collapsed and this time the Blues were relegated after losing the play-offs. Andy Gomarsall missed the matches against Rotherham through injury and later joined Gloucester. He is also profiled as an international.

**B M L Whetstone 2000-02**

Ben Whetstone's total of 121 tries in his Bedford career is the third highest in 125 years of the Blues and his 25 in 26 appearances in 1997-98 was the best return since Derek Wyatt's heyday in the 1970s. He made 282 appearances, playing as an amateur from his first team debut in 1992, then as a professional from 1996 in the All Star team that won promotion. After spending a year at London Irish in 1999-2000, he returned to Bedford to help the club rebuild from the chaos it was plunged into. Ben Whetstone joined from Ely but became Bedford through and through and would have made more than 300 appearances had he not been seriously injured in his second season as captain. He represented the Midlands and the Barbarians and in local radio interviews both Geoff Cooke and Rudi Straeuli said they thought he could have played for England as a centre or winger. He retired through injury in 2005 and in 2011 was a committee member of the Former Players Association and a much valued advisor on player recruitment.

**M J Volland 2002-04**

Matt Volland's signing for the Blues in season 2001-02 signalled a new era in the relationship between Bedford and Northampton, winners of the Heineken Cup in 2000. His arrival with 123 appearances for the Saints under his belt convinced many Bedford supporters that, having survived in level two with a last match of the season draw at Otley, the club meant business. And so it proved with others following and the Blues establishing themselves as a top half of the table team and then as a top four side - with two cup finals at Twickenham, in 2005 and 2006, as well. Matt Volland joined Northampton from Peterborough and made the England 'A' squad as a loose head prop. He made 153 appearances at the Blues before retiring in 2008 when his charisma and popularity among players and fans earned him a role as an assistant coach.

**M C Allen 2004-08**

Matt Allen captained the Blues in all of his four seasons at the club. Though he joined after three years with Cardiff, it was at Northampton, where he made 182 appearances, that he made his reputation as a tough tackling, straight running centre who narrowly missed an England cap but who won a Heineken Cup medal with the Saints in 2000. In fact he was one of six in the Northampton squad for the final who continued their careers for at least a season at Goldington Road. He led Bedford when they beat Plymouth Albion in the Powergen Challenge Shield final in 2005 and when they lost to the Harlequins in the Powergen National Trophy final a year later when they were also runners up in the league. Matt Allen made 104 appearances for Bedford before leaving to become player-coach at Luton in 2008 and then Director of Rugby at the end of season 2009-10.

Matt Allen with the shield at Twickenham in 2005

**D J Richmond 2008-10**

Dan Richmond was the third former Northampton player in a row to captain the Blues and to make more than 100 appearances at Goldington Road - completing his century early in the 2010-11 season. He joined in 2007 having turned out for the Saints 119 times after a debut in 2001- latterly finding his opportunities limited by a future captain and England hooker in the ranks. A karate black belt and a qualified bricklayer who played for Bath U19s before joining the Northampton Academy, he worked part time as a rugby coach at Bedford Modern School and completed an RFU Level Three coaching award in 2010. He led the Blues to third place in National One in his first season and to fourth in the Championship and to the play-off semi finals in his second. In the 2010-11 season he was one of the coaches in the Bedford Academy, helping the Colts to a fourth cup win in five years.

**J G Pritchard 2010 -**

James Pritchard captained the Blues in its 125th season – one of the most successful in its history when the side finished second in the Championship and made the semi finals of the playoffs and the final of the British and Irish Cup. He played mainly at full back or wing but whatever number he wore on his shirt his authority and influence on the team was clear. For him personally, 2010-11 was probably his best in a Bedford career that started when he was signed in 2001 from the Randwick club in Australia. He broke the club points scoring record with 403, the first player ever to pass 400; he passed 300 for the third time, the only one ever to do that, and he joined Andy Finnie as the only Bedford player ever to score 2,000 points in his Bedford career. James Pritchard first broke the club points scoring record with 386 in his second season then left to pursue international honours with Canada before returning in 2006 and making an indelible mark on the history of the Blues. He is also profiled as an international.

# CLUB CAPTAINS

The Blues had many other match day captains who took over when required for whatever reason. In the modern era, they sometimes appointed a Club Captain – again for a variety of reasons such as their respect among other players, loyalty, commitment and their ability to unite and motivate the club as a whole. Since the Centenary season, four such club captains were officially appointed: R M C Greed by the coach Ian Snook in 1992, S Harris by the committee in 1993, B M L Whetstone by Director of Rugby Colin Jackson in 2002 and M J Volland by Director of Rugby Rudi Straeuli in 2004. Messrs Greed, as coach, Whetstone and Volland, as captains, are profiled in the relevant sections.

**S Harris 1993-95**

Steve Harris was one of the bravest of players who, like many throughout its history, regularly put their bodies on the line for Bedford. His was an injury ravaged career between 1984 and 1995 in which he made 158 appearances. He was a natural leader and, as someone held in the highest regard by teammates and supporters, he was appointed – perhaps anointed - club captain to help restore discipline after a small minority hit the headlines for causing post match problems in the town. He was blessed with a wife, Pat, one of the great characters of the era, who cheered on the team with her cries of 'Go On 'Arris' and then charmed the Scrum Hall with her knowledge of the game and charismatic personality. During their time, the social side of the club went from strength to strength. Steve Harris left Bedford for Luton as professionalism dawned and then moved to Port Talbot, his wife's home town, in 2002. Just five years later, the club was stunned to hear of his untimely death at the age of 45 and in August 2007 it staged a memorial match to celebrate his life.

Steve Harris, right, with Leigh Mansell, left and Richard Porter

# OTHER CAPTAINS

The Blues had a second team for many years until the advent of professionalism and then for two seasons from 2002. Until the season 1932-33, it was known as the 'A' team, then it was renamed the Wanderers after another former independent club that operated in the 1890s. Early captains included A Udal, H V Wells, C T Morris, G R Watson and J E Jarvis. The policy was to elect a 'man of stature'. Often he would be required by the first team and another appointed in his place. Before the First World War only the first team captains were recorded in the minutes, but from1920-21, the second team skipper was noted as well.

In the early 1960s, it was decided to institute a third team to provide further support to the first two and they adopted the appropriate name of the Rovers. In 1970-71, a fourth team, later to adopt the name, the Rams, was created. The Rovers and the Rams provided a haven for former first team players on the way down and for others who could only aspire to the first team. But they became an important part of the Blues – almost a club within a club – especially on the social side. They struggled however in the years before professionalism and captains were often appointed on a match basis. The Wanderers did make it to 1996 but after that they became a second XV based on the first XV and a Development side rather than the distinct unit they had been. They too faded away early in the 21st century. What the absence of lower teams at the Blues did though was ensure a stream of players into other clubs in the town and sides like Queens in 1995 and Bedford Athletic in 1998 were to benefit and taste success in cup finals at Twickenham, the 'Ath' later making it for a while into the national leagues.

**Wanderers captains:**

G T Freshwater (1920-21); R G Cocking (1921-23); A Hall (1923-25); R C Adkin (1925-26); R C Adkin and B A Harris (1926-27); C E Spring (1927-28); T I C Bevan (1928-31); J M Bilham (1931-32); O L Lloyd (1932-33); N J Timmins (1933-36); E J C Brown (1936-38); R V Spark (1938-39); B R Black (1946-47); P C Previte (1947-49); H Elliott (1949-50); G S S Gilbert (1950-51); H Payne (1951-52); P J Wootton (1952-56); D R Medd (1956-57); G S S Gilbert (1957-58); R A Lovell (1958-59); A G Robertson (1959-60); H Green (1960-62); P R Carlisle (1962-66); K W Phillips (1966-68); G Davies (1968-70); H Childs (1970-71); M Nurton (1971-72); G Davies (1972-73); R Chadwick (1973-74); M D Fitzgerald (1974-75); B Page (1975-76); J T Mawle and D Hanson (1976-77); S Ingram (1977-81); S Ashton (1981-82); D Mackay (1982-83); S Ashton and A Walford (1983-84); J Clemence (1984-85); A Walford (1985-88), P Stephenson (1988-91), A Tapper (1993-94), M Roach (1994-95), A Tapper (1995-96).

**Rovers captains:**

P J B Davies (1961-62); M Potter (1962-62); M T Dazley (1963-65): K W Phillips (1965-66); B W Stapleton (1966-67); R A Lovell (1967-70); I Bullerwell (1970-71); J Dalzell (1971-72); M Lilley (1972-74); R Luff (1974-75); J Howard (1975-76); I Bullerwell (1976-77); G Davies (1977-79); R J Slaughter (1979-80); S Micklewright (1980-82); S O'Neill (1982-84); D Harris (1984-85); S O'Neill (1985-90).

**Rams captains:**

R G Simmonds (1970-71); C Rogers (1971-74); H Harries (1974-75); P Edmunds (1975-76); D Lang (1976-77); I Dougal (1977-78); J Mumford (1978-79); A P Kirk (1979-80); H B Travis (1980-82); G Davies (1982-84); P Boon (1984-89). I Dougall (1989-90).

# THE INTERNATIONALS

*J G Milton*
*F G Brooks*
*E L Chambers*
*D M Grant*
*R C Stafford*
*C R Davies*
*J C Cook*
*D L K Milman*
*V J Lyttle*
*G A Kelly*
*L F L Oakley*
*A C Towell*

*J F Bance*
*St L H Webb*
*D P Rogers OBE*
*D G Perry*
*G P Frankcom*
*R D Hearn*
*J J Page*
*J P A G Janion*
*W C C Steele*
*A M Jorden*
*W N Bennett*
*R M Wilkinson*

*D M Wyatt*
*J Orwin*
*M C Bayfield*
*P J Paramore*
*S Murray*
*D W O'Mahony*
*D Edwards*
*S Stewart*
*A C T Gomarsall MBE*
*M G Rivaro*
*L Martin*
*J G Pritchard*
*S Tonga'uiha*

Thirty seven players have represented their country while a member of, or contracted to, the Bedford club. In some cases where a player left Bedford but hadn't yet played for his new club his international appearances were recorded as though he was still at Bedford. This became known as the Bayfield principle where M C Bayfield left the Blues in the spring and played for England in the summer before he had turned out for his new club, Northampton, in the autumn of 1991. He presented the first of his 31 England shirts to the Blues. Of course when the sport when professional it was easier. A player was, or was not, contracted to a particular club when he played an international.

Leading the list of internationals is D P Rogers with 34 for England as a Bedford player. He is followed by J G Pritchard with 28 for Canada while contracted to Bedford. The following all represented England unless stated – while at the Blues: D G Perry, 15, W C C Steele, 13 for Scotland, S Murray, 12 for Scotland, J P A G Janion, nine, S Stewart nine for Canada, J Orwin, seven, R D Hearn, six, and R M Wilkinson, six. P J Paramore turned out six times for Samoa while a Bedford player. R C Stafford, D L K Milman, J J Page, G A Kelly, St L H Webb, all made four international appearances for England. J G Milton, E L Chambers, V J Lyttle, Ireland, G P Frankcom and W N Bennett made three. D Edwards made three for Tonga while contracted to Bedford. D M Grant, for Scotland, A M Jorden, M C Bayfield, L Martin for Italy and S Tonga'uiha for Tonga all made two. F G Brooks, C R Davies, Wales, J G Cook, L F Oakley, A C Towell, J F Bance, D M Wyatt and A C T Gomarsall made one international appearance while members of the Bedford club. D W O'Mahony played once for Ireland and M Rivaro once for Italy while they were with the Blues.

**J G Milton, England**

'Jumbo' Milton was a member of the Bedford club while still a pupil at Bedford Grammar School. He was captain of the school team in 1903-04 and played four times that season for Bedford, scoring a try against the Racing Club De France on December 28 and playing against Marlborough Nomads on October 10, Northampton on February 27 and Park House on March 26, 1904. He made his England debut as a forward against Wales at Leicester on January 9, 1904, a 14-14 draw, and was capped twice more that season and then twice more while at the Camborne School of Mines. His brother, C H Milton, was captain of Bedford Grammar School in 1902-03 and he too played for the Bedford club while he was there. He was capped for England against Ireland in 1906 while at the Camborne School of Mines. A third brother, N W Milton, won an Oxford Blue in 1905-06-07 after leaving Bedford Grammar School. The Milton family is unique in the history of English rugby since the father of two international brothers also played for England. Sir William Henry Milton was capped twice at half-back, in 1874 and 1875, and later, in 1888, captained the South African cricket team. J G Milton's Bedford record was played four, scored three points in 1903-04. His England record is v Scotland 1904 and 1905, v Ireland 1904 and 1907 and v Wales 1904 – five caps. He died in 1915.

**F G Brooks, England**

FG Brooks

Freddie Brooks was born in India, of a Rhodesian family and educated with three brothers at Bedford Grammar School where he was captain of the rugby team from 1900 until 1902 and an outstanding athlete. He played on the wing for Bedford while still at school but returned to southern Africa where he so impressed in the Currie Cup competition of 1906 that he was invited to join the Springbok touring team scheduled to visit Great Britain that year. However, the invitation was withheld because it was realised that he didn't quite meet the five year residential qualification. So F G returned to England 'on holiday' and resumed his career at Bedford, playing four more games and scoring four tries in one match against Hampstead Wanderers on November 3, 1906. He played for the South in the England trial against the North and was then selected to play for England against South Africa. F G Brooks gained his one and only England cap against the first ever Springboks at Crystal Palace in front of 40,000 people on December 8, 1906 and scored the second half try that earned England a 3-3 draw. According to the *Bedfordshire Times* of August 28, 1910, he returned home and played for Rhodesia against England at Bulawayo on July 30, 1910, a match Rhodesia lost by 24-11. More likely 'England' were the fourth British Isles tourists to South Africa. F G Brooks became a high ranking civil servant and refereed rugby up until his death in 1948. His Bedford record is played 17, scored six conversions and 19 tries, for 69 points. His England record is v South Africa, 1906 when he scored one try.

**E L Chambers, England**

Ernest Leonard Chambers was educated at Bedford Grammar School and twice, in the season 1903-04, played for the Bedford club while he was there. He won a rugby and an athletics Blue at Cambridge in 1904 and then seems to have joined Blackheath and played county rugby for Kent. He became an assistant master at Uppingham Preparatory School before returning as a master to Bedford Grammar. He played once, officially, for Bedford in 1908-09 and once in 1909-10 but he played for England in 1908 and 1910 and for the East Midlands in 1909. His debut was in the pack in England's 19-0 win over the French at the Stade Colombes, Paris, on January 1, 1908. His second international appearance was in one of the most famous matches of all time. That was the game when England beat Wales, by 11-6, for the first time since 1898, but the game is most remembered as the first international to be played at Twickenham, 'Billy Williams' Cabbage Patch', now the headquarters of the RFU. He also played in the second match at Twickenham, in front of the Prince of Wales and 20,000 people, a 0-0 draw with Ireland on February 12, 1910. E L Chambers served in the First World War as an officer in the Bedfordshire Regiment, the Northumberland Fusiliers and the King's Own Yorkshire Light Infantry. He was awarded the MC and mentioned in despatches in 1917. He died in 1946. His Bedford record is played four times. His England record is v France, 1908, and v Wales and Ireland in 1910.

**D M Grant, Scotland**

D M Grant was educated at the Elstow, or County, School in the Ampthill Road – the same public school where one of the club's founding fathers, 'Pinkie' Booth learned the game. He played for Bedford and the East Midlands while still at the school, making 19 appearances for the Blues in 1909-10 and six more in 1910-11. He was an all round sportsman, representing the school at athletics, cricket and hockey as well as rugby, playing half-back, wing three-quarter or centre. In 1911, he was selected twice for Scotland, making his debut at Inverleith in a 32-10 defeat at the hands of Wales and also playing in a 16-0 defeat by Ireland at the same venue. He left school, moved from the area and joined London Scottish. He emigrated to Canada but returned with the Expeditionary Force in 1915. His Bedford record is played 25 times, scored one conversion and 12 tries. His international record is for Scotland v Wales and v Ireland, in 1911.

**R C Stafford, England**

Richard Calvert Stafford was a brilliant all round athlete and rugby player who had a trial for Bedford when he was a 15-year-old pupil at Bedford Modern School in 1908. He was vice-captain of Bedford in 1910-11 and was elected captain in 1911-12, at the age of 18. At the same age, he made a debut, as a forward, for England at Twickenham on January 20, 1912, in an 8-0 win over Wales. He played in a team that contained the three early greats of English rugby: Adrian Stoop, Ronnie Poulton-Palmer, and C H 'Cherry' Pillman. His second international was in England's 5-0 win over Ireland at Twickenham on February 10, his third in an 8-3 defeat by Scotland at Inverleith on March 16, and his fourth in an 18-8 win at Parc des Princes, Paris, against the French on April 8. That final victory of the season on Easter Monday entitled England to share the championship with Ireland. Dick Stafford died of spinal cancer on December 1, 1912, at the age of 19 – the youngest age at which a full England international has died. The town went into mourning. His Bedford record is played 67 times, scored 106 points, including 32 tries, two conversions, one dropped goal and one penalty. His England record is v Wales, Ireland, Scotland and France in 1912.

### C R Davies, Wales

Cecil Davies played for Bedford for one season while stationed at RAF Henlow. He made his Bedford debut on September 7, 1933, against Mr Palmer's XV in a special match to mark the opening of the new grandstand. He was a forward and came through the Welsh trials that season to win a cap against England at Cardiff Arms Park on January 20, 1934. Wales, who had introduced 13 new players for the match, were beaten in front of 50,000 people by three tries to nil, 9-0, and when the selectors swung the axe, Davies was among those who went. Interestingly, one of those called up for their next match was the Bedford schoolmaster Iorwerth Evans, at the time a member of the London Welsh club. He remembered the dashing RAF pilot who was shot down and killed during the Second World War as an "officer and a gentleman". C R Davies played his final game for Bedford on February 2, 1934, and his record at the club is played 13 times, scored one try. His Welsh record is v England, 1934.

### D L K Milman, England

Dermot Lionel Kennedy Milman, later Sir Dermot, joined Bedford from Cambridge University. He was a back row forward who could dribble and run with the ball at his feet, a prized skill of the era. He made his England debut against Wales at Twickenham on January 16, 1937, in a team containing seven new players. In front of 65,000 people, England won by 4-3, one dropped goal to one try with, it was said, "the aid of the Welsh selectors." D L K missed the rest of that championship-winning international season but returned for England's first three matches of 1938. He played in the 14-8 defeat by Wales at Cardiff Arms Park on January 15, the 50th international between the two teams and then in a 36-14 win over Ireland at Lansdowne Road, Dublin on February 12. His final international was in what became known as Wilson Shaw's match when Scotland won 21-16 in front of 70,000 spectators at Twickenham on March 19. He was a schoolmaster at Epsom College and later Fettes and during the war he served as an officer in many theatres, in France, Belgium, Burma, where he was mentioned in Despatches, and India. He became a British Council Officer serving in South America, Italy and Pakistan from 1946. He made the occasional appearance for the club and so did his brother. His father retired to the town and took a keen interest in the affairs of the club and when he died, in 1962, DLK succeeded him as the eighth Baronet Milman of Levaton in Woodland, Devon (created 1800). His Bedford record is 102 appearances, scoring 39 tries. His England record is v Wales, 1937 and 1938, v Scotland and Ireland 1938.

### J G Cook, England

Gilbert Cook was an Old Bedfordian who joined the club as a centre and place kicker as soon as he left school. He made his Bedford debut in 1929 and became a regular until work took him to Ireland. While there he developed into a wing forward and played in that position on his return to Bedford. Playing in a team that developed into one of the club's greatest, J G was capped for England against Scotland at Murrayfield, on March 20, 1937. England won the game, their first success at Murrayfield, by two tries to a penalty, 6-3, and in doing so made certain of the championship, Triple Crown and Calcutta Cup. Cook missed the conversions and at least one penalty kick. In the England team that day were the famous Wheatley brothers from Coventry and Ray Longland, one of Olney's favourite sons and a former Bedford player who achieved international honours in the colours of Northampton. J G Cook's full Bedford record is played 184 times, scored 450 points, 132 conversions, 37 tries and 25 penalties. His England record is v Scotland 1937.

### V J Lyttle, Ireland

Victor Johnstone Lyttle was born in Belfast in July 1911 and educated at the Methodist College. He played with the Collegians club until 1933 when, having studied photography, he came to England to work for Kodak. He played part of a season for the Harlequins but joined Bedford in 1934, having been invited by one of Kodak's executives E E Blake, later managing director, and President of Bedford. He made a debut for the Blues on the wing against Old Merchant Taylors on February 17, 1934, and soon established himself as a prolific try scorer, becoming one of the few players to score more than 100 tries for the club. He scored three in a match eight times. An Irish trialist with the Collegians, he played in the star-studded Blues teams of the late 1930s, six of whom turned out for the East Midlands in the Mobbs Memorial match against the Barbarians in 1937. It was remembered as the Prince (Obolensky) against the Leprechaun (Lyttle). Both scored a try in the East's 13-3 win. Vic Lyttle made his debut for Ireland against an England side containing D L K Milman at Lansdowne Road, Dublin, on February 12, 1938. England won 36-14. He gained his second cap in a 5-0 win over England at Twickenham in February 1939 and his third in Ireland's 12-3 home win over Scotland. In the final Irish trial of 1939, there were two other Bedford players on the field besides Vic Lyttle - George O'Brien Power and Ellis Walshe. His Bedford record is played 138 times, scored 103 tries. For Ireland, he played v England in 1938 and 1939 and v Scotland in 1939.

### G A Kelly, England

Geoffrey Arnold Kelly was educated at The Perse School, Cambridge, and joined Bedford in 1934-35 from Letchworth. He played for the East Midlands, Eastern Counties and Barbarians and later was a selector and keen committee man for Hertfordshire. He made his Bedford debut at prop against Guy's Hospital on January 25, 1935 and during the war was one of the stalwarts who kept the club going. In 1945-46, the four home countries with France and the New Zealand forces team stationed in Britain were engaged in a special series of International matches known as the Victory series. No caps were awarded but Geoff Kelly was selected for England six times. England's first official international since 1939 took place against Wales at Cardiff Arms Park on January 18, 1947 and he was one of 14 England players to make their debuts in a 9-6 win. He gained a second cap against Ireland at Lansdowne Road on February 8. England were routed 22-0. After one of the worst winters in history, England and Scotland met on a frozen pitch at Twickenham on March 15, 1947. The Bedford player was one of two from either side who were injured and didn't complete the match which ended in a 24-5 win to England. Geoff Kelly earned his fourth cap on January 17, 1948 in a 3-3 draw against Wales in front of 73,000 at Twickenham. His Bedford record is played 151 times, scored 13 tries. His international record is v Scotland, 1947, v Ireland, 1947, v Wales, 1947 and 1948.

### A C Towell, England

Alan Towell made a debut for Bedford in 1946-47 while in the RAF. He then joined Leicester for three seasons, won an England cap and rejoined Bedford when his work as a PE master brought him back to the area. He was capped again – this time as a Bedford player. While at the club he formed a formidable midfield partnership with Leo Oakley. He made his England debut at the Stade Colombes, Paris, on March 29, 1948 in a match won by France by 15-0, at the time the biggest margin between the two countries since matches started in 1906. Leo Oakley was at centre for England's opening match of 1951; Alan Towell was selected for their final match of that season's international campaign. He gained his second cap against Scotland at Twickenham on March 17 and England's 5-3 victory saw them regain the Calcutta Cup but could not save them from the wooden spoon for the second successive season, sharing it with the team they had beaten. Reports praised Towell for "several exciting bursts." The Northampton flanker Don White recalled to the team for the first time since 1948, scored the England try. Alan Towell's record at Bedford is played 126, scored 96 points made up of 25 tries and seven dropped goals. His international record is v France 1948 and v Scotland 1951.

**L F L Oakley, England**

Leo Oakley was an Old Bedfordian who made his Bedford debut on March 27, 1943, against St Mary's Hospital. In the team that day were his partners from Bedford School, Murray Fletcher at scrum half and 'Tich' Haynes at fly half. All three were on leave from university and the entire school back division of 1941 was selected for the match. Leo Oakley was rated as one of the finest centre three-quarters ever to play for the club. Five times he scored three tries in a match and he is one of just ten players in 125 years to have scored five tries in one match. An all round sportsman and champion boxer, he played for the Army, the Barbarians and the East Midlands and represented England in a Service international against Scotland in 1944. The England selectors were keen for him to play on the wing, but Bedford were reluctant to put him there because he was such a potent force in the centre. He was one of ten England players to make a debut against Wales at St Helen's, Swansea, on January 20, 1951. Wales, in contrast, fielded 11 of the 1950 British Lions and the core of their Grand Slam team of the season before and won the match 23-5. A leg injury kept Leo Oakley out of the game in 1951-52 but he made a comeback in 1952-53 until a broken leg on January 10, 1953, finished his playing days. He died in 1981 and a memorial gate at the entrance to the club was named after him. His Bedford record is played 77, scored 168 points made up of 52 tries, three conversions, one dropped goal and one penalty. His international record is v Wales, 1951.

**J F Bance, England**

John Forsyth Bance was educated at Radley College and made a debut for Bedford while a student at Cambridge University in 1945-46. He played 24 times in 1946-47, moved to Norfolk and missed the next season, but played 10 times in 1948-49 and then became a regular who achieved a place in the top 20 appearances of all time. He won wartime colours at Cambridge and a full Blue in 1945, going on to captain Bedford for three seasons and becoming a Barbarian and later President of the East Midlands and President of Huntingdon. He was called up to the England second row as a line out specialist for the match against Scotland at Murrayfield on March 20, 1954. He was one of four England changes from the side that beat Ireland in the preceding match, replacing Peter Yarranton of the Wasps. England ran out winners by 13-3 to secure the Triple Crown for the 11th time and the Calcutta Cup. Scotland collected the wooden spoon for the third consecutive season. John Bance's Bedford record is played 279 times, scored 17 tries and four conversions for 59 points. His England record is v Scotland 1954.

**St L H Webb, England**

St Lawrence Hugh Webb is one of the select few in Bedford's history who captained the club, made over 300 appearances and played for the Barbarians and England. He joined Bedford in 1952-53 as a back row forward but moved to prop and won international recognition in that position. He played in all four England internationals in 1959 and was selected again in 1960 but forced to withdraw. He made his debut at Cardiff Arms Park on January 17 in a 5-0 defeat by Wales. There were 13 newcomers to international rugby on parade in the mud that day. One of them, the Welsh winger Dewi Bebb, scored the winning try. He played his second international at Lansdowne Road against the Irish on February 14 and England won 3-0, Bev Risman landing a penalty. His next was in a 3-3 draw against France at Twickenham on February 28 in a match which revealed "a glorious revival of English forward play." His fourth international was against Scotland at Twickenham on March 21. Again in another low scoring match England failed to produce a try and penalties from Risman and Ken Scotland settled the match. Larry Webb's full record at Bedford is played 336 times and scored 74 tries for 222 points. His England record is v Wales, Ireland, France and Scotland in 1959.

**D P Rogers OBE, England**

Derek Prior 'Budge' Rogers was capped, as a Bedford player, more times than anyone else in 125 years. He scored a try on his England debut at Lansdowne Road, Dublin in an 11-8 defeat by Ireland on February 11, 1961 and never looked back. By the end of his international career – against Wales at Cardiff Arms Park in a 30-9 defeat on April 12, 1969 – he had established a record number of England caps, 34. The previous highest total, 31, had stood to Lord Wakefield of Kendal, William Wavell Wakefield, for 42 years. It had been established between 1920 and 1927. 'Budge' Rogers equalled the total on his international recall in Dublin on February 8, 1969 in a 17-15 defeat by Ireland, and he passed it in England's next game – a 22-8 victory over the French at Twickenham on February 22. In that match, he took over the captaincy for a second spell when Dick Greenwood was injured playing squash the night before the game. He captained England in seven internationals, taking over from his Bedford back row colleague, David Perry, for the 11-6 defeat by Wales on January 15, 1966. He led the side in all four matches that season and again for the second, third and fourth games of 1969. Tony Neary, the flanker who eventually replaced him in the England team and the one who wore the famous number seven shirt when England won the Grand Slam in 1980, with D P Rogers as Chairman of Selectors, established a new record of 43 by the end of his career. The Bedford record of D P Rogers is: played 485 times, scored 126 tries and one dropped goal – at Bath on April 25, 1964. His England record is played 34 times, three tries: v Scotland in 1961, '63, '64, '65, '66, '67 and '69; v Ireland in 1961, '62, '63, '64, '65, '66 and '69; v Wales in 1962, '63, '64, '65, '66, '67 and '69; v France in 1961, '62, '63, '64, '65, '66 and '69; v Australia in 1963 and '67; v New Zealand in 1963, twice, '64 and '67.

**D G Perry, England**

David Perry

David Perry was capped for England 15 times, four as captain and each time 'Budge' Rogers was in the side as well. He made his debut in the 6-5 win over France at Twickenham on February 23, 1963 and played in the final match of the home series that year – a 10-8 win over Scotland – before going on England's tour to New Zealand and Australia. For the second of the defeats against the All Blacks he moved from the number eight position to lock and stayed there for the match at the Sydney Cricket Ground on June 4 when England lost 18-9 to Australia. He returned to number eight for three matches in the 1964 season which included another against New Zealand and he scored a try in a 6-6 draw with Wales at Twickenham on January 18. David Perry took over the England captaincy from Ron Jacobs for the 1965 season and for the four matches that year, he and Rogers were joined by another Bedford player, Geoff Frankcom. His fourth match as captain was against Scotland at Twickenham on March 20, 1965. Queen Elizabeth II was present to see the memorable last-minute length-of-the-field try scored by the Northampton winger Andy Hancock to draw the match 3-3. David Perry played in three of England's matches in 1966 under 'Budge' Rogers and scored a try in the first, against Wales at Twickenham in an 11-6 defeat on January 15. His full Bedford record is played 101 times, scored 115 points, from 37 tries and two conversions. His England record is v Scotland 1963 and '65, v Ireland 1964, '65 and '66, v Wales 1964, '65 and '66, v France 1963, '65, '66, v New Zealand 1963 twice and '64, v Australia 1963. He scored two tries for England.

**G P Frankcom, England**

Geoffrey Peter Frankcom, a centre, started his first class career with Bath and made over 100 appearances for them. He won Blues at Cambridge University in 1961, '63, '64 and played for Bedford after the 1964 Varsity match, making his debut on January 23, 1965 and scoring two tries against Old Millhillians. Pat Briggs had encouraged him to join the club. He attracted attention in the 1963-64 season as the leading try scorer in England, and he was called up to the full international side for four caps in 1965, joining David Perry and 'Budge' Rogers in the England team. He was one of four new three-quarters in the side that lost 14-3 to Wales on January 16, 1965. In his *Book of English International Rugby*, John Griffiths writes "Frankcom ... was the victim of a particularly vicious and totally unnecessary attack by one of the Welsh forwards, and displayed prominent bite marks in the dressing room after the match." He played in England's 5-0 defeat by Ireland on February 13, 1965, in the 9-6 win over France at Twickenham on February 27 and then in that famous 3-3 draw with Scotland on March 20. Geoff Frankcom joined the teaching staff at Bedford School and later entered the RAF where he became a pilot. His full Bedford record is played 59 times, scoring 24 tries and two dropped goals for 78 points. His England record is v Scotland, Ireland, Wales and France in 1965. He was capped once before his Bedford debut and three times after it.

### R D Hearn, England

Robert Daniel Hearn was educated at Cheltenham College, Trinity College, Dublin, and Oxford University where he won a Blue in 1964. He roomed with fellow centre Geoff Frankcom on an Oxford-Cambridge tour of the Argentine and was invited to join Bedford by Pat Briggs. He made his debut on October 21, 1965 in an 18-9 win over Cambridge University and played 12 games that season and 15 the next. Danny Hearn had an Irish qualification as well as an English one. He had been an Irish Universities boxing champion and his grandfather had been Bishop of Cork. He was invited for an Irish trial but David Perry advised him to "hang on" and he was called up by England to face the French at Stade Colombes, Paris, on February 26, 1966. The French won 13-0 and his second international, a 6-3 defeat by Scotland at Murrayfield, secured England the wooden spoon but he kept his place and played in all the home internationals the next season. Danny Hearn, along with Budge Rogers, was selected for the London, Midlands and Home Counties match at Leicester against the touring All Blacks on October 28, 1967. Within minutes of the start he was seriously injured making a tackle and suffered severe spinal injuries that left him paralysed. His rugby career was ended but his fight back was an example of rare courage and he resumed the post at Haileybury School that he had secured, after teaching practice at Bedford School. His Bedford record is played 27 times, scored 21 tries for 63 points. His England record is v France 1966 and '67, v Scotland 1966 and '67, v Ireland 1967, v Wales 1967 for six caps.

### J J Page, England

John Jackson Page was a canny forward-orientated scrum half. Educated at Cambridgeshire High School and Queens College, Cambridge, he made his Bedford debut on February 18, 1967 in a 6-3 defeat at Moseley. He won Blues in 1968, '69 and '70, playing for Bedford in the second term and in vacations. He made his international debut at the start of England Centenary season at Cardiff Arms Park on January 16, 1971. Welsh rugby was in its prime, Barry John was man of the match and England lost 22-6. J P A G Janion, also of Bedford, made his debut in the same match. 'Jacko' Page was at scrum half, with Ian Wright of Northampton at fly half, in English victories over Ireland in Dublin and France at Twickenham. In the championship match against Scotland A R Cowman was his partner. He left Bedford to team up again with Wright at Northampton and later became something of a thorn in the flesh of his former club both in the colours of the Saints and later with Birmingham. He was capped again, as a Northampton player, on March 15, 1975 and played a prominent part in a 7-6 win over Scotland with W N Bennett of Bedford making his debut, A M Jorden at full back and the former Blues winger W C C Steele, then with London Scottish, on the wing for Scotland. 'Jacko' Page's Bedford record is played 53 times, scored 56 points, ten tries, five dropped goals, three penalties and one conversion. His England record is v Scotland, Ireland, Wales and France as a Bedford player in 1971 and v Scotland as a Northampton player in 1975.

### J P A G Janion, England

Jeremy Paul Arthur George Janion was a powerful threequarter who joined Bedford from Saffron Walden. He made a debut in the team that ran in eight tries against Leicester in a 39-5 win on September 6, 1969 and got a hat-trick against London Irish in his second match. He was soon spotted in a star studded team that won The *Sunday Telegraph's* English-Welsh Pennant and was capped 12 times for England, nine times while at Bedford, three while playing for Richmond, seven times as a winger, five as a centre. He started off for England on the wing and made his debut against Wales in Cardiff on January 16, 1971. He played in the three other matches in the home international series of that season and in the special match against Scotland to mark 100 years of internationals and the Centenary international against the RFU President's XV. Jeremy Janion played in the 12-3 defeat by a Welsh team containing ten of the successful 1971 British Lions at Twickenham in January 1972 and in the 23-9 defeat to Scotland that condemned England to defeat in all four home internationals for the first time. He played for England for the last time as a Bedford player in the 18-9 win over South Africa at Ellis Park on June 3, 1972. His last game for Bedford was against Leicester on December 23, 1972 and his full club record is played 76 times, scored 50 tries for 167 points, the try having been increased in value to four points in 1971-72. His full England record is v Wales 1971 and '72, v Ireland and France 1971, v Scotland 1971, twice, and '72, v President's XV 1971, v South Africa 1972, v Australia 1973 and '75, twice.

### W C C Steele, Scotland

Billy Steele was the first Scotsman to represent his country while a member of Bedford since D M Grant in 1911. In 1974 he became the first Bedford player to represent the British Lions since 'Budge' Rogers in 1962. He joined the Blues while stationed locally in the RAF, having already won a Scottish cap against England with Langholm in 1969. He made his Bedford debut on the wing at Leicester on September 5, 1970, in a 14-5 defeat and played regularly until Christmas after which the RAF had first claim on his services. Along with Geoff Frankcom, he represented the RAF against Bedford on March 6 of his first season, with the Blues winning 17-6. Service calls and internationals restricted his appearances in club colours to just 45 in four seasons, turning out for the last time on November 17, 1974, in a 16-6 win over Northampton. He was capped, as a Bedford player, in 1971, '72, and '73 and his final international before he joined London Scottish and earned nine more caps, was against England at Twickenham on March 17. England won 20-13 but Billy Steele scored two tries for Scotland. He missed the 1974 season through injury but returned again in 1975 and 1976 before bowing out of the international arena at Twickenham on January 8, 1977. Billy Steele's Bedford record is 45 appearances, 23 tries for 82 points. His Scotland record is v England 1969, '71, twice, '72, '73, '75, '76, '77, v France 1971, '72, '73, '75, v Wales 1971, '72, '73, '75, '76, v Ireland 1971, '73, '75, '76, v New Zealand 1972, '75.

### A M Jorden, England

Anthony Mervyn Jorden was already capped as an England full back at both Cambridge University and then Blackheath when he joined Bedford at the beginning of the 1974-75 season. He was a double Blue at both rugby and cricket at Cambridge in 1968 and in 1969, was captain of cricket in 1969, and later played for both Essex and Bedfordshire. He made his England debut in a 35-13 defeat by the French in Paris on April 18, 1970. His next appearance, was as a Blackheath player, in an 18-9 defeat by the Irish in Dublin on February 10. He scored in both and then again in the two remaining matches of that year's championship before earning a fifth cap in England's 12-12 draw on their first visit to the French at the new Parc des Princes ground in Paris on March 2, 1974. Tony Jorden was recalled for two further caps, this time as a Bedford player, for the 20-4 defeat by Wales at Cardiff on February 15, 1975 and for the 7-6 win over the Scots at Twickenham on March 15 when his Bedford colleague Neil Bennett made his debut. The next month he featured in the Blues' cup victory over Rosslyn Park.

He was a regular for the next three seasons but retired from the first class game after the opening match of 1979-80 to play junior rugby in Hertfordshire. He became an administrator and later an England selector. Tony Jorden's Bedford record is played 124 times for 352 points, 70 conversions, 39 penalties, 17 tries and nine dropped goals. His England record is v France 1970, '73 and '74, v Ireland 1973, v Scotland 1973 and '75, v Wales 1975. He scored 22 points, five conversions and four penalties.

**W N Bennett, England**

Neil Bennett joined Bedford in 1973-74 after he accepted a teaching post at John Bunyan School. He made his debut for the club at fly half in a 35-15 win over Leicester on September 1, 1973 and was an immediate success. In his first season, he became the first Bedford player ever to score 300 points when he set a new record of 307. Included in that total was another record when he scored 35 points against the Wasps, scoring three tries, one penalty and converting ten times out of a possible 12. In his second season 'Nelly' Bennett played at fly half when Bedford won the cup and he scored 281 points. In his third season, he set another new points record of 351 from 36 matches. In 1977 he secured a new teaching post in Kent and played his last game for Bedford in November of that year having made 103 appearances and set several records. He joined the London Welsh club and teamed up again with Alun Lewis, scrum half in the cup winning side. Neil Bennett made his international debut against Scotland on March 15, 1975 with Tony Jorden at full back, 'Jacko' Page at scrum half and Billy Steele in the Scotland team. In all, he played seven times for England, three as a Bedford player, once as a replacement, and then four times while a member of London Welsh in the Five Nations Championship of 1979. His Bedford record is played 103 times, scored 1,034 points, 34 tries, 173 conversions, 165 penalties and 19 dropped goals. His England record is v Scotland 1975, '76, '79, v Australia 1975, v Ireland, France and Wales 1979. He scored 23 points, two tries and five penalties.

**R M Wilkinson, England**

Robert Michael Wilkinson was one of the very best lineout experts and ball handling lock forwards seen at the Blues. And he was one of just a handful of players in 125 years who captained the club, made more than 300 appearances and played for the Barbarians and England. He made his Bedford debut as a 17-year-old St Albans School pupil on February 1, 1969, and continued his career at Goldington Road when he was available while studying at Cambridge University where he won Blues in 1971, '72 and '73. He played in the Barbarians' famous match against the All Blacks at Cardiff in 1973 and partnered Clive Hooker in Bedford's cup winning team of 1975 before being selected for the tour of Australia in the summer of that year. He made his full England debut in the second Test defeat at Brisbane on May 31, 1975 in a match remembered mainly for what was described as an "unprecedented outburst of thuggery" in which Mike Burton became the first England player to be sent off in an international. Bob Wilkinson made his second England appearance on January 3, 1976 in a 23-6 win over the Australians at Twickenham. His partner in the second row on both occasions against Australia and for the four games of the Five Nations Championship of 1976 was Bill Beaumont, England captain in the Grand Slam side of 1980. He retired some 15 years after his Bedford debut having played 311 times, scoring 37 tries. His England record is v Australia 1975 and 1976, v Wales, Scotland, Ireland and France in 1976.

## D M Wyatt, England

Derek Murray Wyatt scored more tries, 145, than anyone else in the club's 125 years. He was one of the club's most exciting players in one of its most exciting eras and his points total of 686 was beaten by only six others. He joined from Ipswich and made his debut at Pontypool on October 13, 1973, scoring 33 tries on the left wing in 29 appearances in his first season, 30 from 28 in his second, 35 from 36 in his third, 30 from 33 in his fourth and 17 from 26 in his fifth. His 35 tries in the record breaking season of 1975-76 is equal second highest with A D Heard's total in 1908-09. Only H H Morris in 1893-94 scored more, 38. His six tries in one match at Bournemouth on November 3, 1974, equalled a record with H Willett and A D Heard. Three times in all Derek Wyatt scored five tries in a match, five times he scored four and in a record 17 matches, he ran in three. On October 19, 1977, he scored 33 points in a 65-15 win over Cambridge University, three tries, nine conversions and one penalty. Only kickers Neil Bennett, with 35 against Wasps in 1974, and Ali Hepher, 34 against Newbury in 2006, scored more in one match. Derek Wyatt made his England debut as replacement for David Duckham in the first half of the Calcutta Cup defeat at Murrayfield on February 21, 1976. It was his only appearance – though a year later he scored four tries in a match against the USA for which no caps were awarded. He played his final game for Bedford at Bath on April 27, 1978, then joined the Bath club and got into the record books there as well with 29 tries in each of two seasons. Later he studied at Oxford University, winning a Blue, aged 32, in the Centenary Varsity match in 1981, and he became a media personality, publisher, rugby writer and, from 1997 until 2010, the Labour MP for Sittingbourne & Sheppey.

## J Orwin, England

John Orwin had been capped by England seven times when he arrived at Goldington Road from Gloucester at the age of 32 for what most people thought would be the twilight of his career. He'd just led the 'Cherry and Whites' to the Merit Table 'A' title but had such a galvanizing effect at his new club that Bedford, who'd finished bottom in Merit Table 'B,' were soon on the up again. Lauded to the skies by an enthusiastic local press, he soon came to the attention of the selectors again and was invited to a trial where an outstanding performance saw him picked in the second row at the start of the 1988 Five Nations. After the first match in Paris on January 16, he was described there as 'Un monstre magnifique' in spite of the defeat; but the Orwin legend was really born during the final match against Ireland, on March 19, where he took over the England captaincy at half time following an injury to Nigel Melville and suddenly saw a 3-0 deficit turn into a 35-3 win. This was the match where 'Sweet Chariot' the England 'anthem' was adopted as Chris Oti of the Wasps ran in three tries and a section of the crowd sang the song after each one. On the strength of this success, John Orwin was selected as captain for the summer tour of Australia and Fiji and played in the Tests in Brisbane and Sydney. But it was a difficult experience for the 34 year old and eventually he was replaced by Will Carling. John Orwin represented Bedford 75 times between 1986 and 1988. As a Blues player he was capped in 1988 v France, Wales, Scotland, Ireland, twice, and Australia twice. He was the third Bedford forward to captain England.

### M C Bayfield, England

Martin Bayfield with Hayley Lant outside the Times & Citizen office in 1990

Martin Bayfield was the last player born and bred in Bedford to represent England in the first 125 years of the Blues. And for a while he was such a recognizable sight walking the town in his police uniform that when Bedford was mentioned people thought of the statue of John Bunyan in St Peters, the statue of John Howard in the High Street and of the 6'10" officer who played rugby. The son of an executive at Tobler Meltis and a teacher at Bedford High School, he was educated at Bedford School where he was enthusiastically nurtured by a staff who saw another potential international. His height drew him towards a career in the police and having made a debut for the Blues in 1985-86, he joined the Metropolitan Police Rugby Club before returning to the Blues and the Bedfordshire force in 1989-90. Bedford, under John Orwin, had just been promoted but the dream partnership in the second row never played together because Orwin left for pastures new. After two tough seasons it became clear Martin Bayfield would have to move on to achieve his ambition of full England honours; but it was his performances in a struggling Bedford team that saw him selected for the tour to Australia and Fiji and capped twice before he'd actually played for Northampton, His first England shirt became a prized possession at the Blues. Martin Bayfield went on to represent his country 31 times between 1991 and 1996, featuring in two Grand Slams, the 1995 World Cup and partnering the legendary Martin Johnson 18 times. In 1993 he had an outstanding Lions tour in New Zealand and in 1995 he was voted the RFU Player of the Year. After retiring through injury in 1998, he turned to after dinner speaking, at which he achieved great success. He also became a rugby reporter, pundit and TV presenter and featured in the Harry Potter films as the body double for Robbie Coltrane's 'Hagrid' character. He played 56 times for Bedford and 31 times for England, twice while a Bedford player v Fiji and Australia in 1991.

### P J Paramore, Samoa

Peter Junior Paramore would surely have won a poll in which Bedford supporters nominated the most popular player of the first decade of the professional era. And many would rank him among the very best – if not the best for his dynamic game and 'sublime' hands. Even when he wasn't playing, the crowd would chant 'Junior, Junior' as he walked in front of the stand at Goldington Road – even after he'd left. He was held in huge esteem in the wider community as well where people recognized someone proud to be among them. A back row forward who played with a ferocious dignity, he took up rugby only after his family moved to New Zealand when he was 15. There, he made such progress that he was selected for the Western Samoan squad for the 1991 World Cup – the first of three he appeared in. In 1999 in Wales he was in the team that beat the host nation, with Mike Rayer making his debut, at the Millennium Stadium. After the 1995 World Cup in South Africa, he switched to rugby league in Australia and then went on loan to Castleford Tigers in West Yorkshire where he was spotted by Paul Turner – an enthusiast of the sport and someone about to put together a team of All Stars and grafters. His signing started a love affair with Bedford which never waned even when he left for Gloucester days after the sale in 1999. He became an iconic figure there as well but returned after five years for another two at the Blues after Rudi Straeuli tempted him back. He retired following a serious neck injury and in 2006 and took up coaching- first at Luton, then Bournemouth and then, in 2010, Basingstoke. Junior Paramore played 113 times for Bedford and 27 times for his country – six while he was a Bedford player: v Ireland in 1996, Tonga and Fiji in 1997 and Tonga, Fiji and Australia in 1998.

### S Murray, Scotland

Scott Murray played in more international matches than any other Bedford player in the club's first 125 years. He represented Scotland 87 times between November 1997 and September 2007 when he captained his country for the fifth time - against New Zealand in the World Cup. He was a basketball international when he was invited to try rugby at Preston Lodge. Soon he joined Edinburgh Academicals and as the game went professional he was offered terms at Bedford where he became a worthy successor to the club's other second row internationals of the modern era such as Bob Wilkinson, John Orwin and Martin Bayfield. He quickly made his mark at the Blues on and off the field where he was a popular after-match clubhouse star. Having joined Bedford at 20, he won his first full cap at 21 and became a regular in the Scottish side. He was a key figure in the Blues push for promotion to level one and the attempt to stay there. Like many others he determined to hang on at the club for as long as he could but left for the Saracens and made a debut for them at the start of 1999-2000 season. He was a popular figure at Vicarage Road and stayed there until he joined Edinburgh where he played from 2002 until 2007 before taking his skills to France. He played in three World Cups, toured with the Lions in 2001, was Scotland's Player of the Year three times and when he made his 83rd appearance in March 2007 he became his country's most capped player. Scott Murray made 76 appearances for Bedford between 1996 and 1999 and during that time at Goldington Road he played 12 times for Scotland: v Australia and South Africa in 1997, Italy, Fiji, Australia, twice, and South Africa in 1998 and Wales, Italy, England, Ireland and France in 1999.

**D W O'Mahony, Ireland**

Darragh O'Mahony was a deadly finisher – an elusive, smooth-running winger with deceptive pace who could beat an opponent off either foot. At Bedford, he was the natural heir of the club's only other Irish international, Vic Lyttle, who played three times on the wing for his country in the late 1930s. He started playing at the age of six with Cork Constitution, won a rugby scholarship to University College, Dublin, and while there was selected for the World Cup in South Africa in 1995, winning the first of his four caps against Italy before the event started and the second at the quarter final stage of the tournament when Ireland lost 36-12 to France. When the sport went professional he joined Moseley where he set try scoring records in two seasons and earned a third cap; but when that club overstretched itself and went into administration he signed for Bedford where he was an instant success. He played just the one season, 1998-99, before he left to join the Saracens as Bedford, too, came face to face with the reality of professional rugby. One of his great matches was in the last gasp 35-33 win against the Harlequins in which he scored two tries including the winner. That he wasn't in the 47 man Irish squad was a 'criminal waste of talent' wrote David Llewellyn in his match report in *The Independent* of October 12, 1998. He soon was, though, but his appearance against Romania just over a month later was his last. He retired from first class rugby on leaving the Saracens in 2004 and later turned out for his local club, Old Albanians. Darragh O'Mahony played 32 times for Bedford and once for Ireland v Romania in 1998 as a Bedford player.

**D Edwards, Tonga**

David Edwards was one of a number of players recruited by Paul Turner in his second session at Bedford – this time under the Jefferson Lloyd International regime when the club was hanging on to its status and its very existence by a thread. Born in New Zealand, he made a debut as a replacement for Tonga against Australia in September 1998 and then played for them another six times in 1999 before joining the Blues. He was soon off to the World Cup where he played in the 45-9 defeat at the hands of New Zealand in Bristol, the 28-25 win over Italy in Leicester and the 101-10 defeat to England at Twickenham on October 15 in a match remembered as the one where England scored their first World Cup century. He made his Bedford debut at Cambridge University on October 23, 1999, an important date that marked the first match after the regime change and he was mentioned in despatches after a memorable, albeit losing, match against Bath in November. He was injured in the match against Saracens in January and didn't return until the end of April. He played in the first of the play-off matches against Rotherham when the team coach, Alistair Murdoch, left himself out of the line up because sides could field only two 'overseas' players, reckoning that hard tackling back row forwards would have more impact in the away leg. David Edwards played 13 times for the Blues and ten times for Tonga, three – against New Zealand, Italy and England in 1999 - as a contracted Bedford player even though he hadn't actually played for the club!

**D S Stewart, Canada**

Scott Stewart played 64 times for Canada becoming the most capped full back in their history. He appeared in the World Cups of 1991, 1995 and 1999 and represented his country in the World Cup 7s of 1993 and 1997. He learned the game at school in Vancouver and at the University of British Columbia, developing the reputation of a mentally tough character who relished the physical challenge - something he showed in what became known as the Battle of Boet Erasmus when Canada took on the host nation, South Africa, in the 1995 World Cup.

He played in his first international as a 20 year old against the USA in Toronto in September 1989 and by the time he made his Bedford debut at Cardiff in February 1999, after spells at Dax and the Harlequins, he'd been capped 45 times. He arrived with the Blues up for sale and, like many others, did his bit to help it retain its Premiership status in spite of all the issues off the field. In his second season he left for the 1999 World Cup with the club in an even greater crisis but he returned in time to see the light at the end of the tunnel and the subsequent buy-out. At the end of the 1999-2000 season with the club secured, but relegated, he left. However, the Blues pulled out all the stops to persuade him back for one more season - to play at fly half and to take the kicks. Scott Stewart turned out for Bedford 55 times and made nine appearances for Canada while a Bedford player: v Samoa, USA, Tonga, Wales, England, France, Fiji and Namibia in 1999 and Italy in 2000.

**A C T Gomarsall MBE, England**

Andy Gomarsall was the latest in a long line of outstanding scrum halves to emerge from Bedford School and with 35 England caps to his name he was surely the best. When the weekly *Rugby Times* nominated its Premiership team of the first decade of the 21st century, he was at scrum half. He played rugby professionally at the top level from 1992 when he joined the Wasps until 2010, having also turned out for Bedford, Gloucester, Worcester, Harlequins and Leeds along the way. As a schoolboy he made his debut for Bedford in the record 90-3 win over the Old Paulines in 1991. He sprang to prominence on a national level when he led the 1992 England Schools U18s to their first Grand Slam for 11 years and after a glittering procession through the U21s, Students, Emerging Players and the 'A' team he made his England debut against Italy in 1996. After helping Wasps win the 1999 cup, he moved to Bedford at a time when they were struggling for their Premiership survival and very existence. He was captain and top scorer in 1999-2000 but relegation was inevitable and he moved on to Gloucester where he tasted more cup success in 2003. World Cups too. Having been flown out as cover in the 1995 campaign in South Africa, he was a member of the England squad that won the Webb Ellis Trophy in Australia in 2003, hence the MBE, playing twice in the group stages. He is credited with a pivotal role in the England recovery in France in 2007 and started in the final against South Africa. For Bedford, Andy Gomarsall played 26 times, scoring five tries, 12 conversions and 13 penalties. His only international as a Bedford player was against Italy in Rome in March 2000.

**M G Rivaro, Italy**

Marco Rivaro was already an Italian international when he signed for Bedford after the University match of 2000 having come on as replacement in Italy's famous 34-20 win over Scotland in the inaugural Six Nations. He also played in the defeats that year to Wales and Ireland. A law graduate from Genoa, he came to London to continue his studies and his rugby, firstly in London and then in Cambridge. In the 1999-2000 season he turned out in the centre for London Irish, often alongside the popular Bedford threequarter, Ben Whetstone, who also played there for that one season. Legend has it that the Italian coach noticed his ferocious tackling in one match on TV and called him up on the strength of it. In the autumn, he went to study at Hughes Hall, Cambridge, and played in the Varsity fixture against Oxford before rejoining Ben Whetstone – by now captain of the Blues. Cambridge colleague Mike Count also joined. Marco Rivaro played just six times for Bedford and while he was at the club he came on as a replacement for the Italian side, with Luca Martin on the wing, that lost heavily to England at Twickenham in February 2001. It was his last international.

### L Martin, Italy

Luca Martin played 38 times for Italy in a six year spell either side of their joining the Six Nations in 2000. He featured in the centre in their famous win over Scotland in Rome in February of that year. Born in Padua, he started playing for the town's famous Petrarca club – named after the poet and known for its philosophy of trying to prepare players for the wider world as much as for rugby. The great Bergamasco brothers were nurtured there as well. Few foreigners were invited to join - 'unless strictly necessary' - and few local players were encouraged to leave to improve their game. But some did, Luca Martin heading for Begles in France for two seasons from 1998 and then Northampton for two more between 2000 and 2002. He was first capped against France in October 1997 and played in the match against England in the 1999 World Cup. At Northampton, Heineken Cup winners in 2000, his opportunities were limited and in January, 2002 he was loaned to Bedford. He played for the Blues away to Exeter on the 12th, at home to Moseley on the 19th, away to Henley on February 9 and at home to Rotherham on the 23rd – just four times. In between, he played for Italy in the Six Nations against France in Paris on February 2 and against Scotland in Rome on the 16th. He never played for Bedford, Northampton or the full Italian XV again, but went back to Rovigo, captaining the Italian 7s team until 2005 and then rejoined Petrarca in 2006.

### J G Pritchard, Canada

James Pritchard played in more international matches as a Bedford player than anyone else save 'Budge' Rogers. By the end of the 2010-11 Championship season in England he had played 33 times for Canada – 28 of them as a Bedford player – and had scored 332 international points. And he was in such form as captain of the Blues, having just set another record, that more caps looked certain to follow. Add to that 181 appearances and the second highest career total of points in 125 years – including 65 tries - and it's clear he belongs among Bedford's all time greats. Australian born, with a Canadian grandfather and a grandmother from Northamptonshire, he was signed by Colin Jackson from the Randwick club with the reputation of a points machine - and he didn't disappoint, finishing as top scorer in the seven seasons he played up to, and including, 2010-11. In his second, 2002-03, he broke the club record with 386, in league and cup, in just 27 games. His 374 in the league that season was still a record in 2011 when he regained the overall club record with 403. His early success convinced him to try to make the Canada squad for the 2003 World Cup and so he left Bedford to join Prairie Fire in the Canadian Super League. He made his international debut in a non cap match against the New Zealand Maori in July 2003 and then played in three capped matches in a Pan American tournament in Buenos Aires in August before making the World Cup squad and playing against Wales and Tonga in Australia. He joined Plymouth Albion in August 2004 and scored 319 points for them in 29 consecutive appearances. His last match for the Albion was against Bedford in the 2005 Powergen Challenge Shield final at Twickenham where he broke his collarbone in the 16th minute. After three years away and spells in Perpignan and Northampton, James Pritchard returned to Goldington Road for the 2006-07 season and scored 303 points in that campaign. He was recalled to the Canadian team in 2006 setting a new record of 36 points in a match against the USA and then played in all four pool games in the 2007 World Cup in France.

**S L Tonga'uiha, Tonga, Pacific Islanders**

Soane Tonga'uiha served notice in his first season at Bedford that he was something special. And he showed just why in his second. He was an impact player in the Bedford squad that won the Powergen Challenge Shield at Twickenham in 2005. But when it went on to finish second in National One and runners up in the Powergen National Trophy in 2006 he was ranked among the best players in the league. A massive, mobile, ball carrying prop, nicknamed 'Tiny,' he became a great favourite after being recommended by Junior Paramore to Rudi Straeuli who saw in the Tongan someone he could help develop become a world class player. His ball carrying was awesome but he could off load like a back and as his reputation grew so Premiership clubs joined the queue to try to prise him away from the Blues. Northampton won the race to sign him for the 2006-07 season and he, having married Lucy, the daughter of David Jackson the great Bedford number eight and captain of the 1970s, achieved iconic status at Franklin's Gardens as well. In 2010, he was named by most commentators in the Premiership team of the season with Will Greenwood writing in *The Daily Telegraph*: "Offloading in crowds is his speciality. Control among the chaos when he passes and just chaos when he runs". Bedford supporters knew exactly what was meant. That same year he was involved in a contractual tug of war with Saracens after he changed his mind about joining them and re-signed for Northampton after more than 100 first team games for them, going on to feature in the 2011 Heineken Cup Final. He was capped first by the Pacific Islanders against Australia in 2004 and then played against New Zealand and South Africa. He was capped twice for Tonga, against Italy and France, while at the Blues in 2005, and then played in all four of Tonga's games at the 2007 World Cup. He played 49 times for Bedford over two seasons between 2004 and 2006.

Mike Rayer, Alistair Murdoch and Scott Murray at the 2011 Former Players London Lunch

# OTHER INTERNATIONALS

Other players who have been members of the Bedford club have played for their country, some before they joined the Blues, others after they left. Some were internationals and guested for the club, like Basil Maclear, who was educated in the town and played on and off for Bedford between 1896, when he was at school, and 1906. As an officer in the Royal Dublin Fusiliers, he was capped for Ireland 11 times between 1905 and 1907 and accredited as a player at Cork County and Monkstown. The Cambridge Blue G F Redmond played for Bedford at the request of the England selectors in the match at Wasps on April 4, 1970 and then made an England debut in Paris on April 18. He didn't play for Bedford again, nor was he capped again by England.

Some players were very close to a cap – O V Bevan was selected as an A N Other in the late 1930s but had to withdraw because of flu. Others played for England in games where no caps were awarded. Rex Willsher, 'Beef' Dancer, C G Gilthorpe and H R Peel all played in wartime Red Cross, Service or Victory internationals. I G Peck played for England against Fiji at Suva in 1979; M Rennell was selected for the England tour of Canada in 1993. Again no caps were awarded.

The following English, unless stated, internationals have also played for Bedford. The year of their first cap is in brackets.

H H Castens, South Africa (1891), H W Finlinson (1895), G H McAllan, Ireland (1896), P G Jacob (1898), H J Anderson, Ireland (1903), B Maclear, Ireland (1905), F H Palmer (1905), A Hudson (1906), C H Milton (1906), E R Mobbs (1909), W A Stewart, Scotland (1913), G H H P Maxwell, Scotland (1913), A G Bull (1914), Q E M A King (1921), D E John, Wales (1923), R J Longland (1932), K C Fyfe, Scotland (1933), I Evans, Wales (1934), M M Henderson, Scotland (1937), G A Walker (1939), E L Horsfall (1949), R J H Uprichard, Ireland (1950), W G Hook (1951), D A McSweeney, Ireland (1955), P B Glover (1967), B Keen (1968), G F Redmond (1970), N O Martin (1972), L E Weston (1972), M Rafter (1977), N G Youngs (1983), M Bailey (1984), R Underwood (1984), F Clough (1986), N Hadley, Canada (1987), J Probyn (1988), C Innes, New Zealand (1989), P Turner, Wales (1989), M A Rayer, Wales (1991), A Murdoch, Australia (1993), S Alatini, Tonga (1994), D Jones, Wales (1994), R A W Straeuli, South Africa (1994), M Caputo, Australia (1996), R Eriksson, Scotland (1996), J Sleightholme (1996), M Stewart, Scotland (1996), S Brown (1998), D Sims (1998), R Banks, Canada (1999), A Codling (2002), B Hinshelwood, Scotland (2002), J Forster, Wales (2004), C Horsman, Wales (2005), T Varndell (2005), P Tupai, Samoa (2005), P Sackey (2006), N Walshe (2006), R Winters (2007), B Alexander, Australia (2008), D Cole (2009), W Harries, Wales (2010).

By 2010, players were able to move anywhere they were able to secure a contract and a number of those who had played or who were to play for Bedford won caps for countries ranked below the top two tiers by the sports ruling body – the International Rugby Board, established in1886. Those in the top tier in 2010 were the Six Nations countries, the Tri Nations and Argentina. Those in the second tier were: Canada, Fiji, Japan, Romania, Samoa, Tonga and USA.

Bedford players who represented countries ranked by the IRB below the second tier are listed with the date of their first cap where known:

P Berzin, Russia (1982), M Lloyd-Williams, Hong Kong (1983), A Tucker, Zimbabwe (1987), A Mihajlovic, Yugoslavia, R Fredricks, Hong Kong (1997), T Suring, T Otte, P Saffy, all Netherlands, R Subbiani, Arabian Gulf (2003), N Clarke, Hong Kong (2006).

Martin Offiah, one of the greatest rugby league players of all time, also played for Bedford (1996-97) as did Steve McCurrie in the same season. Both represented Widnes, and other clubs, England and Great Britain, Offiah making his GB debut in 1988 and McCurrie in 1993.

# THE BARBARIANS

The Barbarian motto reads: "Rugby is a game for gentlemen in all classes, but for no bad sportsmen in any class." It was coined by one of the earliest Barbarians, the Right Reverend W J Carey, an Old Bedfordian and member of Bedford who later became Bishop of Bloemfontein and then Bishop of Ely.

W J Carey played for the Blues the first time the club played the Barbarians. He was still at Bedford Grammar School when on February 21, 1894, Bedford entertained what was to become the most famous club side in the world and, in front of over 6,000 people at Goldington Avenue, won the match by 7-3. Two other Grammar School boys were in a side captained by Billy Rees – P G Jacob who dropped the goal that won the match and W F Surtees, later to become Bishop of Crediton. The school captain F A Cory actually played for the Barbarians, replacing one of their team who missed the train. W G Druce scored a try for the visitors and G L Hamilton one for Bedford. The Barbarian captain that day was the man who raised a scratch team to start it all in 1890, W P 'Tottie' Carpmael.

Bedford members played against the Barbarians from 1921 onwards in the colours of the East Midlands for the annual Mobbs Memorial Match played in honour of the great Northampton, East Midlands, Barbarian and England centre, Edgar Mobbs who was killed in action at Passchendaele on July 29, 1917. Mobbs was educated at Bedford Modern School and played also for Olney and Bedford. He turned out for the Blues twice – once against New Zealand in 1905. Most of the 'Mobbs' games were staged in Northampton, but those in 1926, 1938, 1949, 1951, 1953, 1955 and 1957 were staged at Goldington Road before it moved permanently to Bedford in 2005 and became a Bedford Blues v Barbarians fixture in 2008.

An invitation to play for the Barbarians was recognised as one of the great honours in the game and, in 2011, 'Budge' Rogers was still the second most 'capped' Barbarian with 25 appearances, five behind Tony O'Reilly of Ireland. Bob Wilkinson was eighth in the list with 23. The following played for Bedford and for the Barbarians, not necessarily while Bedford members. The season of their first appearance is in brackets.

H P Reynolds (1892-93), H W Finlinson (1893-94), F A Cory (1893-94),W J Carey (1894-95), F W Potter (1895-96), M E Finlinson (1901-02), J G Milton (1902-03), C E L Hammond (1903-04), F H Palmer (1903-04), C H Milton (1904-05), H J Anderson (1905-06), B Maclear (1906-07), G A De Smidt (1906-07), E J B Tagg (1908-09), C T Te Water (1909-09), E R Mobbs (1911-12), R V Knight (1911-12), Q E M A King (1913-14), H Willett (1915), A J Osbourn (1915), A G Bull (1915), J C Seagar (1919-20), F H X Gwynne (1919-20), H V Brodie (1925-26), R C Brumwell (1930-31), K C Fyfe (1932-33), R Willsher (1934-35), D L K Milman (1935-36), R J Longland (1935-36), J G Cook (1936-37), G T Dancer (1936-37), J G Rogers (1936-37), M M Henderson (1936-37), V J Lyttle (1937-38), G A Walker (1938-39), C G Gilthorpe (1941-42), G A Kelly (1945-46), H R Peel (1945-46), F M Fletcher (1948-49), L F Oakley (1948-49), J F Bance (1950-51), S H Wilcock (1957-58), L H Webb (1958-59), D P Rogers (1960-61), D G Perry (1961-62), D Coley (1961-62), J Smith (1964-65), G P Frankcom (1964-65), R D Hearn (1966-67), P B Glover (1966-67), P D Briggs (1968-69), B W Keen (1968-69), G D Lilley (1968-69), A M Jorden (1969-70), W C C Steele (1970-71), J P Janion (1970-71), R M Wilkinson (1971-72), N O Martin (1973-74), A K Rogers (1973-74), W N Bennett (1974-75), L E Weston (1974-75), J J Page (1975-76), P D'A Keith-Roach (1975-76), G N Phillips (1978-79), D M Wyatt (1978-79), I G Peck (1980-81), M Bailey (1983-84), I Metcalfe (1984-85), A Keay (1985-86).

From the Centenary season onwards, only players who represented the Barbarians while members of, or contracted to, Bedford were recorded and the season of their first appearance given – though in some cases they had played for the Barbarians earlier while members of other clubs.

M Howe (1987-88), P Alston (1994-95), R Subbiani (1995-96), S Brown (1996-97), J Probyn (1996-97), M Rayer (1996-97), D Sims (1999-2000), J Shanahan (2001-02), J Paramore (2003-04), M Stewart (2003-04), B Whetstone (2003-04), A Page (2005-06), A Brenton (2006-07), O Brown (2006-07), M Allen (2007-08), J Phillips (2007-08), L Roberts (2007-08), J Cannon (2008-09), O Dodge (2008-09), N Walshe (2008-09).

Bob Wilkinson on the ball with Andy Whitehouse and 'Gruff' Mansell in support

# THE LIONS

*G T Dancer* | *D P Rogers OBE* | *W C C Steele*

The same W J Carey who instituted the Barbarians' motto was arguably Bedford's first British Isles tourist. In 1896, the man later to become Bishop of Bloemfontein was a member of the second touring side from Britain to visit South Africa. In the season 1893-94, he had played six times for Bedford, including the famous win over the Barbarians, and later he played twice more, scoring two tries for the club in eight appearances.

He turned out once for Bedford in the 1894-95 season and once in 1896-97. In between, he toured South Africa as a member of the Oxford University club. Later, like many others from the Grammar School, he joined Blackheath, one of the founder members, in 1871, of the Rugby Football Union. Blackheath was a club with strong military links, and one to which the legendary Grammar School coach Hastings Dasent used to recommend many of his charges. Indeed, each year they sent him 15 membership cards for his first XV.

Other Old Bedfordians at the Blackheath club, H H Vassall in 1908 and S W Harris in 1924, were both tourists in British Isles teams, however unrepresentative, though there is no evidence that either ever played for Bedford. Harris was later to become a South African champion at both boxing and ballroom dancing and he also represented that country at Davis Cup tennis.

The XVs at both Bedford School and Bedford Modern were also given membership of Bedford in the Easter term under an agreement known as Rule Four and this throws up some interesting avenues for the statistician to explore. All the same, just three players have represented the British and Irish Lions, while a member of Bedford, one from each of the two public schools and one through the services connection.

**G T Dancer, South Africa, 1938**

The first player to tour with a British Isles team while actually a member of Bedford was the OBM Gerald Thomas Dancer, a prop forward who was never capped by England, though he did play in numerous trials and wartime internationals. 'Beef' was a member of the 1938 party that toured South Africa under the captaincy of Sammy Walker of Belfast Instonians, playing in all three Test matches and scoring a try in the 21-16 win in Cape Town on September 10. The British Isles lost the first Test by 26-12 in Johannesburg and the second by 19-3 in Port Elizabeth. Its overall record was played 23, won 17, lost six. 'Beef' Dancer played in Bedford's star-studded teams of the late 1930s and made 317 appearances, scoring 25 tries, between 1927 and 1948.

Gerry Dancer

**D P Rogers, South Africa, 1962**

'Budge' Rogers

Bedford's second British Lion was its most famous player, 'Budge' Rogers, who was a member of the party, captained by Arthur Smith of Edinburgh Wanderers, that toured South African in 1962. He played wing forward in the first and fourth Test matches in a series the Lions lost with three defeats and one draw. They drew the first 3-3 in Johannesburg, lost the second 3-0 in Durban, the third 8-3 in Cape Town and the fourth 34-14 in Bloemfontein. The side's overall record was played 24, won 15, lost five, and drawn four. Also in the party was R E G 'Dickie' Jeeps of Northampton, a former pupil at Bedford Modern School, later to become chairman of the Sports Council. He played 24 times for England and in 13 Test matches for the British Isles between 1955 and 1962.

**W C C Steele, South Africa, 1974**

Billy Steele

Bedford's third British Lion was their Scottish international William Charles Common 'Billy' Steele, who toured South Africa in 1974 as a member of the unbeaten party captained by Willie John McBride of Ballymena and Ireland. He played on the right wing in the first two Tests of the series, a 12-3 win at Cape Town and a 28-9 win in Pretoria. The Lions won the third Test 26-9 in Port Elizabeth and they drew the final one 13-13 in Johannesburg, having won all 21 other games to become the most successful British Isles team to visit the country since the very first, in 1891, won all 19 games. Billy Steele made ten of his 45 appearances for Bedford in the 1973-74 season. He missed the Home International series in 1974 but recovered from injury in time to earn selection for the tour. A serviceman in the RAF, he was posted away from the Bedford area and didn't play for Bedford again on his return from the tour. He continued his international career as a member of London Scottish.

No other Bedford players toured abroad with British Isles teams while they were actually members of the club. However, in 1977 one of its former players was summoned to join the party in New Zealand as a replacement. A D Lewis, a scrum half then playing for the London Welsh club, arrived in time to play in the last two provincial games of the tour but was not selected for the fourth and final Test match which the Lions, captained by Phil Bennett, lost 10-9 and the series by 3-1. In an era of outstanding Welsh scrum halves, Alun Lewis was never capped for his country. He made his reputation at Bedford after joining in his first year at Cambridge University and made his debut in a 29-9 win at Northampton on November 16, 1974. He played for the club for just one season – his last match was the cup final of 1975 – and his record is played 21, scored 27 points, six tries and a dropped goal. He went on to win Blues at Cambridge in 1975 and 1976.

In 1993, Martin Bayfield, profiled as an international, was selected for the Lions tour to New Zealand, while a member of Northampton, and played in all three Tests. Rory Underwood, who played 63 times for Bedford and scored 25 tries in two seasons between 1997 and 1999, went on Lions' tours in 1989, to Australia, and 1993, to New Zealand, and made six Test appearances. At the time he was a Leicester player. In 2001, Scott Murray, then with Saracens, went on the tour to Australia. He wasn't selected for any of the Tests.

# HEAD COACHES AND DIRECTORS OF RUGBY

*P D Briggs*
*R J Slaughter*
*M D Fitzgerald*
*R M Chadwick*
*I R Snook*
*M Rafter*
*R M C Greed*
*G D Cooke OBE*
*P Turner*
*R A W Straeuli*
*A R Murdoch*
*C S Jackson*
*M A Rayer*

There were just 13 head coaches who were actually recognized as such in the first 125 years of the Blues. Of course over the years there were many people who helped prepare a team for matches but it wasn't until the early 1970s that coaches became part of the management structure at Goldington Road and even then it started with an element of players not wanting to lose the influence of P D Briggs, a previous captain with serious talents as a communicator, thinker, tactician, motivator and trainer.

Managers had been in charge of soccer clubs in the 19th century but until 1946 it was still the Football Association who picked and prepared the England team. In rugby union, though some other countries had coaches, it wasn't until 1969, three years after the impact made by England winning the World Cup at soccer, that the first England rugby union coach was appointed. He was Don White, the former Northampton flanker and captain and, in his retirement, a frequent visitor to Goldington Road.

Traditionally captains had been expected to train their teams and then join a selection panel to help pick the teams. The early coaches too – though they soon learned how to get their way. Many rugby players, of course, were schoolmasters with an interest in teaching sport and they were able to have an input in the preparation of teams – at the captain's behest – though training rarely amounted to very much.

Bedford, based as they were on two rugby playing public schools, always had teachers in their ranks – for one thing because the attraction of posts at the schools was one way to entice players. So it's no surprise that three of the club's first four coaches were trained as teachers and the other was an athlete before he was a rugby player. In time, coaching became a recognized career and all sorts of different titles were used to cover the role. Many clubs appointed a director of rugby for whom coaching, often done by others was just one of the responsibilities of the job. When Martin Johnson became the England 'supremo' in 2008, he was given the title 'manager' and he assumed responsibility for a staff of other specialists – some of whom were coaches. This was the case in soccer and it wasn't hard to see rugby clubs adopting the same model. Profiled here are the people who headed up the coaching structure at Bedford – some of whom were known as coaches; others as directors of rugby.

### PD Briggs 1973-81

Pat Briggs became Bedford's first official coach when he retired from playing and he steered the side he'd captained and helped put together to victory in the cup in 1975 playing his brand of open attacking rugby. Even as a player, his skills were obvious in communication, man management, motivation, tactical awareness, match preparation, fitness and so on. He would discuss tactics, styles of play and set moves at a time when the idea of a club side being coached was virtually unheard of. When he stopped playing through injury, he was asked to carry on with the team and he did so through a golden age attracting some of the best players and creating an exciting brand of rugby with skilful, mobile forwards, dazzling half backs and deadly finishers on the wing. He coached the England U 23s and many thought he would go on to coach England. Once he said that a coach only had a three or four year lifespan; but he was captain for three years and then coach for eight. By 2011, no one had been coach at the Blues longer.

### R J Slaughter 1981-83

Roger 'Tod' Slaughter's mantra as a player, captain and coach was 'fitness, fitness, fitness.' And if his sides could be 'fighting fit' then so much the better. He had been an outstanding athlete under the influence of P J King at Bedford Modern School and he always said that anything he passed on to others in rugby he learned from Mr King at athletics. As captain of the Blues in 1967-68 and in 1968-69, he was, of course, responsible for what passed then for coaching. And his emphasis on fitness, passion and aggression paid off in second half of the season surges in form. "We may not have been brilliant rugby players but we played for the full 80 minutes, we took no nonsense and we all enjoyed ourselves," he often said. He took over as the official coach as the Blues embarked on a difficult period in the 1980s where they tended to lose more games than they won and the sport itself started to change significantly.

### M D Fitzgerald 1983-87

'Brothers in law' Mike Fitzgerald, left, and Richard Chadwick were both coaches at the Blues

Mike Fitzgerald was the classic schoolmaster coach with a prop's knowledge of forward play in particular and a Mountain Ash born Welshman's natural appetite for the game. He moved to Bedford with his family in 1966 and entered the sixth form at Bedford Modern School where he established himself in the XV and later that year started playing at Goldington Road, mainly with the Rovers. He went back to Wales to train as a teacher at the well known rugby nursery that was the Cardiff College of Education before returning to Bedford and becoming a stalwart of the club, making 55 first team appearances. A natural communicator with an engaging smile, he captained the Wanderers in 1974-75 and coached them between 1978 and 1983 before stepping up to the first team. His first season saw a record points against total but his period in charge saw a number of highlights – including a rare double over Northampton in 1985-86 and the Centenary season itself.

**R M Chadwick 1987-89**

Richard Chadwick was another schoolmaster coach who succeeded his 'brother-in-law' – both he and Mike Fitzgerald married daughters of the legendary P J King. A Lancastrian who played for Preston Grasshoppers, he arrived in Bedford in 1971 to take up a teaching post at Bedford Modern School where he stayed until his retirement in 2009. As a student at Loughborough College he came under the influence of the coaching guru Jim Greenwood and he set out to put the principles he learned to good use as a player, schoolmaster and coach himself. He made 101 appearances for the Blues between 1972 and 1980 - starting in the back row and then moving to the centre, the position where he turned out for the team that won the cup in 1975. Though the 1980s were one of the toughest decades, the club saw its fortunes change soon after the introduction of leagues when, on the back of an overall 50-50 record in 1988-89, the Blues earned promotion to level one with Richard Chadwick as coach.

**I R Snook 1989-1992**

Ian Snook was Bedford's first professional coach. And he had all the credentials. He was a New Zealander, a qualified teacher, a first class rugby player, a first class cricketer and he'd been coaching professionally since 1986. His mission, quite simply, was to keep Bedford in Courage League One after their surprise promotion; but it proved to be impossible after the key forward, John Orwin, and the key back, Brian Gabriel, decided to move on at the end of the previous season and the retirement of two senior players Andy Whitehouse and Kevin Canning. Though they battled bravely, the Blues were out of their depth in level one and quickly crashed back down to earth in a season that saw a record number of defeats and points against. Ian Snook was a coach of the new school, well versed in all things modern but quite capable of confusing some players not quite on the same wavelength. He kept the Blues in League Two for two more seasons before continuing a coaching career all over the world.

**M Rafter 1992-95**

Mike Rafter was a legend at Bristol Rugby Club where he played between 1972 and 1984 and was captain for two successful seasons before he retired. Known as 'Rafter the Grafter' he made 17 appearances for England at flanker and was considered unlucky not to go on the Lions tours of 1977 and 1980. He captained Gloucestershire for seven seasons, leading them to County Championships twice. Having qualified as a coach while still playing, he was in charge of the 1985 England Colts and arrived at Bedford for the 1992-93 season with plenty of experience. His side finished seventh in Courage League Two but with leagues being reorganised they were still relegated. They were runners up in League Three in 1993-94 and secured promotion back to level two by finishing top in his final season before he returned to pursue business and other coaching interests in the Bristol area.

**R M C Greed 1995-96**

Richard Greed was Bedford's first club captain and last coach before rugby went fully professional. He joined as a full back from Loughborough University and later in the season 1988-89 he was the player who scored the try in the 15-15 draw at Sale that earned the Blues promotion. He made 51 appearances before moving into coaching where the leadership qualities that convinced Ian Snook to appoint him club captain were put to good use with the Wanderers. Later he worked alongside Mike Rafter and Dick Tilley, who'd made his name with England Schools and Northampton. A master at Bedford School, Richard Greed took over in 1995 with assistance from Peter Cook, the former Nottingham captain. After full time coaches took over at Goldington Road, he went on to coach the England Schools and to continue his career as the master in charge of rugby at Radley College.

**G D Cooke OBE 1996-98**

Geoff Cooke was Director of Rugby in the 'Dream Team' that was put in place following the sale of the club to Frank Warren's Sports Network Europe. He had a pedigree second to none as one of the most successful rugby coaches or managers of the amateur era leading England in 49 internationals between 1987 and 1994 during which time the team won two successive Grand Slams in the Five Nations Championship, were finalists in the 1991 World Cup and won the World Sevens Cup in 1993. He was also manager of the British Lions tour to New Zealand in 1993. Quite simply Bedford couldn't have found anyone with greater credentials. He was charged with securing promotion which he did at the second attempt but left in December 1998 as the financial consequences of the freezing by the courts of Frank Warren's assets continued to bite. He became chief executive at Worcester and later chief executive of First Division Rugby Ltd until 2009. He was awarded the OBE in 1992 for services to rugby.

**P Turner 1996-98 and 1999**

Paul Turner was Director of Coaching in the 'Dream Team' – effectively the hands on coach who also played and captained the side from fly half as he had done when he came to prominence at Sale. In an early interview with the *Bedford Times and Citizen* he promised that his teams would play with smiles on their faces and he didn't disappoint with the side producing some of the best rugby ever seen at Goldington Road until the wheels started coming off. He left 'by mutual consent' in September 1998 and he set off on a coaching odyssey that took him to Saracens, Rugby Lions, Gloucester, Harlequins and Newport Gwent Dragons. He was tempted back to Bedford as Director of Rugby by the Jefferson Lloyd International consortium and to him fell the unedifying task of taking the players to Coventry after the 'sale'. He left again as part of the regime change soon after the supporters' buy-out in October 1999.

**R A W Straeuli 1998-99 and 2004-05**

Rudolf Straeuli was a giant of a South African number eight and a giant personality in the history of the Blues. He took over the playing side when first Paul Turner and then Geoff Cooke left in 1998 and he kept the squad together in some of the darkest days the club had known. Having featured in the World Cup Final of 1995, he was recruited as a player for the 1997-98 campaign and then, as things started to go wrong, he became an inspirational figure to players, officials and supporters, creating the spirit that saw the team survive the relegation play-offs.

He returned to South Africa soon after the club was sold to Jefferson Lloyd International but made a dramatic appearance in support of the buy-out at the meeting at Goldington Road on October 28, 1999. Rudi Straeuli made such rapid progress back home that he became coach of South Africa in 2002 but resigned after the 2003 World Cup. He returned to Bedford as Director of Rugby for the 2004-05 season and led the side to the Powergen Challenge Shield win at Twickenham in 2005 before resuming his career at the Natal Sharks in South Africa.

**A R Murdoch 1999-2000**

Alistair Murdoch was captain of the Blues when they survived the relegation play-offs against Rotherham in 1999 and a player and Director of Rugby when they lost to Rotherham the following year. He had to make the difficult decision to leave himself out of the team for the away leg in 2000 because the team had too many overseas qualified players. Having stepped up as captain in a crisis he took over as head coach when the club was overhauled at the buy-out of 1999 following the attempt to sell the club to Coventry by Jefferson Lloyd International – something he didn't hesitate to speak out against. He was a popular coach who did what he saw as his duty in taking over the reins in a crisis; but playing was where his heart was – on the wing for Australia, in the centre with Ben Whetstone for Bedford and on the wing for Scotland 'A' – and at the end of one of the most difficult seasons in the club's history, he left for Worcester and then moved on to Exeter.

**C S Jackson 2000–04**

Colin Jackson took over as Director of Rugby after relegation and had to start from scratch. The top players left and all the others were automatically out of contract. He was charged with making sure that the club survived in the second level – something he managed with a draw at Otley on the last day of his first season and then more comfortably in his next three. A New Zealander, he was prised from the all conquering Dunstablians of 1999-2000 and brought some core players with him. As an agent he knew how to discover players and recruit them – and among his signings were several who went on to become internationals including James Pritchard, Chris Horsman and Ben Hinshelwood. An excellent communicator, he steadied the ship, he established good relations with Northampton, signing several of their players, and he supported the progress of the youth section. When he left to become Chief Executive of North Otago Rugby, mission accomplished and the Blues back on their feet, the *Bedford Times and Citizen* back page headline read: "Good On Ya, Colin."

**M A Rayer 2005 -**

Mike Rayer's record as a player at Bedford is one of the most spectacular in its history. His main achievement as Director of Rugby was to turn the Blues from a middle of the table team in level two into one regularly in the top four – twice in the top two - and one with a reputation for playing exciting, open, running rugby shown at its best in the successful 2010-11 season. When Paul Turner started to assemble the All Stars of 1996-98, he told *BBC Three Counties Radio* that he was about to sign 'the best player in Wales' and the 21 times capped Mike Rayer, considered the first player to command a transfer fee, didn't disappoint with 62 appearances and points records in each of his two seasons. When the bubble burst he went back to Cardiff to resume his playing career and cut his teeth there in various coaching roles, developing a keen eye for young players in his own image that was to serve him well when the call came to invite him back to Goldington Road. In 2001 he was inducted into the Cardiff Blues Hall of Fame.

Many Bedford players and coaches went on to greater things, several with clubs, districts and regions and two with top tier countries. ABC Davies, a threequarter who played nine times for the Blues in 1970-71 while stationed locally in the RAF, became coach of Nottingham, then part of the England set up in the late 1980s and then coach of Wales between 1991 and 1995. RAW Straeuli whose qualities of inspiration and motivation shone through at Bedford during the crises of the late 1990s became coach of Borders, then Natal Sharks and eventually South Africa between 2002 and 2003.

The coaching team at Bedford, as listed in the match day programme, in season 2010-11 was:
Director of Rugby: M Rayer. Forwards Coach: M Hynes. Backs Coach: N Walshe. Strength and Conditioning Coach: J Bain. Team Manager: R Crowle. Assistant Coach: M Volland. Consultant Physiotherapist: S Jones. Head Physiotherapist: Miss M Evans. Sports Therapist: R Chaplin. Kit Manager: G Davies.

# THE PRESIDENTS

| | | |
|---|---|---|
| *Guy Pym MP* | *L A R Fensome* | *R H Haynes* |
| *E H Dasent* | *E M King* | *H F Rawkins* |
| *S R Wells MP* | *N J Timmins* | *D Fowler* |
| *Lord Luke* | *H Elliott MC* | *A P Goodman* |
| *H W Finlinson* | *D M King* | *G B Willey* |
| *E E Blake* | *H W Nightingale* | *J R Saunders* |
| *A Marshall* | *H Bitton* | *G W Davies* |

There were 21 Presidents in the first 125 years of the Blues - nine of them with Bedford Modern School connections, as pupil or teacher, and four with Bedford School allegiances. There were two MPs, one peer, two brothers, the man who brought the cinema to the town and another who was introduced to the club when he collected sheep droppings from the pitch for his grandfather who was one of the originals. One, Harry Elliott MC, served two terms.

**Guy Pym MP 1886-1914**

The club's first President was the town's MP at the time of its formation, Guy Pym. He held the Bedford seat for the Conservatives from 1895 until the Liberal landslide of 1906. Born in 1841, he was the youngest of a family of 14, whose seat was Hassells Hall, near Sandy. He is minuted as attending all the club's annual meetings up to the outbreak of war in 1914 and supporting it financially. He was Chairman of the Harpur Trust and a life size portrait of him is in their possession. Mr Pym died in 1918 and is the longest serving President in the club's history. Among the landmarks in his term of office were the opening of the first grandstand in 1905 and the Scrum Hall in 1910 as well as matches against the Barbarians and New Zealand.

**E H Dasent 1921-23**

Edward Hastings Dasent was the coach at Bedford Grammar School while a master there between 1883 and 1923, producing many fine players - one of whom, J G Milton, was capped for England while still at the school. Known as 'The Man', he made "Bedford School rugby the envy of all " said E H D Sewell, one of his captains, and author of the book 'Rugger – The Man's Game' (1944) dedicated to Dasent's "esteemed memory". He played for the Bedford Rovers, became President of the East Midlands and served on the Rugby Union for many years. He also became a referee and received praise from the press for his handling of the match between Bedford and Stade de France in Goldington Avenue in 1894 – not for his understanding of the game, but for his ability to speak French.

**S R Wells MP 1923-36**

Sydney Richard Wells was an all round sportsman at Bedford Grammar School where three of his brothers and four of his sons were also educated. He played for the Blues 80 times between 1898 and 1908 as a half back or back row forward. Two of his brothers, Hayward and Harry, both played for the first team. He was an active committee man before becoming President, an office which he also held at the town's rowing and association football clubs. A member of the brewing family, Charles Wells and Sons, he became Conservative MP for Bedford in 1922, turning a Liberal stronghold into a safe seat with a majority of more than 7,000 and holding it for a record 23 years until Labour won it in 1945. He was knighted in 1938 and was Chairman of the Harpur Trust from 1938 until his death in 1956.

**Lord Luke of Pavenham 1936-37**

The former George Lawson Johnston was invited to become the club's fourth President on the resignation of the man later to become Sir Richard Wells. Lord Luke was chairman of the Bovril empire – a high powered business based in London. He bought Pavenham Bury and, in 1934, Odell Castle as a country retreat. He became High Sheriff in 1924, a peer in 1929 and Lord Lieutenant of the County from 1936 until his death in 1943. Active in business and in the House of Lords, he held the office for one year.

**H W Finlinson 1937-38**

Horace William Finlinson, remembered as 'Finny' was the son of Wilkinson Finlinson, headmaster of the Commercial School when it changed its name to Bedford Modern. An Old Modernian himself, he played 38 times for Bedford between 1891 and 1906, and against them in the colours of the Barbarians in 1894 and for Blackheath with whom he made 76 appearances between 1892 and 1898. He was capped three times in 1895 – against Scotland, Ireland and Wales – and each time he wore the England shirt, his Blackheath clubmate W B Thomson, the Modern School's first international, was in the same side. Two brothers A L and M E Finlinson both played for Bedford. 'Finny' became, in 1897, the first captain of the East Midlands. A master at Lancing College with interest in Ornithology and Zoology, he came back to the town on his retirement and became Chairman from 1933 until 1945.

**E E Blake 1938-61**

Ernie Blake was a great figurehead and benefactor and the younger brother of William Blake, Bedford's Chairman between 1927 and 1933. The brothers were the early pioneers of local cinema, taking a gas illuminated projector around the villages in a pony and trap, showing animated photographs in schoolrooms and halls around the turn of the century. Ernest Edgar was born in 1879 and died, aged 82, in 1961 while still President. He started work in his father's photographic firm Blake and Edgar and, with his brother, opened Bedford's first cinema at the Association Hall on the corner of Silver Street and Harpur Street in 1909. In 1910 they opened the Picturedrome on the Embankment and in 1915 the Empire in Midland Road, later to become part of the Granada Group. In 1903 he joined the Kodak company on 45 shillings a week, says C G Peck in *Bedfordshire Cinemas* (1981), and he rose through the ranks to become Chairman by 1946 at £20,000 a year – a huge salary at the time. Rugby was one of the great passions of his life, nurtured at BMS and as a member of the Bedford Wanderers, an independent club which flourished in the late 1890s.

### A Marshall 1962-65

Arthur Marshall took over as President on the death of Ernie Blake and died in office himself having risen to the highest position in rugby. He was the 50th President of the RFU in 1957-58. He was educated at Goldington School and was converted from soccer when he decided to have a go at the Bedford Athletic club in 1921. He moved on to the Blues and was a regular between 1922 and 1933 making 250 appearances in the front row before retiring and turning his skills to official channels. He became secretary of Bedford and in 1937 secretary of the East Midlands. In 1945 he became the East's representative on the Rugby Union and served on many important committees before becoming Vice-President and then President, and then President of the East Midlands and of Bedford. He was the first Bedford player to achieve the Presidency of the RFU and when his son Tony became Bedford captain, the family achieved another record as the only father and son to hold that office. Arthur served on the International Board in 1963-64 and framed the schools' section rules.

### L A R Fensome 1965-68

Aubrey Fensome watched his father Archie play rugby for the Kempston club and decided to follow in his footsteps. He was educated at a non rugby playing school, the Harpur Elementary known as Bates' School. Born in 1900, he was apprenticed as a carpenter and joiner and later took over the family building business. He joined the army under age and on his demob set about joining a rugby club. He went to meetings held to get the Blues going again after the war and was given a game in the front row of the 'A' team. Then he was moved to the centre where he made his debut for the first team in 1921-22 but changed to the wing and took over the position vacated by 'Jim', C A E C Howard on his retirement. He became club captain, 1925-27, but broke his leg in December 1926 just days before he was invited to play in an England trial. He came back, switched to wing forward and retired in 1933 after 196 appearances, scoring 97 tries and modestly describing himself as "not as fast as Rex Alston." Maurice Pugh and R G G Squibbs were among his favourite players. Aubrey Fensome served the club in many offices after his retirement. He also became President of the East Midlands.

### E M King 1968-70

Eric Maltravers King was one of the club's great administrators, becoming fixtures secretary in 1928, club secretary in 1937 and then again from 1945 until his death in 1970. Educated at Bedford Modern School, he was captain of the XV there in 1922 but didn't play other than for the Bank of England on leaving. His father was an early committee man at the club, his uncle a chairman of the Athletic and his brother Don was President when the Blues won the cup in 1975. Eric joined the bank when he left school and it was said that he used to run the club on the 7.15am commuters' train from Midland Road to St Pancras. "Bedford must always remain first class" was his passionate belief – whatever the cost. Eric lived for the Blues and he died supporting them, suffering a heart attack in the stand at Northampton during a charity match in April 1970. Many visiting players and pressmen were grateful to Eric and Molly King for after-match hospitality at the family home.

### N J Timmins 1970-72

Norman Timmins was elected President after serving the club for many years as both player and officer. Educated at Bedford School, he joined the Athletic on leaving in 1923 and played there until 1928 when he was recruited by Peter Perkins who was looking for a man of stature to captain the 'A' team, later to be known as the Wanderers. He made a number of first team appearances but skippered the second side for three years. At the time it included such fine players as Geoff Kelly, Jimmy Grey, Claud Quarry and Percy Scrivener. He became chairman of selectors for six years and with a background in insurance, (he worked at the Sun with Ronnie Eidsforth), he was an invaluable assistant secretary from 1936 until 1971, working closely with Eric King. He said that the best team he saw at Bedford in 60 years was the one brought together just before the Second World War.

### H Elliott MC 1972-74 and 1986-87

Harry Elliott

Harry Elliott was elected President for the club's Centenary celebration season, the first person to hold the office for a second term having been succeeded after a first. By 1986-87, he had completed 50 years with the Blues. He joined as a player in 1936-37 when he moved to the town to take up a post with the Cryselco company from which he retired as director and general manager. His playing career was broken by the 1939-45 war where as Major Elliott, he served with distinction in the Worcestershire Regiment and was awarded the Military Cross for bravery in the Far East. Returning to the club, he made 48 appearances in the second row between 1946 and 1949, later to become Wanderers captain. He was team secretary from 1948 until 1952 and with the retirement of Peter Perkins in 1959 he took over as Chairman, an office which he held for a record 22 years in an era of great strides forward. A popular figure on the first class circuit, he was also President of the East Midlands.

### D M King 1974-76

Donald King was Eric King's younger brother. He had the same family middle name, Maltravers, went to the same school, Bedford Modern, worked like Eric at the Bank of England and married Joan, the sister of Eric's wife, Molly. At school, Eric was the captain of rugby. Donald was the captain of cricket. At the Blues, while Eric was the President when Bedford won the *Sunday Telegraph's* English-Welsh Pennant, Donald was President when Bedford won the RFU Club Competition in 1975. One of Eric's great passions was the Bedford fixture list and after Donald came out of war service in the RAF he started more than 30 years' service as a committee man at the Blues when Eric entrusted him with the state of health of that list.

**H W Nightingale 1976-78**

Harold Walker 'Jack' Nightingale was part of the backroom team at the Blues put together by Peter Perkins and Eric King during the war. As a local businessman, managing director of the fertiliser firm, Alfred Nightingale and Sons, in Duck Mill Lane, he was invited on to the committee. Educated at BMS, most of his sporting prowess was shown on the cricket field. As a member of the ground committee and an expert on fertiliser, he was first asked to take over responsibility for the ground and he served the club for 40 years in such capacities as sponge man, laundry organiser and barman. One of his earliest tasks was to turn up to the Scrum Hall three times a week to light the boilers that heated the six baths so that players could clean up after training and matches. Even as President, he continued to do the most mundane, but essential, daily chores to ensure the smooth running of the club. One of his proudest achievements was in being able to offer employment to Leo Oakley in his family firm.

**H W Bitton 1978-80**

Harry Bitton was the son of a missionary in China. Born in South London in 1914, he was educated at the missionary school, Eltham College, where Scottish international Eric Liddle, a famous sprinter later to become missionary, and A L Gracie were former pupils. He studied maths at Cambridge University in one of their golden eras for rugby and took up a teaching post at Blackpool Grammar School. While a member of the Fylde club, an accident on a mountain put to an end his playing career and convinced him that he should concentrate on coaching. He joined the staff at Bedford Modern School in 1950 and was master in charge of rugby from 1954 until 1960. E E Blake proposed, and L A R Fensome seconded, that the coaches at Bedford Modern and Bedford School be co-opted and so Harry Bitton joined the committee, becoming vice-chairman to Harry Elliott, a man he considered an outstanding administrator.

**R H Haynes 1980-81**

Reginald Herbert 'Tich' Haynes was born in Honey Hill Road, Bedford, educated at Queen's Park School, Bedford School and Oxford University where he won a wartime 'colour'. He was a member of the famous Bedford School teams that included Leo Oakley, Murray Fletcher and Peter, later Sir Peter, Parker. He made his Bedford debut at fly half in the Easter of 1943 and went on to become one of the club greats with an outstanding partnership with his school scrum half Murray Fletcher. He made 155 appearances and his 597 points was once the fourth highest in the club's history: 120 conversions, 58 penalties, 40 tries and 20 dropped goals. He was vice-captain in 1952-3, retired at the end of the season but came back, to be cheered off the field, for a match against Coventry after a late drop out. In the 1949-50 season he had a trial for England. An executive with Kodak, he helped with selection when he finished playing and was team secretary from 1966 until 1970. He held the President's office for just one year, having to stand down when he was posted out of the area.

Celebrations at Twickenham in 2005

Fans at Twickenham

James Pritchard

Billy Twelvetrees

Ollie Dodge

Sacha Harding

Junior Paramore

Mike Howard

Ali Hepher

Ben Whetstone

Karl Dickson

Mr Beefcake Tonga'uiha

East Midlands President Paul McGuckian presents the National Colts Cup to George Messum at Northampton in May 2011

Mouritz Botha, capped by England in August 2011

The 2010-11 squad

Ladies Day in the marquee

Margaret

Paula and Baz

### H F Rawkins 1981-84

Harry Rawkins was born in the brewery house in Dagnell, Bucks in 1913 and moved with his family to the village of Renhold in 1919. He started school at Bedford Modern in 1924 but took little interest there in rugby. When he left, he played in goal for the village soccer team but was advised by a spectator, an injured rugby player, to join Bedford Athletic which he did, later becoming captain. He was then invited to play for the town and made his debut in the second row against the Met Police on March 29, 1937. After a career in insurance, he joined the Bedfs and Herts Regiment in Kempston in 1940 (he always insisted on the spelling 'Bedfs') and retired as a Major in 1968 having turned out for service teams, skippered many of them and become a referee. Gilbert Cook invited him to join the committee at the Blues when he returned home from Germany and he became assistant fixture secretary and a most popular President with an enthusiastic wife, Kay. In 1981-82 he was President of the East Midlands.

### D Fowler 1984-86

The club's President in its 100th year was appropriately the grandson of one of its founder members. Doug Fowler's earliest childhood memories are of collecting sheep droppings before the games at Goldington Road where his grandfather Tommy was the part-time groundsman, having been a player in the club's first season and a member of both of its parent clubs, the Rovers and the Swifts. Tommy had four sons, two of whom played for Bedford. One became a well-known cyclist and the other a racehorse trainer in France. Young Doug operated the clock and ran the line for the second team from the age of 12. He was a county class soccer player at Queen's Park School and played rugby while he was apprenticed at Britannia Works and later at the Igranic and the Athletic. He became director of a number of firms in the electrical business in the north of England and had a Yorkshire trial in 1938. He retired as owner of a printing firm in Bedford and the author of a script on kicking. His father, Ralph, was a Blues player and former classmate at Ampthill Road School of Peter Perkins. Doug Fowler was recruited to the club by Harry Elliott and served as membership secretary, chairman of finance and was a keen force in the new clubhouse project.

### H Elliott MC 1986-87

Harry Elliott was a popular choice to become the club's President in its Centenary season, having previously served in the same office from 1972 until 1974. In 1986, he completed his own half century at the club. In his foreword to '100 Years of the Blues', he captured the mood of members and the state of play perfectly. He wrote: "We reach our Centenary at a difficult time for the club in particular and for the game we love so much in general. Yet those of us with long memories know that this has usually been the case over the years. Rugby football has always been at the crossroads. The Blues, like other clubs, have faced many crises in 100 years. Little worth preserving is without its ups and downs. We have known the greatest success both on the field and off it. We have also known disappointment; yet we have never lost sight of the fact that rugby is about much more....We shall enjoy our Centenary and use it wisely. I believe that we have the people to take us out of our current depression; and at the end of the season we should be in good heart to face our next 100 years....We shall look back in affection at our glorious past yet be well aware of our responsibilities to ensure an exciting future."

**A P Goodman 1987-92**

Tony Goodman

Tony Goodman brought an entrepreneurial flair to the committee room without ever losing sight of what really made a rugby club tick. He had business interests in a number of prominent companies in the area. But having been a player at the Old Haberdashers, Harlequins and the Saracens Wednesday Club it was to the terraces and the Scrum Hall that he was drawn when he moved to Bedford. He bought a piano for the after match sing song and eagerly set up a group known among themselves as the eight before eight club (eight pints before 8pm). He drove many of them to away games in his Rolls Royce. In the bar after a match in Gloucester, he overheard the former England lock John Orwin say he wanted to become a publican when he left the RAF but no one would help him. He said: "I'll help you - if you play for Bedford," and so Orwin joined, became captain, saw the Blues promoted to level one and resurrected his England career into the bargain - so much so that he became captain. Having served on the social committee, Tony Goodman was soon invited to become President and later helped bring others, including coach Ian Snook, to the club. He said that being made President was the greatest and most unexpected honour of his life. He was a generous benefactor and host and a friend to many from all walks of life.

**G B Willey 1992-99**

Bruce Willey

Bruce Willey was a successful local businessman with a military background and a prominent profile on the social scene of Bedfordshire. As Chairman from 1990 until 1992 and President from 1992 until his untimely death in 1999, he was seen as someone with the attributes and authority needed at a difficult time in which the Blues, having tasted an uncomfortable season in the top tier, were soon in the third. The dawn of the professional era gave the club another opportunity to remain first class and Bruce Willey's negotiating skills, tact and good humour helped it make the transition from the amateur era with ease while never taking his eye off the legacy of the past. Many saw him as the person who had already turned around the fortunes of Bedford Rowing Club during his term as President there with the Britannia Cup win at Henley in its Centenary in 1986 just one of the highlights. Educated at Bedford Modern School, Bruce Willey was commissioned in the Royal Artillery. Later he worked in the motor trade and became an auctioneer. He continued to support his old school, serving as President of the former pupils' club between 1987 and1989 and as a governor from 1989 until his death. He and his wife Gill hosted many memorable end of season parties at their home in Podington. In 1998 he was appointed a Deputy Lieutenant for Bedfordshire.

**J R Saunders 2000-03**

John Saunders

John Saunders was the perfect choice to become the 20th President. He took office at a time when the club was finding its feet again following the period of trauma prior to the buy-back of 1999. His appointment showed that Bedford would strive to return to the values that had served it so well over the years. A man with no side, John Saunders represented the traditional rugby man - a tireless worker for the greater good, respected by players, volunteers, officials, administrators and the media. His many roles included Wanderers secretary from 1976 until 1980, first team secretary from 1980 until 1992 and fixture secretary from 1983 until 1995. As a local farmer, his tractors, mowers and other machinery were often used on the Goldington Road pitch and his straw and covers were much appreciated during bad weather. He and his wife, Margaret, an enthusiastic woman of the countryside and a leading light in the teams of ladies who made the players' teas in the Scrum Hall, were famous for welcoming players and their families to their home and to the club. An organised tour of their dairy farm was a must for all young newcomers. Once the *Bedfordshire Times* referred to them as the 'Mother and Father of the Blues'. In 1994, John Saunders was made a Life Member.

**G W Davies 2003 -**

Gareth Davies

Gareth Davies was a popular ambassador for the Blues who brought to the office the authority of a former player, the skill of a school teacher and the love of the club of a genuine fan. He was brought up in the same Welsh village as Carwyn James and Barry John and played at Llanelli, London Welsh and Bedford, the town where he lived for most of his life. He became kit manager in 1991 and, even as President from 2003, he continued in his hands-on role in the 'boot room' at Goldington Road - much like one of his predecessors, Jack Nightingale. Gareth Davies joined Bedford after securing a job at Westfield School. He played 81 games for the first team and many more for the others at the club turning out at some time or other in his career in every position in the backs. In 2011, he was still the holder of the club's record for dropped goals. He made his name as a kicking fly half, and he captained the Wanderers, Rovers and Rams before retiring as a player in 1988. He helped set up the mini section in 1973, served on committees in the amateur days and was team manager from 1998 until 2001. He was made a Life Member in 2001. In 2009, his wife, Marie, became the first woman to be so honoured in the history of the club.

# THE CHAIRMEN

*J W Carter*
*Rev S W Hartley*
*W N Blake*
*H W Finlinson*
*A H Perkins OBE*
*H Elliott MC*
*K W Phillips*
*G B Willey*
*I M Bullerwell*
*F Warren*
*Jefferson Lloyd Int.*
*D Ledsom*
*G S I Irvine*

Before 1921, the office of Chairman, did not exist. In the early days, the captain was expected to take the chair at meetings, but during The First World War, a number of meetings were held at the home of the secretary, Mr Cannon, at 1 Ashburnham Road, the main business of which seems to have been the attempt to get money out of the army for the use of Goldington Road. The most important meeting after the war was the one advertised in the press for August 21, 1919, at the King's Arms in St Mary's Street. It invited members and supporters to come and talk over the affairs and prospects of the club. Its great problem was that the military had hung on to the very end and there was no prospect of playing on the ground that season. The man who was to become the club's first chairman was voted to the chair at that and a number of meetings that followed. The office itself was instituted at the annual meeting of 1921.

**J W Carter 1921-22**

John Walton Carter was the club's first elected Chairman. He served one of the most difficult terms as the Blues tried to get things together again after The First World War. He was no stranger to taking the chair at meetings having been a member of the committee since 1902. He was born in Shefford in 1857 but moved soon after to Bedford where his father J B Carter founded a wholesale business in Lime Street. J W Carter was an ardent Liberal and supporter of Samuel Whitbread, a good speaker, Governor of the Harpur Trust and a member of the Bedford Town Council in 1900. One of the founders of the Bedford Bowling Club, in 1910, he was one of the four businessmen who each agreed to become a guarantor for the loan used to build the new Scrum Hall. Charles Franklin, S R Wells and E H C Inskip were the others. He served for one year only because of ill health and his obituary in the *Bedfordshire Times* in September 1924 said that he would long be remembered as a genial and sympathetic friend and companion and as a public spirited member of the community.

**Rev S V Hartley 1922-27**

The club's second elected Chairman was 'Tonk' Hartley, a teacher of Latin and Maths at Bedford Modern School and the Vicar of Elstow at the same time. Says Andrew Underwood in *Bedford Modern School of the Black and Red* (1981) "In 1945 he succeeded Mr Blackburn as Second Master. His particular sporting interest was rugby and from 1920 until 1928 he was a highly successful coach to the First XV. The 'Tonk' was a bat shaped wooden device of very certain purpose." The Reverend Hartley was born in Yorkshire, educated at Carlisle, Ripon and Oxford and came to Bedford as curate to St Mary's Church in 1915. In 1919 he took up the appointment at Bedford Modern School and was offered the living at Elstow. He was interested in coaching duties at a difficult time at the Blues and as Chairman led the team that was still engaged in rebuilding the club. He was succeeded as coach at BMS by P J King, who he had turned into a hooker at the Blues. At the club the captain and senior players like Albert Joy and Frank Holmes, who built up a strong 'A' team, were responsible for training. The Reverend Hartley died in 1953, aged 66, and one of his sons, Peter, who wrote a book on life in a Japanese prisoner of war camp, took over at Elstow. One of his duties was to officiate at the wedding of Brian McCarthy, a member of the Blues' 300 Club.

**W N Blake 1927-32**

William Norman 'Bill' Blake was the elder brother of Ernie Blake, President of the Blues from 1938 until 1961. He was born in Bedford in 1870, educated privately at Miss Francis' School and rose to become the acknowledged head of the cinema industry in Bedfordshire and neighbouring counties. It is said (C G Peck, 1981) that he took some of the earliest animated photographs ever made in England for which he received recognition at leading exhibitions. The Blake brothers were camera men at Queen Victoria's Jubilee in 1897 and Bill became President of the Cinematograph Association in 1926-27. His great passion, besides the cinema, was rugby football and he joined the Blues committee after the war. He was a great benefactor and popular Chairman who hardly missed an away match. He died in office in September 1932 having already put the wheels in motion for the new stand, the one still in use in 2011. His widow and brother made substantial contributions towards its cost of £1,760 and it was opened, with a plaque inscribed to his memory, by Sir Percy Royds, 29th President of the RFU with a special game against Northampton on September 7, 1933. A keen athlete in his youth, Bill was an early patron of the Camera Club and an active member of the Magpie Pigeon Club, having at the time of his death one of the best hens in the country. He never forgot the early days where he used to watch the Rovers and two years before he died he started the 'Pinkie' Booth Fund.

**H W Finlinson 1933-45**

Horace Finlinson was the club's fourth Chairman. He is profiled as its fifth President.

**A H Perkins OBE, 1945-59**

Arthur Harry 'Peter' Perkins was born at Clapham in 1888 and he completed his education at Bates' School, later the Harpur Central. He 'entered the service of the county' at the age of 14 and when a finance department was set up in 1918, he became County Treasurer, a position he held until his retirement in 1951 when he was awarded the OBE. Outside Shire Hall his main interest was the well being of Bedford Rugby Union Football Club. As a youth, he was a member of the St Cuthbert's soccer club but he was invited to join the committee of the Blues in 1928 and he became one of the greats, living at 101 Goldington Road and accompanied for years by his Great Dane, "Bruf". At the County Hall, he surrounded himself with rugby lovers. The Chairman, Sir Thomas Keens described him as a keen disciplinarian and a glutton for work. At the Blues, he is best remembered as the man who kept the club together during The Second World War. In his distinctive handwriting he wrote to players all over the world in his capacity as team secretary from1939 until 1947. He made certain that players were kept in touch with news of each other, that the club was able to put teams out and, above all, that it didn't suffer the sort of problems it did after The First World War.

**H Elliott MC 1959-81**

Harry Elliott was Chairman for a record 22 years. He is profiled as President from 1972-74, and in the Centenary season.

**K W Phillips 1981-1990**

Ken Phillips

Ken Phillips masterminded the successful Centenary effort at the Blues and represented the Senior Clubs on the RFU at a time when merit tables and leagues were introduced and when professionalism made it to the rugby agenda. He was born in Barnstaple, Devon and educated at Huish's Grammar School, Taunton. Pursuing a career in local government, he became the Bedfordshire County Council Trading Standards Officer. He joined the Blues as a player and made seven first team appearances between 1964 and 1968, captaining the Wanderers between 1966 and 1968. With 'Tod' Slaughter, he was mainly responsible for the honours board in the Scrum Hall and, with Maurice Webb and Doug Fowler, was one of the prime forces in the drive for the new clubhouse. He took over as fixture secretary from Don King and built up a formidable list, he was on the selection committee when the Blues won the cup and he served as team secretary from 1977 until 1980 and vice-chairman to Harry Elliott. He determined to use the Centenary celebrations to encourage members to look back on a glorious past and face the new realities of the future. He set up a Centenary committee in 1981 and it commissioned *100 Years of the Blues* soon after. As rugby prepared itself for a more competitive structure Ken Phillips chaired the Senior Clubs Committee which first recommended the institution of the official merit tables that led to leagues. He sat on the RFU as representative for the Midlands Senior Clubs.

**G B Willey 1990-92**

Bruce Willey succeeded Ken Phillips as Chairman at a difficult time in the club's development following the Centenary and the reality that followed the introduction of leagues. Having served a highly successful term at Bedford Rowing Club, he was seen as someone with the necessary clout and authority to take over; but after two seasons he persuaded Ian Bullerwell to become Chairman and he became President. "Because of his status in the town and contacts in the community he was the perfect person to have on board in any capacity," said Graham Tucker of the Gentlemen of Sharnbrook.

**I M Bullerwell 1992-97**

Ian Bullerwell

Ian Bullerwell was at the helm when the club took the most momentous decision in its history – to sell 90 per cent of itself to the boxing promoter Frank Warren in 1996. As rugby turned professional, he took the call asking if Bedford would be interested, he met the potential investors and then took the issue firstly to the committee and then to the membership at a famous meeting in the County Hotel on June 4 where the motion to sell was overwhelmingly accepted. He had doubts, he had some regrets but in an interview in 2009 he said that he was convinced that the club had to do something drastic at the time or lose its status. In hindsight, he thought, it was all the stronger for its experiences in the difficult times that followed the initial euphoria. And he was right. When things went pear-shaped in 1999, he was blamed by some though it was clearly nothing to do with him. However, it was generally acknowledged that he played a major role in generating support among the business community, especially, for the rescue operation – something confirmed by Geoff Irvine at the 2011 annual meeting when Ian Bullerwell was an important member of the board. He followed in the footsteps of many from Bedford Modern School by serving the club as both player and officer. He joined straight from school in 1966 and soon came under the influence of Alan Lovell in the Rovers and Rams. An injury ended his playing career, so he took up refereeing and was fast tracked by the East Midlands Society. He attained a high profile in the game as a member of the international panel between 1988 and 1991, refereeing the famous match in which Romania beat Wales in Cardiff in 1988.

**F Warren 1997-99**

Frank Warren

Frank Warren was a world famous London based boxing promoter and one of a number of sporting entrepreneurs who decided to invest in rugby when it went professional. Bedford members could hardly believe it when it became clear that he wanted to be involved and to invest unheard of sums into the club through his company Sports Network Europe - recruiting famous managers, coaches and players and setting a target of promotion to the top tier of rugby. Supporters accepted the project wholeheartedly and week after week they sat back and waited for the next sensational announcement. The former head of ITV Sport, Bob Burrows, arrived as chief executive, Geoff Cooke, one of the most respected England coaches, became Director of Rugby and Paul Turner, a highly respected former Welsh international became effectively player-coach. Martin Offiah, a rugby league legend, was one of many stars to turn out for Bedford in a short golden era. Frank Warren was an enthusiastic convert to the sport and did everything he said he would as the Blues swept all before them in 1997-98 to earn promotion to Premiership One. The dream stalled only when his assets were frozen in the courts in a dispute with the American boxing promoter Don King and a judge effectively told him to dispose of his interests in rugby while the case, which in the end he lost, proceeded. One can only imagine what would have happened had he been able to stay on board.

**Jefferson Lloyd International 1999**

There is no question that Frank Warren did his best for Bedford. And more. But he was ordered to sell his interest in the club and concentrate on his core business – and that was putting on boxing promotions; not running a rugby club. Various groups expressed an interest in taking over. Some felt they lacked support and stood aside. In the end, Jefferson Lloyd International, acquired the club for a nominal sum in April 1999. Few knew anything about them; but they were introduced as bona fide investors by, perhaps naive, local supporters who, few doubted, had the club's interest at heart. A board of directors was formed and at least two chairmen named in match day programmes. One of them denied he was chairman and that he ever chaired a meeting. Another, who was never introduced to the media, bore the name of someone who later emerged at Luton Town when John Gurney, who gradually emerged as the man behind the Jefferson Lloyd project, took over there for another hardly believable episode in the life of a long established Bedfordshire sporting institution.

### D Ledsom 1999-2001

Dave Ledsom

Dave Ledsom was the most prominent figure in the buy-out from Jefferson Lloyd International when supporters raised more than half a million pounds in a fortnight to reclaim the club. He was the front man - with internet entrepreneur Mick Kavanagh and local accountant Dave Rawlinson in support. His was the 'establishment' face acceptable to the vendors, the person who was able to represent ordinary supporters, business interests, the local authority and the man in the street who wasn't that interested in rugby but who followed the Blues and who knew what the club meant to the town. Said his successor Geoff Irvine soon after his tragic death in November 2008: "Without his massive influence, Bedford Blues would probably not exist in its present form." Dave Ledsom came from Liverpool and was a soccer fan. He helped set up what became a hugely successful building firm in Bedford and from the very beginning he immersed himself into the community, supporting and sponsoring all sorts of activities. He helped popularise St George's Day and raise vast sums for the 'St George's Day Charity.' He became an officially adopted son of Bedford and one of the most popular personalities at the rugby club. His memorial service was held in the Blues' Marquee, the former players' bar was extended in memory of him and the club administrator, Tony Mills, and the council introduced The Dave Ledsom Civic Award in recognition of his work in the community.

### G S I Irvine 2001 -

Geoff Irvine

Geoff Irvine was a self-made businessman who steered the Blues into a period of stability off the pitch and success on it. He took over from his friend Dave Ledsom once the club had started to find its feet again after the buy-out of October 1999. Right from the start of his term of office he was determined to get the club financially sound, to have local players come into the first team through an academy programme and for the side to play an attractive brand of rugby. He launched a series of rights issues to shareholders, investing heavily himself – on one occasion matching funding to the tune of £250,000. A former pupil at Bedford Modern School, he was an all round and well known local sportsman who was committed to the town to such an extent that at the age of just 24 he was appointed to the board of the 'Eagles', then the town's successful Southern League soccer club. It was an experience that was to serve him well in striving for financial rigour on behalf of organisations whose instincts are to spend and also in appointing the right people to carry out his objectives. His success in turning Bedford into what was described in 2010 by *Rugby Times* as a model club saw him become chairman of the National One, later Championship, clubs, representing them at the RFU and helping shape the way the sport was run below the top tier. Launching an appeal to raise £75,000 for new floodlights at the annual meeting of 2011, he told shareholders that the club was on course to balance the books for the first time since the buy-out.

### Other principal officers

As the club grew, so players handed over duties in administration to others keen and able to perform them. In the first year of the Blues, there was a committee of no more than eight, most of whom were players, but the First World War in particular made it clear that players could not conduct the affairs of the club on their own. By 1986 there were more than 100 positions taken on at least nine committees but by 1996 when the club went professional the volunteer administrator gave way to the paid official. Some, like Graham Radford, the team secretary, carried on in a new role of paid team manager; but most did not.

Principal officers, besides President and Chairman, up to the advent of professionalism in 1996 were:

Secretaries:

A F Dudley (1886-88), J Gilchrist Crossman (1888-91), A Parrott (1891-93), A G Goodison (1893-94), A Parrott (1894-96), A Ingram (1896-98), R Thompson (1898-1902), G C Wood (1902-04), A P Clarke (1904-05), H Willett (1905-08), H C MacNaughton (1908-09), R Willett (1909-10), F W Cannon (1910-20), V F Farr (1920-21); Capt E H G Chambers (1921-22); P W Bandey (1922-24); W P Mayo (1924-28), P W Bandey (1928-30), F G Hore (1930-32), J N White (1932-33), A Marshall (1933-37), E M King (1937-38), H A N Tebbs (1938-42), A Marshall (1942-45), E M King (1945-70), J Jewell (1970-73), L J Bridgeman (1973-77), M L Bridgeman (1977-80), A Mills (1980-86), R Evans (1987-89) A Mills (1989-96).

Assistant Secretaries:

N J Timmins (1936-71), L J Bridgeman (1971-73), J Jewell (1973-77), A K Towersey (1977-85), R Evans (1985-86), A Mills (1987-88), P Smith (1993-96).

Treasurers:

A F Dudley (1886-88), W Brown (1888-89), J Gilchrist Crossman (1889-91), A Parrott (1891-93), A G Goodison (1893-94), W Gilpin (1894-98), F S P Saunders (1898-1903), H B Flook (1903-06), H Nelson Tebbs (1906-12), W H Plewman (1912-20), E H Hime (1920-21), H B Flook (1921-22), W P Mayo (1922-29), B Edgington (1927-42), A Marshall (1942-44), E J C Brown (1944-64), L R Drury (1964-68), D P Southgate (1968-72), J Claridge (1972-76), J F Walker (1976-80), R M Wilkinson (1980-83), P Hulance (1983-86), D Taylor (1989-91), A Knight (1991-96).

Assistant Treasurers:

J G Rogers (1948-49), R G Newell (1949-58), H P E Esnouf (1958-72), D Fowler (1972-73), J Claridge (1976-81), J F Walker (1981-86), K Sheldon (1989-90), G Bygraves (1991-92), P Bowker (1993-1996).

Membership Secretaries:

D Fowler (1972-82), P Hulance (1982-84), B Hire (1984-89), P Smith 1989-96).

Medical Advisors:

Dr H Martin Coombs (appointed in 1931), Dr A J Chillingsworth (1934), Dr G J Griffiths (1936), Dr C V Fraser (1958), Dr W Murdie (1958), Dr B H Hamilton (1967), Dr R E W Main (1967), Dr G A Robson (1977), Dr B Crawford (1991), Dr J Hood (1991), Dr S Lowe (1998), Dr C Baldock (1998), Dr S Short (1998), Dr D Niblett (2000), Dr Sarah Snape (2006).

Legal Advisors:

H N Tebbs (appointed 1929), K G Rose (1952), J Rose (1976), R E Stubbings (1995).

Sponsorship and Advertising Secretaries:

R Forsyth (1989-90), Ms M Garner (1992-96).

Commercial Manager:

R Forsyth (1989-90 and 1991-92).

Administrator:

JR Saunders (1992-96).

Ground Administrator:

**D Shawl (1995-96).**

Fixture Secretaries:

D B Welland (1927-28), E M King (1928-37), A Marshall (1937-38), E M King (1938-56), D M King (1956-73), K W Phillips (1973-83), J R Saunders (1983-96).

Assistant Fixture Secretaries:

P Boon (1986-89), T Beard (1989-95).

Team Secretaries:

First XV: M E Finlinson (1903-04), S R Wells (1907-12), D W Aldridge (1912-13), A V Manton (1913-14), A Leach (1919-21), H H Wood (1921-22), P W Bandey (1922-23), H A Bence (1923-25), S Crawley (1925-28), A Marshall (1928-32), L A R Fensome (1932-36), H R Newton (1936-40), A H Perkins (1940-48), H Elliott (1948-52), G Jenkins (1952-55), T L Lloyd (1955-61), L G Chubb (1961-63), J French (1963-64), R A Lovell (1964-66), R H Haynes (1966-70), M Bridgeman (1970-77), K W Phillips (1977-80), J R Saunders (1980-92), B Fletcher (1992-94), G Radford (1994-96).

Second XV Secretaries:

D B Welland (1925-27), C J Churchill (1927-33), B J Holloway (1933-35), F Holmes (1935-40), P C Previte (1946-47), K Vane-Percy (1947-48), R V Spark (1948-49), P E Green (1949-50), G S S Gilbert (1951-52), I L Williamson (1952-53), R S B Luckman (1953-54), T L Lloyd (1954-57), L Chubb (1957-61), C J Perry (1961-63), M L Bridgeman (1963-64), C Rogers (1964-66), J Jewell (1966-70), M L Bridgeman (1970-73), T Bullerwell (1973-76), J R Saunders (1976-80), S O'Neill (1980-82), A Kirk (1982-83), R Forsyth (1983-84), D Mathews (1984-89), B Fletcher (1989-90), G Brown (1990-91), J Cooley (1991-92), B Fletcher (1992-93), T Wickens (1993-94), D Shawl (1994-95), R Crowle (1995-96).

Rovers Secretaries:

D Bodger (1961-62), M L Bridgeman (1962-63), C Lovell (1963-64), Hilton Elliott (1964-65), J Jewell (1965-68), R A Lovell (1968-74), B R Black (1974-76), M Lilley (1976-77), B R Black (1977-79), I O'Hara (1979-81), A P Kirk (1981-82), K McKenna (1982-84), M Lilley (1984-90), D O'Kane (1992-93), B McGee (1993-94).

Rams Secretaries:

R A Lovell (1970-74), B R Black (1974-79), A P Kirk (1979-82), B Pinsent (1982-85), M Lilley (1985-90).

Colts Secretaries:

D Matthews (1978-84), B Fletcher (1984-87), H Sheard (1987-89).

Colts Managers:

P Roberts (1989-90), Mrs J Bostock (1990-93), Mrs I Britton (1993-2004), T Dancer (2004-2006), M Elliott (2006-2009).

Under 21 Managers:

P Roberts (1990-92), C Baines (1992-93), S Ashton (1993-94).

Development XV manager:

S Spring (1995-96).

Academy Managers:

J Keates (2000-2003), D Ormesher (2003-2008), S Low (2008-2010).

Academy Director:

D Ormesher (2010-)

### Board of directors

From 1996 onwards, the club was run by a board of directors, a chief executive, a director in charge of rugby and a full time professional staff. The club directory for 2010-11 listed the following:

Chairman: G Irvine. Directors: I Bullerwell, R Glasspool, D Gunner, M Howe, P Smith, D Twigden. Chief Executive: A Irvine. President: G Davies. Director of Rugby: M Rayer. Club Doctors: Dr J Hood, Dr D Niblett, Dr S Short, Dr Sarah Snape. Company Secretary: A Buchanan. Rugby Administrator: Mrs D Rayer. Ground Manager: P Beard. Groundsman: N Cooley. Safety Officer: D Muirhead. Marketing Consultant: E Carroll. Press Officer: S Hutchinson. Club Photographer: N Rudgard. Functions Manager: Mrs M White. Shop Manager: Mrs R Beard. Bar Manager: P Day. Club Chaplain: Rev S Plummer

# HONORARY LIFE MEMBERS

*A Hall*
*A J Osbourn*
*F M Millward*
*G U A Read*
*H Nelson Tebbs*
*P W Bandey*
*F G Hore*
*C J Churchill*
*R C Brumwell*
*H Rogers*
*A Fensome*
*F Holmes*
*A W Joy*
*L H E Perks*
*R Eidsforth*
*Dr A J Chillingworth*

*A H Perkins OBE*
*R Willsher*
*R G Furbank*
*E J C Brown*
*E M King*
*L A R Fensome*
*N J Timmins*
*H R Newton*
*J G Cook*
*H W Nightingale*
*D C Riddy CBE*
*D M King*
*H P Esnouf*
*H Elliott MC*
*D P Rogers OBE*
*R H Haynes*

*M Webb*
*Dr C V Fraser*
*K G Rose*
*H F Rawkins*
*K W Phillips*
*R J Slaughter*
*L J Rose*
*Dr D R Main*
*J R Saunders*
*A D Mills*
*G W Davies*
*D Ledsom*
*Mrs M Davies*
*P H Smith*
*G S I Irvine*

Life Members at a Former Players Luncheon in 2005.
Left to right, back row: Dr Bob Main, John Saunders, 'Budge' Rogers, John Rose, 'Tod' Slaughter, Dave Ledsom, Tony Mills.
Middle: Maurice Webb, 'Tich' Haynes, Gareth Davies, Ken Phillips.
Front: Dr Campbell Fraser

Marie Davies, the first female Life Member

# FORMER PLAYERS

In his programme article for the Barbarians match of March 2, 2010 John Cooley, the secretary of the Former Players Association wrote: "Players tend to give everything on the field; but when they come to an age when they retire, they are often lost to the club. This may be because the adrenalin rush on a Saturday afternoon cannot be replaced and some are known not to be good watchers of the game."

For too long, too many players drifted away from Goldington Road when their time was up. They were allowed to go and their experience, commitment and understanding of the club was lost to subsequent teams and regimes. And that meant that a vital source of potential coaches and administrators of the future was lost as well.

Players used to argue that it was their game – they weren't paid and turned out for the love of it. Their voice was heard through captains in the myriad of committees that ran the club. But when they left it was someone else's turn.

Professionalism changed all that. Suddenly former players started to realise that their opinions could carry weight – not just in the bar but in the board room and beyond. Moreover, as commercial interests, supporters and others made certain that their voices were being heard, it began to dawn on former players that they had a contribution to make. And one that bore an authority that could not be ignored – a fact reflected in 2011 with three members, Ian Bullerwell, David Gunner and Mark Howe – on the board of directors at the Blues.

If the game belonged to the players, so did the past; so did the heritage, the history and the legacy. And it was when that heritage was at stake that some people, not least former players, were prepared to risk their reputations to make sure that trophies, jerseys and memorabilia were not lost.

Towards the end of the Gurney era, all sorts of strangers would turn up, make demands and then make off. Supporters thought they were intent on not just stripping the assets but also on taking items of little value on a wider market but things that represented the legacy of the Blues – things that had been collected over more than 100 years.

So a group got together to smuggle treasures out of the club before anyone else could take them. One item that was taken was Martin Bayfield's first international jersey. He himself had the same idea and was horrified to find that it had gone from its place of honour on the wall – only to be told it was safe at the home of a former player.

The club's heritage, was just one concept that convinced some former players that they should take responsibility for it at a time of chaos. Some wanted a voice in the new regime. Most, though, were keener on the social side and supported the desire to keep people at the club when their days on the pitch were over.

Former club Chairman Ian Bullerwell wrote in a tribute to the Blues stalwart and administrator Tony Mills in the match programme of February 21, 2009: "In 1999, having returned from a very hospitable afternoon in the company of old friends in Northampton, we both agreed that it would be beneficial to establish a base for the Former Players Association at the club".

With the green light from the board, the association became more formal and structured and the tractor shed under the scoreboard at the Goldington Avenue end was converted into a lounge where members could meet. The inaugural annual meeting was held there on April 21, 2001 when a constitution was agreed and a committee formed with Ian Bullerwell as

Chairman, Tony Mills as Secretary and Alan Lake as Treasurer. Other members were Gareth Davies, Mike Lilley, and Steve Wells, the latter two and Alan Lake still serving in 2011. Former club committee man Peter Hulance was auditor, handing over in 2010 to former player Gerald Bygraves. By the end of the season 2000-2001 there were 84 members. In 2011 there were more than 300. In 2010, the association opened its own Facebook page and within a year it had more than 100 friends from all over the world. Many were reunited with the club and subsequently became members of the Former Players Association.

Functions for former players had been organised for some time before the association was set up. In April 1995, former players Richard Chadwick and Gareth Davies organised a reunion lunch to celebrate the 20th anniversary of the Canadian tour with Roger Smith travelling from Australia to be present and just one member of the squad unable to attend. Other reunions followed – in 2000, the 25th Canada reunion and in 2001, the 20th USA reunion. In 2005 a dinner to celebrate the 1975 cup triumph was initiated by Ken Phillips and hosted at the House of Commons by Derek Wyatt MP, the club's record try scorer who played and scored in the match at Twickenham.

In 2002, with the help of former players' contributions, the Irvine-Whitlock workforce and other generous gifts a kitchen, dining area and toilet facilities were added and in 2009 an extension to the bar, dedicated to former club Chairman Dave Ledsom and to Tony Mills, was opened after members raised £30,000. A year later Tony Marshall, the then oldest living club captain, unveiled a mural in the lounge depicting rugby through the ages at Goldington Road. It provided a spectacular setting where visiting committees were entertained.

In 2011, golf featured prominently in the association's calendar. Former record points scorer Brian Page organised a tour to France in 2002 which became an annual event. A match against former players of Northampton Saints was established before the annual Mobbs Memorial Match, past players took on current ones each season for the President's Cup and two other golf days were organised each year.

The main aim of the association was to provide a meeting point for former players so that they wouldn't drift away as soon as they hung up their boots. By providing the match day hospitality for visiting committees, staging lunches at Goldington Road, an annual reunion lunch at historic venues in London, barbecues, dinners, balls and concerts, the association was able to support the club with regular financial donations. And with its commitment to heritage, the association asked Neil Roy to produce '125 Years of the Blues' after Keeper of the Records Phil Beard and Tony Mills came up with the idea.

The committee of the Bedford Blues Former Players Association for 2010-11 was:

Chairman: L Mansell, Secretary: J Cooley, Treasurer: A Lake. Other members: P Bowker, J Chandler, J Hinkins, M Lilley, P Simmonds, R Slaughter, M Volland, B Whetstone, S Wells.

Left to right: Mike Lilley, 'Tod' Slaughter, John Cooley, Steve Wells, Leigh Mansell, Matt Volland, Ben Whetstone of the Former Players Association committee

# THE FOLLOWERS

Players, coaches and administrators can ensure the game is played; but it's the supporters who can give it greater meaning and value and it's they who can provide the atmosphere and add to the inspiration. It hasn't always been the case but fans have gradually been acknowledged as an integral part of the Bedford Blues family. And over the years they've performed a vital role not just in making a lot of noise home and away.

When the chips were down in 1999, Followers were to the fore. Peter Smith, then a Trustee and later Chairman, was the person John Gurney chose to tell about his terms for sale. The President, Jackie Markham, made a call to arms on the *BBC's John Gaunt Show* and the association's jungle drums ensured a massive crowd turned up to the grandstand to hear what they were.

Local TV was waiting and the anger of members in emotional interviews made compelling viewing. The message got out. Mr Smith, an officer at the borough council, was able to get key people there involved. The political leader, Shan Hunt, the Mayor Carole Ellis and MP Patrick Hall were soon on board. The whole town was on the case.

The use of the club's internet discussion forum 'Have Your Say' showed exactly how to mobilise the support of a united group of people. One member gave £30,000 to the appeal to buy back the club. Others gave more than they ever thought they would donate to a good cause and they continued to back the club financially through the various rights issues and fundraising initiatives as well as through the gates like all supporters.

The Followers, as Jackie Markham wrote in the programme for a successful 60th anniversary ball in October 2009, were called just that "in order to make it clear that the organisation was there to be involved with transport, not to be involved in the running of Bedford R U F C."

That may still be the situation. But through events like dinners, balls, jackpot tickets, raffles and firework displays, the Followers raised vast sums for vital projects at the club over the years and more than proved their worth. In 2011, Peter Smith was a long standing member of the club's board of directors. One of the bars was named after former Followers' Chairman Jack Pope and the club President was a member. Mrs Markham chaired the shareholder panel that was set up after the buy-out to communicate with the board and with supporters.

In the summer of 1949, Dick Dellow, a reporter on the *Bedfordshire Times*, and Percy Burke, an army captain, wrote to the club asking for permission to form a supporters association. The committee wrote back saying it had no objection. But it was not prepared to sponsor it or to receive gifts.

On July 15, the newspaper reported under the headline: For Rugby Followers: "Bedford rugby enthusiasts are banding themselves together for the purpose of hiring transport to the town's away matches next season. A 35 seater coach will be available in addition to the one organised by Jack Nightingale. Charges will be kept down to cost." The first official coach left for Gloucester on October 7, 1949.

And so the Followers were born. Soon, with another founder member Ted Keep on board they started travelling to away games – not just to watch the rugby but to see the country recovering from the devastating effects of war, often leaving early to visit landmarks like Coventry Cathedral, Kew Gardens and Greenwich en route to Coundon Road, London Welsh and Blackheath.

But providing good value transport was the thing. Mr Keep and his successors ran what often turned into 'magical mystery tours' – often getting lost, sometimes breaking down, once, in 1989, diverting to Northampton for a tour of the town and Franklin's Gardens just to make sure that the locals were aware that Bedford had just secured promotion and would soon be playing in the top league (though not for long as it turned out).

The proud boast was that the Followers would always get you to an away game. In 1975, ten coaches were booked to take fans to Twickenham for the 'cup' final. In 2005, for the Powergen Challenge Shield final, Margaret Appleton and her team sent out 30. In March 2011, Mrs Appleton's husband, Geoff, completed a record of being present at 400 Blues games in succession – including one in Penzance where his wife had to be rushed to hospital just before the match!

Bedford supporters always had a positive reputation. The *Courage Clubs Championship Directory* for 1995-96 noted that their supporters 'deserved success' after a big crowd cheered the team on to promotion from National League Three. Earlier in 1982, Blues fans were voted the best in the country by the magazine *Rugby World* and in 1999 they showed why. On Boxing Day 2010, more than 200 supporters helped clear the pitch of snow and the Bedford fixture was the only Championship game to go ahead with more than 4,000 turning up to see the win over Bristol.

The Followers' first President was the former player and broadcaster, Rex Alston. In the club's Centenary season, Vic Storrow, a former Mayor of the borough, held the office.

The Bedford Rugby Followers Association committee for 2010-11 was:
President: Mrs J Markham, Chairman: P Smith, Vice Chairman: A Tanner, Secretary Mrs J Roberts, Treasurer: G Appleton, Membership and Outings: Mrs M Appleton, Social Secretary: M Clark. Committee members: Mrs H Clark, A Cobley, Ms L Cornish, A Harper-Smith, P Kimber, P Novis, A Randall, B Rylands, Ms A Saxton, Mrs E Tanner, B Townsend.

Since the 2002-03 season, the Followers have held an end of season ball and presented an award to their Player of the Year, who was voted for by members. The player was presented with a trophy to keep and, from 2009-10, a shield in memory of former committee man Nigel Roberts which was kept with other club trophies in the Larry Webb Room.

Winners:
2002-03: James Pritchard; 2003-04: Arthur Brenton; 2004-05: Leigh Hinton; 2005-06: Nic Strauss; 2006-07: James Pritchard; 2007-08: Mouritz Botha; 2008-09 Karl Dickson; 2009-10: Sacha Harding; 2010-11: Paul Tupai.

From the 2004-05 season the Followers presented a bottle of champagne, paid for by the presenter, to their man of the match at away matches and from 1995, the committee chose a Supporter of the Year from among all members bar themselves. In later years, the winner received a trophy to keep and one to hold for a year. It was donated by Margaret and Geoff Appleton in memory of Mrs Terry Hayward, herself a winner in 2004.

Winners:
1995: Philip A Beard; 1996: Hannah Shires; 1997: Gloria Butler; 1998: Harry Hollinrake; 1999: Tim Simmonds; 2000: Geoff Appleton; 2001: Norman and Wendy Flinn; 2002: Mark Poxton and Family; 2003: Mick and Daphne Shotbolt; 2004: Terry Hayward; 2005: John Mitchell; 2006: Kirsty Hull; 2007: Michael Ursell and Jennifer Hull; 2008: Bob Marks; 2009: Tim Soroko; 2010: Tegan Straw, Charlie Clark and Charles Rylands.

# WOMEN AT THE BLUES

When Marie Davies was made the club's first female Life Member in 2009, it was a deserved recognition of the service she had given the Blues over more than 40 years in different roles from supporter, tea lady to match day programme writer. But it was also recognition of the part women in general have played in making the Blues what they were. Without their efforts over the years, it would be unrecognisable from the modern, outward looking, community based, family orientated club that it aspired to be and which was held up as a model for others to follow. In 2010-11, when its reputation was well established in rugby circles, women held several key positions throughout the organisation from the management to the mini section. Of course, they played the game as well – in the thriving Junior Blues and in 2011 five Under 18s and three Under 15s were selected for East Midlands squads.

The old image of women at rugby clubs was of wives, girlfriends, mums and sisters, happy to make the teas and the post match meals – stalwarts like the famous Mrs Brown of the 1960s and 70s and many others throughout history.

But at Goldington Road, certainly since the 1970s, women were prominent in other areas too. Often the strongest opinions in the clubhouse came from people like Kath Thomas who could dominate the Scrum Hall in the days when it was full of internationals in the 1970s. The formidable Mrs Thomas thought nothing of putting a famous player in his place if he'd kicked when she thought he should have run or late tackled one of her favourite players. Missed tackles were even more worthy of her invective.

Pat Harris was wife, cheer leader, trainer, mentor and best friend to her husband, Steve, one of the most popular players of the last 25 years whose untimely death had the toughest of men and women in tears. Players, coaches and supporters knew he was a proud player who put his body on the line week in week out. But only she knew how much her 'Arris had given to the club. As did other wives, girlfriends sisters and mothers of every other player over the years.

With the media demanding different and more interesting stories about soccer and rugby clubs than just the injury scares and groin strains that coaches liked to trot out, women at the Blues often provided that quality and human touch the press expected. Louise Allen, wife of the four term captain Matt, was featured on local TV with her article that appeared in a Followers Newsletter about what it was like waking up on a Sunday morning next to a man whose head was stuck to the pillow with blood.

Often the media preferred stories that had little to do with the actual game. Karen, wife of lock forward Arthur Brenton, went into labour sitting in the front row of the apron of the stand during a match in April 2008 and poor Arthur had to be hauled off out of a lineout after other wives got the message to coaches. "I was going to give them a right earful for bringing me off," said Arthur. It was club doctor Sarah Snape who took charge. Baby Oscar was born that same evening at Bedford Hospital and his first appearance in public was in the national press.

That sort of human interest story helped create the image of the Blues as a genuine family orientated, inclusive club that players and their friends and families would want to come to and that people would want to support. Having female and local stewards after professionals were bussed in during the Premiership years was quite simply a breath of fresh air in the eyes of most supporters.

The Blues always had mothers who helped with their child's team but several followed through into key administrative roles with the Colts, the first two being Jan Bostock and Isabel Britton who were managers from 1990-93 and 1993-2004 respectively. Mrs Britton was still involved when the Colts made it to their first National Cup final in 2004.

In short, many women have played their part throughout the history of the club. Unlike those players who turned out for the first team even for just a few minutes at the end of their one and only match, only a few have been recorded in spite of years of dedication to the cause.

Over the years, several women took on prominent management positions at the Blues. In 2011, Debra Rayer was the club's administrator, one of the only women in such a crucial role in the whole of a male dominated business. She was doing a 'magnificent job' said the Chairman. Ronnie Beard ran the club shop selling replica shirts and branded merchandise that provided an important stream of income and Melissa White looked after hospitality so efficiently that she earned a paragraph all to herself in Chris Harte's *Recollections of a Sportswriter (page 134)*. In 125 years, however, no woman had become coach, chief executive or a member of the board. But by the time the club's story of 150 or 200 years is told that will surely no longer be the case.

Supporters at the 2011 Followers Ball
Picture Mick Ursell

# THE ACADEMY

At the start of the 2010-11 season, the Blues announced that its 27 year old flanker Sacha Harding had been granted a testimonial in recognition of his decade at the club and more than 150 first team games. A former pupil of Hitchin Boys' School, he was invited to join the Bedford Academy at the age of 17 and, after a spell in Australia, he combined a degree course in Business at De Montfort University's Bedford campus with rugby at Goldington Road. He wasn't alone in the first team squad of that 125th season as a player who'd come through the ranks. Will Chudley, Duncan Taylor, Chris Locke and Darryl Veenendaal all featured in successful Academy teams before breaking through and justifying the aims of club Chairman Geoff Irvine. Another Josh Bassett signed a development contract after impressing in one league and one cup match in February, 2011. Academy players Elliot Bale and Steve Smith also turned out for the Blues. One of the guiding principles of the Irvine era was to produce more home grown players for the first team.

The Academy developed out of the Bedford Colts, the Under 19s, and other age group teams. Blues director David Gunner issued a report to shareholders in the year 2000 in which he said that he, Tony Mills, Adrian Skeggs, the first team forwards coach, Phil Roberts, Denis Ormesher and Martin Elliott had been putting together a strategy for junior teams within the professional club. He pointed out that the RFU looked likely to fund academies at premiership clubs but that the Blues had to help themselves because "our own future as a premiership club is by no means certain."

Mr Gunner, a meat baron with a sports reporter's eye and imagination, was a long standing rugby man who'd played in the LX Club at Cambridge University and some of the sides at the Blues. He and his chairman saw the Academy as a crucial part of their 'consortium' project. He went on: "It will comprise Under 17, Under 19 and Under 21 teams each with its own coaching, medical and administration... Links have already been established with Bedford College and De Montfort University so that the educational needs of these young players may be suitably catered for."

Jez Keates, a former Colts captain, was the first manager of the Academy which found a champion in Colin Jackson after his arrival for the 2000-2001 season. Others played important roles. Among them, Jan Bostock, Isabel Britton, Terry Dancer and Martin Elliott were all involved with the Colts. Denis Ormesher and Stuart Low followed as managers. They were also coaches as were Jim Bailey, Eamonn Quinn, Kevin McMillan, John Eastcott, Peter Cook, Alan Brown, Steve Guest, Mark Alderton and in 2010-11 current players Dan Richmond and Ian Vass and former player James Hinkins.

Denis Ormesher, who was manager from 2003 until he was appointed Director of Rugby at Luton in 2008 returned as Director in 2010. He wrote: "We tried to position ourselves as the best non RFU funded Academy in the country. If a player did not make it to one of the Premiership clubs then we could offer him a development route with the possibility of a contract with the Blues." Karl Dickson was one such success story who, after coming through the Academy, played more than 100 games for Bedford and in 2009-10 secured a contract with the Harlequins.

More than 50 years earlier, a side known as the Colts had grown out of former pupils at the Harpur Central School; organised by Jock McCulloch it had loose links with the Blues in the 1950s and then when the boys became over age, it developed into the Swifts.

A Colts side was absorbed into the main Bedford club during the junior and mini boom of the 70s and 80s, with the John Bunyan Schoolmaster Bruce Allen its early guiding light. Phil Evans, John Cooley, Tod Slaughter and Brian Fletcher were among the coaches who, by the Centenary, produced England Colts in Charlie Davison, Paul Alston, Chris Phelps, Scott Walters, Dave Elkington, Alex Tupman and Cameron Glanvill.

Under 19 Colts from the Bedford Academy had great success with four wins in five years in the National Cup – a competition open to those outside the chosen elite and instituted in 1997-98 as part of the East Midlands Centenary celebrations. They were beaten by Leeds (7-25) in the final of 2004 but were winners against Redruth (30-5) in 2007, Nuneaton in 2008 (33-16), Weston Hornets (55-12) in 2010 and Redingensians (38-10) in 2011. And such was their dominance in the competition that rules were expected that would prevent them from entering. The 2010-11 squad:

1. Ben Campbell, 2. Khrys Speed, 3. Curtis Weaver, 4. Matt Dunn, 5. Josh Walker, 6. Andy Ince, 7. Jake McCloud, 8. George Messum (capt); 9. Ali Price, 10. Elliot Bale; 11. Josh Bassett (v.capt), 12. Steve Smith, 13. Alex Awenat, 14. Tom Chellew; 15. De la Rey Veenendaal. Reps: Ollie Clough, Will Allard, Jack Warrior, Sven Meilland, Will Kiddle, Lawrence Rayner, Felix Stretton.

Scorers in the final at Franklin's Gardens. Tries: Price,2, Ince, Smith, Bassett, Veenendaal. Cons: Bale,4.

The Academy management in 2010-11 was: Director: D Ormesher. Coaches: S Guest, M Alderton, D Richmond, I Vass, J Hinkins. Sports Therapist: Miss H Cole, N Allen and Miss A Bridge.

The squad that won the National Colts Cup at Northampton in 2011

If the Academy was a gilt edged route to the Blues then the Junior Section produced hundreds of enthusiastic players with the opportunity to try out originally for the Colts and then for the Academy. In 2010-11 there were flourishing sections playing at Bedford Athletic on Sundays for Mini (U7-U13s), Junior (up to U 17s) and Ladies (U15 and U18) sections. In 2010 the U8s and U13s won their groups in the Bedfordshire Cup and the U17s were runners up in the National Cup.

Pat Briggs and Gareth Davies laid the foundations when in 1973 they invited youngsters between the age of nine and 13 to turn up on Sunday mornings for organised instruction; 150 turned up to their first session. Lloyd Griffiths, Jim Blakemore, Bryan Hire and Terry Barfoot were soon to join them at the beginnings of the nationwide boom in mini rugby and they laid the foundations for a flourishing junior section with a representative later sitting on the club's main committee. John Eastcott had links with Salles, near Bordeaux in France, and the Junior section formed a relationship with the town's rugby club that started in 1978 and lasted for more than 30 years with tours in both directions.

Thousands of youngsters and parents were involved with the Bedford Juniors over the years and, though not everyone carried on playing or organising teams and tournaments, the interest in rugby stayed with many as supporters. Dominic Malone, who played 80 times for the Blues between 2003 and 2007 after rejoining from Northampton, with whom he was a Heineken Cup winner in 2000, started his rugby life in the Bedford mini and junior section. So did Steve Smith and others of the 2011 vintage.

In 2010-11, Nigel Crowe was President, Keith Breeze was Chairman and Alison Bowden was Vice Chairman. Other members of the committee were:

Steve Janes, Paul Moffatt, Donald Andrews, Marcus Buckle, Mark Apps, Steve Minney, Llewellyn John, Bob Ballard, Mary Lipner, Chris O'Dell, Chris Wright, Darren Kerr, Mike Pendleton, Emma Minney, John Eagles.

# 3. FOR THE RECORD

# APPEARANCES

## THE 300 CLUB

*D P Rogers*
*M A Howe*
*R Eidsforth*
*R Willsher*
*F N Barker*
*J Smith*
*St L H Webb*
*R J Slaughter*
*B E McCarthy*
*A J Finnie*
*R A Lovell*
*G T Dancer*
*R M Wilkinson*

Seven members of the 300 club met at a players' reunion in 1986
Left to right, back row: Brian McCarthy, 'Budge' Rogers, Bob Wilkinson, 'Tod' Slaughter, Rex Willsher.
Front row: Jack Smith and Gerry Dancer.
The only other players to make more than 300 appearances are inset, left to right:
Ronnie Eidsforth, Larry Webb, Alan Lovell, Norman Barker, Mark Howe and Andy Finnie

In 125 years of the Blues, more than 2,600 players made at least one appearance for the first team. Nearly 140 players turned out at least 100 times; 43 of them made more than 200 appearances; 20 made 250 or more; 13 more than 300, and just two, D P Rogers and M A Howe, more than 400.

What became known as the 300 Club never met. Of their members Ronnie Eidsforth, Larry Webb and Alan Lovell died before many realised that it existed. Just how exclusive it was can be seen by the absence from its ranks of many of the club's great stalwarts who gave years of service on the field. War, University, National Service and injury all conspired to restrict the first class careers of many fine players. In the early days, there were far fewer matches per season. In some eras it was much easier to get a place in the team than others. From 1976-77 an appearance as a replacement counted. In the professional era, it wasn't unusual for some to play only ten minutes per match - and that counted. Be that as it may, to have made 100 appearances for the first team of a first class club is surely a marvellous achievement. To have made 300 is outstanding.

In the 300 Club, there are three OBs, D P Rogers, R Eidsforth and J Smith, and four OBMs, G T Dancer, R Willsher, R J Slaughter and M A Howe. Junior clubs in Bedford helped develop B E McCarthy (the Swifts), Slaughter and R A Lovell (Queens) and Dancer (Bedford Athletic). Six of the 13 were captains, five were internationals, two of them in wartime; two were Lions. Four of them, Rogers, McCarthy, Slaughter and Lovell all, at some stage of their careers, worked for W H Allen, the engineering firm in Queen's Park, the area Dancer came from. Two of the three backs among the 13 were full backs and one a fly half. Of the ten forwards, six were from the front row union, three were hookers, three were flankers and one a lock.

The six captains, the three full internationals and the two Lions are all profiled under those headings.

**D P Rogers**

'Budge' Rogers heads the list of appearances with 485 in a 20 year career. He was a formidable number seven and is profiled as captain, international and Lion.

**M A Howe**

Mark Howe was the 12th player to become a member of the 300 Club and he went on to become just the second to make 400 appearances in a 20 year career from 1976-77 until 1995-96, recording a total of 478. He was a one club man in a difficult era when the Blues struggled to match the quality of the fixture list they'd built up on the back of outstanding success and he was one of many players who gave their all in the cause of keeping the club 'first class'. He was deputy head boy at Bedford Modern School when the Queen visited the new site in Manton Lane in May 1976 and none of his contemporaries had any doubt that he would make his mark as a gentleman in life and comrade in arms on the rugby field. He would surely have made even more appearances had he not been a farmer's boy having to miss the start of most seasons because of the harvest – especially when he took over the running of the family's 600 acres in the Marston Vale in 1985. That at least gave other hookers a chance for a game. Some of them thought he should play as a flanker but his preference was always for the front row. Off the field, he was an active member of the Rotary Club of Bedford Park - President during the Millenium year, a Trustee of the Marston Vale Trust and a director of the Bedford Blues. He is also profiled as captain.

### R Eidsforth

Ronnie Eidsforth made 374 appearances for the club in a remarkable career at full back, which spanned nearly a quarter of a century. His total became a club record when he passed the 272 achieved by Alf Hall between 1906 and 1925. Before that the record was 237 by H Willett who first played in 1904, G U A Read 183 from 1901, C Franklin, 161, 1901, W Rees 134, 1891, and F W Potter, 128 from 1891. An Old Bedfordian, Ronnie Eidsforth made his debut on January 6, 1925, when he deputised against Coventry for the regular full back C J 'Jack' Churchill. By 1926-27, he had made the position his own and he was a regular choice until 1938-39 when he decided to stand down in favour of a younger man. He was repatriated from a German prisoner of war camp in 1943 and made two wartime appearances for the club. On October 30, 1948, he played his last first team match, deputising for Bill Rose against Rosslyn Park, and showing, according to the press report of the match, all his "old power and judgement". Always of immaculate appearance he scored 433 points in his career and played for Eastern Counties as well as East Midlands.

### R Willsher

Rex Willsher was the Budge Rogers of his day. Only the war prevented him from winning a full cap. Described in the *Bedfordshire Times* as a 'gentleman farmer', his 354 appearances was the fourth highest. He is profiled as captain.

### F N Barker

Fifth in the all-time list of appearances with 347 is Norman Barker, hooker in the cup winning team of 1975 and a very fast forward in the loose. He joined Bedford from Loughborough College and made his debut on September 3, 1966, in a side captained by D P Rogers that lost 14-3 in Leicester. He made 38 appearances out of the 40 matches that season and for the next ten years he averaged 30 a season to achieve probably the fastest 300. His last game was at Moseley for an 18-6 defeat on December 18, 1976, and he handed over to the rising star Mark Howe who became the principal custodian of the number two shirt for the next twenty years. Norman Barker scored 33 tries in his career and played for Leicestershire, East Midlands and Bucks where he was captain in 1973-74. A keen musician in a popular rock group, he taught at schools in the Northampton area and nurtured several notable rugby players including Courtney Lawes.

### J Smith

Jack Smith was once described as a perfect example of 'that rare breed of genuinely amateur bird'. He was an outstanding sportsman at Bedford School and besides being a safe full back for the Blues, he played for the town and captained the county at cricket. Among his sporting achievements are appearances against three countries within a year. He played full back for the Midland Counties against New Zealand at Leicester in December 1963, having played cricket for the Minor Counties against the West Indies in the summer of that year. In June 1964, he represented the Minor Counties against the Australians at the Bury in Bedford. Jack Smith made his debut for the Blues against Leicester in September 1954, the season after his twin brother, Peter, had made the first of his 29 appearances at scrum half. In 343 appearances, he scored 134 points. His son Simon made his Blues debut at fly half in 1982 while captain of Bedford School and the England Schoolboys. He was one of the club's most prolific scorers, reaching 284 points from 36 appearances in his first full season and kicking a then club record of 67 penalties.

### St L H Webb

Larry Webb was a member of a series of formidable front rows at the Blues. His 336 appearances put him seventh in the list. He is profiled as captain and international.

### R J Slaughter

'Tod' Slaughter valued his membership of the 300 Club as highly as any of his many honours at the Blues. He made 334 appearances. He is profiled as captain and coach.

### B E McCarthy

Brian McCarthy was born in Renhold and educated at the Harpur Central School where the Welsh international hooker Iorwerth Evans saw a young man in his own image. On leaving school he joined others from the Central in the Bedford Colts, who had been set up, with loose links at the Blues, by Jock McCulloch. Brian was in the vintage that, when it became over age, formed the new Swifts club that exists today, playing then at Fairhill in Clapham Road and choosing their name after the original club who joined with the Rovers to form the Blues. The *Bedfordshire Times* sub editor, Tom Sobey, was one of its earliest supporters. Brian was captain of the Swifts when he was invited to play for the Wanderers at Goldington Road and he took his chance there making a first team debut against Sale on January 17, 1953. He spent two seasons in the RAF and by the time he played his last first team game in November 1964, he had made 330 appearances at hooker. His close friend was his front row colleague Alan Lovell and each was best man at the other's wedding.

### A J Finnie

Andy Finnie scored more points than any other player in Bedford's 125 year history. By the time he'd completed the last of his 322 games he'd more than doubled the previous record of Brian Page to set a new mark of 2,616. He took over the fly half berth from Simon Smith in a very difficult era when the Blues were trying to sustain a fixture list built up on the back of the success of the 1960s and 70s without the same international class players in their ranks. In his first ten seasons there was just one in which the number of wins exceeded the number of defeats and it was his astonishing place kicking that secured many of those wins – not from in front of the posts but from long range penalties all over the pitch and conversions from the touchlines after hard earned tries. Twice he passed 300 points in a season, once in the third division, and he was the top scorer 11 times. In the record 90-3 win over the Old Paulines in 1991, he landed a record 11 conversions and scored two tries for 30 points in the game. He was a wonderful place kicker yet it was his kicking out of hand where he had few peers at the highest levels of the game. 'Albert' Finnie retired from the first class scene just as professionalism arrived in Bedford. For a while he commentated on the Blues for BBC local radio and then went back to play three more seasons at Stockwood Park in Luton from where he had come in the first place.

### R A Lovell

Alan 'Alf' Lovell was described in a match programme as being made of "the real stuff of rugby". The son of a police officer who later kept the Half Moon public house in Kempston, he came from a family well-known in sporting circles, especially boxing. He was educated at Bedford Road Junior and Senior schools in Kempston before winning a scholarship to Luton Technical College and going on to become a student at W H Allen where he played for the Queens club. He made his first team debut for the Blues when he stood in for John Bance in the second row in a 9-3 win over Nottingham on September 18, 1954. He was called up to fill a vacancy in the front row a fortnight later and made his reputation as a prop in the formidable units of the day. A regular until 1967, appearing in every game for two seasons, he played in sides throughout the club, making the last of his 320 first team outings against Pontypool in October 1972. He became team secretary of the Rovers in 1968, then of the Rovers and Rams in 1970-71, and held those posts until his untimely death at the age of 39 in December 1973. The annual match against the county, instituted in 1974, was named in his honour and funds raised from it helped towards his daughter's education.

### G T Dancer

'Beef' Dancer made 317 appearances. He was the hero of the great pre-war teams upon whom the tough customers of the post-war front rows modelled themselves. He is profiled as a Lion.

### R M Wilkinson

Bob Wilkinson became the eleventh member of the club in December 1983. He played 311 times and is 13th in the list. He is profiled as captain and international but it was as a Barbarian and a member of the 1973 side that beat the All Blacks that made him one of Bedford's most famous players .

The 300 Club was just beyond the range of several other Bedford greats. Roger Perkins, the Olney hooker, kept a Welsh international out of the Bedford team. Ben Whetstone played just twice, through injury, in a season in which he was captain. John Bance, Alf Hall and Arthur Marshall were all captains. Andy Whitehouse and Kevin Canning were stalwarts in one of the club's most difficult eras. Each played more than 250 times.

## MOST APPEARANCES

| Name | Between | Apps |
|---|---|---|
| D P Rogers | 1956-76 | 485 |
| M A Howe | 1976-96 | 478 |
| R Eidsforth | 1924-49 | 374 |
| R Willsher | 1928-49 | 354 |
| F N Barker | 1966-77 | 347 |
| J Smith | 1953-68 | 343 |
| St L H Webb | 1952-65 | 336 |
| R J Slaughter | 1960-78 | 334 |
| B E Mcarthy | 1952-65 | 330 |
| A J Finnie | 1982-96 | 322 |
| R A Lovell | 1954-67 | 320 |
| G T Dancer | 1927-48 | 317 |
| R M Wilkinson | 1968-85 | 311 |
| R Perkins | 1927-38 | 283 |
| B M L Whetstone | 1992-05 | 282 |
| A Whitehouse | 1976-89 | 280 |
| J F Bance | 1945-58 | 279 |
| A Hall | 1906-25 | 272 |
| K Canning | 1978-89 | 253 |
| A Marshall | 1922-33 | 250 |
| R G Furbank | 1938-53 | 249 |
| B K Williams | 1958-67 | 249 |

| Name | Between | Apps |
|---|---|---|
| I G Peck | 1975-88 | 246 |
| C Hooker | 1971-82 | 242 |
| T R Marshall | 1945-59 | 241 |
| M Upex | 1986-97 | 239 |
| P D Briggs | 1962-73 | 238 |
| H Willett | 1904-13 | 237 |
| R C Brumwell | 1924-34 | 232 |
| I Skingsley | 1984-97 | 223 |
| C Rose | 1929-38 | 222 |
| J T Mawle | 1970-82 | 220 |
| P Ralphs | 1943-55 | 214 |
| A J Osbourn | 1908-22 | 213 |
| D Jackson | 1971-79 | 212 |
| W A Sime | 1926-38 | 210 |
| M R Hale | 1947-57 | 209 |
| N R Boult | 1966-73 | 207 |
| B Mackay | 1975-90 | 206 |
| A J Hollins | 1971-81 | 204 |
| A V Manton | 1902-22 | 203 |
| G Bygraves | 1982-91 | 203 |
| T D Thevenard | 1932-41 | 201 |

The 400 Club: 'Budge' Rogers, left, and Mark Howe with Mark's wife Rebekah in 2011

## BETWEEN 100 AND 200

| Name | Between | Apps |
|---|---|---|
| P Jackson | 1955-63 | 197 |
| L A R Fensome | 1921-33 | 196 |
| P S Collingridge | 1948-57 | 196 |
| A Key | 1981-87 | 196 |
| J Chandler | 1985-96 | 191 |
| R Carter | 1955-63 | 189 |
| A R G Else | 1964-72 | 188 |
| B R Black | 1931-48 | 187 |
| J G Cook | 1929-46 | 184 |
| G U A Read | 1901-11 | 183 |
| J G Pritchard | 2001-11 | 181 |
| L R Drury | 1958-68 | 180 |
| A K Towersey | 1968-80 | 179 |
| C Glanvill | 1985-96 | 172 |
| B Page | 1969-78 | 170 |
| N F Reed | 1927-35 | 168 |
| O V Bevan | 1927-47 | 166 |
| P J Green | 1967-74 | 165 |
| L G Ashwell | 1927-35 | 163 |
| W H Whiting | 1948-58 | 163 |
| R Pascall | 1978-93 | 163 |
| C Franklin | 1901-10 | 161 |
| S Binnington | 1981-94 | 158 |
| S Harris | 1984-95 | 158 |
| R H Haynes | 1942-54 | 155 |
| H W Rose | 1945-53 | 154 |
| S Harding | 2002-11 | 154 |
| P Alston | 1982-03 | 153 |
| M J Volland | 1999-08 | 153 |
| D M Wyatt | 1973-78 | 152 |
| G A Kelly | 1934-48 | 151 |
| C H Thompkins | 1921-28 | 150 |
| F M Fletcher | 1942-53 | 148 |
| R Demming | 1972-80 | 147 |
| G N Phillips | 1978-85 | 146 |
| L Mansell | 1989-03 | 145 |
| A Brenton | 2002-08 | 145 |
| T E K Williams | 1926-34 | 142 |
| E A Joy | 1924-32 | 141 |
| C J Bailward | 1972-78 | 140 |
| V J Lyttle | 1933-42 | 138 |
| M Hall | 1944-50 | 138 |
| P S Onyett | 1965-72 | 138 |
| W Rees | 1891-02 | 134 |
| R Porter | 1984-94 | 134 |
| S D Kitchener | 1905-24 | 133 |
| J Hinkins | 1997-08 | 133 |

| Name | Between | Apps |
|---|---|---|
| J Brooks | 2000-06 | 133 |
| R Maclear | 1895-06 | 132 |
| F W Potter | 1891-98 | 128 |
| G Jenkins | 1946-53 | 127 |
| N J Philbrook | 1963-70 | 127 |
| A C Towell | 1946-56 | 126 |
| D J Richmond | 2007-11 | 126 |
| P C Burgess | 1892-98 | 125 |
| B L Arthur | 1966-72 | 125 |
| A M Jorden | 1974-80 | 124 |
| N Bennett | 1981-87 | 124 |
| P Garrett | 1990-96 | 122 |
| L H Nicholson | 1920-27 | 122 |
| H J Simcoe | 1920-30 | 121 |
| A R Alston | 1924-30 | 120 |
| R Thompson | 1889-02 | 117 |
| J Phillips | 2003-08 | 117 |
| R G Cocking | 1908-22 | 116 |
| P H Avery | 1955-61 | 116 |
| D J Small | 1964-72 | 116 |
| F Edwards | 1973-78 | 116 |
| R Winters | 1996-00 | 116 |
| N B Larby | 1923-31 | 115 |
| G Wood | 1986-91 | 114 |
| J O'B Power | 1932-39 | 113 |
| P J Paramore | 1996-06 | 113 |
| A W Joy | 1921-26 | 112 |
| V J Lewis | 1970-74 | 112 |
| C S Nailer | 1905-13 | 111 |
| C J Churchill | 1921-29 | 111 |
| J M Howard | 1972-76 | 110 |
| N Strauss | 2004-08 | 109 |
| L Roberts | 2005-10 | 108 |
| I Vass | 2004-11 | 108 |
| K Dickson | 2004-09 | 107 |
| C C Wood | 1901-08 | 104 |
| C Ashe | 1903-10 | 104 |
| M C Allen | 2004-08 | 104 |
| W N Bennett | 1973-77 | 103 |
| D L K Milman | 1933-46 | 102 |
| D G Perry | 1961-66 | 101 |
| R Chadwick | 1972-80 | 101 |
| M Staten | 2002-07 | 101 |
| O L Lloyd | 1926-34 | 100 |
| R Meadows | 1978-85 | 100 |
| B Gabriel | 1985-92 | 100 |
| B Burke | 2006-11 | 100 |
| O Dodge | 2006-11 | 100 |

### Most appearances in a season

F N Barker holds the record. He made 42 from a possible 45 in 1975-76. He is followed by G N Phillips 41 from 45 in 1980-81, R J Carter 40 from 44 in 1960-61, J M Howard 40 from 45 in 1975-76, J T Mawle 40 from 45 in 1980-81 and M A Howe and G Bygraves who both made 40 appearances in 1986-87 from a possible 43.

### Consecutive appearances

Twenty two players turned out in every game during a season. Three of them, R G Furbank, R J Carter and R A Lovell did so twice. One, A J Osbourn, did so three times. After the Centenary season, only R Underwood (1997-98), J Pritchard (2002-03) and J Brooks (2003-04) managed it – though a number of others turned out in every league and cup match.

The record number of consecutive appearances is 106. It is held by R G Furbank who set the figure between 1947 and 1950. More than 50 consecutive appearances were recorded by:

R G Furbank (1947-50) 106, R A Lovell (1963-65) 98, P Ralphs (1948-50) 86, A J Osbourn (1910-12) 85, B R Black (1933-35) 75, R J Slaughter (1966-68) 60, R J Carter (1957-59) 59, A J Osbourn (1913-19) 55, P Jackson (1957-58) 55, A W Joy (1923-24) 54, J Smith (1964-65) 52.

### Most players in a season

In 1905-06, Bedford fielded 87 players in its 36 matches. In 1897-98 it used 85 for 32 fixtures and in 1920-21, 82 in 25.

### Fewest players in a season

Thirty five, in 2005-06 when there were 31 games, is the lowest number of players to represent the first team in a full season in all matches. Fewer were recorded in the club's earliest years but records from that era are unreliable. In 2008-09, 32 players turned out in 33 league and cup games. Thirty six in a season has been recorded three times - from 34 matches in 1968-69, from 35 in 1969-70 and from 36 in 1974-75.

## The family connection

There was one case in 125 years of the Blues of a father and son both captaining the club, two of twins in the same team, two of a father having two sons to play for the first team as well as himself, three of four brothers all playing, nine of three brothers all making the first team, 20 of father and son and 41 of two brothers - not counting the twins and not necessarily in the same team.

Father and son captain: A and T R Marshall

Father and two sons: Fowler and Marshall

Father and son: Evans, Simcoe, Kitchener, Pugh, Joy, Churchill, Williams, Quarry, Cook, Prigmore, Fletcher, Micklewright, Smith, Phillips, Mansell, Cooley, Rodgers, Abrahams, Youngs, Peck.

Twins in the same team: J and P Smith; S and M Gray

Four brothers: Foster, Maclear, Lacey

Three brothers: Tucker, Udal, Griffith, Wells, Finlinson, Brooks, Helmsley, Bevan, Bilham, Mackay.

Two brothers: Brown, McVittie, Potter, Morris, Pickwoad, Wells, Skinner, Cocking, Milton, Fowler, Grant, Willett, Nailer, Kitchener, Hall, Stafford, Stimson, Howard, Pryor, Joy, Williams, Bovill-Jones, Cook, Rogers, Power, Milman, Blincow, Fielden, Hook, Marshall, Evans, Rogers, Briggs, Higham, Landon, Barker, Bygraves, Glanvill, Elphick, Phillips.

Like father, like son. Guy Fletcher was a Bedford scrum half like his father Murray, left

# INDIVIDUAL RECORDS

## THE LEADING SCORERS

The top five points scorers in the 125 year history of the Blues were all prolific goalkickers - none more so than Andy Finnie, whose career total of 2616 will be very hard to beat, and James Pritchard who was the only other player to pass 2,000. Brian Page and Neil Bennett were the only others to score more than 1,000 points.

Andy Finnie scored more points for the club than anyone else in 125 years

| Name | Apps | Between | Tries | Cons | Pens | DGs | Points |
|---|---|---|---|---|---|---|---|
| A J Finnie | 322 | 1982-96 | 21 | 339 | 556 | 61 | 2616 |
| J G Pritchard | 181 | 2001-11 | 65 | 360 | 332 | - | 2041 |
| B Page | 170 | 1969-78 | 16 | 229 | 214 | 7 | 1182 |
| W N Bennett | 103 | 1973-77 | 34 | 173 | 165 | 19 | 1034 |
| M A Rayer | 62 | 1996-98 | 16 | 189 | 91 | - | 731 |
| D M Wyatt | 152 | 1973-78 | 145 | 38 | 7 | 3 | 686 |
| B M L Whetstone | 282 | 1992-05 | 121 | 10 | 16 | 2 | 679 |
| R H Haynes | 155 | 1942-54 | 40 | 120 | 58 | 20 | 597 |
| S Smith | 71 | 1981-97 | 6 | 47 | 141 | 8 | 565 |
| W A Sime | 210 | 1926-38 | 52 | 144 | 22 | 9 | 546 |
| N J Philbrook | 127 | 1963-70 | 66 | 74 | 58 | 1 | 523 |
| L R Drury | 180 | 1958-68 | 32 | 112 | 52 | 1 | 479 |
| J G Cook | 184 | 1929-46 | 37 | 132 | 25 | - | 450 |
| A K Towersey | 179 | 1968-80 | 112 | 1 | - | 1 | 445 |
| R Eidsforth | 374 | 1924-49 | 7 | 121 | 26 | 23 | 433 |
| D P Rogers | 485 | 1956-76 | 126 | - | - | 1 | 400 |
| L Hinton | 30 | 2004-05 | 10 | 52 | 81 | - | 397 |
| P D Briggs | 238 | 1962-73 | 22 | 62 | 32 | 33 | 387 |
| B K Williams | 249 | 1958-67 | 126 | 1 | - | 1 | 383 |
| H Willett | 237 | 1904-13 | 102 | 9 | - | 10 | 364 |
| H W Rose | 154 | 1945-53 | 17 | 83 | 44 | 4 | 364 |
| A R Alston | 120 | 1924-30 | 96 | 34 | 2 | - | 362 |
| D Coley | 95 | 1962-67 | 15 | 88 | 47 | - | 362 |
| A Hepher | 85 | 2001-06 | 18 | 70 | 40 | 2 | 356 |
| A M Jorden | 124 | 1974-80 | 17 | 70 | 39 | 9 | 352 |
| G U A Read | 183 | 1901-11 | 1 | 123 | 27 | 5 | 350 |
| R C Brumwell | 232 | 1924-34 | 106 | 3 | - | 4 | 340 |
| A D Heard | 74 | 1904-13 | 104 | 5 | 2 | 1 | 332 |
| S Kerridge | 67 | 1978-83 | 8 | 48 | 67 | - | 329 |
| M Nurton | 59 | 1967-71 | 6 | 67 | 55 | 4 | 329 |
| V J Lyttle | 138 | 1933-42 | 103 | - | - | 1 | 313 |
| T D Thevenard | 201 | 1932-41 | 103 | - | - | - | 309 |
| F W Potter | 128 | 1891-98 | 54 | 49 | 4 | 5 | 295 |
| L A R Fensome | 196 | 1921-33 | 97 | - | 1 | - | 294 |
| R Demming | 147 | 1972-80 | 73 | - | - | - | 292 |
| K Canning | 253 | 1978-89 | 73 | - | - | - | 292 |
| M Harris | 31 | 2004-06 | 15 | 61 | 31 | - | 290 |
| H H Morris | 82 | 1892-97 | 71 | 28 | 1 | 4 | 289 |
| M E Finlinson | 76 | 1900-09 | 61 | 31 | 5 | - | 260 |
| N R Boult | 207 | 1966-73 | 82 | - | - | - | 260 |
| P S Collingridge | 196 | 1948-57 | 69 | 11 | 7 | - | 250 |
| P J Green | 165 | 1967-74 | 72 | - | - | - | 250 |

Progressive career points records were:

289 - H H Morris (1892-97), 350 - G U A Read (1901-11), 364 - H Willett (1904-13), 546 - W A Sime (1926-38), 597 – R H Haynes (1942-54), 1182 – B Page (1969-78), 2616 – A J Finnie (1982-96).

## MOST IN A SEASON

Goal kickers dominate the table of players who scored most points in a season with James Pritchard the only one to score more than 400 and more than 300 three times. Neil Bennett, Andy Finnie and Mike Rayer all managed 300 twice and Leigh Hinton once. Pritchard's 403, set on the last day of the 2010-11 season, was the highest total in a season in 125 years. H H Morris, whose record 171 points in 1893-94 lasted for 40 years, was the first of the great scorers to register more tries than goals in his total.

| Name | Season | Apps | Tries | Cons | Pens | DGs | Points |
|---|---|---|---|---|---|---|---|
| J G Pritchard | 2010-11 | 30 | 10 | 73 | 69 | - | 403 |
| L Hinton | 2004-05 | 30 | 10 | 52 | 81 | - | 397 |
| J G Pritchard | 2002-03 | 27 | 13 | 51 | 73 | - | 386 |
| M A Rayer | 1997-98 | 29 | 7 | 88 | 53 | - | 370 |
| M A Rayer | 1996-97 | 33 | 9 | 101 | 38 | - | 361 |
| W N Bennett | 1975-76 | 36 | 6 | 60 | 64 | 5 | 351 |
| A J Finnie | 1994-95 | 31 | - | 43 | 79 | 5 | 338 |
| A J Finnie | 1991-92 | 35 | 3 | 50 | 67 | 6 | 331 |
| W N Bennett | 1973-74 | 30 | 13 | 54 | 46 | 3 | 307 |
| J G Pritchard | 2006-07 | 27 | 12 | 63 | 39 | - | 303 |
| B Page | 1971-72 | 36 | 4 | 65 | 50 | - | 296 |
| A J Finnie | 1993-94 | 30 | - | 44 | 64 | 4 | 292 |
| S Smith | 1982-83 | 36 | 3 | 28 | 67 | 5 | 284 |
| W N Bennett | 1974-75 | 25 | 12 | 46 | 38 | 9 | 281 |
| M Harris | 2005-06 | 20 | 11 | 61 | 31 | - | 270 |
| A J Finnie | 1984-85 | 32 | 4 | 17 | 59 | 8 | 251 |
| J G Pritchard | 2001-02 | 25 | 8 | 42 | 42 | - | 250 |
| J G Pritchard | 2007-08 | 26 | 12 | 35 | 36 | - | 238 |
| J G Pritchard | 2008-09 | 22 | 4 | 55 | 35 | - | 235 |
| B Page | 1969-70 | 29 | 1 | 41 | 44 | 4 | 229 |
| A J Finnie | 1987-88 | 30 | 1 | 36 | 45 | 5 | 226 |
| A J Finnie | 1990-91 | 30 | 3 | 29 | 46 | 6 | 226 |
| J G Pritchard | 2009-10 | 24 | 6 | 41 | 38 | - | 226 |
| S Smith | 1983-84 | 26 | 2 | 13 | 60 | 3 | 223 |
| A J Finnie | 1988-89 | 31 | 1 | 29 | 44 | 9 | 221 |
| N J Philbrook | 1967-68 | 36 | 19 | 38 | 28 | - | 217 |
| B Page | 1970-71 | 28 | 2 | 33 | 46 | 2 | 216 |
| B Page | 1972-73 | 24 | 3 | 39 | 40 | - | 210 |
| L R Drury | 1961-62 | 32 | 6 | 59 | 18 | - | 190 |
| A J Finnie | 1992-93 | 20 | 2 | 26 | 39 | 3 | 188 |
| S Howard | 1998-99 | 28 | 4 | 38 | 28 | 1 | 183 |
| N J Philbrook | 1966-67 | 38 | 21 | 26 | 21 | - | 178 |
| E Barnes | 2003-04 | 22 | 1 | 43 | 28 | 1 | 178 |
| A Hepher | 2005-06 | 28 | 9 | 49 | 9 | 2 | 175 |
| W A Sime | 1933-34 | 35 | 15 | 47 | 7 | 3 | 172 |
| A Yapp | 1998-99 | 31 | 3 | 26 | 28 | 7 | 172 |
| H H Morris | 1893-94 | 29 | 38 | 21 | 1 | 3 | 171 |
| D M Wyatt | 1976-77 | 33 | 30 | 16 | 3 | 1 | 164 |
| D Coley | 1963-64 | 35 | 7 | 41 | 20 | - | 163 |

| Name | Season | Apps | Tries | Cons | Pens | DGs | Points |
|---|---|---|---|---|---|---|---|
| W Twelvetrees | 2008-09 | 31 | 18 | 16 | 13 | - | 161 |
| A J Finnie | 1986-87 | 17 | 4 | 19 | 30 | 4 | 156 |
| I Metcalfe | 1979-80 | 16 | 4 | 31 | 24 | 1 | 153 |
| A M Jorden | 1977-78 | 26 | 5 | 35 | 15 | 5 | 150 |

Progressive season points records were: 171 – H H Morris (1893-94), 172 – W A Sime (1933-34), 190 - L R Drury (1961-62), 217 - N J Philbrook (1967-68), 229 – B Page (1969-70), 296 – B Page (1971-72), 307 - W N Bennett (1973-74), 351 – W N Bennett (1975-76), 361 – M A Rayer (1996-97), 370 – M A Rayer (1997-98), 386 – J G Pritchard ( 2002-03), 397 – L Hinton (2004-05), 403 – J G Pritchard (2010-11).

Simon Smith

Leigh Hinton

Brian Page

'Tich' Haynes

Jim Philbrook

# THE GREAT TRY SCORERS

Ten players scored more than 100 tries in a career at the Blues in its first 125 years with one forward, 'Budge' Rogers, among nine threequarters. With an average of nearly one per match, Derek Wyatt leads the list with 145 tries from 152 appearances in five seasons.

Derek Wyatt scored more tries for the club than anyone else in 125 years

### 50 tries in a career

| Name | Apps | Between | Tries |
|---|---|---|---|
| D M Wyatt | 152 | 1973-78 | 145 |
| D P Rogers | 485 | 1956-76 | 126 |
| B K Williams | 249 | 1958-67 | 126 |
| B M L Whetstone | 282 | 1992-05 | 121 |
| A K Towersey | 179 | 1968-80 | 112 |
| R C Brumwell | 232 | 1924-34 | 106 |
| A D Heard | 74 | 1904-13 | 104 |
| T D Thevenard | 201 | 1932-41 | 103 |
| V J Lyttle | 138 | 1933-42 | 103 |
| H Willett | 237 | 1904-13 | 102 |
| L A R Fensome | 196 | 1921-33 | 97 |
| A R Alston | 120 | 1924-30 | 96 |
| L G Ashwell | 163 | 1927-35 | 92 |
| N R Boult | 207 | 1966-72 | 82 |
| A V Manton | 203 | 1902-22 | 75 |
| St L H Webb | 336 | 1952-65 | 74 |
| R Demming | 147 | 1972-80 | 73 |
| K Canning | 253 | 1978-89 | 73 |

| Name | Apps | Between | Tries |
|---|---|---|---|
| P J Green | 165 | 1967-74 | 72 |
| H H Morris | 82 | 1892-97 | 71 |
| P S Collingridge | 196 | 1948-57 | 69 |
| N F Reed | 168 | 1926-34 | 67 |
| N J Philbrook | 127 | 1963-70 | 66 |
| W H Whiting | 163 | 1948-58 | 65 |
| J G Pritchard | 181 | 2001-11 | 65 |
| R J Slaughter | 334 | 1960-78 | 64 |
| M E Finlinson | 76 | 1900-09 | 61 |
| R Willsher | 354 | 1928-49 | 60 |
| A Hall | 272 | 1906-25 | 58 |
| T E K Williams | 142 | 1926-34 | 55 |
| F W Potter | 128 | 1891-98 | 54 |
| D Jackson | 212 | 1971-79 | 53 |
| W A Sime | 210 | 1926-38 | 52 |
| L F Oakley | 77 | 1942-53 | 52 |
| J P Janion | 76 | 1969-73 | 50 |

The club record of 38 tries in a season stands to H H Morris, one of the Invincibles of 1893-94. He played in every match of a season in which the Blues lost once and drew once in 29 outings. Derek Wyatt, Arthur Heard and Len Ashwell are the only other players to score 30 or more tries in one season, Wyatt doing so a record four times.

### 20 tries in a season

| Name | Apps | Season | Tries |
|---|---|---|---|
| H H Morris | 29 | 1893-94 | 38 |
| A D Heard | 26 | 1908-09 | 35 |
| D M Wyatt | 36 | 1975-76 | 35 |
| DM Wyatt | 29 | 1973-74 | 33 |
| A D Heard | 23 | 1907-08 | 31 |
| L G Ashwell | 26 | 1929-30 | 31 |
| D M Wyatt | 28 | 1974-75 | 30 |
| D M Wyatt | 33 | 1976-77 | 30 |
| A R Alston | 29 | 1927-28 | 29 |
| M E Finlinson | 26 | 1905-06 | 28 |
| A R Alston | 27 | 1926-27 | 27 |
| L A R Fensome | 32 | 1924-25 | 26 |
| V J Lyttle | 28 | 1934-35 | 26 |
| A K Towersey | 33 | 1972-73 | 26 |
| R C Brumwell | 32 | 1931-32 | 25 |
| B M L Whetstone | 26 | 1997-98 | 25 |

| Name | Apps | Season | Tries |
|---|---|---|---|
| H Schmidt | 28 | 2010-11 | 25 |
| M E Finlinson | 26 | 1903-04 | 24 |
| V J Lyttle | 23 | 1935-36 | 24 |
| B K Williams | 35 | 1964-65 | 24 |
| H Willett | 28 | 1906-07 | 23 |
| L G Ashwell | 31 | 1930-31 | 23 |
| L W McLean | 29 | 1951-52 | 23 |
| F W Potter | 19 | 1893-94 | 21 |
| T D Thevenard | 28 | 1935-36 | 21 |
| N J Philbrook | 38 | 1966-67 | 21 |
| J P Janion | 29 | 1967-70 | 21 |
| A K Towersey | 20 | 1975-76 | 21 |
| R Demming | 31 | 1976-77 | 21 |
| B M L Whetstone | 30 | 1996-97 | 21 |
| B K Williams | 34 | 1961-62 | 20 |

### Most points in a match

35 (3t, 10c, 1p): W N Bennett v Wasps (a), April 6, 1974.

34 (3t, 8c, 1p): A Hepher v Newbury (h) April 29, 2006.

33 (3t, 9c, 1p): D M Wyatt: v Cambridge University (h), October 19, 1977.

### Most tries in a match

6: H Willett, v St Thomas Hospital (H), February 16 1907. A D Heard, v Herts Wands (H), November 7 1908. D M Wyatt, v Bournemouth (A), November 3 1974.

5: H Willett, A D Heard (six times), D M Wyatt (three times), H H Morris, L A R Fensome, L G Ashwell, L F L Oakley, R Fletcher, N J Philbrook, J Chandler.

4: A D Heard (8 times), D M Wyatt (five times), A K Towersey (four times), lead the list.

3: D M Wyatt (17 times), A D Heard (14 times), V J Lyttle and A K Towersey (eight times) lead the list.

### Most conversions in a match

11: A J Finnie v Old Paulines (h) December 26, 1991.

10: R Fowler v Civil Service (h) October 12, 1912.

10: W N Bennett v Wasps (a) April 6, 1974.

10: J G Pritchard v Rotherham (h) April 16, 2011.

9: D M Wyatt v Cambridge University (h) October 19, 1977

9: A Hepher v Birmingham & Solihull (a) March 11, 2006

### Most penalties in a match

8: J G Pritchard v Otley (h) November 2, 2002.

7: A J Finnie v Coventry (h), April 23, 1994.

6: A J Finnie v Leighton Buzzard (a) October 26, 1987.

6: A J Finnie v Leicester (a) January 18, 1992.

6: M A Rayer v Rotherham (h) August 30, 1997.

6: J G Pritchard v Cornish Pirates (h) October 9, 2010.

6: J G Pritchard v Worcester (h) October 16, 2010.

### Most dropped goals in a match

3: A M Jorden v Northampton (h), November, 19, 1977.

### Conversions

#### Most in a season:

M A Rayer, 101, 1996-97.

M A Rayer, 88, 1997-98.

J G Pritchard, 73, 2010-11

#### Most in a career:

J G Pritchard, 360.

A J Finnie, 339.

B Page, 229.

**Penalty goals**

Most in a season:

L Hinton, 81, 2004-05.

A J Finnie,79, 1994-95.

J G Pritchard, 73, 2002-03.

Most in a career:

A J Finnie, 556.

J G Pritchard, 332.

B Page, 214.

**Dropped goals**

Most in a season:

G W Davies, 12, 1971-72.

W N Bennett, 9, 1974-75.

A J Finnie, 9, 1988-89.

Most in a career:

A J Finnie, 61.

P D Briggs, 33.

R Eidsforth 23.

Bob Demming

Nick Youngs on the ball with Andy Whitehouse, second left, and Rupert Meadows, right, in support

# TEAM RECORDS

## WIN, LOSE OR DRAW

The record breaking season of 1893-94 is the first in which reliable records are available. And that team of 'Invincibles' which lost just once was the first to score more than 500 points and more than 100 tries. The 1975-76 side was the first to score 1,000 points in a season and the first to register more than 150 tries. The period from 1967-68 to 1979-80 saw 100 or more tries scored in each of the 13 seasons – the longest unbroken sequence in 125 years. Penalty tries, though introduced for obstruction in 1888, weren't always recorded, nor were tries awarded to 'the pack.'

| Season | Played | Won | Lost | Drawn | For | Against | Tries | Cons | Pens | DGs | PTs |
|---|---|---|---|---|---|---|---|---|---|---|---|
| 1886-87 | 20 | 17 | 1 | 2 | | | | | | | |
| 1887-88 | 25 | 22 | 1 | 2 | | | | | | | |
| 1888-89 | 19 | 12 | 2 | 5 | | | | | | | |
| 1889-90 | 13 | 7 | 5 | 1 | | | | | | | |
| 1890-91 | 14 | 8 | 5 | 1 | | | | | | | |
| 1891-92 | 15 | 8 | 4 | 3 | | | | | | | |
| 1892-93 | 17 | 9 | 5 | 3 | | | | | | | |
| 1893-94 | 29 | 27 | 1 | 1 | 520 | 49 | 120 | 50 | 4 | 12 | |
| 1894-95 | 27 | 13 | 13 | 1 | 215 | 128 | 55 | 22 | 2 | 0 | |
| 1895-96 | 32 | 19 | 9 | 4 | 253 | 137 | 65 | 24 | 2 | 1 | |
| 1896-97 | 31 | 20 | 10 | 1 | 301 | 134 | 74 | 29 | 3 | 3 | |
| 1897-98 | 32 | 9 | 19 | 4 | 196 | 191 | 49 | 16 | 3 | 2 | |
| 1898-99 | 32 | 12 | 18 | 2 | 217 | 196 | 56 | 16 | 3 | 2 | |
| 1899-00 | 28 | 15 | 8 | 5 | 179 | 181 | 48 | 15 | 0 | 2 | |
| 1900-01 | 26 | 14 | 9 | 3 | 248 | 119 | 62 | 26 | 2 | 1 | |
| 1901-02 | 26 | 11 | 13 | 2 | 143 | 185 | 36 | 15 | 0 | 2 | |
| 1902-03 | 29 | 18 | 10 | 1 | 307 | 153 | 77 | 31 | 2 | 2 | |
| 1903-04 | 26 | 19 | 6 | 1 | 346 | 106 | 87 | 36 | 3 | 1 | |
| 1904-05 | 29 | 20 | 7 | 2 | 326 | 140 | 76 | 30 | 4 | 4 | |
| 1905-06 | 36 | 20 | 15 | 1 | 451 | 372 | 105 | 52 | 8 | 2 | |
| 1906-07 | 30 | 21 | 9 | 0 | 578 | 169 | 132 | 72 | 7 | 5 | |
| 1907-08 | 32 | 19 | 13 | 0 | 423 | 339 | 103 | 45 | 4 | 3 | |
| 1908-09 | 34 | 19 | 15 | 0 | 447 | 298 | 102 | 50 | 7 | 5 | |
| 1909-10 | 35 | 15 | 19 | 1 | 389 | 373 | 87 | 40 | 8 | 6 | |
| 1910-11 | 33 | 15 | 16 | 2 | 379 | 416 | 81 | 41 | 10 | 6 | |
| 1911-12 | 34 | 20 | 12 | 2 | 470 | 325 | 114 | 41 | 6 | 7 | |
| 1912-13 | 35 | 24 | 9 | 2 | 506 | 249 | 130 | 46 | 8 | 0 | |
| 1913-14 | 35 | 23 | 8 | 4 | 469 | 284 | 120 | 40 | 7 | 2 | |
| 1919-20 | 14 | 6 | 8 | 0 | 114 | 248 | 25 | 9 | 3 | 3 | |
| 1920-21 | 25 | 7 | 17 | 1 | 154 | 434 | 39 | 12 | 3 | 1 | |
| 1921-22 | 36 | 20 | 13 | 3 | 435 | 349 | 106 | 35 | 5 | 8 | |
| 1922-23 | 35 | 21 | 12 | 2 | 368 | 177 | 90 | 29 | 8 | 4 | |
| 1923-24 | 35 | 28 | 5 | 2 | 430 | 211 | 99 | 39 | 13 | 4 | |
| 1924-25 | 35 | 15 | 17 | 3 | 340 | 325 | 90 | 29 | 4 | 0 | |
| 1925-26 | 32 | 20 | 9 | 3 | 513 | 246 | 124 | 53 | 9 | 2 | |

| Season | Played | Won | Lost | Drawn | For | Against | Tries | Cons | Pens | DGs | PTs |
|---|---|---|---|---|---|---|---|---|---|---|---|
| 1926-27 | 36 | 23 | 13 | 0 | 485 | 319 | 124 | 42 | 7 | 2 | |
| 1927-28 | 33 | 25 | 6 | 2 | 467 | 220 | 122 | 36 | 7 | 2 | |
| 1928-29 | 36 | 17 | 17 | 2 | 332 | 327 | 87 | 32 | 1 | 1 | |
| 1929-30 | 34 | 20 | 10 | 4 | 430 | 235 | 110 | 34 | 0 | 8 | |
| 1930-31 | 35 | 27 | 7 | 1 | 445 | 212 | 107 | 38 | 10 | 4 | |
| 1931-32 | 34 | 23 | 11 | 0 | 421 | 229 | 100 | 42 | 9 | 5 | |
| 1932-33 | 34 | 23 | 11 | 0 | 389 | 234 | 93 | 37 | 7 | 9 | |
| 1933-34 | 38 | 27 | 9 | 2 | 547 | 313 | 124 | 53 | 13 | 8 | |
| 1934-35 | 36 | 26 | 8 | 2 | 585 | 220 | 139 | 66 | 8 | 3 | |
| 1935-36 | 32 | 22 | 9 | 1 | 402 | 206 | 100 | 31 | 4 | 6 | |
| 1936-37 | 33 | 23 | 9 | 1 | 407 | 241 | 88 | 36 | 17 | 5 | |
| 1937-38 | 34 | 17 | 14 | 3 | 389 | 214 | 93 | 33 | 12 | 2 | |
| 1938-39 | 32 | 25 | 4 | 3 | 470 | 134 | 102 | 46 | 11 | 5 | |
| 1939-40 | 7 | 5 | 2 | 0 | 59 | 43 | 16 | 4 | 1 | 0 | |
| 1940-41 | 13 | 8 | 4 | 1 | 171 | 99 | 39 | 17 | 4 | 2 | |
| 1941-42 | 8 | 5 | 3 | 0 | 91 | 98 | 20 | 6 | 1 | 4 | |
| 1942-43 | 10 | 8 | 2 | 0 | 179 | 102 | 43 | 17 | 4 | 1 | |
| 1943-44 | 11 | 6 | 5 | 0 | 125 | 85 | 30 | 11 | 3 | 1 | |
| 1944-45 | 10 | 7 | 3 | 0 | 120 | 80 | 27 | 14 | 1 | 2 | |
| 1945-46 | 31 | 17 | 13 | 1 | 412 | 333 | 95 | 41 | 11 | 3 | |
| 1946-47 | 27 | 16 | 9 | 2 | 300 | 215 | 67 | 31 | 11 | 1 | |
| 1947-48 | 35 | 22 | 11 | 2 | 414 | 242 | 86 | 37 | 22 | 4 | |
| 1948-49 | 34 | 23 | 7 | 4 | 462 | 170 | 103 | 42 | 18 | 5 | |
| 1949-50 | 36 | 25 | 10 | 1 | 485 | 208 | 98 | 49 | 23 | 8 | |
| 1950-51 | 33 | 24 | 5 | 4 | 425 | 105 | 90 | 40 | 20 | 5 | |
| 1951-52 | 36 | 28 | 6 | 2 | 454 | 158 | 95 | 47 | 17 | 8 | |
| 1952-53 | 34 | 20 | 10 | 4 | 351 | 243 | 67 | 36 | 18 | 8 | |
| 1953-54 | 33 | 19 | 13 | 1 | 362 | 311 | 76 | 28 | 19 | 7 | |
| 1954-55 | 36 | 17 | 16 | 3 | 325 | 275 | 63 | 23 | 23 | 7 | |
| 1955-56 | 36 | 18 | 16 | 2 | 286 | 321 | 58 | 23 | 13 | 9 | |
| 1956-57 | 38 | 15 | 19 | 4 | 279 | 383 | 66 | 18 | 13 | 2 | |
| 1957-58 | 37 | 18 | 14 | 5 | 314 | 308 | 57 | 25 | 20 | 11 | |
| 1958-59 | 35 | 18 | 14 | 3 | 401 | 306 | 79 | 34 | 29 | 3 | |
| 1959-60 | 37 | 26 | 7 | 4 | 532 | 291 | 111 | 50 | 28 | 5 | |
| 1960-61 | 40 | 22 | 16 | 2 | 371 | 255 | 84 | 28 | 21 | 0 | |
| 1961-62 | 35 | 17 | 15 | 3 | 590 | 381 | 130 | 67 | 18 | 4 | |
| 1962-63 | 28 | 18 | 7 | 3 | 416 | 211 | 88 | 40 | 20 | 4 | |
| 1963-64 | 38 | 26 | 11 | 1 | 622 | 333 | 134 | 62 | 26 | 6 | |
| 1964-65 | 37 | 18 | 17 | 2 | 499 | 440 | 102 | 41 | 26 | 11 | |
| 1965-66 | 35 | 19 | 16 | 0 | 393 | 360 | 80 | 36 | 19 | 8 | |
| 1966-67 | 40 | 23 | 16 | 1 | 417 | 343 | 76 | 39 | 29 | 8 | |
| 1967-68 | 39 | 24 | 12 | 3 | 658 | 442 | 126 | 62 | 44 | 8 | |
| 1968-69 | 34 | 21 | 9 | 4 | 563 | 371 | 109 | 43 | 42 | 8 | |
| 1969-70 | 35 | 28 | 6 | 1 | 637 | 287 | 114 | 56 | 55 | 6 | |
| 1970-71 | 35 | 28 | 7 | 0 | 596 | 331 | 100 | 49 | 54 | 12 | |
| 1971-72 | 39 | 29 | 9 | 1 | 853 | 414 | 130 | 71 | 51 | 12 | |
| 1972-73 | 38 | 19 | 17 | 2 | 723 | 579 | 108 | 57 | 54 | 5 | |
| 1973-74 | 36 | 22 | 12 | 2 | 742 | 539 | 113 | 64 | 51 | 3 | |
| 1974-75 | 36 | 24 | 11 | 1 | 799 | 386 | 116 | 67 | 54 | 13 | |
| 1975-76 | 45 | 26 | 19 | 0 | 1043 | 731 | 151 | 86 | 82 | 7 | |

| Season | Played | Won | Lost | Drawn | For | Against | Tries | Cons | Pens | DGs | PTs |
|---|---|---|---|---|---|---|---|---|---|---|---|
| 1976-77 | 37 | 22 | 15 | 0 | 756 | 531 | 123 | 63 | 41 | 5 | |
| 1977-78 | 39 | 18 | 21 | 0 | 752 | 623 | 132 | 67 | 24 | 6 | |
| 1978-79 | 38 | 17 | 19 | 2 | 664 | 596 | 101 | 52 | 46 | 6 | |
| 1979-80 | 41 | 23 | 17 | 1 | 755 | 554 | 114 | 58 | 54 | 7 | |
| 1980-81 | 45 | 18 | 24 | 3 | 540 | 684 | 74 | 34 | 54 | 5 | |
| 1981-82 | 37 | 12 | 21 | 4 | 486 | 495 | 59 | 27 | 61 | 4 | |
| 1982-83 | 41 | 17 | 23 | 1 | 530 | 668 | 56 | 30 | 76 | 6 | |
| 1983-84 | 42 | 17 | 25 | 0 | 539 | 797 | 61 | 24 | 79 | 4 | |
| 1984-85 | 41 | 18 | 20 | 3 | 546 | 756 | 63 | 27 | 69 | 11 | |
| 1985-86 | 38 | 13 | 23 | 2 | 421 | 851 | 51 | 20 | 50 | 9 | |
| 1986-87 | 43 | 18 | 25 | 0 | 590 | 667 | 70 | 37 | 72 | 6 | 1 |
| 1987-88 | 42 | 22 | 18 | 2 | 723 | 800 | 98 | 52 | 60 | 11 | 3 |
| 1988-89 | 40 | 19 | 19 | 2 | 649 | 693 | 82 | 47 | 57 | 16 | 2 |
| 1989-90 | 40 | 8 | 31 | 1 | 436 | 1120 | 64 | 28 | 36 | 4 | 1 |
| 1990-91 | 36 | 13 | 21 | 2 | 612 | 824 | 89 | 35 | 52 | 6 | 1 |
| 1991-92 | 39 | 18 | 20 | 1 | 730 | 672 | 96 | 59 | 70 | 6 | 0 |
| 1992-93 | 35 | 19 | 14 | 2 | 687 | 601 | 75 | 39 | 74 | 4 | 0 |
| 1993-94 | 37 | 21 | 16 | 0 | 868 | 640 | 98 | 61 | 78 | 4 | 2 |
| 1994-95 | 37 | 24 | 12 | 1 | 900 | 648 | 96 | 61 | 90 | 6 | 1 |
| 1995-96 | 33 | 11 | 21 | 1 | 604 | 938 | 76 | 39 | 43 | 4 | 0 |
| 1996-97 | 37 | 22 | 15 | 0 | 1207 | 862 | 168 | 111 | 42 | 0 | 4 |
| 1997-98 | 33 | 29 | 4 | 0 | 1254 | 588 | 166 | 116 | 63 | 2 | 8 |
| 1998-99 | 39 | 10 | 28 | 1 | 807 | 1174 | 99 | 66 | 57 | 1 | 0 |
| 1999-00 | 34 | 6 | 28 | 0 | 638 | 1147 | 75 | 53 | 48 | 1 | 2 |
| 2000-01 | 30 | 11 | 18 | 1 | 564 | 719 | 71 | 36 | 38 | 3 | 0 |
| 2001-02 | 28 | 12 | 13 | 3 | 688 | 652 | 83 | 48 | 57 | 7 | 2 |
| 2002-03 | 27 | 13 | 13 | 1 | 692 | 787 | 68 | 54 | 73 | 5 | 2 |
| 2003-04 | 29 | 14 | 14 | 1 | 727 | 677 | 87 | 64 | 53 | 0 | 0 |
| 2004-05 | 33 | 22 | 10 | 1 | 855 | 652 | 88 | 62 | 87 | 1 | 1 |
| 2005-06 | 31 | 23 | 7 | 1 | 1098 | 650 | 139 | 117 | 46 | 2 | 5 |
| 2006-07 | 32 | 19 | 11 | 2 | 871 | 600 | 104 | 79 | 54 | 2 | 4 |
| 2007-08 | 34 | 20 | 14 | 0 | 796 | 636 | 92 | 61 | 68 | 2 | 1 |
| 2008-09 | 33 | 24 | 9 | 0 | 978 | 583 | 135 | 73 | 49 | 0 | 0 |
| 2009-10 | 35 | 20 | 14 | 1 | 885 | 706 | 106 | 76 | 66 | 0 | 1 |
| 2010-11 | 38 | 27 | 11 | 0 | 1216 | 713 | 144 | 106 | 87 | 1 | 4 |

**Best record in a season**

(minimum 25 matches, based on percentage of wins to games played)

1893-94: P29, W27, L1, D1.

**Worst record in a season**

1999-2000: P34, W6, L28.

**Most Wins in a season**

29: 1971-72 (from 39);
1997-98 (from 33).

**Most defeats in a season**

31: 1989-90 (from 40).

**Fewest wins in a season**

6: 1999-2000 (from 34).

**Fewest defeats**

1: 1893-94 (from 29).

**Consecutive wins in a season**

1893-94: 21.

**Consecutive matches without defeat**

1893-94: 28 (one draw).

**Longest losing sequence**

14 matches in 1999-2000.

**Longest losing run in a season**

14 matches in 1999-2000.

**Unbeaten at home**

1893-94, 1969-70, 1997-98.

**Most home wins in a season**

1923-24: 26 from 31.

**Most away wins in a season**

1997-98: 12 from 16.

**Biggest win (by margin)**

90-3 v Old Paulines (h), December 26, 1991.

### Heaviest defeat

12-106 v Richmond (h), May 16, 1999.

### Most points in a match

90 v Old Paulines (h), December 26, 1991
80 v Rotherham (h), April 16, 2011
77 v Coventry (h), November 8, 1997

### Most points against in a match

106 v Richmond (h), May 16,1999.
76 v Harlequins, September 25, 1920.
76 v Bath, January 13, 1990.

### Most points for in a season

1254 in 1997-98.

### Most points against in a season

1174 in 1998-99.

### Biggest home wins (by margin)

90-3 (17t, 11c) v Old Paulines, December 26,. 1991.
77-3 (11t, 8c, 2p) v Coventry, November 8, 1997.
74-0 (15t, 7c), v Oxford University, January 22, 1972.

### Biggest away wins

71-7 (12t, 10c, 1p), v Wasps, April 6, 1974.
64-0 (10t, 7c), v Sedgley Park, March 21, 2009.
66-6 (11t, 8c, 2p), v Bournemouth, November 3, 1974.
67-7 (9t, 8c, 2p), v Fylde, December 27, 1997.

### Heaviest home defeats

12-106 (16t, 13c) v Richmond, May 16,1999.
3-68 (12t, 10c), v Leicester, September 3, 1983.
9-58 (9t, 8c, 2p), v Wasps, September 22, 1984.

### Heaviest away defeats

0-76 (17t, 11c, 1p), v Harlequins, September 25, 1920.
0-76 (14t, 10c ) v Bath, January 13, 1990.
9-64 (9t, 8c, 4p), v Leicester, March 10, 1984.

### Most tries for in one match

Home:

17: v Old Paulines, December 26, 1991

16: v Old Alleynians, December 23, 1967.

15: v Upper Clapton, October 27, 1906.

15: v Oxford University, January 22, 1972.

Away:

12: v Wasps, April 6, 1974.

11: v Bournemouth, November 3, 1974.

11: v Taunton, April 19, 1976.

### Most tries against in one match

Home:

16: v Richmond, May 16, 1999.

12: v Leicester, September 3, 1983.

11: v Harlequins, October 15, 1910.

Away:

17: v Harlequins, September 25, 1920.

13: v Harlequins, September 27, 1913.

13: v Northampton, December 27, 1919.

13: v Bristol, January 1, 1983.

13: v Cardiff, April 5, 1986.

Kevin Canning

Ian Skingsley on the ball with Matt Deans in support

# THE OPPOSITION

In their first 125 years, the Blues played 3,873 recorded matches starting against Olney on October 9, 1886 and ending with Bristol on May 7, 2011. Bedford played Northampton (211) more than any other club. Coventry (174), Leicester (146), London Welsh (111) and Moseley (102) are next. The following table shows, in alphabetical order, the clubs on the fixture list for 2010-11, the year of the first game and the record. Home totals are shown in brackets.

| Opponents | First | Played | | Won | | Drawn | | Lost | |
|---|---|---|---|---|---|---|---|---|---|
| Barbarians | 1894 | 5 | (5) | 2 | (2) | - | (-) | 3 | (3) |
| Birmingham & Solihull | 1923 | 33 | (18) | 26 | (16) | 2 | (-) | 5 | (2) |
| Bristol | 1925 | 66 | (34) | 19 | (14) | 1 | (1) | 46 | (20) |
| Cornish Pirates (P&N) | 1958 | 23 | (10) | 8 | (6) | 1 | (-) | 14 | (3) |
| Doncaster | 2005 | 12 | (6) | 7 | (4) | - | (-) | 5 | (3) |
| Esher | 2005 | 7 | (4) | 6 | (4) | - | (-) | 1 | (-) |
| Leinster 'A' | 2011 | 1 | (1) | 1 | (1) | - | (-) | - | (-) |
| London Welsh | 1892 | 111 | (66) | 51 | (34) | 9 | (5) | 51 | (27) |
| Moseley | 1895 | 102 | (50) | 43 | (30) | 7 | (4) | 52 | (16) |
| Neath | 1971 | 12 | (5) | 6 | (5) | - | (-) | 6 | (-) |
| Nottingham | 1893 | 89 | (63) | 57 | (49) | 3 | (1) | 29 | (13) |
| Plymouth | 1898 | 34 | (17) | 24 | (15) | - | (-) | 10 | (2) |
| Rotherham | 1995 | 25 | (13) | 16 | (10) | - | (-) | 9 | (2) |
| Swansea | 1895 | 8 | (3) | 2 | (1) | - | (-) | 6 | (2) |
| Ulster Ravens | 2009 | 2 | (1) | 1 | (1) | - | (-) | 1 | (-) |
| Worcester | 1995 | 13 | (7) | 2 | (2) | - | (-) | 11 | (5) |

Other teams played with date of their first fixture and record in brackets:-

Aberavon (1895 p15 w6 l9), Abercarn (1896 p2 w1 l1), Abertillery (1996 p2 w2), Aldershot Services (1934 p13 w11 l2), Argentine Clubs (1963 p7 w7), Askeans (1991 p3 w3), Aspatria (1898 p2 l2), Auckland (1993 p1 l1).

Bank of England (1926 p6 w5 l1), Barkers Butts (1985 p2 w2), Barking (2003 p1 w1), Bath (1934 p44 w20 d3 l21), Bective Rangers (1895 p3 l3), Bedford & District League (1899 p4 w3 d1), Bedford County School (1886 p4 w4), Bedford Grammar School (1886 p17 w10 d2 l5), Bedford Grammar School Past & Present (1887 p6 w1 d1 l4), Bedford Modern School (1886 p22 w21 d1), Bedfordshire (1910 p20, w18, d1, l1), Bedfordshire Masters (1887 p3 w2 l1), Bedfordshire Police (1993 p1 w1), Bedford Thursday (1922 p1 w1), Bedford United Schools (1904 p1 w1), Berkshire Wanderers (1921 p1 w1), Birkenhead Park (1952 p10 w6 d1 l3), Birmingham University (1925 p2 w1 d1), Blackheath ( 1924 p66 w43 d3 l20), Blackheath 'A' (1894 p2 w1 l1), Blackwell (1924 p17 w15 l2), Bosuns (1970 p2 w2), Bournemouth (1974 p1 w1), Bracknell (2001 p2 w2), Bradford (1950 p4 w4), Bradford & Bingley (1993 p1 l1), H.V.Brodies XV (1926 p1 w1), Bridgend (1974 p3 l3), Bridgwater (1923 p1 w1), British Columbia Clubs (1975 p4 w4), Brockley (1894 p1 w1), Broughton Park (1894 p2 w2), Burton on Trent (1894 p21 w17 l4).

Camborne (1988 p1 w1), Cambridge City (1978 p1 w1), Cambridge Hybrids (1925 p1 w1), Cambridge University (1905 p72 w33 d3 l36), Cambridge University Past & Present (1987 p1 l1), Canterbury NZ (1994 p1 l1), Cardiff (1924 p12 w2 l10), Cardiff Scottish (1923 p1 w1), H.H.Castens (London XV1888 p1 l1), Castres (1999 p2 l2), Catford Bridge (1905 p3 w3), Cheltenham (1924 p5 w2 l3), Chesterfield (1979 p1 w1), Cinderford (1923 p1 w1), Civil Service (1889 p22 w16 d1 l5), Clapham Rovers (1891 p2 w1 d1), Clifton (1994 p2 w2), Combined Services XV (1940 p1 w1), Coventry (1894 p174 w58 d11 l105), Crawshay's XV (1986 p2 l2), Cross Keys (1930 p1 d1), H.Cross XV (1892 p1 l1), Croydon (1897 p5 w2 l3).

Dungannon (1996 p1 w1), Durham University (1952 p3 w2 l1).

Ealing (1891 p8 w8), East Sheen (1888 p1 d1), Eastern Counties (1985 p2 w1 l1), Eastern Suburbs Sydney (1975 p1 l1), Ebbw Vale (1924 p28 w15 d1 l12), Eccles (1900 p12 w8 l4), Edinburgh Academicals (1951 p1 d1), Edinburgh University (1949 p13 w9 l4), Edgeware (1921 p5 w5), Evesham (1985 p1 w1), Exeter (1972 p35 w17 l18).

E.A.Fowlers XV (1887 p1 w1), Fylde (1968 p9 w8 l1).

Gautang Falcons SA (1998 p1 w1), Glamorgan Wanderers (1990 p1 l1), Glasgow HSFP (1964 p2 w2), Glasgow University (1907 p4 w3 l1), Gloucester (1905 p51 w16 d4 l31), Gosforth (1967 p16 w10 l6).

Hospital teams: Charing Cross (1887 p1 w1), Guys (1898 p50 w36 l14), Kings College (1894 p7 w7), London (1894 p53 w39 d2 l12), Middlesex (1888 p13 w9 d1 l3), St Bartholomew's (1893 p34 w27 d1 l6), St George's (1893 p1 w1), St Mary's (1887 p58 w44 d6 l8), St Thomas's (1895 p24 w10 d1 l13), University College (1894 p1 w1).

Halifax (1960 p3 w1 l2), Hammersmith (1899 p4 w4), Hampstead (1892 p3 w3), Hampstead Wanderers (1906 p1 w1), Harlequins (1908 p54 w17 d5 l32), Harlequins 'A' (1996 p1 l1), Harrogate (1974 p6 w6), Hartlepool Rovers (1950 p4 w4), Havant (1993 p2 w2), Hayle (1976 p1 w1), Headingly (1923 p39 w22 d3 l14), R.S.Hellier London XV (1926 p1 w1), Herts Wanderers (1908 p1 w1), Henley (1999 p8 w5 l3), Hinckley(1979 p1 w1), Hon Artillery Co (1888 p3 w3), Huddersfield (1959 p4 w4), Hull Ionians (1992 p1 w1).

Jedforest (1908 p1 l1).

Keble College Oxford (1894 p2 w1 l1), Kelso (1995 p3 w2 l1), Kempston (1887 p6 w6), F.Kendall's London XV (1897 p3 w1 d1 l1), Kensington (1898 p9 w5 d1 l3), Kensington Nomads (1896 p1 w1), Kent Wanderers (1893 p1 l1), Kingston on Thames (1893 p2 w2).

Launceston (2007 p2 w2), Leeds (2000 p6 w2 l4), Leicester (1886 p146 w44 d9 l93), Leicester Stoneygate (1923 p1 w1), Leighton Buzzard (1987 p1 w1), Lennox (1898 p8 w6 l2), Lensbury (1924 p4 w3 d1), Leytonstone (1901 p10 w9 d1), Lichfield (1979 p2 w1 l1), Liverpool (1961 p1 w1), Liverpool SH (1988 p3 w1 l2), Lizards (1928 p1 w1), Llanelli (1897 p13 w3 l10), Llwynpia (1895 p1 w1), London Buccaneers (1899 p5 w5), London Caledonians (1888 p1 w1), London Clergy (1914 p1 w1), London Devonians (1902 p10 w7 d1 l2), London Irish (1899 p73 w39 d4 l30), London Scottish (1935 p56 w24 d2 l30), London University (1923 p6 w6), Loughborough College (1962 p2 w1 d1), Loughborough Students (1986 p7 w5 l2).

Manchester (1936 p38 w32 d3 l3), Marlborough Nomads (1897 p14 w8 d1 l5), Merthyr Tydfil (1897 p1 w1), Metropolitan Police (1933 p34 w20 d4 l10), Monkstown (1896 p2 l2), Morley (1989 p2 l2), Mortlake (1887 p1 w1).

Neath United (1922 p1 w1), New Brighton (1976 p4 w3 l1), Newbury (2006 p8 w8), Newcastle (1995 p8 w3 l5), Newcastle Gosforth (1991 p3 w1 l2), Newport (2000 p2 w1 l1), New Zealand (1905 p1 l1), Norfolk & Suffolk Combined Services (1940 p1 w1), Northampton (1887 p211 w66 d15 l130), Northampton Unity (1886 p1 l1), North Bucks Wanderers (1889 p1 d1), Northern (1978 p2 w1 l1), Northern Wanderers (1903 p4 l4), Norwich (1953 p2 w2), Norwood (1904 p1 w1), Nuneaton (1899 p44 w29 d3 l12).

Occasiords Cambridge (1886 p2 w2), OCTU Sandhurst (1940 p1 w1), Olney (1886 p54 w38 d5 l11), Orrell (1980 p15 w3 d1 l11), H.R.Orrs Cambridge XV (1888 p1 w1), Otley (1939 p21 w14 d2 l5), Oxford (1955 p7 w7), Oxford University (1908 p41 w26 d5 l10), Oxford University Greyhounds (1929 p1 w1).

Old Boys teams: Combined Birmingham OB (1971 p1 w1), Harrogate OB (1923 p1 w1), Old Alleynians (1907 p50 w39 d3 l8), Old Alleynians cum Whitgiftians (1945 p1 w1), Old Bedfordians (1892 p4 w4), Old Bedford Modernians (1928 p1 w1), Old Blues (1907 p29 w19 d1 l9), Old Centrals (1922 p1 w1), Old Charltonians (1909 p1 l1), Old Cranleighians (1924 p14 w10 l4), Old Dovorians (1891 p1 w1), Old Dunstonians (1907 p4 w4), Old Edwardians (1895 p29 w19 d2 l8), Old Elstonians (1890 p1 w1), Old Emanuel (1922 p3 w2 d1), Old Haileybarians (1923 p1 w1), Old Leysians (1891 p23 w15 d1 l7), Old Paulines (1897 p69 w60 l9), Old Merchant Taylors (1905 p44 w25 d2 l17), Old Merchistonians (1909 p4 w2 l2), Old Millhillians (1910 p29 w25 d1 l3), Old Upper Hamians (1902 p1 w1), Old Whitgiftians (1909 p9 w9), UCS Old Boys (1902 p22 w16 l6), Yorkshire School OB (1899 p2 d1 l1).

Park House (1904 p3 w3), Penarth (1904 p11 w7 l4), Penguins (2003 p1 w1), Penycraig (1895 p1 w1), Penzance & Newlyn (1958 p3 w1 d1 l1), Percy Park (1950 p8 w5 l3), Pill Harriers (1923 p1 w1), Pontypool (1909 p24 w9 d2 l13), Portsmouth (1896 p1 w1), Public School Wanderers (1991 p1 w1).

Racing Club de France (1903 p1 w1), RAF (1929 p50 w36 d4 l10), Redruth (1958 p3 w3), W.Rees XV(1900 p1 w1), REME (1946 p1 w1), Richmond (1931 p60 w27 d1 l32), Richmond cum Blackheath (1945 p1 w1), RMA Woolwich (1912 p2 w2), RMC Camberley (1924 p1 w1), D.P.Rogers International XV (1978 p1 w1), Rosslyn Park (1897 p88 w42 d4 l42), Roundhay (1981 p4 w1 d1 l2), Rovigo (1999 p2 w1 l1), Royal Indian Engineering College (1894 p1 l1), Royal Navy (1964 p3 w2 l1), Royal School of Mines (1922 p1 w1), Royal Vetinery College (1889 p3 w3), Rugby (1890 p73 w47 d3 l23), Rushden & Higham (1984 p1 w1).

Sale (1932 p45 w20 d4 l21), Saracens (1899 p28 w12 d2 l14), Sedgley Park (2004 p10 w9 l1), Selkirk (1993 p1 w1), Shandon (1903 p1 w1), Sheffield (1990 p5 w3 l2), T.L.Shoosmith's XV(1888 p1 w1), South Africa 'A' (1996 p1 l1), Southend (1987 p1 w1), South West Districts SA (1997 p1 w1), St Catherine's College Cambridge (1921 p1 l1), St Ives (1958 p2 w1 l1), St Lukes College Exeter (1977 p1 w1), Staines (1997 p1 w1), Stony Stratford (1886 p2 w2), Stourbridge (1994 p1 w1), R.Straeuli's XV (1999 p2 w2), Stratford on Avon (1888 p4 w3 l1), Streatham (1920 p5 w5), Steatham & Croydon (1975 p1 w1), Suffolk County (1926 p1 w1), Surrey Wanderers (1888 p1 w1), Stade Bordelais (1909 p2 w1 l1), Stade Francais (1894 p1 w1), Surbiton (1902 p1 l1).

Tabard (2004 p1 w1), Taunton (1976 p2 w2), Territorial Army (1960 p4 w4), The Army (1954 p4 w4), Thurlow Park (1892 p1 w1), Tonbridge (1909 p2 w1 l1), Trerhebert (1923 p1 w1), Tynedale (2009 p1 w1).

United Engineering College (1900 p1 w1), United Services Aldershot (1934 p1 w1), United Sevices Chatham (1926 p1 w1), United Services Portsmouth (1947 p14 w10 d1 l3), Upper Clapton (1886 p33 w28 d2 l3), USA clubs (1981 p6 w6), UWIC (1996 p1 w1).

Vale of Lune (1985 p4 w3 d1).

Wakefield (1931 p26 w16 l10), Wasps (1892 p42 w23 d3 l16), Waterloo (1970 p27 w17 d2 l8), S.R.Wells XV (1902 p1 w1), West Hartlepool (1991 p5 w2 l3), West Herts (1921 p3 w3), Westleigh (1921 p2 w2), Westminster Bank (1927 p4 w4), Weston Super Mare (1935 p2 d1 l1), West Park SH (1994 p1 w1), Wickham Park (1897 p5 w1 d1 l3), Wilmslow (1974 p2 w2), Wolverton (1890 p2 w1 l1), Wormholt (1894 p4 w3 d1).

Bedford Followers in full flow at Plymouth Albion

The party that toured Canada in 1975

It wasn't until the club established itself in the minds of the press around 1893 that games were reported in full and lists of appearances and scorers given in local newspapers. Early records from the *Bedfordshire Times* and others are incomplete and the idea of a Keeper of the Records was not formally raised until 1949 when Eric King, in his capacity as secretary, suggested that Don Riddy might like to undertake the task. A former player and Old Bedford Modernian whose father was a master baker in Kempston, Mr Riddy received the CBE for services to education in post-war Germany.

Working closely with local reporter Doug Bowker, he laid the foundation for this statistical section from records kept at the *Bedfordshire Times*. He died in 1980 and in quick succession the President of the day, Harry Bitton, Rams captain Howard Travis and *Bedfordshire Times* reporter Neil Roy took on the role before the retired Vauxhall executive Jack Pope emerged. Mr Pope, immersed himself in the post to such an extent that for the next 20 years he became a walking encyclopaedia on all matters to do with Bedford Rugby Union Football Club. He compiled most of the statistics for the Centenary book going back to the same sources as Don Riddy and he carried on until his death in 2002. Phil Beard took on the role from season 2002-03. It was his idea to update the original book.

Though in some cases the opposition and the scores are not known, it was established as best it could be that in 1886-87 there were 20 matches, 17 wins, one defeat and two draws. Home matches were played on the Swifts ground, part of the House of Industry site in Goldington Road.

Just how many players turned out for the club in its first season is unclear. But the following made at least the number of appearances given by the first figure in the brackets. They also scored at least the number of conversions, dropped goals, penalties, and tries. Prior to 1886, schools, universities and clubs often played to their own complicated laws and points scoring systems but after the formation of the Rugby Football Union in 1871, attempts were made to get everyone to accept the same. In 1886, the RFU adopted a system where points were scored for a try, a conversion/goal and a dropped goal. A try was worth one point. It was upgraded to two in 1891, three in 1893, four in 1971 and five in 1992. A conversion/goal was valued at two points in 1886, three in 1891 and two again from 1893. The penalty kick was introduced in 1888 with a value of two points and then three from 1891. A dropped goal was worth three points in 1886, four from 1891 and three from 1948.

Official records were kept in a slightly different form from the Centenary with tries listed first. The convention of referring to players only by the initial of the christian name they used had by now become established in match programmes. Newspapers tended to use only surnames. However, the initials of club captains and officials, where known, are written out in full elsewhere.

# 1886-87

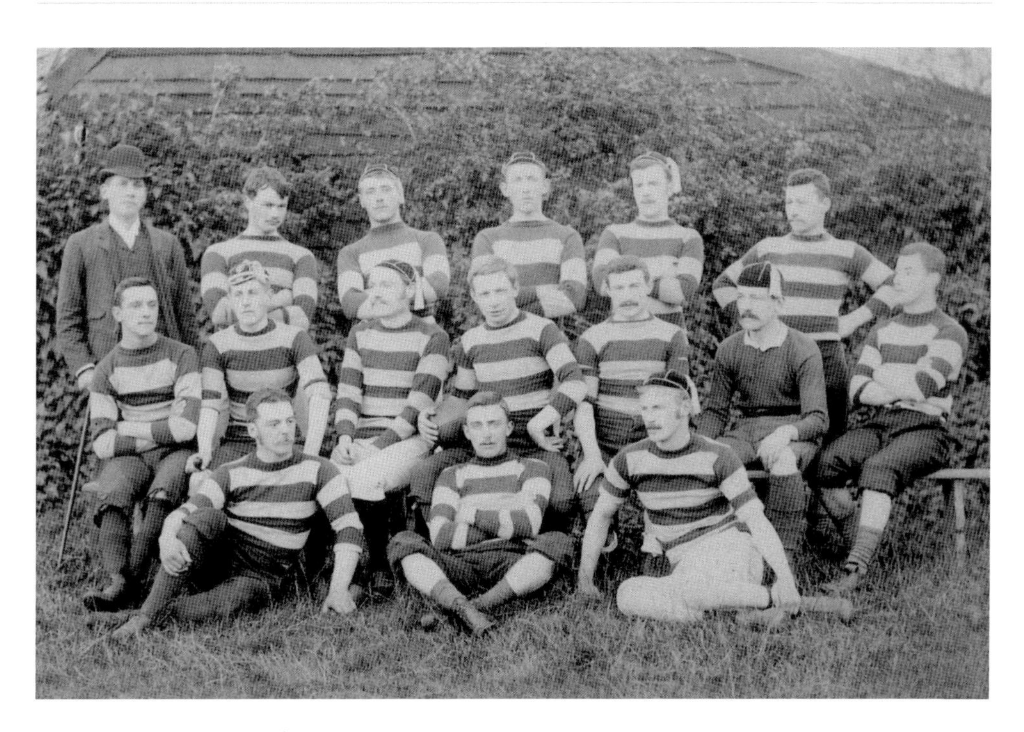

Played 20, won 17, lost 1, drawn 2.

Captain: A Parrott

| October | | | | f | a |
|---|---|---|---|---|---|
| 9 | H | Olney | W | 10 | 3 |
| 16 | H | Stony Stratford | W | 15 | 0 |
| 23 | A | Northampton Unity | W | 5 | 0 |
| 30 | | | | | |
| **November** | | | | | |
| 6 | H | Bedford Mod Sch | W | 1 | 0 |
| 10 | A | Bedford Cty Sch | W | 12 | 0 |
| 13 | | | | | |
| 20 | H | Bedford Gram Sch | W | 8 | 0 |
| 27 | A | Leicester | L | 0 | 10 |
| **December** | | | | | |
| 4 | A | Occasionords (Camb) | W | | |
| 11 | A | Bedford Mod Sch | D | 0 | 0 |
| 27 | H | Upper Clapton | W | | |

| January | | | | f | a |
|---|---|---|---|---|---|
| 1 | | | | | |
| 8 | | | | | |
| 15 | H | Northampton | W | | |
| 22 | H | H Mortlake | W | 20 | 0 |
| 29 | | | | | |
| **February** | | | | | |
| 5 | A | Stony Stratford | W | 8 | 0 |
| 12 | H | Leicester | D | 0 | 0 |
| 19 | H | Occasionords (Camb) | W | | |
| 26 | H | Olney | W | | |
| **March** | | | | | |
| 12 | H | Bedford Gram Sch | W | 5 | 0 |
| 26 | A | Upper Clapton | W | | |

A W Allen (6, 4t), L Bastock (7, 6t), C Bowler (2), Burns (3), A F Dudley (4, 5t), Rev H W Evans (4), Chas Foster (8, 2t), John Foster (9, 3t), Joseph Foster (9, 2t), E O Fowler (1), T Fowler (7, 1t), H Garner (3, 2c, 3t), W J Haffenden (3), T Harris (7), t W E Hawker (2), M Humphrey (1), C H Ireson (3), J B Jones (11, 3c, 5t), W Jones (1), J Moore (3), A Parrott (9, 2t), W B Ranson (3, 7t), F Reeves (2, 1t), W Smith (3), R Steel (3), C Tomlin (2), G Tucker (5, 1t), H Tucker (3), H E Vipan (4), Wright (1).

## 1887-88

Played 25, won 22, lost 1, drawn 2. Captain: A Parrott

| | | | | f | a |
|---|---|---|---|---|---|
| **October** | | | | | |
| 1 | A | Kempston Rovers | W | 5 | 0 |
| 8 | H | Bedford Gram Sch | W | 7 | 3 |
| 15 | H | Leicester | W | 8 | 0 |
| 22 | H | Charing Cross Hos | W | | |
| 29 | H | Northampton Town | W | 8 | 0 |
| **November** | | | | | |
| 9 | A | Bedford Cty Sch | W | 19 | 0 |
| 12 | H | Bedford Mod Sch | W | 7 | 0 |
| 19 | H | Bedfordshire Masters | W | 10 | 1 |
| 23 | H | Bedford Cty Sch | W | 26 | 0 |
| 26 | A | Olney | W | 1 | 0 |
| **December** | | | | | |
| 3 | H | EO Fowlers XV | W | 3 | 0 |
| 10 | H | St Mary's Hosp | W | 10 | 3 |
| 17 | A | Bedford Mod Sch | W | | |
| 24 | H | Bedford Gram Sch P&P | D | | |
| 26 | H | Bedford Gram Sch P&P | W | 9 | 0 |
| **January** | | | | | |
| 5 | A | Northampton | W | 8 | 0 |
| 7 | H | Olney | W | 9 | 0 |
| 12 | A | T L Shoosmiths XV | W | 8 | 0 |
| 18 | H | H H Casten's (Ldn) XV | L | 0 | 16 |
| **February** | | | | | |
| 4 | A | Kempston Rovers | W | 7 | 1 |
| 29 | H | East Sheen | D | 3 | 3 |
| **March** | | | | | |
| 7 | H | H R Orrs (Cam U) XV | W | 3 | 1 |
| 10 | H | Bedford Gram Sch | W | 3 | 1 |
| 17 | H | London Caledonians | W | 12 | 0 |
| 24 | H | Hon Artillery Co | W | 8 | 0 |

Highest points scorer in the club's second season was J B Jones with 23, while J Foster, with six, scored the most tries. The captain, A Parrott, made the most appearances, 15.

A W Allen (2, 3t), J Anderson (1), H A Block (13, 5t), F J Brown (5), W Browne (10, 2t), C Castens (6), H H Castens (1), A F Dudley (3, 1c), Rev H W Evans (11, 5c, 4t), Chas Foster (5, 2c, 3t), James Foster (3), John Foster (12, 6t), Joseph Foster (13 2t), E O Fowler (13, 4t), J M Glubb (1), T Harris (6), M Humphrey (11), C H Ireson (5), E W Jones (6, 10c, 1t), J B Jones (11, 9c, 5t), H S Morris (7, 1t), Mowbray (1), N Oliver (6), F L Orman (2, 1t), A Parrott (15, 2t), Porter (3, 1t), H Simmons (2), R Steel (10, 1t), H E Vipan (11, 3t), W A Williamson (2, 1t).

## 1888-89

Played 19, won 12, lost 2, drawn 5. Captain: A Parrott

| | | | | f | a |
|---|---|---|---|---|---|
| **October** | | | | | |
| 13 | H | Bedford Mod Sch | W | 15 | 0 |
| 17 | H | Leicester | D | 1 | 1 |
| 20 | H | Middlesex Hosp | W | 9 | 3 |
| 27 | H | Bedford Gram Sch | W | 4 | 0 |
| **November** | | | | | |
| 3 | A | St Mary's Hosp | D | 0 | 0 |
| 10 | H | N'pton St James | W | 6 | 3 |
| 21 | H | Bedford Masters | L | 3 | 4 |
| **December** | | | | | |
| 1 | A | Bedford Mod Sch | W | 6 | 0 |
| 15 | A | Leicester | D | 3 | 3 |
| 26 | H | Bed Gram Sch P&P | W | | |
| 29 | H | Bed Gram Sch P&P | W | | |
| **January** | | | | | |
| 12 | H | Olney | W | 2 | 1 |
| 15 | H | N Bucks Wand | D | 6 | 6 |
| 26 | H | St Mary's Hosp | W | 7 | 4 |
| **February** | | | | | |
| 2 | H | Leicester | W | 3 | 1 |
| 9 | H | Surrey Wand | W | 13 | 1 |
| **March** | | | | | |
| 6 | A | Leicester | L | 3 | 4 |
| 16 | H | Bedford Gram Sch | D | 2 | 2 |
| 23 | H | Kempston Rovers | W | 18 | 0 |

A number of players scored two tries with J B Jones also kicking three conversions for eight points, the most recorded in available sources. A Parrott again made most appearances.

H L Bacon (2), Briggs (1), F J Brown (6), W Browne (4), W Bucklow (1), H Cross (1), W Dazeley (1), H W Dickson (3), Rev H W Evans (4, 1c, 2t), Chas Foster (6, 1t), John Foster (6, 1t), Joseph Foster (6), E O Fowler (3), T Fowler (5), T Harris (6), Hogg (1), A E Holt (2), S Howard (1), C H Ireson (1), E W Jones (3, 2c, 1t), J B Jones (4, 3c, 2t), F King (3), Le Mesurier (2), H S Morris (3), Oclee (1, 1t), N Oliver (3), H S Orr (5, 2t), Rhodes (1), A Parrott (6), H Simmons (1), G Steadman (1), R Steel (1), A Suthery (1), F Taylor (1), T L Trethewey (1), H E Vipan (4), H Waller (2).

# 1889-90

Played 13, won 7, lost 5, drawn 1.

Captain: H S Morris

| | | | | f | a |
|---|---|---|---|---|---|
| **October** | | | | | |
| 19 | A | Northampton | W | | |
| **November** | | | | | |
| 2 | H | Royal Vet Col | W | 2 | 0 |
| 9 | H | Bedford Gram Sch | L | 0 | 8 |
| 16 | H | Stratford on Avon | L | 1 | 2 |
| 23 | H | St Mary's Hosp | W | 4 | 0 |
| 30 | H | Civil Service | D | 0 | 0 |
| **December** | | | | | |
| 26 | H | Bed Gram Sch P&P | L | 0 | 11 |
| **January** | | | | | |
| 4 | H | Kempston Rovers | W | 5 | 1 |
| 11 | H | N'pton St James | W | 9 | 0 |
| 18 | A | Stratford-on-Avon | L | 1 | 5 |
| 25 | A | St Mary's Hosp | W | 3 | 0 |
| **February** | | | | | |
| 8 | A | Olney | L | 1 | 5 |
| **March** | | | | | |
| 22 | H | Old Elstonians | W | 9 | 0 |

In 1889-90 a try was still worth one point, a penalty goal became two points and a dropped goal and a goal were worth three. H P Reynolds scored seven points and C Foster three tries.

J Anderson (2), P H Bell (3), C E Combes (2), L Corry-Smith (2), C S Crampton (1), L Dobbin (1), W Dazeley (2), A F Dudley (1), H W Dickson (2), Eckford (1), Chas Foster (7, 3t), Joseph Foster (8, 1t), A Graham (1), T Harris (7), F Hatchell (1), J Hawkins (1), A E Holt (1), P Howard (5), C H Ireson (5), A O Jones (2), J B Jones (5, 1c, 1t), F King (3), W March (4), C McVittie (2), H S Morris (7), R Morris (1), F L Orman (1), A Parrott (3), W M Pool (5), H P Reynolds (2c, 1d), W H Rhodes (1), Rogers (1), H Simmons (1), G A Spencer (1), A E Stone (5, 1c, 1t), Talbot (1), C Tennant (1), R Thompson (2), C Tucker (1), H Tucker (3), A H Turing (4), H E Vipan (6), Williams (1), W Wilson (1).

# 1890-91

Played 14, won 8, lost 5, drawn 1.

Captain: H S Morris

| | | | | f | a |
|---|---|---|---|---|---|
| **October** | | | | | |
| 15 | A | Bedford Mod Sch | W | 7 | 0 |
| **November** | | | | | |
| W | H | Royal Vet Col | W | 8 | 1 |
| 8 | H | Leicester | L | 6 | 7 |
| 12 | A | Bedford Gram Sch | W | 4 | 0 |
| 19 | H | Bedford Mod Sch | W | 7 | 0 |
| 22 | H | Rugby | L | 2 | 6 |
| **December** | | | | | |
| 6 | H | Wolverton | W | 13 | 1 |
| **January** | | | | | |
| 24 | A | Leicester | L | 0 | 6 |
| 31 | H | Ealing | W | 3 | 0 |
| **February** | | | | | |
| 4 | H | Bedford Gram Sch | L | 1 | 3 |
| 7 | H | Bedford Mod Sch | W | 4 | 1 |
| 11 | H | Middlesex Hosp | L | 0 | 1 |
| 21 | H | Old Doverians | W | 3 | 1 |
| **March** | | | | | |
| 13 | A | Wolverton | D | 0 | 0 |

Highest points scorer with 20 and highest try scorer with nine, was W Bryan. The captain, H S Morris, made the most appearances, 11.

H L Bacon (2), P H Bell (1), L G Brown (3), W Bryan (5, 4c, 1d, 9t), H Chapman (1), H Cross (7), A F Crossman (3), A D Clough (2), J J Craig (6), W Dazeley (10), H W Dickson (6, 2t), C Elsee (4), R D Fagan (1), A Forde (1), Chas Foster (10), Joseph Foster (9), T Fowler (8), T Harris (4), F P Hill (3, 2c, 1t), A E Holt (2), F H Holt (5), P Howard (1), C H Ireson (5), A O Jones (1), C L Jones (1), J B Jones (3, 1t), F C D Kendall (1), G D Kettlewell (1), F King (10, 5c), H P G Mawle (1), C G McVittie (6, 2t), H McVittie (1), G C Moore (1), H S Morris (11), J A Page (1), A Parrott (7), H T Pearce (3), H P Reynolds (1), E H D Sewell (1), F Taylor (1), A Thorpe (1), H Tucker (4, 1t), A Udal (1), H E Vipan (9), A C Wheeler (2), H Wilson (1), C G Wright (2).

## 1891-92

Played 15, won 8, lost 4, drawn 3.

Captain: H E Vipan

| | | | | f | a |
|---|---|---|---|---|---|
| **October** | | | | | |
| 17 | H | Old Leysians | L | 5 | 16 |
| 24 | A | Olney | L | 5 | 10 |
| **November** | | | | | |
| 4 | A | Bedford Mod Sch | W | 11 | 0 |
| 7 | A | N'pton St James | W | 7 | 0 |
| 14 | H | St Mary's Hosp | W | 7 | 0 |
| 21 | H | Leicester | D | 0 | 0 |
| 28 | H | Clapham Rovers | D | 0 | 0 |
| **December** | | | | | |
| 5 | H | Bedford Mod Sch | W | 9 | 0 |
| 12 | H | S'ford-on-Avon | W | 5 | 0 |
| 28 | H | Bed Gram Sch P&P | L | 2 | 9 |

| | | | | f | a |
|---|---|---|---|---|---|
| **January** | | | | | |
| 6 | H | Old Bedfordians | W | 9 | 2 |
| 30 | H | Olney | W | 9 | 2 |
| **February** | | | | | |
| 3 | H | Middlesex Hosp | D | 0 | 0 |
| 6 | A | Bedford Gram Sch | L | 0 | 2 |
| **March** | | | | | |
| 5 | | | | | |
| 19 | H | Wormholt | W | 9 | 0 |
| 26 | | | | | |

A try was by now worth two points, a goal five (including the try), a penalty three and a dropped goal four. The highest points scorer was R Rumboll who had six tries in his 18.The captain, H E Vipan, and A F Crossman both played in 14 games.

W Branson (1), L G Brown (2), H Cross (10), A F Crossman (14), A D Clough (6, 1t), P Clough (6, 1t), W Dazeley (12), H W Dickson (1), H W Finlinson (2), Chas Foster (2), Joseph Foster (2), T Fowler (11), A G Goodison (1), A H Griffith (1), W C Griffith (1), C S Hadow (2), D L Hamilton (1), C H Hatchet (6), F C Haydock (1), P Howard (2), C H Ireson (10), W Jesse (3), A O Jones (7, 3c, 1t), G N Jones (10), J B Jones (6, 2t), F King (11, 2t), C B McVittie (4), H S Morris (4), W R Pearce (1,1t), F Popham (9), F W Potter (3, 1c, 1t), W Rees (11), H P Reynolds (6, 2c, 1d, 2t), H Roberts (1), W K Roberts (4, 1t), R Rumboll (7, 2c, 6t), W Rushton (4), E H D Sewell (1, 1c, 1t), E G Sexton (1), H Steadman (3), J H Stewart (1), W Stewart (1), F Swann (1, 1t), R Thompson (4), Trepte (1), H E Vipan (14, 2t), H Waller (2), J Watson (8), C Wingate (1).

## 1892-93

Played 17, won 9, lost 5, drawn 3.

Captain: H E Vipan

| | | | | f | a |
|---|---|---|---|---|---|
| **October** | | | | | |
| 15 | A | Bedford Gram Sch | L | 0 | 14 |
| 22 | A | Bedford Mod Sch | W | 11 | 0 |
| 29 | H | Northampton | D | 2 | 2 |
| **November** | | | | | |
| 5 | A | Olney | D | 0 | 0 |
| 12 | H | London Welsh | W | 5 | 4 |
| 19 | H | Bedford Mod Sch | W | 9 | 0 |
| 26 | A | Leicester | L | 0 | 8 |
| **December** | | | | | |
| 3 | H | H Cross (BGS) XV | L | 0 | 12 |
| 17 | H | Thurlow Park | W | 16 | 0 |

| | | | | f | a |
|---|---|---|---|---|---|
| **February** | | | | | |
| 4 | H | Upper Clapton | D | 0 | 0 |
| 11 | H | Bedford Mod Sch | W | 5 | 0 |
| 18 | H | Olney | W | 7 | 0 |
| 25 | H | Catford Bridge | L | 0 | 12 |
| **March** | | | | | |
| 4 | H | Kent Wanderers | L | 0 | 4 |
| 11 | H | Hampstead | W | 13 | 0 |
| 18 | A | Northampton | W | 7 | 0 |
| 25 | A | Clapham Rovers | W | 4 | 0 |

The highest points scorer was F W Potter with 13 and the highest try scorer was L C Jones with three. F W Potter and W Rees both played at least ten times.

C Alston (1), P C Burgess (9), L G Brown (1), H Campbell (1), C S Crampton (1), H Cross (4), A F Crossman (2), R Crossman (1), W Dazeley (5), F H Edwards (1), F H Finney (1), T Fowler (3), L Cashwell (1), A G Goodison (5), W J Hassell (3), A E Holt (3), F H Holt (1), C H Ireson (7), W Jesse (4), A O Jones (5, 1c, 1d, 2t), L C Jones (7, 3t), F King (5), D H Lewis (7), E McIntyre (8), H H Morris (1, 1c, 1d), H S Morris (3, 1t), W Ottewell (2), W L R Paley (5), Pollard (1), W M Poole (1), F W Potter (10, 3c, 1d), W Rees (10), W H Rhodes (5), H Roberts (1), W K Roberts (6, 1t), E E Skinner (1), F R Smith (4), H Steadman (2, 1t), J H Stewart (4, 1t), L H Swann (2), A Udal (9), H E Vipan (5), H Walker (2), Whitaker (4), H Young (1).

# 1893-94

HH Morris scored 38 tries in the season. His record still stood in 2011. And the team's record with just one defeat and one draw in 29 games was the best in 125 years.

Played 29, won 27, lost 1, drawn 1. F 520. A 49

Captain: W Rees

| | | | | f | a |
|---|---|---|---|---|---|
| **October** | | | | | |
| 7 | A | Olney | W | 13 | 3 |
| 11 | H | Bedford Mod Sch | W | 28 | 5 |
| 14 | H | St George's Hosp | W | 61 | 0 |
| 21 | H | St Bart's Hosp | W | 22 | 0 |
| 25 | A | Bedford Mod Sch | W | 9 | 0 |
| 28 | H | Royal Vet Col | W | 33 | 0 |
| **November** | | | | | |
| 4 | H | Catford Bridge | W | 25 | 3 |
| 8 | H | Bedford Gram Sch | W | 27 | 5 |
| 11 | H | London Welsh | W | 13 | 3 |
| 25 | H | Notts | W | 25 | 0 |
| **December** | | | | | |
| 2 | H | Upper Clapton | W | 8 | 3 |
| 9 | A | K'ston on Thames | W | 13 | 0 |
| 23 | H | Leicester | W | 8 | 6 |
| 26 | H | K'ston on Thames | W | 39 | 0 |
| 30 | A | Leicester | W | 7 | 3 |
| **January** | | | | | |
| 13 | A | Ealing | W | 16 | 0 |
| 20 | H | Northampton | W | 12 | 3 |
| 27 | H | Univ Col Hosp | W | 14 | 0 |
| **February** | | | | | |
| 3 | H | Olney | W | 34 | 0 |
| 5 | H | Stade Francais | W | 22 | 0 |
| 7 | A | Bedford Gram Sch | W | 6 | 0 |
| 10 | A | Northampton | D | 0 | 0 |
| 17 | H | Brockley | W | 38 | 0 |
| 21 | H | Barbarians | W | 7 | 3 |
| **March** | | | | | |
| 3 | A | Upper Clapton | W | 14 | 0 |
| 10 | H | Old Leysians | W | 3 | 0 |
| 17 | H | Hampstead | W | 20 | 0 |
| 24 | H | Wormholt | W | 3 | 0 |
| 26 | A | Coventry | L | 0 | 12 |

Probably because of the astonishing success of the 1893-94 side, newspapers started giving full reports, and for this season only two appearances, one conversion and one try are unaccounted for. The pack is credited with two tries. By now a try was worth three points, a goal five (ie a conversion two), a dropped goal four and a penalty three, and these values stood for many years until the dropped goal was reduced to three points in 1947-48 and the try increased to four in 1971-72. The points record of 171 set by H H Morris stood for 40 years and his 38 tries in one season was still a record in 2011. Three players, the captain W Rees, A H Griffith and H H Morris, played in all 29 matches in the club's most successful season in 125 years where just 49 points were conceded in 29 matches. A crowd estimated at 6,000 saw Bedford beat the Barbarians.

H M Beasley (1), H G Billson (5), E W Brackenbury (11, 1t), C C Brearey (2), L G Brown (1, 2c), P C Burgess (21), W J Carey (6, 1t), F A Cory (2), C S Crampton (1), G Crampton (9), H Cross (17, 2t), F H Edwards (8, 2t), H W Finlinson (2), A G Goodison (24), A H Griffith (29, 1t), E W Griffith (2), G L Hamilton (13, 1t), C A Harris (19, 5c, 5t), E C Harris (1), A J Hawkins (5, 1t), R E T Hogg (2), P G Jacob (13, 4c, 5d, 1p, 10t), A O Jones (3, 1d, 3t), B C N Knight (21, 1d, 4t), D H Lewis (2), A Maclear (4), P C McEwan (6), H H Morris (29, 21c, 3d, 1p, 38t), E McIntyre (2), J Niven (3), F W Potter (19, 4c, 1d, 21t), W Rees (29, 1c), H P Reynolds (1, 2c, 1t), W K Roberts (27, 1d, 5t), F L Rose (1), H Sharman (11, 3t), Statham (1), E G Sexton (3, 1c), J H Stewart (15, 1t), R A Swettenham (6), W F Surtees (4, 2t), R Thompson (26, 9c, 1d, 14t), A Udal (23, 1t), Young (3).

# 1894-95

WK Roberts was one of two captains in the season. An OBM, he became a clergyman and in 1914 raised a team known as London Clergy to play Bedford.

Played 27, won 13, lost 13, drawn 1. F 215, A 128.

Captains: W Rees
W K Roberts

| | | | | f | a |
|---|---|---|---|---|---|
| **October** | | | | | |
| 6 | H | Bedford Mod Sch | W | 23 | 0 |
| 13 | H | Old Leysians | L | 0 | 8 |
| 20 | H | Bedford Gram Sch | W | 13 | 0 |
| 27 | H | Northampton | W | 11 | 0 |
| **November** | | | | | |
| 3 | H | Olney | W | 25 | 0 |
| 10 | A | Rugby | L | 5 | 8 |
| 17 | H | London Hospital | W | 30 | 0 |
| 22 | H | Keble College | L | 0 | 16 |
| 24 | A | Blackheath 'A' | L | 0 | 11 |
| **December** | | | | | |
| 1 | H | Upper Clapton | W | 9 | 0 |
| 8 | H | Rugby | W | 16 | 3 |
| 15 | A | Bedford Mod Sch | W | 11 | 0 |
| 20 | H | R Indian Eng Col | L | 3 | 8 |
| 22 | A | Leicester | L | 3 | 14 |
| 26 | H | Burton on Trent | W | 3 | 0 |

| | | | | f | a |
|---|---|---|---|---|---|
| **January** | | | | | |
| 2 | H | Bective Rangers | L | 3 | 19 |
| 5 | H | St Thomas' Hosp | D | 0 | 0 |
| 19 | A | Swansea | L | 0 | 7 |
| 21 | A | Aberavon | L | 0 | 9 |
| **February** | | | | | |
| 23 | A | Olney | L | 0 | 3 |
| **March** | | | | | |
| 2 | A | Upper Clapton | W | 3 | 0 |
| 16 | A | Northampton | L | 0 | 8 |
| 23 | H | Civil Service | W | 19 | 0 |
| 30 | H | Wormholt | W | 26 | 0 |
| **April** | | | | | |
| 6 | A | Moseley | L | 0 | 6 |
| 15 | A | Coventry | W | 9 | 3 |
| 20 | H | Leicester | L | 3 | 5 |

H H Morris with 18 tries and a total of 58 points was the leading try scorer while W Rees and W K Roberts who were the captains for the season, both played in 26 matches, as did F W Potter.

H M Beasley (12, 1c, 1t), C A Brack (13, 3t), P C Burgess (23), A F Carey (1), A L Carpenter (1), H B Chambers (2), F A Cory (5), C S Crampton (2), G Crampton (24, 1t), H Cross (6), T J Davies (5, 1t), R M Doig (2), N Duckworth (1), F H Edwards (14, 3c, 1p), H W Finlinson (1), E L Hammond (1), E C Harris (7), G H Hodgson (1), P G Jacob (2), C H Jones (1), F Kendall (1), D H Lewis (7), P C McEwan (3), A Maclear (8), L M McVittie (21), C T Morris (8), H H Morris (25, 2c, 18t), W T Morris (8, 2t), C A Pickwoad (10), F W Potter (26, 5c, 1p, 8t), H C Potter (5, 2t), C Redhead (1), W Rees (26), H P Reynolds (2, 4c, 2t), W K Roberts (26, 1t), J L Rose (7), E G Sexton (9, 2t), E E Skinner (1), F R Smith (1), H V Staunton (5, 2c), N V Stoddart (2), J W Stratton (1), W F Surtees (1, 2t), R A Swettenham (11, 4t), C H Taylor (2), T Thomas (2, 5c, 3t), R Thompson (16), F G Thompson (1), G F Tripp (5, 2t), A J Trollope (2), A Udal (23, 3t), E Warden (3), H B Warner (1), F Webb (1), Weighton.

# 1895-96

W Rees, captain in the club's best ever season, played throughout the 1890s

Played 32, won 19, lost 9, drawn 4. F 253, A 137.

Captain: W Rees

| October | | | | f | a |
|---|---|---|---|---|---|
| 5 | A | Olney | L | 0 | 3 |
| 12 | H | Leicester | W | 8 | 3 |
| 19 | H | Upper Clapton | W | 5 | 3 |
| 26 | H | Bedford Gram Sch | W | 3 | 0 |
| **November** | | | | | |
| 2 | A | Bedford Mod Sch | W | 20 | 3 |
| 6 | H | Keble College | W | 5 | 0 |
| 9 | H | Old Edwardians | L | 8 | 13 |
| 16 | A | Moseley | L | 0 | 11 |
| 23 | H | Northampton | W | 5 | 0 |
| 30 | A | Leicester | L | 0 | 13 |
| **December** | | | | | |
| 7 | H | Rugby | W | 14 | 3 |
| 14 | H | Bedford Mod Sch | W | 13 | 5 |
| 21 | H | S'ford on Avon | W | 16 | 5 |
| 26 | H | Burton on Trent | W | 17 | 0 |
| 28 | H | Penycraig | W | 14 | 9 |
| 30 | H | Bective Rangers | L | 0 | 8 |

| January | | | | f | a |
|---|---|---|---|---|---|
| 4 | A | Old Edwardians | W | 7 | 3 |
| 9 | A | Coventry | L | 0 | 13 |
| 11 | H | Olney | W | 6 | 0 |
| 18 | H | Hampstead | W | 30 | 3 |
| 25 | H | Moseley | D | 0 | 0 |
| **February** | | | | | |
| 1 | A | Bedford Gram Sch | D | 0 | 0 |
| 8 | H | London Welsh | W | 3 | 0 |
| 15 | H | Northampton | L | 3 | 16 |
| 22 | H | Coventry | L | 6 | 8 |
| 29 | A | Rugby | L | 0 | 3 |
| **March** | | | | | |
| 7 | H | Blackheath A | W | 14 | 0 |
| 14 | A | Upper Clapton | W | 13 | 3 |
| 21 | H | Civil Service | W | 32 | 3 |
| 28 | H | Wormholt | D | 0 | 0 |
| **April** | | | | | |
| 4 | H | Abercarn | W | 8 | 3 |
| 6 | H | Llwynpia | D | 3 | 3 |

Again H H Morris with 14 tries and 50 points was top scorer. P C Burgess made most appearances, 30. Sixty eight players turned out at least once.

F R Adams (7), H W Barff (2), H M Beasley (10, 1d, 1p, 4t), P M Bennett (2, 1t), E R Bird (1), H Brackenbury (1), P C Burgess (30), R E Burlingham (1), B Cary (1), H C Chambers (1), H N Cobb (2, 1t), C S Crampton (6), G Crampton (24, 2t), H Cross (11), C H Davies (1), T J Davies (1), W S Dawson (1), D H Farrer (2), H W Finlinson (1), A Francis (12, 1t), F M Furness (3), A H Griffiths (1), F A Hamilton (20, 1t), C T Harris (2), E C Harris (6), A E Hodder (12, 1c), R E T Hogg (1), P G Jacob (1), J B Jones (1), F Kendall (10, 10t), V Kirwan (1), D H Lewis (8, 2t), A D Lippert (2), P Maclear (11), R Maclear (1), J Manton (9, 1t), J C Montero (10), C T Morris (7), H H Morris (26, 4c, 14t), W T Morris (8), R C Mullins (2), F L Palmer (1), W De La Passy (4), F W Potter (23, 14c, 1p, 4t), H C Potter (10, 2t), C E Redhead (3), W Rees (29, 1t), F Reynolds (5), W K Roberts (1), J L Rose (4), J Rowland (2), E G Sexton (6, 2t), E J Skinner (8, 3t), N V Stoddart (14, 3t), L H Swann (3, 1t), R A Swettenham (8), A Tankerville (1), R Thompson (13, 1c), B Thwaites (10), A J Turner (2), A Udal (7), H B Warner (8, 3c, 2t), G E Waugh (1), Hayward Wells (6), H V Wells (9, 2t), F Wilkins (1), E Wighton (8), A W Woodyatt (4, 2t).

# 1896-97

Played 31, won 20, lost 10, drawn 1. F 301, A 134.

Captain: F W Potter

| | | | | f | a |
|---|---|---|---|---|---|
| **October** | | | | | |
| 3 | H | S'ford on Avon | W | 17 | 0 |
| 10 | A | Olney | W | 8 | 3 |
| 17 | H | London Welsh | W | 23 | 0 |
| 24 | H | Civil Service | W | 19 | 0 |
| 31 | H | Bedford Gram Sch | W | 8 | 0 |
| **November** | | | | | |
| 7 | H | Bedford Mod Sch | W | 27 | 0 |
| 14 | H | St Thomas' Hosp | W | 8 | 3 |
| 21 | A | Rugby | L | 6 | 13 |
| 26 | H | Monkstown | L | 0 | 3 |
| 28 | H | Coventry | W | 10 | 9 |
| **December** | | | | | |
| 5 | H | Portsmouth | L | 4 | 8 |
| 9 | A | Bedford Mod Sch | W | 12 | 5 |
| 12 | A | Old Edwardians | W | 5 | 0 |
| 19 | H | Leicester | L | 0 | 13 |
| 26 | H | Moseley | W | 3 | 0 |
| 28 | H | Kensington Nomads | W | 15 | 0 |
| **January** | | | | | |
| 2 | H | Rugby | W | 17 | 0 |
| 9 | H | Old Leysians | W | 3 | 0 |
| 16 | H | Upper Clapton | W | 16 | 6 |
| 23 | A | Leicester | L | 5 | 11 |
| **February** | | | | | |
| 13 | H | Olney | D | 0 | 0 |
| 20 | A | Moseley | L | 0 | 24 |
| 27 | H | Croydon | L | 0 | 14 |
| **March** | | | | | |
| 6 | H | Hampstead | W | 33 | 5 |
| 13 | H | Upper Clapton | W | 3 | 0 |
| 20 | H | Wormholt | W | 19 | 0 |
| 27 | H | Wickham Park | L | 3 | 5 |
| **April** | | | | | |
| 3 | H | Broughton | W | 24 | 0 |
| 10 | H | Merthyr Tydfil | W | 13 | 0 |
| 17 | H | Abercarn | L | 0 | 6 |
| 19 | A | Coventry | L | 0 | 6 |

The captain F W Potter made most appearances, 26, scored most tries, nine, and recorded the highest points total, 65. All the season's scorers were recorded in newspapers but appearances were not. There were also four players who appeared under pseudonyms including 'A Baby' and 'Monkey Brand'. Significantly, all four scored. Eighty players made appearances.

E M Baker (1), J G Bayes (12, 1t), H M Beasley (3, 1c, 2t), C Berrill (1), E R Bird (1), P C Burgess (21), Byrde (1), R B Campbell (1), B Cary (1, 1t), Chancellor (2), C E Clements (2), H N Cobb (1), C S Crampton (2), G Crampton (3), H Cross (10), F W R Denny (5), R M Doig (1), R B Finlay (1), H W Finlinson (5), A Francis (17), J M Furness (17, 2t), E C Harris (1), C Harris (1), A E Hodden (9), A Hawkins (1), C M Hogg (1, 2t), R E T Hogg (1), A Ingram (2), W L Jones (2), P G Jacob (4, 2c, 1d, 1p, 2t), F Kendall (10, 1c, 2p, 8t), Kerr (1), Lawrence (1), Lincoln (1), C D Linnell (1), A W D Lippert (7), P C McEwan (1), A Maclear (4), B Maclear (1, 2c, 1t), R Maclear (20, 2c, 1t), H V Margary (2), C T Morris (6), H H Morris (1, 1t), W T Morris (24), J G R Marsh (1), J C Montero (2), G E Mortlock (2), F H Palmer (12, 8t), C B Pennell (1), F W Potter (26, 15c, 2d, 9t), H C Potter (10, 4t), J M Pooley (1), Pryce-Jones (1), Rainsford (1), W Rees (25, 1t), J E Roberts (3), J M Robertson (1), J L Rose (6, 1t), C A Rust (11, 2t), E G Sexton (3, 1t), C M Sharpe (3, 4t), J Simcoe (2), E J Skinner (11, 4t), R Skinner (8, 1t), E Smith (1), N V Stoddart (10, 2c, 2t), J S Swallow (4, 2c, 3t), W Swire (1), R Thomas (4), B Thwaites (22), A J Turner (1), A Udal (14, 2t), G Udal (5), H V Wells (2), H B Warner (4, 2t), A W Woodyatt (2), 'A Baby' (1, 2t), C S Shaw (1, 1c, 2t), 'Snowe' (2, 1c, 2t), 'Monkey Brand' (1, 2t).

# 1897-98

FW Potter was the leading scorer in the season. One of the Invincibles of 1893-94, he was the reserve England full back in 1896 and later headed up the Shanghai Gas Works.

Played 32, won 9, lost 19, drawn 4. F 196, A 191.

Captain: F W Potter

| | | | | f | a |
|---|---|---|---|---|---|
| **September** | | | | | |
| 25 | A | Olney | W | 5 | 3 |
| **October** | | | | | |
| 2 | H | Upper Clapton | L | 3 | 5 |
| 4 | H | Llanelly | L | 3 | 5 |
| 9 | A | Northampton | L | 6 | 9 |
| 16 | H | Marlb'gh Nomads | L | 3 | 8 |
| 23 | H | Rosslyn Park | L | 6 | 9 |
| 30 | H | Olney | D | 3 | 3 |
| **November** | | | | | |
| 6 | A | Rugby | W | 9 | 0 |
| 13 | H | St Mary's Hosp | D | 5 | 5 |
| 20 | H | Moseley | L | 0 | 3 |
| 27 | H | London Welsh | W | 23 | 5 |
| **December** | | | | | |
| 4 | A | Kensington | W | 11 | 0 |
| 11 | H | Old Edwardians | W | 19 | 0 |
| 18 | A | Leicester | L | 0 | 14 |
| 27 | H | Burton onTrent | L | 0 | 3 |
| 30 | H | Old Paulines | L | 8 | 10 |
| **January** | | | | | |
| 1 | H | Leicester | W | 3 | 0 |
| 8 | A | Old Edwardians | L | 0 | 10 |
| 15 | H | Rugby | W | 29 | 0 |
| 22 | A | Moseley | D | 5 | 5 |
| 29 | H | Old Leysians | W | 19 | 3 |
| **February** | | | | | |
| 5 | H | Wickham Park | L | 3 | 4 |
| 12 | H | Olney | L | 5 | 11 |
| 19 | H | Wasps | D | 0 | 0 |
| 26 | H | Croydon | L | 0 | 11 |
| **March** | | | | | |
| 5 | A | Rosslyn Park | L | 3 | 14 |
| 12 | H | Wickham Park | L | 3 | 5 |
| 19 | H | Northampton | L | 0 | 7 |
| 26 | H | Kensington | L | 0 | 6 |
| **April** | | | | | |
| 2 | A | Plymouth | L | 5 | 22 |
| 9 | H | Broughton | W | 14 | 3 |
| 11 | H | Aspatria | L | 3 | 8 |

F W Potter with 11 tries and 55 points was the leading scorer. B Thwaites made most appearances, 28. Eighty five players, a club record, turned out in a difficult season.

H Brackenbury (4), J G Bayes (6), C Berrill (1), W Best (1), J Beinco (1), L Blackstone (1, 1t), S R Bradley (5), P C Burgess (21), H C Butler (2), R B Campbell (5), H N Cobb (1, 1t), H Cole (3), A Collins (6), C E Clements (3), H Cross (7), T Crouch (2), F W R Denny (3, 1t), W J Dixon (2), A Field (2), A L Finlinson (1), H W Finlinson (16, 1t), C L Foster (2), A Francis (13), Genity (1), J R D Glascott (1), G M Griffith (20), H Griffith (5, 1t), P C Groves (2), G Hamilton (1), H W Hodgson (1), C M Hogg (5, 3c, 1p, 1t), R E T Hogg (5), A E Hudson (16), A Ingram (3), P G Jacob (2, 1t), J C Johnston (1), F Jolley (1), J B Jones (1), F Kendall (13, 3c, 6t,), R Kerr (4), W Kerr (1), A M Leggatt (1), C E H Leggatt (3), F H Lewis (2), A W D Lippert (18), R H Loubser (1), G H McAllan (1), A Maclear (15), B Maclear (2), R Maclear (16), D W McPherson (1), J G R Marsh (23), W T Morris (3), G E Mortlock (4), M Mullineux (4), H T Oliver (4), W Owen (1, 1t), H E Perks (2), E H Philbrick (1), F W Potter (21, 6c, 1d, 2p, 11t), H C Potter (9, 2t), Ransford (1), W K Roberts (3), F J Robinson (1), B Sargeant (11, 1t), A E Sargeant (8, 2t), C M Sharpe (24, 1d, 6t), J Simcoe (3, 1t), E J Skinner (10, 4t), R Skinner (7, 1t), F R Smith (1), H Smith (1), H Smyth (11), G E Smyth (13), R Stanley (1), N V Stoddart (5, 1c), R Thompson (9, 3t), H Thorp (1, 1c) B Thwaites (28), A J Turner (7, 1t), W L D Twiss (1), G Udal (5, 1t), G C Wheeler (2), W Wright (1). One pseudonym J Smith (1).

# 1898-99

Bedford Grammar School which became the Town Hall in 1892

Played 32, won 12, lost 18, drawn 2. F 217, A 196.

Captain: J R D Glascott

| October | | | | f | a |
|---|---|---|---|---|---|
| 1 | H | Upper Clapton | W | 11 | 3 |
| 8 | A | Northampton | L | 0 | 19 |
| 15 | H | Marlb'gh Nomads | L | 5 | 7 |
| 22 | H | Rosslyn Park | L | 0 | 8 |
| 29 | H | London Welsh | W | 18 | 3 |
| **November** | | | | | |
| 5 | H | Wickham Park | D | 3 | 3 |
| 12 | H | St Thomas' Hosp | W | 15 | 0 |
| 19 | H | Guy's Hospital | L | 0 | 14 |
| 24 | H | Monkstown | L | 0 | 22 |
| 26 | H | St Bart's Hosp | W | 9 | 3 |
| **December** | | | | | |
| 3 | A | Kensington | L | 6 | 11 |
| 10 | H | St Mary's Hosp | L | 0 | 3 |
| 17 | A | Old Edwardians | L | 3 | 5 |
| 24 | H | Lennox | L | 0 | 3 |
| 26 | H | Burton on Trent | L | 0 | 5 |
| 27 | A | Olney | W | 13 | 0 |
| 31 | A | Moseley | L | 0 | 13 |

| January | | | | f | a |
|---|---|---|---|---|---|
| 2 | H | Bective Rangers | L | 0 | 5 |
| 7 | H | Wasps | W | 8 | 0 |
| 14 | H | Hammersmith | W | 31 | 3 |
| 21 | H | Old Edwardians | W | 6 | 0 |
| **February** | | | | | |
| 11 | H | Olney | L | 6 | 8 |
| 18 | H | Moseley | L | 0 | 11 |
| 25 | A | Croydon | L | 8 | 13 |
| **March** | | | | | |
| 1 | H | Yorkshire Sch OB | D | 3 | 3 |
| 4 | A | Rosslyn Park | L | 4 | 5 |
| 11 | H | Saracens | W | 11 | 5 |
| 18 | H | Northampton | L | 3 | 12 |
| 25 | H | Bedford & Dist Lge | W | 22 | 6 |
| **April** | | | | | |
| 1 | H | P Kendall's Ldn XV | W | 11 | 0 |
| 3 | H | Ldn Buccaneers | W | 21 | 0 |
| 4 | A | Olney | L | 0 | 3 |

Highest try scorer was J S Swallow with 19 in a total of 65 points. J R D Glascott made at least 29 appearances.

Barr (1), J G Bayes (4), A B Benison (12, 1d), Bligh (3), S R Bradley (2), H N C Campbell (7), H W Cole (6), A Collins (1), T Crouch (7, 1t), Rev W M Davison (5), F N Ellaby (2, 1c), F C Evans (5), A L Finlinson (12), H W Finlinson (3), J Foster (1), A Francis (1), J R D Glascott (29, 2c, 1t), G M Griffith (9, 4t), H Griffith (16), A Harris (1), Hopkinson (4, 2c, 1t), A James (1), T W D Jarvis (10), Jenkins (2, 1t), G J Johnstone-Smith (1), H M Kemp (9, 1c, 2t), F Kendall (2, 1t), R H Kerr (2), W Kerr (12), H King (1), C D Linell (6), A W D Lippert (2), A Maclear (27), P Maclear (8), R Maclear (1), E MacLaren (1), D MacPherson (2), J C Montero (1), W T Morris (28, 3t), A E Nesbit (1), A Norris (21), H T Oliver (6, 1t), W B Otterwell (21), W Owen (21, 8t), C B Parson (1), H Passy (1), H C Potter (5, 1t), F J Robinson (2), G G Roff (2), A Russell (3), R Ryder (4, 2t), A E Sargent (1, 1t), F S P Saunders (16), B Severs (19, 7c, 3p, 1t), N V Stoddart (5), D M Stone (1), J S Swallow (26, 2c, 1d, 19t), W Swire (15, 2t), H Talbot (3), R Thompson (18, 1t), B Thwaites (4), A J Turner (1, 1t), G Udal (11, 3t), Hayward Wells (3), H B Wells (3), S R Wells (3), Wilson (1).

## 1899-1900

Played 28, won 15, lost 8, drawn 5. F 179, A 181.

Captain: J R D Glascott

| | | | | f | a |
|---|---|---|---|---|---|
| **September** | | | | | |
| 30 | H | Bedford & District | D | 5 | 5 |
| **October** | | | | | |
| 7 | A | London Irish | W | 11 | 9 |
| 14 | H | Marlborough Nomads | L | 0 | 18 |
| 21 | H | Upper Clapton | W | 14 | 0 |
| 28 | A | Northampton | L | 0 | 29 |
| **November** | | | | | |
| 4 | H | Nuneaton | L | 5 | 8 |
| 11 | H | St Thomas' Hosp | D | 3 | 3 |
| 18 | H | Guy's Hospital | L | 5 | 19 |
| 25 | H | Kensington | L | 4 | 17 |
| **December** | | | | | |
| 2 | H | St Mary's Hosp | W | 8 | 4 |
| 9 | A | Old Edwardians | L | 3 | 6 |
| 23 | H | W Rees' XV | W | 12 | 5 |
| 26 | H | Burton on Trent | W | 8 | 5 |
| 30 | A | Olney | W | 8 | 0 |
| **January** | | | | | |
| 16 | H | St Bart's Hosp | W | 6 | 3 |
| 20 | H | Old Edwardians | W | 9 | 0 |
| 27 | H | Old Leysians | D | 3 | 3 |
| **February** | | | | | |
| 24 | H | Northampton | L | 5 | 14 |
| **March** | | | | | |
| 3 | H | Wasps | W | 6 | 0 |
| 8 | H | Yorkshire Sch OB | L | 8 | 18 |
| 10 | A | Saracens | D | 3 | 3 |
| 17 | H | London Welsh | D | 3 | 3 |
| 21 | H | Utd Eng Col | W | 8 | 0 |
| 24 | H | Kensington | W | 9 | 0 |
| 31 | H | Wickham Park | W | 11 | 6 |
| **April** | | | | | |
| 7 | H | Croydon | W | 8 | 0 |
| 14 | H | Ldn Buccaneers | W | 6 | 3 |
| 16 | H | Eccles | W | 8 | 0 |

Highest try scorers were R Ryder and G Udal with seven. R Ryder was the leading points scorer with 25. J R D Glascott made 26 appearances.

J B Rayes (1), A B Benison (11, 1d, 1t), T Bennett (4), T Billingham (5), J Bryant (7), Capon (1), G Cole (12), F Felts (2), Ferrier (1), A L Finlinson (1), H W Finlinson (5), J Foster (13, 1t), A Francis (1), J R D Glascott (26, 10c, 1t), R C Greller (4, 1t), H Griffith (3), C M Harris (3), R Hunt (1), E Hopkinson (4, 2t), A E Hudson (1, 1c), C J Johnstone-Smith (12), W L Jones (1), R Kerr (4), W Kerr (14), A Maclear (22), R Maclear (9, 2t), O Madden (3, 1t), T L Margary (3), W T Morris (7), A E Nesbit (12), A Norris (1), W Owen (4), E Palmer (1), H E Perks (4), H C Potter (3, 2t), C Randall (12, 1t), C Ransford (6), N Ransford (1), F Redman (8), W Rees (3), A Roberts (1), G C Roff (12, 1c, 3t), F J Robinson (1), B Ryder (1), L D Ryder (6, 2t), R Ryder (13, 2c, 7t), C S Sargent (1), A E Sargent (4, 2t), F S P Saunders (18), E J Skinner (18, 5t), B Severs (1), R Stanley (1, 1t), Stewart (1), J S Swallow (11, 1d, 5t), W Talbot (5), R Thompson (13, 1t), B Thwaites (1), J Tilley (1), A J Trollope (1, 1c), F Tucker (20, 3t), G Udal (22, 7t), G G Warder (3), Watson (1), H B Wells (3), S R Wells (5), Wilson (1).

# 1900-01

Bedford Modern School in 1900

Played 26, won 14, lost 9, drawn 3. F 248, A 119.

Captain: F S P Saunders

| | | | | f | a |
|---|---|---|---|---|---|
| **September** | | | | | |
| 29 | H | London Welsh | W | 22 | 3 |
| **October** | | | | | |
| 6 | A | London Irish | L | 0 | 3 |
| 13 | H | Marlborough Nomads | D | 6 | 6 |
| 20 | H | Upper Clapton | W | 6 | 3 |
| 27 | A | Northampton | L | 5 | 7 |
| **November** | | | | | |
| 3 | H | Bed & Dist Lge | W | 45 | 0 |
| 10 | H | St Thomas' Hosp | W | 30 | 0 |
| 17 | H | Guy's Hospital | L | 3 | 6 |
| 24 | A | Kensington | D | 0 | 0 |
| **December** | | | | | |
| 1 | H | St Mary's Hosp | W | 11 | 0 |
| 8 | H | Hammersmith | W | 21 | 3 |
| 15 | H | Rugby | L | 0 | 8 |
| 22 | H | W Rees' XV | W | 8 | 3 |
| 26 | H | Burton on Trent | W | 14 | 0 |
| 29 | A | Olney | W | 8 | 3 |
| **January** | | | | | |
| 3 | H | Old Paulines | L | 0 | 15 |
| 5 | H | St Bart's Hosp | W | 17 | 3 |
| 19 | H | Nuneaton | D | 5 | 5 |
| **February** | | | | | |
| 9 | H | Olney | W | 16 | 0 |
| 16 | A | Nuneaton | L | 0 | 8 |
| 23 | H | Northampton | L | 3 | 14 |
| **March** | | | | | |
| 2 | H | Wasps | W | 11 | 3 |
| 16 | A | Croydon | L | 0 | 23 |
| 30 | H | Kensington | W | 6 | 0 |
| **April** | | | | | |
| 6 | H | Olney | W | 11 | 0 |
| 8 | H | Eccles | L | 0 | 3 |

B Maclear was the highest points scorer with 31, and, with F H Tucker, the highest try scorer with five. F Redman made most appearances, 26. Certain matches were not recorded in full.

H Beddall (3), T Bennett (2), T B Billingham (5), F G Brooks (3, 2t), W F Bryant (24, 3t), A Chambers (1), A Chibnell (8, 1t), Coates (1), H M Coombs (1, 1t), De Schmitt (3, 1t), G Dobbin (1), J H Evans (1), H Farmer (3), F Felts (1), A L Finlinson (15, 3t), M E Finlinson (3), L Fletcher (3, 1t), J Flower (1), J Foster (21, 1t), G Freer (2), J R D Glascott (15, 7c, 1p, 2t), G M Griffith (2), H W Haines (2), R Hackett (1, 1t), R Hunt (1), A Helmsley (6, 1t), H W Hodgson (3), D A Jones (2), E Kalberer (2), C Lapworth (1), Leather (1), A Maclear (4, 3t), B Maclear (3, 6c, 1d, 5t), R Maclear (9, 1c), Marsden (1), H Maurice (3, 3c), A Mender (1), A Norris (2), G Owen (2), F H Palmer (1), C B Parsons (3), G Paton (4), A Pringle (5, 2t), C Randell (20, 1c, 2t), C Ransford (5), F Redman (26) W Rees (3), J Richards (3), G C Roff (14, 1c, 2t), F G Royds (2), L D Ryder (5, 3t), R Ryder (4), A E Sargeant (5, 1c, 3t), W E M Sargeant (3, 1t), F S P Saunders (23, 1t), E J Skinner (7, 2t), C H Stone (1), H Sutton (1, 1t), R Thompson (11, 2c, 4t), J Tilley (5, 1c, 1p, 4t), A J Trollope (3, 2c, 1t), F H Tucker (23, 5t), G Udal (2), F Udal (6, 3t), G R Watson (8), S R Wells (12, 3t), W Whaley (6).

# 1901-02

The Elstow or County School on the Ampthill Road

Played 26, won 11, lost 13, drawn 2. F 143, A185.

Captain: F S P Saunders

| | | | | f | a |
|---|---|---|---|---|---|
| **September** | | | | | |
| 28 | H | Leytonstone | W | 3 | 0 |
| **October** | | | | | |
| 5 | A | London Irish | L | 0 | 6 |
| 12 | H | Marlborough Nomads | L | 0 | 36 |
| 19 | H | Upper Clapton | L | 0 | 5 |
| 26 | A | Northampton | L | 0 | 32 |
| **November** | | | | | |
| 2 | H | London Hosp | L | 0 | 11 |
| 9 | H | St Thomas' Hosp | W | 21 | 0 |
| 16 | H | Guy's Hospital | L | 0 | 15 |
| 23 | A | Kensington | L | 0 | 16 |
| 30 | H | St Mary's Hosp | W | 9 | 8 |
| **December** | | | | | |
| 7 | H | Hammersmith | W | 11 | 0 |
| 14 | H | Nuneaton | L | 0 | 3 |
| 26 | H | Burton on Trent | W | 19 | 0 |
| **January** | | | | | |
| 2 | H | Old Paulines | W | 11 | 0 |
| 4 | H | London Devonians | W | 11 | 0 |
| 11 | H | Olney | W | 14 | 3 |
| 25 | H | St Bart's Hosp | L | 0 | 3 |
| **February** | | | | | |
| 1 | A | Olney | D | 0 | 0 |
| 22 | H | Surbiton | L | 0 | 8 |
| **March** | | | | | |
| 1 | H | Wasps | D | 3 | 3 |
| 8 | H | London Irish | L | 0 | 8 |
| 15 | H | UCS Old Boys | W | 5 | 3 |
| 22 | H | S R Wells XV | W | 22 | 3 |
| 29 | H | Kempston | W | 9 | 0 |
| 31 | H | Eccles | L | 5 | 8 |
| **April** | | | | | |
| 5 | H | Northampton | L | 0 | 14 |

G U A Read made the most appearances, 25, and scored most points, 35. F G Brooks, with five, was the highest try scorer. One try was credited to both J G Bayes and F S P Saunders and again the match against Burton on Trent on Boxing Day was not fully recorded. Bedford fielded only 14 men in matches against Nuneaton on December 14 and Olney on February 1.

Atkinson (2), A Bayes (7), J G Bayes (23, 2t), H B Beddall (12), C Berrill (1), F G Brooks (3, 5t), W F Bryant (20, 1t), R B Campbell (11), R S Cantrel (1), A Chapman (1), A P Clarke (13, 3t), H P Cocking (1), H M Coombs (9, 1t), C Deane (2), H Dobbs (1), J H Evans (3, 1t), Fenning (1), A L Finlinson (3, 1c, 1t), M E Finlinson (9, 4t), L Fletcher (2, 1t), H B Follitt (2), J Foster (4), C Franklin (2), J R D Glascott (20, 2t), H W Haines (3), C Harris (6), M Harrison (1), E R Hawkins (1), R E Jones (4), C Lapworth (2), A McConnell (3), A Maclear (2), R Maclear (5), C Mandel (13, 1t), H Milton (1), C H Milton (1), E G Morris (1), C H Nicholson (17, 2t), A E Norris (2), G Paton (4), H E Perks (2), Pilling (1), C Randall (23, 1t), G Ransford (3), G U A Read (25, 14c, 1d, 1t), F Redman (6), W Rees (1), A H Roberts (3, 2t), G C Roff (13, 1t), A Sargeant (3, 4t), F S P Saunders (17, 1t), R Skinner (5), R Thompson (1), A J Trollope (4, 1d, 1t), F H Tucker (21, 2t), G R Watson (1), W G Watts (1), C Wells (3), H B Wells (3), S R Wells (4), H Whaley (2), L Wilcox (13), C H Wolfe (2), P Woodland (1), C C Wood (5).

# 1902-03

Played 29, won 18, lost 10, drawn 1. F 307, A 153.

Captain: H B Beddall

| | | | | f | a |
|---|---|---|---|---|---|
| **September** | | | | | |
| 27 | H | Leytonstone | W | 6 | 0 |
| **October** | | | | | |
| 4 | A | London Irish | L | 0 | 19 |
| 11 | H | Marlb'gh Nomads | L | 3 | 6 |
| 18 | H | Upper Clapton | D | 3 | 3 |
| 25 | A | Northampton | L | 3 | 27 |
| **November** | | | | | |
| 1 | A | Rugby | L | 3 | 19 |
| 8 | H | St Thomas' Hosp | L | 3 | 10 |
| 15 | H | Guy's Hosp | L | 5 | 9 |
| 22 | A | Kensington | L | 0 | 3 |
| 29 | H | St Mary's Hosp | W | 8 | 3 |
| **December** | | | | | |
| 13 | H | Old Upper Hamians | W | 9 | 5 |
| 20 | H | Northampton | L | 0 | 8 |
| 26 | H | Burton on Trent | W | 20 | 0 |
| 27 | H | Rugby | W | 16 | 10 |

| | | | | f | a |
|---|---|---|---|---|---|
| **January** | | | | | |
| 10 | A | Upper Clapton | W | 9 | 0 |
| 24 | H | St Bart's Hosp | W | 38 | 0 |
| 31 | H | Wasps | W | 17 | 6 |
| **February** | | | | | |
| 7 | H | Leytonstone | W | 22 | 0 |
| 14 | H | London Hosp | W | 19 | 0 |
| 21 | H | London Irish | W | 3 | 0 |
| 28 | H | London Devonians | L | 0 | 3 |
| **March** | | | | | |
| 7 | H | Kempston | W | 22 | 0 |
| 14 | A | Olney | L | 0 | 5 |
| 21 | H | Kempston | W | 27 | 0 |
| 28 | H | Kensington | W | 14 | 0 |
| **April** | | | | | |
| 4 | H | Shandon | W | 13 | 0 |
| 10 | H | Northern Wan | W | 22 | 6 |
| 11 | H | Olney | W | 11 | 3 |
| 13 | H | Eccles | W | 11 | 8 |

Top try scorer was A P Clarke with 17. His points total of 51 was the highest and he made most appearances, 24. There was a home match with Old Upper Hamians which Bedford won 9-5 but there are no details in official records or newspapers.

Austin (1), Bainbridge (1), A Bayes (10), J G Bayes (14), H B Beddall (17, 1c, 2t), Barker (1), A G Bell (1), F G Brooks (2), W H Brookes (3), W J Bryant (15, 2t), L A L Carter (2), A P Clarke (24, 17t), J H Clarke (9, 10t), H P Cocking (9, 15c 1d, 1p, 4t), H M Coombs (7, 2c, 6t), H W Finlinson (1), M E Finlinson (2, 2c), Follett (1), C Fowler (21, 1c), C Franklin (6, 1t), J R D Glascott (3), T Gooding (1), H Griffith (4), W W Gore (1), S Hancock (14, 4t), R Hanray (4), A Hebden (3), A Helmsley (4, 5t), C R Hoskyn (12), C Lapworth (1), W Mc Connell (13, 4t), R Maclear (8, 1c, 1p, 1t), A V Manton (12, 7t), T Mesa (2), C H Nicholson (5, 5c), C W Nicholson (6), A E Norris (1), Norse (1), C Randall (18, 1c, 3t), W H Robertson (4), F T Royds (2), T Sawer (5, 1t), F S P Saunders (4, 1t), N V Stoddart (7, 1c), F H Tucker (13, 2t), C A Walker (2), C Wallinger (1), S R Wells (12, 1t), C C Wood (18, 3t), P Woodland (5, 2t).

# 1903-04

Played 26, won 19, lost 6, drawn 1. F 346, A 106.

Captain: C R Hoskyn

| | | | | f | a |
|---|---|---|---|---|---|
| **October** | | | | | |
| 3 | A | London Irish | W | 16 | 0 |
| 10 | H | Marlb'gh Nomads | W | 10 | 3 |
| 17 | H | Upper Clapton | W | 16 | 0 |
| 24 | A | Northampton | L | 9 | 31 |
| 31 | H | St Mary's Hosp | W | 17 | 0 |
| **November** | | | | | |
| 7 | H | Rosslyn Park | D | 0 | 0 |
| 14 | H | Olney | W | 5 | 0 |
| 21 | H | St Bart's Hosp | W | 36 | 5 |
| 28 | A | Rugby | L | 0 | 8 |
| **December** | | | | | |
| 5 | H | London Welsh | L | 0 | 13 |
| 12 | H | London Devonians | W | 11 | 0 |
| 19 | H | London Buccaneers | W | 21 | 3 |
| 26 | H | Burton on Trent | W | 48 | 3 |
| 28 | H | Racing Club de France | W | 44 | 0 |

| | | | | f | a |
|---|---|---|---|---|---|
| **January** | | | | | |
| 16 | H | Utd Bedford Schs | W | 29 | 0 |
| 30 | H | Wasps | W | 12 | 0 |
| **February** | | | | | |
| 6 | H | Leytonstone | W | 9 | 0 |
| 20 | H | London Irish | W | 5 | 0 |
| 27 | H | Northampton | W | 6 | 5 |
| **March** | | | | | |
| 5 | H | Rugby | L | 3 | 17 |
| 12 | H | London Hosp | L | 3 | 5 |
| 19 | H | Hammersmith | W | 6 | 0 |
| 26 | H | Park House | W | 11 | 0 |
| **April** | | | | | |
| 1 | H | Northern Wand | W | 10 | 4 |
| 2 | H | Saracens | L | 5 | 6 |
| 4 | H | Eccles | W | 14 | 3 |

M E Finlinson was the highest try scorer with 24, highest points scorer with 75 and, with H P Cocking, he made most appearances, 26.

C Ashe (16, 2t), C B Atkinson (1), A Bayes (4), J G Bayes (11), H C Barber (1), H B Beddall (7), A G Bell (9, 2t), A G Benison (5, 1t), H Bertram (1), F G Brooks (5, 3t), G Brailsford (4), H C Butler (2), R Campbell (4), L A L Carter (4), E L Chambers (2, 1t), A P Clarke (23, 9t), J H Clarke (13, 11t), H P Cocking (26, 20c, 1d, 2p), H M Coombs (11, 5t), L Corry-Smith (2), H W Finlinson (1, 1t), M E Finlinson (26, 1p, 24t), H B Follitt (4, 3t), Forbes (1), C Franklin (22, 2t), W Gore (3), A Helmsley (2), C R Hopkinson (2, 1t), C R Hoskyn (24), G G Keene (3), A Kempter (1), W W Kirkby (1), R M McEwan (3), B Maclear (4, 11c, 7t), R Maclear (14, 3c, 1t), W McConnell (3), C H Milton (7), J G Milton (4, 1t) Montgomery (1), T S Muirshead (7, 1c, 7t), C W Nicholson (4), H C Palmer (3, 1t), B L Peel (1), W A Radice (5, 1t), C Rainsford (1), C Randall (7), A L Rogers (13), T Sawer (5, 1t), G P Symes (1), Tattersal (1), Townsend (2), M T Tudor (13, 1t), A P Wagner (2), G K Wells (1), H B Wells (1), S R Wells (1), W T Webster (1), L H Wilcox (1), C C Wood (14, 1c, 2t).

# 1904-05

Played 29, won 20, lost 7, drawn 2. F 326, A 140.

Captain: A L Rogers

| | | | | f | a |
|---|---|---|---|---|---|
| **September** | | | | | |
| 24 | A | Northampton | W | 8 | 3 |
| **October** | | | | | |
| 1 | H | Norwood | W | 21 | 0 |
| 8 | H | Marlb'gh Nomads | W | 19 | 10 |
| 15 | H | Upper Clapton | W | 22 | 0 |
| 22 | H | Old Leysians | W | 10 | 5 |
| 29 | H | St Bart's Hosp | W | 10 | 0 |
| **November** | | | | | |
| 5 | H | Coventry | W | 5 | 3 |
| 12 | H | Lennox | W | 9 | 3 |
| 19 | H | St Bart's Hosp | W | 10 | 0 |
| **December** | | | | | |
| 3 | H | London Devonians | W | 9 | 0 |
| 10 | A | London Irish | W | 8 | 3 |
| 17 | H | Nuneaton | W | 13 | 0 |
| 27 | H | Ldn Buccaneers | W | 18 | 11 |
| 28 | H | Penarth | L | 3 | 8 |
| 31 | H | Leytonstone | W | 9 | 0 |

| | | | | f | a |
|---|---|---|---|---|---|
| **January** | | | | | |
| 7 | A | Upper Clapton | L | 4 | 14 |
| **February** | | | | | |
| 4 | H | Nuneaton | D | 14 | 14 |
| 11 | H | London Welsh | L | 0 | 10 |
| 18 | H | London Irish | D | 0 | 0 |
| 25 | H | Ealing | W | 24 | 0 |
| **March** | | | | | |
| 4 | H | Rosslyn Park | L | 0 | 17 |
| 11 | H | London Hospital | W | 24 | 0 |
| 25 | H | Old Mer Taylors | W | 13 | 5 |
| **April** | | | | | |
| 1 | H | Olney | W | 11 | 0 |
| 8 | H | Northampton | L | 3 | 17 |
| 15 | A | Coventry | L | 3 | 8 |
| 21 | H | Northern Wand | W | 21 | 3 |
| 22 | H | Burton on Trent | W | 22 | 0 |
| 24 | H | Eccles | W | 13 | 6 |

Most appearances, 27, and most tries, 11, were recorded by H Willett. Highest points scorer was A V Manton, 34. Certain games seem to have been unrecorded.

C Ashe (25, 1t), C B Atkinson (5, 5c, 1t), C Attwood 91), B H Barret (1), A Bayes (2), J G Bayes (19, 1t), A G Bell (9, 2t), Blackburn (1, 1t), Boyce (1), L A N Brooks (1), R B Campbell (10, 5t), L A L Carter (1), A P Clarke (7, 1d, 4t), Clayton (1, 1t), H P Cocking (13, 14c, 1p), H M Coombs (9, 1t), C Downe (6, 1t), N P Draper (1), M E Finlinson (7, 3c, 4t), H T Forbes (4), C Franklin (23, 1c, 1t), W Gore (1), Gouldsbury (2, 1t), G Grant (2), R C Greller (2, 1t), N B Griffiths (1), A T Hannington (15, 1t), M Harrison (1), A D Heard (1), A Helmsley (2), A P Hickie (4), C R Hoskyn (12, 1t), G Keene (1), J Kaye (2), W W Kirby (7, 1t), B Maclear (2, 1c), R Maclear (20, 1c, 1t), Mann (5, 2t), A V Manton (18, 1d, 10t), A E Miller (1), A Morrison (1), N Morrison (5), Morton (1), T S Muirshead (7, 1c, 9t), A Naylor (1), N D T Oliver (12, 1c, 2t), J Pallison (1), F H Palmer (1), J Picton (18, 3t), H Pickwoad (14, 3t), W A Radice (4), G U A Read (18, 3c, 2d, 3p), A L Rogers (22, 1t), T Sawer (2, 1t), O R Walkey (1), S R Wells (2), H Willett (27, 11t), R Willett (1), A H Wood (1), C C Wood (25, 4t), Y Yule (1).

# 1905-06

Played 36, won 20, lost 15, drawn 1. F 451 A 372.

Captain: R Maclear

| | | | | f | a |
|---|---|---|---|---|---|
| **September** | | | | | |
| 16 | H | Olney | W | 17 | 0 |
| 23 | A | Northampton | L | 0 | 10 |
| 30 | H | Stratford-on-Avon | W | 10 | 5 |
| **October** | | | | | |
| 7 | H | Marlb'gh Nomads | W | 9 | 0 |
| 14 | H | Old Leysians | W | 11 | 3 |
| 21 | A | Coventry | L | 5 | 13 |
| 28 | H | Upper Clapton | W | 27 | 3 |
| **November** | | | | | |
| 4 | A | Cambridge Univ | L | 8 | 39 |
| 11 | H | St Mary's Hosp | W | 12 | 3 |
| 15 | H | New Zealand | L | 0 | 41 |
| 18 | H | St Bart's Hosp | W | 13 | 3 |
| 25 | A | Gloucester | L | 5 | 52 |
| **December** | | | | | |
| 2 | H | London Devonians | D | 8 | 8 |
| 9 | H | Coventry | L | 0 | 18 |
| 16 | A | London Irish | L | 0 | 25 |
| 23 | H | Rugby | W | 17 | 3 |
| 26 | H | Burton on Trent | W | 32 | 0 |
| 28 | H | Penarth | L | 3 | 11 |
| 30 | H | Catford Bridge | W | 11 | 8 |

| | | | | f | a |
|---|---|---|---|---|---|
| **January** | | | | | |
| 4 | H | Old Paulines | W | 18 | 3 |
| 6 | H | Old Alleynians | W | 30 | 0 |
| 20 | H | Rugby | L | 10 | 22 |
| 27 | H | Park House | W | 35 | 0 |
| **February** | | | | | |
| 3 | H | Civil Service | L | 5 | 8 |
| 10 | H | London Welsh | L | 8 | 13 |
| 17 | H | London Irish | W | 11 | 0 |
| 24 | H | UCS Old Boys | L | 3 | 10 |
| **March** | | | | | |
| 3 | H | Rosslyn Park | L | 3 | 17 |
| 10 | H | London Hosp | W | 8 | 6 |
| 17 | H | Leytonstone | W | 32 | 0 |
| 24 | A | Leicester | L | 5 | 13 |
| 31 | H | Old Edwardians | W | 18 | 16 |
| **April** | | | | | |
| 7 | H | Northampton | L | 3 | 16 |
| 13 | H | Northern Wand | W | 19 | 0 |
| 14 | H | Streatham | W | 10 | 3 |
| 16 | H | Eccles | W | 45 | 0 |

A record eighty-seven players turned out for the club, many of them guests. M E Finlinson was top try scorer with 28 and leading points scorer with 146. G U A Read, 31, made most appearances.

S Abid (1), H J Anderson (2), C Ashe (17), C B Atkinson (8, 6c, 4t), J G Bayes (3, 1t), A G Bell (5), F B Brooks (8, 3t), L A N Brooks (15, 7t), A C Bryson (1, 1t), R B Campbell (2), H P Cocking (2, 2c), H M Coombs (2), W Drage (1), A P Draper (1), J Dobbs (2, 1t), A Fielder (1, 1t), H W Finlinson (1), M E Finlinson (26, 25c, 4p, 28t), H B Follitt (1), C Fowler (8), C Franklin (17, 1p, 2t), S R Gompertz (3), W W Gore (3, 1t), S C Gouldstring (1), A Grossman (2), M Harrison (1), G J Helmsley (1), H N Helmsley (14, 2t), A D Heard (1), H N Henderson (1), C Hickie (4), C R Hoskyn (1), Howard (1), N Howson (2), C Huckle (1), A Hudson (1), Jase (1), W J Johns (1), G C Keene (4), Killick (1), W W Kirkby (7, 2t), S Kitchener (2), G R Klombis (1), R H Lacey (2), Longland (2), E McEwan (1), B Maclear (5, 6c, 7t), R Maclear (28, 2c), Mann (1), A V Manton (29, 6t), J Mason (1), Miles (1), E R Mobbs (1), C C F Moore (4), E G Morris (1), L G Morrison (11), N D Morrison (1), F L Morton (5), T S Muirshead (7, 1c, 5t), C S Nailer (13, 1t), Nicholls (1), A W B Pallister (10, 1t), Pacey (1), H C Palmer (1), Pegler (1), E Pitling (4), A Plain (1), T H Preston (1), C E Radley (1), W A Radice (24, 1t), G U A Read (31, 9c, 3p), A W Rogers (6), A L Rogers (21, 1t), G Romans (1), A E Sargeant (8, 1t), W M Sargeant (2), T Sawer (18, 5t), G L Stranarth (8), O R Walkey (2), J W Ward (15, 4t), B H Watts (1), H B Wells (3, 1t), S R Wells (14), H Willett (29, 1d, 10t), R Willett (2), C C Wood (8), H V Yule (2).

# 1906-07

Played 30, won 21, lost 9. F 578, A 169.

Captain: C Franklin

| | | | | f | a |
|---|---|---|---|---|---|
| **September** | | | | | |
| 15 | H | Olney | W | 5 | 3 |
| 22 | A | Northampton | L | 5 | 28 |
| 29 | H | Old Edwardians | W | 11 | 5 |
| **October** | | | | | |
| 6 | H | Marlb'gh Nomads | W | 24 | 0 |
| 13 | H | Old Leysians | L | 6 | 8 |
| 20 | A | Coventry | L | 0 | 12 |
| 27 | H | Upper Clapton | W | 61 | 0 |
| **November** | | | | | |
| 3 | H | Hampstead Wand | W | 44 | 0 |
| 10 | H | London Devonians | W | 22 | 10 |
| 17 | H | St Bart's Hosp | L | 0 | 15 |
| 24 | H | Lennox | W | 29 | 8 |
| **December** | | | | | |
| 1 | H | London Welsh | L | 0 | 3 |
| 8 | H | Coventry | L | 0 | 16 |
| 15 | H | London Irish | L | 0 | 3 |
| 22 | H | Old Mer Taylors | W | 15 | 0 |

| | | | | f | a |
|---|---|---|---|---|---|
| **January** | | | | | |
| 3 | H | Old Paulines | W | 29 | 0 |
| 5 | H | Old Alleynians | W | 23 | 6 |
| 12 | H | London Hospital | L | 5 | 11 |
| 19 | H | Catford Bridge | W | 13 | 5 |
| **February** | | | | | |
| 9 | H | UCS Old Boys | W | 21 | 0 |
| 16 | H | St Thomas' Hosp | W | 57 | 0 |
| 23 | H | Old Blues | W | 23 | 3 |
| **March** | | | | | |
| 2 | H | Rosslyn Park | L | 14 | 18 |
| 9 | H | Civil Service | W | 37 | 3 |
| 16 | H | Northampton | W | 9 | 3 |
| 23 | H | Old Dunstonians | W | 49 | 0 |
| 30 | H | Lennox | L | 5 | 6 |
| **April** | | | | | |
| 1 | H | Olney | W | 29 | 0 |
| 6 | H | Streatham | W | 12 | 3 |
| 13 | H | Park House | W | 30 | 0 |

Highest points scorer was C B Atkinson with 92, highest try scorer, with 23, was H Willett who, with his captain C Franklin, made most appearances, 28.

C Ashe (13, 4t), C B Atkinson (19, 16c, 3d, 16t), F B Brooks (16, 16t), F G Brooks (4, 6c, 9t), A C Bryson (4, 1t), R B Campbell (4, 1t), P Cochrane (2), H M Coombs (1), K Coomer (9, 2t), N P Draper (5, 3t), F Fauckler (1), M E Finlinson (1, 1c), H B Follitt (1), C Franklin (28, 9c, 3t), C Gilliland (4, 1t), A W B Gompertz (2), A Hall (4, 2t), A S Helmsley (1), H N Helmsley (7, 1t), C Hickie (2, 1t), R H Lacey (11, 1t), Lloyd-Cardos (1), A V Manton (22, 11t), H MacNaughton (2, 2t), F J Mitchell (2), J C Montero (4), L G Morrison (9), E R Odell (1), A W Pallister (12, 3t), L Pointer (1), E V Peppe (5, 3t), G U A Read (26, 26c, 6p), A L Rogers (19, 1t), W P Rogers (19, 1t), G Royle (1), L Sharman (2, 1t), B F Shippey (5), A C Smith (11), W W Vassall (5, 1c, 1t), J W Ward (21, 1c, 9t), B H Watts (1), E V Wells (9, 2t), S R Wells (19, 2t), H West (1), D L Weir (1), F Whaley (4, 2c), H Willett (28, 3c, 2d, 23t), R Willett (3), C C Wood (26, 1c, 8t).

# 1907-08

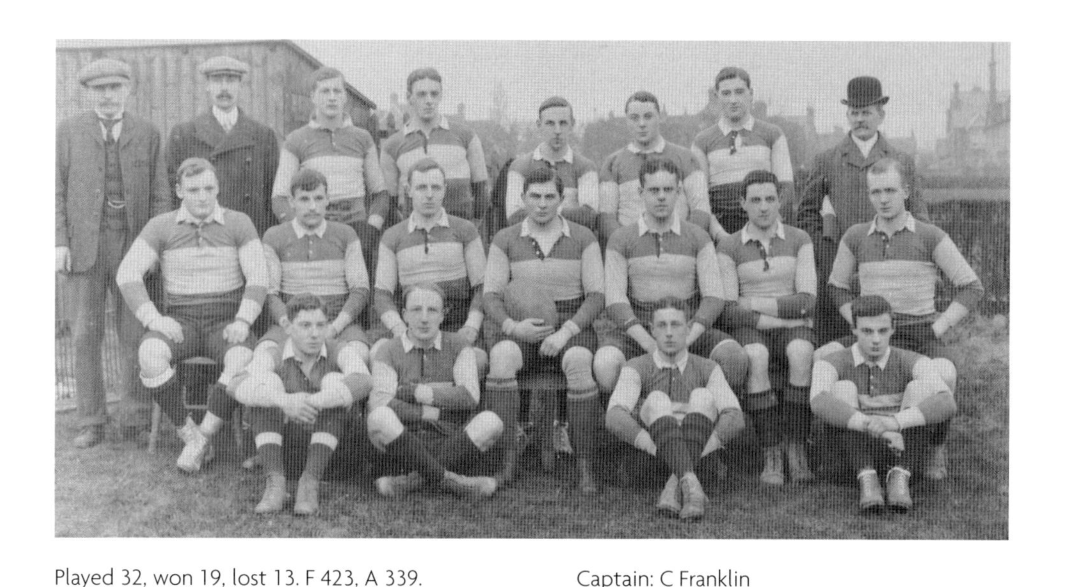

Played 32, won 19, lost 13. F 423, A 339.

Captain: C Franklin

| | | | | f | a |
|---|---|---|---|---|---|
| **September** | | | | | |
| 14 | H | Olney | W | 19 | 8 |
| 21 | A | Northampton | W | 16 | 6 |
| 28 | H | Old Edwardians | W | 16 | 0 |
| **October** | | | | | |
| 5 | H | Marlb'gh Nomads | W | 31 | 3 |
| 12 | H | Rugby | W | 9 | 3 |
| 19 | A | Coventry | L | 0 | 26 |
| 26 | H | Rosslyn Park | W | 13 | 0 |
| **November** | | | | | |
| 2 | H | Notts | W | 15 | 5 |
| 9 | A | Rugby | W | 14 | 0 |
| 16 | H | St Bart's Hosp | L | 3 | 21 |
| 23 | H | Lennox | W | 6 | 0 |
| 30 | A | Notts | L | 5 | 31 |
| **December** | | | | | |
| 7 | H | Coventry | L | 5 | 6 |
| 14 | H | London Hosp | L | 3 | 29 |
| 21 | H | Old Leysians | W | 8 | 0 |
| 26 | H | Burton on Trent | W | 30 | 6 |
| 28 | H | Glasgow Univ | L | 13 | 19 |

| | | | | f | a |
|---|---|---|---|---|---|
| **January** | | | | | |
| 18 | A | Leicester | L | 0 | 40 |
| 25 | A | Cambridge Univ | L | 10 | 28 |
| **February** | | | | | |
| 1 | H | St Mary's Hosp | W | 26 | 0 |
| 8 | H | UCS Old Boys | W | 26 | 0 |
| 15 | H | London Irish | W | 24 | 3 |
| 22 | H | London Welsh | L | 0 | 13 |
| 29 | H | London Devonians | L | 0 | 14 |
| **March** | | | | | |
| 7 | H | Civil Service | W | 15 | 14 |
| 14 | H | Northampton | L | 0 | 15 |
| 21 | A | Moseley | L | 6 | 15 |
| 28 | H | Moseley | W | 21 | 5 |
| **April** | | | | | |
| 4 | H | Streatham | W | 9 | 0 |
| 11 | H | Old Mer Taylors | L | 5 | 21 |
| 18 | H | Rugby | W | 28 | 3 |
| 20 | H | London Buccaneers | W | 47 | 5 |

A D Heard was leading try scorer with 31 and top points scorer with 97. G U A Read made most appearances, 31.

H C Ash (23), R Bailey (3, 1t), C V Birch (3), J Birch (1), A C Bryson (3), H G Burder (23, 3t), A C Chillingsworth (9, 3t), R S Claridge (2), A Colson (3), H W Evans (1), C Fowler (11, 1t), C Franklin (26, 3c, 1p, 3t), H G Gilliland (5, 2t), A W B Gompertz (23, 3c, 9t), A Hall (3), P T Hammington (3), L Hart (1), A D Heard (23, 1d, 31t), H W Helmsley (12, 8t), W J N Hunter (3, 3t), G S Hutton (4, 2t), E N D Jones (1), R H Lacey (27, 1c, 2t,, H MacNaughton (4), J McNeil (10, 2t), W R B McWha (6, 2t), A V Manton (3, 1t), A L Marsh (1), W T Mead (1), A T Miller (6), H Milton (9), F J Mitchell (1), A W B Pallister (2), R S Padraza (10, 1c), T Picton (2), H Powell (1), G U A Read (31, 30c, 3p), S P Rinter (1), W P Rogers (13, 3t), G Royle (20, 1t), L Sharman (1), B F Shippey (4, 2t), A Smith (1), F R S Spalding (4), C C Stimson (16), R D Sutherland (2), E J B Tagg (3), F Tilney (14), A Usher (1), J W Ward (8, 1c, 5t), C T Le Water (2), B H Watts (2), H B Wells (2), S R Wells (8, 1t), G A F Wemyss (8, 1t), H Willett (29, 4c, 2d, 14t).

# 1908-09

Played 34, won 19, lost 15. F 447, A 298.

Captains: A W B Gompertz
H Willett

| | | | | f | a |
|---|---|---|---|---|---|
| **September** | | | | | |
| 12 | H | Olney | W | 21 | 3 |
| 19 | A | Northampton | L | 8 | 21 |
| 26 | H | Old Edwardians | W | 14 | 6 |
| **October** | | | | | |
| 3 | H | Marlb'gh Nomads | W | 34 | 0 |
| 10 | A | Coventry | L | 8 | 17 |
| 17 | H | Harlequins | L | 0 | 13 |
| 24 | H | Ldn Devonians | W | 24 | 11 |
| 31 | H | Notts | W | 14 | 3 |
| **November** | | | | | |
| 7 | H | Herts Wanderers | W | 51 | 0 |
| 14 | H | St Bart's Hosp | W | 16 | 7 |
| 21 | H | London Hospital | L | 0 | 17 |
| 28 | A | Notts | W | 28 | 6 |
| **December** | | | | | |
| 3 | A | Oxford Univ | L | 0 | 43 |
| 5 | H | UCS Old Boys | W | 20 | 0 |
| 12 | H | Coventry | W | 3 | 0 |
| 19 | H | Guy's Hospital | L | 0 | 18 |
| 26 | H | Rosslyn Park | W | 14 | 0 |
| 28 | H | Jedforest | L | 3 | 10 |

| | | | | f | a |
|---|---|---|---|---|---|
| **January** | | | | | |
| 2 | H | Old Alleynians | L | 0 | 10 |
| 9 | H | Leicester | L | 5 | 8 |
| 16 | H | St Mary's Hosp | W | 43 | 3 |
| 23 | H | Cambridge Univ | L | 8 | 10 |
| **February** | | | | | |
| 6 | H | Civil Service | L | 11 | 12 |
| 13 | H | Lennox | W | 6 | 0 |
| 20 | H | London Welsh | L | 3 | 19 |
| 27 | A | London Irish | W | 6 | 3 |
| **March** | | | | | |
| 13 | H | Northampton | L | 3 | 10 |
| 20 | H | Old Charltonians | L | 9 | 21 |
| 27 | H | Old Whitgiftians | W | 18 | 0 |
| **April** | | | | | |
| 3 | H | Old Mer Taylors | W | 11 | 0 |
| 10 | H | Bedford & Dist | W | 42 | 8 |
| 12 | H | Eccles | W | 19 | 8 |
| 13 | H | Stade Bordelais | L | 0 | 8 |
| 17 | H | Streatham | W | 5 | 3 |

A D Heard was again leading try scorer with 35 and top points scorer with 114. H Willett made most appearances, 33.

H C Ash (7), R G Baker (1), H G Burder (25, 4t), C Chambers (1), E L Chambers (1), W Churchman (6, 2t), R G Cocking (30, 2c, 1d), T Crouch (9, 3t), H W Evans (5, 3t), Ferring (2), M E Finlinson (2, 1t), Foster (1), C Fowler (3), C Franklin (22), A W B Gompertz (22, 27c), R W Gosney (13), J Graham (3), A Hall (30, 2t), A D Heard (26, 3c, 1p, 35t), H N Helmsley (1), C Helmsley (3), J S Hickie (2), H Howard (1), W J H Hunter (4, 1t), J Hunter (1), G S Hutton (14, 3t), E N D Jones (7, 1d, 1t), C Knight (1), S Knight (6, 1c, 1d, 4t), R H Lacey (4), A Lacey (2), W Lacey (1), A Leach (1), R Mayes (1), W R B McWha (5, 4t), J McNeil (28, 4t), A V Manton (22, 1c, 9t), A T Miller (1), Mills (1), H Milton (26), S C Nailer (32), N D T Olner (1), J Osbourn (1), A J Osbourn (6), R S Padraza (2, 1t), G U A Read (27, 15c, 5p), R J Ridgeway (4, 1t), G Royle (13, 1t), C C Stafford (8, 2t), R C Stafford (3, 1t), C C Stimson (2), F Tilney (12, 2t), B F Watts (2, 1t), R C Wilkinson (1), H Willett (33, 2d, 13t), R Willett (21, 3t).

# 1909-10

Played 35, won 15, lost 19, drawn 1. F 389, A 373.

Captain: H Willett

| | | | | f | a |
|---|---|---|---|---|---|
| **September** | | | | | |
| 11 | H | Olney | W | 21 | 6 |
| 18 | A | Northampton | L | 3 | 14 |
| 25 | H | Old Edwardians | D | 3 | 3 |
| **October** | | | | | |
| 2 | H | Marlb'gh Nomads | W | 34 | 0 |
| 9 | H | Olney | W | 18 | 8 |
| 16 | A | Harlequins | L | 3 | 23 |
| 23 | H | London Devonians | W | 10 | 6 |
| 30 | H | Rosslyn Park | L | 5 | 11 |
| **November** | | | | | |
| 6 | H | London Irish | W | 13 | 0 |
| 13 | H | St Bart's Hosp | L | 0 | 13 |
| 20 | A | London Hosp | L | 0 | 24 |
| 27 | A | Notts | L | 3 | 5 |
| **December** | | | | | |
| 4 | H | London Welsh | L | 11 | 14 |
| 11 | H | Ealing | W | 20 | 5 |
| 18 | H | Guy's Hospital | L | 5 | 17 |
| 27 | H | Tonbridge | W | 20 | 0 |
| 28 | H | Pontypool | L | 8 | 15 |
| 29 | A | Old Edwardians | L | 5 | 37 |
| 30 | H | Old Merchistonians | L | 0 | 14 |
| **January** | | | | | |
| 1 | H | Old Alleynians | W | 25 | 0 |
| 8 | H | Notts | W | 16 | 3 |
| 15 | H | St Mary's Hosp | W | 28 | 0 |
| **February** | | | | | |
| 3 | H | Oxford Univ | L | 0 | 14 |
| 5 | H | Lennox | W | 11 | 3 |
| 12 | H | Coventry | L | 6 | 12 |
| 19 | H | London Hosp | L | 7 | 25 |
| 26 | H | Old Blues | W | 17 | 5 |
| **March** | | | | | |
| 5 | H | Old Leysians | L | 9 | 11 |
| 12 | H | Northampton | L | 8 | 14 |
| 19 | H | Old Millhillians | W | 21 | 11 |
| 26 | H | Upper Clapton | W | 23 | 12 |
| 28 | H | Eccles | L | 11 | 18 |
| **April** | | | | | |
| 2 | H | Old Mer Taylors | L | 0 | 22 |
| 9 | H | Old Whitgiftians | W | 19 | 0 |
| 16 | H | Streatham | L | 6 | 8 |

F C Hipwell with 14 tries and 54 points topped the scoring lists. S C Nailer made most appearances, 34. The 'pack' is credited with two tries.

C G Ainsworth (2), D W Aldridge (3), H C Ash (3), J Andrews (1), H E Bennett (8, 1t), Birch (1), E L Chambers (1), A Chillingsworth (3), W Churchman (6, 2t), J Clear (1), R G Cocking (24, 7c, 2d, 2p, 2t), H P Cocking (1), P C Cook (2), H M Coombs (1), J Foster (1, 1t), C Franklin (15, 2t), L Garratt (2, 2t), R W Gosney (26, 1t), D M Grant (19, 1c, 9t), C J Gurnhill (3, 2t), A Hall (28, 3t), B Hall (11), C Hall (2), A H B Haylett (8,13c, 1p, 1t), Harrison (2), L S Hart (5), W Hills (4), F C Hipwell (28, 3d, 14t), E N D Jones (1), L Kingston (2), S Knight (26, 7t), C W Lacey (30, 4t), E F Lacey (5, 3t), G H Lacey (1), G Lawson (1), G L Lemmon (1), C Lucas (1), D E Luyt (1), R Mayes (2, 1t), J McNeil (22, 2t), H Milton (2), N P Morrison (5, 1t), S C Nailer (34, 3t), D S O'Brian (2, 2t), A J Osbourn (10), W Owen (2, 1t), R S Padraza (9, 1t), A W B Pallister (2), W H Pemberton (2), L Pointer (2), G U A Read (13, 15c, 1d, 4p), R N Rowbotham (13), L Skempton (1), C C Stafford (3, 1t), R C Stafford (15, 5t), C C Stimson (8, 1t), J P Stimpson (3), W P Thompson (1), F Tilney (24, 2t), A Udal (1), W W Vassall (4, 3t), B H Watts (7), R Welch (1), H Willett (29, 1d, 7t), R Willett (7), Rev S Williams (2).

# 1910-11

Played 33, won 15, lost 16, drawn 2. F 379, A 413.

Captain: H Willett

| | | | | f | a |
|---|---|---|---|---|---|
| **September** | | | | | |
| 3 | H | Bedfordshire RU | W | 23 | 11 |
| 10 | H | Olney | W | 17 | 0 |
| 17 | A | Notts | L | 5 | 24 |
| 24 | A | Northampton | L | 3 | 38 |
| **October** | | | | | |
| 1 | H | Marlb'gh Nomads | W | 24 | 6 |
| 8 | A | Coventry | L | 7 | 25 |
| 15 | H | Harlequins | L | 7 | 47 |
| 22 | H | London Welsh | W | 12 | 6 |
| 29 | H | London Devonians | W | 28 | 0 |
| **November** | | | | | |
| 5 | H | London Irish | W | 16 | 11 |
| 12 | H | St Bart's Hosp | D | 3 | 3 |
| 19 | H | London Hosp | L | 6 | 9 |
| 26 | H | Ealing | W | 57 | 5 |
| **December** | | | | | |
| 3 | H | Leicester | L | 3 | 6 |
| 10 | H | Lennox | W | 7 | 6 |
| 24 | H | UCS Old Boys | W | 14 | 0 |
| 26 | H | Glasgow Univ | W | 7 | 0 |
| 27 | H | Upper Clapton | W | 12 | 5 |
| 31 | H | Civil Service | W | 13 | 5 |
| **January** | | | | | |
| 2 | H | Old Merchistonians | W | 24 | 6 |
| 7 | A | Old Edwardians | L | 8 | 9 |
| 21 | H | Cambridge Univ | L | 3 | 18 |
| 28 | H | Old Millhillians | W | 6 | 5 |
| **February** | | | | | |
| 4 | H | Coventry | D | 8 | 8 |
| 11 | H | Old Edwardians | L | 10 | 14 |
| 18 | A | Old Alleynians | L | 5 | 27 |
| **March** | | | | | |
| 4 | H | Old Blues | L | 12 | 16 |
| 11 | H | Northampton | L | 0 | 14 |
| 25 | H | Rosslyn Park | L | 6 | 11 |
| **April** | | | | | |
| 1 | H | Old Mer Taylors | L | 0 | 29 |
| 8 | H | Old Whitgiftians | W | 16 | 9 |
| 15 | H | Rugby | L | 14 | 19 |
| 17 | H | Eccles | L | 3 | 21 |

A J Osbourn played in all matches, 33. H Willett scored most tries, ten, and R G Cocking scored most points, 89.

G C Ainsworth (2), D W Aldridge (7, 1t), R Brown (1, 1t), H E Bennett (6, 2t), B M Carkeek (2), W Churchman (5, 2t), R G Cocking (29, 27c, 5d, 4p, 1t), H P Cocking (1), E C Cook (1, 1t), G H Corke (1), H A Crouch (4, 1t), H W Evans (3), C Fowler (1), R Fowler (5), C Goldsworthy (10), R W Gosney (3), C J Gurnhill (2), D M Grant (6, 3t), L C Gower (8, 4t), R Haines (6), A Hall (32, 7t), B Hall (29), A D Heard (4, 4t), W Hills (1), F C Hipwell (4), P F Horton (1), J E Jarvis (8), J D King (5, 1c, 1d, 1p), L Kingston (6, 1t), S Knight (20, 7t), C W Lacey (24, 2t), H Lambert (1), L Laville (1), E B Llewellyn (4, 3t), R Mayes (26, 5t), W T Maddock (1), J McNeil (29), P C Melcombe (3), S C Nailer (31, 4t), D S O'Brian (3, 2t), A J Osbourn (33, 4t), R S Padraza (11, 3t), Pasque (1), A S Printer (1), G U A Read (12, 11c, 1d, 3p), R N Rowbotham (7, 2c), Sinbenich (1), H Smith (1), C C Stafford (3), R C Stafford (21, 9t), C C Stimson (11), J P Stimson (1), W P Thompson (2), F Tilney (21), B H Watts (3), C Whiting (1), H Willett (26, 1d, 10t), R Willett (3, 1t).

# 1911-12

Played 34, won 20, lost 12, drawn 2. F 470, A 325.

Captain: R C Stafford

| | | | | f | a |
|---|---|---|---|---|---|
| **September** | | | | | |
| 2 | A | Leicester | L | 3 | 22 |
| 9 | H | Olney | W | 30 | 3 |
| 16 | H | Notts | W | 46 | 3 |
| 23 | A | Northampton | L | 6 | 28 |
| 30 | A | Harlequins | L | 19 | 29 |
| **October** | | | | | |
| 7 | H | St Thomas' Hosp | W | 19 | 13 |
| 14 | A | Rugby | L | 8 | 23 |
| 21 | H | Coventry | L | 3 | 6 |
| 28 | H | Rosslyn Park | W | 14 | 3 |
| **November** | | | | | |
| 4 | H | London Irish | W | 24 | 17 |
| 11 | H | St Bart's Hosp | W | 10 | 7 |
| 18 | A | London Hosp | W | 14 | 6 |
| 25 | A | London Welsh | W | 5 | 3 |
| **December** | | | | | |
| 3 | A | Stade Bordelais | W | 13 | 6 |
| 9 | H | Upper Clapton | W | 30 | 10 |
| 16 | H | Guy's Hospital | L | 6 | 17 |
| 23 | H | Glasgow Univ | W | 27 | 0 |
| 26 | H | Old Paulines | W | 23 | 6 |
| 27 | A | Northampton | L | 11 | 19 |
| 30 | H | Old Merchistonians | L | 6 | 8 |
| **January** | | | | | |
| 6 | A | Old Edwardians | W | 8 | 5 |
| 13 | H | Middlesex Hosp | W | 9 | 0 |
| 27 | H | Old Millhillians | W | 12 | 3 |
| **February** | | | | | |
| 10 | H | Old Edwardians | W | 20 | 13 |
| 17 | H | Old Alleynians | W | 12 | 8 |
| 24 | H | Old Blues | L | 6 | 11 |
| **March** | | | | | |
| 2 | H | Old Leysians | L | 0 | 8 |
| 9 | H | Streatham | D | 0 | 0 |
| 16 | H | London Hospital | D | 3 | 3 |
| 23 | H | London Devonians | W | 17 | 0 |
| 30 | H | Old Mer Taylors | L | 5 | 16 |
| **April** | | | | | |
| 6 | H | Eccles | W | 23 | 3 |
| 8 | H | Upper Clapton | W | 38 | 6 |
| 20 | H | Northampton | L | 0 | 20 |

For the second season, A J Osbourn played in every match, 34, along with A Hall another former Kempston player. A D Heard scored most tries, 17; R G Cocking scored most points, 70.

D W Aldridge (25, 2t), G N Allen (1, 1t), J Andrews (2), Armstrong (4), J Barton (2), D F Beeson (3), R Brownfield (2), A G Bull (1), A Church (1, 1t), F S Clark (1, 1t), J Clear (2), R G Cocking (30, 19c, 5d, 3p, 1t), H P Cocking (1), G N Cork (16, 1d, 2t), Collins (2, 1t), H B Cox (3), Earl (1,1c), C Fowler (2), R Fowler (27), J P Gilliard (1), J A Glaisher (1), L A Godfree (2, 4t), A W B Gompertz (6, 1t), H G Grieson (7, 1t), R G Gurney (3, 2t), A Hall (34, 9t), F Harrison (1, 1t), A D Heard (10, 17t), W H Irving (7, 2t), J E Jarvis (4), J P Jordan (1), R H A Kellie (18, 5t), J D King (6, 11c, 1p), S D Kitchener (27, 4t), H Lansbury (5), R Leslie (2), E B Llewellyn (7, 15c, 1p, 1t), A V Manton (25, 1c, 3t), H Maxey (3), R Mayes (25, 9t), R McMeakin (1), H Melcombe (1), M Milton (5), A Minaham (8, 3t), E R Mobbs (1), H K Nailer (4), A J Osbourn (34, 6t), L P Pacey (20, 1t), R S Padraza (1), A Perkins (2), S R Perry (6, 1t), D F Roberts (1), R H Ross (12, 4t), R N Rowbotham (1), J W Saunders (5), J Seton (2), B F Shippey (1), C C Stafford (6, 1t), R C Stafford (22, 2c, 1d, 14t), C C Stimson (14, 3t), J P Stimson (5), E J B Tagg (2), W P Thompson (2), H Willett (30, 2c, 1d, 12t), W White (1).

# 1912-13

Played 35, won 24, lost 9, drawn 2. F 506, A 249.

Captains: R C Stafford
A V Manton

| | | | | f | a |
|---|---|---|---|---|---|
| **September** | | | | | |
| 7 | H | Olney | W | 17 | 3 |
| 14 | H | London Welsh | W | 16 | 0 |
| 21 | A | Northampton | L | 8 | 19 |
| 28 | H | Harlequins | L | 3 | 31 |
| **October** | | | | | |
| 5 | H | St Thomas' Hosp | W | 32 | 0 |
| 12 | H | Civil Service | W | 56 | 6 |
| 19 | A | Rugby | W | 15 | 8 |
| 26 | H | RMA (Woolwich) | W | 27 | 12 |
| **November** | | | | | |
| 9 | H | St Bart's Hosp | W | 22 | 3 |
| 16 | H | London Hosp | W | 11 | 8 |
| 30 | H | Rosslyn Park | L | 0 | 8 |
| **December** | | | | | |
| 14 | A | Guys Hospital | W | 6 | 5 |
| 21 | H | Ealing | W | 12 | 11 |
| 24 | H | Glasgow Univ | W | 14 | 12 |
| 26 | H | Old Paulines | W | 9 | 0 |
| 28 | H | Old Millhillians | W | 18 | 3 |
| 30 | H | Old Merchistonians | W | 6 | 0 |
| **January** | | | | | |
| 2 | H | Northampton | L | 0 | 5 |
| 4 | A | Old Edwardians | L | 8 | 12 |
| 11 | A | London Welsh | W | 6 | 5 |
| 18 | H | Leicester | L | 9 | 26 |
| 25 | H | Cambridge Univ | W | 9 | 3 |
| **February** | | | | | |
| 1 | A | Oxford Univ | D | 8 | 8 |
| 8 | H | Old Edwardians | W | 35 | 3 |
| 15 | A | Old Alleynians | W | 29 | 0 |
| 22 | H | Old Blues | W | 9 | 0 |
| **March** | | | | | |
| 1 | H | Old Leysians | L | 12 | 29 |
| 8 | H | Streatham | W | 17 | 0 |
| 15 | H | Upper Clapton | W | 11 | 4 |
| 22 | H | Eccles | W | 31 | 0 |
| 24 | H | Leytonstone | W | 15 | 8 |
| 29 | H | Old Mer Taylors | L | 0 | 3 |
| **April** | | | | | |
| 5 | H | Rugby | L | 5 | 8 |
| 12 | H | Catford Bridge | W | 27 | 3 |
| 19 | H | Northampton | D | 3 | 3 |

A J Osbourn, R Fowler and A V Manton all made 32 appearances. A D Heard was again top try scorer with 17 and R Fowler scored most points, 97.

D W Aldridge (25, 1t), A Armstrong (12), C B Atkinson (1, 1c), A Barker (1), H E Bennett (12, 2t), E K Bird (3), J W Bowman (1), A G Bull (1), H G Burder (11, 7t), L A L Carter (15, 9t), W Churchman (2), J Clear (7, 1t) R G Cocking (1), T Collins (1), E C Cook (1), S Curtis (2), A Earl (1), C Fowler (4, 1t), R Fowler (32, 38c, 1d, 6p), J Gilliam (1, 1t), A W B Gompertz (9, 2t), H Hadland (9, 1t), A Hall (27, 9t), A D Heard (9, 2c, 17t), J A Jarvis (1), R H A Kellie (4), E C Kinghorn (9, 4t), C G Kingsley (6, 1t), S D Kitchener (31, 3t), L Laville (1), R S Mackinder (1), A V Manton (32, 5c, 15t), R Mayes (13, 5t), J McNeil (1), F M Millward (31, 5t), M Milton (2), A Mynard (3, 1t), S C Nailer (1), H K Nailer (30, 5t), F C W Newman (14, 11t), A J Osbourn (32, 5t), L P Pacey (22, 3t), D F Roberts (20, 6t), R H Ross (9, 2t), J Seton (4, 1t), F S Smith (5), J Smith (1), R C Stafford (6, 1p, 3t), W A Stewart (1, 4t), J P Stimson (18, 2t), C T Tebbutt (1), A Wade (1), C F Weir (1), H Willett (6, 2t).

# 1913-14

Played 35, won 23, lost 8, drawn 4. F 469, A 284.

Captain: A V Manton

| | | | | f | a |
|---|---|---|---|---|---|
| **September** | | | | | |
| 6 | A | Leicester | L | 8 | 17 |
| 13 | H | Moseley | W | 29 | 3 |
| 20 | A | Northampton | L | 5 | 27 |
| 27 | A | Harlequins | L | 0 | 51 |
| **October** | | | | | |
| 4 | H | Olney | W | 17 | 3 |
| 11 | H | Civil Service | W | 11 | 3 |
| 18 | A | Rugby | L | 3 | 11 |
| 25 | H | RMA Woolwich | W | 14 | 8 |
| **November** | | | | | |
| 1 | H | London Irish | D | 0 | 0 |
| 8 | H | St Bart's Hosp | W | 13 | 10 |
| 15 | A | London Hosp | W | 15 | 14 |
| 22 | A | Moseley | L | 0 | 17 |
| 29 | H | Rosslyn Park | W | 15 | 14 |
| **December** | | | | | |
| 6 | H | Upper Clapton | W | 18 | 6 |
| 13 | H | Guy's Hospital | W | 16 | 8 |
| 20 | A | Old Edwardians | W | 14 | 11 |
| 26 | H | Old Paulines | W | 24 | 8 |
| 27 | H | Rugby | D | 3 | 3 |
| 29 | A | Northampton | W | 9 | 0 |
| **January** | | | | | |
| 3 | H | Old Edwardians | D | 11 | 11 |
| 10 | A | London Welsh | L | 0 | 9 |
| 17 | H | Ealing | W | 28 | 0 |
| 31 | H | UCS Old Boys | W | 33 | 0 |
| **February** | | | | | |
| 5 | H | Oxford Univ | W | 11 | 3 |
| 7 | A | London Irish | L | 0 | 3 |
| 21 | H | Old Blues | W | 6 | 3 |
| 28 | H | Northampton | W | 20 | 5 |
| **March** | | | | | |
| 7 | H | Streatham | W | 6 | 3 |
| 21 | H | Old Whitgiftians | W | 31 | 3 |
| 28 | H | Old Mer Taylors | L | 5 | 9 |
| **April** | | | | | |
| 4 | H | Rugby | W | 18 | 3 |
| 11 | H | Olney | W | 41 | 0 |
| 13 | H | Leytonstone | D | 8 | 8 |
| 16 | H | London Clergy | W | 19 | 10 |
| 18 | H | London Welsh | W | 18 | 0 |

For the third time in four years, A J Osbourn played in every match, 35. Leading try scorer was J Gillam, 17. A Harvey scored most points, 80.

D W Aldridge (2), A Allen (1), J Andrew (1), H E Bennett (6, 4t), J Binyon (2), F Booth (1), R Brownfield (2), A B Bryson (2), L A L Carter (14, 3t), B Catlin (2), A Chillingsworth (1, 1t), H Counsell (5, 1t), J Clear (5), H P Cocking (1), R G Cocking (1), C L Crisp (1), A Earl (1), C Fowler (16, 4c, 3t), R Fowler (4, 2c, 2p), V Farr (3), J Gillam (24, 1c, 17t), R G Gurney (5), H Hadland (21, 4t), A Hall (28, 2c, 11t), A Harvey (29, 23c, 2d, 4p, 5t), D J Hargrieve (1), W Hepple (3), A Huckle (3, 1t), L H Jackson (14), S R Jackson (3, 1c) Q E M A King (2, 2t), C G Kingsley (4, 1t), S D Kitchener (26, 4t), A E Kitchener (2), L A Lagden (3, 1c, 1t), R S Mackinder (24, 1c, 2t), A V Manton (31, 1c, 11t), H Maxey (14), F M Millward (23, 1t), M Milton (12, 5t), F Muddiman (1), A Mynard (1), F C W Newman (29, 15t), F Osbourne (4, 2t), A J Osbourn (35, 2c, 2t), L P Pacey (21, 1t), A Perkins (4, 1t), R Powell (4, 1d, 3t), D F Roberts (9, 2c, 3t), R Royston (13, 1t), J W Saunders (2), J Seton (1), F S Smith (3, 1t), J Smith (3), Rev W W Vassall (22, 5t), A F Wemyss (1), A F Wesley (18, 8t).

# 1919-20

Played 14, won 6, lost 8. F 114, A 248.

Captains: A Hall
A V Manton

| | | | | f | a |
|---|---|---|---|---|---|
| **September** | | | | | |
| 20 | H | Northampton | L | 13 | 21 |
| **October** | | | | | |
| 11 | H | (BMS) Civil Service | W | 16 | 3 |
| 18 | A | Olney | W | 19 | 3 |
| **November** | | | | | |
| 1 | A | London Irish | W | 3 | 0 |
| **December** | | | | | |
| 13 | H | (BMS) Olney | W | 7 | 6 |
| 20 | A | Leicester | L | 0 | 43 |
| 27 | A | Northampton | L | 5 | 40 |
| **January** | | | | | |
| 3 | H | (BS) Streatham | W | 11 | 3 |
| 10 | H | (BS) London Welsh | L | 7 | 14 |
| 17 | A | Rugby | L | 0 | 5 |
| 24 | A | Cambridge Univ | L | 4 | 46 |
| **February** | | | | | |
| 21 | H | (BMS) Old Blues | L | 6 | 8 |
| 28 | A | Northampton | L | 3 | 53 |
| **March** | | | | | |
| 6 | H | (BS) London Irish | W | 20 | 3 |

A Hall and E R Peachey made most appearances, 12. J D King scored most points, 15, and R C Royston, N Gilbert and A Hall all scored three tries. No home matches were played at Goldington Road – (BS) is Bedford School, (BMS) is Bedford Modern School.

R C Adkin (11), Lt Allwood (2), F W J Bannatyne (1), B Bellars (1), J Bennett (2), E A Bethune (1), H L Brocklehurst (3), L Bloxham (1),S D Canvin (8, 1t), Emmerson (1), A G Freshwater (1), H Gilbert (1), N Gilbert (9, 1d, 3t), J J Gracie (8), A Hall (12, 3t), D T Handford (4, 1t), A Harvey (1), Hines (1), C H Hopkinson (4, 2t), W H Hynd (3), W A Ivin (5), E J Jarvis (3, 2t), H L Kilby (3, 2t), J D King (6, 6c, 1p), Capt Laville (1), A Leach (2), E J Lewis (1), C C Lewis (1, 1t), R S Mackinder (4, 1d), A V Manton (1), F W Modlin (6, 1t), H G L Nicholls (3), A J Osbourn (10), E R Peachey (12), E R Perry (4), M Platts (6), E R Plewman (8, 2t), M D Pugh (3), J G Read (6, 2c, 1d, 2p), R R Rose (8, 1t), R C Royston (5, 3t), C C Schmidt (4), J C Seagar (1), H B Y Simpson (2, 1c), R B Smart (1, 1t), J Smith (1), J H Tearle (1), J A Ten-Broeke (10), E P M Walcott (2), C E Welby (1), C L Wemyss (2, 1t), A F Wesley (9, 1t), J R P Willey (1).

# 1920-21

Played 25, won 7, lost 17, drawn 1. F 154, A 434.

Captain: A F Wesley

| | | | | f | a |
|---|---|---|---|---|---|
| **September** | | | | | |
| 4 | H | Nuneaton | W | 17 | 3 |
| 18 | A | Northampton | L | 5 | 25 |
| 25 | A | Harlequins | L | 0 | 76 |
| **October** | | | | | |
| 9 | H | Civil Service | W | 12 | 8 |
| 16 | A | Nuneaton | L | 0 | 32 |
| 30 | H | London Irish | W | 10 | 8 |
| **November** | | | | | |
| 6 | H | St Bart's Hosp | L | 0 | 17 |
| 13 | H | Leytonstone | W | 16 | 10 |
| 20 | H | Old Alleynians | L | 0 | 11 |
| 27 | A | Rugby | L | 0 | 36 |
| **December** | | | | | |
| 4 | H | Upper Clapton | W | 27 | 0 |
| 18 | H | London Hospital | L | 3 | 5 |
| 27 | H | Old Paulines | L | 3 | 21 |
| 28 | A | Coventry | L | 0 | 50 |
| **January** | | | | | |
| 1 | H | Streatham | W | 8 | 6 |
| 8 | A | London Welsh | L | 6 | 15 |
| 22 | H | St Cath's Col (Cam) | L | 6 | 8 |
| 29 | H | Old Whitgiftians | W | 14 | 8 |
| **February** | | | | | |
| 5 | H | Rugby | D | 3 | 3 |
| 19 | H | Old Blues | L | 3 | 22 |
| 26 | H | Northampton | L | 3 | 23 |
| **March** | | | | | |
| 5 | A | London Irish | L | 6 | 16 |
| 12 | H | Olney | L | 0 | 6 |
| 21 | H | Coventry | L | 3 | 5 |
| **April** | | | | | |
| 2 | H | Tonbridge | L | 9 | 20 |

A Hall made most appearances, 24. Highest try scorers were Rev D Hoole and R J J Ireland, six. J D King, with 26, scored most points. A N Other was a Nuneaton player who turned out for Bedford. He was one of 82, including 'A Paddy' who made at least one appearance.

R C Adkin (2), A C Arnold (1), G Arnold (3), A V Askwithe (2), H C Barratt (2), E A Bethune (4), O R Bethune (14), Capt Birch (11, 2t), Bischender (2), S D Canvin (8, 1t), B Catlin (1), Cooper (1), C Ubitt (1), G V Doggett (2), R Drouyn (2), East (1), V Farr (4), A G Freshwater (1), N Gilbert (2), J J Gracie (20, 4t), A Green (4, 1c, 1t), Sgt Greene (2), S/Lt Grey (1), R Grice (1), A Hall (24, 3t), A Harvey (1), F R S Henson (2), Capt E H Hime (1,1t), R E Holloway (2), Rev D Hoole (18, 6t), J Hopkinson (3, 1t), C A E C Howard (3), R J J Ireland (11, 1c, 6t), Jackson-Palmer (2), J D King (12, 8c, 1d, 2p), A Leach (1), E J Lewis (1), Llewyllyn (2, 1t), C A H McDonald (3), A V Manton (5, 2t), W Marshall (2), E Melford-Sharman (1), F M Millward (1), Middleton (1), F Mills (5), F W Modlin (8, 1c), Lt Neale (2), F E Neil (1), H G L Nichol (1), L H Nicholson (6, 1t), T Northern (7), A J Osbourn (23), R S Padraza (2), S Pearson (1), W H Piper (1), A Poppe (1), A Preston (1), M D Pugh (2), R D V Radford (1, 3t), J G Read (1), M F Roberts (1), Rollick (1), R R Rose (3), G W Royle (22, 1t), R C Royston (16, 2t), J W Saunders (13), J Simcoe (1), C Skinner (1), R B Smart (1), J Tancock (2, 1c, 1p, 1t), A F B Taylor (1), R A Taylor (2), J A Ten-Broeke (20, 2t), F C Thody (1), F Thorpe (9,1t), J Tulloch (8), Unwin (1), A F Wesley (5), H Wood (12), F Wright (1), A N Other (1), A Paddy (1).

# 1921-22

Played 36, won 20, lost 13, drawn 3. F 435, A 349.

Captain: L H Nicholson

| | | | | f | a |
|---|---|---|---|---|---|
| **September** | | | | | |
| 17 | H | Northampton | W | 6 | 5 |
| 24 | H | Olney | W | 28 | 20 |
| **October** | | | | | |
| 1 | H | Civil Service | L | 9 | 13 |
| 8 | H | London Irish | W | 23 | 13 |
| 15 | A | Coventry | L | 5 | 41 |
| 22 | H | Edgware | W | 25 | 3 |
| 29 | H | Rosslyn Park | L | 3 | 11 |
| **November** | | | | | |
| 5 | H | St Bart's Hosp | L | 8 | 37 |
| 12 | H | Westleigh | W | 15 | 3 |
| 19 | H | UCS Old Boys | L | 9 | 18 |
| 26 | A | Rugby | L | 0 | 13 |
| **December** | | | | | |
| 3 | H | London Hospital | L | 0 | 13 |
| 10 | H | Leytonstone | W | 20 | 5 |
| 17 | H | Upper Clapton | W | 20 | 6 |
| 20 | A | Old Bedfordians | W | 12 | 6 |
| 24 | H | Ealing | W | 25 | 9 |
| 26 | H | Berkshire Wand | W | 31 | 5 |
| 27 | A | West Herts | W | 16 | 5 |
| 31 | H | Old Paulines | W | 19 | 11 |

| | | | | f | a |
|---|---|---|---|---|---|
| **January** | | | | | |
| 7 | A | London Welsh | L | 5 | 8 |
| 14 | H | Coventry | L | 5 | 8 |
| 21 | H | Streatham | W | 6 | 4 |
| 28 | H | Old Alleynians | D | 9 | 9 |
| **February** | | | | | |
| 4 | H | Old Blues | L | 5 | 6 |
| 18 | H | R School of Mines | W | 9 | 6 |
| 25 | A | Northampton | L | 3 | 30 |
| **March** | | | | | |
| 4 | H | Civil Service | L | 3 | 12 |
| 11 | A | Westleigh | W | 30 | 3 |
| 18 | H | Old Centrals | W | 14 | 3 |
| 24 | H | Old Millhillians | D | 3 | 3 |
| **April** | | | | | |
| 1 | H | Rugby | D | 3 | 3 |
| 8 | H | Old Whitgiftians | W | 14 | 3 |
| 15 | H | West Herts | W | 18 | 0 |
| 17 | H | Edgware | W | 22 | 3 |
| 18 | H | Neath United | W | 7 | 3 |
| 29 | H | Olney | L | 5 | 8 |

C A E C Howard scored most tries, 12, and finished as leading scorer with 42 points. Most appearances were made by F Millward, 35. Seventy nine players were recorded.

R C Adkin (7, 1t), M Arnold (1), G W Baldwin (20, 1c, 1p, 2t), A M Bannatyne (1), N A Basten (1), L Biggie (1, 1t), H W Biggs (4), L H Bloxham (2), T Bovell-Jones (4), W Bovell-Jones (1), H H Brookes (2, 2t), S D Canvin (2, 1t), V Cattell (1), S C Chaplin (7, 1d, 5t), C J Churchill (21, 10c, 1d, 1p, 3t), R L Collett (4, 1t), F W Clarke (2), F G Clifton (13, 11c, 2p), R G Cocking (1), E L W Cumming (28, 1p, 1t), A W Dalgety (1), F C Davis (10, 1t), A Dean (11), G V Doggett (1), R S Drouyn (1), E D Dynes (2), W A Edwards (1), L A R Fensome (5, 1t), I J Fitch (2), J J Gracie (12), E A Grose (8), F H X Gwynne (3, 2t), A Hall (30, 1c, 5t), H Hauberg (1), D K Hayman (4, 1t), E H Hime (9, 4t), M F R Hockliffe (1), M S Holden (1), J C Hopkinson (3, 4t), C A E C Howard (25, 1c, 1d, 12t), R J J Ireland (1), A W Joy (1), L K Kingston (2), E A Lawton (20, 3t), J H E Lansbury (5, 1d), R H Mann (1), A V Manton (3), C Matson (1), V Mathews (10, 3t), G H H Maxwell (2, 1t), C H H Medhurst (2), F Mills (1), F M Millward (35, 2d, 8t), E Minney (5), F W Modlin (1), H G L Nicholls (1), L H Nicholson (26, 1c, 4t), W S North (1, 1t), A J Osbourn (30, 8t),W H Piper (16, 7t), S A Platts (16, 4t), S H Pryor (1), M D Pugh (7, 1c, 1t), J V D Radford (6, 2c, 3t), A Raley (3, 3c, 1d, 1t), R J Raynor (1), R C Reynolds (2), R G Richardson (2, 2c), M H Robinson (1), A C Saint (2), J W Saunders (14, 4t), H B Y Simpson (1), R G G Squibbs (8, 2t), A Stevenson (1), S A D Swannell (17, 4t), J C Taylor (6, 1t), R A Taylor (1), C H Tompkins (9, 1t), H Wood (6, 1t), F Wright (3).

# 1922-23

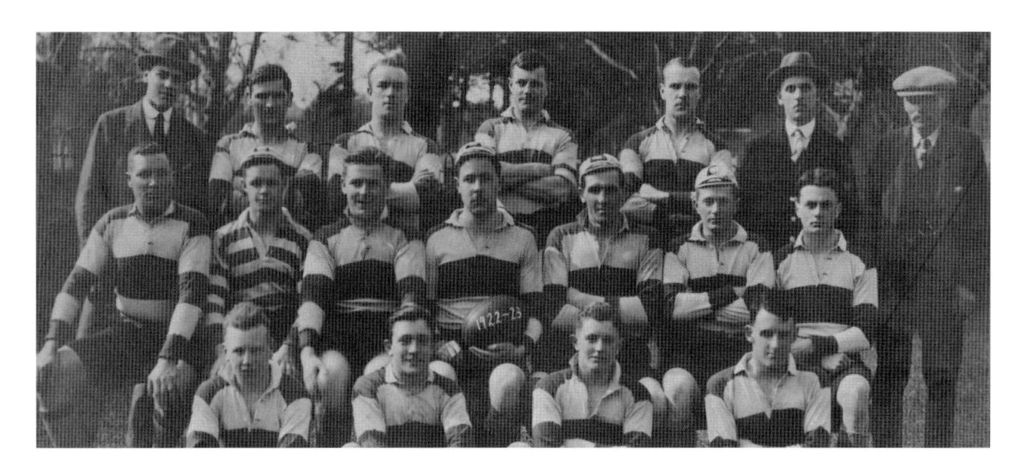


Played 35, won 21, lost 12, drawn 2. F 368, A 177.

Captain: ELW Cumming

| | | | | f | a |
|---|---|---|---|---|---|
| **September** | | | | | |
| 16 | A | Olney | L | 0 | 6 |
| 23 | A | Burton-on-Trent | L | 0 | 13 |
| 30 | A | Northampton | L | 6 | 27 |
| **October** | | | | | |
| 7 | H | Civil Service | W | 19 | 0 |
| 14 | A | Rugby | L | 0 | 11 |
| 21 | H | UCS Old Boys | L | 8 | 11 |
| 28 | H | Burton-on-Trent | W | 6 | 0 |
| **November** | | | | | |
| 4 | A | Wasps | L | 0 | 18 |
| 11 | H | Old Mer Taylors | L | 0 | 3 |
| 18 | H | Rosslyn Park | L | 9 | 11 |
| 25 | H | St Thomas' Hosp | W | 11 | 8 |
| **December** | | | | | |
| 2 | H | London Hosp | W | 24 | 6 |
| 9 | H | St Bart's Hosp | D | 3 | 3 |
| 16 | H | Old Paulines | W | 29 | 3 |
| 23 | H | Old Alleynians | W | 11 | 5 |
| 26 | H | Old Emanuel | D | 3 | 3 |
| 27 | H | Notts | L | 3 | 6 |
| 30 | H | Northampton | L | 0 | 3 |
| **January** | | | | | |
| 6 | H | Streatham | W | 11 | 0 |
| 13 | H | Old Haileyburians | W | 32 | 0 |
| 20 | H | Upper Clapton | W | 28 | 0 |
| 27 | A | Old Alleynians | W | 15 | 3 |
| **February** | | | | | |
| 3 | H | Old Blues | L | 0 | 8 |
| 10 | H | Birmingham | W | 6 | 0 |
| 17 | H | Wasps | W | 23 | 5 |
| 24 | H | London Univ | W | 12 | 0 |
| **March** | | | | | |
| 5 | H | Bridgwater | W | 11 | 6 |
| 10 | H | Rugby | W | 9 | 0 |
| 24 | H | Old Millhillians | W | 16 | 6 |
| 31 | H | Edgware | W | 13 | 3 |
| **April** | | | | | |
| 2 | H | Treherbert | L | 0 | 3 |
| 3 | H | Cardiff Scottish | W | 16 | 0 |
| 7 | H | Leicester Stoneygate | W | 28 | 0 |
| 14 | A | Birmingham | W | 9 | 3 |
| 21 | H | Hon Artillery Co | W | 7 | 3 |

Highest try scorer was L A R Fensome with 12, while M D Pugh, with 37, was the highest points scorer. A W Joy made most appearances, 32.

M Arnold (3), G W Baldwin (1), D G R Bilham (26, 4c, 3p, 2t), S E G Bilham (13), T Bovell-Jones (3, 1t), W Bovell-Jones (6, 1t), J W Bream (2, 1c), H H Brooks (1), H W Biggs (1), J S Carter (1), S C Chaplin (15, 1d, 3t), C J Churchill (24, 8c, 1p, 1t), H Clifton (26), H R Clifton (1, 2t), E R Cooper (1), E L W Cumming (23, 3c, 3p, 1t), C H Curtis (4), D Davidson (1), R M Davies (4, 1t), F C Davis (6), E D Dynes (13, 1d, 4t), J M M Ewing (1), L A R Fensome (28, 12t), S Ferguson (2, 1t), I J Fitch (14, 3t) A G Forrest (2), G E D Foster (4, 1d), A Hall (13, 2t), H Harris (2), E D Hart (8, 1t), M F R Hockliffe (1), C A E C Howard (1), F Hughes (1), H R Jones (1), A W Joy (32, 3t), A B King (1), P J King (5), R F Kitchener (2), S D Kitchener (25, 7t), J H E Lansbury (2), E A Lawton (26, 4t), A Marshall (3, 1t), F M Millward (1), L H Nicholson (26, 2c, 7t), W H Piper (1), M D Pugh (13, 2c, 11t), L Pritchard (1), J G Read (1), R G Richardson (3, 1t), M H Robinson (16, 1c, 4t), R R Rose (1), J W Saunders (9, 2t), H J Simcoe (30, 3t), C G Simpson (2), J B Simpson (20, 4t), H B Y Simpson (1, 1t), R G G Squibbs (4), F K Stranack (8, 1t), S A D Swannell (7, 3t), J Thornelow (1), C H Tompkins (18, 6c, 1p, 2t), H F Two (2, 1t), G L S Vaughan (3), E L Wheeler (2), T P Williams (1), G E V Woods (1, 2c), H F Woof (1), G Wright (3), G A D Young (1).

# 1923-24

Played 35, won 28, lost 5, drawn 2. F 430, A 201.

Captain: S D Kitchener

| September | | | | f | a |
|---|---|---|---|---|---|
| 15 | H | Harrogate OB | W | 17 | 3 |
| 22 | A | Nuneaton | W | 3 | 0 |
| 29 | H | Headingley | W | 6 | 5 |
| **October** | | | | | |
| 6 | H | Civil Service | W | 19 | 5 |
| 13 | H | Northampton | D | 6 | 6 |
| 20 | H | UCS Old Boys | W | 11 | 7 |
| 27 | A | Northampton | L | 0 | 17 |
| **November** | | | | | |
| 3 | H | Coventry | W | 6 | 3 |
| 10 | H | Old Mer Taylors | L | 3 | 6 |
| 17 | H | Rosslyn Park | W | 14 | 3 |
| 24 | H | Pill Harriers | L | 8 | 16 |
| **December** | | | | | |
| 1 | A | Birmingham | W | 6 | 3 |
| 8 | H | Streatham | W | 12 | 8 |
| 15 | H | London Univ | W | 31 | 3 |
| 26 | H | Old Paulines | W | 28 | 14 |
| 27 | H | Cinderford | L | 0 | 8 |
| 29 | H | Notts | W | 8 | 5 |

| January | | | | f | a |
|---|---|---|---|---|---|
| 5 | H | Middlesex Hosp | W | 26 | 0 |
| 12 | H | Old Emanuel | W | 9 | 7 |
| 19 | H | London Irish | W | 10 | 3 |
| **February** | | | | | |
| 2 | H | Old Blues | W | 12 | 11 |
| 9 | H | Birmingham | W | 14 | 0 |
| 16 | H | Wasps | W | 8 | 6 |
| 23 | H | Lensbury | W | 8 | 4 |
| **March** | | | | | |
| 1 | H | Edgware | W | 29 | 8 |
| 8 | H | Blackwell | W | 16 | 4 |
| 15 | H | Olney | W | 14 | 5 |
| 22 | H | Old Millhillians | W | 23 | 12 |
| 29 | H | Upper Clapton | W | 6 | 3 |
| **April** | | | | | |
| 5 | H | Old Cranleighians | W | 22 | 11 |
| 12 | H | Old Whitgiftians | W | 31 | 3 |
| 19 | H | Nuneaton | W | 5 | 0 |
| 21 | H | Old Alleynians | W | 19 | 7 |
| 22 | A | Coventry | D | 0 | 0 |
| 26 | H | Leicester | L | 0 | 5 |

L A R Fensome scored most tries, 18, and most points, 54. A W Joy played in all 35 matches. The total of 28 wins in a season was a record.

F A B Andrews (3, 6c), R C Adkin (2), T S Barker (2), A J Bailey (1), C P Bailey (3), M P Barrow (1), H A Bence (1), L V Bevan (1), S E G Bilham (2), D G R Bilham (4, 1t), J Boswell (1), T Bovell-Jones (2), W Bovell-Jones (2), S D Canvin (3), V Cattell (2), C Clarke (4), C J Churchill (20, 5c, 1d, 1p, 3t), H Clifton (24, 1t), E Collins (1), H C Cookle (1), E L W Cumming (16, 1p, 1t), F C Davis (13, 3t), J M Doak (2), E D Dynes (20, 14c, 3d, 2t), L A R Fensom e (25, 18t), I J Fitch (24, 5t), A G Forrest (5, 1t), T H S Galletly (8, 10t), S Garnett (3), S L Gibbs (4, 1t), J Gilbertson (1), A H Greenwood (13, 1t), E A Grose (1), E D Hart (3), A Hall (3, 1t), J T Handkinson (1), F G Hore (23, 10t), C A E C Howard (1), H Hubbard (1), A W Joy (35, 1t) P Johnson (8, 4t), S D Kitchener (22, 5t), N B Larby (11), E A Lawton (28, 1t), A Marshall (7), H R Newton (1), L H Nicholson (26, 6c, 1p, 9t), H S Parker (2), A O Pollard (2), M D Pugh (2, 1t), L Rabbitt (1), H W Richards (3), R G Richardson (12, 4t), A P B Roberts (15, 3c, 3t), E S Sharman (1), H J Simcoe (29), R B Simpson (2, 3t), C E Spring (2), R G G Squibbs (5, 4t), E A Stone (13, 1t), C H Tompkins (25, 5c, 10p, 2t), H F Two (8, 1t), E F Wakefield (3), A L B Watt (13, 2t), R Wood (1), G E V Woods (1), G A B Young (3).

# 1924-25

Played 35, won 15, lost 17, drawn 3. F 340, A 325.

Captains: F G Hore
AR Alston

| | | | | f | a |
|---|---|---|---|---|---|
| **September** | | | | | |
| 13 | H | Catford Bridge | W | 3 | 0 |
| 20 | A | Burton-on-Trent | L | 3 | 5 |
| 27 | H | Headingley | L | 3 | 5 |
| **October** | | | | | |
| 4 | H | Civil Service | W | 34 | 3 |
| 11 | H | St Thomas' Hosp | W | 19 | 0 |
| 18 | H | Blackheath | W | 11 | 0 |
| 25 | H | RMC Camberley | W | 11 | 8 |
| **November** | | | | | |
| 1 | A | Northampton | L | 0 | 7 |
| 8 | H | Old Mer Taylors | L | 5 | 11 |
| 15 | H | Rosslyn Park | W | 9 | 6 |
| 22 | H | UCS Old Boys | L | 9 | 11 |
| 29 | H | Wasps | W | 20 | 9 |
| **December** | | | | | |
| 13 | A | Coventry | L | 0 | 21 |
| 20 | A | Cheltenham | L | 5 | 21 |
| 26 | H | Old Paulines | L | 8 | 23 |
| 26 | A | Cardiff | L | 6 | 27 |
| 27 | H | Ebbw Vale | L | 0 | 7 |

| | | | | f | a |
|---|---|---|---|---|---|
| **January** | | | | | |
| 3 | H | Coventry | D | 5 | 5 |
| 10 | H | Northampton | L | 0 | 12 |
| 17 | A | Nuneaton | L | 3 | 17 |
| 24 | H | Nuneaton | W | 16 | 10 |
| 31 | H | Blackwell | L | 8 | 18 |
| **February** | | | | | |
| 7 | H | Old Emanuel | W | 20 | 9 |
| 14 | H | Notts | L | 14 | 15 |
| 21 | H | Birmingham Univ | D | 8 | 8 |
| 28 | H | Lensbury | D | 0 | 0 |
| **March** | | | | | |
| 7 | H | Cambridge Hybrids | W | 14 | 10 |
| 14 | H | Old Millhillians | L | 8 | 9 |
| 21 | H | Old Whitgiftians | W | 27 | 3 |
| 28 | H | Upper Clapton | L | 6 | 8 |
| **April** | | | | | |
| 4 | H | Old Cranleighians | W | 14 | 8 |
| 11 | H | Kings Col Hosp | W | 26 | 14 |
| 13 | A | Bristol | L | 10 | 15 |
| 16 | H | Northampton | W | 3 | 0 |
| 18 | H | Burton-on-Trent | W | 12 | 0 |

L A R Fensome and H J Simcoe made the most appearances, 32. The former was also the highest try scorer with 26 and leading overall points scorer with 81.

R C Adkin (4), A R Alston (14, 11t), B A Babb (6, 4t), R D G Barnett (2, 1c, 1t), L V Bevan (1), T Bovell-Jones (4), W Bovell-Jones (6), R C Brumwell (9), C J Churchill (17, 2c), N Clark (1), H Clifton (14), H J Curtis (1), F C Davies (24, 3t), C F Edwards (8), R Eidsforth (2, 1c), L A R Fensome (32, 1p, 26t), I J Fitch (31, 4t), A G Forrest (5, 1c, 1p, 1t), T H S Galletly (14, 7t), A H Greenwood (25, 15c, 3t), F C Greenwood (1), A Hall (4, 1t), J K Hall (4, 1t), E D Hart (2), F G Hore (17, 2t), J Howard (3), P Johnson (1), A W Joy (30, 4t), E A Joy (12), N B Larby (12, 4t), E A Lawton (14, 2t), L Lusty (1), W Lusty (3, 3t), F L Lutter (5), A Marshall (20, 2t), D Mayo (1), F C Mayo (1), H R Newton (1), L H Nicholson (15, 1c, 1t), E A Pearce (10), J L Proudlock (1), L Rabbitt (1), N R Ramsey (1), R C Reynolds (17, 1t), A Riley (3), J Richardson (1), R G Richardson (2), W S Robertson (1), D W Ryley (4), E S Sharman (4), T T Shaw (3), H J Simcoe (32, 2t), C G Simpson (3, 1c), J B Simpson (2), H B Y Simpson (1), F C Sinclair (3), C E Spring (13), E T W Starkie (4), E A Stone (3), R Taylor (12, 2t), J T Thody (1), C H Tompkins (27, 7c, 2p, 4t), J White (1), R Wood (4), G Wright (4).

# 1925-26

Played 32, won 20, lost 9, drawn 3. F 513, A 246.

Captain: L A R Fensome

| | | | | f | a |
|---|---|---|---|---|---|
| **September** | | | | | |
| 5 | H | Catford Bridge | W | 12 | 0 |
| 12 | H | Old Dunstonians | W | 28 | 12 |
| 19 | H | Blackwell | W | 3 | 0 |
| 26 | H | Headingley | W | 28 | 3 |
| **October** | | | | | |
| 3 | H | Civil Service | W | 46 | 3 |
| 10 | H | St Thomas' Hosp | D | 13 | 13 |
| 17 | H | Burton-on-Trent | W | 14 | 5 |
| 24 | H | London University | W | 35 | 0 |
| 31 | A | London Welsh | L | 6 | 12 |
| **November** | | | | | |
| 7 | H | Old Alleynians | W | 19 | 6 |
| 21 | H | Hon Artillery Co | W | 23 | 0 |
| 28 | H | Northampton | L | 0 | 9 |
| **December** | | | | | |
| 12 | H | Lensbury | W | 15 | 8 |
| 19 | H | Nuneaton | L | 3 | 8 |
| 26 | H | Old Paulines | W | 16 | 13 |

| | | | | f | a |
|---|---|---|---|---|---|
| **January** | | | | | |
| 2 | H | Rosslyn Park | L | 10 | 16 |
| 9 | A | Old Alleynians | L | 13 | 16 |
| 23 | H | London Welsh | L | 10 | 22 |
| 30 | H | Blackheath | L | 3 | 13 |
| **February** | | | | | |
| 6 | H | Kings Col. Hosp | W | 9 | 8 |
| 13 | H | St Mary's Hosp | D | 5 | 5 |
| 20 | A | Northampton | D | 6 | 6 |
| 27 | A | Nuneaton | W | 5 | 3 |
| **March** | | | | | |
| 6 | H | Upper Clapton | W | 53 | 3 |
| 13 | H | Old Millhillians | W | 16 | 3 |
| 20 | H | Suffolk County | W | 33 | 3 |
| 27 | H | Old Mer. Taylors | L | 7 | 12 |
| **April** | | | | | |
| 3 | H | London Irish | L | 10 | 16 |
| 5 | H | Bank of England | W | 35 | 11 |
| 10 | H | Old Cranleighians | W | 22 | 8 |
| 17 | A | Burton-on-Trent | W | 5 | 3 |
| 24 | H | Ldn XV (Rex Heller) | W | 10 | 6 |

R C Reynolds played in 31 out of 32 games. L A R Fensome was leading try scorer with 17 and A H Greenwood was leading points scorer with 56.

R C Adkin (2, 1t), A R Alston (13, 3t), B A Babb (15, 11c, 11t), Barbour (1, 2t), E M Bovill (1), H V Brodie (1), R C Brumwell (29, 13t), R H Castle (3, 1t), C J Churchill (18, 3c, 1d, 1p), R D Cotton (7, 4t), O C Crossman (1), F C Davis (15, 10t), E D Dynes (11, 3c, 4t), R Eidsforth (12, 1t), Ewings (1), L A R Fensome (29, 17t), I J Fitch (20, 1t), T H S Galletley (5, 2t), A H Greenwood (28, 19c, 2p, 4t), A F Hamilton-Smythe (2), B A Harris (2), F Harrison (2), F D Hibbert (9, 1d), W D Horne (9, 3t), J Howard (5), P J Howe (1, 1t), A W Joy (14, 1t), E A Joy (29, 4t), Jessop (1), A R Jesty (1), P Johnson (1), Kellett (1, 1t), P J King (5, 1t), N B Larby (22, 1c, 7t), D T Malcomson (2), A Marshall (12, 3t), Maynel (1, 1t), H Moass (2), H R Newton (2), L H Nicholson (25, 4c, 1p, 7t), E A Pearce (2, 2t), J L Proudlock (2), N R Ramsey (2, 1t), R C Reynolds (31, 3t), A Riley (2, 2t), F Robinson (1), T Rose (2), H J Simcoe (24, 4t), G E Spring (2), W H R Street (3), C H Tompkins (21, 12c, 5p, 5t), Wallis (1), C H Williams (5, 2t), W Winter (1), C K Wreford (16), F Wright (1, 2t), G Wright (1), H G Wrighton (2).

# 1926-27

Played 36, won 23, lost 13. F 485, A 319.

Captain: L A R Fensome

| | | | | f | a |
|---|---|---|---|---|---|
| **September** | | | | | |
| 11 | H | Catford Bridge | W | 22 | 3 |
| 18 | H | Blackheath | L | 8 | 13 |
| 25 | H | Headingley | W | 9 | 3 |
| **October** | | | | | |
| 2 | H | Burton-on-Trent | W | 17 | 3 |
| 9 | H | Blackwell | W | 14 | 3 |
| 16 | A | Northampton | L | 3 | 22 |
| 23 | A | Nuneaton | L | 10 | 12 |
| 23 | H | Old Leysians | L | 0 | 23 |
| 30 | H | Utd Services (C/ham) | W | 26 | 3 |
| **November** | | | | | |
| 6 | A | Old Alleynians | W | 5 | 3 |
| 13 | H | Lensbury | W | 20 | 5 |
| 20 | H | Old Millhillians | W | 27 | 5 |
| 27 | H | Old Dunstonians | W | 21 | 3 |
| **December** | | | | | |
| 4 | A | UCS Old Boys | W | 14 | 13 |
| 11 | H | London University | W | 20 | 5 |
| 16 | H | H V Brodie's XV | W | 19 | 15 |
| 18 | H | Blackheath | W | 24 | 3 |
| 27 | H | Old Paulines | W | 30 | 12 |
| 28 | H | Old Bedfordians | W | 14 | 12 |

| | | | | f | a |
|---|---|---|---|---|---|
| **January** | | | | | |
| 1 | H | Rosslyn Park | L | 6 | 15 |
| 8 | H | Notts | W | 14 | 0 |
| 15 | H | Bank of England | L | 10 | 11 |
| 29 | H | London Hospital | L | 9 | 13 |
| **February** | | | | | |
| 5 | A | Guy's Hospital | L | 3 | 17 |
| 12 | H | London Welsh | L | 3 | 5 |
| 19 | H | Old Alleynians | W | 12 | 3 |
| 26 | H | Nuneaton | W | 6 | 3 |
| **March** | | | | | |
| 5 | A | Coventry | L | 6 | 16 |
| 12 | H | Birmingham Univ | W | 34 | 3 |
| 19 | H | Coventry | L | 8 | 14 |
| 26 | A | Burton-on-Trent | W | 13 | 8 |
| **April** | | | | | |
| 2 | H | UCS Old Boys | L | 9 | 13 |
| 9 | H | Northampton | L | 0 | 28 |
| 16 | H | London Irish | W | 12 | 6 |
| 18 | H | Old Cranleighians | W | 21 | 3 |
| 23 | H | Westminster Bank | W | 16 | 0 |

A R Alston was the leading try scorer with 27 and leading points scorer with 87. N B Larby and R C Brumwell made most appearances, 33.

F B Ack (1, 1c), R C Adkin (4), A R Alston (27, 3c, 27t), B A Babb (7, 5t), D G R Bilham (5, 1t), J C Binyon (31, 8t), E M Bovill (2), H V Brodie (10, 1t), H H Brooks (2), R C Brumwell (33, 1d, 11t), L Brown (2), C J Churchill (8, 3c), R D Cotton (2, 1t)), O C Crossman (12, 2c, 5t), M Dent (5, 1t), L Dix (1), E D Dynes (5, 3c, 1t), R Eidsforth (28, 15c, 1d, 4p, 1t), L A R Fensome (16, 9t), I J Fitch (1), H French (1, 2t), B A Harris (5), G M Harrison (4), A C Harwood (5), F D Hibbert (6), F Holmes (3), W D Horne (1), J Howard (1, 1t), F/O Jackson (7), D E John (18, 2t), E A Joy (29, 2t), P J King (6, 1t), N B Larby (33, 1c, 4t), O L Lloyd (4), R Longland (6), Lowe (1), Lucas (1), A Lyell (2), McGauphan (1), D T Malcomson (17, 11c, 1p, 7t), A Marshall (30, 1t), C A Marques (1), L H Nicholson (1), E G Northway (1), W Norwood (3), L Owen (1), E A Pearce (6, 3t), Pennington (1), A H Phypers (3), N R Ramsey (4, 3t), G Reed (1), N F Reed (2, 1t), R C Reynolds (28, 1t), W Ridgway (4), W S Robertson (1), Scott (1), H J Simcoe (2), W A Sime (3, 2t), J B Simpson (9, 2t), C E Spring (2), W R Street (30, 3t), J T Thody (2), C H Tompkins (27, 3c, 2p, 3t), A T A Wallace (2, 1t) C H J Ward (2), J White (3, 3t), Wickes (1), C H Williams (1), D Williams (8, 1t), T E K Williams (2), C K Wreford (1).

# 1927-28

Played 33, won 25, lost 6, drawn 2. F 467, A 210. Captain: A R Alston

| | | | | f | a |
|---|---|---|---|---|---|
| **September** | | | | | |
| 10 | H | Catford Bridge | W | 16 | 8 |
| 17 | H | Blackheath | W | 31 | 8 |
| 24 | H | Headingley | L | 6 | 19 |
| **October** | | | | | |
| 1 | H | Blackwell | W | 11 | 9 |
| 8 | H | UCS Old Boys | W | 15 | 6 |
| 15 | H | London University | W | 26 | 0 |
| 22 | A | Nuneaton | W | 6 | 3 |
| 29 | A | Northampton | W | 6 | 5 |
| **November** | | | | | |
| 5 | H | Old Alleynians | W | 27 | 8 |
| 12 | H | St Thomas' Hosp | W | 19 | 5 |
| 19 | H | Edgware | W | 17 | 0 |
| 26 | H | Old Whitgiftians | W | 27 | 0 |
| **December** | | | | | |
| 3 | H | UCS Old Boys | W | 6 | 3 |
| 10 | H | Notts | W | 12 | 0 |
| 27 | H | Penarth | W | 8 | 6 |
| **January** | | | | | |
| 7 | H | Kings Col Hosp | W | 29 | 8 |
| 14 | A | Old Alleynians | L | 6 | 19 |
| 21 | H | St Mary's Hosp | W | 17 | 3 |
| 28 | H | Old Paulines | W | 12 | 3 |
| **February** | | | | | |
| 4 | H | London Hospital | D | 3 | 3 |
| 11 | H | London Irish | W | 37 | 10 |
| 18 | A | London Welsh | W | 9 | 3 |
| 25 | H | Northampton | D | 0 | 0 |
| 27 | H | Llannelly | L | 0 | 5 |
| **March** | | | | | |
| 3 | A | Coventry | L | 8 | 15 |
| 10 | H | Guy's Hospital | W | 14 | 3 |
| 17 | A | Notts | L | 3 | 24 |
| 24 | H | Nuneaton | W | 22 | 0 |
| 31 | A | Blackwell | W | 11 | 10 |
| **April** | | | | | |
| 7 | H | Olney | W | 24 | 0 |
| 9 | H | Old Bed Modernians | W | 17 | 4 |
| 14 | H | Old Cranleighians | W | 22 | 11 |
| 18 | H | Coventry | L | 0 | 9 |

A R Alston scored most tries, 29, and most points, 102. R C Brumwell and A Marshall both played in 31 games.

A R Alston (29, 6c, 1p, 29t), L G Ashwell (3, 3t), B A Babb (20, 15t), C Barber (2), A Beaumont (1), O V Bevan (2), D G R Bilham (5), E Brooker (7), N E Browning (1), R C Brumwell (31, 2c, 2d, 9t), N Carter (12, 5t), G F Cockell (13), Colquhorn (1, 1t), R D Cotton (27, 11c, 10t, 52pts), J Craig (1), H Davison (1), G T Dancer (2), M Dent (1), B B Dodd (1), E D Dynes (2), R Eidsforth (21, 4c, 1p), H Ewart (1), L A R Fensome (5, 2t), I J Fitch (1), Frieze-Green (1), F Gray (1, 1t), A H Greenwood (1), A C Harwood (16), F D Hibbert (1), A Higgins (2), J N Howard (2), J W Johnstone (8, 5t), W B Jamison (4, 3t), E A Joy (3, 1t), Lang (1), N B Larby (12, 1c, 2t), O L Lloyd (27, 2t), R Longland (4), A Marshall (31, 2t), W Munckley (16), W Owen (1), W F Pearce (1, 1t), R Perkins (9), L H Phypers (7), W Rashleigh (1), N F Reed (19, 12t), G Reed-Lewis (10, 1t), D C Riddy (15, 2t), Rylands (1), W A Sime (4), C E Spring (1), A E Stone (8), H Tebbs (1), C H Tompkins (23, 1c, 3p, 2t), N Varley (20, 1t), C H Williams (30, 11c, 2p, 9t), C K Wreford (6, 1t), F Wright (15, 3t), G Wright (3).

# 1928-29

Played 36, won 17, lost 17, drawn 2. F 332, A 327.

Captain: R C Brumwell

| | | | | f | a |
|---|---|---|---|---|---|
| **September** | | | | | |
| 15 | H | Catford Bridge | W | 12 | 6 |
| 22 | H | Blackheath | L | 6 | 12 |
| 29 | H | Westminster Bank | W | 23 | 11 |
| **October** | | | | | |
| 6 | H | Lizards | W | 14 | 0 |
| 13 | H | Nuneaton | W | 17 | 6 |
| 20 | A | Northampton | L | 3 | 16 |
| 27 | A | Coventry | L | 6 | 9 |
| **November** | | | | | |
| 3 | H | UCS Old Boys | L | 10 | 14 |
| 10 | H | London Welsh | W | 8 | 7 |
| 17 | H | Northampton | L | 0 | 16 |
| 24 | A | Leicester | L | 9 | 27 |
| 24 | H | St Thomas' Hosp | W | 10 | 3 |
| **December** | | | | | |
| 1 | A | Cardiff | L | 5 | 17 |
| 8 | H | Blackwell | L | 6 | 13 |
| 22 | H | London Hospital | L | 3 | 8 |
| 26 | H | Old Paulines | W | 3 | 0 |
| 29 | H | Rosslyn Park | L | 10 | 14 |

| | | | | f | a |
|---|---|---|---|---|---|
| **January** | | | | | |
| 5 | H | Old Alleynians | W | 13 | 0 |
| 12 | H | West Herts | W | 16 | 7 |
| 14 | H | Cardiff | W | 3 | 0 |
| 19 | H | Bank of England | W | 24 | 9 |
| 26 | H | Old Millhillians | L | 6 | 11 |
| **February** | | | | | |
| 2 | H | Old Leysians | W | 11 | 3 |
| 9 | A | London Welsh | L | 0 | 17 |
| 23 | H | Kings Col Hosp | W | 11 | 6 |
| **March** | | | | | |
| 7 | H | Royal Air Force | W | 13 | 3 |
| 9 | H | Burton-on-Trent | W | 22 | 5 |
| 16 | A | Old Alleynians | D | 0 | 0 |
| 23 | H | St Mary's Hosp | W | 23 | 11 |
| 30 | H | Civil Service | L | 11 | 12 |
| **April** | | | | | |
| 1 | H | Moseley | L | 3 | 5 |
| 6 | H | Old Cranleighians | L | 17 | 19 |
| 13 | H | Coventry | L | 0 | 14 |
| 18 | H | Nuneaton | W | 6 | 3 |
| 20 | H | Olney | D | 3 | 3 |
| 27 | H | Northampton | L | 5 | 20 |

A R Alston scored most tries, 12, and most points, 59. R Eidsforth and N F Reed made 33 appearances.

Adams (1, 1t), A R Alston (20, 10c, 1p, 12t), F Alwyn-Lougher (1), L G Ashwell (12, 6t), J C Atkins (1), B A Babb (6, 2t), H A Beale (1), J W Beaumont (8), O V Bevan (1), T I C Bevan (1), D G R Bilham (9, 1t), J M Bilham (21), E M Bovil (1), Cpl Brereton (2), R C Brumwell (18, 9t), F M T Bunney (1), J K Carlton (1), N Carter (13, 1c), C J Churchill (3, 3c), G F Cockell (4), R D Cotton (21, 9t), J Craig (1), F Crompton (2), I Custerson (1), R L Davies (8, 2t), F C Davis (9, 1t), Dodd (1), R Eidsforth (33, 12c), I Evans (6), A H Farr (1), W Grey (3), G M Harrison (2, 1t), A C Harwood (21, 2t), B J Holloway (1), F Holmes (10), W B Hopkins (1), A J Hoskins (1), J W Johnstone (14, 6t), E A Joy (13), O L Lloyd (22, 2t), H H McLeary (1), A Marshall (29, 1t), W Munckley (4), I S Panton (2), F/o Parker (1), R Perkins (26, 1t), A H Phypers (1), L F Phypers (5), M D Pugh (4, 1d, 1t), Pym (1), C H Quarry (11, 1t), G A Redhouse (1), N F Reed (33, 10t), G Reed (4, 1c), G Reed-Lewis (2), D C Riddy (22, 1t), M H Robinson (1), H J Simcoe (2), W A Sime (5, 1t), A E Simmons (2), W H Stapley (21, 3t), W A Tattersall (8), M H Thorogood (2), M A Tulloch (10, 6t), A T A Wallace (1), C H J Ward (3), C H Williams (21, 5c, 6t), T E K Williams (12, 2t).

# 1929-30

Played 34, won 20, lost 10, drawn 4. F 430, A 235.

Captain: R C Brumwell

| | | | | f | a |
|---|---|---|---|---|---|
| **September** | | | | | |
| 14 | H | Catford Bridge | W | 47 | 0 |
| 21 | H | Blackheath | L | 3 | 11 |
| 28 | H | Westminster Bank | W | 21 | 14 |
| **October** | | | | | |
| 5 | H | Blackwell | W | 11 | 0 |
| 12 | A | Moseley | L | 3 | 8 |
| 19 | H | Old Alleynians | W | 25 | 0 |
| 26 | A | UCS Old Boys | W | 8 | 3 |
| **November** | | | | | |
| 2 | H | Oxford U G'hounds | W | 29 | 3 |
| 9 | H | St Mary's Hosp | W | 20 | 3 |
| 16 | A | Northampton | L | 11 | 13 |
| 23 | H | St Thomas' Hosp | W | 33 | 0 |
| 30 | H | Coventry | W | 16 | 13 |
| **December** | | | | | |
| 7 | A | Blackheath | L | 0 | 11 |
| 14 | A | Blackwell | W | 10 | 3 |
| 21 | H | London Hospital | W | 21 | 5 |
| 26 | H | Old Paulines | W | 6 | 0 |
| 28 | H | Rosslyn Park | L | 3 | 11 |
| **January** | | | | | |
| 4 | H | Old Leysians | W | 6 | 5 |
| 11 | H | Moseley | W | 26 | 3 |
| 18 | A | Old Alleynians | D | 6 | 6 |
| 25 | H | UCS Old Boys | W | 22 | 0 |
| **February** | | | | | |
| 1 | H | Royal Air Force | D | 5 | 5 |
| 8 | A | London Welsh | D | 3 | 3 |
| 15 | H | Northampton | L | 0 | 5 |
| 22 | A | Coventry | L | 4 | 24 |
| **March** | | | | | |
| 1 | H | London Welsh | W | 7 | 3 |
| 8 | A | Leicester | L | 3 | 20 |
| 15 | H | Cheltenham | L | 7 | 17 |
| 22 | H | St Bart's Hosp | W | 11 | 8 |
| 29 | H | Old Mer Taylors | L | 11 | 15 |
| **April** | | | | | |
| 5 | A | Nuneaton | W | 15 | 7 |
| 12 | H | Old Millhillians | W | 17 | 3 |
| 19 | H | Cardiff | W | 14 | 7 |
| 21 | H | Cross Keys | D | 6 | 6 |

L G Ashwell scored most tries, 31, and most points, 93. R Eidsforth and R Willsher both made 33 appearances.

A R Alston (17, 15c, 14t), L G Ashwell (26, 31t), F Barr (1), J M Bilham (17), W Brereton (5), R C Brumwell (30, 1d, 15t), F C Carter (1), J R Clarke (7), J G Cook (16, 6c, 3t), R D Cotton (2), H W Coward (18), F C Davis (1), R Eidsforth (33, 13c, 2d, 1t), G Evans (3, 1t), I Evans (1), A H Farr (2), L A R Fensome (8, 1t), K C Fyfe (1), G E Goddard (5), A C Harwood (3), F Holmes (29, 3t), A R Jesty (8, 1t), E A Joy (25), O L Lloyd (9, 1d, 1t), D L MacLean (14, 1d, 8t), A Marshall (29), E A Pearce (1), R Perkins (32, 1t), R Plewman (3), N T Pryor (1), C H Quarry (7), N F Reed (26, 1d, 8t), R H Rodgers (1), C Rose (31, 3t), H J Simcoe (1), A E Simmons (1), A H Southgate (5, 1d, 4t), W H Stapley (27, 5t), W A Tattersall (1), C H J Ward (3), J White (4, 1d), T E K Williams (22, 7t), R Willsher (33, 3t).

# 1930-31

Played 35, won 27, lost 7, drawn 1. F 445, A 212.

| | | | | f | a |
|---|---|---|---|---|---|
| **September** | | | | | |
| 6 | H | Olney | W | 31 | 3 |
| 13 | H | Catford Bridge | W | 20 | 0 |
| 20 | H | Blackheath | W | 11 | 10 |
| 27 | H | Guys Hospital | W | 13 | 0 |
| **October** | | | | | |
| 4 | H | Blackwell | W | 19 | 0 |
| 18 | H | Old Alleynians | W | 17 | 8 |
| 25 | H | Civil Service | W | 21 | 3 |
| **November** | | | | | |
| 1 | H | Coventry | L | 3 | 11 |
| 8 | A | London Welsh | L | 5 | 9 |
| 15 | H | Nuneaton | L | 6 | 12 |
| 22 | H | Northampton | W | 6 | 0 |
| 29 | A | Cheltenham | L | 0 | 6 |
| **December** | | | | | |
| 6 | H | Kings College Hosp | W | 11 | 5 |
| 13 | A | Old Alleynians | W | 8 | 3 |
| 20 | H | London Hospital | W | 22 | 6 |
| 26 | H | Old Paulines | W | 14 | 0 |
| 27 | H | Rosslyn Park | W | 25 | 16 |

Captain: R C Brumwell

| | | | | f | a |
|---|---|---|---|---|---|
| **January** | | | | | |
| 3 | H | Old Millhillians | W | 11 | 0 |
| 17 | H | Old Edwardians | W | 14 | 5 |
| 24 | H | Old Leysians | W | 16 | 0 |
| 31 | A | Coventry | L | 0 | 8 |
| **February** | | | | | |
| 7 | H | Royal Air Force | W | 10 | 0 |
| 12 | H | Westminster Bank | W | 21 | 13 |
| 14 | H | St Bart's Hosp | W | 10 | 3 |
| 21 | A | Northampton | W | 19 | 16 |
| 28 | A | Moseley | D | 5 | 5 |
| **March** | | | | | |
| 7 | H | St Thomas' Hosp | W | 28 | 10 |
| 14 | A | Leicester | L | 0 | 23 |
| 21 | H | Old Mer Taylors | L | 8 | 20 |
| 28 | H | Bank of England | W | 14 | 8 |
| **April** | | | | | |
| 4 | H | Wakefield | W | 14 | 6 |
| 6 | H | Rugby | W | 8 | 0 |
| 11 | H | Old Blues | W | 8 | 0 |
| 16 | H | Wasps | W | 7 | 3 |
| 18 | H | Burton-on-Trent | W | 20 | 0 |

F Holmes appeared in all 35 matches. L G Ashwell scored most tries, 23, and J G Cooke most points, 71. Thirty seven players made at least one appearance.

L G Ashwell (31, 23t), B R Black (1), R C Brumwell (26, 18t), F C Carter (1), J R Clarke (1), J G Cook (28, 16c, 7p, 6t), H W Coward (21, 2t), O C Crossman (2, 1t), R Eidsforth (33, 7c, 2d, 1t), L A R Fensome (15, 1t), G E Goddard (24, 3t), A C Harwood (1), F Holmes (35, 3t), R Jenkins (1), A R Jesty (7, 4t), E A Joy (26, 1t), E M Kellett (1), N B Larby (25, 2t), O L Lloyd (16, 1t), W Madderson (10, 4t), A Marshall (33, 1t), D P Morkel (6, 3t), R Perkins (34), N T Pryor (1), C H Quarry (9) N F Reed (25, 1d, 11t, 37pts), C Rose (33, 2t), W A Sime (23, 1d, 4t), A E Simmons (2), H A Southgate (3, 1t), H A N Tebbs (1), G Turner (1), C H J Ward (1), J White (3, 3t), C H Williams (18, 16c, 3p, 2t), T E K Williams (25, 10t), R Willsher (2).

# 1931-32

Played 34, won 23, lost 11. F 421, A 229.

Captain: R C Brumwell

| | | | | f | a |
|---|---|---|---|---|---|
| **September** | | | | | |
| 12 | H | Catford Bridge | L | 9 | 12 |
| 19 | H | Blackheath | W | 8 | 5 |
| 26 | H | Old Edwardians | W | 17 | 6 |
| **October** | | | | | |
| 3 | H | Moseley | L | 14 | 24 |
| 10 | A | Old Alleynians | L | 0 | 9 |
| 17 | H | St Bart's Hosp | L | 8 | 9 |
| 24 | H | St Mary's Hosp | W | 22 | 0 |
| 31 | A | Richmond | L | 3 | 11 |
| **November** | | | | | |
| 7 | H | Rosslyn Park | W | 16 | 3 |
| 21 | H | Old Blues | L | 3 | 6 |
| 28 | A | Coventry | L | 0 | 14 |
| **December** | | | | | |
| 5 | H | London Hosp | W | 18 | 0 |
| 12 | H | London Welsh | W | 13 | 6 |
| 19 | H | Old Leysians | W | 19 | 5 |
| 26 | H | Old Paulines | W | 22 | 11 |
| 28 | A | Northampton | L | 3 | 15 |

| | | | | f | a |
|---|---|---|---|---|---|
| **January** | | | | | |
| 2 | H | Nuneaton | W | 18 | 10 |
| 9 | H | Kings Col Hosp | W | 20 | 3 |
| 16 | H | Old Millhillians | W | 8 | 3 |
| 23 | H | Old Alleynians | W | 5 | 3 |
| 30 | H | Wasps | W | 8 | 3 |
| **February** | | | | | |
| 6 | H | Royal Air Force | W | 6 | 0 |
| 13 | H | Old Mer Taylors | W | 9 | 0 |
| 20 | H | St Thomas' Hosp | W | 30 | 0 |
| 27 | H | Coventry | W | 10 | 0 |
| **March** | | | | | |
| 5 | H | Northampton | L | 0 | 16 |
| 12 | A | Leicester | L | 0 | 18 |
| 19 | H | Old Whitgiftians | W | 20 | 5 |
| 26 | H | Rugby | W | 13 | 0 |
| 28 | H | Sale | W | 27 | 3 |
| **April** | | | | | |
| 2 | H | UCS Old Boys | W | 14 | 3 |
| 9 | A | Blackwell | W | 20 | 11 |
| 16 | A | Nuneaton | L | 3 | 6 |
| 23 | H | Blackwell | W | 35 | 9 |

R C Brumwell scored most tries, 25; J G Cook most points, 127. W A Sime made most appearances, 33. Forty two players turned out at least once.

L G Ashwell (30, 8t), O V Bevan (8, 2t), D G R Bilham (1), J H Bilham (25), B R Black (1), C Braggins (3), R C Brumwell (32, 1c, 25t), K E Burrows (1), J G Cook (29, 28c, 8p, 9t), O C Crossman (6, 1c, 2t), G T Dancer (29, 1t), R Eidsforth (17, 4d, 1p), A H Farr (4), L A R Fensome (5), G E Goddard (17, 4t), D Hall (1), R C Haynes (2), F Holmes (7), W D Horne (11), E C Howard (3), A R Jesty (5), E A Joy (4), O L Lloyd (6, 2t), B G Longstaff (1), W Madderson (6, 2t), A Marshall (24, 1t), J H Moll (1), G M Neville (2, 1t), R Perkins (27, 1t), C Rawlins (16, 3t) N F Reed (27, 7t), D C Riddy (3), C Rose (32, 1c, 1t), W A Sime (33, 1d, 9t), A E Simmons (25, 3t), R G Smallwood (1), H A Southgate (7, 1c, 2t), N J Timmins (2), G C Turner (1), T E K Williams (30, 12t), R Wise (11, 5t), R Willsher (14).

# 1932-33

Played 34, won 23, lost 11, F 389, A 234.

Captain: A Marshall

| | | | | f | a |
|---|---|---|---|---|---|
| **September** | | | | | |
| 3 | A | Leicester | L | 5 | 10 |
| 10 | H | Catford Bridge | W | 19 | 0 |
| 17 | H | Blackheath | W | 20 | 0 |
| 24 | H | Richmond | W | 21 | 5 |
| **October** | | | | | |
| 1 | A | Moseley | L | 3 | 9 |
| 8 | H | St Mary's Hosp | W | 11 | 6 |
| 15 | H | St Bart's Hosp | W | 3 | 0 |
| 22 | A | Coventry | L | 3 | 8 |
| 29 | H | King's Col Hosp | W | 3 | 0 |
| **November** | | | | | |
| 5 | H | Old Cranleighians | W | 8 | 7 |
| 12 | H | Northampton | L | 3 | 6 |
| 19 | H | Old Blues | W | 9 | 0 |
| **December** | | | | | |
| 3 | H | London Hospital | W | 14 | 0 |
| 10 | H | St Thomas' Hosp | W | 8 | 0 |
| 17 | H | Bank of England | W | 15 | 5 |
| 24 | H | Leicester | W | 13 | 10 |
| 26 | H | Old Paulines | W | 14 | 5 |
| 27 | H | Old Dunstonians | W | 27 | 8 |
| 31 | H | Rosslyn Park | W | 8 | 5 |
| **January** | | | | | |
| 7 | H | Old Edwardians | W | 8 | 3 |
| 14 | H | Coventry | L | 3 | 9 |
| 21 | H | Nuneaton | L | 3 | 6 |
| **February** | | | | | |
| 4 | H | Royal Air Force | W | 15 | 3 |
| 11 | H | Blackwell | W | 19 | 4 |
| 18 | H | Old Mer Taylors | L | 6 | 19 |
| **March** | | | | | |
| 4 | A | Northampton | L | 9 | 28 |
| 11 | H | Old Alleynians | W | 29 | 6 |
| 18 | A | London Welsh | L | 5 | 21 |
| 25 | H | UCS Old Boys | W | 22 | 0 |
| **April** | | | | | |
| 1 | A | Nuneaton | W | 17 | 9 |
| 6 | H | Met Police | L | 3 | 18 |
| 8 | H | Old Leysians | W | 15 | 4 |
| 15 | H | Headingley | L | 16 | 4 |
| 17 | H | Sale | L | 12 | 16 |

G T Dancer and A Marshall both made 33 appearances. N F Reed and T D Thevenard were leading try scorers with 11 and W A Sime scored most points, 58.

L G Ashwell (24, 10t), O V Bevan (2, 1t), J M Bilham (22), B R Black (10), C W Braggins (1), E J C Brown (1), R C Brumwell (18, 5t), K E Burrows (15, 2d, 8t), J R Clarke (5, 1t), J Cook (7, 3c, 2t), G T Dancer (33, 3t), R Eidsforth (24, 5c, 4d, 1t), Emmett (1), L A R Fensome (28), G E Goddard (1, 1t), D Hall (12, 2c, 1t), R C Haynes (5), B J Holloway (1), F Holmes (1), A R Jesty (13, 1t), O L Lloyd (2, 1t), A Marshall (33, 2p, 3t), G M Neville (2, 1t), R Perkins (21, 2t), J O'B Power (1), C G Prigmore (9, 1t), C H Quarry (6), C Rawlins (14, 3t), N F Reed (26, 2d, 11t), A Rogers (1), C Rose (31, 2t), W A Sime (23, 20c, 3p, 3t), A E Simmons (5, 7c, 2p, 1t), S Schofield (18), D A Smith (3), H A Southgate (2), S Stanley (2), T D Thevenard (26, 11t), N J Timmins (7, 5t), G C Turner (3, 1t), T E K Williams (26, 1d, 10t), R Willsher (21, 3t), R G Wise (3, 1t), H W Wood (1).

# 1933-34

Played 38, won 27, lost 9, drawn 2. F 547, A 313.

Captain: W A Sime

| September | | | | f | a |
|---|---|---|---|---|---|
| 2 | A | Leicester | L | 13 | 26 |
| 7 | H | Palmer's XV (N'pton) | W | 10 | 5 |
| 9 | H | Catford Bridge | W | 39 | 11 |
| 16 | H | Blackwell | W | 29 | 13 |
| 23 | H | Blackheath | W | 7 | 0 |
| 30 | A | Richmond | W | 16 | 11 |
| **October** | | | | | |
| 7 | H | Moseley | W | 14 | 5 |
| 14 | H | St Mary's Hosp | W | 8 | 0 |
| 21 | H | St Bart's Hosp | W | 8 | 0 |
| 28 | A | Coventry | L | 10 | 21 |
| **November** | | | | | |
| 4 | H | Old Cranleighians | L | 13 | 14 |
| 11 | A | Northampton | L | 0 | 11 |
| 18 | H | Old Millhillians | W | 14 | 6 |
| 25 | H | St Thomas' Hosp | W | 19 | 0 |
| **December** | | | | | |
| 2 | H | London Welsh | L | 8 | 10 |
| 23 | H | Leicester | W | 20 | 10 |
| 26 | H | Old Paulines | L | 9 | 10 |
| 27 | H | Penarth | L | 4 | 9 |
| 30 | H | London Hospital | W | 15 | 0 |

| January | | | | f | a |
|---|---|---|---|---|---|
| 6 | H | Rosslyn Park | W | 18 | 0 |
| 13 | H | Coventry | W | 5 | 3 |
| 20 | A | Nuneaton | W | 10 | 8 |
| 27 | H | Utd Services (A'shot) | W | 20 | 12 |
| **February** | | | | | |
| 3 | H | Royal Air Force | W | 18 | 14 |
| 10 | H | UCS Old Boys | W | 32 | 11 |
| 17 | H | Old Mer Taylors | W | 10 | 3 |
| 24 | H | Wasps | D | 8 | 8 |
| **March** | | | | | |
| 3 | H | Northampton | W | 13 | 11 |
| 10 | A | Old Alleynians | L | 9 | 27 |
| 17 | H | Notts | W | 32 | 8 |
| 24 | H | Old Leysians | W | 11 | 3 |
| 31 | H | Nuneaton | W | 23 | 10 |
| **April** | | | | | |
| 2 | H | Sale | W | 8 | 3 |
| 3 | H | Wakefield | L | 3 | 13 |
| 7 | H | Old Alleynians | W | 20 | 3 |
| 14 | H | Old Blues | W | 10 | 5 |
| 19 | H | Met Police | W | 14 | 9 |
| 21 | H | Old Edwardians | W | 27 | 0 |

W A Sime scored most points, 172, a new club record which was to last for 28 years. He was also the leading try scorer with 15. B R Black and R Eidsforth both made 36 appearances.

L G Ashwell (31, 11t), O V Bevan (4), J S W Bignall (11), B R Black (36, 1t), E J C Brown (1), R C Brumwell (6, 1t), F C Carter (1), J G Cook (2), E K Cornes (5, 1d, 1p, 2t), G T Dancer (31, 3t), C R Davies (13, 1t), T I Davies (5, 3t), R Eidsforth (36, 5c, 2d, 4p, 1t), A R Ellis (5), D Hall (14, 3t), R C Haynes (27, 9t), E C Howard (1), F Hutton (1), G Jackson (6, 1t), Jameson (1, 2t), A R Jesty (4), D Lincoln (3), G F Llewellyn (4, 1c, 1d, 1t), O L Lloyd (14, 1t), V J Lyttle (9, 9t), D L K Milman (16, 4t), M D Milman (5, 3t), G M Neville (7, 1t), R Panton (1), R Perkins (28), G O'B Power (31, 6t), J O'B Power (4), C G Prigmore (3), N T Pryor (7, 1t), C H Quarry (5), C Rawlins (5, 1t), N F Reed (10, 7t), Reynolds (1), C Rose (32, 2t), D W Russell (1), P W Scrivener (3), W A Sime (35, 47c, 3d, 7p, 15t), A E Simmons (11, 2t), J W Simpson (2), H A Southgate (1), W Spark (1), S Stanley (1), C M Swales (2), T D Thevenard (25, 7t), N J Timmins (2), G C Turner (4), H White (2, 1t), T E K Williams (25, 14t), R Willsher (29, 1d, 10t).

# 1934-35

Played 36, won 26, lost 8, drawn 2. F 585, A 220.

Captain: W A Sime

| | | | | f | a |
|---|---|---|---|---|---|
| **September** | | | | | |
| 1 | A | Leicester | L | 8 | 10 |
| 8 | H | Catford Bridge | W | 48 | 3 |
| 15 | A | Bath | L | 3 | 8 |
| 22 | H | Leicester | L | 5 | 9 |
| 29 | H | Richmond | W | 11 | 8 |
| **October** | | | | | |
| 6 | A | Moseley | L | 7 | 18 |
| 13 | H | St Mary's Hosp | W | 17 | 5 |
| 20 | H | Northampton | W | 15 | 0 |
| 27 | H | St Bart's Hosp | W | 29 | 0 |
| **November** | | | | | |
| 10 | A | Coventry | W | 8 | 3 |
| 17 | H | UCS Old Boys | W | 28 | 11 |
| 24 | H | Bank of England | W | 24 | 5 |
| **December** | | | | | |
| 1 | H | London Hospital | W | 27 | 0 |
| 8 | H | St Thomas' Hosp | W | 13 | 3 |
| 15 | H | Blackwell | W | 33 | 8 |
| 22 | H | Old Blues | D | 3 | 3 |
| 26 | H | Old Paulines | W | 14 | 8 |
| 27 | H | Penarth | W | 19 | 5 |
| 29 | H | Old Millhillians | W | 21 | 0 |
| **January** | | | | | |
| 5 | H | Rosslyn Park | W | 21 | 6 |
| 12 | H | Coventry | W | 8 | 0 |
| 19 | H | Guy's Hospital | W | 24 | 8 |
| 26 | H | Aldershot Services | W | 19 | 9 |
| **February** | | | | | |
| 2 | H | Royal Air Force | L | 9 | 14 |
| 9 | H | Bath | W | 11 | 3 |
| 16 | H | Old Mer Taylors | W | 18 | 6 |
| 23 | H | Wasps | W | 16 | 5 |
| **March** | | | | | |
| 2 | A | Northampton | D | 9 | 9 |
| 9 | H | Old Cranleighians | L | 3 | 11 |
| 16 | A | Guy's Hospital | W | 31 | 0 |
| 23 | H | Old Whitgiftians | W | 20 | 5 |
| 30 | H | London Scottish | L | 3 | 12 |
| **April** | | | | | |
| 6 | H | Old Alleynians | W | 32 | 8 |
| 13 | H | Old Leysians | W | 14 | 6 |
| 20 | H | Sale | W | 11 | 5 |
| 22 | H | Met Police | L | 3 | 6 |

B R Black played in all 36 matches. V J Lyttle was leading try scorer with 26. W A Sime scored most points, 87. Thirty eight players made at least one appearance.

L G Ashwell (6), G R L Abrahams (1), O V Bevan (29, 5t), B R Black (36), D B Coleman (12, 3t), J G Cook (3, 1t), E K Cornes (21, 4c, 2d, 2t), G T Dancer (32, 2t), R Eidsforth (33, 23c, 1d, 3p), A R Ellis (1), A C Harwood (1), R C Haynes (14, 1c, 8t), G Jackson (11), G A Kelly (6), W S Kemble (10, 7t), V J Lyttle (28, 26t), M V McArthur (1), R M Marsh (4, 1t), V May (6, 2t), D L K Milman (26, 14t), A E Osbourn (1), I S Panton (11, 3t), R Perkins (30), G O'B Power (4, 1t), J O'B Power (19, 7t), C G Prigmore (14, 9t), C H Quarry (9), J G Rogers (2), R H Rogers (1), C Rose (33, 2t), S H Saunders (4, 1t), P W Scrivener (22, 2p, 5t), W A Sime (29, 36c, 1p, 4t), A E Simmons (27, 2c, 2p, 4t), J Smalley (1), T D Thevenard (24, 13t), H White (3, 2t), R Willsher (24, 17t).

# 1935-36

Played 32, won 22, lost 9, drawn 1. F 402, A 206.

Captain: W A Sime

| | | | | f | a |
|---|---|---|---|---|---|
| **September** | | | | | |
| 7 | A | Leicester | L | 11 | 30 |
| 14 | H | Bath | W | 26 | 8 |
| 21 | H | Weston Super Mare | L | 7 | 8 |
| 28 | A | Richmond | L | 3 | 11 |
| **October** | | | | | |
| 5 | H | Moseley | W | 20 | 0 |
| 12 | H | St Mary's Hospital | W | 18 | 3 |
| 19 | H | St Bart's Hosp | W | 16 | 3 |
| 26 | A | Blackheath | W | 9 | 3 |
| 26 | H | Old Cranleighians | L | 8 | 18 |
| **November** | | | | | |
| 2 | A | Northampton | W | 9 | 0 |
| 9 | H | Coventry | D | 13 | 13 |
| 16 | H | London Irish | L | 3 | 9 |
| 23 | H | London Hospital | W | 5 | 3 |
| 30 | H | Old Millhillians | W | 11 | 6 |
| **December** | | | | | |
| 7 | H | Rosslyn Park | W | 12 | 0 |
| 26 | H | Old Paulines | W | 10 | 3 |
| 28 | H | Penarth | W | 17 | 9 |
| **January** | | | | | |
| 4 | H | Blackwell | W | 14 | 3 |
| 11 | A | Coventry | L | 0 | 5 |
| **February** | | | | | |
| 1 | H | Old Blues | W | 11 | 9 |
| 8 | A | Bath | L | 3 | 8 |
| 15 | H | Old Mer Taylors | W | 6 | 4 |
| 22 | H | Old Edwardians | W | 12 | 0 |
| 29 | H | Northampton | W | 14 | 11 |
| **March** | | | | | |
| 7 | H | Royal Air Force | W | 16 | 6 |
| 14 | H | Guy's Hospital | W | 28 | 0 |
| 28 | H | London Welsh | W | 14 | 3 |
| **April** | | | | | |
| 2 | H | Leicester | L | 6 | 7 |
| 4 | H | Old Alleynians | W | 29 | 0 |
| 11 | H | Met Police | L | 8 | 9 |
| 13 | H | Sale | W | 26 | 6 |
| 18 | H | Manchester | W | 17 | 8 |

V J Lyttle was the leading try scorer with 24 and leading points scorer with 72. M D Milman made most appearances, 30. Forty six players made at least one.

O V Bevan (26, 6t), B R Black (17, 1t), E J C Brown (1), N E Browning (20, 1c, 1d, 5t), R Clarke (2), D B Coleman (5), J G Cook (1), E K Cornes (1), G T Dancer (23, 2t), A R Dawe (3), R Eidsforth (27, 14c, 1d, 1p), A R Ellis (2), I Evans (6), J E Grey (3), L Gough (1), N Haines (1), R C Haynes (23, 1c, 7t), G Jackson (4), G A Kelly (7), W S Kemble (3), D C Lincoln (1), V J Lyttle (23, 24t), M V McArthur (5), R M Marsh (3, 3t), D L K Milman (18, 7t), M D Milman (30, 2d, 5t), R Moore (2), A D Panton (6), R Perkins (25), J Penson-Whitaker (1), J O'B Power (16, 1c, 2t), C G Prigmore (11, 2t), C H Quarry (4), J G Rogers (16, 4t), C Rose (21, 1t), P W Scrivener (5, 1t), W A Sime (20, 11c, 2d, 2p, 5t), A E Simmons (3), H J Smith (1), T D Thevenard (28, 21t), T Thomas (22, 1t), N J Timmins (1), G A Walker (2), C H Williams (18, 3c, 1p, 1t), H T Williams (2), R Willsher (20, 2t).

# 1936-37

Played 33, won 23, lost 9, drawn 1. F 407, A 241.

Captain: W A Sime

| | | | | f | a |
|---|---|---|---|---|---|
| **September** | | | | | |
| 5 | A | Leicester | W | 18 | 12 |
| 12 | H | Sale | L | 6 | 11 |
| 19 | A | Bath | W | 11 | 10 |
| 26 | H | Richmond | L | 8 | 16 |
| **October** | | | | | |
| 3 | A | Moseley | L | 6 | 10 |
| 10 | H | St Mary's Hosp | W | 14 | 5 |
| 17 | H | St Bart's Hosp | W | 23 | 5 |
| 24 | H | London Scottish | W | 29 | 3 |
| 31 | H | Northampton | W | 4 | 3 |
| **November** | | | | | |
| 7 | A | Coventry | L | 0 | 27 |
| 14 | H | Moseley | L | 5 | 15 |
| 21 | H | London Irish | W | 11 | 0 |
| 28 | H | Old Millhillians | W | 19 | 11 |
| **December** | | | | | |
| 5 | A | Weston Super Mare | D | 6 | 6 |
| 12 | H | London Hospital | W | 9 | 0 |
| 19 | H | Leicester | W | 8 | 3 |
| 26 | H | Old Paulines | L | 0 | 4 |

| | | | | f | a |
|---|---|---|---|---|---|
| **January** | | | | | |
| 2 | H | Rosslyn Park | W | 34 | 8 |
| 9 | H | Coventry | W | 13 | 3 |
| 16 | A | Headingley | W | 11 | 3 |
| 23 | H | Aldershot Services | W | 16 | 0 |
| 30 | A | Sale | L | 6 | 8 |
| **February** | | | | | |
| 6 | H | Old Blues | W | 19 | 9 |
| 13 | H | Bath | W | 11 | 0 |
| 20 | H | Old Mer Taylors | W | 27 | 5 |
| **March** | | | | | |
| 6 | H | Royal Air Force | L | 3 | 17 |
| 13 | H | Guy's Hospital | W | 26 | 3 |
| 20 | A | Northampton | W | 12 | 6 |
| 27 | H | Wakefield | W | 8 | 5 |
| 29 | H | Met Police | L | 0 | 8 |
| **April** | | | | | |
| 3 | H | Old Cranleighians | W | 16 | 9 |
| 10 | H | Old Leysians | W | 19 | 10 |
| 17 | A | Gloucester | W | 9 | 6 |

V J Lyttle scored most tries, 13, W A Sime scored most points, 79, and B R Black made most appearances, 29. Forty three players made at least one.

G L B August (4), O V Bevan (26, 4t), B R Black (29, 1t), R E Blandford (7), N E Browning (8, 1t), A Clarke (1), F W Clarke (3), D B Coleman (26, 8t), J C Cook (10, 4c, 3p, 4t), G T Dancer (28, 3t), A R Dawe (2), R Eidsforth (31, 9c, 3d, 6p,1t), H Elliott (3), T L Garge (24, 1p), J E Grey (2), H W Haines (3), R C Haynes (1, 1t), G Jackson (3), A E P Joy (4), G A Kelly (5, 2t), W S Kemble (2, 1t), V J Lyttle (25, 13t), M V McArthur (2), R M Marsh (22, 9t), D L K Milman (12, 7t), R L Moore (2), A D Panton (1), R Perkins (28), J O' Power (26, 8t), P C Previté (13, 4c, 2p), C G Prigmore (7, 2t), C H Quarry (5, 1t), H F Rawkins (1), A Rogers (1), J G Rogers (15, 3t), C Rose (8), P W Scrivener (16, 3t), G F Sharman (1), W A Sime (23, 19c, 2d, 5p, 6t), R Spark (1), T D Thevenard (26, 9t), T Thomas (11), R Willsher (27).

# 1937-38

Played 34, won 17, lost 14, drawn 3. F 389, A 214.

Captain: W A Sime

| September | | | | f | a |
|---|---|---|---|---|---|
| 4 | A | Leicester | W | 18 | 12 |
| 11 | H | Headingley | L | 5 | 10 |
| 18 | H | Bath | W | 14 | 3 |
| 25 | A | Richmond | W | 11 | 0 |
| **October** | | | | | |
| 2 | H | Moseley | W | 19 | 6 |
| 9 | H | Blackwell | W | 19 | 3 |
| 16 | A | Northampton | D | 3 | 3 |
| 23 | H | Gloucester | L | 5 | 9 |
| 30 | H | St Mary's Hosp | L | 6 | 15 |
| **November** | | | | | |
| 6 | H | Coventry | D | 3 | 3 |
| 13 | A | Moseley | L | 0 | 8 |
| 20 | H | London Irish | L | 9 | 10 |
| 27 | H | London Scottish | L | 0 | 3 |
| **December** | | | | | |
| 4 | H | St Bart's Hosp | W | 16 | 0 |
| 11 | H | London Hospital | W | 23 | 3 |
| 18 | H | Leicester | W | 3 | 0 |
| 27 | H | Old Paulines | W | 27 | 11 |

| January | | | | f | a |
|---|---|---|---|---|---|
| 1 | H | Notts | W | 36 | 0 |
| 8 | A | Coventry | L | 3 | 14 |
| 15 | A | Gloucester | L | 8 | 9 |
| 22 | H | Aldershot Services | W | 23 | 8 |
| 29 | H | Sale | L | 6 | 14 |
| **February** | | | | | |
| 5 | H | Old Blues | L | 7 | 10 |
| 12 | A | Bath | L | 0 | 3 |
| 19 | H | Old Mer Taylors | W | 11 | 3 |
| 26 | H | London Welsh | D | 6 | 6 |
| **March** | | | | | |
| 5 | H | Royal Air Force | L | 8 | 13 |
| 12 | A | Guy's Hospital | W | 11 | 0 |
| 19 | H | Old Edwardians | W | 18 | 6 |
| 26 | H | Northampton | L | 0 | 6 |
| **April** | | | | | |
| 2 | H | Old Alleynians | W | 16 | 3 |
| 9 | H | Old Millhillians | W | 24 | 3 |
| 16 | H | Met Police | L | 6 | 11 |
| 18 | H | Old Leysians | W | 25 | 6 |

T D Thevenard scored most tries, 15, and most points, 45. Forty seven players turned out. R Eidsforth made most appearances, 31.

G L B August (4), O V Bevan (14, 2t), B R Black (23), A S C Blincow (1), Brown (2), F Carter (1), F W Clarke (7), D B Coleman (27, 6t), J G Cook (19, 6c, 2p, 1t), D W Cook (1), G T Dancer (22, 1t), R Eidsforth (31, 10c, 1d, 3p), A Frame (3), C G Gilthorpe (1), L Gough (2, 1t), J E Grey (1), E N Grieve (9, 3t), J C Hatch (1), S G Irving (1), G Jackson (2), A E P Joy (25, 1c, 3t), G A Kelly (18, 4t), C H Lincoln (1, 2t), V J Lyttle (25, 13t), D L K Milman (13, 1t), R L Moore (4), A D Panton (3, 1t), K V Percy (5, 2t), R Perkins (23), J O'B Power (28, 1c, 6t), P C Previte (12, 4c, 4p, 1t), C G Prigmore (2, 1t), A K Rogers (29, 2t), J G Rogers (30, 12t), C Rose (1), P W Scrivener (5, 2t), W A Sime (12, 11c, 3p, 3t), H J Smith (7), R Smyth (7, 1t), R Spark (11), M E Staples (11, 1d), T D Thevenard (28, 15t), T Thomas (4), R Warner (1), E H Walshe (2, 2t), W G Western (2, 1t), R Willsher (29, 7t).

# 1938-39

Played 32, won 25, lost 4, drawn 3. F 470, A 134.

Captain: J G Cook

| | | | | f | a |
|---|---|---|---|---|---|
| **September** | | | | | |
| 3 | A | Leicester | W | 18 | 0 |
| 10 | H | Old Edwardians | W | 40 | 3 |
| 17 | A | Bath | D | 0 | 0 |
| 24 | A | Richmond | W | 26 | 6 |
| **October** | | | | | |
| 1 | A | Gloucester | W | 12 | 7 |
| 8 | H | Old Cranleighians | W | 14 | 0 |
| 15 | A | Moseley | L | 7 | 13 |
| 22 | H | London Scottish | W | 6 | 3 |
| 29 | H | Northampton | W | 10 | 3 |
| **November** | | | | | |
| 5 | A | Coventry | W | 16 | 8 |
| 12 | H | Moseley | D | 0 | 0 |
| 19 | H | St Bart's Hosp | W | 37 | 0 |
| 26 | H | Old Millhillians | W | 19 | 0 |
| **December** | | | | | |
| 3 | H | St Mary's Hosp | W | 37 | 0 |
| 10 | A | Bristol | W | 18 | 9 |
| 17 | H | Aldershot Serv | W | 21 | 5 |
| 31 | H | Rosslyn Park | W | 15 | 5 |

| | | | | f | a |
|---|---|---|---|---|---|
| **January** | | | | | |
| 14 | H | Coventry | W | 23 | 6 |
| 21 | H | Gloucester | W | 11 | 6 |
| 28 | A | Sale | L | 3 | 8 |
| **February** | | | | | |
| 4 | H | Manchester | D | 11 | 11 |
| 11 | H | Bath | W | 3 | 0 |
| 18 | H | Old Mer Taylors | L | 6 | 10 |
| 25 | A | London Welsh | W | 9 | 0 |
| **March** | | | | | |
| 4 | H | Royal Air Force | L | 0 | 14 |
| 11 | H | Guy's Hospital | W | 23 | 3 |
| 18 | A | Northampton | W | 9 | 3 |
| 25 | H | Notts | W | 23 | 3 |
| **April** | | | | | |
| 1 | H | Plymouth Albion | W | 9 | 0 |
| 8 | H | Met Police | W | 5 | 3 |
| 10 | H | Otley | W | 26 | 5 |
| 15 | A | Headingley | W | 13 | 0 |

R Willsher made most appearances, 29. Thirty eight players made at least one. T D Thevenard scored most tries, 16, and J G Cook scored most points 67.

G L B August (4), O V Bevan (28, 4t), B R Black (17, 1t), F W Clarke (4), D B Coleman (23, 3t), J G Cook (23, 23c, 2p, 5t), A E Cook (9, 2c, 3p, 1t), G T Dancer (19, 1t), R Eidsforth (2), J Facer (2), R G Furbank (3), J E Grey (28, 1c, 5d), D Hall (2), H J Irens (19, 18c, 6p, 3t), W F Jones (1, 1t), A E P Joy (16, 4t), G A Kelly (22, 1t), F E Lovelace (3), V J Lyttle (19, 15t), B J McMaster (24, 6t), D L K Milman (6, 4t), G O'B Power (20, 3t), J O'B Power (19, 6t), C G Prigmore (9, 1t), C H Quarry (1), H F Rawkins (4, 2c), J G Rogers (23, 8t), C F Sharman (1), H J Smith (1), R Smyth (25, 5t), R Spark (3), M E Staples (20, 2t), R Stephens (1), T D Thevenard (25, 16t), T Thomas (2), E H Walshe (17, 8t), W G Western (6), R Willsher (29, 2t).

## 1939-40

Played 7, won 5, lost 2. F 59, A 43.

| November | | f | a |
|---|---|---|---|
| 25 H Cambridge Univ | W | 6 | 4 |
| **December** | | | |
| 16 H Northampton | W | 15 | 0 |
| 26 H Old Paulines | W | 6 | 5 |
| **March** | | | |
| 16 H Harlequins | W | 8 | 7 |
| 23 A Rosslyn Park | W | 13 | 11 |
| 30 A Northampton | L | 8 | 11 |
| **April** | | | |
| 20 H Met Police | L | 3 | 5 |

T W Cranfield scored most tries, seven, and most points, 25. Forty two players made appearances. T D Thevenard and R Kenny played in all seven games.

O V Bevan (6), B R Black (2), S Blincow (1), N E Browning (1), D B Coleman (5), A E Cook (1), J G Cook (4, 1c), T W Cranfield (4, 2c, 7t), D M Craven (1), G T Dancer (4), A Dawes (1), J A Eddington (1), F Fox (1), R G Furbank (1), C R Fielden (1), J E Grey (1), D Hall (1), T Hinde (5), H J Irens (2, 1p, 1t), A E P Joy (1), G A Kelly (6), R Kenny (7, 3t), R U F Kynaston (1), F H Lovelace (1), B J McMaster (4, 1t), J Moll (2), E R Oates (3), J Paul (1), J Penson –Whitaker (1), C S Powell (3), G O'B Power (3), P C Previte (5, 1c), C G Prigmore (1), H F Rawkins (2), J G Rogers (3, 1t), R A B Rogers (1, 1t), A E Simmons (1), M E Staples (1), T D Thevenard (7, 1t), P M Vasey (2), E H Walshe (2), R Willsher (6, 2t).

## 1940-41

Played 13, won 8, lost 4, drawn 1. F 171, A 99.

| October | | f | a |
|---|---|---|---|
| 19 H OCTU Sandhurst | W | 14 | 6 |
| 26 H Cambridge Univ | W | 11 | 3 |
| **November** | | | |
| 2 A Rosslyn Park | D | 3 | 3 |
| 23 A St Mary's Hosp | L | 3 | 12 |
| **December** | | | |
| 7 H Met Police | W | 21 | 5 |
| 21 H Comb Services XV | W | 40 | 0 |
| **February** | | | |
| 1 A Cambridge Univ | W | 15 | 13 |
| 15 H St Bart's Hosp | W | 18 | 14 |
| **March** | | | |
| 8 H Guy's Hospital | L | 16 | 19 |
| 13 A Northampton | L | 10 | 13 |
| 22 H Rosslyn Park | W | 12 | 0 |
| 29 H St Mary's Hosp | L | 3 | 11 |
| **April** | | | |
| 5 H Northampton | W | 5 | 0 |

T D Thevenard scored most tries, ten. C R Fielden scored most points, 36. Fifty two players made appearances. C G Prigmore made most, 13.

Ball (1, 1t), O V Bevan (8, 1t), Berridge (1), P Brangwin (1), A L Briggs (3), K C Kanspin (8), J Churcher (3, 1t), M Clarke (3), D B Coleman (1), J G Cook (6, 1c), T W Cranfield (1, 3c), R E Crichton (2, 2t), G T Dancer (5, 2t), W Davis (1), G Dawson (1), T C Downond (2), C R Fielden (6, 12c, 2p, 2t), R Horsfall (8), Hughes (1), G A Kelly (10), R Kenny (12, 2t), R U F Kynaston (2), Landon (1), V J Lyttle (4), R Long (1), R M Marsh (1), W E Marsh (5, 6t), J W Miller (2), D L K Milman (4, 1t), C McIver (1), R Perry (3, 1t), C S F Powell (1), P C Previte (9, 1c, 2p, 1t), C G Prigmore (13, 2d, 2t), H F Rawkins (2), P E Reeve (1), T S Roberts (1), R A B Rogers (1), J G Rogers (1, 1t), P W Scrivener (1), G F Sharman (1), A E Simmons (7), T D Thevenard (12, 10t), Tomlinson (1), W R Tookey (8), Townsend (1), P M Vasey (3), P H Waterkeyn (1, 1t), R Willsher (10, 3t), C H Wilson (8, 1t), J A Withnell (3, 1t), P Wooding (1).

## 1941-42

Played 8, won 5, lost 3. F 91, A 98.

| Date | H/A | Opponent | Result | f | a |
|---|---|---|---|---|---|
| **October** | | | | | |
| 25 | H | Cambridge Univ | W | 14 | 10 |
| **November** | | | | | |
| 1 | A | Rosslyn Park | W | 24 | 21 |
| 29 | A | St Mary's Hosp | L | 0 | 18 |
| **December** | | | | | |
| 6 | H | Oxford Univ | W | 16 | 6 |
| **February** | | | | | |
| 21 | H | St Bart's Hosp | W | 12 | 10 |
| **March** | | | | | |
| 14 | H | Guy's Hospital | W | 14 | 10 |
| 21 | H | Rosslyn Park | L | 5 | 10 |
| 28 | H | St Mary's Hosp | L | 6 | 13 |

R Hook scored most tries, seven, and most points, 37. Forty two players made appearances. R Willsher and R Kenney made the most, eight.

B R Black (1), A S C Blincow (2), D A Brown (6, 1p), Clark (1), P W Cobb (2), J G Cook (7, 1c, 1t), T W Cranfield (1), R E Crichton (3), Cundy (1), G T Dancer (3) Flack (1), C R Fielden (1), Harris (1), R Hook (6, 2c, 3d, 7t), E L Horsfall (6, 2t), E C Howard (1), D J Knight (1), Jagger (1), Jones (1), R Kenney (8, 1t), G A Kelly (6, 1t), R U F Kynaston (3, 2t), W Lewis (2), V J Lyttle (5, 1d, 3t), McArthur (1), B J McMaster (1), R Perry (3), Pollentine (3), G O'B Power (1), C G Prigmore (2), H F Rawkins (6, 2t), P S Reeve (3), R A B Rogers (3), R P Sinclair (1), D H W Thomas (3), W R Tookey (6), Waring (1), Whatmore (1), Whitney (3, 2t), Williams (1, 1t), R Willsher (8), Williams (1, 1c).

## 1942-43

Played 10, won 8, lost 2. F 179, A 102.

| Date | H/A | Opponent | Result | f | a |
|---|---|---|---|---|---|
| **October** | | | | | |
| 24 | H | Cambridge Univ | W | 24 | 9 |
| 31 | A | Rosslyn Park | L | 9 | 16 |
| **November** | | | | | |
| 21 | H | London Hospital | W | 20 | 3 |
| 28 | A | St Mary's Hosp | W | 17 | 8 |
| **December** | | | | | |
| 5 | A | Oxford Univ | W | 22 | 10 |
| **February** | | | | | |
| 6 | A | Cambridge Univ | L | 8 | 14 |
| 20 | H | St Bart's Hosp | W | 8 | 6 |
| **March** | | | | | |
| 13 | H | Guy's Hospital | W | 9 | 4 |
| 20 | H | Rosslyn Park | W | 29 | 19 |
| 27 | H | St Mary's Hosp | W | 33 | 13 |

H G Hay scored most tries, ten, and most points, 30. Fifty four players made appearances, G A Kelly and R Willsher making ten.

Bartram (2), Bell (2), O V Bevan (1), Brown (1, 1t), Candler (1), Clarke (1, 1t), G T Dancer (8, 1t), C Doyle (2), C R Fielden (3, 5c, 1t), F M Fletcher (2), Gardner (1), M Harding (5, 6c, 2p, 3t), Harrison (2), H G Hay (9, 10t), R H Haynes (2, 3t), B J B Hazell (1), R Hook (2, 1t), W G Hook (1, 1t), E L Horsfall (1), Hughes (1), R Kenney (8, 1c, 2t), G A Kelly (10, 1t), D V Knight (3, 2t), R U F Kynaston (1), E Mathews (3), Mapp (1), H V McArthur (1), B J McMaster (4), Mellor (1, 1t), Moore (1), L F Oakley (1, 2c, 1p, 1t), Oldroyd (3, 2t), L C Osbourne (1), P Parker (2), H R Peel (7, 4t), Perkins (1), M Pearce (1), L Pollard (1), H F Rawkins (4), P E Reeve (1), T S Roberts (1, 1t), R A B Rogers (2), R P Sinclair (1), Shabot (1), C C Sherriff (3, 1d, 1t), Smith (1), P Snelling (7), W R Tookey (4, 1c), G A Turner (7), P M Vasey (5, 2c,1p, 1t), P Wildman (2), Williams (1), R Willsher (10, 5t), G A White (1).

## 1943-44

Played 11, won 6, lost 5. F 125, A 85.

| | | | f | a |
|---|---|---|---|---|
| **October** | | | | |
| 23 | H | Cambridge Univ | L | 3 | 11 |
| 30 | A | Rosslyn Park | W | 16 | 6 |
| **November** | | | | |
| 20 | H | London Hospital | W | 24 | 3 |
| 27 | A | St Mary's Hosp | W | 9 | 0 |
| **December** | | | | |
| 4 | H | Oxford Univ | W | 32 | 3 |
| **January** | | | | |
| 8 | H | Guy's Hospital | W | 14 | 11 |
| **February** | | | | |
| 5 | A | Cambridge Univ | L | 8 | 9 |
| 26 | H | Middlesex Hosp | L | 3 | 12 |
| **March** | | | | |
| 11 | A | Guys Hospital | W | 9 | 0 |
| 18 | H | Rosslyn Park | L | 0 | 21 |
| 25 | H | St Mary's Hosp | L | 7 | 9 |

Top try scorers were T W Cranfield and F T Naylor with four. G A White scored most points, 23. Sixty eight players made appearances. G A Kelly, R Kenney and H R Peel all played nine times.

J F Ashby (1), W A Baker (2), D M Bale (1, 1t), O V Bevan (4), R S Bingham (1), S Blincow (2), J R Bridger (5), Chalmer (1), F W Clarke (5), Cole (1), J G Cook (3), G Coulson (1, 1t), Craddock (1), T W Cranfield (2, 4t), M D Crickman (1, 1t), G T Dancer (3, 1t), R Eidsforth (2), C R Fielden (1), F M Fletcher (1), R G Furbank (2, 1t), G Gee (1), B Golding (2), D A B Garton-Sprenger (1), J E Grey (1), F Hanford (1), R H Haynes (2), J R Hazelgrove (1), D E Hennessey (1), W Houston (1), E L Horsfall (1), J Ivor (1), J B R Jenkins (1), E Jones (1), P Jones (2), A E P Joy (3), G A Kelly (9, 2t), R Kenney (9, 3t), D V Knight (2, 1t), J H Langham (2), J J Lloyd (1), P Marshall (1, 1t), D L K Milman (3), R Morris (2), F T Naylor (4, 4t), C W Neale (1), R Newsham (1), P Parker (1), P B Parrish (2), H R Peel (9, 1t), P Previte (1), P Ralphs (1), H F Rawkins (2, 1t), C S G Roberts (6, 1t), C C Sherriff (1, 1t), T Simmonds (3), C S Smith (I), R E Snell (1, 1t), Studman (1), A Thomas (1), W R Tookey (5), P Usher (1), P M Vasey (7, 1d), G A White (3, 4c, 2p, 3t), J G White (6, 7c, 1p, 1t), P Wildman (3, 1t), J Williams (1), R Willsher (8), T Wright (2).

## 1944-45

Played 10, won 7, lost 3. F 120, A 80.

| | | | | f | a |
|---|---|---|---|---|---|
| **October** | | | | | |
| 28 | H | Cambridge Univ | W | 8 | 3 |
| **November** | | | | | |
| 4 | A | Rosslyn Park | L | 15 | 17 |
| 18 | H | St Mary's Hosp | W | 19 | 3 |
| 25 | H | London Hosp | W | 24 | 0 |
| **December** | | | | | |
| 9 | A | Oxford Univ | W | 12 | 8 |
| **February** | | | | | |
| 10 | A | Cambridge Univ | L | 8 | 24 |
| **March** | | | | | |
| 3 | H | Rosslyn Park | L | 3 | 8 |
| 10 | H | Guy's Hospital | W | 10 | 6 |
| 17 | A | St Mary's Hosp | W | 9 | 5 |
| 24 | H | Middlesex Hosp | W | 12 | 6 |

J G Cook scored most points, 26. H R Peel scored most tries, four. R Willsher played in 49 of the club's 59 wartime matches and was captain in most of the games.

R H Bankishire (2), O V Bevan (3), J Bridger (4), Brumskill (1), D O C Butt (1), J G Cook (7, 10c, 1p, 1t), G T Dancer (6), W M Dunn (1), J Fairgrieve (1), M Fielden (2), R G Furbank (2, 2t), G Hale (1), M Hall (3), R F Hill (1), E L Horsfall (1, 1t), B Hume (1), J Ilett (1), P A Jones (1), G A Kelly (9, 1t), W Kelly (1), R Kenney (9, 2t), S Kitchener (2, 1t), W Lewis (1), E M Lewis (1), C Lincoln (5, 2t), D Lincoln (1), D B S Markham (2), P Mills (2), F T Naylor (8, 1d, 3t), J Paine (1, 1d), B Parrish (1), H R Peel (10, 1c, 4t), P Previte (1), H F Rawkins (1), H A K Rowland (2), R E Snell (9, 2t), J R Steele (1), R H Thomas (1), W R Tookey (5, 1t), G Toplas (7), J G White (1), R Willsher (7, 2t), D J Winger (1), T Wright (9, 3c, 3t), W G Wright (1).

## 1945-46

Played 31, won 17, lost 13, drawn 1. F 412, A 333.

Captain: R Willsher

| | | | | f | a |
|---|---|---|---|---|---|
| **September** | | | | | |
| 29 | H | Richmond/B'kheath | W | 28 | 9 |
| **October** | | | | | |
| 6 | H | O Alley's/O Wh'tians | W | 35 | 10 |
| 13 | H | Middlesex Hosp | L | 6 | 11 |
| 18 | H | Cambridge Univ | W | 24 | 8 |
| 20 | H | London Hospital | W | 15 | 12 |
| 27 | A | London Scottish | L | 11 | 14 |
| **November** | | | | | |
| 3 | H | Coventry | L | 3 | 22 |
| 10 | H | Bristol | L | 3 | 26 |
| 17 | A | Northampton | D | 11 | 11 |
| 24 | H | London Irish | W | 6 | 5 |
| **December** | | | | | |
| 1 | H | Oxford Univ | L | 15 | 25 |
| 8 | H | Old Blues | W | 18 | 5 |
| 15 | H | Old Mer Taylors | L | 9 | 10 |
| 22 | H | Leicester | W | 6 | 3 |
| 26 | H | Old Paulines | W | 11 | 0 |
| 29 | H | Rosslyn Park | L | 6 | 17 |

| | | | | f | a |
|---|---|---|---|---|---|
| **January** | | | | | |
| 5 | H | St Bart's Hosp | W | 9 | 0 |
| 12 | A | Coventry | L | 0 | 17 |
| 26 | H | Notts | W | 22 | 8 |
| **February** | | | | | |
| 2 | H | Manchester | W | 20 | 6 |
| 9 | H | REME | W | 30 | 0 |
| 16 | A | Cambridge Univ | W | 23 | 6 |
| 23 | H | London Welsh | L | 11 | 12 |
| **March** | | | | | |
| 9 | A | Guy's Hospital | W | 17 | 8 |
| 16 | A | Leicester | L | 9 | 10 |
| 23 | H | St Mary's Hosp | W | 10 | 4 |
| 30 | H | Northampton | W | 10 | 8 |
| **April** | | | | | |
| 4 | H | Coventry | L | 8 | 22 |
| 13 | H | Met Police | L | 3 | 19 |
| 20 | H | Aldershot Serv | L | 8 | 16 |
| 22 | H | Wakefield | W | 25 | 9 |

In the first post war season, Bedford started with a full programme. R Willsher continued as captain and with R G Furbank made most appearances, 28. Highest try scorer was M M Henderson with ten. J G Cook scored most points, 64. Sixty three players made at least one appearance.

J Archer (12, 6t), W Baker (3), J Bance (2, 1t), O V Bevan (3, 1t), R S Bingham (15, 1t), Booth (1), J G Cook (19, 23c, 2p, 4t), T W Cranfield (4, 4c, 1p), R E Crichton (2, 1t), Craven (1), G T Dancer (24, 1t), S Danes (3), Daniel (1, 1t), A Dawes (1), Dempsey (1), R Dillingham (1), R Eidsforth (7, 2c, 2d, 3p), C R Fielden (17, 7c, 4p, 5t), F A Fielden (3), G Mc F D Fleming (5), R G Furbank (28, 7t),C G Gilthorpe (7, 1p, 1t), J E Grey (7), M Hall (23, 4t), R H Haynes (1, 1t), R Harries (1, 1t), P Heanue (3, 2t), M M Henderson (21, 10t), L Hollins (1), E L Horsfall (1), V A Hubbard (1), A E P Joy (7, 1c, 1t), G A Kelly (15), R Kenney (1, 1t),C H Lincoln (26, 2c, 5t), Logan (3), D B S Markham (11, 6t), P Marshall (11, 4t), T R Marshall (3, 1t), L W McLean (12, 4t), J M Meadows (2), D L K Milman (4, 1t), Nagler (2), D Parker (3), R C Parker (2), H R Peel (8, 2c, 2t), Penney (1), Perry (3, 1t), P Previte (13, 3t), P Ralphs (17, 6t), P Reeve (1), R W Richardson (2), H W Rose (11, 1d, 2t), S Haddock (3), R Smyth (25, 5t), J Stewart (6, 4t), R H Thomas (1), W R Tookey (10), Tilbury (2), R J H Uprichard (2), C H Vallence (1), P Wildman (2), R Willsher (28, 2t).

# 1946-47

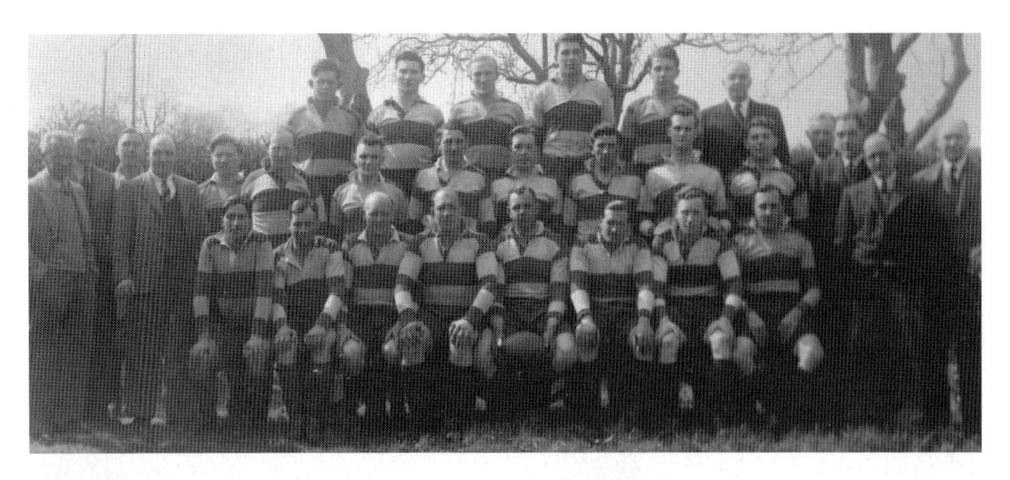

Played 27, won 16, lost 9, drawn 2. F 300, A 215.

Captain: R Willsher

| | | | | f | a |
|---|---|---|---|---|---|
| **September** | | | | | |
| 7 | A | Leicester | L | 0 | 12 |
| 14 | H | Headingley | W | 11 | 3 |
| 21 | H | Met Police | D | 3 | 3 |
| 28 | H | Richmond | W | 33 | 3 |
| **October** | | | | | |
| 5 | H | London Irish | W | 15 | 0 |
| 12 | H | London Hosp | W | 11 | 5 |
| 19 | H | O Cranleighians | W | 35 | 5 |
| 24 | A | Cambridge Univ | L | 0 | 6 |
| 26 | H | London Scottish | W | 11 | 9 |
| **November** | | | | | |
| 2 | A | Coventry | L | 6 | 14 |
| 9 | A | Bristol | L | 13 | 14 |
| 16 | H | Northampton | D | 11 | 11 |
| 23 | H | Middlesex Hosp | W | 9 | 3 |
| 30 | H | Old Millhillians | W | 13 | 5 |

| | | | | f | a |
|---|---|---|---|---|---|
| **December** | | | | | |
| 7 | H | Old Blues | W | 21 | 5 |
| 14 | H | Notts | W | 13 | 6 |
| 26 | H | Old Paulines | L | 12 | 19 |
| 28 | H | Rosslyn Park | W | 8 | 7 |
| **January** | | | | | |
| 4 | A | US Portsmouth | W | 6 | 0 |
| 11 | H | Coventry | L | 6 | 17 |
| 18 | H | Harlequins | W | 22 | 15 |
| **March** | | | | | |
| 22 | H | Leicester | L | 0 | 9 |
| 29 | A | Plymouth Albion | L | 0 | 8 |
| **April** | | | | | |
| 5 | H | Moseley | W | 3 | 0 |
| 7 | H | Otley | W | 11 | 0 |
| 12 | H | St Bart's Hosp | W | 21 | 10 |
| 19 | A | Gloucester | L | 6 | 26 |

H W Rose made most appearances, 25 and scored most tries, seven. C H Lincoln was highest points scorer with 34. Sixty players turned out at least once.

A C W Abrahams (7, 1t), J F Bance (24, 4c, 6t), E Barringer (3), O V Bevan (1), R Bird (1), B R Black (11), Bradford (1), D J W Bridge (1, 2t), T W Cranfield (12, 3c, 3p, 3t), G T Dancer (18, 1t), D Davies (1), H T Davis (1, 1t), W Dimmick (1), H Edwards (2), H Elliott (6), D Fensome (4), C R Fielden (20, 4c, 1p), F M Fletcher (2), G Mc F D Fleming (5, 1t), R G Furbank (24, 4t), P S Gleave (2), K Grive (1), M Hall (20, 5t), M M Henderson (22, 5t), G Jenkins (3, 5t), A B Jones (1), A E P Joy (2, 1p), G A Kelly (9), C K M Kirby (2, 2c, 2p, 1t), J Langham (3), C H Lincoln (22, 14c, 2p), R Lloyd-Davies (1, 2c, 1t), M A L Locket (5), G U Lyle (1), P Marshall (6), L W McLean (5, 5t), J M Meadows (5), D B S Markham (1), E Mullinger (3, 1t), Parsons (1), Lt Peyton-Jones (1), L Pollard (3), C S F Powell (3), P Previte (7, 2c, 2p), Ralston (1, 1t), F/Lt Rees (1), P Reeve (10, 4t), R A B Rogers (8, 2t), H W Rose (25, 1d, 7t), J J H Rymer (1, 3t), R Salmon (1), R Smyth (20, 2t), R M Snell (1), J Stewart (6, 2t), R H Thomas (12, 1t), W R Tookey (1), A C Towell (3), R J H Uprichard (1, 1t), R Willsher (23), E H Walshe (7, 1t).

# 1947-48

Played 35, won 22, lost 11, drawn 2. F 414, A 242.

Captain: R G Furbank

| | | | | f | a |
|---|---|---|---|---|---|
| **September** | | | | | |
| 6 | A | Leicester | L | 3 | 22 |
| 13 | H | London Irish | L | 3 | 9 |
| 20 | H | Met Police | W | 17 | 3 |
| 27 | A | Richmond | D | 6 | 6 |
| **October** | | | | | |
| 4 | H | Gloucester | W | 22 | 6 |
| 11 | H | Plymouth Albion | W | 27 | 7 |
| 18 | A | Guy's Hospital | L | 3 | 9 |
| 23 | H | Cambridge Univ | W | 11 | 6 |
| 25 | A | London Scottish | L | 8 | 19 |
| **November** | | | | | |
| 1 | H | Coventry | L | 3 | 11 |
| 8 | H | Bristol | W | 4 | 3 |
| 22 | H | Middlesex Hosp | W | 18 | 0 |
| 29 | A | Blackheath | W | 10 | 3 |
| **December** | | | | | |
| 6 | H | London Hosp | W | 15 | 4 |
| 13 | A | Moseley | L | 5 | 11 |
| 20 | H | St Mary's Hosp | W | 14 | 8 |
| 26 | H | Old Paulines | L | 0 | 9 |
| 27 | H | Rosslyn Park | W | 10 | 4 |

| | | | | f | a |
|---|---|---|---|---|---|
| **January** | | | | | |
| 3 | H | US Portsmouth | W | 16 | 3 |
| 10 | A | Coventry | W | 16 | 11 |
| 17 | H | Notts | W | 11 | 0 |
| 24 | H | Old Blues | W | 17 | 8 |
| 31 | H | Oxford Univ | L | 3 | 10 |
| **February** | | | | | |
| 7 | H | Manchester | W | 22 | 3 |
| 14 | H | O Cranleighians | W | 25 | 3 |
| 28 | A | Headingley | W | 16 | 3 |
| **March** | | | | | |
| 6 | H | Royal Air Force | W | 13 | 7 |
| 13 | A | Harlequins | W | 15 | 0 |
| 20 | H | Northampton | L | 3 | 25 |
| 27 | H | Old Alleynians | L | 6 | 8 |
| 29 | H | St Bart's Hosp | W | 39 | 6 |
| **April** | | | | | |
| 3 | H | Leicester | W | 6 | 0 |
| 8 | A | Northampton | L | 3 | 11 |
| 10 | H | Old Millhillians | W | 24 | 4 |
| 17 | H | London Welsh | D | 0 | 0 |

R G Furbank, the captain, played in all 35 matches. Fifty one players made at least one appearance. F M Fletcher and R H Haynes were the leading try scorers with eight and H W Rose scored most points, 132. D Riddy was appointed as the club's first Keeper of the Records.

J P Arnold (2), E Barringer (1), B R Black (2), T W Cranfield (3, 2c, 1p, 1t), G T Dancer (27, 3t), D W Dawson (13, 4t), H Elliott (30, 2t), J P Farmer-Wright (6), D Fensome (1), G Mc F D Fleming (1), F M Fletcher (28, 8t), A C B Ford (4, 2t), R G Furbank (35, 2t), J C Hacker (4), M R Hale (5), M Hall (28, 7t), R H Haynes (29, 4c, 3d, 8t), M M Henderson (27, 1t), G Hill (2), B Holmes (2), P H Hosea (1, 1t), G Jenkins (7, 2t), P G Jessop (5), A E P Joy (17, 2t), G A Kelly (19, 1t), W S Knight (21, 1t), D Knopp (1), J M Langham (10, 1t), C H Lincoln (14, 2t), J V Lyle (1), T R Marshall (3, 1t), P Marshall (7), L W McLean (15, 5t), R S Miller (2), F Mullinger (4), P Parker (12, 4t), L Pollard (1), P Previte (4), P Ralphs (20, 4t), P E Reeve (9), R A B Rogers (14, 7t), H W Rose (32, 31c, 1d, 21p, 1t), G S Smith (2), R Smyth (7, 5t), V Strother (1), D Studman (2), J M L Thomas (4), R H Thomas (5, 1t), W R Thomas (15, 8t), R Willsher (19, 2t), J C Wooding (1).

# 1948-49

Played 34, won 23, lost 7, drawn 4. F 462, A 170.

Captain: R G Furbank

| | | | | f | a |
|---|---|---|---|---|---|
| **September** | | | | | |
| 4 | A | Leicester | W | 21 | 3 |
| 11 | H | Notts | W | 18 | 6 |
| 18 | H | Old Mer Taylors | W | 39 | 8 |
| 25 | H | Richmond | L | 9 | 11 |
| **October** | | | | | |
| 2 | A | Gloucester | D | 6 | 6 |
| 9 | H | London Irish | L | 3 | 14 |
| 16 | H | Guy's Hospital | W | 8 | 3 |
| 23 | H | London Scottish | D | 8 | 8 |
| 28 | A | Cambridge Univ | L | 3 | 21 |
| 30 | H | Rosslyn Park | W | 17 | 0 |
| **November** | | | | | |
| 6 | A | Coventry | L | 6 | 9 |
| 13 | A | Bristol | L | 6 | 8 |
| 20 | H | Northampton | W | 6 | 0 |
| 27 | H | Moseley | W | 3 | 0 |
| **December** | | | | | |
| 4 | H | Old Blues | W | 26 | 0 |
| 11 | H | Met Police | W | 19 | 3 |
| 18 | H | St Mary's Hosp | W | 12 | 8 |
| 27 | H | Old Paulines | W | 32 | 0 |

| | | | | f | a |
|---|---|---|---|---|---|
| **January** | | | | | |
| 1 | A | US Portsmouth | W | 16 | 6 |
| 8 | H | Coventry | W | 5 | 3 |
| 15 | H | Leicester | W | 3 | 0 |
| 22 | A | Rosslyn Park | W | 19 | 9 |
| 29 | A | Oxford Univ | D | 8 | 8 |
| **February** | | | | | |
| 12 | A | London Welsh | L | 0 | 5 |
| 19 | H | London Hosp | W | 28 | 3 |
| 26 | A | Plymouth Albion | W | 9 | 0 |
| **March** | | | | | |
| 5 | H | Royal Air Force | L | 3 | 5 |
| 12 | H | Harlequins | D | 3 | 3 |
| 19 | A | Northampton | W | 11 | 3 |
| 26 | A | Blackheath | W | 9 | 3 |
| **April** | | | | | |
| 2 | H | Headingley | W | 24 | 3 |
| 9 | H | Old Millhillians | W | 36 | 3 |
| 16 | H | St Bart's Hosp | W | 20 | 0 |
| 18 | H | Wakefield | W | 26 | 8 |

R G Furbank again played in every match, 34, as did P Ralphs. L F Oakley was highest try scorer with 18. R H Haynes scored most points, 109. Forty five players made appearances. A dropped goal was reduced from four to three points.

P Adkins (4), J Archer (14, 6t), J P Arnold (1,1t), J F Bance (10), P S Collingridge (20, 9t), T W Cranfield (2), D W Dawson (9, 1t), L V Dilley (20, 5t), R Eidsforth (2, 1c), H Elliott (11), D Fensome (4), F M Fletcher (28, 3t), R G Furbank (34, 1c,1p,1t), G S S Gilbert (4), M R Hale (22, 3t), M Hall (31, 7t), P Heanue (17, 1t), M M Henderson (28, 7t), R F Hill (29), R J Horlick (1), R H Haynes (23, 20c, 5d, 10p, 8t), G Jenkins (25, 7t), G Jessop (9, 1t), W S Knight (3), D Knopp (3), J M Langham (2), T R Marshall (1), P M Maxey (1), J M Meadows (1), F Mullinger (2), L W McLean (6, 2t), L F Oakley (23, 18t), J Paine (1), P Parker (10, 6t), D Parren (1), P Ralphs (34, 8t), P E Reeve (5, 1t), H W Rose (31, 20c, 7p, 1t), R V Spark (1), B Stoker (3, 1t), R H Thomas (1), D Vaughan (6), K Webster (1), W H Whiting (15, 6t), R Willsher (1).

# 1949-50

Played 36, won 25, lost 10, drawn 1. F 485, A 208.

Captain: R G Furbank

| | | | | f | a |
|---|---|---|---|---|---|
| **September** | | | | | |
| 3 | A | Leicester | W | 16 | 6 |
| 10 | H | Notts | W | 53 | 0 |
| 17 | H | Old Mer Taylors | W | 29 | 3 |
| 24 | A | Richmond | W | 9 | 3 |
| **October** | | | | | |
| 1 | H | Gloucester | W | 28 | 0 |
| 8 | H | London Irish | W | 17 | 9 |
| 15 | A | Guy's Hospital | W | 12 | 3 |
| 22 | A | London Scottish | L | 3 | 6 |
| 27 | H | Cambridge Univ | W | 8 | 6 |
| 29 | H | London Welsh | L | 0 | 3 |
| **November** | | | | | |
| 5 | H | Edinburgh Univ | L | 3 | 9 |
| 12 | H | Bristol | W | 17 | 5 |
| 26 | A | Moseley | W | 5 | 0 |
| **December** | | | | | |
| 3 | H | Old Blues | W | 13 | 5 |
| 10 | H | Coventry | L | 3 | 14 |
| 17 | A | St Mary's Hosp | W | 6 | 3 |
| 24 | A | Blackheath | W | 6 | 5 |
| 26 | H | Old Paulines | W | 34 | 8 |
| 31 | H | Rosslyn Park | L | 6 | 16 |

| | | | | f | a |
|---|---|---|---|---|---|
| **January** | | | | | |
| 7 | H | U S Portsmouth | W | 19 | 6 |
| 14 | A | Coventry | L | 0 | 11 |
| 21 | H | St Bart's Hosp | W | 17 | 0 |
| **February** | | | | | |
| 4 | H | Manchester | W | 13 | 8 |
| 11 | A | Headingley | D | 6 | 6 |
| 18 | H | London Hospital | W | 16 | 5 |
| 25 | H | Plymouth Albion | W | 18 | 3 |
| **March** | | | | | |
| 4 | H | Royal Air Force | W | 11 | 6 |
| 11 | A | Harlequins | L | 0 | 8 |
| 18 | H | Northampton | L | 3 | 8 |
| 25 | H | Blackheath | W | 21 | 6 |
| **April** | | | | | |
| 1 | H | Middlesex Hosp | W | 33 | 3 |
| 8 | A | Hartlepool Rov | W | 18 | 3 |
| 10 | A | Percy Park | L | 6 | 9 |
| 15 | H | Old Millhillians | W | 24 | 0 |
| 20 | A | Northampton | L | 3 | 17 |
| 22 | H | Met Police | W | 9 | 5 |

R G Furbank again made most appearances, 34. He completed a record of 106 consecutive matches before breaking the sequence to play for the East Midlands. L F Oakley was the highest try scorer with 16. R H Haynes was leading points scorer with 97. Thirty eight players made appearances.

P Adkin (16, 6c, 1t), J P Arnold (18, 1c, 3t), J F Bance (32, 1t), R T Bingham (1), A J Bruce (2), P S Collingridge (31, 13t), A G Coomb (3), H Elliott (1), F M Fletcher (24, 1d, 5t), R G Furbank (34, 6c, 3p, 1t), G S S Gilbert (14), J Goodwin (8, 1t), M R Hale (32, 1c, 3t), M Hall (33, 7t), R H Haynes (25, 17c, 10p, 6t), M M Henderson (1), D Hill (7, 2t), R F Hill (14), D Huff (1), M James (12, 2t), G Jenkins (33, 9t), T R Marshall (15, 3t), L W McLean (1), J R Mee (12), P G Miller (11, 2t), G Mullinger (3), L F Oakley (26, 1c, 1d, 16t), P Parker (32, 9t), D Parren (11), H Payne (3), P Ralphs (33, 7t), H W Rose (28, 17c, 1d, 10p, 5t), B M Steval (1), J Taylor (8), R H Thomas (1), W H Whiting (1), W D Wood (2), P Wootton (10, 2t).

# 1950-51

Played 33, won 24, lost 5, drawn 4. F 425, A 105.

Captain: G Jenkins

| Date | Venue | Opponent | Result | f | a |
|---|---|---|---|---|---|
| **September** | | | | | |
| 2 | A | Leicester | W | 14 | 11 |
| 9 | H | Notts | W | 24 | 9 |
| 16 | H | Headingley | W | 24 | 0 |
| 23 | H | Old Whitgiftians | W | 42 | 0 |
| 30 | W | Richmond | W | 5 | 0 |
| **October** | | | | | |
| 7 | A | Gloucester | L | 0 | 8 |
| 14 | H | London Irish | W | 21 | 3 |
| 21 | H | Guy's Hospital | W | 24 | 0 |
| 26 | A | Cambridge Univ | W | 10 | 0 |
| 28 | H | London Scottish | W | 28 | 3 |
| **November** | | | | | |
| 4 | A | London Welsh | W | 3 | 0 |
| 11 | A | Bristol | W | 6 | 0 |
| 18 | H | Northampton | W | 6 | 0 |
| 25 | H | Moseley | W | 5 | 0 |
| **December** | | | | | |
| 2 | H | Old Blues | W | 19 | 3 |
| 9 | H | Met Police | L | 0 | 3 |
| 26 | H | Old Paulines | W | 20 | 3 |
| **January** | | | | | |
| 6 | A | US Portsmouth | W | 15 | 3 |
| 13 | H | Coventry | D | 9 | 9 |
| 20 | H | Leicester | L | 11 | 15 |
| 27 | A | Oxford Univ | W | 11 | 3 |
| **February** | | | | | |
| 3 | H | Manchester | D | 6 | 6 |
| 10 | H | Old Alleynians | W | 19 | 6 |
| 24 | A | Plymouth Albion | W | 10 | 0 |
| **March** | | | | | |
| 3 | H | Royal Air Force | L | 3 | 5 |
| 10 | H | Harlequins | L | 0 | 3 |
| 17 | A | Northampton | D | 6 | 6 |
| 24 | A | Edinburgh Univ | W | 25 | 0 |
| 26 | A | Edinb'gh Academicals | D | 3 | 3 |
| 31 | H | Leicester | W | 3 | 0 |
| **April** | | | | | |
| 7 | H | Hartlepool Rovers | W | 27 | 0 |
| 14 | A | Coventry | W | 6 | 0 |
| 21 | H | Bradford | W | 20 | 3 |

Thity eight players made at least one appearance. R G Furbank again made most, 32. P S Collingridge scored most tries, 16. R H Haynes scored most points, 103.

M E Allen (3), R Anderson (4, 1c, 2p), J F Bance (30, 1t), J R Beadon (12, 1t), G Bennett (12), P S Collingridge (26, 16t), A G Coomb (4), J Goodwin (2), E Evans (15, 5t), G Mc F D Fleming (2), F M Fletcher (20, 1t), R G Furbank (32, 1c, 2t), G S S Gilbert (18, 1t), M R Hale (30), R H Haynes (22, 23c, 3d, 13p, 3t), B J B Hazell (4), D Hill (14, 3t), P B L Hoppe (2), N P Huntley (13, 1t), G Jenkins (26, 9t), T R Marshall (16), P M Maxey (2), L W McLean (7, 1t), J R Mee (8), P G Miller (3), G Mullinger (1), L F Oakley (12, 7t), P Parker (29, 14t), D Parren (7), H Payne (1), P Ralphs (31, 9t), H W Rose (21, 15c, 5p), B M Steval (2, 1t), J Taylor (1), A C Towell (25, 2d, 8t), D A Wells (10), W H Whiting (23, 6t), P Wootton (5, 1t).

# 1951-52

Played 36, won 28, lost 6, drawn 2. F 454, A 158.

Captain: J F Bance

| | | | | f | a |
|---|---|---|---|---|---|
| **September** | | | | | |
| 1 | A | Leicester | W | 6 | 3 |
| 8 | H | Notts | L | 0 | 3 |
| 15 | H | London Irish | W | 16 | 3 |
| 22 | H | Met Police | W | 25 | 0 |
| 29 | A | Richmond | W | 11 | 5 |
| **October** | | | | | |
| 6 | H | Gloucester | W | 19 | 9 |
| 13 | H | Old Mer Taylors | W | 11 | 0 |
| 20 | A | Guy's Hospital | W | 13 | 3 |
| 25 | H | Cambridge Univ | W | 6 | 5 |
| 27 | A | London Scottish | W | 8 | 3 |
| **November** | | | | | |
| 3 | H | Coventry | L | 3 | 6 |
| 10 | H | Bristol | W | 6 | 5 |
| 17 | A | Northampton | L | 0 | 8 |
| 24 | A | Moseley | W | 9 | 3 |
| **December** | | | | | |
| 1 | H | Aldershot Serv | W | 19 | 5 |
| 8 | H | Middlesex Hosp | W | 22 | 3 |
| 15 | H | St Mary's Hosp | W | 23 | 0 |
| 22 | H | Old Alleynians | W | 14 | 11 |
| 26 | H | Old Paulines | W | 9 | 8 |
| 29 | H | Rosslyn Park | L | 0 | 14 |
| **January** | | | | | |
| 5 | H | US Portsmouth | L | 3 | 5 |
| 12 | A | Coventry | L | 5 | 15 |
| 19 | H | Leicester | W | 5 | 3 |
| 26 | H | Oxford Univ | W | 13 | 3 |
| **February** | | | | | |
| 16 | H | London Hosp | W | 17 | 0 |
| 23 | A | Sale | W | 18 | 5 |
| **March** | | | | | |
| 1 | H | Royal Air Force | W | 8 | 3 |
| 8 | H | Harlequins | W | 20 | 5 |
| 15 | H | Northampton | W | 11 | 0 |
| 22 | H | Blackheath | D | 6 | 6 |
| **April** | | | | | |
| 5 | H | Plymouth Albion | W | 14 | 3 |
| 12 | H | St Bart's Hosp | W | 37 | 10 |
| 14 | H | Durham Univ | W | 8 | 3 |
| 19 | H | Old Blues | W | 34 | 0 |
| 23 | A | Notts | D | 0 | 0 |
| 26 | H | Birkenhead Park | W | 35 | 0 |

R H Haynes was again leading points scorer with 142. L W McLean scored most tries 23, and E Evans made most appearances, 34. Forty four players turned out at least once. The 28 wins in a season equalled the record of 1923-24.

R Anderson (7, 3c, 3p), J F Bance (30, 1t), G Bennett (8), P S Collingridge (19, 10t), A G Coomb (1), S Dalgleish (1), D Evans (1), E Evans (34, 9t), P Evans (2), G Mc F D Fleming (3), F M Fletcher (26, 1t), R G Furbank (28, 3c, 2t), G S S Gilbert (28), M D Graham (3), M R Hale (22, 1t), R H Haynes (28, 32c, 7d, 13p, 6t), P Heanue (18, 1t), J C Heathcote-Hacker (10, 1c), D Hill (4, 1c), P B L Hoppe (11), R J Horlick (1), N P Huntley (33, 1t), G Jenkins (33, 5t), T R Marshall (20, 4c, 1p, 3t), M J O Massey (5), L W McLean (29, 23t), J R Mee (13), P G Miller (1), P Parker (4), H Payne (1), P Ralphs (33, 6t), D Spence (3), J Taylor (1), A W Thorpe (3, 2t), A C Towell (23, 1d, 5t), R J H Uprichard (1), J H Valentine (2), D A Wells (4), W H Whiting (32, 17t), J Willey (1), I L Williamson (2), P J Wooding (2), P Wootton (5), D R Wynn-Williams (4, 4c, 1t).

# 1952-53

Played 34, won 20, lost 10, drawn 4. F 351, A 243.

Captain: J F Bance

| | | | | f | a |
|---|---|---|---|---|---|
| **September** | | | | | |
| 6 | A | Leicester | L | 10 | 16 |
| 13 | H | Headingley | W | 21 | 8 |
| 20 | H | Notts | W | 3 | 0 |
| 27 | H | Richmond | L | 9 | 11 |
| **October** | | | | | |
| 4 | A | Gloucester | W | 14 | 6 |
| 11 | A | Bristol | L | 6 | 11 |
| 18 | H | Guy's Hospital | W | 16 | 0 |
| 23 | A | Cambridge Univ | L | 11 | 4 |
| 25 | H | London Scottish | W | 22 | 0 |
| **November** | | | | | |
| 1 | H | Met Police | D | 6 | 6 |
| 8 | H | Moseley | D | 6 | 6 |
| 15 | H | Northampton | L | 3 | 8 |
| **December** | | | | | |
| 13 | A | St Bart's Hosp | W | 13 | 3 |
| 20 | A | St Mary's Hosp | D | 0 | 0 |
| 26 | H | Old Paulines | W | 15 | 0 |
| **January** | | | | | |
| 3 | A | US Portsmouth | L | 5 | 21 |
| 10 | H | Coventry | L | 6 | 13 |
| 17 | H | Sale | W | 14 | 8 |
| 24 | H | Leicester | L | 3 | 18 |
| 31 | A | Oxford Univ | W | 11 | 8 |
| **February** | | | | | |
| 7 | A | London Welsh | D | 8 | 8 |
| 14 | H | Old Mer Taylors | W | 8 | 0 |
| 21 | H | London Hosp | W | 18 | 0 |
| 28 | A | Plymouth Albion | W | 5 | 3 |
| **March** | | | | | |
| 7 | H | Royal Air Force | L | 6 | 27 |
| 14 | H | Harlequins | W | 8 | 5 |
| 21 | A | Northampton | W | 8 | 6 |
| 28 | A | Blackheath | W | 11 | 8 |
| **April** | | | | | |
| 4 | H | Percy Park | W | 17 | 11 |
| 6 | H | Hartlepool Rovers | W | 5 | 3 |
| 11 | A | Coventry | L | 6 | 11 |
| 16 | H | Durham Univ | W | 13 | 9 |
| 18 | H | Lichfield | W | 23 | 5 |
| 25 | H | Bradford | W | 21 | 0 |

R H Haynes was top scorer with 98 points. L F Oakley scored ten tries. Fifty two players made appearances. T R Marshall made most, 32.

R Anderson (1), J F Bance (27, 1t), G Bates (3), L Chubb (2), P S Collingridge (11, 4t), R A Collinge (1), A G Coomb (22, 4t), S Dalgleish (1), M Davison (2), L V Dilley (3), D Evans (9, 2t), L Evans (8), F M Fletcher (17, 3d, 1t), R G Furbank (26, 2c, 1p, 1t), P C Gibb (1), G S S Gilbert (20), M R Hale (26), R H Haynes (22, 22c, 2d, 12p, 4t), P Heanue (5), P B L Hoppe (15), R J Horlick (7, 2t), N P Huntley (12), G Jenkins (1), D C Kingsley (12, 6c, 1d, 3p), K Mallett (2), T R Marshall (32, 7t), M J O Massey (2), B E McCarthy (17, 1t), L W McLean (2), J R Mee (16, 3t), M S Meeson (2), G Micklewright (6, 1t), P G Miller (15, 6c, 1d, 1p, 1t), L F Oakley (15, 10t), D J Pack (1), S Powell (1, 1t), P Ralphs (29, 8t), H W Rose (6, 1p, 1t), W Shepherd (1), D Spence (9), L Stocks (1), J Taylor (2), B Thomas (2), R F Thomas (2), A C Towell (20, 1d, 3t), J H Valentine (1), P White (1), W H Whiting (28, 8t), St L H Webb (27, 4t), D A Wells (6), I L Williamson (2), P Wootton (8).

# 1953-54

Played 33, won 19, lost 13, drawn 1. F 362, A 311.

Captain: J F Bance

| | | | | f | a |
|---|---|---|---|---|---|
| **September** | | | | | |
| 5 | A | Leicester | L | 6 | 12 |
| 12 | H | Met Police | W | 29 | 24 |
| 19 | H | Notts | W | 18 | 3 |
| 26 | A | Richmond | L | 8 | 14 |
| **October** | | | | | |
| 3 | H | Gloucester | L | 6 | 13 |
| 10 | H | London Hospital | W | 11 | 9 |
| 17 | A | Guy's Hospital | L | 9 | 14 |
| 22 | H | Cambridge Univ | L | 3 | 33 |
| 24 | A | London Scottish | L | 3 | 20 |
| **November** | | | | | |
| 7 | H | Edinburgh Univ | L | 11 | 18 |
| 14 | H | Old Mer Taylors | W | 9 | 5 |
| 21 | A | Northampton | L | 3 | 16 |
| 28 | H | Manchester | W | 19 | 0 |
| **December** | | | | | |
| 5 | A | Coventry | W | 9 | 8 |
| 12 | H | Old Blues | W | 11 | 6 |
| 19 | H | St Mary's Hosp | W | 3 | 0 |
| 26 | H | Old Paulines | W | 11 | 3 |
| **January** | | | | | |
| 2 | H | US Portsmouth | W | 17 | 0 |
| 9 | H | Old Alleynians | W | 18 | 5 |
| 16 | A | Sale | W | 14 | 3 |
| 23 | H | Leicester | W | 22 | 5 |
| **February** | | | | | |
| 20 | A | Moseley | L | 17 | 19 |
| 27 | H | Plymouth Albion | W | 19 | 0 |
| **March** | | | | | |
| 6 | H | Royal Air Force | W | 9 | 8 |
| 13 | A | Harlequins | L | 6 | 14 |
| 18 | H | The Army | W | 9 | 8 |
| 20 | H | Northampton | L | 0 | 11 |
| 27 | H | Blackheath | D | 0 | 0 |
| **April** | | | | | |
| 3 | H | Bristol | L | 3 | 8 |
| 10 | H | Coventry | W | 13 | 11 |
| 17 | H | Bradford | W | 27 | 0 |
| 19 | H | Rugby | W | 14 | 0 |
| 24 | A | Bath | L | 5 | 21 |

W H Whiting scored most tries, 18, and most points, 54. P G Miller, B E McCarthy and St L H Webb made most appearances, 31. Fifty four players made at least one.

J F Bance (26, 1t), J Barrow (1), G Bates (1), F Brookman (17, 9c, 8p), P S Collingridge (12, 6t), A G Coomb (5, 1c), J B Davies (11), T W Davies (18, 3t), L V Dilley (5), D Evans (1), M J Feasey (7, 2t), G Franklin (2), P C Gibb (3), G S S Gilbert (5), J S Graham (15, 9c, 5p, 2t), M R Hale (30), R E Hardham (1), A J Hawkins (2), P J Harris (4), R H Haynes (1, 2c, 1t), P B L Hoppe (1), R J Horlick (4), D C Kingsley (4, 1p), T L Lloyd (6), E G Lucas (1), T R Marshall (27, 2t), J C Mackenzie (11, 2t), B E McCarthy (31, 1t), M J O Massey (9), J R Mee (16, 2t), G Micklewright (19, 13t), P G Miller (31, 3c, 6d, 2p), B R Mills (2), J B Norwood (9), M J Nicholson (1), D J Pack (4), N B Pinnington (6), S Powell (7, 3t), D Price (7), P Ralphs (7, 1t), J Smith (3), P Smith (3, 1t), B M Steval (1), R O Stevenson (1), B Stokes (1), R F Thomas (11), A C Towell (24, 1d, 5t), J H Valentine (1), St L H Webb (31, 7t), P White (1), W H Whiting (28, 18t), B Wilks (4, 1c, 2p, 1t), T Wynn-Jones (7, 3t), D R Wynn-Williams (9, 3c, 1p, 1t).

## 1954-55

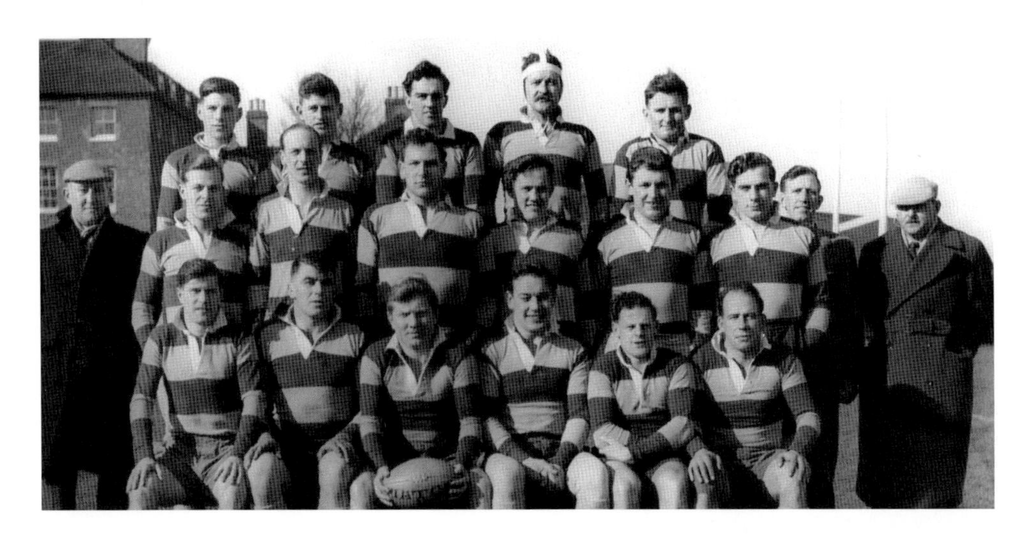

Played 36, won 17, lost 16, drawn 3. F 325, A 275.

Captain: A C Towell

| September | | | | f | a |
|---|---|---|---|---|---|
| 4 | A | Leicester | L | 8 | 17 |
| 11 | H | Met Police | W | 21 | 8 |
| 18 | H | Notts | W | 9 | 3 |
| 25 | L | Richmond | L | 3 | 13 |
| **October** | | | | | |
| 2 | A | Gloucester | D | 6 | 6 |
| 9 | H | London Hospital | W | 19 | 0 |
| 16 | H | Guy's Hospital | W | 6 | 0 |
| 23 | H | London Scottish | D | 6 | 6 |
| 27 | A | Cambridge Univ | L | 3 | 25 |
| 30 | H | London Univ | W | 14 | 6 |
| **November** | | | | | |
| 6 | H | Old Mer Taylors | L | 6 | 8 |
| 13 | H | Rosslyn Park | L | 6 | 12 |
| 20 | H | Northampton | W | 6 | 3 |
| 27 | H | Manchester | W | 20 | 6 |
| **December** | | | | | |
| 4 | H | Coventry | L | 14 | 16 |
| 11 | H | Middlesex Hosp | W | 19 | 0 |
| 18 | H | St Mary's Hosp | W | 13 | 0 |
| 27 | H | Old Paulines | W | 24 | 0 |
| 28 | H | Penarth | L | 3 | 12 |

| January | | | | f | a |
|---|---|---|---|---|---|
| 1 | A | US Portsmouth | W | 17 | 9 |
| 8 | H | Old Alleynians | W | 14 | 5 |
| 22 | H | Leicester | L | 0 | 9 |
| 29 | A | Oxford Univ | L | 3 | 10 |
| **February** | | | | | |
| 5 | A | London Welsh | W | 11 | 6 |
| 12 | H | Headingley | L | 3 | 11 |
| **March** | | | | | |
| 5 | H | Royal Air Force | D | 3 | 3 |
| 12 | H | Harlequins | W | 6 | 0 |
| 19 | A | Northampton | L | 0 | 3 |
| 26 | A | Blackheath | L | 6 | 9 |
| **April** | | | | | |
| 2 | A | Bristol | L | 0 | 13 |
| 9 | H | Durham Univ | L | 3 | 9 |
| 11 | H | Old Blues | L | 0 | 9 |
| 16 | A | Coventry | L | 0 | 14 |
| 20 | H | Moseley | W | 28 | 14 |
| 23 | H | Bath | W | 16 | 5 |
| 30 | H | Birkenhead Park | W | 9 | 5 |

W H Whiting scored most tries, eight. F Brookman was leading points scorer with 99. D Price and B E McCarthy both made 34 appearances. Fifty one players turned out at least once.

B Bainton (3), J F Bance (32, 1t), G Bates (1), O Bergh (5), F Brookman (25, 12c, 1d, 18p, 6t), P G Campbell (8, 1t), R G Churchill (10, 2t), P S Collingridge (18, 2c, 3p, 1t), A G Coomb (20, 3c, 6t), T W Davies (6, 1t), J P Flavell (5, 2t), E Floyd (3, 2t), G Franklin (2), D Green (10), M Godwin (1), M R Hale (18), R Harris (1), A R King (1), A Lamb (1), R A Lovell (21), T R Marshall (27, 6c, 1p, 6t), B E McCarthy (34), D J McPherson (1), R Meadows (1), M Meeson (1), G Micklewright (33, 7t), P G Miller (11, 4d), M J Mynott (5, 1p), W K Nicholas (23, 1d, 5t), P Nicol (8), J B Norwood (17, 1t), R A Pinnington (6, 1t), K R Pledger (4), D M Pugh (3), D Price (34, 2t), P Ralphs (9), A R Ramsey (1), A G Robertson (2), B Robins (25, 1t), R Sanstrom (3, 1t), J W Seamark (7), A J Shepherd (4, 2t), P Smith (9, 1t), J Smith (5), B Stapleton (1), J E Stuart (2), G Thomas (1), A C Towell (26, 1d, 4t), St L H Webb (22, 2t), W H Whiting (23, 8t), P Wootton (1).

# 1955-56

Played 36, won 18, lost 16, drawn 2. F 286, A 321.

Captain: T R Marshall

| | | | | f | a |
|---|---|---|---|---|---|
| **September** | | | | | |
| 3 | A | Leicester | W | 20 | 11 |
| 10 | H | Met Police | W | 21 | 6 |
| 17 | H | Notts | W | 30 | 8 |
| 24 | A | Richmond | L | 0 | 16 |
| **October** | | | | | |
| 1 | H | Gloucester | W | 5 | 3 |
| 8 | H | Oxford RFC | W | 12 | 3 |
| 15 | A | Guy's Hospital | W | 8 | 0 |
| 22 | A | London Scottish | L | 3 | 17 |
| 27 | H | Cambridge Univ | L | 9 | 18 |
| 29 | H | London Hospital | W | 6 | 3 |
| **November** | | | | | |
| 5 | H | Edinburgh Univ | W | 8 | 6 |
| 12 | H | Old Mer Taylors | W | 3 | 0 |
| 19 | A | Northampton | L | 0 | 8 |
| 26 | H | Aldershot Services | W | 24 | 3 |
| **December** | | | | | |
| 3 | A | Coventry | L | 8 | 13 |
| 10 | H | Old Alleynians | W | 24 | 6 |
| 17 | H | St Mary's Hosp | W | 6 | 3 |
| 24 | H | Leicester | D | 0 | 0 |
| 26 | H | Old Paulines | W | 10 | 0 |
| 27 | H | Penarth | L | 0 | 14 |
| 31 | H | Rosslyn Park | W | 3 | 0 |
| **January** | | | | | |
| 7 | H | US Portsmouth | W | 16 | 12 |
| 14 | A | Sale | L | 0 | 13 |
| 21 | H | Manchester | W | 6 | 3 |
| 28 | H | Oxford University | D | 3 | 3 |
| **March** | | | | | |
| 3 | H | Royal Air Force | L | 0 | 38 |
| 10 | A | Harlequins | L | 0 | 14 |
| 17 | H | Northampton | L | 3 | 8 |
| 24 | H | Blackheath | W | 14 | 6 |
| 31 | A | Edinburgh Univ | L | 3 | 11 |
| **April** | | | | | |
| 2 | A | Percy Park | L | 11 | 18 |
| 7 | H | Bristol | L | 5 | 10 |
| 14 | H | Coventry | W | 5 | 0 |
| 18 | A | Moseley | L | 6 | 14 |
| 21 | A | Bath | L | 8 | 19 |
| 28 | A | Birkenhead Park | L | 6 | 14 |

G Micklewright scored most tries, eight, G Watts scored most points, 58, J F Bance made most appearances, 33. Fifty seven players turned out. T R Marshall, as captain, became the first son of a former captain to skipper the side.

B Abrahams (2), P H Avery (10), J F Bance (33), R J Bennett (2), O Bergh (3), F Brookman (3, 2c), A M Brannan (1), P G Campbell (1), R J Carter (3), M J Chadwick (7), R G Churchill (3), P S Collingridge (18, 2c, 2t), W R Dalzell (1), K Davies (8), T W Davies (2), M J Feazey (2), J Flavell (14, 3t), G Franklin (13), A Goodwell (1), D Green (4), M R Hale (16), R A Hepworth (5, 1t), P Hosea (1), K Hughes (10, 3t), P Jackson (30, 2t), E Jefferies (3), M J Laing (18, 3t), R A Lovell (21, 1t), E G Lucas (7), T R Marshall (30, 3t), B E McCarthy (15), L W McLean (1), J McLeod (12), D R Medd (8), G Micklewright (23, 8t), P G Miller (22, 5c, 4d, 1p, 2t), W K Nicholas (25, 4c, 3d, 1t), D Nicol (5, 1t), K D Patten (1), R Pinnington (1), D Price (28, 4t), G Prigmore (2), A G Robertson (3), B Robins (1), B Robinson (1), J W Seamark (29, 2c, 1d, 1p, 6t), A J Shepherd (14, 1p, 3t), P Smith (1), B Stapleton (2), A C Towell (5, 1d), P Voyce (1), G Watts (15, 8c, 10p, 4t), St L H Webb (27, 5t), W H Whiting (4, 1t), S H Wilcock (14, 5t), D G Wood (3), A G Yirrell (4).

# 1956-57

Played 38, won 15, lost 19, drawn 4. F 279, A 383.

Captain: St L H Webb

| | | | | f | a |
|---|---|---|---|---|---|
| **September** | | | | | |
| 1 | A | Leicester | W | 11 | 8 |
| 8 | H | Met Police | W | 12 | 8 |
| 15 | H | Notts | W | 30 | 3 |
| 22 | H | Richmond | W | 16 | 3 |
| 29 | H | Birkenhead Park | L | 3 | 5 |
| **October** | | | | | |
| 6 | A | Gloucester | L | 3 | 6 |
| 13 | H | London Hosp | W | 22 | 3 |
| 20 | H | Guy's Hospital | W | 11 | 6 |
| 24 | A | Cambridge Univ | L | 6 | 11 |
| 27 | H | London Scottish | L | 0 | 17 |
| **November** | | | | | |
| 3 | H | Old Alleynians | W | 17 | 0 |
| 10 | H | Old Mer Taylors | D | 9 | 9 |
| 17 | H | Northampton | L | 0 | 6 |
| 24 | H | Old Millhillians | L | 0 | 25 |
| **December** | | | | | |
| 1 | H | Manchester | D | 3 | 3 |
| 8 | H | St Thomas' Hosp | W | 20 | 0 |
| 15 | H | St Mary's Hosp | W | 8 | 6 |
| 22 | A | Coventry | L | 3 | 13 |
| 26 | H | Old Paulines | L | 0 | 6 |
| 29 | H | Rosslyn Park | L | 0 | 3 |
| **January** | | | | | |
| 5 | A | US Portsmouth | D | 3 | 3 |
| 12 | H | Sale | L | 3 | 26 |
| 19 | H | Leicester | D | 3 | 3 |
| 26 | A | Oxford Univ | L | 3 | 26 |
| **February** | | | | | |
| 2 | A | London Welsh | L | 0 | 8 |
| 9 | H | Headingley | W | 8 | 3 |
| 16 | H | Moseley | L | 0 | 8 |
| 23 | A | Plymouth Albion | L | 0 | 9 |
| **March** | | | | | |
| 2 | H | Royal Air Force | W | 6 | 3 |
| 9 | H | Harlequins | L | 6 | 37 |
| 16 | A | Northampton | L | 10 | 35 |
| 23 | A | Blackheath | L | 14 | 16 |
| 30 | H | Aldershot Services | W | 20 | 9 |
| **April** | | | | | |
| 6 | A | Bristol | L | 0 | 34 |
| 13 | H | Coventry | L | 0 | 3 |
| 20 | H | Percy Park | W | 9 | 8 |
| 22 | H | Rugby | W | 11 | 3 |
| 27 | H | Bath | W | 9 | 8 |

Highest points scorer was P S Collingridge with 50 which included the highest try total, eight. P Jackson made most appearances, 37. Fifty seven players turned out at least once.

M G Allison (9, 2t), E Arnold (3, 1c), P H Avery (26, 1c, 2p), J F Bance (33, 4t), L V Barber (2), R G Bass (1), A M Brannan (6, 1p), D Brooks (5, 1t), B Cain (2), R Carter (13, 1t), M J Chadwick (1, 1t), P S Collingridge (31, 7c, 4p, 8t), D Cook (2), W R Dalzell (3), A Doncaster (12, 3t), G Evans (1), J Flavell (20, 4t), G Fox (10), G Franklin (33, 1t), J French (1), G S S Gilbert (2), M Godwin (1), M R Hale (8, 1t), M Hayes (1), J D Heaton (12, 4c, 4p, 2t), R Hepworth (20), P Jackson (37), G John (3), E Jefferies (8, 3t), M J Laing (16, 1t), R A Lovell (8, 1t), E G Lucas (2, 1t), T R Marshall (23, 2t), B E McCarthy (1), R Meadows (2, 1t), G Micklewright (11, 2t), W K Nicholas (17, 3c, 2d, 2p, 4t), B J Norwood (3), K D Patten (14, 3t), R A Pinnington (1), B Phillips (4), D Price (14), G Prigmore (23, 2t), A G Robertson (1), D P Rogers (3), J W Seamark (5, 1t), J Smith (9), P Smith (10), B Stapleton (2), A W Thorpe (1), P Voyce (24, 4t), St L H Webb (32, 7t), J Whiting (7, 2c, 1t), S H Wilcock (8, 4t), H Wright (2), A G Yirrell (7), K Youds (13, 1t).

# 1957-58

Played 37, won 18, lost 14, drawn 5. F 314, A 308.

Captain: St L H Webb

| | | | | f | a |
|---|---|---|---|---|---|
| **September** | | | | | |
| 7 | A | Leicester | L | 5 | 11 |
| 14 | H | Met Police | W | 8 | 3 |
| 21 | H | Notts | W | 17 | 6 |
| 28 | A | Richmond | L | 11 | 21 |
| **October** | | | | | |
| 5 | H | Gloucester | D | 9 | 9 |
| 12 | H | London Hospital | W | 9 | 6 |
| 19 | H | Guy's Hospital | W | 14 | 8 |
| 24 | H | Cambridge Univ | D | 3 | 3 |
| 26 | A | London Scottish | W | 11 | 6 |
| **November** | | | | | |
| 2 | H | Old Mer Taylors | W | 19 | 8 |
| 9 | H | Edinburgh Univ | W | 8 | 6 |
| 16 | A | Northampton | L | 3 | 14 |
| 23 | A | Coventry | L | 3 | 11 |
| 30 | H | Old Alleynians | W | 21 | 6 |
| **December** | | | | | |
| 7 | H | Manchester | W | 8 | 5 |
| 14 | H | St Thomas Hosp | W | 9 | 6 |
| 21 | A | St Mary's Hosp | D | 0 | 0 |
| 26 | H | Old Paulines | W | 22 | 9 |
| 28 | H | Rosslyn Park | L | 3 | 5 |

| | | | | f | a |
|---|---|---|---|---|---|
| **January** | | | | | |
| 4 | H | US Portsmouth | W | 14 | 3 |
| 11 | A | Sale | L | 10 | 32 |
| 18 | H | Leicester | D | 6 | 6 |
| **February** | | | | | |
| 1 | H | London Welsh | L | 3 | 8 |
| 15 | A | Moseley | L | 6 | 16 |
| 22 | H | Rugby | W | 5 | 0 |
| 27 | H | Oxford Univ | W | 8 | 0 |
| **March** | | | | | |
| 1 | H | Royal Air Force | L | 3 | 15 |
| 8 | A | Harlequins | W | 8 | 6 |
| 15 | H | Northampton | L | 6 | 9 |
| 22 | H | Blackheath | L | 3 | 8 |
| 29 | H | Aldershot Services | W | 11 | 8 |
| **April** | | | | | |
| 5 | A | Redruth | W | 11 | 9 |
| 7 | A | Penzance & Newlyn | L | 3 | 6 |
| 8 | A | St Ives | L | 10 | 13 |
| 12 | H | Bristol | L | 0 | 9 |
| 19 | H | Coventry | W | 18 | 11 |
| 26 | A | Bath | D | 6 | 6 |

Highest points scorer was J D Heaton with 117 which included the highest try total, 16. P Jackson played in all 37 matches. Forty three players made appearances.

M G Allison (9, 1t), E Arnold (13), P H Avery (8, 1t), L V Barber (23, 4t), R G Bass (1), F R Booth (20, 1t), A M Brannan (14, 7c, 2d, 3p), J Burke (3), B Cain (16), R Carter (35, 3t), D Cook (8, 1d, 1t), J Croker (13), G H Gullen (12, 1t), W R Dalzell (4), A Doncaster (11, 3t), K Duchars (21), H Eden (2), J Flavell (5), G Franklin (13, 1t), G S S Gilbert (3), J D Heaton (25, 12c, 2d, 13p, 16t), W K Hepworth (4), P Jackson (37), R A Lovell (12), T R Marshall (26, 2t), B E McCarthy (22), D A McSweeney (2, 1t), J Morgan (3), W K Nicholas (14, 3d, 3p, 2t), D J Pack (1), B Phillips (1), D M Pugh (8, 1t), J Pyke (4), D P Rogers (33, 2t), P Rowlands (18, 4c, 1d, 1p, 7t), J Seamark (2), J Smith (32, 2c, 2d), B Stapleton (5, 1t), P Voyce (26, 1t), J Watson (1), St L H Webb (34, 6t),W H Whiting (8, 1t), K Youds (3).

# 1958-59

Played 35, won 18, lost 14, drawn 3. F 401, A 306.

Captain: P Voyce

| | | | | f | a |
|---|---|---|---|---|---|
| **September** | | | | | |
| 6 | A | Leicester | L | 11 | 20 |
| 13 | H | London Irish | L | 14 | 16 |
| 20 | H | Notts | W | 11 | 6 |
| 27 | H | Richmond | L | 0 | 8 |
| **October** | | | | | |
| 4 | A | Gloucester | L | 3 | 13 |
| 11 | H | London Hospital | W | 17 | 0 |
| 18 | H | Guy's Hospital | W | 32 | 3 |
| 22 | A | Cambridge Univ | L | 3 | 11 |
| 25 | H | London Scottish | L | 16 | 17 |
| **November** | | | | | |
| 1 | H | Old Mer Taylors | W | 20 | 0 |
| 8 | H | Old Blues | W | 24 | 5 |
| 15 | H | Northampton | D | 0 | 0 |
| 22 | A | Coventry | L | 0 | 23 |
| 29 | H | Old Alleynians | W | 20 | 5 |
| **December** | | | | | |
| 6 | H | Manchester | W | 14 | 9 |
| 13 | H | Aldershot Services | W | 25 | 0 |
| 20 | H | St Mary's Hosp | L | 9 | 10 |
| 26 | H | Old Paulines | W | 30 | 0 |
| 27 | A | Rosslyn Park | W | 8 | 0 |
| **January** | | | | | |
| 24 | H | Met Police | W | 11 | 0 |
| 31 | A | Oxford Univ | L | 8 | 13 |
| **February** | | | | | |
| 7 | A | London Welsh | W | 14 | 3 |
| 14 | H | Headingley | L | 0 | 24 |
| 21 | H | Moseley | L | 9 | 14 |
| 28 | H | Rugby | W | 11 | 0 |
| **March** | | | | | |
| 7 | H | Royal Air Force | D | 0 | 0 |
| 14 | H | Harlequins | W | 22 | 16 |
| 21 | A | Northampton | L | 0 | 20 |
| 28 | A | Blackheath | W | 11 | 3 |
| 30 | H | Huddersfield | W | 12 | 8 |
| **April** | | | | | |
| 4 | A | Bristol | L | 11 | 24 |
| 11 | H | Coventry | W | 13 | 6 |
| 18 | A | Bath | D | 6 | 6 |
| 22 | H | Leicester | W | 11 | 9 |
| 25 | A | Birkenhead Park | L | 5 | 14 |

St L H Webb was the highest try scorer with 13, J D Heaton scored most points, 76. R Carter played in all 35 matches. Forty four players made appearances. The pack was credited with two tries.

M G Allison (9, 1d, 1t), R Atkins (3), P H Avery (33, 6t), J Bardner (1), J D Bell (20, 6t), F R Booth (2), A M Brannan (6, 6c, 8p, 1t), B Cain (20, 3t), R Carter (35, 4t), D Cook (3), J Croker (10, 1t), L R Drury (18, 1t), K Duchars (4), R Everdell (12, 1t), G Franklin (1), R Goodwin (18, 3t), H Green (7), J D Heaton (19, 11c, 1d, 12p, 5t), P Hutton (6), P Jackson (2), A A Johnson (9, 7c, 6p), M J Laing (15, 3t), R A Lovell (26), T R Marshall (18, 1t), B E McCarthy (34, 2t), P McGovan (3, 1t), W K Nicholas (3), P A Pettigrew (1), J Pretsell (7), D M Pugh (8, 1t), A G Robertson (10, 1p, 1t), D P Rogers (33, 9t), P Rowlands (5, 4c, 2t), J Smith (23, 5c, 1d, 2p, 1t), P Smith (3, 1t), B Stapleton (5, 1t), P Voyce (12,1t), J Watson (6, 2t), St L H Webb (27, 13t), S H Wilcock (3, 1c), B K Williams (29, 4t), D A Worker (10, 1t), R N Wynn-Williams (1), K Youds (5, 1t).

# 1959-60

Played 37, won 26, lost 7, drawn 4. F 532, A 291.

Captain: P H Avery

| | | | | f | a |
|---|---|---|---|---|---|
| **September** | | | | | |
| 5 | A | Leicester | W | 20 | 11 |
| 12 | H | Rosslyn Park | D | 3 | 3 |
| 19 | H | Notts | W | 10 | 6 |
| 26 | A | Richmond | L | 8 | 11 |
| **October** | | | | | |
| 3 | H | Gloucester | D | 8 | 8 |
| 10 | H | London Hosp | W | 32 | 5 |
| 17 | A | Guy's Hospital | W | 12 | 9 |
| 22 | H | Cambridge Univ | W | 18 | 16 |
| 24 | A | London Scottish | L | 3 | 8 |
| 31 | H | Old Alleynians | W | 44 | 3 |
| **November** | | | | | |
| 7 | H | Edinburgh Univ | W | 14 | 9 |
| 14 | H | Old Mer Taylors | D | 3 | 3 |
| 21 | A | Northampton | L | 0 | 26 |
| 28 | H | Coventry | W | 11 | 3 |
| **December** | | | | | |
| 5 | H | Manchester | W | 23 | 0 |
| 12 | A | Coventry | D | 3 | 3 |
| 19 | A | St Mary's Hosp | W | 17 | 0 |
| 26 | H | Old Paulines | W | 52 | 8 |

| | | | | f | a |
|---|---|---|---|---|---|
| **January** | | | | | |
| 2 | H | US Portsmouth | W | 19 | 9 |
| 9 | A | Sale | L | 6 | 21 |
| 23 | H | Met Police | W | 8 | 3 |
| 30 | H | Oxford Univ | W | 3 | 0 |
| **February** | | | | | |
| 6 | H | London Welsh | L | 3 | 9 |
| 13 | A | Headingley | W | 8 | 0 |
| 20 | A | Moseley | L | 9 | 11 |
| 27 | H | Rugby | W | 16 | 11 |
| **March** | | | | | |
| 5 | H | Royal Air Force | W | 14 | 6 |
| 12 | H | Harlequins | W | 22 | 8 |
| 19 | H | Northampton | W | 13 | 8 |
| 26 | H | Blackheath | W | 13 | 5 |
| **April** | | | | | |
| 2 | H | Bristol | W | 12 | 9 |
| 7 | H | Territorial Army | W | 16 | 15 |
| 9 | H | Aldershot Services | W | 30 | 11 |
| 16 | H | Oxford RFC | W | 22 | 8 |
| 18 | H | Halifax | L | 6 | 13 |
| 23 | H | Bath | W | 14 | 3 |
| 27 | H | Leicester | W | 17 | 9 |

L R Drury scored most points, 76. B K Williams scored most tries, 18. P Jackson made most appearances, 36. Forty seven players made appearances.

M G Allison (18, 4c, 1d, 12t), R Atkins (3), P H Avery (30, 1c, 7t), L V Barber (18, 11t), J Barker (2), R G Bass (2), J M Bell (31, 15t), A M Brannan (5, 5c, 1d, 4p), B Cain (22, 4t), A D Care (1), P R Carlisle (2, 1c, 1p), R Carter (34, 4t), J Croker (2), L R Drury (19, 17c, 1d, 9p, 4t), K Duchars (4), K Evans (1), R Everdell (4), G Franklin (2), D Gee (7, 1d), H Green (2), P Jackson (36, 3t), A A Johnson (2), G A Jones (3), S Kelly (1, 1p), A J A Lewin (1), R A Lovell (26), B E McCarthy (34), P E McGovan (2,1t), M G McNay (1), D R Medd (25, 2t), B Morris (3, 3c, 1t), P A Pettigrew (9, 17c, 7p,2t), J Pretsell (15), D M Pugh (1), J L Rees (8), K Rimmer (4, 2t), D P Rogers (33, 14t), W Simpson (4), J Smith (32, 1c, 1d, 3p), P Smith (3), B Stapleton (19, 1t), C F Sykes (1), B S Taylor (1), S M Vaughan (10, 1c,1p), P Voyce (13), St L H Webb (26, 9t), B K Williams (33, 18t).

# 1960-61

Played 40, won 22, lost 16, drawn 2. F 371, A 255.

Captain: B K Williams

| | | | | f | a |
|---|---|---|---|---|---|
| **September** | | | | | |
| 3 | A | Leicester | D | 9 | 9 |
| 10 | H | Met Police | W | 17 | 6 |
| 17 | H | Notts | W | 22 | 6 |
| 24 | H | Richmond | L | 3 | 8 |
| **October** | | | | | |
| 1 | A | Gloucester | L | 6 | 11 |
| 8 | H | London Hosp | W | 20 | 5 |
| 15 | H | Guy's Hospital | W | 24 | 9 |
| 19 | A | Cambridge Univ | L | 14 | 16 |
| 22 | H | London Scottish | W | 3 | 0 |
| 29 | H | Aldershot Services | L | 0 | 3 |
| **November** | | | | | |
| 5 | H | Old Mer Taylors | L | 0 | 11 |
| 12 | H | Oxford RFC | W | 18 | 3 |
| 19 | H | Northampton | L | 5 | 14 |
| 26 | A | Coventry | L | 3 | 5 |
| **December** | | | | | |
| 3 | H | Manchester | W | 8 | 0 |
| 10 | H | Old Millhillians | W | 6 | 0 |
| 17 | H | St Mary's Hosp | W | 21 | 0 |
| 24 | H | Old Alleynians | W | 11 | 5 |
| 26 | H | Old Paulines | W | 9 | 3 |
| 27 | H | Penarth | W | 12 | 3 |
| 31 | H | Rosslyn Park | W | 8 | 0 |

| | | | | f | a |
|---|---|---|---|---|---|
| **January** | | | | | |
| 7 | A | US Portsmouth | L | 3 | 5 |
| 14 | H | Sale | W | 16 | 10 |
| 21 | H | Leicester | L | 0 | 6 |
| 28 | A | Oxford Univ | L | 0 | 3 |
| **February** | | | | | |
| 4 | A | London Welsh | L | 0 | 8 |
| 11 | H | Headingley | L | 8 | 16 |
| 18 | H | Moseley | W | 13 | 0 |
| 25 | H | Rugby | W | 11 | 0 |
| **March** | | | | | |
| 4 | H | Royal Air Force | D | 8 | 8 |
| 11 | A | Harlequins | L | 6 | 10 |
| 18 | A | Northampton | L | 6 | 21 |
| 25 | A | Blackheath | W | 11 | 0 |
| **April** | | | | | |
| 1 | H | Liverpool | W | 11 | 3 |
| 3 | H | Wakefield | W | 14 | 3 |
| 8 | A | Bristol | L | 3 | 17 |
| 15 | H | Coventry | W | 14 | 8 |
| 19 | H | Territorial Army | W | 14 | 6 |
| 22 | H | Bath | L | 5 | 6 |
| 29 | A | Birkenhead Park | W | 9 | 8 |

R Carter played in all 40 games, having achieved a maximum in 1958-9 as well. Highest try scorer was B K Williams with 16. L R Drury scored most points, 69. Forty four players turned out at least once.

B Abrahams (11, 1t), P Aldis (6), M G Allison (5, 3c, 1p), P H Avery (9), L V Barber (16, 7t), J Bardner (3, 1t), R G Bass (1, 1t), J M Bell (35, 13t), B Cain (9), P R Carlisle (6, 1t), R Carter (40, 1t), J Cook (2), R Dick-Cleland (4), L R Drury (18, 15c,10p,3t), K Duchars (13), J L Evans (24, 2t), R Everdell (1), G Franklin (1), H Green (8), M Greenhow (12, 8t), D Harries (9, 2t), P Jackson (37, 4t), G A Jones (37, 3t), R King (5), A J A Lewin (7, 2t), R A Lovell (38, 3t), J Martin (2), B E McCarthy (39, 1t), D R Medd (33, 1t), L Morgan (1), P A Pettigrew (2), K Rimmer (1), C Rogers (1), D P Rogers (26, 9t), R J Slaughter (7, 1p), G L Smart (3, 1t), J Smith (35, 9c, 6p), B Stapleton (22), P J Turner (2), S M Vaughan (8, 1p), A Walkey (1), St L H Webb (26, 4t), B K Williams (33, 1c, 1p, 16t), A J Winstanley (1).

# 1961-62

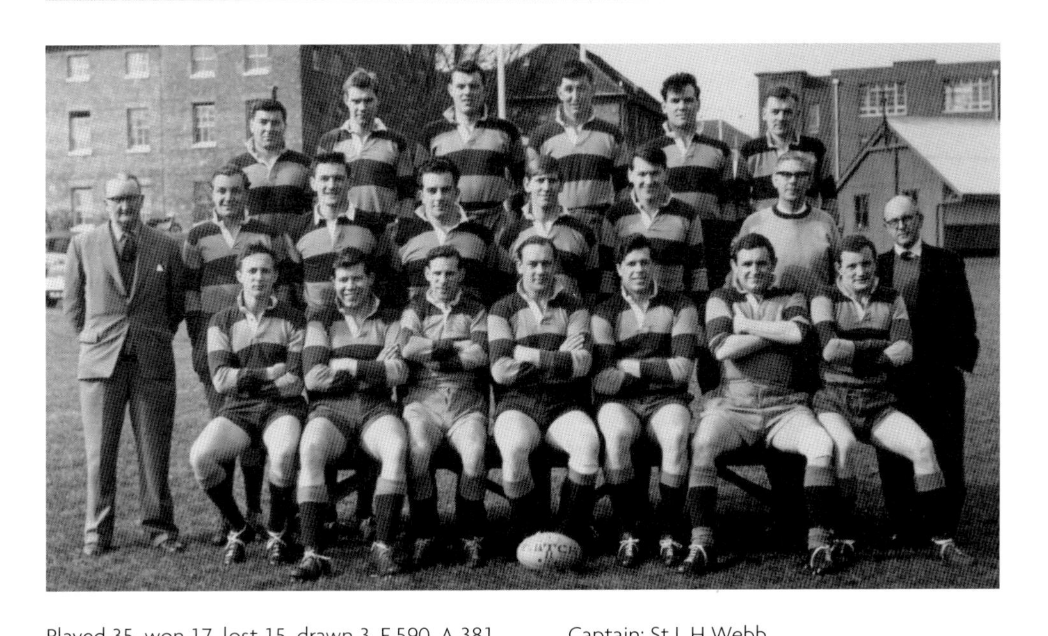

Played 35, won 17, lost 15, drawn 3. F 590, A 381.

Captain: St L H Webb

| | | | | f | a |
|---|---|---|---|---|---|
| **September** | | | | | |
| 2 | H | Leicester | W | 21 | 13 |
| 9 | H | Met Police | W | 16 | 11 |
| 16 | H | Notts | W | 35 | 3 |
| 23 | A | Richmond | L | 11 | 34 |
| 30 | H | Gloucester | L | 11 | 17 |
| **October** | | | | | |
| 7 | H | Oxford RFC | W | 51 | 0 |
| 14 | H | London Hospital | W | 53 | 3 |
| 21 | A | Guy's Hospital | W | 18 | 16 |
| 28 | A | London Scottish | L | 6 | 27 |
| **November** | | | | | |
| 4 | H | Edinburgh Univ | W | 33 | 0 |
| 9 | H | Cambridge Univ | L | 5 | 11 |
| 11 | H | Old Mer Taylors | W | 12 | 0 |
| 18 | A | Northampton | L | 3 | 31 |
| 25 | A | Coventry | L | 15 | 23 |
| **December** | | | | | |
| 2 | H | Manchester | W | 27 | 8 |
| 9 | H | Old Millhillians | W | 52 | 3 |
| 16 | H | St Mary's Hosp | L | 11 | 19 |
| 23 | H | Old Alleynians | W | 41 | 0 |

| | | | | f | a |
|---|---|---|---|---|---|
| **January** | | | | | |
| 13 | A | Sale | L | 3 | 8 |
| 20 | A | Leicester | L | 0 | 19 |
| 27 | H | Oxford Univ | D | 6 | 6 |
| **February** | | | | | |
| 3 | H | London Welsh | L | 5 | 6 |
| 10 | A | Headingley | L | 3 | 6 |
| 17 | A | Moseley | L | 3 | 11 |
| 24 | H | Rugby | W | 11 | 3 |
| **March** | | | | | |
| 3 | H | The Army | W | 11 | 5 |
| 10 | A | Harlequins | L | 9 | 14 |
| 17 | H | Northampton | L | 3 | 16 |
| 24 | H | Blackheath | W | 18 | 9 |
| 31 | H | Coventry | W | 16 | 11 |
| **April** | | | | | |
| 7 | H | Bristol | W | 20 | 9 |
| 14 | A | Bath | W | 29 | 0 |
| 21 | A | Pontypool | D | 5 | 5 |
| 23 | A | Ebbw Vale | L | 11 | 18 |
| 28 | H | Birkenhead Park | D | 16 | 16 |

L R Drury set a new club record points total of 190. B K Williams was the top try scorer with 20 and he also made most appearances, 34. Thirty nine players made at least one.

B Abrahams (31, 5t), P Aldis (22, 8t), M G Allison (2, 2t), L V Barber (20, 1d, 10t), J Bardner (4), R G Bass (1), J M Bell (11, 7t), P R Carlisle (5), R Carter (28, 2t), L R Drury (32, 59c, 18p, 6t), K Duchars (6), C Ferguson (1), G Franklin (2), H Green (5, 5c), D Harries (10, 7t), F C Inglis (16, 6t), P Jackson (16, 1t), G A Jones (1), B Keeble (10), R King (1), A J A Lewin (19, 1c, 3t), R A Lovell (30, 5t), W Mathews (19, 2t), B E McCarthy (33, 1t), D R Medd (19, 4t), M S Palmer (9, 1d), D J Perry (27, 2c, 14t) P A Pettigrew (2), P Quarry (6), M Roberts (3), C Rogers (2), D P Rogers (18, 18t), R J Slaughter (15, 3t), J Smith (31, 2d, 2t), R Smith (2), B Stapleton (7), P J Turner (2), St L H Webb (23, 4t), B K Williams (34, 20t).

# 1962-63

Played 28, won 18, lost 7, drawn 3. F 416, A 211.

Captain: D G Perry

| | | | | f | a |
|---|---|---|---|---|---|
| **September** | | | | | |
| 1 | A | Leicester | L | 13 | 18 |
| 8 | H | Met Police | W | 28 | 11 |
| 15 | H | Notts | W | 32 | 3 |
| 22 | H | Richmond | W | 19 | 8 |
| 29 | A | Gloucester | L | 13 | 17 |
| **October** | | | | | |
| 6 | H | Loughb'gh College | D | 11 | 11 |
| 13 | H | London Hospital | W | 27 | 0 |
| 20 | H | Guy's Hospital | W | 32 | 5 |
| 24 | A | Cambridge Univ | L | 3 | 18 |
| 27 | H | London Scottish | L | 0 | 22 |
| **November** | | | | | |
| 3 | H | Old Mer Taylors | W | 12 | 8 |
| 10 | A | Ebbw Vale | W | 10 | 3 |
| 17 | H | Northampton | D | 3 | 3 |
| 24 | H | Coventry | L | 3 | 6 |

| | | | | f | a |
|---|---|---|---|---|---|
| **December** | | | | | |
| 1 | H | Manchester | W | 6 | 0 |
| 15 | A | St Mary's Hospital | D | 6 | 6 |
| 22 | H | Old Alleynians | W | 11 | 5 |
| **January** | | | | | |
| 29 | H | San Isidro (Argentina) | W | 6 | 0 |
| **March** | | | | | |
| 9 | H | Harlequins | W | 6 | 3 |
| 16 | A | Northampton | W | 16 | 11 |
| 23 | A | Blackheath | L | 5 | 8 |
| 30 | H | Oxford RFC | W | 25 | 3 |
| **April** | | | | | |
| 6 | A | Bristol | W | 11 | 8 |
| 13 | H | Bradford | W | 39 | 0 |
| 15 | H | Huddersfield | W | 25 | 6 |
| 20 | A | Coventry | L | 3 | 11 |
| 25 | H | Territorial Army | W | 42 | 14 |
| 27 | H | Bath | W | 9 | 3 |

B K Williams again scored most tries, 17. D Coley was the leading points scorer with 116. Thirty nine players made appearances. J Smith played in all 28 games.

B Abrahams (14, 1t), P Aldis (2, 1t), L V Barber (1), F R Booth (9), J Bridges (16, 3t), B Bridgman (1), P D Briggs (1), M Buck (5), B Cain (1), P R Carlisle (1), R Carter (2), D Coley (24, 31c, 13p, 5t), J Cooley (21, 1d, 5t), W R Dalzell (2), L R Drury (26, 1c, 6p, 4t), J French (1), H Green (1), D Harries (5, 1t), R Hewitt (3, 1t), F C Inglis (27, 12t), P Jackson (2), A J A Lewin (16, 8t), M Lord (7, 8c, 1d, 1p, 2t), R A Lovell (26, 2t), W Matthews (26, 4t), B E McCarthy (27, 2t), W Murray (1), D G Perry (17, 5t), D P Rogers (12, 4t), R J Slaughter (22, 5t), J Smith (28, 2d, 1t), R Smith (2), D P Southgate (1), B Stapleton (3), L Tatham (16, 1t), B W Warren (2), St L H Webb (21, 4t), G Wheeler (1), B K Williams (27, 17t).

# 1963-64

Played 38, won 26, lost 11, drawn 1. F 622, A 333.

Captain: D P Rogers

| September | | | | f | a |
|---|---|---|---|---|---|
| 7 | A | Leicester | L | 0 | 9 |
| 14 | H | London Irish | W | 41 | 9 |
| 18 | H | Civil Serv | W | 16 | 5 |
| 21 | H | Notts | W | 19 | 3 |
| 25 | H | Met Police | D | 8 | 8 |
| 28 | A | Richmond | W | 20 | 3 |
| **October** | | | | | |
| 5 | H | Gloucester | L | 6 | 14 |
| 12 | H | London Hospital | W | 53 | 14 |
| 19 | H | Guy's Hospital | W | 23 | 11 |
| 24 | H | Cambridge Univ | L | 12 | 17 |
| 26 | A | London Scottish | L | 3 | 19 |
| **November** | | | | | |
| 2 | H | Old Mer Taylors | W | 6 | 3 |
| 9 | H | Edinburgh Univ | W | 33 | 3 |
| 16 | A | Northampton | W | 19 | 14 |
| 23 | A | Coventry | L | 11 | 27 |
| 30 | H | Old Alleynians | W | 14 | 0 |
| **December** | | | | | |
| 7 | A | Manchester | L | 0 | 14 |
| 14 | H | Old Millhillians | W | 42 | 0 |
| 26 | H | Old Paulines | W | 32 | 2 |
| 28 | A | Rosslyn Park | L | 6 | 18 |

| January | | | | f | a |
|---|---|---|---|---|---|
| 4 | H | Bristol | W | 21 | 12 |
| 11 | A | Sale | L | 11 | 13 |
| 25 | H | Oxford Univ | W | 24 | 5 |
| **February** | | | | | |
| 1 | H | London Welsh | L | 6 | 14 |
| 8 | A | Headingley | W | 14 | 9 |
| 15 | H | Rugby | W | 12 | 11 |
| 22 | H | Ebbw Vale | W | 5 | 3 |
| 29 | A | Moseley | W | 11 | 9 |
| **March** | | | | | |
| 7 | H | Royal Navy | W | 9 | 6 |
| 14 | A | Harlequins | W | 9 | 6 |
| 21 | H | Northampton | W | 21 | 6 |
| 30 | H | Glasgow HSFP | W | 8 | 5 |
| **April** | | | | | |
| 4 | A | Wasps | L | 0 | 6 |
| 11 | H | Blackheath | W | 24 | 6 |
| 18 | H | Coventry | W | 18 | 11 |
| 22 | H | Territorial Army | W | 45 | 6 |
| 25 | A | Bath | L | 9 | 4 |
| 29 | H | Leicester | W | 11 | 8 |

D Coley was the leading scorer with 163 points. D P Rogers scored most tries, 16. Forty two players made appearances. R A Lovell played in all 38 games.

J Bardner (8, 6t), P D Briggs (10, 4c), J Bridges (33, 5t), B Bridgman (9, 3t), J Bryant (3), M Buck (6, 1t), P R Carlisle (4, 4c, 1p), G Carter (4), R Castle (2, 1t), D Coley (35, 41c, 20p, 7t), J Cooley (21, 6t), I Cox (7, 1t), W R Dalzell (9), A Doherty (6, 1t), L R Drury (32, 9c, 4p, 9t), R Fennemore (4), G Franklin (1), J French (1), H Green (4, 1t), R Hewitt (5,1t), F C Inglis (15, 7t), M Jenner (1), A J A Lewin (22, 5t), M Lord (25, 1c, 1p, 11t), R A Lovell (38 3t), W Matthews (33, 3c, 13t), B E McCarthy (37), R Pengelly (1), D G Perry (23, 6t), N J Philbrook (1, 1t), P Roberts (2), C Rogers (4), D P Rogers (29, 1d, 16t, 51pts), R J Slaughter (15, 3t), P H Spray (3, 1t), J Smith (36, 1d, 2t), B Stapleton (1), L Tatham (14, 4d), B W Warren (5), St L H Webb (27, 8t), G Wheeler (5, 2t), B K Williams (29, 14t).

# 1964-65

Played 37, won 18, lost 17, drawn 2. F 499, A 440.

Captain: D P Rogers

| | | | | f | a |
|---|---|---|---|---|---|
| **September** | | | | | |
| 5 | A | Leicester | L | 6 | 9 |
| 12 | A | London Irish | D | 17 | 17 |
| 19 | H | Notts | L | 14 | 17 |
| 26 | H | Richmond | L | 5 | 23 |
| **October** | | | | | |
| 3 | A | Gloucester | L | 9 | 19 |
| 10 | H | Penarth | W | 23 | 3 |
| 17 | H | Guy's Hospital | W | 27 | 3 |
| 21 | A | Cambridge Univ | L | 6 | 17 |
| 27 | H | London Scottish | L | 9 | 13 |
| | A | Old Mer Taylors | W | 32 | 6 |
| **November** | | | | | |
| 7 | H | Rosslyn Park | W | 14 | 6 |
| 14 | A | Ebbw Vale | W | 13 | 6 |
| 21 | H | Northampton | L | 9 | 27 |
| 28 | H | Coventry | D | 3 | 3 |
| **December** | | | | | |
| 5 | H | Manchester | W | 33 | 0 |
| 12 | H | Met Police | L | 9 | 19 |
| 19 | H | St Mary's Hospital | W | 19 | 5 |
| 26 | H | Old Paulines | W | 8 | 3 |

| | | | | f | a |
|---|---|---|---|---|---|
| **January** | | | | | |
| 2 | A | Bristol | L | 3 | 18 |
| 9 | H | Sale | W | 15 | 9 |
| 16 | H | Leicester | L | 3 | 22 |
| 23 | H | Old Millhillians | W | 11 | 6 |
| **February** | | | | | |
| 6 | A | London Welsh | L | 5 | 20 |
| 13 | H | Headingley | W | 17 | 5 |
| 17 | H | Royal Air Force | W | 33 | 16 |
| 20 | H | Moseley | W | 25 | 6 |
| 27 | H | Rugby | L | 9 | 11 |
| **March** | | | | | |
| 6 | H | The Army | W | 29 | 11 |
| 13 | H | Harlequins | L | 16 | 26 |
| 19 | A | Northampton | L | 6 | 15 |
| 27 | A | Blackheath | L | 13 | 24 |
| **April** | | | | | |
| 3 | H | Wasps | W | 6 | 0 |
| 10 | H | Pontypool | W | 16 | 8 |
| 13 | A | Coventry | L | 3 | 20 |
| 17 | H | Saracens | L | 6 | 15 |
| 19 | H | Old Alleynians | W | 8 | 6 |
| 24 | H | Bath | W | 19 | 6 |

B K Williams was the leading try scorer with 24, and D Coley, leading points scorer with 80. Forty eight players made appearances. Again, R A Lovell played in every match.

B Abrahams (3), J Bardner (27, 3t), J Betterley (1), J Bridges (18, 5t), B Bridgman (1), M Bridgman (1), P D Briggs (28, 5c, 7d, 2p, 4t), M Buck (11, 1c, 1t), R Butt (2, 1t), P R Carlisle (2), G Carter (4), M Coley (7, 1t), D Coley (28, 16c, 13p, 3t), J G Cook (8), I Cox (10), A Doherty (6, 1t), L R Drury (8, 1t), A R G Else (18, 1t), R Fennemore (4, 1t), R Fletcher (16, 11t), G P Frankcom (10, 1d, 8t), G Franklin (8), W D Hale (11, 1t), R F Hewitt (5, 2t), C F W Higham (23), J R S Higham (3), F C Inglis (4, 2t), A J A Lewin (18, 2t), G Lilley (3), M Lord (20, 14c, 1d, 5p, 2t), R A Lovell (37, 3t), B E McCarthy (6), M Murray (1), D G Perry (18, 7t), N J Philbrook (16, 5c, 6p, 3t), K W Phillips (1), C Rogers (3), D P Rogers (24, 5t), R J Slaughter (20, 5t), J Smith (36, 2d, 2t), D J Small (6, 1t), P H Spray (2), B Stapleton (1), B W Warren (21, 1t), St L H Webb (13, 1t), G Wheeler (4), M Woodward (3), B K Williams (35, 24t).

# 1965-66

Played 35, won 19, lost 16. F 393, A 360.

Captain: D G Perry

| | | | | f | a |
|---|---|---|---|---|---|
| **September** | | | | | |
| 4 | H | Leicester | W | 11 | 6 |
| 11 | H | London Irish | W | 11 | 3 |
| 18 | H | Notts | W | 27 | 19 |
| 25 | A | Richmond | L | 6 | 30 |
| **October** | | | | | |
| 2 | H | Gloucester | L | 8 | 11 |
| 9 | A | Pontypool | W | 10 | 6 |
| 16 | H | Guy's Hospital | W | 25 | 13 |
| 21 | H | Cambridge Univ | W | 18 | 9 |
| 23 | A | London Scottish | L | 9 | 11 |
| 30 | H | Oxford RFC | W | 16 | 3 |
| **November** | | | | | |
| 6 | H | Edinburgh Univ | W | 17 | 6 |
| 13 | H | Old Mer Taylors | W | 33 | 3 |
| 20 | A | Northampton | W | 8 | 0 |
| 27 | A | Coventry | L | 8 | 11 |
| **December** | | | | | |
| 4 | H | Met Police | W | 3 | 0 |
| 11 | H | Old Alleynians | W | 43 | 0 |
| 18 | A | Rosslyn Park | L | 3 | 8 |
| **January** | | | | | |
| 1 | H | Bristol | L | 0 | 14 |
| 8 | A | Sale | W | 9 | 3 |
| 29 | H | Oxford Univ | W | 20 | 8 |
| **February** | | | | | |
| 5 | H | London Welsh | L | 3 | 11 |
| 12 | A | Headingley | W | 9 | 0 |
| 17 | A | Leicester | L | 5 | 9 |
| 19 | H | Moseley | L | 6 | 16 |
| 26 | H | Rugby | L | 11 | 19 |
| **March** | | | | | |
| 5 | H | Royal Navy | L | 11 | 21 |
| 12 | A | Harlequins | L | 6 | 12 |
| 26 | A | Blackheath | L | 6 | 13 |
| **April** | | | | | |
| 2 | A | Wasps | W | 11 | 9 |
| 9 | H | Manchester | L | 3 | 6 |
| 11 | H | Wakefield | W | 5 | 3 |
| 16 | H | Coventry | L | 5 | 15 |
| 23 | H | Ebbw Vale | W | 14 | 3 |
| 27 | H | Northampton | W | 10 | 8 |
| 30 | A | Bath | L | 3 | 51 |

P D Briggs was the leading points scorer with 130. N J Philbrook scored most tries, 15. Forty four players made appearances. M Buck played in all 35 games.

J D Bardner (15), J Betterley (4, 1t), P D Briggs (25, 29c, 6d, 13p, 5t), M Buck (35, 1t), R Butt (5), P R Carlisle (2), M Coley (4), D Coley (4), M Cosby (3), I Cox (6, 1t), A Doherty (7, 1t), L R Drury (10, 2c, 1p, 7pts), A R G Else (23), R Fletcher (19, 1t), G P Frankcom (19, 7t), G Franklin (13), R D Hearn (12, 13t), R Hewitt (1), C F W Higham (22), J R S Higham (11), M Keenan (1), A Kerr (9), A J A Lewin (16, 3t), M Lord (2, 2p), R A Lovell (30), M Marson (9, 1t), B Mulhall (11, 1t), P S Onyett (2), D G Perry (16, 5t), N J Philbrook (27, 5c, 1d, 3p,15t), K W Phillips (5), J D Poustie (5), C Rogers (1, 1t), D P Rogers (20, 5t), R J Slaughter (27, 4t), J Smith (31, 1d, 1t), J Strong (3), P Taylor (1), W Tierney (4), B W Warren (28), L E Weston (1, 1t), G Wheeler (7), M Woodward (4), B K Williams (26, 12t).

# 1966-67

Played 40, won 23, lost 16, drawn 1. F 417, A 343.

Captain: D P Rogers

| September | | | | f | a |
|---|---|---|---|---|---|
| 3 | A | Leicester | L | 3 | 14 |
| 8 | H | Northampton | L | 0 | 6 |
| 10 | A | London Irish | W | 11 | 3 |
| 17 | H | Notts | W | 24 | 0 |
| 24 | H | Richmond | W | 17 | 8 |
| **October** | | | | | |
| 1 | A | Gloucester | L | 3 | 9 |
| 8 | H | Pontypool | L | 6 | 12 |
| 15 | A | Guy's Hospital | L | 6 | 9 |
| 19 | A | Cambridge Univ | L | 3 | 6 |
| 22 | H | London Scottish | L | 11 | 19 |
| 29 | H | Oxford RFC | W | 16 | 6 |
| **November** | | | | | |
| 5 | H | Oxford Univ | W | 6 | 5 |
| 12 | H | Met Police | L | 8 | 14 |
| 19 | H | Northampton | W | 9 | 0 |
| 26 | A | Coventry | L | 9 | 30 |
| **December** | | | | | |
| 3 | H | Manchester | W | 11 | 0 |
| 17 | A | St Mary's Hosp | W | 27 | 6 |
| 24 | H | Old Alleynians | W | 26 | 3 |
| 26 | H | Old Paulines | W | 21 | 12 |
| 27 | H | Penarth | W | 8 | 6 |
| 31 | H | Rosslyn Park | D | 5 | 5 |

| January | | | | f | a |
|---|---|---|---|---|---|
| 7 | A | Bristol | L | 3 | 15 |
| 14 | H | Sale | W | 10 | 5 |
| 21 | H | Leicester | W | 14 | 9 |
| 28 | A | Oxford Univ | W | 14 | 0 |
| **February** | | | | | |
| 4 | A | London Welsh | W | 5 | 3 |
| 11 | H | Headingley | L | 3 | 18 |
| 18 | A | Moseley | L | 3 | 6 |
| 25 | H | Rugby | W | 11 | 8 |
| **March** | | | | | |
| 4 | H | Royal Air Force | W | 8 | 6 |
| 11 | H | Harlequins | L | 11 | 17 |
| 25 | A | Percy Park | W | 19 | 8 |
| 27 | A | Gosforth | W | 17 | 0 |
| **April** | | | | | |
| 1 | H | Wasps | W | 24 | 0 |
| 5 | H | D Rosario (Argentina) | W | 14 | 12 |
| 8 | H | Blackheath | W | 6 | 3 |
| 15 | H | Coventry | L | 8 | 17 |
| 22 | A | Ebbw Vale | L | 3 | 16 |
| 27 | A | Northampton | L | 5 | 21 |
| 29 | H | Bath | W | 9 | 6 |

N J Philbrook scored most points and most tries, 178 and 21. He, with F N Barker and R J Slaughter, also played in most matches, 38. Forty four players made appearances.

B L Arthur (17, 1t), J D Bardner (2), F N Barker (38, 2t), R E Barker (4), J M Bell (1), J C Bicknell (23), N R Boult (36, 6t), P D Briggs (30, 4c, 6d, 3p, 1t), M Buck (19), R Butt (1), D Coley (4, 1p), M Coley (6, 1t), M Cosby (15), I Cox (1, 1t), J Dalzell (1), G Davies (3, 1d), L R Drury (16, 9c, 4p, 3t), A R G Else (29), J Feek (3), R Fletcher (18, 7t), G P Frankcom (30, 1d, 9t, 30pts), W D Hale (10), R D Hearn (15, 8t), R A Lovell (5), M Marson (11, 1t), B Mulhall (2), P S Onyett (14), D O'Regan (12, 1t), J J Page (3, 1t), J Parker (2), N J Philbrook (38, 26c, 21p, 21t), D P Rogers (26, 1t), O Saunders (1), R J Slaughter (38, 3t), J Smith (33), R Smith (10, 1t), P Taylor (9), W Tierney (12, 2t), B W Warren (25), L E Weston (14, 2t), G Whitaker (1), G Wheeler (17, 3t), S H Wilcock (1), B K Williams (3, 1t).

# 1967-68

Played 39, won 24, lost 12, drawn 3. F 658, A 442.

Captain: R J Slaughter

| September | | | | f | a |
|---|---|---|---|---|---|
| 2 | H | Leicester | L | 8 | 24 |
| 9 | H | London Irish | W | 8 | 3 |
| 16 | H | Notts | W | 25 | 3 |
| 23 | A | Richmond | L | 3 | 29 |
| 30 | H | Gloucester | L | 5 | 18 |
| **October** | | | | | |
| 4 | H | Belgrano (Argentina) | W | 22 | 15 |
| 7 | A | Pontypool | L | 13 | 14 |
| 14 | H | Gosforth | W | 14 | 11 |
| 21 | H | Guy's Hospital | L | 0 | 8 |
| 25 | H | Cambridge Univ | W | 23 | 14 |
| 28 | A | London Scottish | L | 8 | 11 |
| **November** | | | | | |
| 4 | H | Edinburgh Univ | L | 8 | 20 |
| 11 | H | Old Mer Taylors | W | 18 | 6 |
| 18 | A | Northampton | L | 3 | 6 |
| 25 | A | Coventry | L | 12 | 27 |
| **December** | | | | | |
| 2 | H | Manchester | W | 34 | 0 |
| 16 | H | St Mary's Hosp | W | 47 | 3 |
| 23 | H | Old Alleynians | W | 66 | 9 |
| 26 | H | Old Paulines | W | 21 | 6 |
| 27 | H | Penarth | W | 25 | 6 |
| 30 | A | Rosslyn Park | L | 11 | 16 |

| January | | | | f | a |
|---|---|---|---|---|---|
| 4 | H | Royal Air Force | W | 16 | 3 |
| 6 | H | Bristol | W | 17 | 8 |
| 19 | A | Leicester | D | 3 | 3 |
| 27 | H | Oxford Univ | W | 19 | 11 |
| **February** | | | | | |
| 3 | H | London Welsh | W | 9 | 8 |
| 10 | A | Headingley | D | 14 | 14 |
| 17 | H | Moseley | W | 14 | 12 |
| 24 | A | Rugby | W | 19 | 17 |
| **March** | | | | | |
| 2 | H | The Army | W | 22 | 8 |
| 9 | A | Harlequins | L | 9 | 21 |
| 16 | H | Ebbw Vale | W | 28 | 11 |
| 23 | H | Blackheath | W | 28 | 11 |
| 30 | H | Northampton | D | 5 | 5 |
| **April** | | | | | |
| 6 | A | Wasps | W | 8 | 6 |
| 13 | H | Fylde | W | 31 | 9 |
| 15 | H | Glasgow HSFP | W | 20 | 6 |
| 20 | H | Coventry | L | 13 | 27 |
| 27 | A | Bath | W | 9 | 3 |

N J Philbrook set a new record points total of 217. He became the first Bedford player to pass 200 in one season. He was also the leading try scorer, with 19. Forty seven players made appearances. F N Barker and N R Boult both made 37.

B L Arthur (33, 5t), J D Bardner (4), F N Barker (37, 4t), R E Barker (7, 2t), J M Baron (2), J C Bicknell (22, 1t), P D Briggs (32, 7c, 2d, 2p, 7t), N R Boult (37, 13t), B M Byrne (7, 1t), P R Carlisle (1), M Cosby (25), J Dalzell (2), G Davies (12, 2d, 2t), S Dawkins (2), A Doherty (26, 12t), L R Drury (1, 1t), B Eccles (4, 3t), A R G Else (22), J M Farrow (8), R Fletcher (4), P B Glover (14, 1d, 8t), P J Green (5, 1t), R Hewitt (1), A E Landon (25, 6t), P Langford (9, 2t), G D Lilley (3, 1t), M Lord (3, 1t), M D Nurton (20, 14c, 2d, 13p, 1t), P S Onyett (13, 1t), D O'Regan (5, 1t), J J Page (8, 1c, 1d, 1p, 2t), L V Palmer (7, 1t), J Parker (2), M Parry-Jones (25, 5t), N J Philbrook (36, 38c, 28p, 19t), K W Phillips (1), D P Rogers (21, 7t), R J Slaughter (34, 8t), W R Slee (14), D J Small (21, 9t), J Smith (9, 2c), R Smith (3), G Tier (1, 1t), W Tierney (2), J Walmsley (12), L E Weston (1), G Wheeler (3).

# 1968-69

Played 34, won 21, lost 9, drawn 4. F 563, A 371.

| | | | | f | a |
|---|---|---|---|---|---|
| **September** | | | | | |
| 7 | A | Leicester | L | 15 | 16 |
| 14 | A | London Irish | W | 18 | 11 |
| 18 | H | Wasps | W | 9 | 5 |
| 21 | H | Notts | W | 37 | 6 |
| 28 | H | Richmond | L | 3 | 16 |
| **October** | | | | | |
| 5 | A | Gloucester | W | 22 | 21 |
| 12 | H | Pontypool | W | 20 | 9 |
| 19 | A | Guy's Hospital | W | 20 | 15 |
| 23 | A | Cambridge Univ | L | 5 | 19 |
| 26 | H | London Scottish | W | 19 | 6 |
| **November** | | | | | |
| 2 | H | Old Mer Taylors | W | 24 | 9 |
| 9 | A | Gosforth | W | 17 | 9 |
| 16 | A | Northampton | L | 11 | 14 |
| 23 | H | Coventry | W | 17 | 5 |
| 30 | H | Old Alleynians | W | 21 | 0 |
| **December** | | | | | |
| 7 | H | Manchester | W | 15 | 6 |
| 21 | A | St Mary's Hosp | W | 26 | 9 |
| 26 | H | Old Paulines | W | 34 | 0 |

Captain: R J Slaughter

| | | | | f | a |
|---|---|---|---|---|---|
| **January** | | | | | |
| 4 | A | Bristol | L | 6 | 13 |
| 11 | H | Sale | W | 14 | 5 |
| 25 | A | Oxford Univ | D | 14 | 14 |
| **February** | | | | | |
| 1 | A | London Welsh | L | 14 | 31 |
| 13 | H | Royal Air Force | W | 9 | 6 |
| **March** | | | | | |
| 1 | H | Royal Navy | W | 12 | 9 |
| 4 | H | C Uni De Buenos Aires | W | 12 | 3 |
| 8 | H | Harlequins | D | 6 | 6 |
| 14 | A | Moseley | L | 3 | 25 |
| 22 | A | Blackheath | L | 11 | 25 |
| 29 | H | Northampton | L | 9 | 13 |
| **April** | | | | | |
| 5 | H | Percy Park | W | 15 | 11 |
| 7 | H | Huddersfield | W | 52 | 0 |
| 12 | A | Ebbw Vale | D | 11 | 11 |
| 19 | A | Coventry | D | 11 | 11 |
| 26 | H | Bath | W | 31 | 12 |

M D Nurton was the highest scorer with 125 points. N R Boult scored most tries, 18. Thirty six players made appearances. A R G Else played 33 times.

B L Arthur (18, 5t), F N Barker (32, 6t), R E Barker (23, 2t), J C Bicknell (11, 1c, 1t), N R Boult (30, 18t), P D Briggs (27, 13c, 4d, 12p), R Butt (5), H Childs (5), M Cosby (28, 2t), N Cowley (1), J Dalzell (2), G Davies (28, 6c, 3p, 10t), A R G Else (33, 1t), R Fletcher (8, 2t), P J Green (31, 14t), D Hart (3, 1t), R Hewitt (5, 2t), A E Landon (16, 6t), G D Lilley (4, 1t), M Lord (4, 1p, 1t), J J Page (14, 3d, 2p, 2t), R Mann (2, 1t), R J McLean (3), M D Nurton (26, 22c, 1d, 23p, 3t), P S Onyett (21, 1t), J Parker (2), D P Rogers (19, 6t), J Rosenthal (8), R J Slaughter (31, 9t), D J Small (21, 4t), R Smith (20, 2t), P Taylor (8, 1p). W Tierney (8, 5t), A K Towersey (4,1c, 3t), R M Wilkinson (3), G Wheeler (6, 1t).

# 1969-70

Played 35, won 28, lost 6, drawn 1. F 637, A 287.

Captain: P D Briggs

| | | | | f | a |
|---|---|---|---|---|---|
| **September** | | | | | |
| 6 | H | Leicester | W | 39 | 5 |
| 13 | H | London Irish | W | 40 | 6 |
| 20 | H | Notts | W | 12 | 5 |
| 27 | A | Richmond | W | 27 | 14 |
| **October** | | | | | |
| 4 | H | Gloucester | W | 17 | 8 |
| 11 | A | Pontypool | W | 12 | 9 |
| 18 | H | Ebbw Vale | W | 17 | 16 |
| 22 | H | Cambridge Univ | D | 17 | 17 |
| 25 | A | London Scottish | W | 17 | 9 |
| **November** | | | | | |
| 1 | H | Edinburgh Univ | W | 41 | 6 |
| 8 | H | Guy's Hospital | W | 22 | 6 |
| 15 | H | Northampton | W | 23 | 6 |
| 22 | A | Coventry | L | 9 | 22 |
| 29 | H | Gosforth | W | 3 | 0 |
| **December** | | | | | |
| 6 | H | Manchester | W | 6 | 3 |
| 13 | A | Saracens | L | 3 | 14 |
| 20 | H | St Mary's Hosp | W | 29 | 0 |
| 26 | H | Old Paulines | W | 42 | 8 |
| 27 | A | Rosslyn Park | L | 6 | 9 |

| | | | | f | a |
|---|---|---|---|---|---|
| **January** | | | | | |
| 3 | H | Bristol | W | 17 | 16 |
| 10 | A | Sale | W | 9 | 3 |
| 17 | A | Leicester | L | 5 | 6 |
| 23 | A | Northampton | W | 16 | 11 |
| 31 | H | Oxford Univ | W | 19 | 0 |
| **February** | | | | | |
| 7 | H | London Welsh | W | 11 | 3 |
| 21 | H | Moseley | W | 17 | 8 |
| 28 | H | Rugby | W | 40 | 0 |
| **March** | | | | | |
| 14 | A | Harlequins | W | 11 | 8 |
| 28 | A | Fylde | W | 14 | 6 |
| 30 | A | Waterloo | W | 13 | 11 |
| **April** | | | | | |
| 4 | A | Wasps | W | 12 | 0 |
| 11 | H | Blackheath | W | 48 | 14 |
| 18 | H | Coventry | W | 9 | 6 |
| 25 | A | Bath | L | 6 | 20 |
| 28 | A | Northampton | L | 8 | 12 |

B Page set a new points record for a season with 229. J P Janion was the leading try scorer with 21. P D Briggs and C R Landon made most appearances, 33. Thirty six players turned out at least once.

B L Arthur (28, 5t), F N Barker (28, 6t), R E Barker (27, 1t), N R Boult (28, 14t), P D Briggs (33, 1d, 3t), I Bullerwell (1, 1t), R Butt (3), H Childs (3, 2t), M Cosby (10), G Davies (2, 1t), A R G Else (30, 3t), P J Green (19, 13t), D Hart (29), J Humphreys (1), J P Janion (29, 21t), P D' A Keith-Roach (1), A E Landon (7), C R Landon (33, 3t), M Lord (2), M D Nurton (6, 15c, 11p, 2t), P S Onyett (28, 5t), B Page (29, 41c, 4d, 44p, 1t), J J Page (19, 4t), J Parker (5), N J Philbrook (9, 7t), G R Redmond (1), D P Rogers (25, 4t), J Rosenthal (1), C Scott (1), R J Slaughter (15, 4t), D J Small (32, 6t), R Smith (17, 1t), R I Thomas (13, 5t), A K Towersey (2, 2t), R Westley (2, 1d), R M Wilkinson (8).

# 1970-71

Played 35, won 28, lost 7. F 596, A 331.

Captain: P D Briggs

| | | | | f | a |
|---|---|---|---|---|---|
| **September** | | | | | |
| 5 | A | Leicester | L | 5 | 14 |
| 12 | A | London Irish | L | 3 | 15 |
| 15 | H | Bosuns | W | 11 | 3 |
| 19 | H | Notts | W | 18 | 11 |
| 26 | H | Richmond | W | 30 | 6 |
| **October** | | | | | |
| 3 | A | Gloucester | W | 21 | 11 |
| 10 | H | Pontypool | W | 40 | 0 |
| 17 | A | Ebbw Vale | W | 19 | 8 |
| 24 | H | London Scottish | W | 17 | 5 |
| 31 | A | Gosforth | W | 9 | 3 |
| **November** | | | | | |
| 7 | H | Old Mer Taylors | W | 40 | 11 |
| 14 | A | Guy's Hospital | W | 18 | 9 |
| 21 | A | Northampton | L | 3 | 27 |
| 28 | H | Coventry | W | 9 | 5 |
| **December** | | | | | |
| 5 | A | Manchester | W | 37 | 3 |
| 12 | H | Saracens | W | 17 | 6 |
| 19 | A | Moseley | W | 25 | 17 |

| | | | | f | a |
|---|---|---|---|---|---|
| **January** | | | | | |
| 9 | H | Sale | W | 22 | 6 |
| 15 | A | Neath | L | 11 | 20 |
| 23 | A | Oxford Univ | W | 32 | 6 |
| 30 | H | Northampton | W | 11 | 8 |
| **February** | | | | | |
| 6 | A | London Welsh | L | 3 | 29 |
| 13 | H | Headingley | L | 12 | 17 |
| 20 | H | Cambridge Univ | W | 21 | 6 |
| 27 | A | Rugby | W | 6 | 3 |
| **March** | | | | | |
| 6 | H | Royal Air Force | W | 17 | 6 |
| 13 | H | Harlequins | L | 17 | 19 |
| 20 | H | Comb Birmingham OBs | W | 27 | 3 |
| 27 | A | Blackheath | W | 8 | 6 |
| **April** | | | | | |
| 3 | H | Wasps | W | 17 | 3 |
| 10 | H | Huddersfield | W | 18 | 3 |
| 12 | H | Rosslyn Park | W | 17 | 12 |
| 17 | A | Coventry | W | 12 | 11 |
| 24 | H | Bath | W | 11 | 8 |
| 28 | H | Leicester | W | 12 | 11 |

B Page was leading points scorer with 216. N R Boult scored most tries, 17. P S Onyett made most appearances, 33. Thirty eight players turned out for the first team.

B L Arthur (20, 1t), C Barber (8, 1t), F N Barker (31, 1t), R E Barker (14), N R Boult (32, 17t), P D Briggs (29, 7d), R Butt (2), R Coad (1), A Davies (9, 4t), G Davies (3), M Douch (14, 5t), A R G Else (25, 3t), M D Fitzgerald (1), P J Green (25, 10t), D Hart (28, 4t), J P Janion (23, 12t), A E Landon (17, 2t), R C Landon (19, 2t), P Langford (5, 1t), V J Lewis (23, 3t), J T Mawle (2), B Mead (4), M Nurton (7, 16c, 1d, 8p), P S Onyett (33, 5t), B Page (28, 33c, 2d, 46p, 2t), J J Page (10, 1d, 1t), J Parker (1), J Richardson (3), A K Rodgers (17), D P Rogers (26, 7t), M Shirley (3, 1t), R J Slaughter (21, 4t), D J Small (1), R Smith (2), W C C Steele (16, 10t), R I Thomas (6), A K Towersey (7, 1d, 3t), R M Wilkinson (9).

# 1971-72

Played 39, won 29, lost 9, drawn 1. F 853 A 414

Captain: P D Briggs

| | | | | f | a |
|---|---|---|---|---|---|
| **September** | | | | | |
| 4 | H | Leicester | W | 35 | 16 |
| 11 | H | London Irish | W | 31 | 3 |
| 15 | A | Wasps | L | 20 | 22 |
| 18 | H | Notts | L | 3 | 6 |
| 25 | A | Richmond | W | 24 | 16 |
| **October** | | | | | |
| 2 | H | Gloucester | L | 3 | 16 |
| 9 | A | Pontypool | D | 25 | 25 |
| 16 | A | Cambridge Univ | W | 11 | 3 |
| 17 | A | Rugby * | W | 17 | 12 |
| 23 | A | London Scottish | L | 12 | 15 |
| 30 | H | Gosforth | W | 34 | 12 |
| **November** | | | | | |
| 6 | H | Waterloo | W | 28 | 4 |
| 13 | H | Edinburgh Univ | W | 64 | 0 |
| 20 | H | Northampton | W | 12 | 9 |
| 27 | A | Coventry | W | 15 | 11 |
| **December** | | | | | |
| 4 | H | Manchester | W | 35 | 9 |
| 11 | A | Saracens | L | 10 | 22 |
| 18 | H | Moseley | W | 24 | 13 |
| 27 | H | Old Paulines | W | 50 | 6 |
| **January** | | | | | |
| 1 | H | Bristol | W | 18 | 9 |
| 8 | A | Sale | W | 21 | 7 |
| 16 | A | Leicester | W | 19 | 10 |
| 22 | H | Oxford Univ | W | 74 | 0 |
| 25 | A | Moseley * | L | 9 | 16 |
| 29 | A | Northampton | L | 6 | 10 |
| **February** | | | | | |
| 5 | H | London Welsh | L | 3 | 9 |
| 12 | A | Headingley | W | 10 | 4 |
| 19 | H | London Scottish | W | 24 | 10 |
| 26 | H | Rugby | W | 23 | 7 |
| **March** | | | | | |
| 4 | H | Royal Air Force | W | 17 | 15 |
| 11 | H | Fylde | W | 16 | 0 |
| 19 | H | San Isidro (Argentina) | W | 18 | 15 |
| 25 | A | Exeter | W | 29 | 14 |
| **April** | | | | | |
| 1 | H | Ebbw Vale | W | 23 | 20 |
| 3 | A | Rosslyn Park | W | 28 | 20 |
| 8 | H | Blackheath | W | 19 | 13 |
| 15 | H | Coventry | L | 7 | 11 |
| 22 | H | Percy Park | W | 26 | 0 |
| 29 | A | Bath | W | 10 | 4 |

* RFU Club Competition.

B Page set a new points scoring record for a season of 296 and the team total of 853 was a record as well. Twenty nine wins in a season was another record. A try was increased in value to four points from three in 1971-72 and P J Green scored most, 19. Forty one players made appearances, V J Lewis making most, 38. The RFU Club Competition was introduced.

B L Arthur (9), F N Barker (35, 1t), R E Barrett (19, 7t), G Bird (1), N R Boult (30, 11t), P D Briggs (17, 2t), R Butt (1), G Davies (16, 12d, 2t), M Douch (4, 4t), A R G Else (8), M D Fitzgerald (15), P J Green (29, 19t), T Harry (7, 1t), D Hart (25, 6t), A J Hollins (7), C Hooker (3), D Jackson (37, 10t), J P Janion (16, 13t), A E Landon (29, 1c, 3t), R C Landon (2, 2t), P Langford (6), V J Lewis (38, 3t), R A Lovell (1), M Manning (2), J T Mawle (23), I McLaren (1, 4c), P S Onyett (27, 1t), B Page (36, 65c, 50p, 4t), J Parker (1), J Richardson (3), P Roberts (3, 1c, 1p), A K Rodgers (2), D P Rogers (26, 8t), R J Slaughter (34, 10t), D J Small (35, 5t), R Smith (1), W C C Steele (8, 4t), R Thomas (5, 1t), A K Towersey (12, 7t), B Waite (2, 2t), R M Wilkinson (9, 1t).

# 1972-73

Played 38, won 19, lost 17, drawn 2. F 723, A 579.

Captain: V J Lewis

| | | | | f | a |
|---|---|---|---|---|---|
| **September** | | | | | |
| 2 | A | Leicester | L | 6 | 25 |
| 9 | A | London Irish | W | 14 | 10 |
| 16 | H | Notts | D | 12 | 12 |
| 23 | H | Richmond | L | 16 | 18 |
| 26 | H | Rugby * | W | 50 | 10 |
| 30 | A | Gloucester | L | 13 | 47 |
| **October** | | | | | |
| 7 | H | Exeter | W | 26 | 23 |
| 14 | H | Pontypool | L | 6 | 13 |
| 21 | A | Ebbw Vale | L | 16 | 23 |
| 28 | H | London Scottish | W | 25 | 12 |
| **November** | | | | | |
| 4 | A | Waterloo | W | 32 | 0 |
| 18 | A | Northampton | L | 7 | 21 |
| 25 | H | Coventry | L | 0 | 18 |
| **December** | | | | | |
| 2 | H | Manchester | W | 29 | 0 |
| 9 | H | Saracens | W | 28 | 7 |
| 16 | A | Moseley | L | 6 | 17 |
| 23 | H | Leicester * | L | 17 | 21 |
| 26 | H | Old Paulines | W | 18 | 4 |
| 30 | H | Rosslyn Park | W | 12 | 7 |

* RFU Club Competition

| | | | | f | a |
|---|---|---|---|---|---|
| **January** | | | | | |
| 6 | A | Bristol | W | 4 | 3 |
| 13 | H | Sale | L | 12 | 15 |
| 21 | H | Leicester | W | 37 | 9 |
| 27 | A | Oxford Univ | W | 65 | 17 |
| **February** | | | | | |
| 3 | A | London Welsh | D | 29 | 29 |
| 10 | H | Headingley | W | 20 | 6 |
| 17 | H | Cambridge Univ | W | 23 | 4 |
| 24 | A | Rugby | W | 26 | 15 |
| **March** | | | | | |
| 3 | H | Royal Air Force | W | 52 | 4 |
| 10 | H | Harlequins | L | 16 | 23 |
| 16 | A | Neath | L | 16 | 26 |
| 24 | A | Blackheath | W | 26 | 24 |
| 31 | H | Northampton | L | 7 | 14 |
| **April** | | | | | |
| 7 | H | Wasps | L | 3 | 6 |
| 14 | A | London Scottish | L | 11 | 20 |
| 17 | A | Coventry | L | 14 | 52 |
| 21 | A | Percy Park | L | 11 | 13 |
| 23 | A | Gosforth | W | 14 | 11 |
| 28 | H | Bath | W | 4 | |

B Page with 210 was again the highest points scorer. A K Towersey scored most tries, 26. Forty three players made appearances, F N Barker made most, 35.

C J Bailward (10, 1t), C Barber (4, 1t), F N Barker (35, 5t), F Bennett (13, 1t), N R Boult (14, 3t), P D Briggs (6), R Butt (1), R Chadwick (8, 1t), J R Cooley (24, 4t), N Cook (9, 1t), G Davies (7, 3c, 4d, 2p), C Davies (3), R Demming (11, 6t), M D Fitzgerald (12), G Fletcher (1), P J Green (33, 7t), D Hanson (5, 1t), D Hart (9), A J Hollins (24, 8t), C Hooker (8, 2t), J M Howard (16, 13c, 9p, 5t), D Jackson (31, 6t), J P Janion (8, 4t), B Keen (12), A E Landon (24, 5t), P Langford (1), V J Lewis (34), R A Lovell (1), M Manning (9, 2c, 3p, 1t), N O Martin (26, 6t), J T Mawle (11), B Mead (1, 1d), A D Mills (3), B Page (24, 39c, 40p, 3t), A K Rodgers (24), D P Rogers (26, 3t), R J Slaughter (15), R Smith (3), W C C Steele (11, 6t), R Thomas (1), A K Towersey (33, 26t), S Wells (14, 1t), R M Wilkinson (5).

# 1973-74

Played 36, won 22, lost 12, drawn 2. F 742, A 539.

Captain: D P Rogers

| September | | | | f | a |
|---|---|---|---|---|---|
| 1 | H | Leicester | W | 35 | 15 |
| 8 | H | London Irish | W | 34 | 26 |
| 15 | A | Notts | D | 16 | 16 |
| 22 | A | Richmond | L | 6 | 22 |
| 29 | H | Gloucester | W | 37 | 15 |
| **October** | | | | | |
| 6 | H | Gosforth | L | 0 | 32 |
| 13 | A | Pontypool | L | 3 | 23 |
| 20 | H | Ebbw Vale | W | 27 | 6 |
| 24 | A | Cambridge Univ | W | 25 | 16 |
| 27 | A | London Scottish | L | 13 | 29 |
| **November** | | | | | |
| 3 | H | Waterloo | W | 39 | 6 |
| 10 | A | Loughborough Colls | W | 16 | 0 |
| 17 | H | Northampton | W | 16 | 6 |
| 24 | A | Coventry | W | 11 | 9 |
| **December** | | | | | |
| 8 | A | Harlequins | L | 7 | 9 |
| 15 | H | Moseley | L | 12 | 43 |
| 22 | A | Saracens | W | 18 | 16 |
| 26 | H | Old Paulines | W | 43 | 6 |
| 29 | A | Rosslyn Park | W | 13 | 11 |

| January | | | | f | a |
|---|---|---|---|---|---|
| 5 | H | Bristol | D | 10 | 10 |
| 12 | A | Sale | L | 6 | 23 |
| 19 | A | Leicester | L | 6 | 20 |
| 26 | H | Oxford Univ | W | 51 | 10 |
| **February** | | | | | |
| 2 | H | London Welsh | W | 14 | 10 |
| 9 | A | Headingley | L | 9 | 16 |
| 16 | H | Rugby | W | 19 | 12 |
| 23 | A | Bridgend | L | 20 | 23 |
| **March** | | | | | |
| 2 | H | Royal Air Force | W | 22 | 12 |
| 9 | H | Harlequins | W | 13 | 3 |
| 23 | H | Blackheath | W | 42 | 6 |
| 30 | A | Northampton | L | 7 | 22 |
| **April** | | | | | |
| 6 | A | Wasps | W | 71 | 7 |
| 13 | H | Wilmslow | W | 15 | 8 |
| 15 | A | Harrogate | W | 17 | 7 |
| 20 | H | Coventry | L | 17 | 25 |
| 27 | A | Bath | W | 32 | 19 |

W N Bennett set a new points record of 307, becoming the first Bedford player to score more than 300 in a season. D M Wyatt was leading try scorer with 33. Thirty eight players made appearances. D Jackson made most, 35.

C J Bailward (27, 1t), F N Barker (32, 3t), W N Bennett (30, 54c, 3d, 46p, 13t), R Chadwick (1), J R Cooley (15), D Cross (1), C Davies (4), G Davies (2, 1c, 2p), R Demming (6, 1t), E F Edwards (4), M D Fitzgerald (8), P J Green (24, 8t), D Hanson (18, 1c), A J Hollins (27, 5t), C Hooker (33, 3t), J M Howard (24, 5t), D Jackson (35, 4t), B Keen (32, 3t), A E Landon (2), V J Lewis (17), M Lilley (1, 1t), R Luff (1), M Manning (1), N O Martin (13, 2t), J T Mawle (18, 1t), B Mead (3), A D Mills (2), T Mortimer (2), B Page (10, 4c, 2p, 2t), D P Rogers (31, 5t), R J Slaughter (9), R Smith (17), W C C Steele (10, 3t), K Stevenson (8), A K Towersey (27, 17t), S Wells (9, 3t), R M Wilkinson (7), D M Wyatt (29, 4c, 1p, 33t).

# 1974-75

Played 36, won 24, lost 11, drawn 1. F 799, A 386.

Captain: D P Rogers

| | | | | f | a |
|---|---|---|---|---|---|
| **September** | | | | | |
| 7 | A | Leicester | L | 12 | 19 |
| 14 | A | London Irish | W | 24 | 0 |
| 21 | H | Nottingham | W | 25 | 16 |
| 28 | H | Richmond | L | 9 | 15 |
| **October** | | | | | |
| 5 | A | Gloucester | L | 9 | 15 |
| 12 | H | Pontypool | W | 7 | 3 |
| 20 | A | Ebbw Vale | L | 12 | 34 |
| 23 | H | Cambridge Univ | W | 19 | 7 |
| 26 | H | London Scottish | W | 15 | 10 |
| **November** | | | | | |
| 3 | A | Bournemouth * | W | 66 | 6 |
| 9 | A | Cheltenham | W | 15 | 3 |
| 16 | A | Northampton | W | 29 | 9 |
| 23 | H | Coventry | L | 16 | 19 |
| 30 | A | Waterloo | W | 37 | 7 |
| **December** | | | | | |
| 7 | H | Manchester | W | 29 | 7 |
| 14 | A | Harlequins | D | 13 | 13 |
| 21 | A | Moseley | L | 16 | 22 |
| 26 | H | Old Paulines | W | 67 | 7 |
| 28 | H | Rosslyn Park | L | 16 | 20 |

| | | | | f | a |
|---|---|---|---|---|---|
| **January** | | | | | |
| 4 | A | Bristol | L | 3 | 9 |
| 11 | H | Sale | W | 19 | 4 |
| 18 | H | Leicester | W | 23 | 9 |
| 25 | A | Rugby | W | 21 | 4 |
| **February** | | | | | |
| 1 | A | London Welsh | W | 17 | 6 |
| 8 | H | Sale * | W | 23 | 3 |
| 22 | H | Blackheath | W | 28 | 13 |
| **March** | | | | | |
| 1 | H | Royal Air Force | W | 51 | 0 |
| 8 | H | Gosforth * | W | 12 | 6 |
| 15 | H | Saracens | L | 3 | 6 |
| 22 | A | Blackheath | L | 7 | 24 |
| 29 | H | Harrogate | W | 35 | 16 |
| 31 | H | Streatham & Croydon | W | 34 | 3 |
| **April** | | | | | |
| 5 | H | Coventry * | W | 13 | 6 |
| 12 | H | Northampton | W | 40 | 16 |
| 19 | A | Coventry | L | 6 | 17 |
| 26 | T | Rosslyn Park * | W | 28 | 12 |

* RFU Club Competition – Winners.
T – Final at Twickenham.

W N Bennett was again leading points scorer with 281. D M Wyatt scored most tries, 30. Thirty six players made appearances. C Hooker played in every match. The committee of the day decided that details of the 74-6 win against Bedfordshire on September 4 – the first Alan Lovell Memorial Match - should not count in the records.

C J Bailward (30, 2t), F N Barker (22), W N Bennett (25, 46c, 9d, 38p, 12t), R Chadwick (10, 5t), J R Cooley (11, 5t), C Davies (5), G Davies (5, 1d, 1p), R Demming (20, 8t), E F Edwards (34, 5t), P Evans (3), M D Fitzgerald (6), G Fletcher (3), D Hanson (2), M Hempstead (9), A J Hollins (25, 6t), C Hooker (36, 3t), J M Howard (30, 1c, 1d, 2p, 4t), S Ingram (1), D Jackson (18, 3t), A Johnson (20, 2t), A M Jorden (23, 3c, 1d, 3p, 2t), B Keen (16, 1t), A D Lewis (21, 1d, 6t), D Ling (2, 1t), M Manning (1), J T Mawle (3), B Page (11, 17c, 9p, 1t), R Rendell (1), D P Rogers (31, 1t), R J Slaughter (1), R Smith (9), A K Towersey (20, 8t), S J Turner (1, 1t), S Wells (27, 8t), R M Wilkinson (31, 1t), D M Wyatt (28, 1p, 30t).

# 1975-76

Played 45, won 26, lost 19. F 1,043, A 731.

Captain: J M Howard

| September | | | | f | a |
|---|---|---|---|---|---|
| 6 | H | Leicester | W | 24 | 12 |
| 13 | H | London Irish | W | 29 | 11 |
| 20 | A | Nottingham | W | 18 | 15 |
| 27 | A | Richmond | L | 0 | 10 |
| **October** | | | | | |
| 4 | H | Gloucester | W | 18 | 10 |
| 6 | A | Llanelli | L | 6 | 40 |
| 11 | A | Pontypool | W | 21 | 15 |
| 18 | H | Ebbw Vale | W | 15 | 14 |
| 22 | H | Cambridge Univ | L | 9 | 28 |
| 25 | A | London Scottish | L | 4 | 40 |
| **November** | | | | | |
| 1 | H | Neath | W | 12 | 3 |
| 8 | H | E Suburbs/Sydney | L | 18 | 19 |
| 10 | H | Llanelli | L | 12 | 28 |
| 15 | H | Northampton | L | 15 | 18 |
| 22 | A | Coventry | W | 16 | 11 |
| 29 | H | Waterloo | W | 23 | 10 |
| **December** | | | | | |
| 6 | H | Manchester | W | 37 | 15 |
| 13 | A | Cardiff | L | 18 | 40 |
| 17 | A | Northampton * | L | 6 | 9 |
| 20 | H | Moseley | W | 15 | 6 |
| 26 | H | Old Paulines | W | 41 | 17 |
| 27 | A | Rosslyn Park | L | 7 | 19 |

* John Player Cup. † Alan Lovell Memorial

| January | | | | f | a |
|---|---|---|---|---|---|
| 1 | H | Nuneaton | W | 23 | 0 |
| 3 | H | Bristol | L | 15 | 21 |
| 10 | A | Sale | W | 18 | 10 |
| 17 | A | Leicester | L | 18 | 28 |
| 24 | H | Rugby | W | 42 | 12 |
| **February** | | | | | |
| 7 | H | London Welsh | L | 9 | 12 |
| 14 | A | Headingley | W | 23 | 12 |
| 22 | H | Cheltenham | W | 61 | 18 |
| 28 | H | Bridgend | L | 12 | 13 |
| **March** | | | | | |
| 6 | H | Royal Air Force | W | 54 | 16 |
| 13 | H | Harlequins | L | 11 | 12 |
| 21 | H | British Columbia | W | 36 | 10 |
| 24 | A | Saracens | L | 6 | 10 |
| 27 | H | Blackheath | W | 54 | 12 |
| 31 | A | Northampton | W | 30 | 12 |
| **April** | | | | | |
| 3 | A | Wasps | L | 6 | 23 |
| 7 | H | Bedfordshire † | L | 25 | 29 |
| 10 | H | New Brighton | W | 66 | 18 |
| 6 | A | Hayle | W | 47 | 15 |
| 17 | A | St Ives | W | 25 | 4 |
| 19 | A | Taunton | W | 65 | 9 |
| 24 | A | Bath | L | 7 | 35 |
| **May** | | | | | |
| 1 | H | Coventry | W | 26 | 10 |

W N Bennett set a new points record for a season of 351. The team's 1,043 points for was a record as was the points against total of 731. The number of defeats, 19, equalled the record of 1909-10 and 1956-57. D M Wyatt scored 35 tries, the highest total since A D Heard's 35 in 1908-09 and H H Morris's 38 in 1893-4. Forty two players made at least one appearance. F N Barker played in 42 of the 45 matches – another record. The RFU Club Competition became known as the John Player Cup after its first sponsor.

C J Bailward (38, 4t), F N Barker (42, 3t), W N Bennett (36, 60c, 5d, 64p, 6t), I Boon (5), P Boulding (1), R Butt (5, 5t), R Chadwick (28, 3t), J R Cooley (2), J Cross (4), C Davies (4), G Davies (2, 1t), J Davies (12, 4t), R Demming (1), E F Edwards (31, 2t), P Evans (15, 2t), M D Fitzgerald (5), G Fletcher (15), T R Glover (13, 1t), D Hanson (7, 1t), C Heron (1, 1t), A J Hollins (23, 4t), C Hooker (37, 6t), J M Howard (40, 1c, 4t), S Ingram (7, 1t), D Jackson (26, 10t), A M Jorden (27, 5c, 3p, 5t), B Keen (39, 6t), R Luff (1), B Mackay (8, 2t), M Manning (1, 1t), J T Mawle (27, 2t), S Maxwell (16, 5t), B Page (20, 20c, 1d, 15p, 3t), I G Peck (3), D P Rogers (23, 2t), R J Slaughter (20, 6t), R Thomas (1), J Thompson (4, 1t), A K Towersey (20, 21t), S Wells (6, 1t), R M Wilkinson (23, 3t), D M Wyatt (36, 1d, 35t).

## 1976-77

Played 37, won 22, lost 15. F 756, A 531.

Captain: R M Wilkinson

| | | | | f | a |
|---|---|---|---|---|---|
| **September** | | | | | |
| 4 | A | Leicester | L | 13 | 34 |
| 11 | A | London Irish | L | 13 | 27 |
| 18 | H | Nottingham | W | 43 | 15 |
| 25 | H | Richmond | W | 30 | 16 |
| **October** | | | | | |
| 2 | A | Gloucester | L | 14 | 35 |
| 9 | H | Pontypool | W | 25 | 15 |
| 16 | A | Ebbw Vale | L | 11 | 13 |
| 20 | A | Cambridge Univ | L | 10 | 14 |
| 23 | H | London Scottish | L | 16 | 22 |
| 30 | A | New Brighton | W | 14 | 10 |
| **November** | | | | | |
| 6 | H | Sale | W | 15 | 0 |
| 13 | H | Birmingham | W | 18 | 15 |
| 20 | A | Northampton | L | 9 | 25 |
| 27 | H | Coventry | W | 37 | 24 |
| **December** | | | | | |
| 18 | A | Moseley | L | 6 | 18 |
| 21 | H | Rosslyn Park | W | 25 | 0 |
| 27 | H | Old Paulines | W | 62 | 6 |
| **January** | | | | | |
| 1 | A | Bristol | L | 4 | 15 |
| 8 | A | Rugby | W | 13 | 10 |
| 14 | H | Leicester | W | 18 | 0 |
| 22 | H | Hartlepool Rovers * | W | 17 | 10 |
| 29 | H | Northampton | W | 23 | 6 |
| **February** | | | | | |
| 5 | A | London Welsh | L | 10 | 13 |
| 12 | H | Rosslyn Park * | W | 20 | 3 |
| 19 | H | Aberavon | L | 7 | 19 |
| 26 | A | Swansea | L | 16 | 17 |
| **March** | | | | | |
| 4 | H | Royal Air Force | W | 30 | 0 |
| 12 | A | Waterloo * | L | 25 | 27 |
| 19 | H | Saracens | W | 22 | 13 |
| 26 | A | Blackheath | W | 22 | 12 |
| **April** | | | | | |
| 2 | H | Wasps | W | 10 | 6 |
| 9 | H | Harrogate | W | 15 | 7 |
| 11 | A | Nuneaton | L | 25 | 26 |
| 16 | A | Coventry | W | 16 | 12 |
| 23 | A | Neath | L | 12 | 28 |
| 27 | H | Bedfordshire † | W | 46 | 3 |
| 30 | H | Bath | W | 44 | 15 |

* John Player Cup. † Alan Lovell Memorial

D M Wyatt scored most points, 164, most tries, 30, and made most appearances, 33. Replacements were now allowed in club rugby and these count in the records as a full appearance. Forty players made at least one.

C J Bailward (25, 1t), F N Barker (15, 2t), W N Bennett (12, 13c, 2d, 17p, 3t), I Boon (3), P Boulding (4), J N C Breakey (20, 2t), K B Cairns (29, 1t), S Callum (17, 5t), R Chadwick (8, 2t), N J Chinneck (21, 7t), J R Cooley (5), J Cross (28), C Davies (10, 1t), G Davies (1), R Demming (31, 21t), E F Edwards (28, 6t), M D Fitzgerald (6), G Fletcher (31, 1d, 5t), D Hanson (2), C Heron (11, 3t), A J Hollins (26, 5t), C Hooker (1), M Howe (12, 1t), M C Humberstone (1, 1c), S Ingram (4, 1t), D Jackson (29, 8t), C Jones (4, 1t), A M Jorden (31, 27c, 1d, 17p, 3t), B Mackay (11, 1t), J T Mawle (14), A D Mills (7), B Page (5, 6c, 4p), I G Peck (7), R J Slaughter (8), J Thompson (5, 1t), A K Towersey (8, 4t), I Vinter (21, 7t), A Whitehouse (1), R M Wilkinson (27, 2t), D M Wyatt (33, 16c, 1d, 3p, 30t).

# 1977-78

Played 39, won 18, lost 21. F 752, A 623.

Captains: R M Wilkinson
D Jackson

| | | | | f | a |
|---|---|---|---|---|---|
| **September** | | | | | |
| 3 | H | Leicester | W | 38 | 19 |
| 10 | A | London Irish | L | 6 | 7 |
| 17 | A | Nottingham | W | 21 | 6 |
| 24 | A | Richmond | W | 12 | 11 |
| **October** | | | | | |
| 1 | H | Gloucester | W | 33 | 6 |
| 8 | A | Pontypool | L | 9 | 21 |
| 15 | H | Ebbw Vale | W | 18 | 10 |
| 19 | H | Cambridge Univ | W | 65 | 15 |
| 22 | A | Llanelli | L | 9 | 53 |
| 29 | H | St Lukes Col Exeter | W | 28 | 14 |
| **November** | | | | | |
| 5 | A | Birmingham | W | 21 | 10 |
| 12 | A | Aberavon | L | 11 | 19 |
| 16 | H | Rugby | W | 39 | 15 |
| 19 | H | Northampton | W | 9 | 3 |
| 26 | H | Coventry | L | 3 | 29 |
| **December** | | | | | |
| 3 | H | Neath | W | 21 | 0 |
| 10 | A | Harlequins | L | 9 | 13 |
| 17 | H | Moseley | W | 14 | 3 |
| 23 | H | Bristol | L | 3 | 9 |
| 26 | H | Old Paulines | W | 49 | 12 |
| 31 | A | Rosslyn Park | L | 10 | 20 |

| | | | | f | a |
|---|---|---|---|---|---|
| **January** | | | | | |
| 2 | A | London Welsh | L | 9 | 17 |
| 7 | H | Cardiff | L | 7 | 15 |
| 14 | A | Sale | L | 9 | 26 |
| 20 | A | Leicester | L | 6 | 12 |
| 28 | A | Waterloo * | L | 4 | 10 |
| **February** | | | | | |
| 25 | H | Birmingham | W | 41 | 3 |
| **March** | | | | | |
| 1 | H | Banco de la N (Argen) | W | 30 | 7 |
| 4 | H | Northern | L | 9 | 37 |
| 11 | H | Rosslyn Park | L | 14 | 24 |
| 17 | H | Saracens | W | 19 | 10 |
| 25 | H | Blackheath | W | 16 | 0 |
| 27 | H | Nuneaton | W | 64 | 9 |
| **April** | | | | | |
| 1 | A | Wasps | L | 4 | 15 |
| 8 | A | Northampton | L | 9 | 12 |
| 9 | H | D P Rogers' XV | L | 32 | 35 |
| 15 | A | Coventry | L | 4 | 24 |
| 22 | H | Broughton Park | L | 19 | 27 |
| 27 | A | Bath | L | 28 | 45 |

* John Player Cup

A M Jorden scored most points, 150. D M Wyatt scored most tries, 17. Forty three players made appearances. A J Hollins, 34, made the most. More than 20 defeats in a season were recorded for the first time.

S Ashton (20, 2t), C J Bailward (10, 1t), I Boon (2), P Boulding (18), J N C Breakey (17, 4t), L Byrne (1), K B Cairns (24, 3t), R Chadwick (32, 11t), N J Chinneck (12), B Collie (4), M Coyle (3, 1t), C Davies (4), R Demming (27, 14t), G Denton (8, 1t), E F Edwards (18, 1t), G Fletcher (9), E Forrester (15, 4t), A J Hollins (34, 6t), C Hooker (28, 3t), M Howe (27, 4t), M C Humberstone (15, 8c, 3p, 9t), S Ingram (4), D Jackson (33, 12t), C Jones (8, 5t), A M Jorden (26, 35c, 5d, 15p, 5t), A Keay (1), M Lloyd-Williams (1, 1t), B Mackay (12), M Manning (4, 2c), J T Mawle (16), A D Mills (1), D Murray (2), B Page (7, 4c, 4p), I G Peck (28, 4t), A K Rodgers (3), R J Slaughter (2), J Thompson (6), A K Towersey (15, 11t), I Vinter (23, 4t), A Whitehouse (24, 3t), R M Wilkinson (28, 5t), D M Wyatt (26, 18c, 1d, 2p, 17t), N G Youngs (2).

# 1978-79

Played 38, won 17, lost 19, drawn 2. F 664, A 596.

Captain: R M Wilkinson

| | | | | f | a |
|---|---|---|---|---|---|
| **September** | | | | | |
| 2 | A | Leicester | L | 12 | 37 |
| 6 | A | Rugby | L | 14 | 15 |
| 9 | H | London Irish | L | 15 | 23 |
| 16 | A | Nottingham | L | 0 | 9 |
| 23 | H | Richmond | W | 21 | 19 |
| 27 | H | Bedfordshire † | W | 20 | 19 |
| 30 | A | Gloucester | L | 10 | 14 |
| **October** | | | | | |
| 1 | H | Exeter | W | 23 | 12 |
| 14 | H | Pontypool | L | 9 | 24 |
| 21 | A | Ebbw Vale | L | 20 | 32 |
| 25 | A | Cambridge Univ | L | 13 | 23 |
| 28 | A | Llanelli | L | 13 | 28 |
| **November** | | | | | |
| 4 | H | Birmingham | W | 34 | 13 |
| 11 | H | Aberavon | W | 18 | 7 |
| 17 | A | Northampton | L | 0 | 10 |
| 24 | H | Coventry | L | 17 | 22 |
| **December** | | | | | |
| 2 | A | Neath | L | 7 | 8 |
| 9 | A | Harlequins | D | 13 | 13 |
| 16 | A | Moseley | L | 8 | 26 |
| 23 | H | Waterloo | D | 7 | 7 |
| 26 | H | Old Paulines | W | 44 | 6 |
| 30 | H | Rosslyn Park | L | 7 | 22 |
| **January** | | | | | |
| 20 | H | Leicester | W | 10 | 8 |
| **February** | | | | | |
| 2 | H | London Welsh | L | 15 | 21 |
| 10 | H | Cambridge | W | 73 | 0 |
| 24 | A | Wakefield * | W | 27 | 12 |
| **March** | | | | | |
| 2 | H | Royal Air Force | W | 26 | 12 |
| 10 | H | Birkenhead Park * | W | 16 | 8 |
| 17 | H | Saracens | W | 4 | 0 |
| 20 | H | Rugby*** | W | 27 | 14 |
| 24 | H | Leicester * | L | 12 | 22 |
| 31 | H | Northampton | L | 0 | 42 |
| **April** | | | | | |
| 7 | H | Hinckley*** | W | 24 | 6 |
| 14 | A | Harrogate | W | 13 | 8 |
| 16 | H | Nuneaton | W | 27 | 3 |
| 21 | A | Coventry | L | 10 | 21 |
| 22 | H | Chesterfield*** | W | 42 | 9 |
| 28 | H | Bath | L | 13 | 21 |

† Alan Lovell Memorial. * John Player Cup. *** Midland Clubs Qualifying Championship.

N G Youngs scored most points, 105. G N Phillips was the leading try scorer with 13 and he also made the most appearances, 35. Fifty players turned out at least once.

S Ashton (11), R Barrett (9), I Boon (7), P Boulding (3), J Brigden (3), K B Cairns (28, 2t), S Callum (1, 2t), K Canning (1), R Chadwick (10, 2t), N Chesworth (5, 2p, 1t), N Chinneck (6), M Cook (1), M Coyle (2), S Darville (3), R Davies (9, 1d), R Demming (24, 10t), G Denton (5), G Fletcher (1), E Forrester (7, 1t), N Greensmith (23, 2d, 4t), A J Hollins (24, 6t), C Hooker (32, 1t), M Howe (32, 5t), M C Humberstone (10, 11c, 15p, 4t), S Ingram (5, 1t), D Jackson (13), C Jones (7, 4t), A M Jorden (16, 2d, 1p, 2t), A Keay (1), A Keep (2, 1t), S Kerridge (13, 10c, 5p, 2t), B Mackay (25, 12c, 11p, 4t), D Mackay (3), M Manning (12, 1t), N O Martin (7), J T Mawle (15, 2t), R Meadows (2), I Metcalfe (3, 1p, 1t), A D Mills (1), D Murray (1), R Pascall (21, 1t), I G Peck (12, 2c, 3p), G N Phillips (35, 13t), S Roache (1), J Thompson (8), A K Towersey (29, 9t), I Vinter (19, 1t), A Whitehouse (18, 3t), R M Wilkinson (30, 7t), N G Youngs (22, 17c, 1d, 8p, 11t).

# 1979-80

Played 41, won 23, lost 17, drawn 1. F 755, A 554.

Captain: N O Martin

| | | | | f | a |
|---|---|---|---|---|---|
| **September** | | | | | |
| 1 | H | Leicester | L | 12 | 34 |
| 2 | H | Lichfield | W | 19 | 6 |
| 8 | A | London Irish | L | 18 | 22 |
| 15 | H | Nottingham | W | 32 | 12 |
| 22 | A | Richmond | W | 26 | 3 |
| 26 | H | Bedfordshire † | W | 19 | 3 |
| 29 | H | Gloucester | L | 4 | 9 |
| **October** | | | | | |
| 6 | H | Exeter | W | 26 | 9 |
| 13 | A | Pontypool | L | 10 | 41 |
| 20 | H | Ebbw Vale | W | 25 | 18 |
| 24 | H | Cambridge Univ | L | 12 | 20 |
| 27 | A | Llanelli | L | 13 | 36 |
| **November** | | | | | |
| 3 | H | Birmingham | W | 39 | 16 |
| 10 | A | Aberavon | L | 4 | 7 |
| 14 | H | Rugby | W | 31 | 3 |
| 17 | H | Northampton | L | 7 | 17 |
| 23 | A | Coventry | L | 3 | 17 |
| **December** | | | | | |
| 1 | H | Neath | W | 25 | 15 |
| 8 | A | Harlequins | L | 13 | 15 |
| 15 | H | Moseley | W | 23 | 12 |
| 22 | A | New Brighton | W | 24 | 17 |
| 26 | H | Old Paulines | W | 62 | 0 |
| 29 | H | Rosslyn Park | W | 10 | 6 |
| **January** | | | | | |
| 5 | H | Bristol | L | 7 | 14 |
| 12 | A | Sale | D | 0 | 0 |
| 26 | H | Wasps * | W | 6 | 3 |
| **February** | | | | | |
| 2 | H | Swansea | L | 7 | 10 |
| 9 | A | Headingley | W | 27 | 7 |
| 16 | H | London Scottish | L | 15 | 21 |
| 23 | A | London Scottish * | L | 9 | 14 |
| 29 | H | London Welsh | L | 15 | 18 |
| **March** | | | | | |
| 8 | H | Richmond | W | 22 | 15 |
| 15 | A | Saracens | W | 15 | 9 |
| 19 | H | Rosaria (Argentina) | W | 8 | 6 |
| 22 | H | Blackheath | W | 22 | 9 |
| 29 | A | Northampton | L | 3 | 19 |
| **April** | | | | | |
| 5 | H | Harrogate | W | 43 | 6 |
| 7 | A | Nuneaton | W | 31 | 6 |
| 12 | A | Wasps | W | 23 | 16 |
| 19 | H | Coventry | W | 29 | 21 |
| 26 | A | Bath | L | 16 | 22 |

† Alan Lovell Memorial. * John Player Cup.

I Metcalfe was the leading points scorer with 153. N G Youngs scored most tries, 14. Forty six players made appearances. A Whitehouse made most, 39.

S Ashton (35, 1t), N Aynsey (1), J Blount (16, 8t), K B Cairns (11), K Canning (10, 8t), R Chadwick (4, 1t), N Chesworth (13, 2c, 1p, 4t), M Coyle (1), J Cross (3), S Darville (5), R Demming (27, 13t), G Denton (6), R Eales (4), E Forrester (2), G Fletcher (1, 1t), J Graves (9, 9t), N Greensmith (7), A J Hollins (13, 2t), C Hooker (28, 1t), M Howe (34, 6t), M C Humberstone (6, 4c, 1d, 10p, 3t), S Ingram (5), A M Jorden (1), S Kerridge (22, 18c, 19p, 4t), A Keay (1), M Lloyd-Williams (26, 7t), M Manning (13, 1t), N O Martin (35, 2t), J T Mawle (17), R Meadows (16), I Metcalfe (16, 31c, 1d, 24p, 4t), J Parsons (6, 2t), R Pascall (32), I G Peck (2, 2t), G N Phillips (34, 5t), M Phillips (2), P Sutton (2), R Thompson (21, 5d, 1t), P Thomson (2), A K Towersey (2, 1t), I Vinter (33, 6t), A Waller (11, 1t), A Whitehouse (39, 2t), R M Wilkinson (10, 5t), M Wood (1), N G Youngs (32, 3c, 14t).

# 1980-81

Played 45, won 18, lost 24, drawn 3. F 540, A 684.

Captain: G M Phillips

| | | | | f | a |
|---|---|---|---|---|---|
| **September** | | | | | |
| 3 | A | Rugby | W | 27 | 6 |
| 6 | A | Leicester | L | 6 | 43 |
| 10 | A | Stockwood Park | W | 25 | 6 |
| 13 | H | London Irish | W | 21 | 12 |
| 20 | A | Nottingham | L | 3 | 13 |
| 24 | H | Bedfordshire † | W | 26 | 0 |
| 27 | H | Richmond | W | 19 | 3 |
| **October** | | | | | |
| 4 | A | Gloucester | L | 3 | 32 |
| 11 | H | Pontypool | L | 9 | 19 |
| 15 | H | Bosuns | W | 34 | 28 |
| 18 | A | Ebbw Vale | L | 6 | 35 |
| 22 | A | Cambridge Univ | L | 11 | 19 |
| 25 | H | Llanelli | W | 25 | 10 |
| **November** | | | | | |
| 1 | A | Birmingham | W | 27 | 6 |
| 8 | H | Aberavon | L | 12 | 19 |
| 15 | A | Northampton | W | 15 | 7 |
| 22 | H | Blackheath | L | 4 | 12 |
| 26 | H | Coventry | W | 7 | 4 |
| 29 | H | New Brighton | L | 6 | 14 |
| **December** | | | | | |
| 6 | A | Neath | L | 7 | 21 |
| 13 | A | Harlequins | L | 3 | 20 |
| 20 | A | Moseley | L | 6 | 22 |
| 26 | H | Old Paulines | W | 45 | 3 |
| 27 | H | Orrell | L | 3 | 17 |
| **January** | | | | | |
| 1 | A | London Welsh | L | 0 | 34 |
| 3 | A | Bristol | L | 4 | 16 |
| 10 | H | Sale | W | 19 | 9 |
| 24 | A | Moseley * | L | 0 | 25 |
| 31 | A | Rosslyn Park | L | 4 | 20 |
| **February** | | | | | |
| 6 | H | London Welsh | W | 16 | 10 |
| 14 | H | Headingley | L | 4 | 10 |
| 21 | A | London Scottish | L | 6 | 20 |
| 28 | H | Roundhay | D | 22 | 22 |
| **March** | | | | | |
| 6 | H | Royal Air Force | W | 28 | 3 |
| 14 | H | Harlequins | W | 21 | 10 |
| 21 | A | Saracens | D | 3 | 3 |
| 25 | A | Coventry | D | 9 | 9 |
| 28 | A | Blackheath | L | 6 | 12 |
| **April** | | | | | |
| 4 | A | Cardiff | L | 12 | 40 |
| 8 | H | Northampton | W | 6 | 3 |
| 11 | H | Wasps | L | 7 | 43 |
| 18 | A | Exeter | L | 7 | 12 |
| 20 | H | Nuneaton | W | 4 | 3 |
| 25 | H | Bath | L | 3 | 6 |
| **May** | | | | | |
| 2 | A | Waterloo | W | 9 | 3 |

† Alan Lovell Memorial. * John Player Cup.

J Graves scored most tries, 13, and most points, 143. Forty nine players made appearances, the captain G N Phillips making most, 41. He led the team on its tour of the USA. Twenty four defeats in a season was a record.

N Ackhurst (17, 1t), S Ashton (17, 1t), W Barker (31, 4t), G Bignell (3), P Boulding (26), D Bruce-Lockhart (10), K Canning (23, 7t), P Carter (7, 3c, 1d, 7p), N Chesworth (24, 11c, 1d, 17p), J Clemence (13), M Coyle (2), S Darville (2), C Davison (19, 5t), G Denton (9), P Dixon (1), R Eales (12, 1t), P Eggleton (3), G Fletcher (14, 2d, 1t), E Forrester (2), S Gibbons (4), J Graves (33, 14c, 21p, 13t), B Gray (1), G Griffiths (1), N Heath (1), A J Hollins (1), C Hooker (18, 1t), M Howe (37, 3t), M C Humberstone (8, 2p, 1t), J Humphreys (1), S Ingram (8, 1t), S Kerridge (11, 6c, 7p, 2t), M Lilley (2), M Lloyd-Williams (19), B Mackay (31, 2t), J T Mawle (40), R Meadows (14, 1t), G Noble (1),R Pascall (39, 2t), G Philip (1), G N Phillips (41, 5t), C Roberts (2), J Sargeant (24, 8t), J Temperley (2), R Thompson (4, 1d), P Thomson (5, 1t), A Whitehouse (33), R M Wilkinson (35, 4t), J Worton (9), N G Youngs (27, 10t).

# 1981-82

Played 37, won 12, lost 21, drawn 4. F 486, A 495.

Captain: J T Mawle

| September | | | | f | a |
|---|---|---|---|---|---|
| 5 | H | Leicester | L | 4 | 28 |
| 12 | A | London Irish | L | 3 | 15 |
| 16 | A | Wasps | L | 12 | 19 |
| 19 | H | Nottingham | W | 19 | 6 |
| 23 | H | Bedfordshire † | W | 20 | 3 |
| 26 | A | Richmond | L | 6 | 16 |
| October | | | | | |
| 3 | H | Gloucester | L | 9 | 19 |
| 10 | A | Pontypool | L | 19 | 26 |
| 14 | H | Rugby | W | 43 | 3 |
| 17 | H | Ebbw Vale | W | 4 | 3 |
| 21 | H | Cambridge Univ | L | 13 | 28 |
| 24 | A | Llanelli | L | 6 | 29 |
| 31 | H | Waterloo | L | 6 | 16 |
| November | | | | | |
| 7 | H | Birmingham | W | 24 | 3 |
| 14 | A | Aberavon | W | 18 | 8 |
| 21 | H | Northampton | W | 12 | 7 |
| 28 | A | Coventry | L | 11 | 25 |
| December | | | | | |
| 5 | H | Neath | W | 15 | 6 |

† Alan Lovell Memorial. * John Player Cup

| January | | | | f | a |
|---|---|---|---|---|---|
| 1 | A | London Welsh | D | 9 | 9 |
| 2 | H | Bristol | L | 9 | 21 |
| 23 | H | Gosforth * | L | 3 | 14 |
| 30 | H | Rosslyn Park | L | 7 | 9 |
| February | | | | | |
| 5 | H | London Welsh | D | 3 | 3 |
| 13 | A | Headingley | L | 0 | 4 |
| 20 | H | London Scottish | L | 6 | 9 |
| 27 | H | Fylde | W | 34 | 9 |
| March | | | | | |
| 5 | H | Royal Air Force | W | 44 | 0 |
| 10 | H | Wasps | L | 14 | 15 |
| 17 | H | Coventry | L | 13 | 25 |
| 20 | A | Saracens | W | 13 | 3 |
| 27 | H | Blackheath | L | 6 | 20 |
| 28 | A | Northampton | D | 16 | 16 |
| April | | | | | |
| 2 | H | Cardiff | L | 10 | 13 |
| 9 | H | Exeter | W | 18 | 10 |
| 12 | A | Nuneaton | D | 10 | 10 |
| 17 | A | Northampton | L | 13 | 17 |
| 24 | A | Bath | L | 14 | 28 |

S Kerridge with 136 was the leading points scorer. K Canning scored most tries, nine. Forty six players made appearances. The captain J T Mawle made most, 34.

N Ackhurst (4), S Ashton (26), M Bailey (12, 7t), S Bain (6, 2t), W Barker (18, 2t), N Bennett (13), S Binnington (6), P Boulding (13), K Canning (27, 9t), N Chesworth (7, 5c, 5p), J Clemence (17, 7c, 4d, 15p), S Darville (4), C Davison (4, 1t), G Denton (3), R Eales (24, 2t), D Elkington (2, 1t), E Forrester (23, 1t), K Green (2), B Gray (2), C Hooker (18), M Howe (27, 2t), S Ingram (3), R Kendall (3), S Kerridge (17, 14c, 36p), A Key (18, 3t), B Mackay (21), D Mackay (11). G Mansell (19), J T Mawle (34), A McGahey (11), S Micklewright (9, 1t), D Murray (1), R Pascall (20, 3t), I G Peck (30, 6t), Geo Philip (6), G N Phillips (11), J Sargeant (21, 4t), B Shannon (6, 1t), S Smith (1, 1c, 1p, 1t), N Thompson (1), R Thompson (1), M Tobin (4, 4p, 2t), S Walters (1), A Whitehouse (30, 2t), R M Wilkinson (29, 6t), N Wilson (4, 3t).

# 1982-83

Played 41, won 17, lost 23, drawn 1. F 530, A 668.

Captain: I G Peck

| | | | | f | a |
|---|---|---|---|---|---|
| **September** | | | | | |
| 4 | A | Leicester | L | 15 | 28 |
| 8 | A | Rugby | W | 23 | 9 |
| 11 | H | London Irish | W | 17 | 10 |
| 18 | A | Nottingham | W | 30 | 10 |
| 22 | H | Bedfordshire † | W | 37 | 3 |
| 25 | H | Richmond | L | 6 | 28 |
| **October** | | | | | |
| 2 | A | Gloucester | L | 9 | 12 |
| 9 | H | Pontypool | W | 16 | 15 |
| 16 | A | Ebbw Vale | L | 6 | 16 |
| 20 | A | Cambridge Univ | W | 23 | 0 |
| 23 | A | Llanelli | L | 6 | 46 |
| 30 | H | Wasps | L | 3 | 19 |
| **November** | | | | | |
| 6 | A | Birmingham | W | 18 | 3 |
| 13 | H | Aberavon | W | 29 | 12 |
| 20 | A | Northampton | L | 13 | 22 |
| 27 | H | Coventry | L | 6 | 9 |
| **December** | | | | | |
| 4 | A | Neath | L | 0 | 23 |
| 8 | H | Royal Air Force | W | 25 | 3 |
| 11 | H | Harlequins | W | 3 | 0 |
| 18 | H | Moseley | D | 6 | 6 |
| 27 | H | Orrell | L | 6 | 16 |

| | | | | f | a |
|---|---|---|---|---|---|
| **January** | | | | | |
| 1 | A | Bristol | L | 0 | 61 |
| 3 | H | Old Paulines | W | 16 | 3 |
| 8 | H | Sale | L | 10 | 19 |
| 14 | H | Leicester | L | 3 | 13 |
| 22 | H | Saracens * | W | 21 | 0 |
| 29 | A | Rosslyn Park | L | 12 | 21 |
| **February** | | | | | |
| 12 | H | Headingley | L | 4 | 14 |
| 19 | A | London Scottish | W | 17 | 3 |
| 26 | H | Bristol * | L | 10 | 20 |
| **March** | | | | | |
| 4 | H | London Welsh | L | 6 | 28 |
| 12 | A | Wilmslow | W | 24 | 4 |
| 18 | H | Saracens | L | 4 | 7 |
| 26 | A | Blackheath | L | 16 | 18 |
| **April** | | | | | |
| 1 | A | Exeter | W | 22 | 6 |
| 4 | H | Nuneaton | W | 7 | 6 |
| 9 | H | Northampton | W | 19 | 16 |
| 16 | A | Waterloo | L | 9 | 28 |
| 20 | A | Coventry | L | 3 | 57 |
| 23 | H | Gosforth | L | 15 | 24 |
| 30 | H | Bath | L | 15 | 30 |

† Alan Lovell Memorial. * John Player Cup.

S Smith was the leading scorer with 284 points. His total included 67 penalty goals, a club record. W Barker scored most tries, seven. Fifty six players made appearances. K Canning made most, 39.

K Albone (16), C Alcock (16), P Alston (1), P Argent (3), S Ashton (7), S Bain (10), W Barker (21, 7t), R Barker (7), A Bathie (2), N Bennett (19, 2t), S Binnington (7, 2t), N Blofeld (1. 1t), G Bygraves (11), K Canning (39, 6t), P Catling (9), D Collins (14, 1t), R Chrome (12, 1t), S Darville (2), C Davison (3), G Denton (3), R Eales (28, 2t), D Elkington (1), A Finnie (6, 2c, 9p), G Fletcher (2), E Forrester (20, 6t), W Green (1), G Griffiths (1), D Henderson (28, 2t), M Howe (5, 1t), T Ibbett (1), R Kendall (3), S Kerridge (4), A Key (36, 6t), M Lee (1), I Macaskill (2), B Mackay (26, 3t), D Mackay (3, 1t), G Mansell (28), A McGahey (33, 4t), D McLeod (1), R Meadows (24, 1t), S Micklewright (4), J Moses (4), I G Peck (38, 1d, 2t), C Phelps (1), G N Phillips (6), D Pimblett (2), J Sargeant (8, 1t), S Smith (36, 28c, 5d, 67p, 3t), N Thompson (2), S Walters (1), A Whitehouse (36, 1t), G Wilcox (1), R M Wilkinson (29, 2t), N Wilson (2), S Yuill (4, 1t).

# 1983-84

Played 42, won 17, lost 25. F 539, A 797.

Captain: I G Peck

| | | | | f | a |
|---|---|---|---|---|---|
| **September** | | | | | |
| 3 | H | Leicester | L | 3 | 68 |
| 10 | A | London Irish | L | 9 | 19 |
| 17 | H | Nottingham | L | 6 | 18 |
| 21 | H | Bedfordshire † | W | 15 | 9 |
| 25 | A | Richmond | W | 19 | 3 |
| **October** | | | | | |
| 1 | H | Gloucester | W | 14 | 6 |
| 8 | A | Pontypool | L | 25 | 27 |
| 12 | H | Rugby | W | 26 | 9 |
| 15 | H | Ebbw Vale | W | 13 | 6 |
| 18 | H | Cambridge Univ | W | 20 | 16 |
| 22 | A | Roundhay | L | 6 | 19 |
| 29 | A | Wasps | L | 4 | 44 |
| **November** | | | | | |
| 5 | H | Birmingham | W | 22 | 3 |
| 12 | A | Aberavon | L | 7 | 26 |
| 19 | H | Northampton | L | 9 | 15 |
| 26 | A | Coventry | L | 7 | 21 |
| **December** | | | | | |
| 3 | H | Neath | W | 21 | 9 |
| 10 | A | Harlequins | W | 10 | 9 |
| 14 | H | Royal Air Force | W | 27 | 6 |
| 17 | A | Moseley | L | 6 | 24 |
| 23 | A | Orrell | L | 3 | 25 |
| 26 | H | Old Paulines | W | 50 | 0 |
| 31 | H | Rosslyn Park | W | 22 | 9 |
| **January** | | | | | |
| 2 | A | London Welsh | L | 16 | 17 |
| 7 | H | Bristol | L | 6 | 20 |
| 14 | A | Sale | L | 3 | 18 |
| 28 | A | London Irish * | L | 7 | 15 |
| **February** | | | | | |
| 3 | H | London Welsh | L | 4 | 19 |
| 11 | A | Headingley | L | 7 | 16 |
| 17 | H | London Scottish | L | 3 | 16 |
| 25 | A | Bridgend | L | 7 | 63 |
| **March** | | | | | |
| 3 | H | Swansea | W | 19 | 13 |
| 10 | A | Leicester | L | 9 | 64 |
| 18 | A | Saracens | W | 12 | 3 |
| 24 | H | Blackheath | W | 13 | 7 |
| 31 | A | Northampton | L | 3 | 10 |
| **April** | | | | | |
| 6 | A | Cardiff | L | 4 | 48 |
| 11 | H | Coventry | L | 10 | 12 |
| 14 | H | Gosforth | W | 15 | 12 |
| 21 | H | Exeter | W | 29 | 17 |
| 23 | A | Nuneaton | L | 9 | 13 |
| 28 | H | Coventry | L | 19 | 23 |

† Alan Lovell Memorial. * John Player Cup

S Smith again scored most points, 223. Highest try scorers were K Canning and G Philip, seven each. Fifty three players made appearances. A Key made most, 39. Points against, 797, was a record as was the number of defeats, 25.

C Alcock (6), P Alston (10, 2t), S Ashton (2, 1t), S Bain (6), R Barker (3), W Barker (19, 1t), A Bathie (29), N Bennett (33, 5t), A Berry (4, 2t), S Binnington (9, 2t), N Blofeld (1), G Bygraves (35), K Canning (33, 7t), M Canning (2), P Catling (28, 1t), R Chrome (31, 1t), J Clemence (1), G Comb (4), P Cray (1), S Darville (1), C Davison (3), I Dougal (1), R Drage (10, 4p, 1t), R Eales (20, 2t), D Elkington (4, 1t), A Finnie (11, 11c, 15p, 2t), J Flint (7), D Harris (3), K Hopkins (4), M Howe (30, 3t), J Keates (1, 1t), A Key (39, 4t), D Lowther (5), B Mackay (32, 1t), G Mansell (1), J McCreath (2), R Meadows (23, 1t), S Mellor (1), J Moses (34, 1t), A Nicholl (1), I G Peck (38, 1d, 3t), G Philip (21, 7t), D Pimblett (1), A K Rodgers (1), S Searl (1), J Sharpe (3), S Smith (26, 13c, 3d, 60p, 2t), A Walford (12, 1t), S Walters (4), R White (6), A Whitehouse (33, 5t), R M Wilkinson (25, 1t), K Wyles (6, 3t).

# 1984-85

Played 41, won 18, lost 20, drawn 3. F 546, A 756. Captain: I G Peck

| | | | | f | a |
|---|---|---|---|---|---|
| **September** | | | | | |
| 1 | A | Leicester | L | 12 | 38 |
| 5 | A | Rugby | W | 15 | 3 |
| 8 | H | London Irish | W | 18 | 15 |
| 15 | A | Nottingham | L | 3 | 32 |
| 19 | H | Bedfordshire † | W | 10 | 6 |
| 22 | H | Rushden & Higham * | W | 51 | 0 |
| 23 | H | Richmond | L | 6 | 19 |
| 29 | H | Wasps | L | 9 | 58 |
| **October** | | | | | |
| 6 | A | Gloucester | L | 10 | 22 |
| 13 | H | Pontypool | L | 15 | 31 |
| 20 | A | Ebbw Vale | L | 3 | 15 |
| 27 | H | Roundhay | W | 17 | 15 |
| 28 | A | Norwich | W | 14 | 6 |
| **November** | | | | | |
| 3 | A | Oxford Univ | W | 32 | 10 |
| 10 | H | Aberavon | W | 15 | 6 |
| 14 | A | Cambridge Univ | W | 8 | 3 |
| 17 | A | Northampton | L | 7 | 22 |
| 24 | H | Coventry | W | 19 | 15 |
| **December** | | | | | |
| 1 | H | Barkers Butts * | W | 10 | 4 |
| 8 | H | Harlequins | D | 10 | 10 |
| 12 | H | Royal Air Force | W | 30 | 9 |
| 15 | H | Moseley | L | 16 | 35 |
| 22 | H | Orrell | L | 9 | 40 |
| 26 | H | Old Paulines | W | 34 | 3 |
| 29 | A | Rosslyn Park | L | 12 | 29 |
| **January** | | | | | |
| 1 | A | London Welsh | L | 6 | 38 |
| 19 | A | Leicester | L | 0 | 20 |
| 26 | H | Waterloo * | L | 6 | 7 |
| **February** | | | | | |
| 2 | A | Swansea | L | 12 | 48 |
| 23 | H | Cambridge Univ | D | 3 | 3 |
| **March** | | | | | |
| 2 | A | Birkenhead Park | W | 28 | 11 |
| 9 | A | Wasps | L | 3 | 58 |
| 15 | H | Saracens | W | 12 | 4 |
| 23 | A | Blackheath | W | 10 | 9 |
| 30 | H | Vale of Lune | D | 7 | 7 |
| **April** | | | | | |
| 6 | H | Waterloo | W | 11 | 0 |
| 8 | H | Northampton | L | 12 | 28 |
| 13 | A | Gosforth | L | 6 | 20 |
| 20 | A | Birmingham | L | 15 | 19 |
| 24 | H | Nuneaton | W | 16 | 9 |
| 27 | H | Eastern Counties | L | 14 | 29 |

† Alan Lovell Memorial. * John Player Cup.

A Finnie was the leading points scorer with 251. G Philip, with 15, was the leading try scorer. Fifty players made appearances. A Key made the most, 38, and missed just nine possible appearances in reaching 100.

C Alcock (24), P Alston (11, 2t), N Ansell (4, 1t), T Atter (4, 2t), R Barker (3), A Bathie (1), N Bennett (32, 5t), A Berry (1), S Binnington (5, 2t), G Bygraves (36, 1t), K Canning (33, 9t), M Canning (28, 1t), P Catling (37), J Clemence (2), G Comb (11), S Darville (2), D Elkington (8, 1t), A Finnie (32, 17c, 8d, 59p, 4t), J Flint (1), R Glenister (1), A Graveney (1), S Harris (25, 2t), M Howe (35, 1t), D Jancey (1), A Key (38, 2c, 1p, 6t), B Mackay (33, 2t), R Malir (8, 1t), G Mansell (3), R Meadows (20), S Mellor (12), D Mitchell (1, 1t), J Moses (21, 1t), I G Peck (33, 1t), G Philip (34, 15t), G N Phillips (19, 1t), D Pimblett (3), R Porter (10), A K Rodgers (1), S Searle (1), I Skingsley (1), P Stephenson (3, 1t), W Tall (9), R Thompson (9, 8c, 3d, 9p, 1t), J Turnbull (1), D Twigden (7, 1t), A Walford (6), R White (8), A Whitehouse (11), R M Wilkinson (3), K Wyles (1).

# 1985-86

Played 38, won 13, lost 23, drawn 2. F 421, A 851.

Captains: I G Peck
A M Key

| | | | | f | a |
|---|---|---|---|---|---|
| **September** | | | | | |
| 7 | H | Leicester | L | 6 | 52 |
| 14 | A | London Irish | L | 9 | 31 |
| 18 | H | Bedfordshire † | D | 12 | 12 |
| 21 | H | Nottingham | L | 10 | 52 |
| 28 | A | Evesham * | W | 13 | 9 |
| **October** | | | | | |
| 2 | A | Richmond | L | 15 | 19 |
| 5 | H | Gloucester | L | 6 | 34 |
| 12 | A | Pontypool | L | 0 | 53 |
| 19 | H | Ebbw Vale | L | 3 | 9 |
| 26 | H | Broughton Park * | L | 10 | 37 |
| 30 | H | Rugby | L | 16 | 18 |
| **November** | | | | | |
| 2 | H | Oxford Univ | W | 3 | 0 |
| 9 | A | Waterloo | L | 7 | 28 |
| 16 | H | Northampton | W | 24 | 20 |
| 23 | A | Coventry | L | 6 | 40 |
| 30 | A | Nuneaton | W | 17 | 10 |
| **December** | | | | | |
| 7 | H | Gosforth | L | 3 | 13 |
| 11 | H | Royal Air Force | W | 20 | 19 |
| 14 | A | Harlequins | L | 7 | 27 |
| 21 | A | Moseley | L | 3 | 42 |
| 26 | H | Old Paulines | W | 26 | 0 |
| **January** | | | | | |
| 1 | H | Bradford/Bingley | W | 13 | 0 |
| 4 | H | Bristol | L | 6 | 26 |
| 11 | A | Sale | L | 7 | 17 |
| 18 | A | Leicester | L | 3 | 33 |
| 25 | H | Northern | W | 21 | 18 |
| 31 | H | London Welsh | W | 16 | 13 |
| **February** | | | | | |
| 22 | A | Taunton | W | 10 | 7 |
| **March** | | | | | |
| 8 | H | Birkenhead Park | W | 16 | 7 |
| 12 | H | Coventry | L | 7 | 17 |
| 16 | A | Saracens | L | 0 | 24 |
| 19 | H | Loughborough Stds | D | 9 | 9 |
| 22 | H | Orrell | L | 0 | 25 |
| 29 | H | Rosslyn Park | L | 4 | 6 |
| 31 | A | Northampton | W | 22 | 16 |
| **April** | | | | | |
| 5 | A | Cardiff | L | 28 | 68 |
| 12 | A | Wasps | L | 11 | 31 |
| 19 | H | Birmingham | W | 32 | 9 |

† Alan Lovell Memorial. * John Player Cup.

A Finnie was again the leading points scorer with 132. K Canning scored most tries, ten, and R Malir played most games, 32. Fifty five players made at least one first team appearance. Three penalty tries were awarded in the season – a record. The 851 points against was also a record.

C Alcock (4), M Bayfield (9), N Bennett (15, 2t), A Berry (1), A Binnington (17, 6t), W Boffey (1), G Bygraves (27), K Canning (29, 10t), P Catling (13, 1t), J Chandler (10, 1t), J Clemence (1), G Comb (16), S Darville (9, 1t), P Ellam (11, 2t), D Finlayson (5,1t), A Finnie (26, 6c, 7d, 33p), J Flint (9), I Fowler (2, 1t), B Gabriel (7), C Glanville (7), B Gray (2), S Harris (6), M Howe (28, 1t), D Jancey (3), L Jefferies (18), J Keates (3), A Key (27, 14c, 2d, 17p, 2t), B Mackay (5), R Malir (32), S Mellor (9), R Millard (8), D Mitchell (21, 2t) J Moses (11, 1t), G Nichols (3), S Parkhouse (1), I G Peck (25, 1t), G Philip (8, 2t), R Porter (27), S Purdy (1), A Rodgers (2), R Russell (10), S Searle (7, 2t), I Skingsley (4), P Stephenson (9, 1t), W Tall (24), N Thompson (1), A Tupman (1), J Turnbull (8, 1t), D Twigden (27, 6t), A Walford (10, 1t), R White (6), A Whitehouse (30, 2t), A Whittle (1), J Woodhouse (1), K Wyles (4).

# 1986-87

Played 43, Won 18, Lost 25. F 590, A 667.

Captain: A M Key

| | | | | f | a |
|---|---|---|---|---|---|
| **September** | | | | | |
| 3 | A | Rugby | W | 23 | 9 |
| 6 | A | Leicester | L | 10 | 22 |
| 10 | H | Wasps | L | 3 | 12 |
| 13 | H | London Irish • | W | 12 | 6 |
| 20 | A | Nottingham | L | 7 | 12 |
| 21 | H | Crawshay's XV | L | 6 | 31 |
| 27 | H | Richmond • | L | 9 | 15 |
| **October** | | | | | |
| 4 | A | Gloucester | L | 12 | 22 |
| 11 | H | Pontypool | W | 12 | 4 |
| 15 | A | Cambridge Univ | W | 21 | 15 |
| 18 | A | Ebbw Vale | L | 15 | 19 |
| 25 | H | Llanelli | L | 9 | 18 |
| **November** | | | | | |
| 1 | A | Oxford Univ | W | 15 | 10 |
| 8 | H | Waterloo • | L | 9 | 23 |
| 12 | H | Bedfordshire † | W | 13 | 6 |
| 15 | A | Northampton • | L | 9 | 15 |
| 22 | H | Coventry | L | 7 | 15 |
| 26 | H | Loughborough Stds | W | 18 | 12 |
| 29 | A | Birmingham | W | 9 | 0 |
| **December** | | | | | |
| 6 | A | Roundhay | L | 12 | 13 |
| 10 | H | Royal Air Force | W | 15 | 6 |
| 13 | H | Harlequins | L | 10 | 22 |
| 20 | H | Moseley | L | 18 | 34 |
| 27 | A | Rosslyn Park • | L | 12 | 15 |

| | | | | f | a |
|---|---|---|---|---|---|
| **January** | | | | | |
| 1 | A | London Welsh • | W | 16 | 0 |
| 3 | A | Bristol | L | 6 | 37 |
| 24 | A | Bristol * | L | 3 | 33 |
| **February** | | | | | |
| 7 | A | Vale of Lune | L | 3 | 15 |
| 14 | H | Headingley • | L | 0 | 8 |
| 21 | A | London Scottish | L | 13 | 16 |
| 28 | H | Southend | W | 24 | 0 |
| **March** | | | | | |
| 4 | H | Nuneaton | W | 25 | 3 |
| 8 | H | Cambridge Univ P&P | L | 36 | 54 |
| 14 | A | Liverpool St Helens • | L | 16 | 23 |
| 20 | H | Saracens • | W | 18 | 14 |
| 22 | A | Old Paulines | W | 12 | 6 |
| 25 | A | Coventry | L | 3 | 17 |
| 28 | A | Blackheath • | W | 12 | 0 |
| **April** | | | | | |
| 5 | H | Cardiff | L | 6 | 36 |
| 11 | A | Gosforth • | L | 10 | 21 |
| 18 | H | Morley | W | 33 | 10 |
| 20 | H | Northampton | W | 21 | 12 |
| 25 | H | Bath | W | 47 | 6 |

• John Smiths Merit Table 'B' - 9th.
* John Player Cup. † Alan Lovell Memorial.

A Finnie was the leading scorer for the third consecutive season with 156 points. K Canning and A Fitzgerald were the top try scorers with eight each. M Howe and G Bygraves made the most appearances, 40. Fifty seven players turned out for the club. Official records were kept in a slightly different form.

R Barker (6), N Bennett (12), S Binnington (29, 3T), N Blakemore (2), W Boffey (4), P Burnhill (12), G Bygraves (40, 1T), K Canning (37, 8T), J Chandler (12, 2T), J Davidson (16, 1T), P Ellam (20, 3T, 1P), D Finlayson (1), A Finnie (17, 4T, 19C, 30P, 4D), A Fitzgerald (24, 8T), I Fletcher (2), J Flint (1), I Fowler (3), D Frankcombe (2), B Gabriel (15, 3T, 5C, 5P, 1D), S Gilbert (2), C Glanvill (14), S Harris (10, 4T), S Hifle (1), M Howe (40, 2T), D Jancey (1), A Jasczak (32, 4T), J Keates (2), A Key (38, 3T, 7C, 25P), R Malir (15, 3T), G Mansell (1), I Marshall (1), P McCarthy (14), I. McGregor (1), A Moffatt (2), J Moses (5), G Nicholls (1), J Orwin (28, 3T), I Peck (25, 4T), G Philip (8), R Porter (1), S Purdy (6), R Russell (6), S Searle (1), R Sheard (1, 1T, 1P), I Skingsley (5, 1T), P Stephenson (12), R Thompson (15, 6C, 10P, 1D), A Tupman (13, 1T), J Turnbull (16, 3T), M Upex (3), A Walford (3), M Whitcombe (19, 2T), R White (24), A Whitehouse (12), D Wood (3, 1T), G Wood (22, 5T), M Wright (17).

# 1987-88

Played 42, Won 22, Lost 18, Drawn 2. F723, A 800.

Captain: J Orwin

| | | | | f | a |
|---|---|---|---|---|---|
| **September** | | | | | |
| 2 | H | Rugby | W | 30 | 20 |
| 5 | H | Leicester | L | 9 | 29 |
| 12 | A | London Irish • | D | 12 | 12 |
| 16 | A | Wasps | L | 12 | 22 |
| 19 | H | Nottingham | W | 12 | 10 |
| 26 | H | Barkers Butts * | W | 35 | 4 |
| 30 | H | London Welsh • | D | 6 | 6 |
| **October** | | | | | |
| 3 | H | Gloucester | W | 12 | 10 |
| 10 | H | Blackheath • | W | 6 | 0 |
| 14 | H | Cambridge Univ | W | 20 | 8 |
| 17 | H | Ebbw Vale | L | 13 | 18 |
| 26 | A | Leighton Buzzard * | W | 24 | 6 |
| 31 | A | Nuneaton | W | 24 | 12 |
| **November** | | | | | |
| 7 | H | Oxford Univ | W | 19 | 12 |
| 14 | A | Waterloo | L | 4 | 27 |
| 18 | H | Bedfordshire † | W | 12 | 3 |
| 21 | H | Northampton • | W | 17 | 16 |
| 28 | A | Coventry | L | 13 | 61 |
| **December** | | | | | |
| 2 | H | Loughborough Stds | W | 26 | 11 |
| 5 | H | Gosforth • | L | 16 | 25 |
| 12 | A | Harlequins | L | 0 | 54 |
| 19 | A | Moseley | L | 0 | 37 |
| 26 | H | Old Paulines | W | 58 | 6 |

| | | | | f | a |
|---|---|---|---|---|---|
| **January** | | | | | |
| 2 | H | Bristol | L | 3 | 25 |
| 9 | A | Sale | L | 6 | 54 |
| 16 | A | Leicester | L | 9 | 42 |
| 23 | H | Bristol * | L | 4 | 21 |
| **February** | | | | | |
| 6 | H | Vale of Lune | W | 16 | 13 |
| 13 | A | Headingley • | W | 13 | 7 |
| 20 | H | London Scottish • | W | 21 | 9 |
| 27 | H | Rosslyn Park • | W | 15 | 3 |
| **March** | | | | | |
| 5 | A | Orrell | L | 9 | 17 |
| 12 | H | Birmingham | W | 59 | 12 |
| 20 | A | Saracens • | L | 4 | 33 |
| 26 | A | Richmond • | L | 25 | 28 |
| **April** | | | | | |
| 1 | A | Camborne | W | 30 | 10 |
| 2 | A | Penzance & Newlyn | W | 49 | 4 |
| 4 | A | Exeter | W | 16 | 9 |
| 9 | H | Roundhay | L | 18 | 21 |
| 13 | A | Northampton | L | 6 | 23 |
| 23 | A | Bath | L | 7 | 35 |
| 30 | H | Liverpool SH • | W | 33 | 25 |

• Courage League Two - 5th.
* John Player Cup. † Alan Lovell Memorial.

A Finnie was again the leading scorer with 226 points and J Chandler the top try scorer with nine. C Glanvill, P Ellam and G Wood each played in 36 matches. Fifty five players made at least one appearance.

S Batty (28, 11T, 6C, 2P), A Berry (1), S Binnington (21, 2T), N Blakemore (6), G Buck (1), M Burman (1), G Bygraves (7), J Chandler (32, 9T), S Cunningham (8, 2T, 5C, 9P, 4D), S Darville (2), J Davidson (19, 1T), P Dunne (7, 2T), P Ellam (36, 5T), A Finnie (30, 1T, 36C, 45P, 5D), I Fletcher (2), J Fletcher (7, 3T), D Fordham (2), D Frankcombe (4), B Gabriel (33, 7T, 5C, 2P), S Gilbert (6), C Glanvill (36, 6T, 1D), P Hall (1), S Harris (23, 6T), K Houghton (3) M. Howe (31, 1T), D Jackson (1), D Jancey (20, 7T), J Keates (7), M Longdon (2), P McCarthy (24, 1D), I McGregor (3, 1T), A Mynard (2, 1T, 2P), J Orwin (17, 1T), I Peck (3), G Philip (1), R Porter (30, 2T), S Purdy (2), S Richardson (3), I Skingsley (22, 8T), P Stephenson (4), T Taylor (6, 2T), A Tucker (16, 4T), J Turnbull (1), S Turner (2), D Twigden (9, 4T), M Upex (16), A Walford (5, 1T), A Walne (3), R White (21, 1T), R White (7, 2T), A Whitehouse (9), P Wilson (3), D Wood (6), G Wood (36, 5T), M Wright (24, 3T).

# 1988-89

Played 40, Won 19, Lost 19, Drawn 2. F 649, A 693. Captain: J Orwin

| | | | | f | a |
|---|---|---|---|---|---|
| **September** | | | | | |
| 3 | A | Leicester | L | 10 | 40 |
| 10 | A | Gosforth • | W | 17 | 16 |
| 17 | H | Abertillery | W | 25 | 14 |
| 24 | H | London Scottish • | W | 9 | 6 |
| **October** | | | | | |
| 1 | A | Gloucester | L | 16 | 25 |
| 8 | A | Headingley • | D | 7 | 7 |
| 12 | A | Cambridge Univ | W | 9 | 7 |
| 15 | H | Bath | L | 10 | 16 |
| 22 | H | London Irish • | L | 15 | 21 |
| 26 | A | Rugby | W | 21 | 13 |
| 29 | H | Loughborough Stds | W | 16 | 7 |
| **November** | | | | | |
| 1 | A | Oxford Univ | W | 12 | 6 |
| 5 | H | Nuneaton * | W | 16 | 0 |
| 12 | H | Coventry • | W | 19 | 9 |
| 19 | A | Saracens • | L | 10 | 50 |
| 26 | A | Northampton • | L | 3 | 42 |
| 30 | H | Bedfordshire † | W | 30 | 3 |
| **December** | | | | | |
| 3 | A | Rosslyn Park | L | 12 | 30 |
| 7 | H | Royal Air Force | L | 18 | 26 |
| 10 | H | Harlequins | W | 25 | 4 |
| 17 | A | Moseley | L | 19 | 24 |
| 26 | H | Old Paulines | W | 68 | 4 |
| 30 | A | Bristol | L | 4 | 34 |

| | | | | f | a |
|---|---|---|---|---|---|
| **January** | | | | | |
| 7 | H | Wakefield | W | 17 | 13 |
| 14 | H | Richmond • | W | 15 | 3 |
| 20 | H | Leicester | L | 3 | 13 |
| 28 | H | Nottingham * | L | 3 | 6 |
| **February** | | | | | |
| 4 | H | Fylde | W | 22 | 16 |
| 11 | A | Liverpool SH | L | 6 | 24 |
| 18 | H | Orrell | L | 22 | 31 |
| 25 | A | Coventry | L | 3 | 6 |
| **March** | | | | | |
| 4 | H | Waterloo | L | 12 | 15 |
| 11 | A | Blackheath • | W | 13 | 12 |
| 18 | A | Nottingham | L | 0 | 55 |
| 25 | A | Morley | W | 48 | 22 |
| 27 | H | Northampton | L | 7 | 18 |
| **April** | | | | | |
| 1 | H | Wasps | L | 14 | 26 |
| 8 | H | London Welsh • | W | 18 | 6 |
| 22 | A | Sale • | D | 15 | 15 |
| 29 | H | Eastern Counties | W | 40 | 8 |

• Courage League Two – 2nd (P).
* Pilkington Cup. † Alan Lovell Memorial.

A Finnie was the leading points scorer for the fifth consecutive season with 221 and K Canning top try scorer with nine. M Upex played 34 times and 53 players appeared in one or more matches.

R Barrington (1, 1T), S Batty (17, 7T), S Binnington (20, 2T), N Blakemore (4), G Bygraves (14), K Canning (21, 9T), J Chandler (29, 1T), T Clarke (6, 1T), G Colleran (20, 4T), S Cunningham (16, 5T, 9C, 1P, 1D), I Deterte (3, 1T), F Du Bois (2), A Finnie (31, 1T, 29C, 44P, 9D), A Fitzgerald (2, 1T), J Fletcher (3), D Frankcombe (17, 2T), B Gabriel (30, 6T, 1P), S Gilbert (1), C Glanvill (17, 1T), S Glover (14, 2T), R Greed (4, 1T, 1D), R. Hall (2), S Harris (10, 7T), K Houghton (26, 1T), M Howe (23), A Jasczak (10), J Keates (3), D Kemball (1), A Lees (2), M Lilley (1), H Lourens (3, 1T), J Mackay (1), P McCarthy (15, 1T), I Marshall (2), C Nicholl (4), D Niven (12, 2T), J Orwin (30, 1T), R Porter (13, 2T), G Simpkins (4, 2T), I Skingsley (30, 6T), T Taylor (7, 1T), D Twigden (7, 2T), M Upex (34), P Van Eden (2, 1T), S Vaudin (26, 5T, 9C, 11P, 5D), A Walford (2), A Walne (1), S Walters (18, 2T), K Warburton (6, 1T), D Ward (23), G Watt (1), A Whitehouse (4), G Wood (32, 2T).

# 1989-90

Played 40, Won 8, Lost 31, Drawn 1. F 436, A 1120.

Captain: M A Howe

| | | | | f | a |
|---|---|---|---|---|---|
| **September** | | | | | |
| 2 | H | Metropolitan Police | W | 16 | 15 |
| 9 | H | Saracens • | L | 3 | 22 |
| 13 | H | Northampton | L | 20 | 22 |
| 23 | A | Leicester • | L | 3 | 60 |
| 30 | H | Wasps | L | 6 | 57 |
| **October** | | | | | |
| 4 | H | Loughborough Stds | L | 10 | 16 |
| 7 | A | Fylde | W | 21 | 3 |
| 14 | H | Harlequins • | L | 8 | 71 |
| 18 | H | Cambridge Univ | L | 6 | 44 |
| 21 | A | London Irish | L | 7 | 28 |
| 26 | A | Gloucester • | L | 6 | 37 |
| **November** | | | | | |
| 11 | H | Orrell • | L | 7 | 25 |
| 18 | A | Nottingham • | L | 16 | 47 |
| 25 | H | Moseley • | L | 0 | 34 |
| 29 | H | Bedfordshire † | W | 31 | 4 |
| **December** | | | | | |
| 2 | H | Vale of Lune | W | 16 | 7 |
| 6 | H | Royal Air Force | L | 15 | 16 |
| 9 | A | Harlequins | L | 10 | 57 |
| 16 | H | Rosslyn Park | L | 16 | 21 |
| 23 | A | Metropolitan Police | D | 15 | 15 |
| 26 | H | Old Paulines | W | 31 | 12 |
| 30 | H | Blackheath | L | 3 | 15 |

| | | | | f | a |
|---|---|---|---|---|---|
| **January** | | | | | |
| 6 | A | Wakefield | L | 17 | 37 |
| 13 | A | Bath • | L | 0 | 76 |
| 19 | H | Leicester | L | 0 | 54 |
| 27 | H | Richmond * | L | 7 | 12 |
| **February** | | | | | |
| 2 | H | Rugby | L | 6 | 20 |
| 17 | H | London Scottish | W | 14 | 7 |
| 24 | H | Coventry | L | 11 | 23 |
| **March** | | | | | |
| 3 | A | Waterloo | L | 7 | 25 |
| 10 | H | Wasps • | L | 9 | 44 |
| 17 | H | Gosforth | W | 8 | 4 |
| 21 | H | Nuneaton | W | 25 | 11 |
| 24 | H | Nottingham | L | 3 | 24 |
| 31 | A | Rosslyn Park • | L | 12 | 45 |
| **April** | | | | | |
| 7 | A | Headingley | L | 14 | 22 |
| 14 | H | Sheffield | L | 3 | 11 |
| 16 | A | Northampton | L | 7 | 37 |
| 21 | A | Glamorgan Wands | L | 21 | 24 |
| 28 | H | Bristol • | L | 6 | 16 |

• Courage League One– 12th (R).

* Pilkington Cup. † Alan Lovell Memorial.

A Moffatt was the leading points scorer with 49 and four players, J Chandler, D Frankcombe, I Skingsley and D Twigden each scored five tries. D Frankcombe made 32 appearances. Sixty three players made one or more. The points against total of 1120 was a record for a season as was the number of defeats, 31.

P Allen (2, 1T), R Amphlett (4, 1T), G Bartlett (2), S Batty (4), M Bayfield (23, 1T), A Baxondale (2), A Berry (7, 1T), S Binnington (12, 2T), N Blakemore (6), D Bygraves (4), G Bygraves (27, 1T), J Chandler (26, 5T), T Clarke (19, 3T), J Cullen (6, 1T), I Drury (12, 3T), J Egan (12, 3T), A Finnie (7, 3C, 6P, 1D), S Fletcher (1), D Fordham (1), D Frankcombe (32, 5T), N Freeman (1), R Frost (8, 2T, 8C, 7P, 1D), C Glanvill (13, 1P), J Glanvill (2), S Glover (28, 1T), I Goslin (2), R Greed (31, 3T, 3C, 7P), M Hanson (5), S Harris (19, 3T), K Houghton (21), M Howe (31, 5T), A Jasczak (4) A. Jones (1), P Kemble (3), A Lees (4), B Mackay (2), L Mansell (2), P McCarthy (20, 2P, 1D), A Moffatt (12, 11C, 8P, 1D), D Niven (1), C Parke (1, 1T), G Patterson (13, 1T, 1C), R Porter (24, 1T), G Simpkins (29, 3T, 1C), P Simmonds (4 ,1T), I Skingsley (18, 5T), P Stephenson (6, 2T), R Stone (1), R Stidulph (1), A,Swain (3), D Tanner (5), T Taylor (6), J Turnbull (1), D Twigden (19, 5T). M Upex (31, 1T), S Vaudin (12, 1C, 5P), A Walford (10, 1T), D Ward (1), G Watt (2), G Williams (1), S Williams (11, 1T), G Wood (10, 1T), D Wyre-Roberts (1).

# 1990-91

Played 36, Won 13, Lost 21, Drawn 2. F 612, A 824.

Captain: G Wood

| | | | | f | a |
|---|---|---|---|---|---|
| **September** | | | | | |
| 1 | A | Leicester | L | 6 | 57 |
| 8 | H | London Welsh | W | 24 | 0 |
| 15 | A | Aberavon | L | 8 | 44 |
| 22 | A | Wakefield • | L | 0 | 27 |
| 28 | A | Northampton | L | 7 | 50 |
| **October** | | | | | |
| 2 | H | Loughborough S | W | 15 | 7 |
| 6 | H | London Irish • | L | 18 | 19 |
| 13 | A | Richmond • | L | 17 | 28 |
| 20 | H | Plymouth Albion • | W | 10 | 9 |
| 23 | A | Cambridge Univ | L | 0 | 29 |
| **November** | | | | | |
| 3 | A | Harrogate * | L | 0 | 16 |
| 10 | A | Rugby • | L | 3 | 28 |
| 17 | H | Sale • | D | 10 | 10 |
| 24 | H | Lichfield | L | 20 | 25 |
| **December** | | | | | |
| 1 | H | Wasps | L | 9 | 22 |
| 5 | H | Royal Air Force | W | 20 | 16 |
| 15 | H | Nottingham | L | 14 | 28 |
| 22 | H | Moseley | L | 16 | 22 |
| 26 | H | Old Paulines | W | 46 | 6 |

| | | | | f | a |
|---|---|---|---|---|---|
| **January** | | | | | |
| 5 | H | Liverpool SH | L | 10 | 27 |
| 12 | A | Waterloo | D | 13 | 13 |
| 18 | H | Leicester | L | 7 | 41 |
| 26 | A | Nuneaton | W | 21 | 4 |
| 30 | H | Bedfordshire † | W | 41 | 4 |
| **February** | | | | | |
| 2 | H | Rosslyn Park | L | 13 | 25 |
| 6 | A | Orrell | L | 19 | 63 |
| 23 | H | London Scottish | W | 44 | 14 |
| **March** | | | | | |
| 2 | H | Metropolitan Police | W | 35 | 29 |
| 9 | A | Blackheath • | W | 16 | 12 |
| 23 | H | Coventry • | L | 7 | 9 |
| 30 | H | Morley | L | 27 | 35 |
| **April** | | | | | |
| 1 | H | Northampton | W | 44 | 22 |
| 6 | H | London Scottish • | W | 21 | 16 |
| 13 | A | Newcastle/Gosforth • | L | 7 | 22 |
| 20 | A | Sheffield | L | 28 | 35 |
| 27 | H | Headingley • | W | 16 | 10 |

• Courage League Two– 8th. * Pilkington Cup.
† Alan Lovell Memorial.

A Finnie was once again the leading scorer with 226 points. He also made the most appearances, 30. T Young was top try scorer with 15. Fifty nine players appeared in one or more matches.

R Amphlett (5), J Ashworth (3), M Bayfield (24, 2T), A Berry (1), J Brain (5), M Burman (7), J Busby (1), G Bygraves (6), J Chandler (11, 2T), S Clithero (2, 2T) A Cooke (1), I Crossan (2, 1T, 1C, 4P), R Drew (2, 4T), J Egan (13, 2T), A Finnie (30, 3T, 29C, 46P, 6D), J Fordham (1), N Freeman (1), W Furnell (29, 3T), P Garrett (11, 1T), S Gilbert (3, 1T), C Glanvill (26, 5T, 1C, 1P), S Glover (28, 8T), R Greed (8, 1T), J Halkett (3, 1T), R Hansen (4), S Harris (12, 1T), C Hogg (1) K Houghton (15, 1T), M Howe (14, 1T), A Jasczak (12), D Jones (3), M Jones (1, 2T), A Lees (1), L Mansell (14), P McCarthy (2), K McGovan (2), R Millard (14), B Miller (1), M Morris (2, 1T), R Pascall (6), N Patterson (9), G Porteous (3), R Porter (21, 1C), M Rennell (25, 7T), G Simpkins (15, 2T), R Simmons (1), I Skingsley (19, 4T), A Smith (15), J Taylor (2), T Taylor (20, 2T), V Turner (11, 4T), M Upex (4), C Venn (1), A Walne (8, 1T), D Ward (4, 1T), G Watt (9, 1T), G Williams (18, 9T, 3C, 1P), G Wood (14, 1T), T Young (29, 15T).

## 1991-92

Played 39, Won 18, Lost 20, Drawn 1. F 730, A 672.

Captain: R E Pascall

| | | | | f | a |
|---|---|---|---|---|---|
| **September** | | | | | |
| 1 | A | Vale of Lune | W | 21 | 15 |
| 7 | H | Leicester | L | 18 | 25 |
| 14 | H | Public School Wands | W | 39 | 17 |
| 21 | H | Aberavon | W | 22 | 15 |
| 28 | A | Rosslyn Park | D | 6 | 6 |
| **October** | | | | | |
| 2 | H | Loughborough S | W | 37 | 10 |
| 5 | H | Northampton | L | 15 | 23 |
| 12 | H | Nottingham | W | 15 | 11 |
| 19 | A | Bristol | L | 3 | 22 |
| 22 | H | Cambridge Univ | W | 14 | 13 |
| 25 | H | Askeans | W | 29 | 12 |
| **November** | | | | | |
| 1 | A | Coventry | L | 3 | 16 |
| 9 | A | Sheffield * | W | 30 | 13 |
| 16 | H | Wakefield • | L | 6 | 25 |
| 23 | A | Liverpool SH • | W | 22 | 6 |
| 30 | H | Harlequins * | L | 3 | 33 |
| **December** | | | | | |
| 7 | H | West Hartlepool • | L | 6 | 30 |
| 14 | A | Plymouth Albion • | L | 9 | 24 |
| 18 | H | Royal Air Force | L | 13 | 16 |
| 21 | A | Wasps | L | 9 | 24 |
| 26 | H | Old Paulines | W | 90 | 3 |

| | | | | f | a |
|---|---|---|---|---|---|
| **January** | | | | | |
| 4 | H | Moseley • | L | 8 | 9 |
| 11 | A | Sale • | L | 6 | 16 |
| 18 | A | Leicester | L | 24 | 45 |
| 25 | H | Hull Ionians | W | 24 | 10 |
| 29 | H | Bedfordshire † | W | 49 | 6 |
| **February** | | | | | |
| 1 | H | Orrell | L | 10 | 22 |
| 8 | A | Nottingham | L | 7 | 42 |
| 15 | A | London Irish | L | 9 | 22 |
| 22 | H | London Welsh | W | 27 | 4 |
| 29 | A | London Scottish • | L | 0 | 38 |
| **March** | | | | | |
| 6 | H | Harrogate | W | 27 | 3 |
| 14 | H | Blackheath • | W | 52 | 10 |
| 18 | H | Rugby | W | 12 | 10 |
| 28 | A | Coventry • | L | 13 | 19 |
| **April** | | | | | |
| 4 | H | Waterloo • | W | 25 | 4 |
| 11 | H | Newcastle Gosforth • | W | 9 | 4 |
| 18 | A | Northampton | L | 6 | 30 |
| 25 | A | Morley • | L | 12 | 19 |

• Courage League Two– 10th.
* Pilkington Cup. † Alan Lovell Memorial.

Once again A Finnie was the leading scorer with 331 points. M Rennell was top try scorer with 12. Three players, A Finnie, L Mansell and M Upex each played in 35 games. Fifty eight players appeared in one or more matches. The 90-3 defeat of the Old Paulines was a record.

P Alston (6), R Amphlett (1,1T), A Bartlett (1, 3T), G Bartlett (11), S Binnington (17, 3T), T Burbridge (5), J Brain (27), B Brock (2), J Chandler (25, 2T), D Clift (7, 1T), S Clithero (5, 1T), M Denney (1, 1T), J Egan (5), D Fayle (3, 1T), A Finnie (35, 3T, 50C, 67P, 6D), W Furnell (6, 1T), B Gabriel (15, 8T, 4C, 1P), P Garrett (13), C Glanvill (29, 3T), J Glanvill (1, 2T), S Gleye (1), A Gomarsall (1, 2T), M Graham (8), R Greed (8), S Harris (14, 5T), M Howe (11, 1T), C Innes (4, 3T), A Jasczak (5), G Kimber (18, 3T), A Lees (1), L Mansell (35, 2T), D McGavin (7), K McGovern (2), R Millard (11, 3T), C Park (1), R Pascall (30, 3T), N Patterson (24, 2T), G Porteous (7), R Porter (2), M Rees (16, 2T), M Rennell (28, 12T, 1P), I Robertson (1), M Sharp (5, 1T), I Skingsley (29, 4T), G Simpkins (2), C Simpson (2, 1T), A Smith (5), G Stewart (2, 1T), R Stone (1, 1T), T Taylor (16, 4T), J Thame (1), J Turnbull (6, 1T), V Turner (16, 5T), D Trueman (1), M Upex (35, 1T), C Venn (2), G Williams (26, 3T, 5C, 1P), T Young (14, 6T).

# 1992-93

Played 35, Won 19, Lost 14, Drawn 2. F 687, A 601.

Captain: P Alston

| | | | | f | a |
|---|---|---|---|---|---|
| **September** | | | | | |
| 5 | A | Harrogate | W | 35 | 11 |
| 12 | H | London Welsh | W | 39 | 3 |
| 19 | A | Moseley • | D | 9 | 9 |
| 26 | A | Wakefield • | L | 3 | 27 |
| **October** | | | | | |
| 3 | H | Richmond • | W | 22 | 16 |
| 10 | A | Rosslyn Park • | W | 16 | 13 |
| 17 | A | Harlequins | W | 30 | 27 |
| 24 | H | Fylde • | W | 24 | 12 |
| 31 | A | Loughborough Stds | L | 13 | 22 |
| **November** | | | | | |
| 7 | H | Askeans * | W | 21 | 12 |
| 13 | A | Cambridge Univ | L | 11 | 17 |
| 21 | H | Sale • | D | 9 | 9 |
| 28 | A | Rugby * | L | 14 | 27 |
| **December** | | | | | |
| 5 | A | Northampton | L | 16 | 33 |
| 12 | H | Wasps | W | 13 | 9 |
| 16 | H | Royal Air Force | W | 17 | 10 |
| 19 | A | Rugby | L | 10 | 12 |
| **January** | | | | | |
| 2 | A | Rosslyn Park | W | 20 | 9 |
| 9 | A | Waterloo • | L | 8 | 28 |
| 15 | H | Leicester | L | 13 | 16 |
| 23 | H | Bristol | L | 6 | 41 |
| 27 | H | Bedfordshire † | W | 25 | 16 |
| 30 | A | Askeans | W | 20 | 12 |
| **February** | | | | | |
| 6 | A | Orrell | L | 3 | 20 |
| 13 | H | Nottingham • | W | 15 | 9 |
| 20 | A | West Hartlepool | L | 14 | 27 |
| 27 | A | Saracens | L | 11 | 20 |
| **March** | | | | | |
| 5 | H | Selkirk | W | 23 | 19 |
| 13 | A | Blackheath • | L | 12 | 16 |
| 19 | H | London Scottish | W | 35 | 15 |
| 27 | H | Coventry • | W | 30 | 15 |
| **April** | | | | | |
| 3 | A | Newcastle Gosforth • | L | 13 | 19 |
| 10 | H | Saracens | W | 55 | 23 |
| 17 | H | Sheffield | W | 57 | 17 |
| 24 | H | Morley • | W | 25 | 10 |

• Courage League Two– 7th (R).

* Pilkington Cup. † Alan Lovell Memorial.

A Finnie was again leading scorer with 188 points. M Rennell and P Moss scored the most tries, nine, in a season when the value of a try was increased from four to five points. P Alston played in the most matches, 33. Forty eight players made at least one appearance.

P Allen (4, 1T), P Alston (33, 2T), R Barrington (7, 1T), E Bastow (3, 1P), P Berzin (3, 2T), S Binnington (11, 1T), J Brain (14), J Chandler (24, 4T, 1C), M Deans (9), M Denney (5), A Finnie (20, 2T, 26C, 39P, 3D), P Garrett (19, 5T), S Harris (2), K Houghton (2), M Howe (24, 1T), A Hunn (5, 2T), D James (1), M Jones (12, 1D), D Malone (1), L Mansell (32, 4T), N Marment (13, 7C, 21P), D McGavin (5), K McGovern (1), A Mortimore (2), P. Moss (32, 9T, 1C, 7P), R Pascall (15), N Patterson (5), R Porter (2), K Plummer (2), M Rennell (22, 9T), M Sharp (4), B Simmonds-Dance (2), I Skingsley (24, 3T), A Smith (2), T Smith (27, 1T), A Tapper (2), T Taylor (27, 6T), J Thame (18, 5T), J Turnbull (11, 1T), V Turner (23, 6T), R Tushingham (6, 4C, 6P), M Upex (27, 1T), S Weathers (3), B Whetstone (22, 6T), T White (1, 1T), A Wilcox (2), G Williams (1), T Young (7, 2T).

# 1993-94

Played 37, Won 21, Lost 16. F 868, A 640.

Captain: P Alston

| | | | | f | a |
|---|---|---|---|---|---|
| **September** | | | | | |
| 4 | H | Moseley ° | L | 19 | 20 |
| 11 | H | Richmond ° | W | 23 | 16 |
| 18 | A | Sheffield* | W | 25 | 24 |
| 22 | H | Beds Police ° | W | 64 | 0 |
| 25 | H | Liverpool SH ° | W | 55 | 3 |
| **October** | | | | | |
| 2 | H | Loughborough Stds ° | W | 40 | 6 |
| 9 | H | Llanelli ° | W | 31 | 7 |
| 16 | A | Bradford & Bingley * | L | 15 | 23 |
| 23 | A | Rosslyn Park | W | 17 | 12 |
| 26 | H | Cambridge Univ ° | L | 13 | 15 |
| 30 | H | Fylde | W | 23 | 12 |
| **November** | | | | | |
| 6 | A | Havant | W | 20 | 14 |
| 13 | H | Redruth | W | 22 | 3 |
| 17 | H | Auckland NZ ° | L | 3 | 51 |
| 27 | A | Saracens ° | L | 13 | 50 |
| **December** | | | | | |
| 4 | H | Morley | W | 25 | 10 |
| 11 | H | Richmond | L | 12 | 19 |
| 18 | H | Southend ° | W | 50 | 6 |
| 27 | H | Old Paulines ° | W | 83 | 12 |

| | | | | f | a |
|---|---|---|---|---|---|
| **January** | | | | | |
| 1 | A | London Welsh ° | L | 10 | 40 |
| 3 | A | Blackheath | L | 9 | 34 |
| 15 | A | Coventry | L | 10 | 17 |
| 22 | H | London Scottish ° | W | 14 | 3 |
| 29 | A | Fylde | L | 6 | 20 |
| **February** | | | | | |
| 4 | H | Saracens ° | L | 19 | 22 |
| 12 | H | Havant | W | 27 | 12 |
| 19 | H | Exeter | W | 18 | 14 |
| 26 | A | Redruth | W | 33 | 14 |
| **March** | | | | | |
| 5 | A | Nottingham ° | L | 25 | 32 |
| 12 | H | Blackheath | W | 6 | 0 |
| 18 | H | Rugby ° | L | 21 | 32 |
| 26 | A | Morley | L | 17 | 18 |
| **April** | | | | | |
| 2 | H | Rosslyn Park | W | 28 | 13 |
| 9 | A | Richmond | W | 26 | 20 |
| 16 | H | Bath ° | L | 13 | 18 |
| 23 | H | Coventry | W | 21 | 15 |
| 30 | A | Exeter | L | 12 | 13 |

Courage League Three– 2nd. ° Friendly.
* Pilkington Cup.

A Finnie was again the leading points scorer with 292. P Alston and V Turner were top try scorers with twelve. P Alston made the most appearances with 34. Fifty five players appeared for the club.

P Allen (16, 1T), P Alston (34, 12T, 1C), S Basra (7), S Binnington (4, 1T), P Blunt (1), J Bostock (1), N Broughton (2, 1T), J Chandler (7, 4T), M Cooke (5, 1T), M Cook (4, 2T), J Cooley (2), M Deans (30, 8T), J Egan (3), D,Elkington (14, 1T), A Finnie (30, 44C, 64P, 4D), I Fletcher (2), P Garrett (26, 4T), C Glanvill (19, 4T), R Glenn (1), D Goodwin (1), P Hales (3), M Hancock (20, 4T), S Harris (11), K Houghton (9, 1T), M Howe (19, 3T), D James (2), P Kemble (3), S Kench (3), L Mansell (23, 2T), D McGavin (2), A Mortimore (3), P Moss (17, 2T, 2C), R Porter (4), M Rafter (1), M Sharp (21), K Simpson (12, 1T), I Skingsley (26, 6T), R Subbiani (29, 7T), C Taffs (3, 2T), A Tapper (7, 4C, 13P), T Taylor (3, 1T), J Thame (1), J Turnbull (14, 3T), V Turner (32,12T) R Tushingham (4, 1T, 10C,1P) M Upex (18) B Whetstone (30, 9T) K Webster (1), T Webster (6), A Wilcox (6, 2T), J Wilkinson (5, 1T), C Wilson (4), C Wright (9), M Wright (4), D Wyre-Roberts (20, 2T).

# 1994-95

Played 37, Won 24, Lost 12, Drawn 1. F 900, A 648.

Captain: P Alston

| | | | | f | a |
|---|---|---|---|---|---|
| **September** | | | | | |
| 3 | A | Moseley ° | W | 26 | 25 |
| 10 | A | Rugby ° | L | 9 | 25 |
| 17 | H | Clifton | W | 19 | 5 |
| 24 | A | Richmond | W | 16 | 14 |
| **October** | | | | | |
| 1 | H | Morley | W | 45 | 8 |
| 4 | H | Oxford Univ ° | W | 24 | 16 |
| 8 | A | Stourbridge * | W | 35 | 17 |
| 15 | A | Rosslyn Park | W | 31 | 13 |
| 22 | H | Blackheath | W | 12 | 3 |
| 25 | A | Cambridge Univ ° | L | 13 | 30 |
| 29 | A | Exeter | W | 19 | 3 |
| **November** | | | | | |
| 5 | A | West Park * | W | 40 | 14 |
| 7 | H | Canterbury NZ ° | L | 14 | 23 |
| 12 | H | Harrogate | W | 39 | 13 |
| 19 | A | Llanelli ° | L | 7 | 33 |
| 26 | A | Northampton ° | W | 21 | 19 |
| 30 | H | Royal Air Force ° | W | 42 | 16 |
| **December** | | | | | |
| 3 | H | Gloucester ° | W | 16 | 14 |
| 10 | H | Sale ° | W | 25 | 21 |
| 17 | A | Aspatria * | L | 6 | 32 |
| 26 | H | Bedfordshire ° | W | 54 | 0 |
| 31 | H | London Welsh ° | W | 51 | 5 |
| **January** | | | | | |
| 7 | A | Otley | L | 6 | 12 |
| 14 | A | Clifton | W | 21 | 18 |
| 21 | A | London Scottish ° | L | 10 | 37 |
| 28 | H | Nottingham ° | L | 9 | 10 |
| **February** | | | | | |
| 4 | A | Saracens ° | L | 19 | 36 |
| 17 | H | Leicester ° | L | 10 | 26 |
| 25 | A | Morley | L | 9 | 28 |
| **March** | | | | | |
| 11 | H | Rosslyn Park | W | 31 | 5 |
| 17 | H | Kelso ° | W | 57 | 24 |
| 25 | A | Blackheath | D | 12 | 12 |
| **April** | | | | | |
| 1 | H | Exeter | W | 23 | 10 |
| 8 | H | Otley | W | 32 | 11 |
| 12 | H | Rugby | L | 17 | 35 |
| 15 | A | Harrogate | W | 59 | 15 |
| 29 | H | Richmond | W | 21 | 20 |

Courage League Three – 1st (P).
° Friendly. * Pilkington Cup.

A Finnie was again the top points scorer with 338. His 79 penalties was a record. J Simons was the leading try scorer with 15. P Alston again made the most appearances, 35. Fifty six players made one or more.

P Allen (15, 1T), P Alston (35, 6T), C Astley (1), S Basra (33), L Bennett (1), N Beytell (6), D Bradshaw (1), J Chandler (7, 1T), F Clough (20, 3T), M Cook (20, 6T), J Cooley (11), M Deans (24, 7T), J Egan (3), A Elvidge (1), J Farr (26, 2T), A Finnie (31, 43C, 79P, 5D), P Garrett (25, 2T), J Gaylard (2, 1T), C Glanvill (10), A Goldsmith (9, 4T), D Godwin (1), J Graves (1, 4C, 3P), S Harris (26, 5T), T Heaver (1), K Houghton (8, 1T), T Howard (2), M Howe (15, 2T), P Kemble (5), S Kench (2), A Mortimore (3), M Oliver (2), M Redrup (2 ,1T) M Rennell (4) M Roach (4, 1T) C Roberts (3) I Robertson (1) M Sharp (22) J Simons (19, 15T), K Simpson (2), I Skingsley (23, 3T), R Stidolph (3), R Subbiani (20, 8T), N Swanson (1), A Tapper (5, 3T, 14C, 8P), J Thame (8), R Thompson (11, 1T), J Thorpe (1), J Turnbull (5, 2T), V Turner (16, 5T), M Upex (29), M Vincent (1), B Whetstone (30, 14T, 1D), G Witheat (3, 1T), C Wright (1), M Wright (2), D Wyre-Roberts (20, 1T).

# 1995-96

Played 33, Won 11, Lost 21, Drawn 1. F 604, A 938.

Captain: P Alston

| | | | | f | a |
|---|---|---|---|---|---|
| **September** | | | | | |
| 2 | H | Rosslyn Park ° | W | 20 | 13 |
| 9 | A | Wakefield | L | 23 | 32 |
| 16 | H | Waterloo | D | 10 | 10 |
| 23 | H | Blackheath | W | 21 | 18 |
| 30 | A | Newcastle | W | 30 | 23 |
| **October** | | | | | |
| 7 | H | Northampton | L | 17 | 49 |
| 10 | A | Oxford Univ ° | L | 27 | 41 |
| 14 | A | London Scottish | L | 10 | 50 |
| 21 | H | London Irish | L | 29 | 46 |
| 28 | A | Moseley | L | 18 | 27 |
| **November** | | | | | |
| 4 | H | Nottingham | W | 20 | 12 |
| 11 | H | Wakefield | W | 20 | 13 |
| 17 | A | Gloucester ° | L | 15 | 63 |
| 25 | A | London Welsh ° | L | 24 | 28 |
| **December** | | | | | |
| 2 | H | Wasps ° | W | 21 | 15 |
| 16 | H | Rotherham ° | W | 41 | 22 |
| 23 | H | Worcester * | W | 27 | 12 |

| | | | | f | a |
|---|---|---|---|---|---|
| **January** | | | | | |
| 6 | A | Blackheath | L | 8 | 23 |
| 13 | A | Waterloo | L | 24 | 48 |
| 19 | A | Leicester ° | L | 13 | 38 |
| **February** | | | | | |
| 2 | H | Saracens ° | L | 11 | 23 |
| 10 | H | Bristol * | L | 0 | 37 |
| 14 | H | Cambridge Univ ° | W | 36 | 24 |
| 24 | H | Harlequins 'A' ° | L | 5 | 22 |
| **March** | | | | | |
| 1 | A | Kelso ° | L | 12 | 27 |
| 9 | H | Newcastle | L | 6 | 24 |
| 15 | H | Dungannon ° | W | 44 | 17 |
| 23 | A | Northampton | L | 0 | 48 |
| 30 | H | London Scottish | W | 21 | 19 |
| **April** | | | | | |
| 6 | A | London Irish | L | 13 | 25 |
| 13 | H | Moseley | L | 8 | 23 |
| 20 | H | Bath ° | L | 19 | 36 |
| 27 | A | Nottingham | L | 11 | 30 |

Courage League Two-10th. ° Friendly. * Pilkington Cup.

A Finnie was top points scorer for the 11th time with 122 and M Oliver scored the most tries, 13. P Garrett played the most matches, 28. Forty seven players made at least one appearance.

P Allen (14, 2T), P Alston (19, 6T), S Basra (16, 1T), N Beytell (2), P Brunsden (1), J Chandler (8,2T), M Coe (1), F Clough (12, 2T), M Cook (25, 4T, 2P, 1D), J Cooley (2), M Deans (19, 3T) J Farr (5, 2T) A Finnie (16, 1T, 24C, 20P, 3D), P Garrett (28, 1T) J Gaylard (1) C Glanvill (1), A Goldsmith (8, 5T), T Howard (1), M Howe (3), B Hyde (7, 1T), P Kemble (5), A Mortimore (9), M Oliver (26, 13T, 1C), S Osman (3), M Redrup (9, 2T, 1C) , M Rennell (8, 3T), M Roach (21, 1T), C Roberts (14), I Robertson (1), M Sharp (19), J Simons (10, 5T), P Simmonds (6, 1T), K Simpson (2, 1T), K Simpson (21), I Skingsley (14, 2T), S Smith (7, 5C, 13P), R Stidolph (1) R Stone (20, 8T), R Subbiani (10, 4T), A Tapper (8, 8C, 8P), R Thompson (25, 1T), M Upex (24, 1T), B Whetstone (20, 4T), G Witheat (25), G Williams (3), C Wright (3), M Wright (8).

# 1996-97

Played 37, Won 22, Lost 15. F 1207, A 862.

Captain: P Turner

| | | | | f | a |
|---|---|---|---|---|---|
| **August** | | | | | |
| 24 | H | Ebbw Vale ° | W | 33 | 17 |
| 31 | A | U.W.I.C. AW | W | 39 | 24 |
| **September** | | | | | |
| 7 | H | Nottingham | W | 41 | 23 |
| 14 | A | Blackheath | L | 3 | 11 |
| 21 | H | Richmond | L | 17 | 44 |
| 29 | A | Rugby | W | 34 | 6 |
| **October** | | | | | |
| 5 | H | Wakefield | W | 25 | 19 |
| 12 | A | Waterloo | W | 34 | 11 |
| 19 | H | Rotherham | W | 44 | 30 |
| 26 | A | Newcastle | L | 12 | 49 |
| **November** | | | | | |
| 2 | H | Moseley | W | 64 | 9 |
| 4 | H | South Africa 'A' | L | 27 | 41 |
| 9 | A | London Scottish | W | 27 | 26 |
| 16 | H | Coventry | W | 30 | 23 |
| 22 | H | Northampton | L | 3 | 61 |
| 29 | H | Abertillery AW | W | 64 | 14 |
| **December** | | | | | |
| 4 | H | Royal Air Force ° | W | 60 | 10 |
| 7 | A | Aberavon AW | L | 12 | 32 |
| 13 | H | Leicester ° | L | 22 | 45 |
| 21 | A | Orrell * | L | 31 | 34 |
| 28 | A | Nottingham | W | 36 | 13 |

| | | | | f | a |
|---|---|---|---|---|---|
| **January** | | | | | |
| 18 | H | Rugby | W | 57 | 6 |
| 26 | A | Richmond | L | 33 | 34 |
| 31 | H | Kelso ° | W | 74 | 8 |
| **February** | | | | | |
| 8 | A | Wakefield | W | 29 | 17 |
| 14 | H | South West D (SA) ° | W | 24 | 17 |
| 22 | H | Blackheath | W | 72 | 18 |
| **March** | | | | | |
| 2 | H | Aberavon AW | L | 17 | 19 |
| 8 | H | Waterloo | W | 38 | 6 |
| 14 | H | Gloucester ° | W | 58 | 19 |
| 22 | A | Rotherham | W | 32 | 11 |
| **April** | | | | | |
| 5 | H | Newcastle | W | 34 | 28 |
| 12 | A | Moseley | L | 34 | 40 |
| 19 | H | London Scottish | L | 14 | 28 |
| 26 | A | Coventry | L | 10 | 30 |
| **May** | | | | | |
| 7 | H | Bristol PREM | L | 11 | 20 |
| 12 | A | Bristol PREM | L | 12 | 19 |

Courage League Two - 4th. ° Friendly.
* Pilkington Cup. AW Anglo Welsh Competition.
PREM Premiership Play-Off.

M Rayer was the top points scorer with 361, a club record in all matches, which included 101 conversions – another record. He also played in the most matches, 33. B Whetstone scored the most tries, 21. The points for total of 1207 was also a record. Fifty eight players made at least one appearance. Four penalty tries were awarded.

P Allen (12, 2T), S Basra (3), C Bajak (4, 3T), F Bibby (3), C Boyd (11, 2T), S Brown (25, 6T), S Cassidy (6), M Cook (10,1T), S Crossland (7, 4T), M Curry (1), M Deans (11, 4T), D Edwards (6, 3T), J Farr (7, 1T), N Hadley (15, 3T), P Hewitt (26, 9T), G Higginbotham (2), B Hyde (14, 2T), A Kelly (1), P Kemble (6), S Kemp (1, 2T), G Lavin (2), G Luck (2), L Mansell (8, 2T), J Marshall (6, 3T), A Matchett (4, 1T), N McCarthy (10), S McCurrie (22, 2T), A Mortimore (1), S Murray (20, 6T), M Offiah (22, 13T), M Oliver (24, 6T), R O'Neill (6, 5T), J Paramore (24, 11T), M Pepper (17, 2T), M Pechey (13, 9T), H Pfluger (11, 4T, 3C, 2P), S Platford (10, 2T), J Probyn (29, 6T), M Rayer (33, 9T, 101C, 38P), M Rennell (3, 1T), N Roussouw (1), B Ryan (1), R Scott (1) P Simmonds (22, 1T), K Simpson (2), I Skingsley (8, 2T), O Slack (1), S Smith (1), R Stone (17, 7T), R Straeuli (11), A Tapper (2 ,1T, 6C, 1P), R Thompson (10), P Turner (28, 3T, 1C), M Upex (18, 2T), B Whetstone (30, 21T), R White (10), G Williams (2, 2T, 1P), R Winters (25, 1T).

# 1997-98

Played 33, Won 29, Lost 4. F 1254, A 588.

Captain: P Turner

| | | | | f | a |
|---|---|---|---|---|---|
| **August** | | | | | |
| 30 | H | Rotherham | W | 18 | 11 |
| **September** | | | | | |
| 13 | A | Exeter | W | 32 | 17 |
| 20 | H | London Scottish | W | 45 | 33 |
| 27 | A | Coventry | W | 22 | 15 |
| **October** | | | | | |
| 4 | H | Waterloo | W | 34 | 17 |
| 11 | A | Moseley | W | 35 | 16 |
| 18 | H | West Hartlepool | W | 22 | 9 |
| 25 | A | London Scottish | W | 22 | 15 |
| **November** | | | | | |
| 1 | H | Staines • | W | 76 | 15 |
| 8 | H | Coventry | W | 77 | 3 |
| 19 | H | Cambridge Univ ° | W | 53 | 22 |
| 29 | A | London Scottish * | W | 52 | 26 |
| **December** | | | | | |
| 6 | A | Richmond * | W | 30 | 17 |
| 13 | A | Waterloo | W | 28 | 14 |
| 20 | H | Moseley | W | 32 | 16 |
| 27 | A | Fylde | W | 67 | 7 |
| **January** | | | | | |
| 3 | A | Northampton • | L | 26 | 31 |
| 17 | H | Fylde | W | 50 | 14 |
| 25 | H | Gautang Falcons SA ° | W | 31 | 18 |
| 31 | H | Orrell | W | 47 | 22 |
| **February** | | | | | |
| 7 | H | Blackheath * | W | 70 | 5 |
| 14 | A | Wakefield | W | 24 | 13 |
| 28 | A | Gloucester ° | W | 32 | 20 |
| **March** | | | | | |
| 7 | A | Blackheath | W | 37 | 13 |
| 11 | H | Bristol * | W | 37 | 20 |
| 14 | H | Wakefield | W | 36 | 10 |
| 21 | H | Sale * | W | 31 | 20 |
| 28 | A | Orrell | W | 29 | 16 |
| **April** | | | | | |
| 3 | N | Gloucester * | L | 25 | 33 |
| 11 | A | Rotherham | L | 17 | 18 |
| 18 | H | Exeter | W | 16 | 3 |
| 25 | H | Blackheath | W | 72 | 31 |
| **May** | | | | | |
| 2 | A | West Hartlepool | L | 29 | 48 |

Allied Dunbar Premiership Two – 1st (P). * Cheltenham & Gloucester Cup, N - Final at Northampton.
° Friendly. • Tetley Bitter Cup.

M Rayer was the leading scorer with 370 points, beating his own club record set the season before. B Whetstone was top try scorer with 25, the best return for more than 20 years. R Underwood played in all 33 games. Forty seven players appeared at least once. A record number of eight penalty tries were awarded. The points for total of 1254 was a record.

P Anglesea (8, 3T), C Astley (1), C Boyd (27, 1T), S Brading (9, 2T), S Brown (12, 1T), S Crabb (17, 6T), J Cullen (15, 1T), A Davis (4), M Deans (23, 6T), A Duke (1), J Ewens (8, 4T), J Forster (31, 19T), M George (1), N Hadley (2), N Hatley (22, 2T), P Hewitt (10, 2T), D Hinkins (20, 1T), J Hinkins (3, 1T), S Howard (9, 2T, 2C), A Kardooni (22), M Kirkby (5, 7T), R Kirke (18, 2T), S McCurrie (2), A Murdoch (21, 12T), S Murray (30, 7T), M. Oliver (2, 1T), R O'Neill (2, 1T), J Paramore (25, 10T), M Pechey (16, 4T), H Pfluger (12, 4T, 16C, 9P), S Platford (25, 2T), J Probyn (4), M Rayer (29, 7T, 88C, 53P), J Richards (15, 1T), P Simmonds (14), N Smith (1), R Stone (9, 4T), R Straeuli (15, 2T), R Thompson (4), J Thorpe (2), P Turner (18, 4T), R Underwood (33, 10T), J Wells (13), B Whetstone (26, 25T, 1D), D Whiston (5, 1T), R Winters (30, 5T), A Yapp (25, 2T, 1C, 1P, 1D).

# 1998-99

Played 39, Won 10, Lost 28, Drawn 1. F 807, A 1174. Captain: A R Murdoch

| | | | | f | a |
|---|---|---|---|---|---|
| **September** | | | | | |
| 5 | H | Cardiff ° | L | 10 | 27 |
| 12 | A | Sale | L | 21 | 39 |
| 19 | H | London Scottish | W | 24 | 16 |
| 26 | H | Leicester | L | 23 | 32 |
| **October** | | | | | |
| 3 | A | Bath | L | 19 | 57 |
| 10 | H | Harlequins | W | 35 | 33 |
| 17 | A | Northampton | L | 29 | 34 |
| 21 | A | Wasps | L | 19 | 35 |
| 24 | H | Newcastle | L | 22 | 29 |
| **November** | | | | | |
| 1 | A | Richmond | L | 32 | 38 |
| 7 | A | Gloucester | L | 21 | 31 |
| 15 | H | Saracens | L | 20 | 25 |
| 21 | A | London Irish | L | 19 | 30 |
| 29 | A | Coventry * | L | 12 | 13 |
| **December** | | | | | |
| 12 | H | West Hartlepool | L | 10 | 23 |
| 15 | H | Coventry * | W | 39 | 12 |
| 20 | H | Swansea ° | L | 14 | 28 |
| 26 | A | Leicester | L | 0 | 26 |
| 31 | A | Saracens | L | 13 | 44 |

| | | | | f | a |
|---|---|---|---|---|---|
| **January** | | | | | |
| 5 | A | Newcastle | L | 23 | 34 |
| 10 | H | Henley • | L | 22 | 29 |
| 23 | H | Bath | L | 17 | 30 |
| **February** | | | | | |
| 7 | A | Cardiff ° | L | 14 | 57 |
| 13 | H | Wasps | W | 25 | 23 |
| 21 | A | Rugby * | W | 22 | 19 |
| 27 | H | Sale * | L | 7 | 18 |
| **March** | | | | | |
| 5 | A | Moseley * | W | 28 | 14 |
| 13 | A | London Scottish | W | 24 | 15 |
| 21 | H | Newcastle * | D | 27 | 27 |
| 27 | H | Gloucester | W | 19 | 15 |
| **April** | | | | | |
| 11 | N | Gloucester * | L | 9 | 24 |
| 17 | A | Harlequins | L | 16 | 29 |
| 20 | A | Swansea ° | L | 31 | 46 |
| 24 | H | Northampton | L | 31 | 42 |
| **May** | | | | | |
| 5 | A | West Hartlepool | W | 39 | 0 |
| 8 | H | London Irish | L | 21 | 36 |
| 16 | H | Richmond | L | 12 | 106 |
| 20 | A | Rotherham PREM | L | 11 | 19 |
| 23 | H | Rotherham PREM | W | 27 | 19 |

Allied Dunbar Premiership One – 13th.
° Friendly. * Cheltenham & Gloucester Cup.
N - Final at Northampton. • Tetley Bitter Cup. PREM Premiership Play-Off.

S Howard was the leading points scorer with 183. R Underwood was the top try scorer with 15. J Richards made the most appearances, 35. Fifty eight players turned out. The points against total of 1174 was a record.

J Abrahams (4), R Ashforth (7), S Basra (1), J Beardsmore (6), C Boyd (30), S Brading (2), R Candlin (2), C Cano (8), N Clarke (1), J Cockle (30, 2T), A Codling (8), M Culclough (1), M Cook (1, 2T), S Crabb (9), A Davis (12, 2T), M Deans (6), A Duke (17), Earl (1), R Elliott (15, 1T), P Elphick (8), J Ewens (25, 10T), Enyon (1), J Forster (34, 14T), W Fuller (1), L Gibbons (2), D Harris (21), C Harrison (30, 2T), V Hartland (21), N Hatley (12), P Hewitt (4), J Hinkins (6, 1T), S Howard (28, 4T, 38C, 28P, 1D), A Hudson (1), Jones (1), M Kirkby (2), M Mainwaring (2), A Murdoch (30, 5T), S Murray (26), A Olver (11, 2T), D O'Mahony (32, 13T), A Ozdemir (17), J Paramore (20, 6T), B Pegna (1), Reynolds (1), J Richards (35, 1T), P Simmonds (2), S Stewart (14, 1T, 1C), R Straeuli (9), R Underwood (30, 15T), R Ward (3), B Watts (1), J Wells (6, 5T), B Whetstone (27, 7T, 1C, 1P), H Whitford (1), R Winters (31), Wood (1) A Yapp (31, 3T, 26C, 28P, 7D), D Zaltzman (26, 3T).

# 1999-2000

Played 34, Won 6, Lost 28. F 638, A 1147.

Captain: A C T Gomarsall

| | | | | f | a |
|---|---|---|---|---|---|
| **September** | | | | | |
| 4 | H | Northampton | L | 17 | 34 |
| 10 | A | Bristol | L | 25 | 40 |
| 17 | H | Oxford Univ ° | W | 29 | 5 |
| 25 | A | London Irish | L | 8 | 29 |
| **October** | | | | | |
| 1 | A | Saracens | L | 15 | 39 |
| 23 | A | Cambridge Univ ° | W | 32 | 9 |
| 30 | A | Leicester | L | 12 | 61 |
| **November** | | | | | |
| 6 | H | Bath | L | 24 | 28 |
| 13 | A | Harlequins | L | 10 | 11 |
| 20 | H | Newport * | W | 28 | 18 |
| 28 | A | Rovigo * | W | 33 | 24 |
| **December** | | | | | |
| 4 | H | Northampton | L | 17 | 41 |
| 11 | H | Castres * | L | 25 | 60 |
| 18 | A | Castres * | L | 6 | 56 |
| 26 | A | Sale | L | 3 | 22 |
| 29 | H | Gloucester | L | 6 | 18 |

| | | | | f | a |
|---|---|---|---|---|---|
| **January** | | | | | |
| 3 | H | Saracens • | L | 9 | 33 |
| 9 | H | Rovigo * | L | 10 | 20 |
| 15 | A | Newport * | L | 19 | 44 |
| 22 | A | Northampton | L | 16 | 38 |
| 25 | H | Harlequins | L | 25 | 28 |
| **February** | | | | | |
| 12 | A | Bath | L | 22 | 32 |
| 27 | A | Newcastle | L | 20 | 23 |
| **March** | | | | | |
| 11 | H | Leicester | L | 22 | 32 |
| 26 | A | Wasps | L | 8 | 62 |
| **April** | | | | | |
| 8 | H | Newcastle | W | 32 | 22 |
| 16 | H | Saracens | L | 29 | 57 |
| 22 | A | London Irish | L | 23 | 33 |
| 26 | H | Wasps | L | 7 | 21 |
| 29 | H | Bristol | L | 19 | 57 |
| **May** | | | | | |
| 6 | A | Gloucester | L | 16 | 60 |
| 14 | H | Sale | L | 37 | 50 |
| 24 | A | Rotherham PREM | L | 20 | 40 |
| 28 | H | Rotherham PREM | W | 14 | 0 |

Allied Dunbar Premiership One – 12th (R). * European Shield. ° Friendly, • Tetley Bitter Cup. PREM Premiership Play-Off.

A Gomarsall was the leading points scorer with 76 and P Sackey scored the most tries, 11. Fifty two players made at least one appearance; R Winters, with 30, made the most. The overall record of six wins and 28 defeats in a season was the worst in 125 years of the Blues – expressed as a percentage of wins to games played (minimum 25).

J Abrahams (3), R Banks (25, 5T), P Beal (11), A Black (25, 2T), G Bowen (5, 4C, 2P), W Brant (4), N Broughton (6, 2T), N Buoy (1), R Candlin (3, 1T), M Caputo (3), J Cockle (5), J Connolly (9, 5T), A Davies (16 1T), C Eagle (29, 1T), R Earnshaw (1), D Edwards (12, 3T), R Elliott (8), J Elphick (5, 1T, 1P), P Elphick (10, 1T), R Eriksson (17, 1T), R Faiers (2), A Gomarsall (25, 3T, 12C, 13P), D Harris (23, 4T), C Harrison (17, 1T), V Hartland (14), P Hewitt (8), J Hinkins (3), D Hughes (11, 1T, 3C, 3P), A Hurford (1), A Johnson (6), D Jones (4), M Kwisick (19, 1T), A McLean (19, 6T), A Murdoch (15, 3T), A Olver (27, 2T), R O'Neill (13, 1T), C Pearson (11, 3T), C Richards (15, 7C, 5P), F Rossigneux (27, 4T), G Ruskin (1), P Sackey (24, 11T) D Sims (13), O Slack (5), K Stewart (14, 1T), S Stewart (23, 2T, 13C, 10P, 1D), R Thompson (10, 14C, 14P), G Truelove (29, 4T), M Volland (2), M Webber (9), P Williams (1), R Winters (30, 4T), D Zaltzman (15, 1T).

# 2000-2001

Played 30, Won 11, Lost 18, Drawn 1. F 564, A 719.

Captain: B M L Whetstone

| | | | | f | a |
|---|---|---|---|---|---|
| **September** | | | | | |
| 9 | H | Henley | L | 31 | 34 |
| 16 | A | London Welsh | W | 20 | 14 |
| 23 | H | Birmingham & Solihull | L | 17 | 20 |
| 30 | A | Worcester | L | 25 | 31 |
| **October** | | | | | |
| 3 | A | Oxford Univ ° | L | 10 | 17 |
| 7 | H | Orrell | W | 27 | 0 |
| 14 | A | Leeds | L | 6 | 42 |
| 21 | H | Sedgley Park • | W | 45 | 15 |
| 28 | H | Manchester | W | 20 | 8 |
| **November** | | | | | |
| 4 | H | Saracens • | L | 24 | 54 |
| 14 | H | Cambridge Univ ° | W | 22 | 17 |
| 19 | H | Moseley | W | 28 | 14 |
| 25 | A | Waterloo | W | 20 | 11 |
| **December** | | | | | |
| 2 | H | Otley | W | 16 | 15 |
| 16 | H | Waterloo | W | 37 | 9 |
| **January** | | | | | |
| 6 | H | Coventry | L | 15 | 20 |
| 13 | A | Moseley | L | 17 | 24 |
| 27 | A | Coventry | L | 22 | 39 |
| **February** | | | | | |
| 4 | A | Manchester | L | 13 | 22 |
| 10 | H | Leeds | L | 3 | 48 |
| 24 | A | Orrell | L | 14 | 15 |
| **March** | | | | | |
| 3 | A | Exeter | L | 13 | 39 |
| 10 | H | Worcester | L | 14 | 32 |
| 24 | A | Wakefield | L | 7 | 56 |
| 31 | H | London Welsh | W | 23 | 18 |
| **April** | | | | | |
| 8 | H | Wakefield | W | 19 | 18 |
| 14 | A | Henley | L | 10 | 18 |
| 21 | H | Exeter | L | 11 | 33 |
| 25 | A | Birmingham & Solihull | L | 18 | 19 |
| 28 | A | Otley | D | 17 | 17 |

National One - 11th. ° Friendly. • Tetley Bitter Cup.

B Whetstone was the leading points scorer with 111. J Hinkins, with 12, was top try scorer. Forty three players appeared in one or more matches. B Whetstone, J Shanahan and B Hinshelwood each played 30 times.

J Abrahams (3), C Bajak (21, 9T), P Barnard (4), J Brooks (28, 1T), D Browne (17), R Candlin (10), P Clarke (20, 2T), M. Cook (3,1T), H Crane (15, 3T), M Count (7), A Davis (13), M Devin (6), P Elphick (14, 2T), R Fredricks (9), A Fox (14, 1T), A Hennessey (13), P Hewitt (2), J Hinkins (28, 12T), B Hinshelwood (30, 6T, 1C, 2P), R Jackson (4), R Jewell (6), L Mansell (24), M McLoughlin (1), M Ormesher (1), T Otte (12), M Rivaro (6), J Ross (10, 1T), J Rudd (17, 6T), J Shanahan (30, 7T, 6C, 4P, 3D), M Sharp (6, 2T), M Skillecorn (20), S Stewart (18, 21C, 17P), J Summers (16), T Suring (1), C Thomas (23, 5T), M Wallwork (19, 1C), D Ward (25), J Wells (3, 1T), B Whetstone (30, 10T, 8C, 15P), L White (27, 2T), D Whitehead (11), H Whitford (22, 1T), P Williams (4).

# 2001-02

Played 28, Won 12, Lost 13, Drawn 3. F 688, A 652.

Captain: B M L Whetstone

| | | | | f | a |
|---|---|---|---|---|---|
| **September** | | | | | |
| 1 | A | Rugby | D | 32 | 32 |
| 8 | H | Exeter | W | 36 | 27 |
| 15 | A | Moseley | L | 45 | 46 |
| 22 | H | Manchester | W | 21 | 10 |
| 29 | A | Birmingham & Solihull | D | 19 | 19 |
| **October** | | | | | |
| 6 | H | Henley | W | 44 | 9 |
| 13 | H | Wakefield • | L | 19 | 22 |
| 20 | A | Rotherham | L | 13 | 53 |
| **November** | | | | | |
| 1 | A | Cambridge Univ ° | L | 15 | 30 |
| 10 | A | Coventry | D | 15 | 15 |
| 17 | H | Worcester | L | 11 | 20 |
| 24 | H | London Welsh | W | 39 | 27 |
| **December** | | | | | |
| 1 | A | Otley | L | 10 | 26 |
| 8 | H | Bracknell | W | 27 | 10 |
| 29 | A | Wakefield | L | 6 | 18 |
| **January** | | | | | |
| 12 | A | Exeter | L | 13 | 18 |
| 19 | H | Moseley | W | 36 | 25 |
| 26 | A | Manchester | W | 24 | 12 |
| **February** | | | | | |
| 2 | H | Birmingham & Solihull | W | 23 | 10 |
| 9 | A | Henley | W | 37 | 25 |
| 23 | H | Rotherham | L | 31 | 36 |
| **March** | | | | | |
| 1 | H | Rugby | W | 25 | 15 |
| 9 | A | London Welsh | L | 20 | 26 |
| 16 | H | Coventry | W | 29 | 24 |
| 30 | A | Worcester | L | 22 | 46 |
| **April** | | | | | |
| 6 | H | Otley | L | 17 | 22 |
| 13 | A | Bracknell | W | 41 | 7 |
| 27 | H | Wakefield | L | 18 | 22 |

National One - 6th. ° Friendly. • Powergen Cup.

J Pritchard was the leading points scorer with 250 and J Shanahan top try scorer with 11. S Bell, with 27, made the most appearances. Forty players represented the club.

S Alatini (6, 3T), C Bajak (21, 9T), S Bell (27, 4T), J Brooks (20), P Clarke (22), M Cook (24, 3T), M Dawson (12, 3T), C Du Plessis (9) F Fichot (26, 8T) A Fox (25, 2T), S Gray (6), L Gunnell (11), D Hankinson (1), A Hepher (2, 1P), J Hinkins (10, 5T), C Horsman (26, 5T), E Jennings (20, 1T), S Lincoln (25, 4T), A Llewellyn (11), M Loxton (4, 2T), L Mansell (5), L Martin (4), M Meenan (22, 2T, 6C, 4P, 5D), A Mihajlovic (1), J Pritchard (25, 8T, 42C, 42P), H Quigley (3), P Rollason (23, 1T), J Ross-Ryan (20, 1T), P Saffy (2), J Shanahan (23, 11T, 2D), M Sharp (2), G Seely (2, 2T), P Simmonds (6), C Thomas (23, 2T), M Volland (22), B Whetstone (2, 2T), L White (19, 4T), H Whitford (19, 1T), B Williams (2), R Williamson (1).

# 2002-03

Played 27, Won 13, Lost 13, Drawn 1. F 692, A 787.

Captain: M J Volland

| | | | | f | a |
|---|---|---|---|---|---|
| **August** | | | | | |
| 31 | H | Moseley | W | 21 | 15 |
| **September** | | | | | |
| 7 | A | Plymouth Albion | L | 29 | 49 |
| 14 | H | Wakefield | W | 47 | 14 |
| 22 | A | Rotherham | L | 6 | 51 |
| 28 | H | Rugby | W | 37 | 13 |
| **October** | | | | | |
| 5 | A | Worcester | L | 10 | 69 |
| 12 | H | Coventry | L | 26 | 28 |
| 19 | A | Halifax • | L | 17 | 27 |
| 26 | A | Orrell | L | 23 | 43 |
| **November** | | | | | |
| 2 | H | Otley | W | 24 | 16 |
| 16 | A | Exeter | L | 12 | 28 |
| 23 | H | Manchester | W | 54 | 28 |
| **December** | | | | | |
| 7 | H | Birmingham & Solihull | W | 19 | 7 |
| 14 | A | London Welsh | W | 26 | 24 |
| **January** | | | | | |
| 18 | A | Wakefield | L | 18 | 24 |
| **February** | | | | | |
| 1 | A | Rugby | W | 35 | 23 |
| 8 | H | Worcester | L | 9 | 45 |
| 16 | A | Moseley | W | 51 | 31 |
| 19 | H | Orrell | L | 26 | 37 |
| 22 | A | Coventry | W | 25 | 22 |
| **March** | | | | | |
| 8 | H | Rotherham | L | 13 | 40 |
| 15 | A | Otley | L | 32 | 41 |
| 23 | H | Plymouth Albion | W | 31 | 16 |
| 29 | H | Exeter | L | 23 | 32 |
| **April** | | | | | |
| 12 | A | Manchester | W | 35 | 22 |
| 19 | H | London Welsh | W | 19 | 18 |
| 26 | A | Birmingham & Solihull | D | 24 | 24 |

National One -7th. • Powergen Cup.

J Pritchard featured in every match, setting a new club record of 386 for league and cup points (374 and 12) scored in a season. He was also the leading try scorer with 13. Forty three players made an appearance. P Beard was appointed Hon. Keeper of the Records following the death of J Pope. The total of 27 matches in a season was the lowest since 1946-47 when there was also 27.

P Alston (4), L Anker (14, 2T), P Baird (19, 5T), J Ball (2), E Barnes (23, 3T, 5D), S Bell (4), A Brenton (21, 1T), J Brooks (9), S Brown (16, 6T), M Cornish (20, 1T), F Fichot (21, 4T), A Fox (17, 3T), M Gray (3), S Gray (19, 1T), L Gunnell (6), S Halsey (7), D Hankinson (3), C Hannon (16), S Harding (3), N Harris (1), A Hepher (7, 1T), N Hill (1), A Holloway (16, 1T), T Kirk (21, 2T), S Lincoln (7), L Mansell (2), M Mansfield (2, 2T), M Ormesher (1), A Orugboh (8), J Pritchard (27, 13T, 51C, 73P), H Quigley (5), C Richards (16, 2T, 3C), P Rollason (9), K Ronaki (27, 3T), J Ross-Ryan (24, 4T), P Saffy (9), M Staten (25, 6T), K Todd (9), M Volland (19, 1T), D Wheatley (1), B Whetstone (24, 6T), L White (21, 1T), H Whitford (16).

# 2003-04

Played 29, Won 14, Lost 14, Drawn 1. F 727, A 677.

Captain: M J Volland

| | | | | f | a |
|---|---|---|---|---|---|
| **September** | | | | | |
| 6 | H | Manchester | W | 29 | 15 |
| 13 | A | Wakefield | L | 23 | 27 |
| 20 | H | Worcester | L | 20 | 31 |
| 27 | A | Plymouth Albion | W | 24 | 15 |
| **October** | | | | | |
| 4 | A | Barking • | W | 46 | 14 |
| 11 | H | Exeter | W | 47 | 24 |
| 18 | H | Nuneaton • | W | 39 | 15 |
| 26 | A | Bristol | L | 14 | 20 |
| **November** | | | | | |
| 1 | A | Penzance & Newlyn • | L | 19 | 21 |
| 8 | H | Penzance & Newlyn | W | 39 | 7 |
| 22 | A | Coventry | L | 19 | 23 |
| 29 | H | Otley | W | 22 | 15 |
| **December** | | | | | |
| 6 | A | Orrell | L | 24 | 57 |
| 13 | H | Henley | W | 45 | 20 |
| 20 | A | Birmingham & Solihull | L | 5 | 22 |
| 27 | H | London Welsh | L | 19 | 22 |

| | | | | f | a |
|---|---|---|---|---|---|
| **January** | | | | | |
| 10 | A | Manchester | W | 47 | 19 |
| 17 | H | Wakefield | W | 29 | 8 |
| 24 | A | Worcester | L | 5 | 43 |
| 31 | H | Plymouth Albion | L | 6 | 26 |
| **February** | | | | | |
| 7 | A | Exeter | L | 10 | 21 |
| 14 | H | Bristol | W | 30 | 16 |
| 28 | A | Penzance & Newlyn | D | 20 | 20 |
| **March** | | | | | |
| 19 | H | Coventry | W | 24 | 20 |
| 27 | H | Birmingham & Solihull | W | 38 | 26 |
| **April** | | | | | |
| 3 | A | Otley | L | 17 | 27 |
| 10 | A | London Welsh | W | 30 | 25 |
| 17 | H | Orrell | L | 22 | 55 |
| 24 | A | Henley | L | 15 | 23 |

National One -7th. • Powergen Cup.

E Barnes was the leading points scorer with 175 and B Whetstone top try scorer with 12. Thirty seven players turned out. J Brooks played in all 29 games.

L Anker (22, 3T), P Baird (14, 5T), J Ball (13), E Barnes (22, 1T, 43C, 28P), S Brady (13, 2T), A Brenton (28, 2T), J Brooks (29, 2T), S Brown (10, 1T), M Gray (2), S Gray (3), S Halsey (2), S Harding (3), A Hepher (25, 6T, 18C, 25P), S Hepher (20, 6T), J Hinkins (19, 3T), A Holloway (9), T Kirk (26, 7T), S Lincoln (5), M Loxton (8, 1T) D Malone (25, 4T, 2C), M Mansfield (8), A Orugboh (22), J Phillips (1, 2T), M Price (3, 1T), H Quigley (21, 2T), C Rainbow (23, 4T), P Rollason (7), K Ronaki (20, 9T), J Ross-Ryan (23), P Saffy (21, 4T), J Sleightholme (1), M Staten (23, 5T), M Stewart (26, 1T), M Volland (28, 1T), B Whetstone (23, 12T, 1C), L White (25, 2T), H Whitford (10, 1T).

# 2004-05

Played 33, Won 22, Lost 10, Drawn 1. F 855, A 652. Captain: M C Allen

| | | | | f | a |
|---|---|---|---|---|---|
| **September** | | | | | |
| 11 | H | Henley | W | 49 | 23 |
| 18 | A | Otley | W | 34 | 6 |
| 25 | A | Exeter | L | 21 | 42 |
| **October** | | | | | |
| 2 | H | Orrell | D | 14 | 14 |
| 9 | A | London Welsh | W | 46 | 24 |
| 12 | H | Cambridge Univ ° | W | 24 | 14 |
| 16 | H | Tabard • | W | 52 | 13 |
| 23 | H | Sedgley Park | W | 13 | 8 |
| 31 | A | Penzance & Newlyn | L | 19 | 30 |
| **November** | | | | | |
| 6 | H | Halifax • | W | 40 | 10 |
| 13 | A | Plymouth Albion | L | 9 | 19 |
| 20 | H | Birmingham & Solihull | W | 41 | 8 |
| 27 | H | Exeter • | W | 23 | 18 |
| **December** | | | | | |
| 5 | A | Bristol | L | 6 | 37 |
| 11 | H | Coventry | W | 26 | 16 |
| 18 | A | Northampton • | L | 8 | 41 |
| 27 | H | Nottingham | W | 33 | 13 |

| | | | | f | a |
|---|---|---|---|---|---|
| **January** | | | | | |
| 3 | A | Rotherham | W | 26 | 24 |
| 8 | A | Henley | W | 43 | 10 |
| 15 | H | Otley | W | 26 | 13 |
| 22 | H | Exeter | L | 20 | 39 |
| 29 | A | Orrell | W | 29 | 18 |
| **February** | | | | | |
| 12 | H | Rotherham | L | 12 | 17 |
| 19 | H | London Welsh | L | 16 | 17 |
| 26 | A | Sedgley Park | W | 23 | 12 |
| **March** | | | | | |
| 5 | A | Birmingham & Solihull •• | W | 15 | 7 |
| 12 | H | Penzance & Newlyn | L | 23 | 28 |
| 26 | A | Nottingham | W | 20 | 12 |
| **April** | | | | | |
| 2 | H | Plymouth Albion | W | 39 | 21 |
| 9 | A | Birmingham & Solihull | W | 29 | 18 |
| 16 | T | Plymouth Albion •• | W | 14 | 13 |
| 23 | H | Bristol | W | 33 | 20 |
| 30 | A | Coventry | L | 29 | 47 |

National One - 7th. ° Friendly. • Powergen Cup. •• Powergen Challenge Shield. T – Final at Twickenham - Winners.

L Hinton was the leading points scorer in league and cup with 397 (347 and 50), a new club record. His total of 81 penalties was another record. He was also the top try scorer, with ten, and, with N Strauss, made the most appearances, 30. Fifty five players represented the club.

L Alden (1), M Allen (22, 3T), J Armitage (1), J Ball (10), W Bester (2), E Binham (11, 1T), S Booth (2), S Brady (26, 5T), A Brenton (27, 2T), J Brooks (18, 1T), S Brown (11, 2T), M Burton (2), M Comb (7), A Dalgleish (3), K Dickson (7, 1T), J Graham (5), S Griffiths (2), K Hallett (2, 1T, 7C, 1P, 1D), M Hampson (3), S Harding (4), M Harris (11, 4T), A Hepher (23, 2T, 3C, 5P), J Hinkins (16, 2T), L Hinton (30, 10T, 52C, 81P), M Holford (2), C Johnson (26, 1T), B Lewitt (26, 6T), M Loxton (2, 1T), E Malloy (2), D Malone (20, 3T), M Mansfield (1), C Moir (22, 2T), M Mrdjenovich (3, 2T), A Orugboh (2), E Palladino (1), J Paramore (25, 3T), A Phillips (11, 1T), J Phillips (27, 4T), M Price (4), C Rainbow (7), M Rossam (1), J Ross (20, 3T), T Ryder (1), W Saayman (8, 1T), M Staten (25, 5T), M Stewart (16, 2T), N Strauss (30, 2T), B Sturgess (1), T Tombleson (1), S Tonga'uiha (20, 4T), J Van Wyk (4), I Vass (30, 9T, 1D), M Volland (27), B Whetstone (18, 5T), H Whitford (2).

# 2005-06

Played 31, Won 23, Lost 7, Drawn 1. F 1098, A 650.

Captain: M C Allen

| | | | | f | a |
|---|---|---|---|---|---|
| **September** | | | | | |
| 3 | A | Otley | D | 16 | 16 |
| 10 | H | Doncaster | W | 47 | 17 |
| 17 | H | Sedgley Park | W | 34 | 13 |
| 24 | A | London Welsh | W | 40 | 24 |
| **October** | | | | | |
| 1 | H | Cornish Pirates | W | 31 | 12 |
| 8 | H | Rotherham | W | 24 | 16 |
| 22 | A | Nottingham | W | 25 | 10 |
| 29 | H | Birmingham & Solihull | W | 35 | 18 |
| **November** | | | | | |
| 5 | H | Blackheath • | W | 61 | 0 |
| 19 | A | Plymouth Albion | L | 23 | 28 |
| 26 | H | Esher • | W | 57 | 17 |
| **December** | | | | | |
| 3 | H | Harlequins | L | 20 | 26 |
| 10 | A | Newbury | W | 50 | 17 |
| 17 | H | Exeter | W | 28 | 13 |
| 27 | A | Coventry | W | 31 | 24 |

| | | | | f | a |
|---|---|---|---|---|---|
| **January** | | | | | |
| 2 | H | Otley | W | 42 | 24 |
| 7 | A | Otley • | W | 14 | 13 |
| 14 | A | Doncaster | W | 24 | 17 |
| 21 | A | Sedgley Park | W | 45 | 29 |
| 28 | H | London Welsh | W | 38 | 17 |
| **February** | | | | | |
| 12 | A | Cornish Pirates | L | 21 | 26 |
| 18 | A | Rotherham | W | 31 | 9 |
| 25 | H | Nottingham | L | 21 | 26 |
| **March** | | | | | |
| 4 | A | Exeter • | W | 37 | 35 |
| 11 | A | Birmingham & Solihull | W | 68 | 16 |
| 25 | H | Plymouth Albion | W | 34 | 28 |
| **April** | | | | | |
| 1 | A | Exeter | L | 23 | 26 |
| 9 | T | Harlequins •• | L | 23 | 39 |
| 15 | H | Coventry | W | 40 | 27 |
| 22 | A | Harlequins | L | 36 | 45 |
| 29 | H | Newbury | W | 79 | 22 |

National One - 2nd. • Powergen National Trophy. •• Powergen National Trophy Final at Twickenham - Runners Up.

M Harris was the leading points scorer with 270 and the top try scorer with 11. J Phillips made the most appearances, 30. Only 35 players turned out for the team – a record given that statistics in the first two seasons are unreliable.

M Allen (28, 8T), J Brooks (29, 1T), S Brady (29, 7T), A Brenton (29, 1T), M Comb (22, 1T), K Dickson (14, 4T), J Graham (14), S Harding (18, 5T), K Hallett (12, 3T, 2C, 1P), M Harris (20, 11T, 61C, 31P), A Hepher (28, 9T, 49C, 9P, 2D), J Hinkins (22, 8T), C Johnson (25, 9T), P Kendall (11, 4T), A Kettle (16, 6T), E Lewis (13, 5T), T Luke (23, 3T, 5C, 5P), D Malone (24, 2T), C Moir (25, 8T), O Montgomery (2), A Page (20, 8T), J Paramore (19, 3T), A Phillips (13), J Phillips (30, 1T), M Price (11, 2T), C Rainbow (17, 5T), L Roberts (23, 5T), J Ross (7), M Staten (18, 6T), N Strauss (25, 6T), M Taylor (1), S Tonga'uiha (29, 8T), M Volland (16), D Ward (1), C Whitehead (4).

# 2006-07

Played 32, Won 19, Lost 11, Drawn 2. F 871, A 600.

Captain: M C Allen

| | | | | f | a |
|---|---|---|---|---|---|
| **September** | | | | | |
| 2 | H | Birmingham & Solihull | D | 29 | 29 |
| 9 | A | Moseley | L | 37 | 44 |
| 16 | H | Sedgley Park | W | 41 | 7 |
| 23 | A | Newbury | W | 34 | 19 |
| 30 | H | Exeter | W | 22 | 10 |
| **October** | | | | | |
| 7 | A | Waterloo | W | 42 | 13 |
| 14 | H | Leeds | W | 25 | 21 |
| 22 | A | Cornish Pirates | L | 5 | 34 |
| 28 | H | Coventry | W | 38 | 8 |
| **November** | | | | | |
| 4 | A | Otley | W | 31 | 21 |
| 12 | A | Nottingham | L | 28 | 29 |
| 18 | H | Rotherham | L | 32 | 34 |
| 25 | A | Birmingham & Solihull | L | 27 | 34 |
| **December** | | | | | |
| 2 | H | Moseley | W | 34 | 10 |
| 9 | A | Sedgley Park | L | 8 | 10 |
| 16 | H | Newbury | W | 29 | 15 |
| 26 | H | London Welsh | W | 35 | 15 |
| 30 | A | Plymouth Albion | L | 8 | 22 |
| **January** | | | | | |
| 6 | H | Doncaster | W | 9 | 6 |
| 13 | A | Exeter | L | 10 | 35 |
| 20 | H | Rotherham • | W | 31 | 21 |
| 27 | H | Waterloo | W | 49 | 3 |
| **February** | | | | | |
| 4 | A | Leeds | L | 0 | 31 |
| 10 | H | Exeter • | D | 13 | 13 |
| 24 | A | Coventry | W | 24 | 17 |
| **March** | | | | | |
| 10 | H | Otley | W | 66 | 8 |
| 17 | H | Nottingham | W | 14 | 10 |
| 31 | A | Rotherham | L | 20 | 26 |
| **April** | | | | | |
| 4 | H | Cornish Pirates | W | 41 | 10 |
| 7 | A | London Welsh | W | 47 | 10 |
| 21 | H | Plymouth Albion | W | 30 | 13 |
| 28 | A | Doncaster | L | 12 | 22 |

National One - 7th. • EDF Energy National Trophy.

J Pritchard scored the most points, 303, and was also the leading try scorer with 12. B Patston made the most appearances, 31; thirty nine players made at least one.

M Allen (25, 4T), B Alexander (23, 2T), S Brady (22, 2T), A Brenton (13, 1T), R Broadfoot (29, 5T, 13C, 14P), M Botha (11), O Brown (11), B Burke (7, 3T), D Cole (22, 3T), M Comb (28, 1T), P Cook (9), G Cooke (3), K Dickson (26, 5T), O Dodge (18, 6T), J Graham (10, 1T), K Hallett (3, 1P), S Harding (26, 7T), J Hinkins (9, 1T), C Johnson (16, 5T), P Kendall (6), A Kettle (24, 5T), E Lewis (17, 4T), D Malone (11), C Moir (16, 4T), A Olver (18, 1T), A Page (24, 5T), B Patston (31, 3T, 3C, 2D), J Percival (14, 2T), B Pienaar (20, 2T), J Phillips (26, 3T), M Price (15), J Pritchard (27, 12T, 63C, 39P), L Roberts (15, 4T), M Staten (10, 3T), N Strauss (29, 6T), T Varndell (2, 2T), M Volland (23, 1T), C Whitehead (28), T Youngs (10, 1T).

# 2007-08

Played 34, Won 20, Lost 14. F 796, A 636.

Captain: M C Allen

| September | | | | f | a |
|---|---|---|---|---|---|
| 1 | A | Newbury | W | 37 | 22 |
| 8 | H | Esher | W | 31 | 29 |
| 16 | A | Nottingham | L | 16 | 31 |
| 22 | H | Northampton | L | 23 | 34 |
| 29 | A | Exeter | L | 6 | 27 |
| **October** | | | | | |
| 5 | H | Coventry | W | 24 | 16 |
| 13 | H | Plymouth Albion | W | 13 | 10 |
| 21 | A | Cornish Pirates | L | 18 | 19 |
| 27 | A | Sedgley Park | W | 24 | 20 |
| **November** | | | | | |
| 3 | A | London Welsh | W | 23 | 10 |
| 10 | H | Moseley | W | 62 | 17 |
| 17 | H | Doncaster | L | 14 | 16 |
| 24 | A | Rotherham | L | 25 | 28 |
| **December** | | | | | |
| 1 | H | Launceston | W | 43 | 16 |
| 8 | A | Birmingham & Solihull | W | 13 | 10 |
| 15 | H | Newbury | W | 24 | 7 |
| 22 | A | Esher | L | 30 | 35 |
| 29 | H | Nottingham | L | 26 | 27 |

| January | | | | f | a |
|---|---|---|---|---|---|
| 5 | A | Northampton | L | 9 | 35 |
| 12 | A | Otley • | W | 22 | 8 |
| 19 | H | Exeter | W | 14 | 12 |
| 26 | A | Coventry | W | 24 | 19 |
| **February** | | | | | |
| 2 | H | Sedgley Park • | W | 42 | 20 |
| 9 | A | Plymouth Albion | W | 13 | 6 |
| 16 | H | Cornish Pirates | L | 15 | 17 |
| 23 | H | Northampton • | L | 8 | 32 |
| **March** | | | | | |
| 1 | A | Sedgley Park | W | 22 | 7 |
| 8 | H | London Welsh | W | 22 | 0 |
| 18 | H | Barbarians † | L | 19 | 34 |
| 22 | A | Moseley | W | 43 | 5 |
| 29 | A | Doncaster | L | 3 | 11 |
| **April** | | | | | |
| 5 | H | Rotherham | W | 56 | 17 |
| 19 | A | Launceston | W | 22 | 18 |
| 26 | H | Birmingham & Solihull | L | 10 | 21 |

National One - 6th. • EDF Energy National Trophy.
† Mobbs Memorial Match.

J Pritchard was again the leading points scorer with 238 and was joint top try scorer, with A Page, on 12. K Dickson, J Phillips and D Richmond appeared in every league and cup match. Forty seven players made at least one appearance, 38 in league and cup. From 2008, the Mobbs Memorial Match became a Bedford fixture against the Barbarians rather than an East Midlands one.

M Allen (29, 2T), M Botha (31, 3T), A Brenton (27, 3T), A Brown (2), B Burke (26, 3T), M Cecere (23, 2T), W Chudley (10, 1T), P Clarke (2), D Cole (12, 1T), M Comb (13), B Daynes (2), K Dickson (33, 9T), O Dodge (10, 4T), J Elrick (26, 5T, 22C, 25P), B Fortuna (18), J Graham (22), S Harding (29, 2T), W Harries (1), S Harrison (1), D Hawksworth (4), D Hemingway (1), J Hinkins (16, 2T), M Howard (1), J Lumby (7, 1T), A Lyon (11), R McKay (25, 1T), B McNamee (1), C Moir (19, 1T), C Mundy (10), R Noonan (4), R Owen (9), A Page (26, 12T), A Parkin ( 1), B Patston (26, 2T, 4C, 7P, 2D), J Phillips (33, 1T), B Pienaar (21, 4T), J Pritchard (26, 12T, 35C, 36P), D Richmond (33, 6T), L Roberts (28, 8T), J Russell (3), G Sammons (22, 1T), C Short (1), D Smith (1), N Strauss (25, 2T), W Twelvetrees (1), M Volland (16), T Youngs (14, 4T).

# 2008-09

Played 33, Won 24, Lost 9. F 978, A 583.

Captain: D J Richmond

| | | | | f | a |
|---|---|---|---|---|---|
| **August** | | | | | |
| 30 | H | Manchester | W | 62 | 0 |
| **September** | | | | | |
| 7 | A | Rotherham | W | 33 | 10 |
| 13 | H | Newbury | W | 53 | 12 |
| 20 | A | London Welsh | W | 32 | 23 |
| 27 | H | Exeter | L | 23 | 26 |
| **October** | | | | | |
| 3 | A | Coventry | W | 26 | 3 |
| 11 | H | Otley | W | 37 | 12 |
| 18 | H | Sedgley Park | W | 53 | 7 |
| 26 | A | Nottingham | L | 7 | 15 |
| **November** | | | | | |
| 1 | H | Cornish Pirates | L | 6 | 26 |
| 9 | A | Leeds | L | 8 | 19 |
| 15 | H | Plymouth Albion | W | 37 | 9 |
| 22 | A | Doncaster | L | 21 | 50 |
| 28 | H | Moseley | W | 17 | 15 |
| **December** | | | | | |
| 6 | A | Esher | W | 18 | 13 |
| 13 | A | Manchester | W | 25 | 5 |
| 20 | H | Rotherham | W | 32 | 18 |
| 27 | A | Newbury | W | 34 | 0 |
| **January** | | | | | |
| 3 | H | London Welsh | L | 32 | 33 |
| 10 | A | Exeter | L | 21 | 40 |
| 17 | A | Tynedale • | W | 30 | 23 |
| 24 | H | Coventry | W | 23 | 9 |
| 31 | A | Otley | W | 23 | 17 |
| **February** | | | | | |
| 14 | A | Exeter • | L | 11 | 12 |
| 21 | H | Nottingham | W | 23 | 16 |
| **March** | | | | | |
| 8 | A | Cornish Pirates | W | 6 | 5 |
| 14 | H | Leeds | W | 27 | 24 |
| 21 | A | Sedgley Park | W | 64 | 0 |
| 28 | A | Plymouth Albion | W | 31 | 14 |
| **April** | | | | | |
| 4 | H | Doncaster | W | 42 | 20 |
| 7 | H | Barbarians † | L | 45 | 76 |
| 11 | A | Moseley | W | 26 | 23 |
| 25 | H | Esher | W | 50 | 8 |

National One - 3rd.
• EDF Energy National Trophy.
† Mobbs Memorial Match

J Pritchard was again the leading points scorer with 235 and W Twelvetrees scored the most tries, 18. G Gillanders appeared in all 32 league and cup games. Forty two players turned out in at least one match, 32 in league and cup.

H Allen (1, 1T), M Botha (31, 7T), P Boulton (29, 1T), A Brown (1), B Burke (28, 4T, 1C, 1P), J Cannon (17), M Cecere (30), W Chudley (9), I Davey (20, 15T), B Davies (12, 1P, 2C, 1D), B Daynes (17, 1T), A Dempsey (1), K Dickson (27, 14T), O Dodge (23, 13T), S Falvey (1), A Fenner (1, 3C), T Foden (1), G Gillanders (32, 7T), J Graham (15), S Harding (27, 3T), W Harries (25, 12T), S Hobson (1), M Howard (29, 3T), P Hoy (6), J Knight (5, 2T), W Lawson (1), C Locke (11, 2T), G Micans (1), R McKay (29, 6T), R Owen (21, 10T), B Pienaar (5), J Pritchard (22, 4T, 55C, 35P), D Richmond (30, 3T), L Roberts (20, 2T), G Sammons (19), D Taylor (2, 1T), P Tupai (27, 3T), W Twelvetrees (31, 18T, 16C, 13P) I Vass (27, 1T), D Veenendaal (1, 2T), S Walsh (26), N Walshe (27, 1C).

# 2009-10

Played 35, Won 20, Lost 14, Drawn 1. F 885, A 706.

Captain: D J Richmond

| | | | | f | a |
|---|---|---|---|---|---|
| **September** | | | | | |
| 5 | A | Doncaster | W | 26 | 12 |
| 12 | H | Coventry | W | 42 | 6 |
| 19 | A | Plymouth Albion | W | 38 | 3 |
| 26 | H | Bristol | L | 5 | 6 |
| **October** | | | | | |
| 3 | A | London Welsh | L | 17 | 28 |
| 10 | H | Birmingham & Solihull | W | 53 | 25 |
| 17 | A | Rotherham | W | 27 | 25 |
| 25 | A | Nottingham | L | 29 | 30 |
| 31 | H | Exeter | L | 11 | 20 |
| **November** | | | | | |
| 8 | A | Cornish Pirates | L | 24 | 25 |
| 13 | H | Moseley | W | 23 | 7 |
| 20 | A | Ulster Ravens • | L | 3 | 29 |
| 28 | H | Llanelli • | W | 36 | 24 |
| **December** | | | | | |
| 4 | A | Coventry | D | 15 | 15 |
| 12 | H | Plymouth Albion | L | 16 | 19 |
| 18 | A | Bristol | L | 16 | 37 |
| 26 | H | London Welsh | W | 30 | 23 |

| | | | | f | a |
|---|---|---|---|---|---|
| **January** | | | | | |
| 2 | A | Birmingham & Solihull | W | 49 | 10 |
| 16 | H | Nottingham | W | 51 | 19 |
| 23 | A | Exeter | L | 19 | 42 |
| 30 | H | Cornish Pirates | W | 19 | 16 |
| **February** | | | | | |
| 6 | A | Moseley | W | 26 | 19 |
| 13 | A | London Welsh • | L | 13 | 26 |
| 20 | H | Doncaster | L | 12 | 23 |
| 27 | H | Aberavon • | W | 17 | 15 |
| **March** | | | | | |
| 2 | H | Barbarians † | W | 50 | 14 |
| 5 | A | Moseley • | W | 23 | 0 |
| 13 | H | Rotherham | W | 33 | 26 |
| 20 | A | Plymouth Albion * | W | 10 | 9 |
| 27 | H | Bristol * | W | 17 | 16 |
| **April** | | | | | |
| 4 | A | Cornish Pirates * | L | 18 | 22 |
| 10 | H | Cornish Pirates * | W | 42 | 18 |
| 18 | A | Bristol * | L | 32 | 41 |
| **May** | | | | | |
| 1 | H | Plymouth Albion * | W | 35 | 19 |
| 8 | A | Exeter ** | L | 8 | 37 |

Championship – 4th. * Playoffs – 2nd Group A.
** Playoff semi final. • British and Irish Cup - 3rd Pool C.
† Mobbs Memorial Match.

J Pritchard was again the leading points scorer with 226 and L Fielden scored the most tries, 15. M Dorrian played in every Championship match and made most appearances, 33. Forty one players turned out at least once, 37 in league and cup. The 'away' fixture against Birmingham and Solihull was played at Bedford because of the weather and pitch conditions in Solihull.

H Allen (1,1T), C Brightwell (7, 2T), P Boulton (31) , A Brown (7), B Burke (17, 5T), M Cecere (11), W Chudley (23, 3T), I Davey (26, 8T), B Davies (23, 2T, 15C, 11P), B Daynes (7, 1T), O Dodge (24, 6T), M Dorrian (33, 8T, 19C, 16P), O Farrell (1,1P), L Fielden (28, 15T), G Gillanders (25, 4T), C Goodman (27, 3T), S Harding (24, 3T), J Harlock (28), J Harris (1), C Hircock (1), M Howard (17), J Knight (14, 2T), M Kohler (1, 1T), B Lewitt (27, 3T), M Lilley (3), C Locke (27, 3T), G Micans (1), J Pritchard (24, 6T, 41C, 38P), A Rae (32, 2T), D Richmond (30), L Roberts (22, 5T), D Seal (26), J Sharp (2, 1C), J Short (1), H Spencer (11), D Taylor (22, 9T), P Tupai (29, 7T), I Vass (29, 2T), D Veenendaal (7), S Walsh (31, 5T), N Walshe (23).

# 2010-11

Played 38, Won 27, Lost 11. F 1216, A 713.

Captain: J G Pritchard

| | | | | f | a |
|---|---|---|---|---|---|
| **August** | | | | | |
| 26 | H | Plymouth Albion | W | 51 | 3 |
| **September** | | | | | |
| 5 | A | Rotherham | L | 16 | 19 |
| 11 | H | Esher | W | 31 | 9 |
| 18 | A | Doncaster | W | 29 | 24 |
| 25 | H | Moseley | W | 41 | 12 |
| **October** | | | | | |
| 3 | A | Bristol | W | 23 | 16 |
| 9 | H | Cornish Pirates | W | 32 | 25 |
| 16 | H | Worcester | L | 18 | 28 |
| 24 | A | Nottingham | W | 24 | 13 |
| 29 | H | London Welsh | W | 19 | 16 |
| **November** | | | | | |
| 7 | A | Birmingham & Solihull | W | 31 | 18 |
| 13 | H | Rotherham | W | 37 | 10 |
| 20 | A | Esher | W | 53 | 15 |
| 27 | H | Doncaster | W | 35 | 7 |
| **December** | | | | | |
| 4 | A | Moseley | W | 22 | 15 |
| 11 | H | Ulster • | W | 36 | 22 |
| 26 | H | Bristol | W | 39 | 22 |
| **January** | | | | | |
| 2 | A | Cornish Pirates | L | 13 | 22 |
| 8 | A | Worcester | L | 0 | 32 |

| | | | | f | a |
|---|---|---|---|---|---|
| **January** | | | | | |
| 15 | H | London Welsh • | W | 44 | 14 |
| 19 | A | Neath • | W | 13 | 6 |
| 29 | H | Nottingham | W | 47 | 19 |
| **February** | | | | | |
| 5 | A | London Welsh | L | 22 | 25 |
| 8 | A | Swansea • | W | 43 | 9 |
| 11 | H | Birmingham & Solihull | W | 52 | 0 |
| 19 | A | Plymouth Albion | W | 27 | 24 |
| 26 | H | Moseley • | W | 28 | 15 |
| **March** | | | | | |
| 5 | H | Leinster A • | W | 50 | 15 |
| 12 | A | Rotherham | W | 58 | 15 |
| 20 | H | Cornish Pirates | L | 18 | 31 |
| 27 | A | Doncaster | W | 17 | 16 |
| **April** | | | | | |
| 2 | H | Doncaster * | L | 31 | 33 |
| 10 | A | Cornish Pirates * | L | 22 | 33 |
| 16 | H | Rotherham * | W | 80 | 19 |
| 19 | H | Barbarians † | L | 35 | 43 |
| 23 | H | Worcester •• | W | 43 | 27 |
| **May** | | | | | |
| 1 | A | Worcester ** | L | 22 | 23 |
| 7 | A | Bristol ••• | L | 14 | 17 |

Championship – 2nd. * Playoffs – 2nd Group B. ** Playoff semi final. • British and Irish Cup - 1 st Pool C. •• British and Irish Cup semi final. ••• British and Irish Cup final. † Mobbs Memorial Match.

J Pritchard was again the leading points scorer with 403 (275 in the Championship and 128 in the cup), a new club record and the first time any player passed 400 in a season. H Schmidt scored the most tries, 25, the best return since B Whetstone's 25 in 1997-98. A Rae and G Gillanders played in most games, 36. Gillanders and M Dorrian played in all 29 Championship matches. Fifty players turned out at least once, 38 of them in league and cup.

H Allen (1), E Bale (2, 1C), D Barrell (1, 1T), J Bassett (6, 2T), T Bax (1), T Bedford (33, 3T, 1C) R Boot (11), P Boulton (27, 1T), A Brown (2,1T), B Burke (22, 4T, 3C), D Carstens (1), W Chudley (31, 7T), J Clark (25, 2T), O Cooper-Miller (1), O Dodge (25, 9T), M Dorrian (35, 4T, 18C, 10P), O Farrell (3, 1C, 2P), S Flatman (1), W Fraser (9, 3T), G Gillanders (36, 5T), C Goodman (26, 2T), S Harding (20, 4T), M Howard (34, 3T), M Kohler (1), G Kruis (6), J Leszczuk (1), B Lewitt (12, 1T), C Locke (12), R Long (1), G Messum (1), L Ovens (19), H Peck (1), J Pritchard (30, 10T, 73C, 69P), A Rae (36, 5T), D Richmond (33, 5T), H Schmidt (28, 25T), D Seal (33, 1T), J Sharp (21, 2T, 2C, 3P, 1D), J Short (8, 4T), S Smith (2, 1T), H Staff (1, 1T), D Taylor (18, 7T), E Thrower (27, 17T, 7C, 3P), S Tomes (31,1T), P Tupai (31, 4T), I Vass (22), D Veenendaal (26, 3T), S Walsh (27, 3T), N Walshe (16, 2T), J Wray (13, 1T).

# 5. POSTSCRIPT

Players and supporters on the pitch after the promotion clinching win against Richmond in April 1995.

The Blues Book Club:

Forwards coach Martin Hynes with some of the supporters who helped with this book.

Left to right: Jeff Cox, Phil Beard, Terry Stark, Marie Davies, Mick Meadows, Matt Webb, Dave Brown, Jackie Markham, Martin Hynes, Sam Roberts, Jane Roberts, Geoff Appleton, Phil Novis, Nigel Rudgard, Neil Roy.

Insets: Peter John Gates and Mike Green.

Picture: Elaine Rudgard.

# PITY THE POOR SCRIBE

No book, however grand its objectives, can possibly do justice to the thousands of people, players, committee, supporters and helpers of all sorts who have created the 125 year history of the Blues. This book has been written from a privileged position – the press box and the archives of local newspapers in particular. Many former players, committee men and supporters have helped in compiling it. None of them should be held responsible for errors, omissions or bias.

"Pity the poor scribe" wrote *Doug Bowker* when the mother of a player rebuked him for not mentioning the lad in his report. So humble apologies to any mother's son not given his due for what he did on or off the pitch – or any mother not given hers.

Bowker wrote in *100 Years of the Blues*. "I remember an early game at Richmond when I went into the Blues dressing room afterwards and helped haul the jersey off Alan Lovell. It was almost welded to him with muck and sweat, and when at last it tore free, the scrapes and bruises were starting to show through.

"How and why did he and his like give all for no reward? A cynic would say the answer lay in the bar afterwards. I preferred to believe he was playing his head off for his colleagues and for Bedford.

"If Alan and his fellows could cope with the bar the place often threatened to get me into trouble. After all, 4pm is no time to start drinking, and the team needed three or four pints to put back what they'd lost. Trying to keep pace interspersed with phoning reports to the Sunday newspapers was a precarious operation.

"It always surprised me that (a) players read my reports and (b) took notice of them. I remember Mike Lord once tearing into me for splashing Bob Fletcher's name all over the paper for scoring five tries when it should have been his for making the breaks to leave the winger simple run-ins. Dear 'Tod' Slaughter always complained that I kept hundreds off the gates if I didn't laud the team to the skies.

"I remember once being grateful to the team secretary Lin Lloyd when I was being given a pretty torrid time. "It's all right for you lot. You can say what you like but Doug has to write something and be open to everyone's criticism." Pity the local scribe. Lin was a great boost to the team at low periods. It would always be better next season when a number of internationals were due to join (usually of the 'Chinese' variety)."

How can anyone put into adequate words what captains, players and everyone else did over 125 years? Most did it all for nothing; but even those who thought they were going to be handsomely paid did things way beyond the call of duty. Rudi Straeuli convinced players not to leave or go on strike when things went pear-shaped. Did we do justice to those who kept going? What about those who kept the place together as amateurs in other eras. How about forwards in general – like those who did the hard work for Karl Dickson to set up the position and for Ali Hepher to land the famous dropped goal that won the day 37-35 at Exeter in the Powergen National Trophy semi final of 2006? They hardly got a mention - but forwards throughout history will understand. What about those who stayed in the background? And those coaches who actually did the coaching without a grand title? And what about all those who have pumped money into the club expecting no return: the supporters, the helpers, the mums and dads of the minis and juniors? They all did their bit to create the legacy of the Bedford Blues. It was impossible to do justice to everyone. But we did our best.

Perhaps the final word - and an answer to a crucial question - should come from a former player. Barrie Williams followed in the footsteps of his father TEK Williams and his uncle CH Williams who played in the mid 1920s. He made a debut in 1958 and scored 126 tries in 249 appearances before retiring in 1966. In 1960-61, fifty years before the Blues reached their 125th anniversary, BK Williams was Bedford's captain. In 2010-11 he was still a staunch supporter and, having been a county tennis and squash player, he was still turning out for the Hertfordshire over 70s tennis team and still going on skiing holidays. He wrote about the laws, the players and of their approach to the game. And he concluded:

Barrie Williams in the stand at Goldington Road in March 2011. He was the Bedford captain in 1960-61.

"I am certainly not saying the individual skills of 50 years ago were not as good as those of today's players, but the league structure has led to a tremendous leap in fitness and all round skills.

"This has been achieved not only by the player himself but by the provision of equipment, facilities and professional support staff which could only be dreamed of in the past. Today's player is bigger, stronger, fitter and so much better prepared than those who played 50 years ago. We might have trained twice a week but without much guidance or coaching. Our diet wasn't questioned and our Saturday evenings were spent at the bar. We would turn up for a match sometimes 30 minutes or less before kick off and our warm up would be in the changing room with the captain setting out the game plan minutes before the team ran on to the pitch. Our half time pep talk was in the middle with a piece of orange each."

He went on: "The pitch at Bedford has changed beyond recognition. The slope was still there 50 years ago but in the winter months the bottom corner was often like a quagmire and forward battles raged there for ages. Today the surface is as good as anything in the country."

Groundsman Norman Cooley in May 2011. In his playing days he was one of the most famous sportsmen in town – a Bedfordshire Minor Counties cricketer and a stalwart at the Eagles, Bedford Town FC.

So would he have made the team 50 years on? Would he have scored 126 tries at the rate of one every two games in the modern professional era? "I'd like to think so," he said. "But I'm not sure I'd be too happy sitting on a bench and not getting my 80 minutes of rugby every Saturday afternoon. That's what would worry me most if I played today."

And just say he could skipper a team of all the players he'd seen in Bedford colours since his debut in 1958. Just imagine the selectors put him on the right wing and told him to pick the rest of the team. Who would he want in his side? He thought for a week and on March 5, 2011 – the day right winger Handre Schmidt scored his third hat-trick of the season with four tries against Leinster A – he came up with (from one to 15):

*Larry Webb (1952-65), Norman Barker (1966-77), John Brooks (2000-06); Bob Wilkinson (1968-1985), Scott Murray (1996-98); 'Tod' Slaughter (1960-78), 'Budge' Rogers (1956-76), Junior Paramore (1996-2006); Paul Turner (1996-98), Tony Lewin (1959-66); Derek Wyatt (1973-78), Billy Twelvetrees (2008-09), Geoff Frankcom (1964-67), Barrie Williams (1958-67); Mike Rayer (1996-98). Replacements: Soane Tonga'uiha (2004-06), Mark Howe (1976-96), Jason Forster (1997-99), Ian Peck (1975-88), Mike Lord (1962-70), Danny Hearn (1965-67) and James Pritchard (2001-11).* Now there's a talking point.

And his favourite player from those 50 years: Scott Murray.

John Brooks

Former players switched on the new floodlights at Goldington Road on August 19, 2011 at the pre-season match against Saracens.

The lights were installed following a £75,000 appeal that was launched at the annual meeting in March. The players were invited to do the honours as members of the team that represented the Blues in the match against Llanelli in 1975 to mark the installation of the club's original lights.

Left to right: Neil Bennett, Danny Hanson, Brian Page, Brian Keen, Derek Wyatt, Norman Barker, Chris Bailward, Bob Wilkinson, Foster Edwards and 'Budge' Rogers.

Most of the Blues squad for their new campaign lined up for photographer Nigel Rudgard for the pre-season friendly against Saracens.
Alex Rae was appointed captain while James Pritchard was on World Cup duty for Canada.

Looking to the future: Former players, current players, officials and supporters look forward optimistically to the new season while celebrating 125 years of the Blues.
Nigel Rudgard took this photograph of the 'Royal Box' area in a packed Charles Wells stand at the pre-season friendly against the Saracens on August 19, 2011.

# AUTOGRAPHS